SO-BOE-539

GRACE W. WEINSTEIN writes the monthly "Your Money" column for *Good Housekeeping* and is also a frequent contributor to *McCall's, Ladies Home Journal, Glamour,* and *Money.* Her previous books include *Men, Women, and Money,* available from NAL Books, *Children and Money: A Guide for Parents,* available in a Plume edition, *Money of Your Own,* available from Dutton, and *Life Plans: Looking Forward to Retirement.*

The Lifetime Book of Money Management

Revised Edition

GRACE W. WEINSTEIN

A PLUME BOOK

NEW AMERICAN LIBRARY

NEW YORK AND SCARBOROUGH, ONTARIO

PLUME TRADEMARK REG. U.S. PAT. OFF. AND FOREIGN COUNTRIES
REG. TRADEMARK—MARCA REGISTRADA
HECHO EN HARRISONBURG, VA., U.S.A.

SIGNET, SIGNET CLASSIC, MENTOR, ONYX, PLUME, MERIDIAN and NAL BOOKS
are published *in the United States* by New American Library,
1633 Broadway, New York, New York 10019,
in Canada by The New American Library of Canada Limited,
81 Mack Avenue, Scarborough, Ontario M1L 1M8

Designed by Barbara Huntley

Library of Congress Cataloging in Publication Data

Weinstein, Grace W.
  The lifetime book of money management.

  Includes index.
  1. Finance, Personal. I. Title.
HG179.W439 1987   332.024   86-28644
ISBN 0–452–25893–6

First Plume Printing, February, 1987

1 2 3 4 5 6 7 8 9

PRINTED IN THE UNITED STATES OF AMERICA

FOR STEVE

Preface
to the
Revised Edition

The world of personal finance changes, in large ways and small, even faster than seems possible.

There have been two major changes since the 1984 edition of *The Lifetime Book of Money Management:* (1) That edition was written when inflation was at an all-time high and when interest rates were at a peak of about 18 percent. Today inflation has subsided and lower interest rates mean that drastically different techniques are required if you are to make the most of your money. (Both editions, in fact, tell you what to do under various inflation and interest-rate scenarios; in this edition, the emphasis has shifted.) (2) Tax "reform," even when advertised as "simplification," changes the rules across the financial board and makes our financial lives more complicated than ever. Just the prospect of tax reform, as it hangs over our heads, complicates our lives in a variety of ways. Even when major tax legislation is passed, as in late 1986, the process never ends. Tax law is constantly subject to change. No book is definitive, therefore, and you should always consult your own tax adviser.

There have, of course, been other significant changes. Adjustable mortgages, brand-new in the early 1980s, came in an almost infinite variety; today, with the mortgage market far more standardized, I have found it necessary to completely rewrite Chapter 13, Financing a House Today. Bank deregulation and a proliferation of new financial services have meant substantive changes in the chapters on cash management. Lifestyles have continued to change: Later marriage and later childbearing mean more singles and more two-income couples; a longer life span means ever more need for retirement planning.

Through it all, however, the message of the first edition remains constant: the critical importance of managing your money well. This book is meant to help you do so.

Acknowledgments

Appreciative thanks go to a great many people and organizations, too many to list. I would like to single out the following, however, with special thanks for their special help.

- Stanley H. Beckerman of Oppenheim, Appel, Dixon & Co.
- Jerome Manning, Esq., of Stroock & Stroock & Lavan
- Robert Waldron of the American Council of Life Insurance
- Robert Leider of Octameron Associates
- Barry M. Kilzer of the Oakland Financial Group
- Judith Avner of the NOW Legal Defense & Education Fund
- Walter Walsh and F. J. "Pete" Leo of The Bankers Life
- Michael S. Johnson, University of New Orleans
- James N. Kendall of the United States League of Savings Institutions.

Thanks, too, to Dan Frank, editor, for taking over as a competent and caring shepherd, to Ted Johnson for copy-editing above and beyond the call of duty, and to Claire M. Smith, literary agent and friend, for being there.

Acknowledgments for the Revised Edition

Appreciative thanks, again, to the splendid souls listed above. And acknowledgments anew to the following equally splendid and helpful people:

- Alex Kubiacyzk and Diane Orvos of the American Council of Life Insurance and the Health Insurance Association of America
- Joseph M. Re of Octameron Associates
- Aivars Ziedins of Ziedins & Company
- Elizabeth Christy of the National Association of Home Builders
- Elizabeth Johnson of the National Association of Realtors
- Eli Warach and Julian Block of Prentice Hall

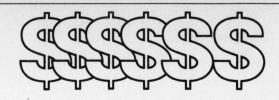

Contents

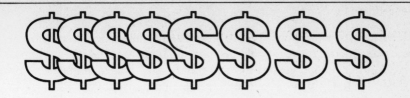

Introduction

Managing your money well may be the single most important thing you can do today.

Galloping inflation seems to be, at least temporarily, under control. Interest rates, which reached unprecedented levels in 1981 and 1982, have subsided. But prices are still rising at such a rate that even two-income families with sizable and steady paychecks are having trouble making ends meet. More and more people in this turbulent economy no longer have the luxury of steady paychecks. Buying a house, or sending children to college, or putting money aside for your own retirement may seem more and more an impossible dream.

Personal money management problems are, of course, a reflection of the unnerving changes taking place in the once-conservative world of finance. The interest rates that you can earn on your own savings, a steady 5 or 5.5 percent for years, have recently resembled an out-of-control roller coaster. And just as you got used to receiving double-digit rates of return and began to count on that interest income to meet the rising cost of living, rates came tumbling down. At the same time, the interest rates that you must pay when you borrow money, when you take out a mortgage, finance a car, or take a consumer loan, went way up and have come down to a much smaller degree.

Many of the rules of the financial game have changed, turned upside down by new players in a new ball park. It isn't possible, for example, to talk simply about "savings" and "checking" as alternate forms of cash management when a wide variety of multipurpose accounts now exist. It's almost impossible to differentiate between stockbrokers and bankers when they are equally willing to offer you a checking account or sell you securities. It's no longer possible to declare that a specific percentage of income, and no more, should be spent on housing. And it's not appropriate to offer advice geared to the "traditional" nuclear family to today's single-person, single-parent, or live-together households.

In the topsy-turvy world in which we live, you may believe that successful money management is a myth. It's not. You *can* learn to make the most of what you have, to make your assets grow, and to achieve your goals. In order to do so, you don't have to be an economist, or even to understand how the economy works, although it probably won't hurt if you do. You do have to invest the time to learn as much as you possibly can about the practical ins and outs of personal finance. You have to learn enough to be willing to make decisions, to take action. And you have to know *how* to take action, to apply the practical know-how to your own life, at the stage of life you're in right now, the stage you're approaching, and the stage on the most distant horizon.

Money management, in short, is not a quick fix. It's not a one-answer-fits-all solution. The answer you need to a particular financial problem has to be an answer tailored to you. It has to recognize both your temperament (do you gleefully take risks, or shudder at the thought?) and your position in the cycle of life (are you financially responsible for yourself alone? or for the well-being of small children and/or dependent parents?).

This book will show you how to make the most of the money you have, at your current stage of life and at all the stages that lie ahead. It offers useful guidance whether you are single (living alone or with others) or married (in a traditional nuclear family or a contemporary one of any size or shape). It provides advice to you as city-dweller or suburbanite, as a single-income household or multi-income unit. It provides detailed information on what it costs to live in different parts of the United States. Whether you want to establish credit or keep your debt load manageable, find some money to invest or pick the right tax shelter, choose the best life insurance policy or finance a car or pay as little income tax as possible, this book will help.

You'll find an overview of the life cycle in Chapter 1, followed by specific chapters on specific topics from budgeting through retirement planning. Within each chapter specific information is linked to life stages, because the investments you make at 35, as just one example, are seldom the investments you will want to make at 60. Your needs across the board —in housing, life and health insurance, even the kind of car you buy— change with your age and with the configuration of your life at various ages. Within each chapter, too, you'll find nuts-and-bolts financial information buttressed by the experiences of real people and by questions and answers on specific points. Read Chapter 1 now, then the chapters of immediate concern in your own financial planning; refer to other chapters as the need arises. Each chapter is part of the whole. Each stands alone.

Details may change: Interest rates will go up or down, laws and tax codes will be amended, the regulations that govern financial institutions will be tightened or loosened according to the whims of government and the sometimes contradictory opinions of "experts." But the information set forth here, tailored to your own individual situation, should serve you well for some time to come.

The Lifetime Book of Money Management

WHERE ARE YOU NOW AND WHERE ARE YOU GOING?

Life Cycle Planning

★ Sherry is 23 and engaged to be married. She has grown up in a society shaped by affluence and molded by inflation. Sherry, as a result, shares some attitudes and expectations common to her peers: She'll start married life in an apartment, but she'll have a home of her own, because that's what people do. She'll go into debt to buy that home, and to acquire other possessions as well, because that's also what people do. Why pay cash today, after all, when tomorrow's dollars will be worth less and less?

★ Rob is Sherry's father. At 47, he is doing well with his own accounting firm. His early years were shaped by his parents' experience of the Depression, but his own youth was lived in the economic boom that followed World War II. He thinks his parents' frugality excessive, but can't quite accept the free-spending ways of his children's generation. Rob is, in fact, somewhat concerned about his own approaching retirement. He's afraid continually rising prices will make it increasingly difficult to live on a limited income.

★ Fred is 74 and recently retired. He married and became a father during the Great Depression of the 1930s, at a time when he was grateful for a Civil Service desk job instead of the law school he had always wanted but could not afford. His whole life has been shaped by the memories of those years: of his father losing a prosperous business, of neighbors out of work, of his own struggles to make ends meet and raise a growing family. The children are long since grown, and Fred and his wife, Trudy, have been financially comfortable for quite a few years. But old memories are hard to shed. Fred is still reluctant to buy on credit, still scrupulous in keeping track of expenditures. He suspects it's simply too late to change.

The traditional life sequence—school, job, marriage, child-rearing, back to being a couple as children leave the nest, back to being alone as one spouse dies—has its counterpart in monetary terms: Income rises gradually from young adulthood through the child-rearing years, remains relatively stable from the middle years until retirement, then stays fixed or actually declines after retirement and in widowhood. Outgo, in the same sequence, starts low, rises for the setting-up-housekeeping expenses of early marriage, declines briefly, rises sharply with the arrival of children and still more sharply with the college years, and falls off abruptly as children leave the nest. The ascending lines, if this pattern were to be graphed, would be roughly parallel—except that the peak of outgo, associated with the growing family, frequently occurs ten full years earlier than the peak of income, which is attained in the middle years.

But this neat sequence is no longer universal. Young adults marry later, or not at all. Married couples often defer parenthood, and one in ten married couples do not have children at all. Four in ten marriages dissolve long before widowhood. The divorced remarry, form new families, and face the expenses of those new families against the backdrop of continuing expense for the existing family. All of these demographic changes reshape the face of society. They also affect the financial planning of the people involved.

Wherever you are in the life cycle, whether you're following a traditional sequence or charting a new path, you can make your money work for you. Whatever your temperament, too, you can manage your money well. Look at the following sequence in terms of the financial tasks you face at different ages.

Financial Planning Throughout the Life Cycle

AGES 13–17

- Learn to budget through handling an allowance.
- Develop financial understanding by working for pay.
- Begin to think about future career options.

AGES 18–24

- Establish household.
- Train for career.
- Identify long-range goals.
- Begin to attain financial independence.
- Start a savings program.
- Establish a credit identity.
- Begin to invest.
- Purchase insurance.
- Develop a financial record-keeping system.

AGES 25–40

- Provide for childbearing and child-rearing costs.
- Provide for expanding housing needs.
- Expand career goals.
- Manage increased need for credit.
- Invest for capital growth.
- Build an education fund.
- Expand insurance to meet expanding needs.
- Write a will; name guardian for children.
- Involve every member of the household in financial management.

AGES 41–54

- Continue career development.
- Diversify investments.
- Provide greater income for growing needs.
- Continue to build education funds, provide education for children.
- Begin to develop estate plan.
- Explore retirement goals.
- Review and revise will as necessary.

AGES 55–64

- Evaluate and update retirement plans.
- Concentrate on income-producing investments.

- Review insurance and reduce coverage where not needed.
- Decide where to live in retirement.
- Meet responsibilities for aging parents.
- Review estate plan.

AGES 65 AND OVER

- Reevaluate budget to meet retirement needs.
- Investigate part-time employment and/or volunteer work for retirement.
- Review will.
- Write a letter of instructions to accompany will.
- Share financial management and household management tasks with spouse.

Now look at the following life stages in terms of where you are now, where you expect to be, and where you hope to be. Then apply the money management techniques in this book, and you'll be able to take charge of your financial fortunes.

Financial Planning for Singles

The rise in the number of people who live alone is one of the major changes in living patterns of our era. In 1960, one-person households accounted for 15 percent of all American households; by 1985 the percentage had risen to a startling 23 percent.

The Young Adult

Your income may be low today, compared with your anticipated income in the future, but your needs, as a single adult, should also be lower. This is the time, therefore, to build a cushion for the years ahead. It may be tempting to spend virtually your entire salary on self-indulgence, on travel and stereos and entertainment (especially if you're living with your parents or sharing expenses with a roommate). But you'll do much better in the long run if you anticipate the spending needs you will face in the stages to come. If you build a savings plan by setting aside at least 10 percent of your take-home pay in the highest-yielding investments you can safely tackle (see Chapter 6 on risk vs. return), you'll be more than independent. You'll be free, free to leave one job and move on to another, free to live the way you want to live, and eventually, if not right now, in a place of your own.

If you're a young adult who plans to remain single and childless, you can plot the growth of rising income without charting against it the rising cost of family obligations. This can mean a significant difference in the way you save and how. Risk-bearing investments may suit your style, for example, while they might be totally out of the question for the parents of young children. At the same time, you'll have to ensure a secure future without relying on anyone else.

Q. My daughter is fiercely independent, has been since high school days. Now that she's out of college, she won't take any help from us at all. Yet she lives in a neighborhood that makes me fear for her safety. Is there any way we can get her to accept help?

A. Your daughter's fierce independence may be healthier than clinging dependence at this stage. While most young adults shed parental ties gradually, many find it very important to prove themselves by refusing all help. When this is the case, they usually become more flexible once they've made their point. You'll probably find that your daughter will welcome a smoothing of the way later on. Meanwhile, if you're actually concerned for her safety, see if you can make a business arrangement with her. She might accept a loan, complete with her written promise to repay and your assurances that you will accept repayment, in order to move to better quarters.

The Mature Single

If you're thrust into singlehood in your middle years, after fifteen or twenty or however many years of marriage (see p. 17), you will have to restructure your financial life as well as your emotional life. You'll be ahead of the game if you've paid attention to financial matters right from the start, if you've owned property, established credit, made independent investments.

If you are an older adult and have been alone for a lifetime, you've probably ordered your financial affairs to your liking; you've had decades of training. If you're alone in the later years because of divorce or widowhood, however, you may have a lot to learn about money management. You may have to look at fixed or diminishing income in a time of rising costs, and plan accordingly.

Financial Planning for Live-Togethers

Lots of people have roommates, of the same sex or the opposite, for reasons of companionship as well as economy but with no romantic implication. Others have romance in mind as well. In 1979, 1.3 million households (or more than 1.5 percent of all households) consisted, in Census Bureau jargon, of "unrelated couples of the opposite sex." By

1984 there were 1.9 million such households, 30 percent of which contained at least one live-in child.

If you are sharing a household with someone, you have to decide some basic questions: who owns what, who buys what, who pays for what, and who is left holding the bag when one of you decides to call it quits. These questions need answers if yours is a strictly platonic arrangement, if you are roommates for convenience. But they get very sticky indeed if your relationship is complicated by romance. Then what you have is all the economic and emotional realities of marriage, without the protection provided by law. This is when you must establish your own safeguards.

Some couples draw up a contract, a legal document that spells out the responsibilities and obligations of each partner. A contract can forestall legal battles should you come to an angry parting of the ways. The simplest agreement, if you want to waive all financial claims on each other, might state:

—that neither of you has an obligation to support the other,

—that neither of you has any intention to share earnings or property with the other,

—that any property acquired while you live together belongs to the purchaser thereof.

If you do intend to be mutually responsible, your contract should spell out that intent. If you want your partner to inherit your belongings should you meet a sudden mishap, write a will. Husbands and wives have some automatic rights of inheritance; live-togethers do not. (Be sure to write a will, whether or not your living arrangements are sanctified by law, if you have a dependent child.)

If you and your partner have different intentions and expectations as you start out together, it would be a good idea to reach an understanding of each other's position. But what if you're allergic to contracts? What if you're living together, instead of getting married, precisely because you don't want your relationship sullied by the law? Then, at the very least, be aware of what you're doing and talk through your financial arrangements.

OWNERSHIP

This should be your first consideration. To forestall confusion and distress if you do break up (the landlord may not let you back in to claim your stereo if your ex-partner changes the lock on the door), keep track of ownership as you go along. Specify, in writing, who owns what. Did you buy the stereo while your partner purchased the dining-room set? Write it down. Did you contribute jointly to the purchase of a car? Write it down. Did one of you buy the stereo, or the car, while the other took care of food and rent and utilities for a number of months? Write that down too.

KEEPING ACCOUNTS

This can be a murky area. Should you pool your incomes? keep joint bank accounts? buy property together? It depends, of course, on your relationship. But it also depends on some cold, hard financial facts of life.

With a joint account, either partner has full access to the total account. That's fine, as long as the relationship lasts. But you might want to consider trust accounts instead, in which each partner has limited access to the other's money. Or, to keep things simple, you might maintain a joint household account for your joint living expenses and separate accounts for your personal expenses. Unless your incomes are roughly the same, by the way, identical contributions to your joint account might not be appropriate. Consider, instead, contributing an equivalent proportion of your individual earnings. That will leave each of you about the same proportion of your income for personal expenditures.

Whether you see living together as a permanent arrangement or as a temporary one, try to look ahead. Take advantage of reduced living costs (two don't live quite as cheaply as one, but they do live more cheaply together than alone), and establish a savings plan for the future. Organize your financial life for what might be as well as for what is, and you'll be able to take control of your life.

Financial Planning for the Newly Married

Jeff and Anne both come from traditional middle-class families. Both fathers were breadwinners; both mothers were homemakers. But Jeff's father turned over his weekly paycheck and his mother paid all the bills, balanced the accounts, and made many of the spending decisions. Anne's father, by contrast, doled out weekly allowances to both wife and children and made all the major family spending decisions himself. Jeff expects Anne to make her own decisions; she, instinctively, consults him before she buys more than groceries. He doesn't understand why she does, and she doesn't understand why he gets irritated.

Such differences may very well show up in your marriage. One of you may be hooked on saving even at the expense of comfort, while the other prefers to save what's left over after making life comfortable. One of you may believe that all income is joint income and should be put in a common pot, to be drawn on as needed; the other may insist on separate ownership and separate responsibility. One of you may be a scrupulous record-keeper, while the other is far more casual.

Most of these differences will probably be resolved over a period of time, some by adopting one partner's viewpoint and some by compromise. And, gradually, you should develop a team approach to most money matters. If you don't always agree, and you probably won't, you will still develop an acceptable set of procedures for day-to-day money management. (If you don't, your marriage is going to be in trouble.)

In developing these procedures, you'll come face to face with your expectations about spending. You probably expect to live well because both of you are earning. But if you live up to the level of those earnings —with frequent dinners out, expensive trips, a car or two—you may find that expectations outstrip reality. If you live up to the level of those earnings without a thought for the future, you're setting the stage for future conflict over money.

You'll also come face to face with your individual attitudes about the source of your income. Even among today's two-income couples, it's possible to find interesting variations on the theme of whose money is whose. It all comes down to the fact that the spouse who controls the purse strings (or is perceived to do so) is the spouse who rules the roost.

Who Makes the Decisions?

When young couples earn roughly similar amounts and have similar career expectations, the game of whose money is whose is psychological more than strictly financial. But it is still real. Is his income supposed to cover the household budget, while hers goes for the "extras" that make life fun? Is she supposed to run the household out of her salary, while his goes for the big-ticket items like travel and recreation? Who, really, makes the spending decisions?

Caroline Bird, in *The Two-Paycheck Marriage* (Rawson, Wade, 1979), describes several variations:

- "Pin money" couples play down the wife's earnings in the interests of traditional male supremacy; these couples (there aren't as many of them as there used to be) relegate the wife's income in attitude if not in fact to frivolous purchases.

- "Earmarker" couples are what Bird calls "neo-traditionalists." They cope with the threat of a wife's income by setting it aside for specific goals, for a vacation trip or a down payment on a house or college tuition for the kids.

- "Pooler" couples put all their money together, although they don't necessarily claim equal say in spending decisions. One may still be the senior partner, the other the junior.

- "Bargainer" couples are the true radicals. With separate accounts for individual earnings, they scrupulously divide financial responsibilities.

As you start out together, it will help your financial planning to understand where you and your spouse stand in attitudes and expectations. It will also help if you address practical matters right from the start. If you're both earning, how will you handle your respective salaries? What kind of bank account will you establish? Who will pay the bills and balance the checkbook? Who will hold title to the property you acquire together? Read the chapters on banking, investments, and housing before you leap to joint ownership on all your possessions; it isn't always a good idea. And don't let a romantic glow prevent you from tackling these practical financial questions; tackling them now may preserve the romance later on.

Marriage as an Economic Partnership

Jane and Edward, a Wisconsin couple, agreed to use her income to support the household while they invested his for their future. They did so for fourteen years. Then, in 1970, they were divorced. Edward claimed that the house and all the investments belonged solely to him, since they had been purchased with his earnings and were held in his name. Jane was horrified. She would have saved some of her own earnings had she not thought they were working together. Moreover, as she told the court, he couldn't have made the investments at all without her assumption of his legal responsibility to support the family. The court was not impressed. It held that Jane and Edward's intention to save the money for both of them was not enough to give her a legal right to any of the money.

If Jane and Edward's case came before a Wisconsin court today, this could not happen. Many state laws with respect to marital ownership of property have changed, and more are changing. So far, however, most of the changes deal with the disposition of property after divorce (see pp. 18–19). Most laws are silent with respect to property ownership during an ongoing marriage. You may view your marriage as an economic partnership, but the state may not. You'll find out only if your marriage ends. But be aware, as you start out together, that the state in which you live is a third party to your marriage. Keep the state in its proper role, that of inactive and invisible partner, by maintaining your financial affairs with care. Keep track of who earns what, and who buys what, and you'll have the documentation you may someday need.

The National Conference of Commissioners on Uniform State Laws, in its draft of a Uniform Marital Property Act, speaks of the need for defining "interspousal economic relationships" during marriage. Right now, the Conference points out, "a linear diagram of marriage would have a beginning, and end, and something in-between. For most of us, the in-between *is* the marriage. Yet the framers of laws have tended to be exclusively concerned with the beginning and the end."

The Committee on the Uniform Marital Property Act, with the belief that the end of marriage by either divorce or death will be far less traumatic if economic relationships during marriage are clearly delineated, recommends that states adopt legislation holding that:

■ Property acquired during marriage by a couple, by the personal effort of either, is property to be owned by both and defined as "ours," as "marital property."

■ Property brought into the marriage or acquired afterward by gift is not marital but individual property. Any *appreciation* in its value remains individual property (the house your father leaves you becomes more valuable and you sell it; the appreciated value is yours); any *income* from the property becomes marital property (you rent out the house, and the rental income belongs to both you and your spouse).

■ Either spouse can deal as an owner with most marital property—buying, selling, entering into contracts, and so on.

■ Spouses have the right to create their own "marital property agreement" and may contract to do so. Both must agree in writing to any such contract.

The drafters of the Uniform Marital Property Act suggest that economic rewards stemming from the personal efforts of each spouse during marriage should be owned in equal shares. "It is seen as a system of elemental fairness and justice that those who share the work of establishing and maintaining a marriage should share equally in the acquisitions of that marriage."

Wisconsin has adopted the Uniform Marital Property Act, as of early 1986, and several other states have it under consideration.

As you start out together, too, keep your eye on the future. Right now, your living costs are probably on the low side. You don't need as much living space as a couple with children, for instance, so your housing budget may be minimal. You're young and, probably, healthy, so medical costs are few. You do have housekeeping setup costs, for furniture and such, but these purchases can be spread over time. With two incomes, your discretionary spending power may be at its highest point for the next twenty years. Enjoy that discretionary spending power—but use it, too, to invest in your future.

Standard advice used to call for a working wife to save all or most of her earnings, against the inevitable day when she became a full-time homemaker. That day is no longer inevitable. You may not intend to become a full-time homemaker, whether or not you ever intend to have children. You should, nonetheless, establish a savings plan with a significant portion of your combined income. Those savings can be drawn on to pay the heavy cost of child care if you do have a baby and then return to work. They can cushion the financial shock if you intend to return to work and then, as a growing number of young mothers are doing, decide to stay home for a while instead. They can even come in handy, without children at all, if one of you is laid off or simply wants a change of career. And those savings can help to maintain your standard of living against a rising cost of living and, invested wisely, secure your future.

Financial Planning for Parents

The only type of household which lost ground during the decade of the '70s, the Census Bureau reports, is the married-couple-with-children household; there were 1.3 million fewer such families in 1985 than in 1970. Proportionately, such family units fell from 40.3 percent of the population in 1970 to 28 percent in 1985. In part this drop reflects the growing number of older couples who no longer have children at home. But it also reflects the growing number of young couples who are choosing to defer parenthood or to forego it altogether.

Parenthood today, in other words, is often a deliberate choice and not necessarily an automatic corollary of marriage. That choice is made on a number of grounds, the least of which is probably economic. Still, if you decide to have children, economic considerations soon gain importance. Children cost a lot, both to have and to raise. It's best to be prepared.

The Costs of Having Children

Economists consider the costs of having children in terms of both direct maintenance costs and what they call "opportunity costs." The direct costs are all those out-of-pocket costs that mount up from the time a child is conceived until the day that child turns 18 (college costs are another kettle of fish). Direct costs are examined in some detail on p. 14. Opportunity costs are less tangible but no less real: They are losses of opportunities for economic betterment, opportunities lost because of the presence of children.

Mothers who go right back to work after a maternity leave of several weeks may not suffer reduced income (although they will face higher direct outlays for child care), but mothers who drop out of the labor force for several years forgo both income and career advancement. Missing out on an annual after-tax income of $10,000 adds up to $50,000 in the five years until your child starts kindergarten (assuming the unlikely situation of no promotions and no raises).

The money spent on child-rearing, moreover, whether you forgo income or not, is not available for spending on an enhanced life-style or for investing to cushion your future. This can require both a psychological adjustment and a financial one. Two incomes may have been enabling you to keep up with inflation while living the life you want to lead. When one of those incomes is curtailed or when a great deal of money is spent on a third member of the family, other expectations have to be reduced.

The sum of direct and opportunity costs varies by geographic region (it generally costs more, for some reason, to raise children on the West Coast), by educational level (the better-educated mother usually earns more and therefore loses more if she steps out of the work force), and by economic level (the more you earn, the more you're likely to spend on your children). But you do effect some savings if you have more than one child; the per-child costs are reduced as your family increases.

In general, when direct and opportunity costs are added together (with opportunity costs based on a mother's working half-time, which is probably no longer realistic), population economist Thomas J. Espenshade of the Urban Institute concluded that the total economic cost of raising a child to the age of 18 in 1980, excluding college, ranged from slightly more than $100,000 at the low-income level to nearly $140,000 for middle-income families. In mid-1986, depending on where you live and on your income level, total costs may be considerably higher. Let's see how the direct costs break down.

CHILDBEARING

Birth is the first budgetable expense. In 1982 the Health Insurance Association of America came up with a total of almost $3,000: $1,451 for three days in the hospital and $642 for medical expenses (add $150 for an anesthesiologist, if you use one), and $851 for a layette and nursery furnishings (excluding furniture). Add another $1,000 if you're among the one in five having a cesarean delivery.

Your direct outlay will be lower, despite skyrocketing medical costs, if you're covered by hospital and medical insurance that includes maternity benefits. But your costs may be higher, possibly much higher, if you don't have maternity coverage, if you live in a region where hospital and medical care is more expensive, and if the birth is complicated. Your costs will also be higher if you want more variety in maternity clothes or indulge yourself in buying the baby's layette.

CHILD-REARING

The cost of rearing your children from birth to age 18 depends in part on where you live. Direct costs in 1985 ranged from $38,027 for the 18 years for a rural but nonfarm family in the Midwestern states to $100,004 for an urban family in the West, covering food, clothing, housing, medical care, education, and transportation. These costs are in current dollars. Inflation, assuming an annual rate of 5 percent, will greatly increase the dollar cost. Table 1 is a detailed breakdown of what child-rearing cost in one region for a child born in 1966 and what it's likely to cost for one born in 1984. Adjust for inflation to get current costs.

Cost estimates of child-rearing, as Table 1 indicates, include a child's share of the family's overall costs for such things as housing and transportation as well as direct expenditures on behalf of the child. If you have a child, therefore, your out-of-pocket costs won't necessarily increase by these annual totals. And when a child leaves home you won't have this much money added to your discretionary spending power.

One important ingredient—child care—is not included in these estimates. An occasional baby-sitter can cost a few hundred dollars a year. But you can't go back to work with an occasional baby-sitter. The cost of full-time care ranges from $20 to $50 a week for family day care (a group of children tended in a caregiver's home), to $75 or $85 a week for a child care center, to $100 to $300 a week, plus room and board, for a live-in caregiver. Specific costs depend on where you live, but the arithmetic yields some staggering annual totals. (Some child-care costs, of course, are tax-deductible; see Chapter 23.)

You'll also need more living space as your family grows, you'll start thinking about protecting your family through life insurance, and you'll run up sizable medical bills or (unless you have employer-paid group health insurance) sizable health insurance premiums, since even healthy children need regular checkups and inoculations. Your children will need more and more clothes to fit rapidly growing bodies and will consume more and more food to make those bodies grow.

Child-rearing always costs more than parents anticipate, with more of the family income going to meet fixed costs than in any other stage of the life cycle. If you're prepared, it may be easier.

Q. I think our 10-year-old daughter should have regular spending money. My husband prefers to screen every request for money. Who is right?

A. You are. Children need regular spending money so that they can learn to budget, to plan ahead, and to take responsibility for spending wisely. If you make all their decisions for them, children don't get the necessary practice in handling money. Let them make small mistakes now, with small sums, and they'll be less likely to make big mistakes later on, when they have money of their own. This allowance checklist may be helpful:

- Be consistent. Children need to know what they are getting and when, or they can't make budgetary decisions.

TABLE 1: Current dollar estimates of cost of raising a child born in 1966 and in 1984 at the moderate cost level in the urban North Central region.

Year	Age of child (years)	Total	Food at home	Food away from home	Cloth-ing	Hous-ing	Medi-cal care	Educa-tion	Trans-por-tation	Other
COST OF RAISING A CHILD BORN IN 1966										
1966	Under 1	$1,316	$194	0	$66	$539	$70	0	$267	$180
1967	1	1,397	238	0	69	555	75	0	275	185
1968	2	1,372	245	0	118	508	79	0	247	175
1969	3	1,448	257	0	125	541	85	0	257	183
1970	4	1,620	310	$50	130	580	90	0	270	190
1971	5	1,688	317	53	134	606	96	0	284	198
1972	6	1,829	321	55	190	598	99	$43	287	236
1973	7	2,027	460	59	197	624	103	44	296	244
1974	8	2,254	528	66	211	697	112	47	330	263
1975	9	2,463	572	73	221	772	126	51	361	287
1976	10	2,713	695	78	229	820	138	53	397	303
1977	11	2,886	736	84	239	877	151	56	424	319
1978	12	3,366	831	109	357	971	164	70	478	386
1979	13	3,827	1,023	122	373	1,090	179	76	548	416
1980	14	4,282	1,105	135	397	1,262	199	83	645	456
1981	15	4,698	1,185	147	418	1,406	220	94	724	504
1982	16	5,469	1,371	155	592	1,562	244	107	832	606
1983	17	5,643	1,385	162	607	1,598	265	118	852	656
TOTAL 1966–83		50,298	11,773	1,348	4,673	15,606	2,495	842	7,774	5,787
COST OF RAISING A CHILD BORN IN 1984										
1984	Under 1	$4,312	$571	0	$142	$1,876	$278	0	$866	$579
1985	1	4,664	736	0	149	1,970	292	0	910	607
1986	2	4,561	773	0	254	1,819	307	0	832	576
1987	3	4,789	812	0	266	1,910	322	0	874	605
1988	4	5,327	979	$172	279	2,005	338	0	918	636
1989	5	5,593	1,028	181	293	2,105	355	0	964	667
1990	6	6,118	1,044	190	426	2,095	373	$166	1,012	812
1991	7	6,678	1,352	199	448	2,200	391	174	1,062	852
1992	8	7,012	1,419	209	470	2,310	411	183	1,115	895
1993	9	7,364	1,490	220	494	2,425	432	192	1,171	940
1994	10	8,031	1,863	231	518	2,547	453	202	1,230	987
1995	11	8,431	1,956	242	544	2,674	476	212	1,291	1,036
1996	12	9,456	2,099	305	826	2,911	500	222	1,456	1,137
1997	13	10,175	2,449	321	867	3,057	525	234	1,528	1,194
1998	14	10,685	2,572	337	911	3,210	551	245	1,605	1,254
1999	15	11,217	2,700	354	956	3,370	578	258	1,685	1,316
2000	16	12,933	3,174	371	1,391	3,663	607	270	1,953	1,504
2001	17	13,581	3,333	390	1,461	3,846	638	284	2,050	1,579
TOTAL 1984–2001		140,927	30,350	3,722	10,695	45,993	7,827	2,642	22,522	17,176

Note: Table assumes child is in the family of a husband and wife with no more than five children. Prices are current in the years specified, rounded to nearest $1; future prices are inflated from 1983 constant dollar estimates at an annual rate of 5 percent, rounded to nearest $1.
(Source: United States Department of Agriculture)

- Set the allowance amount in consultation with your child, and evaluate it regularly.

- Be realistic in determining the amount; remember inflation. While you don't want your child to have too much money, too little means there will be nothing to buy and nothing (except frustration) to be learned.

- Be sure that the allowance, whatever pre-allocated sums it includes (bus fare and the like), also includes some "bubble-gum money," a discretionary sum that the child can spend without explanation; this is the real learning tool.

- Keep the allowance separate from your child's responsibility to perform household chores or to do his or her best in school; don't use the allowance to punish misbehavior. Money has enough emotional links; using it this way within the family reinforces those links and undercuts objective lessons in money management.

- Be flexible. Don't bail your child out regularly or you will undercut the purpose of the allowance, but don't be rigid either. If your child manages well most of the time, occasional extra help may be in order.

COLLEGE COSTS

The cost of higher education lagged behind the rate of inflation during the 1970s but has more than caught up in the last couple of years. Fees for tuition and room and board doubled at virtually all schools between 1970 and 1980, with the College Board reporting annual mean national costs for a four-year private college in the 1985–86 school year at $9,659. Some schools, notably the prestigious Ivy League institutions, cost considerably more. Others, including some outstanding state universities, cost a good deal less. Wherever your child attends college, you'll be paying the bills with after-tax dollars, and you're bound to feel the pinch. Disposable personal income does, as a rule, rise along with inflation, but to many parents it never seems to rise fast enough.

You'll find detailed plans for projecting college costs and meeting them in Chapter 20, but you'll come out ahead if you count them in, from the beginning, as part of the cost of child-rearing.

Financial Planning for Divorce

Marriages used to end primarily by death, only occasionally by divorce. Not today. Today the reverse is true, and more marriages end by legal dissolution than by death. Divorce may take place at any age or stage, from newly married to senior citizen. Whenever it happens, if it does, it has a significant impact on your current financial situation and on the planning you must do for the future. The legal fees for the divorce itself are just the first step.

Distribution of Assets

Be sure that you remember all your assets as you give thought to divorce, and make a list before you see your lawyer. Some commonly overlooked items:

- The cash value of whole life insurance
- Vested pension benefits
- Prepaid taxes

Q. My husband and I have agreed to an amicable divorce after twelve years of marriage. We've agreed about the way our property is to be divided. Do I have to use a lawyer? Or is it okay to fill out the forms in a "do-it-yourself" divorce kit that I've seen on sale?

A. You don't have to use a lawyer, if you don't own much property and you agree on everything, but you might be wise to consult one before proceeding. You may agree on the distribution of assets, but have you thought about sorting out the value in life insurance policies? What about pension accumulations? What about the tax implications of your agreement? You may be haunted in later years by a distribution you make now, if you don't secure legal advice. If you have children, don't even consider a do-it-yourself divorce; conflicts over custody and child-support payments can develop far into the future. If you don't have children, a consultation with an able lawyer will tell you if your case is as simple as it seems.

COMMUNITY PROPERTY STATES

If you've lived in one of the eight community property states (Arizona, California, Idaho, Louisiana, Nevada, New Mexico, Texas, or Washington) or in Wisconsin, there is a presumption that all property acquired during marriage is jointly held. This joint ownership does not include property which one of you inherited or which was acquired before the marriage. Even in these states, however, where everything appears to be clear-cut, there are often complications. If a down payment was made on a house by one partner, with money brought into the marriage by an inheritance, is the house community property? Or is just the appreciated value of the house, above the initial purchase price, considered community property? State laws differ, even among community property states ("fault" is at issue in some jurisdictions, when it comes to divorce settlements), and judges have a fair amount of latitude in making decisions.

"TITLE" STATES

Although almost every state now has some form of equitable distribution law (see below), Mississippi, in mid-1985, still clings to the traditional common law concept of title, in which legal title to the property is the deciding factor. If title to securities is in one spouse's name, for instance, it doesn't matter whose money was used to make the purchase; that spouse is presumed to be the owner and will retain the asset at divorce.

EQUITABLE DISTRIBUTION

In the vast majority of states which now have laws with equitable distribution provisions, marital property is divided according to both its source and the need of the parties without regard to title. If the divorce goes to trial, the judge may consider a number of factors: the length of the marriage, the contribution of each spouse to the building of assets (including the asset of one spouse's business or professional career), the employability of the respective spouses, who has custody of children, and so on.

"Equitable," when all these factors come into play, is not the same as "equal." Don't expect a fifty-fifty split. In many instances wives are receiving less than they would have under old laws. Accurate record-keeping is now more essential than ever so that you can document, if necessary, a down payment on a house made through a gift from your parents or the fact that your spouse's professional career was made possible through your sacrifice of career options.

Equitable distribution, although it deals only with distribution of assets at the dissolution of a marriage, goes a long way toward converting marriage from a strictly social partnership to an economic partnership. But it also means that the previously absolute duty of a husband to support his wife and a father to support his children has been repealed. A wife in an equitable distribution state, whether or not she has worked outside the home, is generally presumed to be capable of economic equality. She may receive temporary maintenance, but she will be expected to become self-supporting. Conversely, the wife may now owe maintenance payments to her husband.

The division of assets, in any case, is only the beginning.

Starting Over

Making a new start, once the property is divided and the decree is final, has financial ramifications, too. Two households now have to be supported on an income that previously may have had to stretch to meet the needs of one family. A nonearning partner must learn to become economically self-sufficient, a task easier for younger divorcées than for older ones. A single parent has extensive financial obligations with often meager financial resources. Credit must be obtained, insurance needs met, investments handled.

A Second Marriage

Remarriage is not without its financial constraints. A man may still have to provide financial support for the children of a first marriage while bringing up the children of a second marriage. Either spouse may owe maintenance payments to a first partner, even after marriage to a second.

With serial marriages, and larger and larger extended families, there are sometimes extended financial obligations. If your second wife remained on good terms with the mother-in-law of her first marriage, and that mother-in-law is now ill and alone, will you support your wife's desire to help her out? If your husband grants a business loan which he can ill afford to a brother-in-law from his first marriage, will you feel that you and your children are unfairly deprived?

Some of these problems and some of the problems related to property settlement in divorce may be resolved in advance if you sign an antenuptial ("before marriage") contract, spelling out mutual rights and obligations. It's difficult, of course, to anticipate divorce while in a happy marriage. It's even more difficult to contemplate divorce as a possible stage of life before you marry at all. But in the overall scheme of financial life planning, it's important to contemplate all the possible scenarios. If Act II turns out to contain a divorce, you'll be better prepared if you've thought ahead as you've acquired assets and established title to them.

Financial Planning for the Empty Nest

You thought it would never happen, but it has: The last college tuition bill has been paid, the last child has moved out. Now you can look forward to a number of years—typically thirteen or more years—in an empty nest. That nest is probably pretty well feathered; with more women in their forties and fifties working outside the home and with the income of men at a lifetime peak, income per family member is higher than ever. This income peak comes, for most people, just as outgo is reduced. Costs related to child-rearing, by and large, are finished. The mortgage may also be paid up, and housing costs reduced. Major purchases, for appliances and the like, have long since been made and are now limited to replacement items and luxury items.

With higher income and reduced family obligations, now might be the time to alleviate any creeping midlife restlessness: to make a career change, to go back to school, to take a year off to recharge your batteries. With proper financial planning, it can be done.

But there are still some potential areas of financial strain in these middle years.

Grown Children

Your children's continued demands, financial and/or emotional, may put a strain on your pocketbook and on your marriage. Some young adults continue to demand parental support; some, finding the going rough in the outside world, move back into the parental home. Others, of course, won't take help that you really want them to have. You have to take stock of your own family constellation. At the same time, however, you've earned your financial independence and should not be reluctant to say so. Think twice before you permit an adult child to expect regular support. Think twice, too, if you're hanging on and refusing to let go. Adult children need to grow up; you're not doing them any favors if you keep the apron strings tied.

Aged Parents

New obligations to parents frequently surface at about the time children are ready to stand alone. With lengthening life spans, in fact, you may find yourself responsible for elderly grandparents. Here, too, there's a double bind. The elderly, like the young, are better off if they are independent. Don't encourage a parent to move in with you just because that parent has been widowed. Don't assume responsibility for decisions that parents can make for themselves.

An Added Income

When a wife returns to paid employment in the middle years, as often happens today, it can create financial strains even while it produces augmented family income. The biggest problem can stem from the increased tax bite. The second paycheck is piled on top of the existing one, says the New York State Society of Certified Public Accountants, and may be taxed at the higher rate on the combined income (see p. 475).

If you or your spouse returns to work after a period of remaining at home, be sure to figure the net income after related costs. Look at commuting, clothing, and lunch expenditures, as well as the tax bite, before deciding what you'll do with all the "extra" money. It may take a couple of years before going back to work appears financially worthwhile.

Financial Planning for the Later Years

While inflation has put the squeeze on people with fixed incomes, the retirement years are seldom the problem many people anticipate. Many expenses do go down. In addition to reduced household expenses—your mortgage is probably paid up—you can probably count on reduced outlays for clothing, for transportation, and for incidentals. Just eliminate commuting, daily lunches out, office attire, and the occasional office gift or contribution, and you may be ahead several thousand dollars a year.

Retirement

You may not retire for twenty or more years, but planning ahead, long before you actually retire, is the key to successful living in retirement. Whether you stay in the same job you've held these many years or make a midlife career switch, you'll want to give some thought to the lower-income years ahead. You should divert as much current income as you can into high-yielding investments, and shelter some from taxes, if you're eligible, in an Individual Retirement Account. Then, shortly before you retire: Cut back on expenses, to approximate retirement income. Make any necessary major purchase—buy a new winter coat, if you'll need one, or have the house reroofed—while income is still coming in. Arrange for continuation of your health insurance coverage or buy supplemental insurance. Refer to Chapter 22 for details on health insurance and to Chapter 24 for information on estate planning. Retirement planning is covered in detail in Chapter 25.

Widowhood

If you're married, prepare your spouse to live alone as you approach retirement. One of you has probably paid the bills and kept the books and decided how much insurance to buy and where to invest, just as one of you has probably assumed the tasks of dealing with appliance repairmen and storing out-of-season clothes and changing a fuse when it needed changing. One of you probably knows where all the filed checks are, and the income tax records, and the safe deposit key.

Go through the house and go through your financial affairs, now, and give your partner a crash course in survival skills. It's bad enough to cope with the inevitable grief when one of you is left alone. It's intolerable to also have to cope with day-in, day-out details of living that you know nothing about.

KEY POINTS

- Your spending patterns are shaped by your temperament, your stage of life, and the economic climate in which you live as well as by the amount of money you have and the skill with which you manage that money.

- The stages of your life, from youth through old age, can be plotted in monetary terms.

- Anticipating life's stages enables you to plan ahead and to stay in charge of your financial affairs.

- You can do a great deal with the money you have. You can make your money work for you, no matter how much or how little you have, if you make financial plans and follow through.

2

Budgets and Record-Keeping

Before you develop an investment strategy, analyze your insurance needs, or even decide which banking services to use, you have to come to grips with how much money you have and how you use that money. Then you can look at how much money you expect to have and plan to use that money in the best possible way. That best possible way won't be according to some abstract principle; it will be the way that suits *you* best.

Taking charge of your finances so that your money will work for you entails both analysis and record-keeping, both long-term plans and here-and-now action. The first step is to identify your personal goals and objectives. Then you can ensure success by periodically monitoring your cash flow, assessing your net worth, and keeping systematic records—all in the interest of accumulating your assets and making them work for you.

Goals and Objectives

What do you want out of life? Other than keeping your head above water and a balance in your bank account, what do you want to be able to do? A lot of people never stop to look ahead, too caught up in day-to-day living to determine where they are going. You have to be farsighted to develop a workable financial plan. You have to set up a three-part program, consisting of goals, objectives, and action:

Goals are an expression of your values, a long-range look ahead at what is most important to you. What is your financial destination?

Enough money to open your own business? to buy a house? to send your children to college? to travel around the world? to quit working and play tennis? to endow a favorite charity? to ensure a comfortable retirement? Whatever your financial goal or goals, you have to identify each one clearly before you can take any action.

Objectives are a step-by-step path to your goal. Once you've clarified a long-term goal, a goal that may take many years to reach, you can break it down into specific attainable objectives.

Action, the hard core of your financial program, is the here-and-now day-to-day behavior that will make both objectives and goals possible.

For example: You are in your late forties. The nest is empty and the children are out of college and on their own. You've decided that your primary goal, right now, is to ensure a worry-free retirement. That's a worthy goal, but it's both vague and long-term. It needs to be reduced to manageable objectives. Your specific objectives might include the establishment of an adequate cash reserve, income-producing investments, and ventures for long-term capital gain. The action you take to meet those objectives and thereby meet your long-term goal might include setting up a budget to monitor spending, reducing expenditures across the board to free funds for investment, and securing good financial advice.

The same breakdown of goals, objectives, and action can help you to clarify all of your financial planning. But it can't be undertaken in a vacuum. You'll also want to look at decision-making and the art of communication.

Making Decisions

Decision-making should be purposeful. Sidestepping decisions doesn't work; it simply leads to decision-making by default. If you do nothing about finding a new job, you've made a decision, conscious or unconscious, to stick with the one you have. If you do nothing about seeking out a solid investment for some spare funds, you've made a decision, conscious or unconscious, to leave your funds where they are.

No decision has to be forever. Circumstances change, *you* change, and your decisions will change as well. That's the point of life cycle planning: to make the decisions appropriate at each stage of life.

If you're married or living in any sort of permanent relationship, however, don't do your financial planning alone. Two of you will have to live with the system you devise, and two of you had better be involved in devising it. Two of you will have to work together in setting both the goals and objectives and the course of action which both of you will have to follow. Think through your personal goals, and share them with your partner. Be sure that you share the same goals or, at least, that you understand each other.

Decisions in a partnership are made in a variety of ways: by mutual agreement, by accommodation (that is, agreeing to disagree), by compromise, or by concession.

Mutual agreement may be preferable, but it isn't always possible. You may agree on some things, disagree on others. Consensus is more likely, however, if you openly discuss your goals and objectives. Don't assume that your partner's goals are the same as yours, or allow your partner to make assumptions about you. Don't be like the couple shocked to find out that *he* had always assumed they would retire to a little cottage in snow-covered Vermont while *she* had always known they were retiring in the sunny South. Talk to each other.

THE BRAINSTORMING TECHNIQUE

When you do talk to each other and reach an impasse, it's time for a new form of discussion. Brainstorming is a tried-and-true method in which you put forth all the possible solutions to a particular question, not just the two solutions you've both fixed on, in the quest for an answer that will suit you both. There is probably a third place you'd both like to live; you don't have to limit your choice to one or the other.

If you're brainstorming about investment possibilities, for instance, because you're conservatively inclined and your spouse feels it's worth some risk for potential gain, run through every type of investment that comes to mind, from a savings account to an oil-and-gas-exploration deal. An even-tempered verbal free-for-all—don't interrupt each other, don't raise your voices, and don't discard any suggestion as too preposterous —will place a wide-ranging menu of alternatives up for consideration. Then, when your imaginations are exhausted and the list is complete, evaluate each item in terms of personal preference.

If one of you has strenuous objections to investing in diamonds, drop that thought right away. If one of you is violently opposed to putting money in oil exploration, don't do it. If one of you is absolutely certain that money in a savings account is money wasting away, drop this idea too. Measure the remaining alternatives in terms of how they will meet your previously determined joint goals and objectives. Look at the consequences of each alternative: Is there a reasonable chance of making a profit on this investment? Will money have to be tied up for a long time on that one, too long a time for comfort? What are the tax implications? What's the actual degree of risk? Will you still be speaking to each other if the investment doesn't pan out? Then, and only then, make your decision.

THE "PLANNING BOARD" TECHNIQUE

When you have a few thousand dollars to invest, and suspect that you'll be making other investments later on, you can take turns suiting each other's wishes. But what if you're committing your lifetime savings and making a choice that will be difficult to reverse? What if you're at odds, for example, about where to live in retirement?

The Kidds, for instance, knew they wanted to move. They'd never much liked the industrial town to which his business had brought them thirty-two years ago. They'd made the best of it, but now their children lived elsewhere, their friends were retiring and pulling up stakes, and they were ready to move on as well. But where to? He had always loved their vacation cottage in Vermont, with its quiet fishing lakes and winter solitude. She detested winter and, moreover, was eager to live closer to the children.

One way the Kidds might clarify their own priorities and resolve differences of opinion is to make a planning board of all the options. In this procedure, suggested by Sidney Simon of the University of Massachusetts, you make out a slip of paper for each of your housing choices. The slips should include every possibility, not only housing types ("condominium" or "cottage" or "rental apartment") but location ("Florida" or "Vermont" or "the town where I grew up" or "a college town where I can take classes"). Write out the slips over a period of days or weeks or months, while you gather information about all your options, and collect them in an envelope. Then make a date to open the envelope and review the slips of paper. Place them in order of their importance to you. It sounds simple, but writing out the choices and physically arranging them before you actually does clarify their relative importance.

This can work for you, as an individual. It works best for a couple if you make duplicate slips of paper as you go along. Then, when the envelope is opened, you each arrange the slips in the order of your personal preference. A comparison can then be made. If moving back to your hometown is on the bottom of both your lists, that choice is quickly dropped. If you can't find a good compromise and you're still at odds, try arguing each other's point of view. If you want Florida, try making the case for Vermont, and have your spouse step in your shoes. Sooner or later, you'll come to a meeting of the minds.

While this book is about finances, and this chapter is about setting goals and implementing them, it's vitally important to make decisions via open communication before you try to develop a financial strategy.

Your Financial Plan

When their last child graduated from college and left the nest, the Links sold their suburban home and moved to Manhattan. With $185,000 in hand from the sale of the house plus $95,000 in joint annual income, the 58-year-old couple felt that the time had come for some well-deserved self-indulgence. But $2,100 in rent, $390 a month for parking two cars in Manhattan's high-rent district, dinners out virtually every night of the week, and an impulse expenditure of $20,000 for a boat soon put both their bank account and their marriage in distress. The Links sought financial counseling. By preparing an income-outgo statement (which they had never done before), they discovered that they had annual expenditures of $16,000 over and above annual income. Analysis also showed the need to minimize taxes, along with the need to plan for retirement. The counselor made some specific suggestions—such as chartering the boat on occasional weekends to see if this would be an appealing post-retirement activity. But the key to saving both pocketbook and marriage was the simple process of sitting down and taking a good hard look, together, at their finances.

Your personal financial plan has to support what you (and your partner, if you have one) really want to do—not what someone else thinks is good for you. There are no hard-and-fast rules for what proportion of your income should go for what. But there are recognized guidelines which will help you to put your financial house in order. The guidelines include:

- Making a budget

- Assessing your net worth

- Keeping adequate records

Budgeting Without Pain

There are definite advantages to keeping a budget. You'll see exactly where you are, in terms of current income and outgo. You'll then be able to adjust your outgo to match your income, and trim any excess spending so that you can save for up-and-coming expenditures. You'll be able to stop the dribbling away of money in nonproductive and nongratifying ways, the kind of dribbling away that inevitably occurs when you're not keeping track. You'll be able to zero in on your personal goals and objectives and make your dreams come true.

Despite these advantages—and you're probably nodding your head in agreement as you read—most people want nothing to do with the whole tedious process. But budgets, despite their reputation, need not be dull and forbidding. Simply remember: A budget is a tool to help you stay on top of your financial affairs. You can and you should develop and use a budget that you can live with, a budget that will serve you instead of the other way around. Here are some varieties to consider:

A Look over Your Shoulder

One budget technique involves looking back, without looking ahead. This essentially short-term exercise allows you to see where your money is going. Then you can decide if where it's going is where you want it to go. If it is, fine; if not, you can mend your ways.

This technique may prove effective if you constantly find yourself in the position of having $30 in your pocket on Monday and $6 on Tuesday, and no recollection of what happened in between. Simply record, faithfully and without exception, every single penny you spend. Carry a small notebook and write down every newspaper, bus fare, haircut, paperback book, and cup of coffee as well as every business lunch, bag of groceries, and item of clothing. Do this for a month and you'll have a clear picture of where the money goes. Then, without the need to continue the record-keeping indefinitely, you can cut back on the silly little expenditures that add up without giving you much pleasure.

The Set-Aside Budget

This goal-oriented exercise is keyed to well-honed motivation. If you are determined to buy a new car or to vacation in the Orient, decide how much you'll need. If you'll need $2,000 for a down payment on the car you want to buy a year from now, you'll need to set aside $166 a month until then (actually less if you're going to put the money into an interest-earning vehicle, as you will, instead of in a cookie jar). If the car is super-important to you, you'll take that $166 off the top of your take-home pay each month and put it aside for the car. Don't let anything interfere with your goal; simply erase that $166 from your take-home pay, as if you took a cut in salary, and arrange the rest of your spending accordingly.

This budget can help you to reach a specific objective, but it does have some limitations. If you're operating close to the margin to begin with, it's not going to help you very much to cut back still further. It leaves no cushion for emergencies, unless you've already got a comfortable savings account. It won't help you keep pace with inflation. And it's essentially a limited venture, not the kind of tool that will help you control all your financial affairs.

Envelopes, Jars, and Piggy Banks

In this slightly more all-inclusive version of the set-aside budget you'll allocate all your take-home pay according to category. If you convert a weekly paycheck to cash, for instance, you'll then put the needed dollars into an envelope (or whatever) designated according to need: rent, food, gasoline, lunches, savings, and so on. You may find yourself eating gasoline money from time to time, as you borrow from one envelope or another, but that's okay if it all comes out right in the end.

This kind of budget is essentially an operating tool, not a planning tool. It can help you to control your spending, but it may not help you with a key element of a good financial plan: accumulating resources for the future. To do this, you'll have to go to a bit more trouble.

A Cash Flow Forecast

The most useful budget is one that identifies current income and outgo and projected income and outgo. It takes some effort, but if you take a few hours to set up a detailed cash flow forecast, and then spend half an hour every month keeping it up to date, you'll get a firm grip on your financial affairs. This cash management approach, while it may seem complicated at first glance, can be approached in a simple step-by-step way. Use the sample Income-Outgo Worksheet on p. 31 as a guide.

INCOME

Start by identifying your current income. On a single sheet of paper, list all your definite sources of income: salary, interest, dividends, royalties, commissions, rents—anything you know you'll have in hand in the course of the year. Put down the annual totals. You can break them down to a monthly basis later on. Use after-tax, take-home income to work with, because it's spendable income that you're allocating.

On a separate sheet (or on the same sheet, in a parallel column), identify your projected income a year from now. Don't count uncertain income in either column. You may work regular overtime but, unless it's contractually guaranteed, it could stop. You may have been the happy recipient of a year-end bonus every year for the last six years, but this too could come to an unhappy end. You may have received an annual cash gift from your father, as he disposes of his estate during his lifetime, but he could find another use for his money. Such income, which you may or may not actually receive, should be designated for extra savings or allocated for luxuries. Enjoy it, in other words, but don't count on it.

OUTGO

On another sheet of paper identify your current outgo, by category, on an annual basis. Pull together current figures from your checkbook and charge account records. Then identify anticipated expenditures in the same areas a year from now. Convert your annual figures to monthly ones, so that you can allocate funds ahead of time for an annual insurance premium or a semiannual tuition bill. Round all figures to the nearest $5, too, to make the task easier.

Set up your outgo categories in descending order, from fixed to variable. Start with those expenses that are both fixed and absolutely

INCOME-OUTGO WORKSHEET

MONTHLY INCOME	This year	Next year
Salary		
Your own	_____	_____
Your spouse's	_____	_____
Bonuses	_____	_____
Commissions	_____	_____
Tips	_____	_____
Interest	_____	_____
Dividends	_____	_____
Rental property	_____	_____
Royalties	_____	_____
Social Security	_____	_____
Pension benefits	_____	_____
Profit-sharing	_____	_____
Annuities	_____	_____
Life insurance benefits	_____	_____
Other	_____	_____
TOTAL	_____	_____

MONTHLY OUTGO	This year	Next year
FIXED EXPENSES		
Housing (mortgage or rent)	_____	_____
Household insurance	_____	_____
Medical care, including health insurance	_____	_____
Other insurance	_____	_____
Taxes	_____	_____
Installment purchases (automobile and others)	_____	_____
Savings	_____	_____
VARIABLE EXPENSES		
Food, at home and out	_____	_____
Home maintenance and repairs	_____	_____
Utilities and fuel	_____	_____
Telephone	_____	_____
Clothing	_____	_____
Transportation	_____	_____
Entertainment/ recreation	_____	_____
Travel and vacations	_____	_____
Clubs and organizations	_____	_____
Hobbies	_____	_____
Gifts and contributions	_____	_____
OPTIONAL EXPENSES		
Housing (a second home or a major home improvement)	_____	_____
Transportation (a second car)	_____	_____
Extended travel (two months in Europe?)	_____	_____
Other (a boat? a recreational vehicle?)	_____	_____
TOTAL	_____	_____

essential: housing (rent or mortgage payments), insurance, taxes (other than those withheld), savings (yes, savings are essential and should be a fixed off-the-top portion of your income). Then list the variable but essential categories: food (both at home and out), housing repair and maintenance, utilities, clothing, medical care, transportation. Don't forget pocket money for lunches, haircuts, bus fare, and the like. Next come not-so-essential items (in economic, not emotional, terms): entertainment, recreation, travel, contributions, gifts, hobbies. Rank these flexible expenditures in order of their importance to you, before you decide how much you'll spend in each category. A midwinter vacation may seem extravagant, an extra to be ruthlessly cut back in the interests of a balanced budget, but if that vacation is the only thing that will keep you sane you may choose to cut back in other areas instead.

You can also look at outgo in terms of "definite," "maybe," and "wouldn't-it-be-nice." "Definite" expenditures, fixed and variable, include the essential items listed above. "Maybe" items include entertainment and recreation, travel and vacations, clubs and organizations, hobbies and sports, gifts and contributions. The "wouldn't-it-be-nice" category includes all your heart's desires, the things you'd do if only you had the money and the things you will be able to do if you make a budget and stick to it: a vacation home in the country, a trip around the world, a recreational vehicle, a boat, a complete redecoration of your home.

Q. How can I possibly budget? I work in sales and on commission, and never quite know what the year's income will be or even a given month's. Yet I have to pay my rent on a regular basis. My income has gone up each year of the last five, but I'm not secure enough to believe that it will necessarily continue to rise; it could go down if I have a bad year or if I get sick. How can I allocate my money for current expenses and plan ahead for the future?

A. You need an extra dose of self-discipline. Try to set aside some money from each check you receive, no matter how difficult it may be, to cover the times when there may be no checks at all. You have to build up a cushion of savings to tide you over the slow periods as well as to cover any personal crises or emergencies. Set up your personal budget, first, by charting your income over a period of six months to a year. Then build up your savings by spending an amount no more than midway between your lowest monthly income and your average monthly income. As your savings increase, along with your confidence that your earnings will stay about a certain predictable level, you'll be able to spend more.

But don't forget taxes. If income tax is not withheld, you'll have to file quarterly estimates and have enough cash on hand to pay these estimates. You can also make taxes work for you: If a large year-end fee will dramatically increase your taxes, consider splitting it between two calendar years. What's important for the salaried, moreover, is even more important for you: Keep accurate records of all your income and all your outgo, especially your business-related, tax-deductible outgo.

Monitoring Your Cash Flow

If you take your cash flow forecast a step further and monitor your actual spending, you can see what changes you must make, on a month-to-month basis, to stay on top. Figure 1 shows a cash flow chart developed by New York's Citibank. To make such a chart for yourself, list each allocation category across the top of a sheet of paper. Under each category, set up two columns: debit and credit. The debits will be the amount you actually spend in each category each month; the credits represent your annual forecast figure divided by twelve. The amounts won't come out even each month, but you'll carry over any accumulated surplus or deficit and start each month with the net amount then available.

FIGURE 1: Cash flow chart.

HOUSING		HOME ENERGY MAINTENANCE/ PHONE		TAXES		INSURANCE	
Debit	Credit	Debit	Credit	Debit	Credit	Debit	Credit
___	___	___	___	___	___	___	___
___	___	___	___	___	___	___	___
___	___	___	___	___	___	___	___

LOAN PAYMENTS		TRANSPORT		SAVINGS		MEDICAL		INVESTMENTS	
Debit	Credit	Debit	Credit	Debit	Credit	Debit	Credit	Debit	Credit
___	___	___	___	___	___	___	___	___	___
___	___	___	___	___	___	___	___	___	___
___	___	___	___	___	___	___	___	___	___

EDUCATION		POCKET MONEY		FOOD/LIQUOR		HOME APPLIANCES/ FURNISHINGS		CLOTHES	
Debit	Credit	Debit	Credit	Debit	Credit	Debit	Credit	Debit	Credit
___	___	___	___	___	___	___	___	___	___
___	___	___	___	___	___	___	___	___	___
___	___	___	___	___	___	___	___	___	___

VACATION/ RECREATION		GIFTS/ CONTRIBUTIONS	
Debit	Credit	Debit	Credit
___	___	___	___
___	___	___	___

If you spend a lot on clothing in April, for instance, as you build up your spring wardrobe, you'll probably exceed your monthly allocation for clothing. But since you probably won't spend as much in May, once your wardrobe has been brought up to date, you can catch up then and come out even. In other categories, such as food and housing, your actual spending should come out close to your estimate. If it doesn't, over a period of several months, you've got to make some adjustments to avoid serious trouble.

Keeping track of expenses in this specific debit-credit way will show you where your budget is working and where it is not. You may have to raise your annual forecast in one category and cut back in another. A child might be sent to camp for two weeks instead of four, for instance, to free money for other family needs. Or you may decide to cut back on restaurant meals in order to send a child to camp.

You'll also change your spending patterns as you move into different stages of life; recognizing those changes and taking advantage of them is essential. Children outgrow camp and start to stay at home instead; perhaps they even find a summer job. What happens to the camp money then? Is it absorbed, unnoticed? Or do you make a deliberate decision about what to do with it? Life cycle planning enables you to look ahead, to anticipate freed money that can then be used for other purposes, and to anticipate and meet the costs associated with a new life stage. Those costs may be part of obligations to others (college for your children, support for your aged parents). They may also represent obligations to yourself (a new career direction which requires time out for training, a festive celebration of your twenty-fifth wedding anniversary). Cash flow forecasting combined with a monitoring system will give you the clearest financial portrait of all.

Budget Tips

Whichever form of budget you decide is best for you:

- Review it regularly to be sure it's up-to-date and serving your needs.

- Plan for large once-a-year expenses by allocating one-twelfth of the necessary sum each month.

- Include adequate provision for taxes. Unless you're on straight salary with no outside income, you'll probably owe some extra income tax. If you'll owe $500 or more in tax, over and above the amount withheld from your salary, you may have to pay an estimated quarterly tax. See Chapter 23 for details.

- Put an inflation factor in your budget. If you bring home $30,000 in after-tax income, you'll need an additional $2,400 to compensate for an inflation rate of 8 percent. If you figured on 5 percent inflation for the year and designed your budget to absorb an increase of only $1,500, an 8 percent rise would leave you $900 in the hole—$900 that would have to come out of long-term savings or put you into debt. So, beyond your provisions for systematic savings, try to calculate an inflation factor. The best bet is to use the inflation rate for the preceding year as you do your personal forecast.

Net Worth

A budget will help you control your spending on a month-to-month or even year-to-year basis. But a budget shouldn't stand alone. The best way to measure your financial progress is through assessing your net worth and charting its changes over the years. Net worth represents the success with which you are converting income into assets. A net worth statement will signal your ability to handle more debt. And it will indicate whether or not you are keeping pace with inflation.

Your personal or family net worth, simply put, is the sum of all assets minus the sum of all liabilities. Put another way, it's what you would have if you sold everything you own and paid back everything you owe. Here is a sample Net Worth Worksheet to use as a guide:

NET WORTH WORKSHEET

CURRENT ASSETS		CURRENT LIABILITIES	
Checking accounts	————	Mortgage (balance due)	————
Savings accounts	————	Taxes	————
Certificates of deposit	————	Debts (including installment	
U.S. Savings Bonds (current		loans)	————
value)	————	Insurance premiums	————
Life insurance (cash value)	————	Charge account balances	————
Securities (market value)	————	Charitable pledges	————
Annuities (surrender value)	————	Other	————
Pension (vested interest)	————	TOTAL LIABILITIES	————
Real estate (market value)	————		
Business interests (market		Subtract total liabilities from	
value)	————	total assets:	
Residence (market value)	————	Total assets:	————
Furnishings, jewelry, automo-		− Total liabilities:	————
bile, etc. (current market		= TOTAL NET WORTH	————
value)	————		
Other	————		
TOTAL ASSETS	————		

ASSETS

Start by listing your liquid assets: cash on hand, savings and checking accounts, deposits in money market funds, the cash value of life insurance policies, the market value of securities. Include the current value of certificates of deposit, savings bonds, money owed you by others—and don't forget the security deposit on your apartment, if you're a tenant. Then tally the current market value (not what you paid for the property, but what you could get if you sold it) of your home, car, jewelry, appliances, coin or art collections, etc.

LIABILITIES

Then total everything you owe: mortgages, outstanding loans, charge account balances, insurance premiums, tuition payments, taxes due. Don't forget yet-to-be-paid medical bills or charitable pledges. Subtract your total liabilities from your total assets and you'll have your net worth.

If the liabilities add up to more than the assets, you've got a negative net worth—and some major changes to make in the way you manage your money. Make those changes by going back to your operating budget. See if you can eliminate some spending and build up your savings. If you can't manage to save at least 5 percent of your after-tax income (and that's a bare minimum) you'll have to take harsher measures. Cut out your use of credit, rearrange your style of living, and get down to basics.

If your net worth is positive, that's good. But is it working for you in the best way possible? Can you do better?

Analyze Your Net Worth

The net worth figure alone won't tell you very much. If you analyze the figure and compare it with succeeding years, however, you'll be using the information to improve your financial position. You might even set a target and measure your increased net worth against that target.

Your analysis, at least once a year, should include the kind of questions a corporation would ask itself. For example:

IS YOUR NET WORTH GROWING MORE THAN THE ANNUAL RATE OF INFLATION?

The first time you perform this exercise, you'll have to estimate, but in the future you can be precise. Compare the year-to-year change in net worth; if the percentage increase is less than the rate of inflation in your area, you are falling behind in terms of purchasing power. You can find out the local inflation rate by calling the nearest office of the Bureau of Labor Statistics. Once you have the figure, multiply the total value of your assets by the inflation rate to find out the dollar rate of increase you need.

Your net worth may grow without deliberate action on your part. Staying on the job may increase your assets in the form of built-up pension benefits. Making monthly mortgage payments reduces your debt and increases your net worth by increasing the equity in your home. But this kind of accidental growth won't help you in the battle against inflation. Take deliberate action and you can make your net worth grow in significant ways.

You can consciously build your net worth by investing savings, reinvesting the income that your investments produce, and enjoying capital appreciation. To do this, first you have to save enough to invest, then you have to invest it wisely. You have to balance your investments among those that produce income and those that are more likely to produce capital growth; see Chapter 6 for details.

You may also wind up with a reduction in net worth from one year to the next if assets produce little or no income or capital appreciation, if you allow yourself to be overburdened by expensive short-term liabilities, or if you simply spend too much and save too little for new investment.

The remaining steps in your net worth analysis will help you pin down the cause of increase or decrease in your net worth. They will help you change the mix of your assets and liabilities to achieve more growth.

WHAT IS THE RATIO OF ASSETS TO LIABILITIES?

According to the Federal Reserve Board, the typical American has about $6 in assets for every $1 in debt. Just what ratio is right for you, however, depends on your age and income potential. If you are still moving toward your peak earning years, you can assume greater liabilities because you know that you'll be in a position to pay them off. If you are nearing retirement, you should try to increase assets and reduce liabilities.

The right ratio for you also depends on your temperament. You can assume more debt in the expectation of potentially greater gain, as long as it won't lead to chronically sleepless nights.

WHAT IS THE RATIO OF SHORT-TERM LIABILITIES TO LONG-TERM LIABILITIES?

Although debt is no longer intrinsically "bad" in late-twentieth-century America, some kinds of debt are still better than other kinds. Long-term debt, used to finance the purchase of assets that will create more wealth, is good; an outstanding example is long-term mortgage debt. Short-term interest-bearing debt, if it is used to finance day-to-day living costs, is bad because it produces no return; an example is the use of charge accounts and credit cards to purchase groceries.

Interest charges, moreover, are steep. Paying interest on everyday items reduces the amount of money you have to save and to invest in productive assets. Even though the interest you pay on consumer debt is, at this writing, tax-deductible, you'll still generally be ahead of the game if you keep short-term debt to a minimum.

WHAT IS THE RATIO OF FIXED TO LIQUID ASSETS?

Fixed assets, such as your house or a collection of antique silver, increase in value but are hard to tap; you have to find a willing buyer before you can turn such assets into cash. With inflated housing prices you may find that as much as half of your net worth is tied up in your equity in your home. Yet you need some funds readily available as operating expenses and for emergencies. Liquid assets are those that can be converted quickly to cash, such as bank accounts and securities.

The appropriate split between fixed and liquid assets, for you, depends on age, income, and personal preference. It also depends on the degree to which you are cushioned in other ways. If, for instance, you are adequately covered by medical insurance, disability insurance, unemployment insurance, and a second income in the household, you may not need more than two to three months' income on hand in a savings account or money market fund. If you're single, between jobs, and/or without insurance coverage, you'll be safer with at least a six-month cushion.

However much cushion you decide you need, don't invade that amount to cover short-term debts or to splurge on a trip to Europe. The need for cash can be both urgent and unexpected. One man, for instance, recently started a management job with excellent fringe benefits. But he had not yet received his hospitalization insurance card when he was rushed to the hospital with bleeding ulcers. Without the proof of insurance, the hospital was firm: A check for $1,500 would precede admission.

Working with Your Net Worth

Now that you've drawn up your net worth statement and analyzed it in terms of your own situation and your own goals, don't put it aside and forget it. Bring it up to date at regular intervals (as often as quarterly if inflation surges once again) to see if:

- Your investments are keeping up with inflation or ought to be replaced.
- Your insurance coverage is adequate.
- Your overall net worth is outpacing inflation for real growth.

Keeping Track

Now that you have drawn up budget sheets and net worth statements, what are you going to do with them? What do you usually do with bills, receipts, and financial records of all kinds? Are you the stash-them-in-a-shoebox type? Or do you have organized folders, by year and by category, so that you can find records when you need them?

Clearly, organization is better than chaos. But most of us shy away from organizing just as we shy away from budgets. The former, like the latter, need not be difficult. You simply have to decide what to keep and where.

You'll find some motivation for the task if you ask yourself these questions:

- What would happen if your home were burglarized or destroyed by fire? Would all your important records disappear along with your possessions?

- Who, besides you, knows where to find important information on family assets and obligations?

- How easy would it be for any other member of your family to figure out your record-keeping system?

What to Keep

A rule of thumb: Keep the papers you will need to document facts for as long as those facts might be questioned.

Some things have to be kept virtually forever: records on a home purchase and home improvements, because they will substantiate a tax claim when the house is sold; buy and sell documents on securities, paintings, rare coins, and other assets whose sale may have tax consequences; old tax returns themselves so that you have a record of your affairs over the years. Insurance policies should be retained for several years after the expiration date, in case a delayed claim is filed. And you'll want to keep your budget sheets and net worth statements to chart your progress over the years.

Other records need to be kept for limited periods of time. Any papers that document a tax deduction (other than those related to capital gains or losses, detailed above) should be kept for a minimum of three years after the filing of that return; that's the usual audit period for federal income tax returns. (State laws on tax audits vary; check with local authorities to determine appropriate record-keeping periods. And remember: In cases of fraud, all bets are off. Both the IRS and local tax authorities can investigate suspected fraud years later.) Tax records to be kept for at least three years include bills for medical services, bills substantiating home office deductions or business travel, records of casualty or theft losses, and so on.

Other bits and pieces of the paper storm that drifts through your life may be discarded almost immediately. Bills from gasoline companies and department stores, for instance, may be disposed of as soon as your payment is accurately credited. Credit card statements showing finance charges need no longer be kept; consumer interest, under the 1986 tax law, is no longer a tax-deductible item.

Q. I've always filed my canceled checks, along with the bank statement, by month and year. Now I have several boxes of canceled checks to review before I can figure out which are the tax-related items to keep and which I can throw away. Is there a better way of doing this?

A. As you reconcile each month's bank statement, sort your canceled checks by category. Then store them in files labeled by tax-related category: medical bills, home improvements, and so on. Keep the rest, filed by month, for a year or until you're sure you won't need to prove that you've paid a bill; then discard. This method has two advantages: You'll have all your tax records properly filed, and you'll reduce the avalanche of paper you would otherwise keep on hand.

Where to Keep It

A rule of thumb: Keep irreplaceable papers in the safest possible location; keep current files where it's easy and convenient to work with them; keep back records out of the way but accessible.

SAFEKEEPING FOR IRREPLACEABLE DOCUMENTS

A safe deposit box is the best place for papers that are either extremely valuable or difficult to replace, such as birth and marriage certificates, deeds, titles, and securities. But check with your bank before you place your will or your life insurance policies in safe deposit. In many states a box is sealed upon the death of the owner, and, while access may be obtained specifically for the purpose of locating a will, it may take time and add unnecessary trouble at a difficult moment.

If you don't have a safe deposit box, a fireproof box is the second-best location for these papers. Look for a metal box labeled as to its fire resistance, but don't expect it to be burglarproof as well.

CURRENT FILES

You might try an accordion file, with a pocket for each month of the year or for each category, for such items as bills to be paid and receipts for those recently paid, premium notices, bank statements, and your ongoing budget sheets. Other items to keep on hand: insurance policies, warranties, mortgage statements, credit card data, employment and health records, and a list of what's in your safe deposit box.

INACTIVE RECORDS

Anything over three years old, as a rule, belongs either with your permanent (but inactive) records or in the wastebasket. Your yearly net worth statements, tax returns for prior years, and the documentation for those returns can be tucked away in an attic or closet, out of the way yet accessible if you need them.

You can keep your papers wherever you like, but the key to organization is knowing where they are. So make up a list of exactly what you have. Key the list so that the location of every document will be clear. Whether it's in the upper-left-hand desk drawer in your bedroom, in the fireproof box in the basement, or in the safe deposit box at your local bank, you (or, when it comes to that, whoever is handling your affairs) will know exactly where everything is. You might end up with a list something like this:

INVENTORY OF VALUABLES

Bank books (**D**)
Safe deposit key (**D**)
Tax records (**A**)
Insurance policies (*****)
Savings bonds (**B**)
Appliance warranties (**K**)
Copy of will (*****)

KEY
D: desk drawer
A: accordion file, bedroom
B: bank vault
K: drawer next to sink, in kitchen
* fireproof box, bedroom closet

Make another list and itemize, by number, every insurance policy, credit card, and savings bond. Duplicate both lists; keep one copy at home and one in your safe deposit box.

KEY POINTS

- Identify your goals and objectives, and plan a course of action to meet those goals and objectives, and you'll take the essential first step toward successful money management.

- Use a budget to help adjust outgo to income, to track your spending, and to ensure that you use your money in the ways that matter most to you.

- Draw up a net worth statement each year to see if you're making progress toward your personal objectives.

- Organize your financial records.

PUTTING YOUR
MONEY TO WORK:
CASH MANAGEMENT

Checking Accounts

★ You're single, just out of school, with a brand-new job. Where should you open your new checking account? And should that account be an interest-earning NOW account?

★ As a two-income couple you divide the responsibility for household expenses. Should you, then, pay those expenses out of a single joint checking account? Or should you maintain separate individual accounts?

★ With children approaching the teen years you're stepping up your college savings program, using certificates of deposit at your neighborhood savings and loan. Is this the best place for this money?

Your personal financial plan will change over time to meet your changing needs. Wherever you are in life, however, whether you're currently building a nest egg to buy your first house or, mortgage payments finished, are looking ahead to retirement, there are three building blocks to your personal financial plan: managing your cash on hand, investing for capital growth, and extending your resources through judicious use of credit. Managing your cash comes first.

The basic tools of cash management are checking and savings accounts. Both are available at a variety of traditional financial institutions: commercial banks, savings and loan associations, mutual savings banks, and credit unions. Both, in somewhat different form, are also becoming available at other institutions.

Commercial banks are sometimes called full-service banks because, originally established to serve business, they offer an entire range of financial services. If, for instance, you need to transfer cash overseas, you may have to go to a commercial bank. If you want a financial institution to manage a trust, you may turn to a commercial bank.

Savings and loan associations and **mutual savings banks** (the "thrifts"), by contrast, have traditionally provided personal financial services: home mortgages, home improvement loans, college loans, money orders, and so on.

Credit unions are nonprofit cooperative institutions, organized by people who have a "common bond." That bond most often is a place of employment; it may also be a club or church or community group. Credit unions often pay more interest on deposits and charge less on loans than other institutions. Although credit unions are expanding their services— with credit cards and NOW accounts and Individual Retirement Accounts—many are small and may not have the funds to make home mortgages or other sizable loans.

These distinctions, particularly those between banks and thrifts, used to be sharp and clear. Banks were the only place to find checking accounts and credit cards and trust services. Thrifts were the place to go for home mortgages. Both offered savings accounts, but thrifts could pay slightly more in interest (in order to encourage the deposits that would then be available for home mortgages). Credit unions were a good place for an auto loan but were legally prohibited from making mortgage loans, offering revolving lines of credit, and paying interest on checking. Many of the restrictions have now been lifted and many of these distinctions, although not all, have blurred.

As brokerage houses, credit card issuers, and large retail establishments start to offer competing financial services, traditional financial institutions will change still more. Today's revolution in financial services may dramatically affect the way in which you manage your cash. Here's what's afoot:

Deregulation

In the aftermath of the Depression of the 1930s, banks and thrifts were subject to extensive regulation. That regulation has been firmly in place for decades, and only now, with the passing of the formidably titled Depository Institutions Deregulation and Monetary Control Act of 1980, is being modified. Among other things, the Monetary Control Act:

- Authorized banks and thrifts everywhere to offer interest-bearing checking (NOW) accounts.

- Permitted thrifts to write consumer loans, handle trusts, and issue credit cards.

- Scheduled a six-year phase-out, concluded in 1986, of interest ceilings and of the interest differential between banks and thrifts.

In addition, many savings and loan associations now have subsidiaries through which customers can buy and sell securities. More, spurred by competitive pressures, are expected to offer this service. And a form of interstate banking is growing apace with the spread of networks of automatic teller machines.

While deregulation can spark competition among financial institutions, deregulation does not always work in favor of the consumer. When 30-month "Small Saver" certificates, for instance, were subject to a federally imposed interest ceiling, most institutions offered the maximum allowable interest. When the ceiling was removed, a number of institutions offered less. As financial institutions have greater freedom to set their own rules, consumers need to be increasingly alert.

NON-BANK BANKS

Unregulated and sometimes seemingly unrelated industries, meanwhile, are crossing the border into banklike financial services. Some examples:

. . . Sears Roebuck and Co., long a major extender of consumer credit and a seller of insurance, has moved into stock brokerage and sales of real estate.

. . . Merrill Lynch Pierce Fenner & Smith, one of the country's largest brokerage firms, offers money market funds with check-writing privileges, debit cards, and personal loans; it also sells homes, insures mortgages, and helps executives move from one city to another.

These are just two examples of what some observers are calling the financial supermarket of the future, the place where you'll be able to do just about anything and everything connected with money: make deposits and withdrawals, write checks, take a loan or get a credit card, buy insurance or securities or a house.

But will you want to secure all these services under one roof? There are disadvantages as well as advantages:

- Right now, if you take a loan in a bank where you do your checking and saving, that bank can tap your account if you are delinquent on the loan. The bank can't do it if your savings account is elsewhere. What will happen if all your financial transactions are in one centralized location?

- Right now, too, some people are concerned about a loss of privacy on financial transactions. If your entire financial profile—where you live, what you've borrowed, who you've paid—is centrally located, are you in danger of a real invasion of privacy?

How to Decide Which Institution to Use

The key things to evaluate are services, cost, convenience, size, and stability.

SERVICE

Look, first, at the services offered. All institutions may be permitted to offer various services; not all institutions may choose to do so. What's the point of building your reputation as a good customer so that you can secure a college loan for your child if the place where you do your checking and saving doesn't choose to write college loans? Find out before you open your account what services are offered. The list will change from time to time, but the current list will give you a fairly good idea of where the institution stands in the competitive scheme of things.

Q. When I applied for a loan, the bank wanted me to authorize automatic deductions from my savings account to repay the loan. Must I do so?

A. No. You may arrange for automatic deductions if you find this a convenient way to repay the loan, but you don't have to do so. If you default on the loan, however, the bank can take the money from your checking or savings account in that bank.

COSTS

Costs count too. Financial institutions in general are pricing services realistically, to meet the increasing costs of doing business. (It isn't just rising costs in general; the Federal Reserve Board is now charging banks and thrifts, for example, for services that used to be free.) But the definition of "realistically" may vary; one institution may charge $5 to stop payment on a check, another may charge $15. Ask the institution for a schedule of charges. And ask how customers are notified when charges change.

CONVENIENCE

Convenience is also a factor, although too many people rate it first. The fact that the bank or thrift is located near your home or your workplace may not be as important as the speed and courtesy with which personnel respond to customers. Take a look, some lunchtime, at the length of lines and the way they are handled.

But accessibility is important. There may be little reason to stick with a bank after you've moved to another neighborhood. If you do, in fact, after it's no longer convenient to get there, you may find yourself holding on to checks longer than you should before depositing them.

SIZE

The size of the institution may make a difference. Large institutions may be able to offer more services; smaller ones may be more responsive to you as an individual, more willing to call you if a mistake is detected in your account rather than levying an automatic charge. But large banks can be human and small banks can offer extensive services. The only way to be sure is to ask.

STABILITY

The stability of the institution, more difficult to judge, also matters. Many banks and thrifts ran into a great deal of difficulty in the high-interest years of 1980–82. Locked into long-term low-interest mortgage loans on the incoming side and forced to pay then-current high yields on the outgoing side, many seemingly stable institutions foundered and had to be salvaged by merger with others. More recently, banks and thrifts have foundered under the weight of unwise commercial loans. For the customer, the key point here is federal insurance. Deposits in federally insured institutions, whether banks or thrifts or credit unions, are insured up to $100,000. For safety's sake, don't keep more than that in one account under one name.

In this era of serious questions about the stability of financial institutions, a look at your bank's "statement of condition" or, if it is publicly owned, its annual report to stockholders is a good idea. Richard E. Band of the newsletter *Personal Finance* suggests that you look specifically at the institution's liquidity (accessible funds preferably more than 50 percent of deposits) and capital strength (net worth 5 percent or more of assets).

Q. I have several accounts in a savings and loan: individual savings and checking, a Christmas Club, time deposits, and a retirement account. I also have a joint account with my wife and a trust account for my son. How much insurance do I have?

A. All of your individual accounts are insured by the Federal Savings and Loan Insurance Corporation (in a bank it would be the Federal Deposit Insurance Corporation) for a *total* of $100,000 (except Individual Retirement Accounts, which are separately insured up to $100,000); if your accounts add up to more than this, you might think about moving some of them to another institution. Your joint account and your trust account are each separately insured, because of their different form of ownership, to $100,000. This insurance, by the way, applies only to the closing of the institution, not to loss sustained in any other way.

Evaluating a Credit Union

Most of the criteria that apply to banks and thrifts may also be applied to credit unions. There are, however, some additional points to check before putting money into a particular credit union. The Credit Union National Association suggests:

- Make sure that the credit union is insured. Deposits in all federally chartered credit unions are insured, just as deposits in banks and thrifts are, up to $100,000. Most state-chartered credit unions are also insured. But several states do not require insurance.

- Ask members about the credit union's reputation. If you hear complaints about processing mistakes or bad service, the credit union may be inadequately managed. Small credit unions often save money by relying on volunteer labor; that labor may be more or less competent.

- Look at financial statements. The ratio of operating expenses to total income should not exceed 30 percent. And a hefty proportion—50 to as much as 80 percent—of members' deposits should be recirculated in the form of loans.

Types of Checking Accounts

Checking accounts are used to transfer funds. The money you should keep in your checking account, therefore, is money you plan to use in the very near future to make purchases or pay bills. Unless you have an interest-earning checking account (more on this in a moment) you'll be wasting money by keeping idle cash in a checking account. Any extra money, any money not immediately needed, should be earning interest.

There are several types of checking accounts:

Special accounts are for people who don't write many checks. You can keep as little as you like in this type of account, but you'll pay a per-check fee and often a monthly fee as well.

Regular accounts do not have per-check or monthly fees, but they do require that you keep a minimum balance, sometimes a sizable minimum balance, in the account.

Reserve or overdraft checking is an extension of regular checking to include a permanent line of credit; you can't bounce a check if you have overdraft checking because you will be automatically incurring a loan instead. You'll also automatically become liable for interest on the loan, because this form of checking account is actually an extension of credit (see Chapter 9).

NOW (Negotiated Order of Withdrawal) accounts are technically savings accounts on which funds can be drawn; the credit union equivalent is called a share draft account. Both actually function as interest-earning checking accounts. Although it's better to earn interest than to leave funds idle, NOW accounts are not necessarily the right answer for everyone. (So-called "Super-NOW" accounts, which were allowed to offer higher interest rates, have been eliminated. All interest-earning checking accounts are now simply NOW accounts.)

SHOULD YOU OPEN A NOW ACCOUNT?

Interest on checking, at first glance, sounds like a gift. But it's a gift with strings attached. NOW accounts are expensive to administer, and costs are being passed on to the consumer. Before you open a NOW account, therefore, you owe it to yourself to ask some hard questions:

- What minimum balance will you have to maintain to forestall service charges? Minimum balance requirements have been inching up since the first heady days when every financial institution was competing for NOW account customers. But it's still possible to find minimum balance requirements of $500 or less. (At some commercial banks, by contrast, the minimum balance requirement may be as much as $3,000—although some banks will count all of your accounts, including time deposits, toward that minimum.)
- Could you earn higher interest elsewhere on the minimum balance required? In simple interest terms (for ease of comparison), $1,000 in a NOW account at 5.25 percent would earn $52.50 for the year. The same $1,000 in a money market fund (see p. 79) at 8 percent would earn $80.
- What charges will the bank impose if the balance falls below the required minimum? Maintenance fees, when this happens, typically run $3 to $7 a month, although some institutions assess a per-check charge of 10¢ or 15¢ instead. Some do both. And some also stop paying interest if the balance falls below a designated amount.
- What interest rate is the institution offering? Some pay higher interest on accounts with larger balances. And some have "stair-step" rates so that differing amounts of interest are earned on money within a single account.
- How and when is the balance calculated? It will cost you more if your banker uses what is called a "minimum balance" requirement; in this case, charges will be imposed and/or interest will cease if the balance dips below the required minimum on any one day. You'll have a bit more flexibility if the bank goes by the "average monthly balance," because there won't be any charges unless the daily average balance for the entire month falls below the minimum.

Should you open a NOW account? If you customarily maintain a sizable balance in your checking account, the answer may be yes. If you don't keep much money in checking, you could wind up paying more in service charges than the interest your account will earn. Think about your own checking needs before you decide. Think about consolidating accounts, because, with deregulation, financial institutions are likely to pay higher rates of interest on larger accounts. And definitely shop around, comparing both yields and fees. Now that the federal government has stepped offstage, competing institutions may indeed compete.

Using a Checking Account

Whichever type of checking account you decide is right for you, there are some things you should know:

Writing Checks

Checks are the equivalent of cash. Unless they are written carefully and endorsed properly, they may be cashed for the wrong amount or by the wrong person.

When you write a check, use a pen (and not the variety with erasable ink). Start as far to the left as possible in writing the amount in words, and fill in any unused space with a line. Start right next to the $ sign in filling in the amount in numbers, and don't leave excessive space between numbers or someone could fill in some extra digits. Make a record of each check—its amount, date, and purpose—just as soon as you write it. (If you're in the habit of carrying loose checks, with no stub on which to make an entry, record the check on some piece of paper and then transfer the entry to your checkbook as soon as you return home.) If you make a mistake while writing a check, don't cross it out. Tear up the check. And be sure to write VOID across that space in your check register.

Keep your checks, canceled checks, and checkbook in a safe place and notify your bank if they are missing. A dishonest person could make good use of your account number and samples of your signature.

Endorsing Checks

An endorsement transfers ownership of the funds represented by the check. If you simply sign your name on the back of a check made out to you, anyone may cash it. If you place a restriction on the endorsement, however, the bank must honor the restriction. You might write "For deposit only" followed by your account number and signature (and should do so if you are depositing checks by mail); with this endorsement the check must be deposited to your account. Or, if you want to transfer the funds to someone else, you may write "Pay to the order of" and the person's name, followed by your own signature. That person may then, in turn, make the check payable to someone else by endorsing it appropriately but, whatever he or she does, your responsibility is at an end.

In any endorsement your name must be written, exactly as it appears on the check, across the left side of the back of the check. If the spelling is incorrect, write it the way it appears and then write it again, correctly, below.

Balancing Your Checkbook

Always balance your checkbook within a few days after receiving your monthly statement. If you catch an error (and financial institutions do make errors) it will be much easier to correct at the outset. Many institutions, in fact, ask customers to notify them of any errors within a specified time; errors can often be corrected later, but it becomes more difficult.

The last number on your statement should be the same as the number in your checkbook for that date. If it's not the same, there are three possible reasons:

- One or more checks, written by you earlier, have not yet been returned for payment.

- One or more deposits may not have been credited.

- You or the bank has made a mistake in arithmetic.

Any or all of these things should be easy to catch. Yet balancing a checkbook is a task that throws a lot of people for a loop. (I've known people to change banks rather than reconcile a hopelessly fudged-up checkbook.) Don't let it throw you. Just follow this step-by-step method:

1. Put your returned checks in sequence by number or by date (some banks now provide statements with checks in sequence).

2. Match the returned checks against those in your checkbook. Make a list of any checks still outstanding.

3. Subtract any outstanding checks from the balance shown on your statement.

4. Check off the deposits shown on the statement against those in your checkbook. Add any deposits made after the statement date to the balance shown on your statement.

5. The balance shown on your statement plus any additional deposits minus any outstanding checks should equal the current balance you have in

your checkbook. If it does not, check your arithmetic. And use a banker's trick if a stubborn checkbook won't balance: See if you can divide the disparity by nine. If you can, if your total is off by 45 or by 81 or by any other number divisible by nine, a simple transposition of numbers is at fault; somewhere along the way you wrote 123 when you meant to write 132 or made a similar transposition. If you can't balance your checkbook despite your best efforts, don't overlook the possibility that the bank may have made a mistake. After rechecking your arithmetic, report the error to the bank without delay.

BALANCING AN INTEREST-EARNING NOW ACCOUNT

Follow the same procedure described above. Then add any interest earned on your account and subtract any service charges. You're less likely to become overdrawn on a NOW account, since additional funds are deposited in your account in the form of interest. But don't count on that interest until it is actually credited to your account. Otherwise, if you let your account drop below the required minimum balance even for a day or two (depending on the policy of the institution, which you should know), you may be sadly surprised.

WHEN THE BANK KEEPS THE CANCELED CHECKS

Some banks and thrifts have stopped returning canceled checks. In a practice called *truncation,* or *check safekeeping,* the institution will keep canceled checks on file and supply you with copies you may need for such things as tax-return documentation. As a regular practice, instead of canceled checks, you get a very detailed monthly statement. Even without canceled checks to work with, however, you need to balance your checkbook. Without the checks themselves, it becomes more important than ever to keep accurate records of the checks you write. Some institutions will help in this regard by providing you with a checkbook which makes carbonless copies of checks as you write them. (So far, check safekeeping is optional and you can still get your checks returned if you want them. With some institutions, however, you'll pay a monthly fee for the privilege.)

When a Check Bounces

If, for some reason, you don't have enough money in your account to cover a check you've written, you'll face both embarrassment and a service charge from your bank. (You may even face a service charge if you deposit someone else's check and it bounces—a good reason for depositing checks promptly.) You can avoid the embarrassment, however, if you can get an agreement from your bank to notify you if it appears that a check will bounce. The bank can flag your record card so that any bank employee will know that you should be called. (This is one of the services to ask about when you open your account.)

You can avoid both embarrassment and service charges, however, if you (1) enter every check you write (and, on a joint account, get your partner to do so as well), (2) balance your account promptly each month so that you'll know your balance at all times, and (3) understand that we live in an electronic age and that it's no longer safe to write a check one day and deposit funds to cover it two days later—your check may, embarrassingly, clear in the meantime. It also helps if you understand the operating regulations banks impose (see below).

Q. My monthly mortgage payments include property tax and homeowner's insurance premiums, which my bank is supposed to pay as they come due. But it is consistently late in making the payments. I've received an overdue tax notice from my town, and my homeowner's insurance was actually allowed to expire. Is there anything I can do?

A. Sit down with an officer of the bank and discuss the problem. Offer to pay these bills yourself directly and send the bank proof of payment; this will reduce the institution's paperwork, so agreement may be quickly forthcoming. If not, however, and the bank continues to be negligent, contact the institution's president. If you still get nowhere, write to the appropriate regulatory agency. For a federally chartered savings and loan, write to Supervisory Agent, Federal Home Loan Bank Board, One World Trade Center, Floor 103, New York, NY 10048. For a state-chartered bank or savings and loan association, write to your state banking commission. For a federally chartered bank, write to the Federal Reserve Board.

Using Your Deposited Funds

You may think that once you've deposited funds to your account you can safely write checks on those funds. But you may or may not be right. Unless you live in a state which has restricted "check hold" times (or unless Congress has acted by now, and imposed federal rules), you may find your bank waiting at least a week for a deposited check to clear. During this time you can't write any checks on those deposited funds without running the risk of a bounce (technically, in this case, writing checks on uncollected funds, also subject to a charge). Ask, before you establish your account, what the bank's regulations are in this respect. Ask if other accounts or certificates of deposit you hold in the same institution may be used as collateral for uncleared deposits. If not, and if you need the funds available, try converting a check to cash before you deposit it—and tell the bank that you will be drawing against those funds.

Note: If you borrow a deposit slip to make a deposit, *cut out* any account number other than your own. You can't simply cross it out because the magnetic characters will be read by a computer and your money may be deposited to someone else's account.

Stopping a Check

A persuasive door-to-door salesman has talked you into buying an elaborate set of pots and pans. You've signed a contract, and given him a check. Now, after he's left, you've had second thoughts. What do you do?

The first thing you do is notify the company, in writing, that you've changed your mind about the purchase (consumer protection laws give you three days, after a purchase in your home, to change your mind and cancel the contract). The second thing you do, just to be on the safe side, is stop payment on your check. You do this by notifying your bank, first by telephone and then in writing, that you want the check stopped. With that notification the bank should refuse to release the funds if the check is presented for payment.

But the bank incurs expenses in stopping a check, and you can expect those expenses to be passed on to you. Most institutions charge $10 to $20. So take advantage of the stop-payment privilege if you've really made a mistake, but don't use it lightly. And do find out, when you open your account, what this charge will be.

Note: Be sure to ask how long a stop-payment order is effective. If the check has not come in during this period, you may want to renew the order. (Many banks will not honor a check more than 90 days old for payment, but some will. And some tellers make mistakes.)

Automatic Payroll Deposit and Telephone Transfer

You may, at most institutions, make arrangements for automatic deposit of payroll and Social Security checks. This can be a great convenience, and also an aid to regular deposits.

You may also, at many institutions, arrange by telephone to have funds transferred from your savings account to your checking account. This, too, can be a great convenience, since you can keep funds earning interest until they are needed. If you have a market rate account (see page 81) or have combined your savings and checking accounts into an interest-earning NOW account, this transfer privilege may, of course, be unnecessary.

Q. My employer uses a payroll deposit program under which my paycheck is automatically deposited in the bank he has designated. I prefer my own bank and do not feel I should have to pay a transfer or service fee to his bank. What can I do?

A. Direct deposit programs like this one were, until a couple of years ago, limited to the single institution in which they were established. Today, with 95 percent of the nation's banks linked to an automated clearinghouse through which funds can be transferred by wire, all you should have to do is go into your own bank and say you want to arrange automatic transfer from your employer's bank to your bank. There should be no charge for this service.

Joint Accounts

You and your spouse open a joint checking account so that you can pool your earnings and each write checks as necessary. You and your college-student son or daughter have a joint checking account so that you can handle banking chores at home while the child handles them at school. You and your elderly parent have a joint checking account so that you can manage your parent's affairs. You are single and so is your brother; you open a checking account together so that the money will automatically belong to the one who survives the other.

Are any or all of these joint accounts a good idea?

Joint accounts do offer convenience. But they also have some disadvantages:

- All the money in the account legally belongs to either one of the joint owners. Either one of you, therefore, can empty the account. Husbands and wives have done this to each other when a marriage turns sour. Children have done it to parents.

- Even when the relationship remains both joyous and honest, joint ownership may not always run smoothly. During your lifetime, you must be sure to enter every check you write. After death, the surviving co-owner may be temporarily short of funds because some states (not all) require that an account be frozen for a time when one co-owner dies. You may be able to gain access, but it may be difficult.

- Estate taxes pose the last hurdle. The Internal Revenue Service has always assumed that the total sum in a joint account belongs to the first to die. The total, accordingly, was counted in the valuation of the estate for estate tax purposes . . . *unless* the other co-owner could conclusively prove that the funds belonged to him or to her. This was true even on joint accounts held by husband and wife, until the passage of the 1981 Economic Recovery Tax Act. Now you and your spouse, in far more equitable treatment, will each be assumed to own half of any joint asset. But the old rules still hold for joint accounts with other people. If you have a joint account with a brother or a niece because you want that relative to have the money after your death without any estate taxes, it won't work. Keep the account to yourself and leave the money to your relative in your will.

Q. We have been married for four years and are both working. Should we pool our earnings in a single joint account? And what should we do when I stop working, as I plan to do next year, to have a baby?

A. Many marriages run smoothly with every penny merged in joint accounts. But it's a good idea, both psychologically and financially, to maintain separate accounts as well. With an individual account you won't be stuck if your spouse leaves or dies. More important, assuming that you live happily ever after, you'll retain a sense of independence—and the ability to buy him a gift without his knowing what it cost. You may also want to take care of your own personal expenses without explanation. Put aside some of your own earnings now, in a separate account. And when you stop working, arrange for enough household allowance to keep your separate account alive.

TIPS ON CHECKING

- As financial institutions compete for your dollars, you owe it to yourself to compare carefully. Look at service, costs, convenience, and stability.

- Open a checking account as soon as you have bills to pay on a regular basis; funnel all income and outgo through a checking account and you'll keep track of your cash flow.

- Don't keep much money in a checking account that does not pay interest, but don't open an interest-earning account unless you will earn enough to offset any fees you will pay.

- Keep accurate records and balance your checkbook promptly.

Savings Accounts, Time Deposits, and Other Bank Services

The passbook savings account has been the basis of American thrift for generations. Long before checking accounts became universally acceptable, savings accounts were widespread. Today, even when higher yields are available elsewhere, a great many people maintain some of their cash savings, if not all, in a savings account at a neighborhood bank or thrift. Parents pass the message on to children, who are encouraged to deposit both earnings and cash gifts in a savings account.

Q. My 11-year-old daughter never wants to put money in her savings account. She says, if she does, the money just "gets stuck." How can I encourage her to save?

A. Children have to learn how to spend before they can appreciate the wisdom of saving. They have to see what small amounts of money can do before they will understand that saving large amounts makes it possible to do more. Your daughter may be rebelling because her money really does get stuck. Do you ever let her take money out of the savings account? You should, because savings aren't meant to be a dead end. They're meant to be a useful tool. Take your daughter to the bank, if you haven't done so yet, and let her handle a transaction for herself. Give her a sense of participating in the banking process and she should be more interested.

Compound Interest

Your money grows in a savings account because interest is added to the principal on deposit on a regular basis. Interest is *compounded* when, at the end of each interest period, it is calculated on the sum of both principal and interest already in the account. This compounding is what makes the "effective annual yield" on a savings account greater than the stated rate of interest (see Table 1).

TABLE 1: The power of compound interest.

If you deposit $1,000 and add nothing more to it, this is what you'll have at various interest rates, compounded annually:

Years	6%	8%	10%	12%	14%
1	1,060	1,080	1,100	1,120	1,140
2	1,124	1,166	1,210	1,254	1,300
3	1,191	1,260	1,331	1,405	1,482
4	1,262	1,360	1,464	1,574	1,689
5	1,338	1,469	1,611	1,762	1,925
6	1,419	1,587	1,772	1,974	2,195
7	1,504	1,714	1,949	2,211	2,502
8	1,594	1,851	2,144	2,476	2,853
9	1,689	1,999	2,358	2,773	3,252
10	1,791	2,159	2,594	3,106	3,707

The power of compound interest alone will just about double your money in nine years at 8 percent, compounded annually. Even when interest rates were much lower, the power of compound interest could be impressive. Benjamin Franklin, according to the American Bankers Association, left $5,000 to the residents of Boston in 1791, with the understanding that it should be allowed to accumulate for a hundred years. By 1891 the $5,000 had grown to $322,000. A school was built, and $92,000 was set aside for a second hundred years of growth. In 1960, this second century fund had reached $1,400,000. As Franklin put it, in anticipation: "Money makes money and the money that money makes makes more money."

If you want to determine how long it will take your money to double at various rates of interest, use what bankers call the Rule of 72. Divide the quoted rate of return into 72 and you'll have the number of years required to double your money at that rate of interest, assuming that interest is compounded annually (see Table 2). When interest is compounded more frequently, as it often is, your money will double faster.

Interest Rates

Interest rates on savings accounts had long been regulated by law, but all federally imposed interest rate ceilings have now been removed. The removal of regulatory rate ceilings, however, does not necessarily mean

TABLE 2: The Rule of 72.

If you divide 72 by the rate of interest on your savings, you'll know how long it will take to double your money if interest is compounded annually:

Rate of interest	Years it takes to double money	Rate of interest	Years it takes to double money
8%	$72 \div 8 = 9.0$ years	14%	$72 \div 14 = 5.1$ years
9	$72 \div 9 = 8.0$	15	$72 \div 15 = 4.8$
10	$72 \div 10 = 7.2$	16	$72 \div 16 = 4.5$
11	$72 \div 11 = 6.5$	17	$72 \div 17 = 4.2$
12	$72 \div 12 = 6.0$	18	$72 \div 18 = 4.0$
13	$72 \div 13 = 5.5$	19	$72 \div 19 = 3.8$

an increase in the interest rates that financial institutions will pay. All it means is that they may set their own rates. Some, eager to attract and keep customers, will raise rates. Others will not. Some, as interest rates decline to new lows, may drop interest rates below the old regulated levels.

When rates are going up, some may raise rates on new accounts but not on existing ones; if this happens to you, close your old account and open a new one. Some customers don't think it's worth the bother to switch from a low-paying institution to one more in tune with the times. Such customers may be right if, in return, they receive other services, such as free checking. Otherwise, such laziness makes little sense. You work hard for your money; you should keep your money working hard for you.

Some institutions pay a higher rate on statement savings, in order to encourage their use (they cost less to administer), than on passbook accounts. With a statement account you don't have a passbook. Instead you receive a monthly computerized record of deposits, withdrawals, and interest payments, much like a checking account statement. Look for an institution that pays a competitive rate, whichever kind of account you prefer.

FINDING THE BEST RATE

We've seen that all savings accounts are not equal. But even those that appear to be equal may not be. Finding the best interest rate for your savings account funds, in short, is not simply a matter of going to the institution with the highest advertised rate. You have to dig a little deeper:

■ Penalties and service fees can reduce your yield. Some banks impose service charges for low-balance accounts; others allow only one free withdrawal from a small savings account in a given month, then charge a fee for each withdrawal. Some banks charge a fee if an account is closed before it's been open for six months or a year.

■ The more often interest is compounded, the more money you earn. Daily compounding pays more than quarterly compounding, and quarterly compounding pays more than annual compounding. Here's the difference: A 5.25 percent savings account, compounded annually, yields 5.25 percent. The same account, compounded daily, yields 5.47 percent. (However, even when a bank compounds interest on a daily basis it may add the interest to your account on a quarterly basis. If you close out such an account in mid-quarter, you'll lose interest for the entire quarter. You'll do best when interest is calculated from day of deposit to day of withdrawal.)

■ You will earn more if interest is computed on all the money you keep in the account rather than on just the lowest balance you have in the account during the interest period. There are actually four methods an institution might use in determining the balance in your account:

Low balance, as its name implies, credits interest only on the lowest balance in your account during the quarter.

FIFO—first-in, first-out—credits interest from the day of deposit to the end of the interest period but charges withdrawals to either the opening balance or the first deposit.

LIFO—last-in, first-out—deducts each withdrawal from the most recent deposit and then calculates the interest, so that earlier deposits accrue interest longer.

Day of deposit to day of withdrawal lets you earn interest on the exact amount in your account each day.

The following example shows the difference:

Assume that you have a passbook account at 5 percent a year with interest compounded and credited quarterly. You begin the year with a $5,000 balance, withdraw $4,000 on February 1, deposit $10,000 on March 1, and withdraw $1,000 on March 31. Table 3, from a *Consumers Guide to Banking* prepared by the Committee on Banking, Housing and Urban Affairs of the United States Senate, shows what happens under each method of computation.

Losing Your Savings

The power of compound interest works for you only as long as you keep your savings account active. You don't have to make constant transactions, but you do have to do *something* every couple of years—make a deposit or withdrawal, present your passbook to the bank or thrift to have interest credited, simply write a letter saying that you are alive and well—or you may well find your name on one of those lengthy published lists of "lost" depositors. If your name does appear on one of those lists

TABLE 3: How interest earned can vary when the balance in a savings account is computed by different methods.

	Deposits	Withdrawals	Balance
Jan. 1			$5,000
Feb. 1		4,000	1,000
Mar. 1	10,000		11,000
Mar. 31		1,000	10,000

Computation method	Interest earned on account	Amount of interest
Low balance	$1,000 for 1 quarter (1,000 × 5% ÷ 4) =	$12.50
FIFO	$10,000 for 1 month (10,000 × 5% ÷ 12) =	41.66
LIFO	$1,000 for 1 quarter (1,000 × 5% ÷ 4) =	12.50
	$9,000 for 1 month (9,000 × 5% ÷ 12) =	37.50
	TOTAL	50.00
Day of deposit to day of withdrawal	$5,000 for 1 month (5,000 × 5% ÷ 12) =	20.83
	$1,000 for 1 month (1,000 × 5% ÷ 12) =	4.16
	$11,000 for 1 month (11,000 × 5% ÷ 12) =	45.83
	TOTAL	70.82

after a period of inactivity in your account (the precise period varies from state to state, but it can be as short as a couple of years) and if you fail to respond, your money will be turned over to the state under the "law of escheat."

It isn't just vagabonds who can lose their property this way. According to reports in late 1979, the dormant accounts of two movie stars and the then governor of California had been turned over to the state. Interested observers thought that these particular depositors should have been easy to find.

Should you be inattentive enough to lose an account this way, you can still reclaim your property from the state. But you will need documentary proof of your ownership. And interest stops accumulating, in most states, at the point at which the property is transferred to the state. Don't let this happen to your hard-earned savings.

Q. When my husband was a little boy his uncle opened a savings account for him. The bank book never turned up after his uncle's death, and we don't even know the name of the bank. Is there any way we can trace the account? And could my husband still get whatever money is in the account?

A. Write to the Controller's Office (usually in the state capital) of the state in which the account was located (probably the state where the uncle lived at the time). Give the name and address of the person who opened the account, your husband's name, and the year in which you think the account was opened. If the state can locate the account (states keep permanent records and will make every effort to do so) your husband can still claim the funds. Interest, however, probably stopped accruing when the state took over.

There's another penalty for the inattentive. Long before funds are turned over to the state, some banks and thrifts stop paying interest on dormant accounts. Others levy service charges. (There seem to be service charges these days for too much activity and for too little. I wonder if anyone has identified how much banking is just right?) Congressional hearings in 1980 focused attention on this practice and evoked a considerable protest from consumer advocates. A star witness was a 12-year-old Minnesota boy whose entire $5 account had been wiped out by service charges; the boy and his parents were never told of this particular bank practice. Moral: Pay attention to your bank accounts, and keep them active.

Bank Failure

Until the 1930s, if a bank or savings institution failed its depositors would lose some or all of their money, but for more than half a century individual banks and thrifts have protected their depositors by one form or another of deposit insurance. There's federal insurance on banks from the Federal Deposit Insurance Corporation (FDIC), on savings institutions from the Federal Savings and Loan Insurance Corporation (FSLIC), and on credit unions from the National Credit Union Share Insurance Fund. All insure deposits up to $100,000 in any one person's name; you may have several accounts in the same institution, each insured, if the accounts are in different forms (such as a joint account and an IRA). All are backed by the U.S. government and all are safe. State insurance plans and private deposit insurance, carried by some institutions, are a bit riskier in an era of institutional instability.

Special-Purpose Accounts

In addition to regular savings accounts, banks and thrift institutions offer accounts for systematic saving, trust and custodial accounts, and various high-earnings accounts. These are described below; see Chapter 5 for still other types, based on the money market.

Club Accounts

Many banks and thrifts offer Christmas/Hanukah Clubs; many also offer Vacation Clubs or other special-purpose savings accounts. For years such accounts paid no interest. Many people used them, nonetheless, for the week-by-week saving they encouraged. Today club accounts usually do pay interest, although the interest may be less than that on a regular savings account.

If you feel that you need the discipline of a regular coupon book to make you save, by all means use one of these accounts. But keep in mind that you can encourage yourself to save in other ways as well. You might try automatic payroll deductions. You might even try a "coupon book" of your own devising; just put a savings account deposit slip in with the bills you pay and write out a deposit every time you pay your bills. You'll be surprised how the savings add up.

Trust Accounts

Savings accounts may also be opened by you "in trust for" someone else, such as a minor child. You control the account during your lifetime (and pay any income taxes due on the interest); the proceeds are payable directly to your beneficiary upon your death. Since you control the account, you may change that beneficiary at any time. You may also close the account.

Custodial Accounts

A custodial account is also a means of transferring your assets to someone else, but without the same degree of flexibility. Once you set up a custodial account, the funds in that account legally belong to the person named. Interest earned on the account is taxable to that person—except that investment earnings over $1,000, in the account of a child under age 14, are taxed at the parent's rate.

You might, for instance, establish a custodial account for a child's college funds (see Chapter 20) or to help support an elderly parent. As custodian, you have access to the account and can determine how it is to be invested (you might, for instance, want a higher-interest time deposit instead of passbook savings), but you won't be able to withdraw the funds except to use for the child's or parent's benefit.

If you serve as the custodian on funds that you give, the account will be included in your estate—and possibly subject to estate tax—if you die before your parent or before your child reaches legal age. A way around this: Name a trusted relative as custodian, then proceed as before.

Time Deposits

Time deposits (TDs) or certificates of deposit (CDs) are another form of savings account offered by traditional financial institutions. There is a wide variety available, in intervals from a single week to many years and in amounts from $100 to $10,000 and more.

The universal ingredient of these accounts is your commitment to leave your money on deposit with the institution for a fixed period of time in exchange for a rate of interest which is often higher than that paid on regular savings. In early 1982, when the maximum interest rate on regular savings accounts was still 5.5 percent, some time deposits were paying over 14 percent. In 1986, rates are lower, but it's not surprising that these accounts are very attractive to many people.

There are things to know, however, before you buy:

- The interest rate on these accounts is fixed for the life of the certificate. If interest rates are coming down, that's a good time to lock in a higher yield. If, however, interest rates are continuing to climb, you might be better off with your money in a money market fund or account.

- Maximum yield is achieved when interest is compounded. If it's not, and you want the particular time deposit anyway, see if you can either withdraw the interest periodically or have it automatically transferred to a regular savings account, where it will compound.

- Interest rates vary considerably, and you may find the best rate in another city. Long-distance banking can make sense on a time deposit, but you should be sure that the institution is covered by federal deposit insurance.

- You can usually withdraw your money before the maturity date, but only with a penalty. The specific penalty depends on rules set by the individual institution. Don't buy a certificate without understanding the rules on early withdrawal. Don't buy one with money you know you're going to need. And don't buy one at an institution that won't permit withdrawal even with a penalty.

Q. Several years ago I deposited $1,000 in an 8-year certificate that was paying 8 percent. Then interest rates went up a lot. But the thought of all the penalties for early withdrawal kept me from cashing in the certificate early and buying one at a higher rate. Would I have come out ahead if I had traded? Or should I have stayed put?

A. Always base this kind of decision on the penalty your bank will impose, the proceeds from the early redemption, the break-even point with the new certificate, and your potential gain—a calculation your bank may even help you to do. In general, if a certificate still has more than half its length to run, the odds are that it will be worthwhile to make the switch. But find out exactly what penalty your bank will charge on early redemption (assuming that it will let you redeem the certificate early). And you do have to do the arithmetic.

■ Institutions have different procedures when maturity dates roll around. Most, but not all, will notify you in advance. Some will automatically roll the account over into a new time deposit of equal length unless you notify them within a specified time (often ten days) that you want the funds. Find out which procedure your bank follows. And keep a record of maturity dates.

Repurchase Agreements

As part of a competitive push to attract deposits, some banks and thrifts offer "money funds" (they go by different names at different institutions) to the small investor. These funds are actually repurchase agreements or "repos." If you buy a repo you are technically making a loan to the institution, with its promise to repay backed by a portfolio of U.S. government or government-agency obligations. Repos may be purchased for as little as $1,000, with repayment date set anywhere from 7 to about 89 days after purchase. There usually are no penalties for early withdrawal; if a better deal comes along you're able to take it. But (there's always a but) there are some disadvantages:

■ Unlike time deposits and other traditional vehicles offered by banks and thrifts, repurchase agreements are not federally insured.

■ Should the institution run into financial trouble, the underlying obligations would be sold in order to repay investors. The value of those securities fluctuates, and it is possible that you could sustain a loss.

With the introduction of insured market rate accounts repos are no longer widely available, but they are still being offered by some institutions. Sometimes, in fact, they are offered as part of a broad package of financial services.

Other Bank Services

Both banks and thrifts offer a great many services beyond checking and savings accounts. As deregulation takes hold, and financial institutions move into such customer service areas as stock brokerage, the service smorgasbord will become still more extensive. Right now, however, you can find all or most of the services discussed below at your neighborhood bank or thrift.

Loans

One of the reasons it makes good sense to do most of your banking in one place is to establish a reputation as a good customer—a reputation that can help you secure a loan.

Banks and thrifts offer many types of loans. There are those dedicated to a particular purpose: a mortgage, a home improvement loan, an automobile loan, a college loan. Most of these are secured loans—the mortgage is backed by the house, the auto loan by the car. But you can also get personal or unsecured loans at a bank or thrift. Details will be found in Chapter 9, on credit.

Always consider the value of your savings as collateral for a loan before taking out another form of loan. If, for instance, you need to withdraw a substantial amount shortly before interest will be credited to your account, you can take a passbook loan for that amount and come out ahead.

Bank Cards

Bank cards, such as Visa and MasterCard, are nationally available and issued by both banks and thrifts. You don't have to have an account at a particular institution in order to get a bank credit card, but it sometimes helps, especially if you are establishing a credit record for the first time. Details on bank credit cards will also be found in Chapter 9.

Safe Deposit Boxes

Boxes of various sizes may be rented for the safekeeping of valuables. Rates are moderate and may, if the box is used to store items that produce taxable income (such as securities), be tax-deductible. Securely located in the institution's vault, safe deposit boxes are accessible only to the person whose signature is on file and who has the key necessary to open the box. It takes two keys to open each box, one retained by the vault attendant and the other by the box owner. Neither will work alone.

What should be kept in a safe deposit box? A good rule of thumb is to keep valuable items (seldom-worn jewelry, securities, etc.) and difficult-to-replace items (birth and marriage certificates, the deed to your house, etc.) in a box. An equally good rule is *not* to keep items that will be needed right after the safe-renter's death (the original of the person's will, life insurance policies, a cemetery deed or burial instructions) in that person's safe deposit box. The box will probably be sealed at the death of its owner and, although it may be opened to remove documents such as these, you may have to get a court order to do so. Laws vary from state to state, so check the rules before you rent your safe deposit box.

Check the rules, too, before you rent a box jointly, even with your spouse. In many states the box will be sealed upon the death of the first co-owner, until the tax authorities are satisfied. A better idea: Rent the box in one partner's name, with the other named as deputy with permission to enter. You'll have equal access, but you'll avoid the possible complications of joint ownership.

Q. Recent news of a vault break-in, where the contents of many safe deposit boxes were stolen, made me wonder: How safe are these boxes? Is the bank responsible if a theft does take place?

A. A safe deposit box in a bank vault is undoubtedly the safest place for your important documents and valuable possessions. But break-ins do occasionally occur. A few banks carry special insurance against this risk, but most don't; they are not responsible for a loss—as the small print on the safe deposit agreement will tell you. Your own homeowner's policy will cover loss up to its limits (such as $1,000 for jewelry) just as if the loss took place at your home. If you want additional coverage, consult your insurance agent; you may be able to purchase insurance specifically for the contents of your safe deposit box.

Traveler's Checks

Many banks, as a convenience to customers, sell traveler's checks. When you buy traveler's checks, usually for a nominal fee of $1 per $100 of checks (although some banks offer traveler's checks free to customers while others have occasional special promotions during which the checks are free), you sign each one in the presence of the seller. Then, when you use each check, you sign it again so that the two signatures can be compared. Traveler's checks are a convenient and safe way to carry currency when you travel.

But there's little point in keeping extra traveler's checks on hand after you return home. You've paid for them, after all, so the only beneficiary of your failure to use them is the issuing company.

Certified Checks

A certified check is a personal check stamped "Certified" by your bank after funds are set aside from your account to cover the amount. You will probably have to pay a service charge to secure this guarantee, but a certified check may be required, for instance, when you take title to a house.

Cashier's Checks

A cashier's check is a similar guarantee of payment, useful if you don't have a checking account. In this case you pay the bank and it then makes payment out of its own funds. When you purchase this service, you specify the person or company to whom the check is to be made out. And you should keep a carbon or stub for your records.

Q. My daughter moved to another state and, on my suggestion, secured a cashier's check to open her new bank account. We both thought that doing it this way would enable her to write checks right away. Instead, her checks bounced. What went wrong?

A. When a new account is opened with a certified or cashier's check (sometimes even with cash), many banks insist on waiting a week or so to make sure both the check and the depositor are legitimate. To secure immediate access to funds in a new location, do one of three things: Buy enough traveler's checks, before you move, to cover immediate needs and to open a new account; ask your current bank to wire fund's directly to the new bank; or use your current bank's cash machine in your new town. In any case, keep your present account in force until all outstanding checks have cleared. Then you can have the balance wired to your new bank and credited to your account.

Money Orders

Money orders are a means of transferring small sums of money without using either cash or a personal check. Like a check, the money order shows the name of the purchaser, the name of the person who is to receive the payment, and the amount to be paid. You buy a money order by paying the issuing bank the face amount plus a small fee.

United States Savings Bonds

Banks and thrifts sell and redeem U.S. Savings Bonds. These bonds (also often available through regular payroll deductions) offer a systematic way of saving small amounts. The interest on Series EE bonds accumulates and is paid at redemption; the interest rate has been raised over the years and is currently a variable yield tied to an index of 5-year Treasury bonds. The interest on Series HH bonds, a fixed-income bond which is often used for retirement income, is payable semiannually by check.

Other investments may earn more but you may find U.S. Savings Bonds, especially the popular EE series, a convenient and secure way to invest. If you are interested in Series EE bonds, these are the things you should know:

- Series EE bonds are now issued at a minimum purchase price of $25; this bond is worth $50 at maturity.

- Although bonds are designed as a long-term investment, you are not locked in. Bonds may be redeemed at any time after six months from issue date, although the interest rate will be lower.

- The bonds are exempt from state and local income taxes; if you live in a high-tax state, this could add appreciably to your yield.

- The earned interest is subject to federal income tax, but the tax on EE bonds may be deferred, if you choose to do so, until you redeem the bonds. *Note:* If you are buying bonds for a child, it may be wise to declare the tax right from the beginning. Buy the bonds in the child's name. Then file a federal income tax form on behalf of the youngster in the first year (keep the form until the bonds are redeemed); there will be no tax due unless the child has other income, but you will establish the intent to pay the tax and no further forms need be filed. If your child already owns bonds on which no tax form has ever been filed, you may file a form now and pay the tax on the interest earned up to this point. It's worth doing before your youngster leaves school for full-time employment, and a higher tax bracket.

- Although Series EE bonds are issued with a maturity date, the date on which full interest becomes payable, maturity dates have usually been extended. The oldest bonds, E bonds issued during World War II, paid interest for a total of forty years. If you have older bonds which no longer earn interest, cash them in—or swap them for HH bonds and defer paying tax on the accrued interest.

- You may buy Series EE bonds as an individual, as an individual with a named beneficiary, or as a co-owner. If you have either a beneficiary or a co-owner, then the bonds will not be part of your estate for probate purposes; they will still be counted, however, in calculating whether estate tax is due.

Q. My late father bought a number of U.S. Savings Bonds in both our names. Is the value taxable as part of his estate? Or do the bonds simply belong to me, with no estate tax due?

A. You automatically became the sole owner of the bonds upon your father's death. You may then keep the bonds as they are, have them reissued in your name alone or with another co-owner or beneficiary, or cash them in immediately. Whatever you choose to do, the value of the bonds (their redemption value on the date of his death) is included in your father's gross estate, and estate taxes may be due. Income taxes are something else. The income tax liability on all the interest the bonds ever earned will pass to you, and will be payable when you redeem the bonds, unless the executor of your father's estate chooses to pay the tax due on the interest earned until his death. If this is done, then you will owe income tax only on the interest earned from the date of your father's death until you redeem the bonds.

- Bonds should be kept in a safe place, such as a safe deposit box. And you should keep a written record of the bonds you own. If you lose a bond, however, you may be able to secure a replacement. Write to the Bureau of the Public Debt, 200 Third St., Parkersburg, WV 26101. The more information you can supply—the denomination of the missing bond or bonds, the year of purchase, etc.—the faster you will receive a reply.

Life Insurance

Over-the-counter life insurance (Savings Bank Life or SBLI), frequently less expensive than comparable insurance available elsewhere, has been sold in mutual savings banks in Massachusetts, New York, and Connecticut for many years. Now another plan, Savers Life Insurance, is being offered through savings and loan associations across the country. See Chapter 21 for details.

Retirement Plans

You may set up a retirement plan for yourself at your bank or thrift or credit union via an Individual Retirement Account if you are eligible (see Chapter 25), or if you are self-employed, you may open a Keogh Plan. These tax-deferred accounts may take almost any form, including time deposits.

A great many financial institutions, including insurance companies and brokerage firms and mutual funds, are vying for your retirement dollars. Shop around to determine which plan is best for you (see Chapter 25 for details), but don't overlook your neighborhood bank or thrift as you do.

KEY POINTS

- With nonregulated rates of interest being paid by financial institutions, you have more choice than ever when it comes to making your savings grow.
- Small amounts of extra cash still belong in a regular savings account, earning interest but accessible if needed.
- Larger amounts of cash should be put in a market-rate account, either in a bank or thrift or a money market mutual fund.
- Special-purpose accounts, such as Christmas Clubs or custodial accounts, can help you put money aside for specific purposes.

- Time deposits, with set maturity dates, allow you to lock in a fixed rate of return, a good maneuver when interest rates in general are falling and when you're sure you won't need the money before the maturity date.

- Other bank services—from consumer loans to safe deposit boxes to U.S. Savings Bonds—may fit into your financial plan at one time or another.

A New Era
in Banking

Automation has enabled financial institutions to expand their services in a big way. Many of these developments are good for consumers; others have hidden pitfalls. Here's a sampling of what's available and what you should know:

Automatic Teller Machines (ATMs)

Perhaps the most visible symbol of the electronic age, these teller machines stand on street corners, in office-building lobbies, and in supermarkets across the United States.

To use an ATM you must have a card and a personal identification number, both issued by your bank or thrift. You can use the card, together with the code number, to make a deposit, to transfer funds from one account to another, or to make a cash withdrawal. If you need cash at an hour when banks are closed, the ATM can be particularly convenient.

CAUTION IS REQUIRED

But you must be careful in using an ATM:

- Select an identification number that you can easily remember (so you won't have to write it down anywhere) but one that other people won't guess. A favorite aunt's birthdate might be a good choice. Don't share the number, or someone else might be able to tap your account. Don't even let anyone look over your shoulder while you're using the machine. Be unfriendly, if necessary, but insist on privacy.

- Be doubly sure to enter every single transaction in your checkbook. Keep an accurate running tally, along with the machine-issued transaction records (be sure they're accurate before you leave the machine), and reconcile your statement promptly. Report any errors to the bank without delay.

- Notify the bank or thrift immediately if your card is lost or stolen. Federal rules limit your liability to $50 as long as you notify the bank within two business days after you learn of the loss or theft; after this two-day period, your liability escalates sharply.

When automatic teller machines were new, they malfunctioned fairly often. When they were first introduced, too, they were particularly vulnerable to crime. Today both mechanical and security aspects have been greatly improved. Nonetheless, you should be careful. If the machine is in a locked area, don't be polite and hold the door open for others; it's locked for a reason. If you make a cash deposit at a machine and the machine malfunctions, it may be virtually impossible to trace the transaction and get proper credit; make deposits by check at the machine and save cash deposits for a trip to the bank.

Paying Bills by Telephone

Over 300 banks and thrifts in the United States have some form of automatic bill-paying available to their customers. In one form, not strictly involving the telephone, you can give your bank a list of regular payments to be made on a monthly basis. Or, using the telephone, you either (1) speak to an operator and identify yourself with a personal identification number or (2) tap a code directly from a touch-tone telephone into the bank's computer. Either way, the bank will then pay the bills you have authorized.

If you choose to pay bills this way, you won't get back your canceled checks but you will get a detailed descriptive statement that spells out whom you paid and when, in the order in which you authorized payment. If your bill-paying is from a NOW or regular savings account, moreover, you'll earn interest on your money until the bills are paid. You also, of course, do away with the tedious task of writing checks.

Automatic bill-paying isn't usually free. Typical charges call for a per-item fee of 10¢ or 15¢ and/or a minimum balance of $250 to $300. Compare this to the cost of first-class postage if you would otherwise pay your bills by mail.

Some people are fearful of telephone bill-paying, fearful that they will lose control of their accounts. But specific authorization for each bill, plus a personal customer code, keeps you in charge.

But there are still some problems to be resolved before automatic bill-paying is totally worry-free. Problem number one: Because bill-paying by telephone entails different procedures—you're not returning a bill stub with a check—some businesses find it expensive to process. Some even refuse to do so. Some banks, moreover, will make automatic payments only to companies on a predetermined list and not, for instance, to out-of-state companies. So you won't be able to pay all your bills by telephone just yet, even if you want to do so; you'll still have to use your checkbook. Problem number two: The process is not yet fully automatic, and your bank may simply write a check and mail it for you. Be sure you authorize payment far enough in advance of the due date so that you don't incur interest charges when the bank's check is slow to arrive.

Banking at Home

Paying bills by telephone is, of course, banking at home. But the use of video screens takes the process a step further.

At its best, this use of computers encompasses more than just banking. At most banks with the service, customers can authorize payment of bills, check the balance in a checking or savings account, or see how much credit is available on a Visa card—all by dialing the bank's computer and getting a visual display on a home television screen or monitor. Customers of Bank One in Columbus, Ohio, can also use the system to find out what's doing in Columbus or to look up encyclopedia information, while customers of Chase Manhattan Bank in New York City can call up weekly summaries of tax-related news. Most computer banking services cost several dollars a month; they may not be worthwhile unless the service matches your banking needs.

Debit Cards

The traditional credit card enables you to make purchases, be billed for them later, and pay for them still later. The marvel of electronic funds transfer, however, makes it possible to pay for purchases instantly with a debit card used to draw funds from your bank account. (Until more merchants have the electronic technology, however, the card is used to authorize a transfer of funds; the transfer itself is not quite instant.)

The debit card is, in fact, a substitute for a check. It provides access to your account. Unlike a check, however, it may be accepted without a hassle in places where you are a stranger. Debit cards (occasionally called deposit access cards) are issued by the major credit card companies (Visa and MasterCard) and may be acquired from your local bank or thrift. A monthly or annual fee may be charged.

While a debit card has some advantages for people who don't like credit (you don't "borrow" and there's no bill at the end of the month) and for people who travel a great deal, it does rob you of the "float"— that interval between a purchase by check or by credit card and the actual transfer of funds from your account to pay for the purchase. The float on a check may be just a few days. On credit card purchases it may be as long as two months. Either way, during the interval your money is working for you.

If you do use a debit card, remember to keep a written record of your transactions. Use of the card is equivalent to writing a check, but without a checkbook entry.

A debit card, in another sense, is like cash. If you buy something with a credit card and it proves defective, you can withhold payment until the matter is set to rights. If the merchant has already been paid, you've lost a negotiating edge.

The Money Market as a Tool of Cash Management

Although the basic tools of cash management for most people are still savings and checking accounts, no discussion of cash management in the 1980s would be complete without a description of the money market.

The money market has been around for a long time. It's the highly charged area of high finance where corporations invest. It's called the money market because the investments are in money: in government obligations, corporate debt, and other high-yielding, short-term, and liquid investments. Individuals could always invest in the money market too, but only with a minimum sum of $100,000, more than most of us have.

Now, in the last few years, the money market has become accessible to ordinary mortals. One step was the money market certificate (MMC) at banks and thrifts, a 6-month certificate tied to the rate on Treasury bills. Time deposits (of any length) are no longer tied to any specific index, but interest rates do change and can be charted alongside money market rates. Time deposits, as noted, require locking up your funds for a fixed period of time. A better bet for most people, especially when interest rates are either static or moving upward, is either the money market mutual fund or its new cousin, the insured money market deposit account. In both, your money is always accessible. There are no fixed terms for deposit and therefore no penalties for "early" withdrawal. But there are differences. Let's take a closer look at money market mutual funds and money market deposit accounts.

Money Market Mutual Funds

A money market fund is a mutual fund that invests in the money market. Mutual funds (see p. 107) are professionally managed investment pools; they can invest in anything: stocks, bonds, commodity options, gold, etc. A money market fund invests in money, in large-denomination short-term securities otherwise available only to big investors. It affords small investors, by pooling their funds, the chance to get in on the high returns previously available only to the big players. It took people a little while to catch on, but money market funds, in a few short years, have become the biggest phenomenon to come down the cash management pike. With returns averaging about 11 percent from 1981 to 1985, it's little wonder that assets in money market funds jumped from about $4 billion in 1977 to some $208 billion in 1985. Rates dropped sharply in 1986, but money market funds are still widely used.

Money market funds have definite advantages when it comes to cash management:

- Most money market funds are "no-load" funds; they have no sales charge or commission, just a small built-in administrative fee.

- Most money market funds offer check-writing privileges, although in many cases a check must be written for at least $500. That can include your mortgage, taxes, insurance bills, tuition . . . and a monthly payment to your checking account to take care of smaller bills. When you write a check on a money market fund, you earn full interest until that check clears. When the interest rate is well above savings account rates, as it has been, that can add a pretty penny to the family treasury—and give you a chance to keep pace with inflation.

- The exact return on a money market fund is never guaranteed. But the rate is reported in the newspapers, generally on a weekly basis. When the rates go below your expectations, you can pull out without penalty.

- Many money market funds are part of a "family" of funds, with stock and bond funds, growth and income funds, managed by the same company. Most such families have telephone-switching privileges, so that if interest rates come down and you want to move some or all of your funds out of the money market and into, for instance, a stock fund, all it takes is a phone call.

- Money market funds, unlike money market deposit accounts, are generally not insured. Most observers, however, feel that most funds are safe. If you're extra-cautious, in any case, you can put your cash in a money fund that invests only in US government obligations. If such a fund goes under, it will do so only with the country itself.

SELECTING A MONEY MARKET MUTUAL FUND

Money market funds are not all alike. You'll want to evaluate the minimum required initial deposit and subsequent deposits, the minimum amount for which checks may be written, the accessibility of information via toll-free telephone lines. Risk is also important. Look at the following factors before you decide which fund is for you:

- The composition of the fund's portfolio. While most funds invest in the same things—Treasury bills and notes, commercial paper, banker's acceptances, certificates of deposit, repurchase agreements, and guaranteed loans—some of these investments are riskier than others. Safest are government securities; riskiest are deposits in foreign currencies. Unless a fund is invested entirely in U.S. government issues, diversification is important. You'll find the fund's composition in its prospectus; the precise composition varies from day to day, but this will indicate the fund management's investment philosophy.

- Maturity of the fund's holdings. Some stick to 30 days, others go out to 60 days or more. When interest rates are dropping, longer maturities preserve higher yields. When rates are rising, shorter maturities take full advantage of the upward trend. In general, a steady cash turnover means that even heavy redemptions won't cause an excessive drain on the fund. Maturities are found both in the prospectus and in newspaper fund listings.

Money Market Deposit Accounts

Financial institutions are now authorized to compete directly with the money market mutual funds via money market deposit accounts. These accounts typically have minimum deposit requirements, usually as low as $1,000, and are insured by the federal government's FDIC (for banks) and FSLIC (for savings institutions).

Before you transfer all your savings from a money market mutual fund into an insured money market deposit account, here are the things you should know:

- All your money in a money market mutual fund earns interest at the same rate. This is generally true even if your balance falls below the minimum required to open the account. Banks and thrifts, on the other hand, often have "tiered" or "stair-step" rates in which higher interest rates are paid on higher balances. Some banks and thrifts also charge fees for maintaining the accounts.

- Most money market mutual funds permit unlimited check-writing, although checks may have to be for $500 or more. Banks and savings institutions don't usually specify the size of an individual check drawn on a money market deposit account, but are required to limit the number of checks per month to three.

- Interest rates paid by funds change daily; those paid by banks and savings institutions may change daily or be guaranteed for as long as a month. Banks and thrifts may pay any interest rate they choose; some will pay more than others.

Asset Management Accounts

Money market funds do a lot of things for a lot of people. But they do have certain limitations, notably the limitation on the size of checks you write. There's an account that removes that disadvantage, while adding other advantages. Started in 1977 by the brokerage house of Merrill Lynch Pierce Fenner & Smith, the new account is called a Cash Management Account. Other brokerage firms and some banks are offering similar accounts, under different names, but the CMA remains the model.

The CMA is built around a money market fund. (There are actually three money market funds in the CMA: a diversified fund, a tax-exempt fund, and a government securities fund. You have your choice.) It also includes a brokerage account with margin privileges (the ability to purchase securites with borrowing power—see p. 115), a debit card, and a coordinated monthly statement showing all your financial transactions during the month: purchases and sales of securities, checks written, deposits made, dividends credited, etc.

The CMA (and its brethren) is a total money management system: There is no idle cash because any amounts which might otherwise be temporarily left idle, such as dividends on securities left with the broker, are swept automatically into the money market fund. Loans are granted automatically, after all the money in the account is utilized. Checks may be written for any amount at all. The annual fee for all this, at most firms, is about $50.

But there is one drawback: Many asset management accounts, although not all, require initial deposits of $10,000 to $20,000, in any combination of cash and securities, although later balances may drop below this level. A lot of people don't have $10,000 or $15,000 or $20,000 to commit. Even if you do, you may want to think twice about an asset management account. Its combination of services may be excellent, but unless you will use most if not all of those services, the annual fee may not be worthwhile.

KEY POINTS

- Use new financial services—such as automatic teller machines and debit cards—with care; written records become doubly important when you're dealing with electronic gadgetry and instant access to your accounts.

- Take advantage of higher money market rates when you have enough extra cash for a minimum deposit. Some money market mutual funds and money market deposit accounts require as little as $500 to start; more complex asset management accounts may require as much as $20,000

- Compare fees carefully on both financial services and market rate accounts; be sure the advantages are worth the cost.

PUTTING YOUR MONEY TO WORK: INVESTMENTS

Investment
Strategy

Are you saving to buy a house? to open a business? to put children through college? to finance a trip around the world? to ensure a comfortable retirement? to build up the estate you'll leave for your heirs?

Your savings goal is important. But your savings method also depends on a number of variables: How many years do you have between now and the achievement of your particular purpose? Are you investing for the long term or the short? How much risk can you afford to take, both in terms of your own temperament and in terms of the number of people dependent on you? Can you manage your own investment, or will you count on the advice and information you glean from others? What is the investment climate? Are you putting investment dollars to work in a time of galloping inflation? during a recession? in a period of economic uncertainty?

Finding the Money to Invest

Before you skip this chapter, on the grounds that while you're strenuously holding your head above water you can't possibly find money to invest, think again. Here are some possibilities:

- Do you have money in passbook savings or money market accounts? How much money? Once you have the equivalent of three to six months' earnings on hand for emergencies (two to three months' earnings is probably sufficient if you are well insured and a two-income family), any excess should be put where it will grow.

  Note: Money market funds, described in Chapter 5, are not an investment. Like savings accounts, although recently paying far more in interest, money market funds are a base for emergency funds and a parking place for temporarily idle cash. Your capital won't grow in a money fund (although it won't do badly when interest rates are high) and should not be left there indefinitely as a substitute for another investment.

- Do you have a whole life insurance policy with accumulated cash value, with borrowing privileges at a low rate of interest? What better reason to borrow than to increase your capital and thereby provide for your family?

- Could you get along if your employer suddenly imposed a salary cutback of $1,000 a year? You could, because you'd have to. You can also get along if you impose a similar salary reduction on yourself, and put the money to work.

- Can you do without some purchases you were planning to make? If you invest the money you were planning to spend on redecorating the house, for example, you may come out much further ahead.

- Can you, conversely, sell no-longer-used possessions and raise some money? Many people have attics, basements, and garages crammed with outgrown toys, clothes, even appliances. It's possible to raise several hundred dollars, or more, at a well-organized garage sale.

- Would you borrow money to buy a car? You could also consider borrowing money to invest—if you carefully evaluate the degree of risk. The interest you pay is tax-deductible, as long as you don't invest borrowed money in tax-exempt securities. "Leverage," the use of borrowed funds, increases your potential gain and your potential loss.

Do not, however, stretch your resources beyond the point of prudence in the search for investment capital. Don't invest money that you'll need if your car breaks down or if a family member is temporarily unemployed. Investment funds should be funds you can, at least for the short term, do without.

Q. I've been told that you need at least $1,000 to invest. I can never scrape that much together at one time. Is there any way to buy stock, for example, with $50?

A. You can invest with as little as $25, in a couple of ways. You could, for instance, discipline yourself to put a fixed amount into a savings account each month, until you have a few hundred dollars ($1,000 isn't necessary). You could join a brokerage firm's small investors' program. Merrill Lynch has a Sharebuilder Plan under which stocks may be purchased for as little as $25 (gold or silver for as little as $100), with commission discounts from 15 to 40 percent, and automatic dividend reinvestment. You could start an investment club, with friends, and pool $20 or $25 apiece each month for investment.

Information about investment clubs is available from the National Association of Investment Corp. (NAIC), 1515 E. Eleven Mile Rd., Royal Oak, MI 48067.

If you can't get a group together, or aren't sure about joining a club, NAIC also has a program for individual investors. For a nominal $5 service charge on each stock purchase, NAIC will enroll you in a dividend reinvestment program at any of a number of corporations. You make the choice and, once enrolled, can invest amounts of your choice at intervals of your choice.

Who Is Investing These Days?

Over 47 million individual men and women, according to the New York Stock Exchange, own shares in American corporations. A great many—fully 17 percent of all individual investors in 1985—invest solely through common stock mutual funds. More and more, in fact, choose this indirect route to stock ownership.

Here are some interesting current statistics about investors:

- Investors are getting younger. In 1975 the median age of all shareholders was 52½. In 1985 the median age was 44. Newer investors are younger still, with a median age of 34.

- Investment portfolios are changing. A typical adult shareholder in 1975 owned $10,000 worth of stock. By 1980, the median portfolio size was $4,000, reflecting the fact that a great many young new shareowners started out with small investments, and also the fact that some affluent investors sought other investment vehicles to cushion adverse economic developments. By mid-1985, median portfolio size rose to $6,200, growth at least partially attributable to the performance of the market itself during the year.

- The median household income of shareholders rose from $19,000 in 1975 to $36,800 in 1984. Median income for all American households was $11,200 in 1975 and $22,400 in 1984.

Before You Invest

Don't leap into the stock market (or any other investment vehicle) just because you have a few spare dollars. First, be sure that you have a financial cushion appropriate to your circumstances. In addition to readily accessible cash (whether in savings accounts or money market funds), be sure that you have adequate insurance. Most important: medical coverage and the disability insurance that will replace your income if you are laid up. Then analyze your investment temperament, your investment objectives, and the investment climate.

Your Investment Temperament

Two people, at the same age, with the same assets, and the same invest-ment objectives, may reach totally different investment decisions based on the amount of risk they are willing to take. Arthur T. and Keith J., for instance, each have two children in junior high school, each plan to send those children to college, and each can save about $3,000 a year. Arthur will put his $3,000 a year into certificates of deposit at the local savings and loan; Keith will purchase the common stock of high-technology com-panies. Both say that they want their capital to grow. But Arthur is conservative; he wants no chance of loss. He also suspects that he lacks the time, and the inclination, to pay attention to the market. He'll settle for capital growth through the compounding of interest. Keith, on the other hand, is willing to take some risk for the sake of potentially greater capital appreciation. He likes the sense of participation he gets from watching the market and getting in and out as appropriate.

Wise investing stems from matching your own temperament and needs to your investment goals. The range of investment possibilities is enormous, from the totally risk-free vehicle of government issues to the high-flying realm of options and straddles. In between there are stocks and bonds and real estate and collectibles of all kinds, with varying de-grees of risk.

As a general rule, the degree of profit that you can make is related to the degree of risk that you are willing to take. But, although it's not as pleasant to think about, potential loss is also related to the degree of risk. What's the point of a high-risk gamble if you won't be able to sleep at night? What's the value if you might be depriving your children of their education instead of improving their chances? Take a look at your own temperament, and your equanimity in the face of loss, before you invest at all.

Your Investment Objectives

Before you shift any money from savings to investments, think about your investment objectives. Think about the desired end result: college? a vacation home? retirement funds? And think about the means to that end; think about your investments in terms of current income, capital growth, and tax advantages.

CURRENT INCOME

You can get current income from a number of investments, some more secure than others. Beyond your insured savings account, look at U.S. Treasury bills, notes, and bonds; at other U.S. Government Agency ob-ligations; at money market funds, especially (if absolute safety is a concern) at money market funds investing solely in Treasury issues. Blue-chip stocks and corporate bonds, bought individually or via a fund, may also be considered for current income.

CAPITAL GROWTH

Capital growth occurs when you invest in something that appreciates in value, so that your underlying principal grows. You'll usually derive current income as well, in the form of dividends or interest, but the income may be lower when the opportunities for growth are greater. Capital growth can be obtained in relatively safe investments and in riskier ones, along a range from common stocks to real estate. The riskiest—such as options and commodities (see pp. 130–32)—have the highest potential for profit, and for loss. They are highly speculative and not appropriate for the average investor.

TAX CONSIDERATIONS

Some investments, including most municipal bonds, are totally exempt from federal income taxes. Others, such as real estate or oil and gas leases, are temporarily sheltered from income taxes. Such investments are generally appropriate only for people in higher tax brackets. Don't get carried away with the idea of putting one over on Uncle Sam and eluding income taxes unless you are in a bracket in which it makes sense to do so. See Chapter 8 for details.

Whether or not tax-exempt and tax-sheltered income is right for you, there are tax considerations when you invest. Interest and dividends are taxable as ordinary income. Under the 1981 tax law there is no longer a difference in tax treatment between wage income and investment income; the maximum tax rate on either one is exactly the same.

From 1982 through the end of 1985, you could exclude $750 ($1,500 on a joint return) in dividends from qualified public utilities which you had reinvested. Shares had to be held for at least one year after acquisition in order to qualify for the exclusion. When shares bought through dividend reinvestment are sold, all proceeds are fully taxable as if the purchase price had been zero.

Profits from the sale of investments are taxed at the ordinary income tax rate. Previously, the long-term capital gains rate was a maximum of 20 percent (where 50 percent was the maximum income tax rate, applied to 40 percent of the gain), and could be considerably less (see Table 1). For 1987 alone, when there are five transitional tax brackets, short-term gains will be taxed at the same rate as ordinary income while long-term gains will be subject to a maximum tax of 28 percent. Losses may be applied against gains for the year, but if total losses exceed total gains,

TABLE 1: Marginal federal tax rates on long-term capital gains.

1985 Rates		1986 Rates	1985 Rates		1986 Rates
UNMARRIED			JOINT RETURNS		
$ 8,850–11,240	6.40%	$ 9,170–11,650	$ 7,910– 12,390	5.60%	$ 8,200– 12,840
11,240–13,430	7.20	11,650–13,920	12,390– 16,650	6.40	12,840– 17,270
13,430–15,610	8.00	13,920–16,190	16,650– 21,020	7.20	17,270– 21,800
15,610–18,940	9.20	16,190–19,640	21,020– 25,600	8.80	21,800– 26,550
18,940–24,460	10.40	19,640–25,360	25,600– 31,120	10.00	26,550– 32,270
24,460–29,970	12.00	25,360–31,080	31,120– 36,630	11.20	32,270– 37,980
29,970–35,490	13.60	31,080–36,800	36,630– 47,670	13.20	37,980– 49,420
35,490–43,190	15.20	36,800–44,780	47,670– 62,450	15.20	49,420– 64,750
43,190–57,550	16.80	44,780–59,670	62,450– 89,090	16.80	64,750– 92,370
57,550–85,130	19.20	59,670–88,270	89,090–113,860	18.00	92,370–118,050
85,130 and over	20.00	88,270 and over	113,860–169,020	19.60	118,050–172,250
			169,020 and over	20.00	172,250 and over

(Source: Prudential-Bache Securities)

then losses in 1987 and thereafter may be applied to offset up to $3,000 of ordinary income. There is no longer a distinction between long-term and short-term gains or losses.

It's important to look at taxes in developing your investment strategy. It's equally important not to let tax considerations dominate your investment decisions. All other things being equal, make an investment because it's a good investment without regard to tax advantages. All other things being equal, sell a stock (or other investment) when it's time to sell, before you sustain further losses. All other things are *not* equal, of course, when it's almost the end of the year and it will make a lot of difference to record the transaction in a different calendar year. Look at all the relevant factors before making any investment decision.

The Investment Climate

Assess the investment climate every time you're ready to invest. Periods of high inflation tend to depress the price of most common stocks, and fixed-income securities such as bonds become competitive with stocks as interest rates rise. If you can afford to invest for the long term, it may therefore be wise to buy common stocks when prices are low—even if they may go lower still. Periods of galloping inflation make inflation hedges, such as real estate and gold coins, very attractive. But people with large sums tied up in such tangible assets may view the ebbing of inflation with alarm. When inflation does ebb, fixed-rate securities, such as bonds and Treasury notes, become more attractive—especially to investors able to lock in relatively high rates right before the decline.

Periods of interest-rate volatility knock most calculations out of the ball park; the message then: Stay liquid.

Whatever you do, however, try to stay away from follow-the-pack psychology. The day that all your friends are talking about buying oil stocks is the day *not* to buy oil stocks. The day that the evening news commentators chortle about the new highs reached by the Dow-Jones Index is *not* the day to decide to get into the stock market. Either buy when prices have been declining steadily (don't worry about waiting for the absolute bottom), or put consistent sums of money into investments over a period of time so that your purchases will average out. For more on investment strategy, see pp. 93–97.

Meanwhile, don't bury your head in the sand. Be aware of the world around you and adjust your investments accordingly. If interest rates are very high, pull your money out of low-interest savings and put it in a money market mutual fund. If the money market comes down to pass-book rates or below, as it has done before, put your money back into insured savings. Shift varying proportions of your investment portfolio to and from stocks and bonds as appropriate. Above all, stay reasonably liquid so that you can be flexible.

Note: Marketability is not synonymous with liquidity. Common stocks may be sold easily at any time, but if you need to sell them when the market is down you will suffer a loss.

An Individual Investment Plan

★ Donna and George have $20,000, saved from current income, to invest. They are both 29 years old, both lawyers, earning a combined annual income of $69,000. They are still paying off college loans, however, and the $20,000 represents all their assets. They have no children, but expect to start a family within a couple of years.

★ Alison and Tom have $20,000 to invest, money they recently inherited from Tom's uncle. They are in their mid-thirties and have three children; their annual income is $28,700 and they have $3,500 in scraped-together savings.

The amount of money available for investment at a given time is clearly not the only factor to consider. Donna and George, while they plan to start a family, also have the kind of professional incomes that make repeated investments likely. They foresee no immediate need for their cash, and can afford to take a moderate amount of risk. Alison and Tom, on the other hand, have what is probably a one-shot opportunity to invest a significant sum. Without this money, they will find it very difficult to send their children to college. They need to be conservative in their approach to investment.

Your personal investment plan should be based on careful evaluation of where you are and where you want to go, with reevaluation at regular intervals. Look at yourself right now. Are you young, without dependents? Then as long as you earn enough to live comfortably and to save something for the future, you can probably take reasonable risks in the pursuit of capital growth. If you're middle-aged, without dependents, your biggest concern may be sheltering some of your income from taxation. If you have a family, you will probably want to protect that family by being conservative in your investments. And when you reach retirement age, safety of principal and the highest possible income will be of paramount concern.

Before you start to tailor your own investment plan, look back at your net worth statement and your financial forecast. Then look at the following factors:

- Your current age
- Your state of health
- Present annual income (from all sources)
- Anticipated annual income five years from now (from all sources)
- Anticipated windfalls (inheritances, etc.)
- Current expenses, both fixed and discretionary
- Anticipated expenses
- Provision for emergencies (savings accounts, insurance)
- Amount currently available to invest
- Amount anticipated as available for investment
- Investment objectives:
  a. Short-range
  b. Long-range
- Tentative investment decisions:
  a. How much can you risk?
  b. How much are you willing to risk?
  c. How much must have a guaranteed return?

A Balanced Portfolio

Whether you'll aim primarily for income, growth, or tax advantage depends on your age and stage of life as well as your attitude toward risk and the amount of money you have to invest. Through the first half of life, for most people, capital growth is a primary target. In the second half, with the retirement years on the horizon, protection of income often becomes more important. At any age, however, you don't want all of your eggs in one basket. Diversify your investments, and do so in several ways:

- Among the objectives of income, growth, and tax advantages, as appropriate

- Among different investment vehicles, via one or more mutual funds or on your own
- Among different sectors of the economy, government and corporate

THE INVESTMENT TRIANGLE

One approach to investing divides investment dollars into three parts:

- Conservative "foundation" dollars: your home, bank accounts, insurance, government and municipal bonds, annuities
- Growth investments: stock, corporate bonds, mutual funds, and some tax shelters
- Risk investments: speculative stocks, commodities, stock options, raw land

When you're younger, you can afford to risk more (but never all) of your investment dollars. As you become older, especially as you move toward retirement, the balance should tip more toward conservative investment. But age is only one factor. Within each category the balance will shift among investment possibilities according to your objectives, your income, and the degree of risk you are willing to assume.

★ Donna and George, young professionals with no dependents, might keep 5 percent of their investment money in a money market fund for ready access, put 30 percent into established growth company stocks for security, and put 65 percent into the stocks of smaller companies with likelihood of growth. Their primary objective: appreciation.

★ A 50-year-old with two children in college and one still at home would balance his portfolio differently. He might put 10 percent into a money market fund, and divide the rest equally among intermediate-term corporate bonds, high-yield stocks, and established growth company stocks. Objective: to maintain current income and build funds toward retirement.

★ At 68, a retiree might balance his portfolio with 10 percent in the money market, 10 percent in growth company stocks, 30 percent in high-yield stocks, and 50 percent in long-term bonds. Objective: high income and low risk.

These proportions are appropriate only for these people. They'll be different for you, and will vary with the investment climate and with your temperament, as well as with your age. There are no fixed rules.

An Investment Strategy for Beginners

James B. Cloonan, founder of the American Association of Individual Investors, suggests that investors who stay in the market over time reduce their risks. He suggests this strategy for a long-term investment in common stock:

1. Start by putting your money into no-load common stock mutual funds (see p. 107), until you have $10,000 to $15,000 invested.

2. Then develop a portfolio of at least seven different stocks of approximately equal dollar amounts. Do so one stock at a time, with the remaining money kept in the mutual fund.

3. Select stocks of small and medium-sized companies whose profits can reasonably be expected to grow. You'll be a winner if one company among your seven goes from being a medium-sized company to being a successful giant. If you initially buy the stock of very large established companies, you can't expect this kind of growth.

4. About four years before the accumulated wealth will be needed, whether for the purchase of a house or for a child's education, begin to sell. Sell one-quarter of the portfolio in each of the four years. Reinvest the proceeds in shorter-term, low-risk investments which will be available when the money is needed.

5. Instead of liquidating the investments, if retirement is on the horizon, begin to convert them to low-risk, interest-paying investments.

Reevaluate Your Portfolio

Dr. Cloonan recommends holding stock for several years, through at least one business cycle. But most investors err in the other direction: they buy and then sit, ignoring changes in the business climate or the company or their own affairs that would make it advisable to sell. Don't make this mistake. Don't invest unless you're willing to pay attention, willing to reevaluate your portfolio from time to time, and willing to make changes.

If you take a passive stance you might find yourself in the position of one of these investors, cited by the New York Stock Exchange:

★ David M. bought a promising new issue when it was selling for $20 a share. The company prospered and grew and the stock increased in value until it was selling at $200 and paying a steady dividend of $4 a share. David was pleased. He was reluctant to sell, however, because he still had faith in the company's continued growth and because of the capital gains tax he would have to pay. But he didn't stop to think that although he was receiving a 20 percent return based on his cost, his return on current value was only 2 percent. When he reviewed his portfolio with his broker, he learned that the stock was considered to be overvalued at its current price and that peak growth probably had been attained. He sold the stock.

★ In 1961 Mrs. K.'s husband died, leaving her a yearly income of approximately $4,000 from securities. Most of the income came from one large holding, relatively secure, but providing a fairly low yield. After the settlement of the estate, Mrs. K. sat back, content to live on the steady flow of income without investigating alternative forms of investment. Her major holding appreciated only slightly in value over the years, while the yield remained about the same. Inflation, however, steadily devoured a substantial portion of her buying power. She has begun to find it necessary to dip into capital; reinvestment in a higher-yielding security could have made all the difference.

WHEN TO SELL

Investment strategy includes deciding when to sell as well as when to buy. Too many small investors hold stocks indefinitely, afraid to admit that they've made a mistake. Losses on paper somehow seem easier to take than losses in dollars—even if sticking with paper makes the losses greater. You'll find it easier to sell if you make two basic decisions at the time you buy:

■ Decide how much you expect the stock to rise and decide that you will sell when it reaches the targeted amount, even if it appears likely to continue rising.

■ Decide how much of a loss you are willing to accept, and sell if the stock declines to that amount, even if you think it likely to rebound (see Table 2). Set a framework for your stock, the top and bottom limits you can live with, and sell if it reaches either limit. You can make the sale auto-

---

TABLE 2: Gain needed to recoup losses.

The longer you hold a losing stock, the farther behind you get. Simple arithmetic shows that it makes sense to cut your losses early. As this table illustrates, the odds that you'll recover a loss worsen rapidly if the loss gets to be larger than about 10 percent.

Size of loss (%)	Gain needed to break even (%)	Size of loss (%)	Gain needed to break even (%)
5	5.3	40	66.7
10	11.1	50	100.0
15	17.6	60	150.0
20	25.0	70	233.3
25	33.3	80	400.0
30	42.9	90	900.0

(Source: *Personal Finance*)

matic, and avoid temporizing, by leaving an order with your broker to sell at a specific price.

Even if you've purchased mutual fund shares with an eye to professional management, you should reevaluate your portfolio at regular intervals. You might want to review your financial holdings thoroughly every year. You also might want to review them when external or internal events dictate. The New York Stock Exchange offers these lists of factors that should prompt review:

A CHECKLIST OF EXTERNAL EVENTS

- Substantial advance or decline in the stock market
- Change in tax laws
- International monetary upheaval
- Change in business regulatory laws
- Change in attitudes of regulatory agencies
- A shift from inflation to deflation, or the reverse
- Political change
- New international trade agreements, or foreign trade restrictions

CHECKLIST OF PERSONAL CIRCUMSTANCES

- Getting married
- Having a baby
- Receiving an inheritance
- Providing support for parent(s)
- Moving into a higher tax bracket
- Having children enter college
- Making a substantial business investment
- Being widowed or divorced
- Becoming a grandparent
- Retiring

CHECKLIST OF CHANGES IN OUTLOOK OF COMPANIES WHOSE SHARES YOU OWN

- Significant change in price of stock
- New management

- Increased or decreased earnings
- New competitive factors
- New products
- Mergers or acquisitions
- Antitrust or other government actions
- Increase, decrease, or omission of dividends
- New bond issue
- Diversification
- Purchases or sales by institutions.

Q. There was a lot of recent publicity about the failure of a stock brokerage firm. What happens to such a firm's customers?

A. Few brokerage firms fail. When one does, its customers are usually protected by the Securities Investor Protection Corporation (SIPC), which covers stocks, bonds, notes, and certificates of deposit but not commodities or commodity options. Securities registered in a customer's name are returned. Then remaining cash and securities held by the firm are distributed among customers on a pro rata basis. Finally, remaining claims are settled by SIPC to a maximum of $500,000 per customer, of which no more than $100,000 may be for cash. It can take many months to settle, however, and there is no protection against market ups and downs while customer assets are frozen. A word of warning: While you can't really ascertain the financial stability of your brokerage firm, be alert to repeated bookkeeping errors and excessively slow execution of orders. These may be a signal to find a new broker.

Managing Your Investments

Once you've thought about your investment objectives and promised yourself to reevaluate your investments on a regular basis, you need to keep yourself informed.

General Information

Before you invest at all, you should find out what investment is all about. This book will help. In addition, you might look at general information distributed by the securities industry. The New York Stock Exchange, for instance, puts out a six-booklet "Investment Information Kit," available for $7 from the NYSE Publication Section, 11 Wall Street, New York, NY 10005. The NYSE also distributes, free, an Individual Investors Directory listing NYSE member organizations which welcome individual investors.

Good general information is also available through an investment course or seminar. Your local adult education program or community college probably offers such courses. So do stockbrokerage firms, although the advice may be somewhat self-serving and may need to be taken with a grain of salt. Women will find special courses designed for them.

Publications

There are a great many publications offering investment advice, ranging from glossy magazines available on most newsstands to special-interest newsletters available only by subscription. If you're at all serious about your investments, you should scan such publications as the *Wall Street Journal, Barron's, Business Week,* and *Forbes.* They'll tell you about the economic climate, about industry trends, and about the outlook for specific companies.

You may also want to subscribe to one or more newsletters or advisory services. Be aware, though, that "experts" frequently disagree. No one really knows when an inflationary period is ending or beginning; no one can guarantee that a particular investment will move up or down in value. All any of the advisers can do is read the economic signals and react with their own set of assumptions and expectations. So read their advice, but analyze it in light of (1) your own feelings about the economy and (2) your own individual investment strategy.

Company News

When you've narrowed your investment possibilities, ask for research reports on particular companies from your stockbroker. Then, once you do invest, you'll be bombarded with news and information from the company or companies in which you're participating. Read the material. Pay attention to what the figures say. Pay particular attention to the company's quarterly and annual reports.

READING AN ANNUAL REPORT

Amid the dry prose and columns of figures in an annual report lie some crucial messages: Is this company doing well? Are sales increasing? Are earnings on the rise?

In order to decipher these messages, these clues to whether you should invest in the company in the first place or remain an investor from year to year, you have to review certain key elements of the report:

- The company's *balance sheet* shows its year-end financial position, just as your net worth statement shows your position at a specific time. It shows the company's assets (cash on hand and in the bank, marketable securities, accounts receivable, inventories, and property, plants, and equipment) and its liabilities (accounts payable and notes payable, accrued expenses, and federal income taxes payable). It also shows stockholders' equity, the corporation's net worth after subtracting all its liabilities.

- The company's *income statement,* sometimes called the earnings report or statement of profit and loss, is like your cash flow statement; it shows the record of operating activities over the course of the year. It matches the revenues received against all the costs incurred in running the company. The result: a net profit or loss for the year. The very first item—net sales or operating revenues—is most important. Compare this figure against the comparable figure for previous years to see how the company is doing.

- The *independent accountant's report,* usually tucked in the back of the report, simply states that an audit has been conducted and that statements have been prepared in accordance with generally accepted accounting principles. If there are any reservations expressed in the auditor's report, be careful. This is the time to read the footnotes.

- The *footnotes* in a financial report frequently contain extremely important information. It may be in the footnotes that you'll find such details as changes in the company's method of depreciating fixed assets, changes in the value of stock outstanding because of stock dividends and splits, details of stock option plans for officers and employees, and contingent liabilities representing pending claims or lawsuits.

One year's annual report of one company will be informative but won't tell you nearly enough. You'll want to compare this year's figures against those for previous years; some companies make it easy by including five-year or ten-year tables in their annual reports. You may also want to compare the company's earnings against the earnings of comparable companies, particularly those in the same industry.

You can supplement this very brief explanation of annual reports by securing an excellent free guide from Merrill Lynch Pierce Fenner & Smith at their local offices. Or write to MLPF & S, Market Communications, 800 Scudder Mill Rd., Plainsboro, NJ 08540, and ask for a copy of "How to Read a Financial Report."

Q. In cleaning out some old trunks that belonged to my mother, I came across some old stock certificates. The company doesn't seem to be in existence anymore. How can I find out if the shares are worth anything?

A. You may be able to trace the company and find out if it or a successor company has any assets on which the certificates have a claim. If your stockbroker can't locate the company, write to the secretary of state of the state in which the company was incorporated or to the transfer agent; this information should be on the certificate. If this fails, and the security is or was listed on the New York Stock Exchange (11 Wall Street, New York, NY 10005), the Exchange may be able to help you. Unlisted securities may sometimes be traced through the National Association of Securities Dealers, 77 Water St., New York, NY 10005. If all this fails, you may contact a firm that specializes in tracing old securities; the New York Stock Exchange can send you a list. A typical fee is $20 to $25 for a research report on a single company. Never send the original document when you write for information; send a photocopy. And hold on to your finds in any case; old stock certificates with no other value may be worth several dollars as antiques.

Professional Management vs. Self-Management

Are you going to put in the time it takes to intelligently buy and sell securities? Are you going to read annual reports and financial statements, follow your securities in the daily paper, and keep yourself informed? Or are you going to do what a great many people do, and put your money into investments which you will then file and forget? There is something to be said for long-range investment against in-and-out trading. But there is also a lot to be said for management of investments rather than neglect.

If you're not going to take the time to become well informed and to keep on top of your investments, look to professional management. If you're well-to-do, with a portfolio worth at least $100,000, you can hire investment counsel . . . although you'd still better pay attention to what that counsel is doing with your money. If you're middle- to upper-middle-income, interested in capital growth and in tax advantages, you might consider consulting a financial planner for review of your entire financial situation. Be careful, however, about relying on the purchase recommendations of a planner who earns all his income from commissions. If you're middle-income, with no more than a thousand or so to invest at a time (and those times possibly few and far between), your professional management may best be accomplished by joining a group. That group may be a mutual fund or a unit investment trust or (with a little more investment capital) a real estate limited partnership. You'll give up some of the possibility of enormous gain, but you'll also relinquish much of the risk of significant loss. And if you pick your group well, you'll be in good hands . . . although you've still got to pay attention.

Stockbrokers

A stockbroker, whether you use outside investment advice or not, acts as your intermediary in buying and selling stock. He or she can also represent you in a wide variety of other investment transactions—so many today, as brokerage firms move into real estate and insurance as well as options, commodities, stocks and bonds, that knowledge and experience in some areas may be sketchy. You pay the broker a commission for each transaction, a commission that makes brokers less than objective advisers. So while you can obtain very useful information from your broker and from the brokerage firm's research staff, you may not want to rely entirely on the broker's opinion. It is your money, and you're the only one who really cares what happens to it.

SELECTING A STOCKBROKER

Select a stockbroker the same way you would select any professional adviser. Ask friends and your other advisers (your lawyer or your accountant or your banker) for their recommendations. Then interview several candidates before you make a decision. Try to find out:

- The extent (both length and breadth) of the broker's experience. Ideally, you want a broker with several years of experience, one who has worked through market ups and downs and knows how to deal with both. You also want a broker who will admit to inadequate knowledge and who will refer you to a specialist when referral is appropriate. Your broker may be skilled in stock trades and may be able to put you into a money market fund, but he or she may not know much more about real estate syndication than you do.

- The type of clients he or she customarily handles. If most of them make larger transactions than you expect to make, who do you think will get most of the broker's attention?

- Just what the broker expects to do for you. The first thing he or she should do is ask you a lot of questions, about your financial situation and your investment objectives. Steer clear of any broker who makes immediate recommendations before knowing much about you. If the broker does ask the right questions, then go further. Will he call you when an interesting opportunity comes along? Will he call you when it's time to sell, as well as when he would like you to buy?

Give a broker a fair chance, and enough time. But always feel free to change stockbrokers if your investment goals are not compatible. And definitely consider a change if you suspect that your broker is "churning" your account, buying and selling with excessive frequency. Any profits you might make will be eaten up by commissions on a churned account, and the only one to come out ahead will be the broker.

Q. My broker lost a lot of money for me by recommending stocks which were far too risky for someone in my circumstances—recently divorced and responsible for two small children. Is there anything I can do to get my money back?

A. You must realize two things: No stock market investment guarantees that you will make money; and you didn't have to follow your broker's recommendations. The final decision about what to buy was always up to you. Nonetheless, if you believe that you lost money because your broker was either incompetent or unethical (brokers are not supposed to push inappropriate investments), you can either sue the broker or take your case to an industry arbitration panel. (For operational problems, such as accounting snafus, your first step is to contact the branch manager of the brokerage firm.) The National Association of Security Dealers, the New York Stock Exchange, the American Stock Exchange, and some of the regional exchanges have inquiry, compliance, and arbitration panels. If your dispute involves less than $5,000, in fact, you may ask for arbitration by mail. Write to the Arbitrator's Office, New York Stock Exchange, 11 Wall Street, New York, NY 10005.

DISCOUNT STOCKBROKERS

You have a right to expect some attention from a full-service stockbroker: research, telephone calls, even some hand-holding. If you don't need any of this, if you're capable of your own investment decisions, then you might want to consider using a discount stockbroker and saving 30 to 70 percent on brokerage commissions. The size of the discount depends on two things: the fees set by the firm and the size of the transaction. Minimum fees set by some firms could wipe out any saving on small transactions.

Some discount brokers are strictly telephone order-takers. Others are now offering some additional services: an individual to work with, a telephone alert when a stock reaches a predetermined price, a money fund for idle cash. Some run investment seminars, some offer margin accounts (see pp. 115–17). And some are moving beyond stock transactions to offer bonds, commodities, and so on. Research, however, is still generally not available except from full-service brokerage firms. Decide what service you need and want, and shop around for the best price.

Note: You may be able to buy securities (often at discounted commissions) at the same place you keep your savings account, if your bank or savings and loan is one that has moved into the brokerage field. While government regulations still draw distinct lines between banks and brokerage firms, alliances are being formed that cross the lines and offer you far more flexibility.

COMMISSIONS

You'll pay less to a discount stockbroker, by and large, than to a full-service broker. But a lot depends on the size of each transaction and on how many transactions you make. "Round lots" of 100 shares always cost less in commissions than "odd lots," at any broker. But a purchase of 100 shares is still a small transaction, one on which commissions may be roughly equivalent at full-service and discount firms. A purchase of several hundred shares, on the other hand, will probably cost significantly different sums. Brokerage commissions were deregulated in 1975 and every firm sets its own rates, making it essential to shop around.

But don't blindly go to just any broker advertising discounts. Some discount brokers base commissions on the dollar amount of the order, and are generally less expensive when you buy low-priced stocks. Some base commissions on the number of shares purchased, and are generally less expensive when you buy higher-priced stocks. Whichever you use (and you might use both, for different types of purchases, if you are a frequent investor), be sure to compare rate schedules. And be wary of advertised discounts; some ads refer back to pre-1975 regulated rates in claiming big savings.

Some sophisticated investors use both a full-service broker, for the times when they want advice, and a discount broker, for trades initiated on their own. It isn't quite cricket, however, to take information and advice from one broker and then give the commission to another.

Q. I recently bought my first shares of stock. Can I deduct the broker's commissions on my income tax return?

A. No. Commissions aren't deductible while you hold the stock, although they do reduce any taxes due when you sell the stock. At that time you subtract the commission from your profit (or add it to your loss) to determine the taxable amount, if any.

KEY POINTS

- Investments are an essential part of your lifelong financial plan; try to set aside money for investments as part of your regular budget.
- Before you invest at all, establish a readily available financial cushion of up to six months' income.

TABLE 3: Your investment choices.

Investment Medium	Overall degree of risk	Approximate yield	Appreciation/ depreciation of capital	Liquidity	Maturity	Tax aspects	Professional assistance required	Minimum investment required
Savings accounts (passbook, statement, club)	Very low	Low	Generally not possible	Can be withdrawn at any time	N/A	Interest income is fully taxable subject to certain exclusions or deferrals	None	None
Time deposits and certificates	Very low	Generally moderate	Generally not possible	Can be withdrawn at any time but usually with penalty for early withdrawal	70 days to 10 years	Interest income is fully taxable subject to certain exclusions or deferrals	None	Varies but usually $500
Common stocks	Moderate to high	Varies	Possible	Varies, depending if stock is publicly traded or closely held	N/A	Dividends and capital gains (on sale) taxable as ordinary income	Generally moderate to substantial	Varies with range of stock prices
Corporate bonds	Generally moderate	Generally moderate	Potential increases with the term of maturity	Varies, depending on volume of trading and if issue is publicly traded	Up to 30 years	Income taxes payable on interest, capital gains on sale	Moderate	Usually $1,000
Municipal bonds	Moderate	Low to moderate	Potential increases with the term of maturity	Varies with size of issue and market or region	Up to 30 years	Generally exempt from federal and some state income taxes, capital	Moderate	Usually $5,000 but sometimes as low as $100 or $500

Investment							
Treasury bills, bonds, and notes	Very low to moderate	Moderate	increases with the term of maturity	week, generally very liquid	to 30 years	income taxes payable on interest exempt from state taxes, capital gains on sale	moderate	$1,000 for notes and bonds, $10,000 for Treasury bills
Money market funds	Low to moderate	Moderate to high	Generally not possible	Very liquid	N/A	Income taxes on interest (unless tax-exempt fund); and on capital gains on sale	None	Varies but usually $500–$1,000
Other mutual funds	Moderate to high	Varies	Varies with type of fund	Generally very liquid	N/A	Taxation of income depends on types of assets held in the funds	Moderate	Varies
Real estate	Moderate to high	Depends on nature of investment and its respective market	Quite possible	Generally limited	N/A	Some income sheltered by expenses, depreciation and tax credits; capital gains on sale	Generally moderate to substantial	Varies
Tax shelters	Generally high	Depends on nature of shelter	Quite possible	Varies	N/A	Same as real estate	Generally moderate to substantial	Varies but usually $5,000, some now available for Keogh and IRAs at $1,000 levels

(Source: Reston Financial Services, a Prentice-Hall Company)

■ Before you invest in any particular vehicle, evaluate it in terms of your investment temperament, your investment objectives, and the investment climate.

■ Look at individual investments in terms of risk, liquidity, maturity, and tax aspects. Table 3 summarize these and other aspects of various investment vehicles.

■ Tailor your investment plan, and balance your portfolio, in accordance with your age, income, and responsibilities; reevaluate your plan, and your portfolio, at regular intervals.

7

Investment Vehicles

You can achieve your investment objectives with a variety of self-managed investment vehicles. You'll probably invest in more than one vehicle at one time, in fact, and vary your investment mix as your needs and your objectives change.

Mutual Funds

Mutual funds are pooled investments with professional management. Via a mutual fund, you can invest in common stock, corporate bonds, tax-free bonds, options, even (via money market mutual funds) money itself. You can invest for income, for growth, for safety. You can use mutual funds to get started as an investor. And you can use mutual funds, throughout your investment life, as an efficient way to diversify and balance your portfolio.

Types of Funds

Here are some of the ways to meet your investment goals via mutual funds (the objectives of each fund must be spelled out in its prospectus):

- If you want safety of principal coupled with high current income in a long-term investment, try an *income fund,* investing in corporate bonds and/or high-dividend-paying stocks.

- If you're more interested in capital growth, to offset inflation or to build assets before retirement, look at *growth funds,* investing in high-quality common stocks. Over the past several years, the Investment Company

107

Institute reports, equity funds with dividends and capital gains reinvested have kept their shareholders comfortably ahead of the Consumer Price Index—at a time when individual common stocks generally lagged behind.

- For still greater growth (coupled with greater risk), try *aggressive growth* stock funds, sometimes called "performance" or "maximum capital gains" funds, concentrating in speculative issues or specialized industries such as gold or oil exploration.

- If you want both long-term growth of capital and current income, look at a *balanced fund,* investing in a balanced portfolio of fixed-income securities (bonds and/or preferred stocks) and common stocks. With more conservative investment policies than typical growth funds, most balanced funds do not move either up or down very rapidly. Each fund, however, has a different approach to providing a balance and to the degree of risk it will assume. Or, you might consider splitting your investment dollars between two separate funds with clearly defined objectives.

- If your goal is safety of principal, current income, and instant liquidity, try a *money market fund,* investing in short-term money market instruments such as certificates of deposit, corporate commercial paper, and so on. For a still-greater guarantee of safety (although, perhaps, slightly lower rates of return) look at money market funds that invest solely in government obligations.

- For tax-exempt income, safety of principal, and instant liquidity, the right vehicle might be a *tax-exempt money market fund,* investing in municipal notes and bonds, tax anticipation notes, and similar items. The average maturity on tax-free funds is about 70 days, instead of the 30-day average on taxable funds, so these funds are slightly less responsive to changing interest rates and may be an excellent choice when rates are falling. However, yields can be considerably lower on a tax-exempt money fund than on a general-purpose money fund. Look at your tax bracket and comparative yields before you leap to the magnet of tax exemption.

- For tax-exempt return on a longer-term basis, there are *tax-exempt funds,* investing in state and local bonds. Interest is generally exempt from federal income taxes, and from state taxes in the state in which the obligation is issued.

Whatever your goals, a mutual fund has distinct advantages. It affords diversification, reducing your risk by investing in many different securities. You can't manage this much diversification on your own unless you have significant sums to invest. It gives your money professional management, the skills and talents of full-time managers. It promises liquidity; shares can always be redeemed at current net asset value.

Investment Strategy with Mutual Funds

You can make the most of your mutual fund investments if you:

Select a "family" of funds with free exchange-by-telephone privileges so that you can switch your investments as circumstances dictate. *The No-Load Fund Investor,* a newsletter available by subscription (P.O. Box 283, Hastings-on-Hudson, NY 10706), recommends selecting a family by, first, analyzing the type and quality of its stock funds, because this is where differences in performance are most apt to appear. Then look at the variety of fixed-income funds available. Is there a tax-free as well as a taxable bond fund? Then review the group's money market funds; performance may be similar, but preferred groups have three types—general-purpose, government-only, and tax-free.

Don't plan on frequent trades. Mutual funds are not the same kind of trading vehicles as individually purchased stocks and bonds. You might sell a stock because it has gone up as much as you had hoped, but a fund can continue to grow as long as the stock market gains. Mutual funds, with one exception, should be considered long-term investments (but not indefinite; you should still keep an eye on performance and sell, or switch to another fund, if yields drop consistently). The exception: aggressive growth funds. These funds may be the best way for the average investor to invest in the stock of small, likely-to-grow companies, but they are extremely volatile and should be sold as soon as performance begins to decline.

Elect automatic reinvestment. This option allows you to put fund dividends and/or capital gain distributions back into the fund to buy new shares and thereby build up new holdings. Note that reinvested dividends, like dividends you take in cash, are taxable as ordinary income.

Diversify your investment in mutual funds, just as you would in any other investment. Invest regularly, over time, to dollar-cost-average. And consider investing in two to four funds with different investment objectives. These two to four funds may be within the same fund group, if you have chosen wisely, thereby minimizing costs and inconvenience.

Picking a Fund

In addition to funds designated by investment objectives, there are a great many special funds. Some stick to one industry (e.g., chemicals). Some are organized along geographic lines (e.g., investment in the Far East). Some are "index" funds, owning all the stocks reported by one market index (such as Standard & Poor's 500) and intended to reflect the performance of the market as a whole. And some are "socially conscious" funds, investing in companies that make some contribution to the well-being of the world. Special-interest funds may follow different strategies to meet different investment objectives.

There are also significant differences among funds in purely practical terms. In addition to investment vehicles and goals, and investment performance (compared over five to ten years), outlined above, here are some of the major points to consider.

LOAD OR NO-LOAD?

Is the fund "load" or "no-load"? That is, does it charge an initial sales fee or not? Funds offered through a stockbroker or other agency are more likely to charge a sales fee, while those offered directly to the public via newspaper ads and direct mail are more likely to be of the no-load variety.

Stock funds are more often load funds, with a sales charge typically 8.5 percent of the initial investment. Money market funds, on the other hand, are more likely to be of the no-load variety. A new hybrid or "low-load" category of funds charges up to 3.5 percent, while other funds have "back-end" fees or loads at the time you sell. There are both load and no-load funds in each fund category. Newspaper listings of mutual fund quotations show "N.L." under "Offer Price" to designate no-load funds. Performance is often comparable, but you should realize that part of your money is not working for you when you go into a load fund.

Note: The load is a sales commission. All funds—load and no-load—charge annual management fees, usually 0.5 percent to 1 percent of the fund's net asset value.

A list of some 370 no-load funds, with details on their investment goals, is available for $2 from the No-Load Mutual Fund Association, 11 Penn Plaza, Dept. GW86, New York, NY 10001. Information about mutual funds in general (load and no-load), as well as lists of particular funds with particular goals (municipal bond funds, high-technology stock funds, and so on), is available free from the Investment Company Institute, 1600 M St., NW, Washington, DC 20036.

WHAT CONVENIENCES AND PRIVILEGES DOES THE FUND OFFER?

Ask these questions before you invest:

- How easy is it to purchase shares? What is the minimum purchase amount? the minimum amount accepted for subsequent deposits? Is there an automatic reinvestment program? You can open accounts by mail, telephone, or bank wire, depending upon the particular fund. Some will accept automatic deductions from a savings or checking account.

- How easy is it to withdraw your money? Shares may be redeemed by letter, telephone, bank wire, or check, depending on the particular fund. The singular advantage of money market funds has been the ability to write a check (usually in a minimum amount of $500) directly on your money in the fund. Many mutual funds, however, offer withdrawal plans under which shareholders may secure payments at regular intervals; this can be useful for retirement income.

Q. I had no trouble with my mutual fund until I wanted to close out the account. Now they require a signature guarantee, not a notarized signature but a guarantee, before I can get my money. I don't have a stockbroker, and I don't use a commercial bank. Where can I get a signature guarantee?

A. Your savings and loan may be able to arrange a signature guarantee through an affiliated commercial bank. Or you might find a local commercial bank willing to accommodate you even if you are not a depositor. Not all mutual funds have this requirement, and it might be better, next time, to invest in one that does not.

■ Is there an exchange privilege? by telephone? Many funds belong to a "family," a group of funds with different investment vehicles and objectives, and allow investors to switch among the funds as investment objectives or conditions change. Find out, in advance, if there is a charge for the transfer. Find out, too, if there is any limit on the number of times that you may transfer funds.

■ How good is customer service? Many funds offer toll-free telephone numbers, but can you get through, or is the line always busy? This may seem trivial, but can be a point of real aggravation.

Taxes on Mutual Funds

The ownership of mutual funds has tax considerations both during ownership and when you sell your shares:

As a share owner you may receive dividends and/or capital gains distributions. Dividends, whether you take them or reinvest them, must be reported as ordinary income. Capital gains distributions, as the fund profits from buying and selling securities, are generally received and reported annually. Under the 1986 tax law, capital gains distributions are also reported as ordinary income.

When you sell your shares, you may have either a capital gain or a capital loss. If you buy into the fund at one time and sell all your shares at one time, your arithmetic is simple. If you've bought in over a period of time and want to sell only a portion of your shares, your calculations become more complicated. If you keep careful records as you go along, however, you'll be able to sell specific shares, selecting long- and short-term capital gains or losses, to your tax advantage.

Note: Capital gains or losses must be reported when you exchange shares within a family of funds. According to the IRS, such a transaction is a sale and a purchase.

Unit Investment Trusts

All of the mutual funds described above are open-end pooled investments, managed on a regular basis to meet the declared objectives and able to shift their portfolios to meet changing market conditions. There's another type of pooled investment, the unit investment trust. Such a trust is a closed-end unmanaged portfolio, unmanaged because the portfolio—and the interest rate—is fixed at the time of purchase and subsequently runs its course until maturity. That maturity date might be six months from purchase date if the trust invests in certificates of deposit. It might be twenty or thirty years in a trust that invests in corporate bonds.

Trusts are sold in minimum units of $1,000, with sales charges ranging from 2 to 5.5 percent. Interest on the trust is paid by check, often monthly; in many trusts there is also a reinvestment privilege which enables you to compound your return.

Unit investment trusts are always sold with a load—that is, your broker gets a commission. Although unit investment trusts offer the advantages of professional portfolio selection, diversification, and simplicity, it is often more expensive to buy and sell a unit investment trust than it is to buy and sell either individual bonds or CDs or an open-end mutual fund. Don't look at trusts as trading vehicles, therefore, but as a long-term investment.

Common Stock

When you buy one or more shares of common stock you are buying a portion of the corporation that issues the stock; you are becoming an owner. You're not much of an owner, of course, and are not going to be making any management decisions, although you will be asked to cast a vote either in person, at the annual meeting of the corporation, or by mail, via a proxy. But your fortunes will prosper or decline along with the fortunes of the company, with both the price of the stock itself and the dividends it pays subject to change.

What Are Stocks Worth?

Simply put, a share of stock is worth whatever someone is willing to pay for it. The buying and selling of common stock is based purely on supply and demand. The initial shares of a corporation's stock are sold by the corporation, to raise money. After that, for the most part, shares are sold by investors and bought by other investors.

One measure that investors use to determine a stock's value is the *price-to-earnings ratio.* This P/E ratio is the price of a share of stock divided by the company's annual earnings per share. A stock selling for $50 a share and earning $5 a share, for instance, is said to be selling at a price/earnings ratio of 10. This figure is also called the multiple. Whatever it's called, it's most useful as a means of comparing various securities or the same security over time.

The *yield* is another important figure, reflecting dividends as a percentage of the current price of the stock. A stock with a current market value of $40 a share paying dividends at the rate of $3.20 is said to yield 8 percent ($3.20 divided by $40).

The P/E, the yield, and other important information can be found in the stock market reports in your daily newspaper. Under the headings New York Stock Exchange Composite Index or American Stock Exchange, you'll find detailed information about each stock traded on each exchange. Separate listings are run for over-the-counter stocks, often but not always the stocks of smaller companies, in a different format.

Here's a sample stock quotation, for Mobil Corporation (terminology may vary slightly in different newspapers):

52 WEEK				YIELD	PE	SALES				
High	Low	Stock	Div	%	Ratio	100s	High	Low	Last	Change
32	20¾	Mobil *s* 2.00		8.8	4	3748	22⅝	21⅞	22⅝	¾

- The first two figures, the *52-week high* and *low,* reflect the stock's highest and lowest values over the preceding year.

- After the name of the stock, you'll find a column for its *dividend.* This figure is in dollars and represents the annual dividend, based on the latest declared dividend.

- The *yield* is the percentage return represented by the annual dividend at the current price of the stock.

- The *P/E ratio,* as explained above, is the number of times by which the latest 12-month earnings figure for the company must be multiplied to obtain the current stock price.

- *Sales 100s* refers to the volume of sales for the day. There were 374,800 shares of Mobil traded on the day in the chart. A *z* preceding the volume figure means the sales are quoted in full.

- Stock prices are stated in dollar amounts, with increments of one-eighth. The *high, low,* and *last* figures refer to the stock's prices on the particular trading day. Mobil's high was 22⅝ ($22.62); its low for the day was 21⅞ ($21.87), and its closing price, at the end of the day's trading, was 22⅝. The change for the day, +¾, is the difference—plus, minus, or no change—between the day's last reported price and the previous closing price.

There are other symbols in the tables. A small *s,* like the one following "Mobil," refers to the fact that the stock has split and the price has been adjusted accordingly. When a stock splits—when, for instance, your 100 shares at $50 are now 200 shares worth $25 apiece—your holdings don't actually increase in value. The fact that a corporation has declared a stock split, however, implies that the company is doing well and its stock is becoming more valuable. This, in turn, may create more demand for the stock and drive the price up.

An *x* in front of the sales volume figure means that the stock is selling *ex-dividend.* That is, a dividend declared during this period will be paid to the seller and not to the buyer. This is usually a period of just a few days, after a dividend is declared but before it is actually paid.

Q. My husband and I have bought some securities in joint ownership, with right of survivorship. Is this really a good idea?

A. Jointly held assets can reduce administrative costs and speed settlement of the estate of the first to die. But jointly owned securities can also be a big headache. You both have to agree to a sale, for instance, precluding rapid action in the face of market shifts if one of you is ill or out of town. After one of you dies, the securities may bypass probate, but the survivor will face enormous amounts of paperwork in reregistering the stocks individually. Just as an example, one major corporation lists these required forms (all of which must be submitted with signature guaranteed by banker or broker):

- A security "power" form, with the survivor's Social Security number and signature, and the serial numbers of the securities held

- A death certificate, available from the funeral director

- An affidavit of legal residence of the deceased stockholder for one year prior to death, together with affirmation that all debts, taxes, and claims against the estate have been paid; this document must be notarized

- An inheritance tax waiver or, depending on the state, consent to transfer stock ownership

All in all, it's probably preferable to own securities on an individual basis.

Stock Market Averages

Listen to news broadcasts each day and you'll hear the ups and downs of the stock market referred to, more often than not, in terms of the Dow-Jones Industrial Average. What is this index? And what does it tell you about the state of the economy? about whether or not to invest?

The Dow-Jones Industrial Average measures the performance of the thirty largest and most prestigious industrial concerns in America. It therefore represents, for many people, the health of the American economy.

But the Dow is just one among several stock market averages. Others, some observers believe, provide a more accurate measure. The Standard & Poor's Index, for instance, measures the performance of 500 companies. The New York Stock Exchange Index and the American Stock Exchange Index measure the market value of stocks traded on the respective exchanges. And the NASDAQ (National Association of Securities Dealers Automated Quotations) Index reflects activity on the over-the-counter market.

Over the long haul, the measures should be relatively similar. In the short run, because they measure different groups and types of securities, one index may differ greatly from another. For your purposes, as an average investor, the Dow and the others will serve you best if you remember the following points:

- An index is a measure of movement in stock prices. Part of your yield, however, comes from dividends. You should keep both in mind in evaluating any stock for purchase or retention.

- Each index represents an average. On any given day, certain stocks within the measured group will rise while others will fall. Don't worry too much about day-to-day fluctuations; keep your eye on long-range trends.

- While an index may measure economic trends, your specific concern must be with your own portfolio. You should track the performance of your own securities and create your own index to guide your investment decisions.

Buying Stock

Most stock purchases are made on a cash basis. That is, the order is placed and payment is due, in full, within five days. After payment is made, you may choose to receive the stock, registered in your name. Or you may leave the stock with your broker, registered in "street name," for safekeeping. The latter course works well for frequent traders but makes little sense if you will buy the stock and hold it for long periods.

BUYING ON MARGIN

You may also elect to leverage your purchase, increasing your potential profit (or loss), by buying on margin. When you buy securities on margin, you are buying on credit according to rules laid down by the Federal Reserve Board, the New York Stock Exchange, and your own broker. Those rules say that you can buy shares of stock, for example, with only part of the amount necessary to buy with cash; the difference is borrowed from your broker and secured with the stock itself. Margin requirements are changed periodically by the Federal Reserve Board. When margin is set at 50 percent (as it is in mid-1986), you can buy $10,000 worth of stock with a cash outlay of $5,000. You don't have to put up any more money unless the value of your stock drops below a specified amount. The New York Stock Exchange, at this writing, has a 25 percent requirement (or, in this example, $2,500); many brokerage firms have more stringent requirements for additional cash. Look at this example:

You've made a $10,000 purchase with $5,000. If you then sell the stock for $12,000, the broker immediately receives the $5,000 you borrowed from him. You are entitled to $7,000 (your initial $5,000 plus the $2,000 in appreciation), minus commissions and interest on the loan. If your stock declines in value, you've got a different situation. Now you have to decide whether to sell or to hold on. If you sell for $8,000, you will receive $3,000 (the $8,000 minus the $5,000 loan), minus commission and interest. If you don't sell, and the stock continues to drop, you may well face a *margin call,* a request for more money (or additional securities as collateral) so that you will continue to meet the 25 percent rule. If you don't meet a margin call, your broker can sell your stock.

There are several lessons in this example:

- You can increase your yield (or your loss) by buying on margin, as you can with any leveraged purchase. If you bought that $10,000 worth of stock with your own $10,000 and it went to $12,000, you'd have made $2,000, or 20 percent. If you put up just half of the purchase price ($5,000), however, your yield doubles, to 40 percent. The same principle works when you lose. You can lose money when you trade stocks on a cash account, but you can lose far more when you trade on margin.

- It is difficult to make a profit on small margin purchases. The interest you will pay on the loan itself (depending on how much you borrow and how often you do so) will probably start at 0.75 percent above what the broker pays to borrow the money from the bank; in 1986, interest rates on margin accounts were in the neighborhood of 10 percent. This loan interest (although it is tax-deductible) plus commissions (larger, proportionately, on a small purchase) can easily equal or even exceed the appreciation on a small investment.

- Your broker may urge you to enhance your profits by buying on margin. Before you do so, realize that you enhance your risks as well. Buying on margin is a good technique for gamblers; it holds too many pitfalls for the conservative investor.

Q. I'm thinking about buying some securities on margin, but don't want to leave my family with a significant debt if I should die when the stocks are down in value. Is there a solution?

A. Your estate would be responsible for debts in your margin account as for any other debts. Life insurance is the solution for any debt which concerns you and which would trouble your survivors. If you don't have enough other life insurance, your broker can probably sell you "margin life," a form of term insurance specifically designed for this situation. Upon your death it would first pay your broker any amounts due on your margin account, then pay any balance to your beneficiaries. Compare the rates on this term insurance with the rates on other term insurance, and see which best meets your needs.

Dividend Reinvestment

Whether you are a conservative investor or enjoy the risks of speculation, you can benefit from participating in dividend reinvestment plans. Under these plans, offered by a rapidly growing number of corporations, you can choose to have your dividends applied to the purchase of additional shares. There are several advantages:

■ Dividend reinvestment is a convenient way to put small sums to work, sums you might otherwise fritter away without noticing.

■ Even when commissions are charged—and some companies absorb the cost—the commissions tend to be lower than they would otherwise be on small purchases because your funds are pooled with those of other investors.

■ Dividend reinvestment is a form of automatic *dollar cost averaging*. This is a system of stock purchase under which you purchase small amounts of stock at regular intervals, some at higher prices and some at lower ones, thereby averaging your purchase cost.

Assuming that you have made a good choice to begin with, you can compound your profits by participating in the dividend reinvestment plan. I would suggest doing so unless you are relying on your stock dividends for current income. You can also withdraw from a reinvestment plan at any time, and sell part or all of your accumulated shares, so you might consider participating even if you are approaching the years when you might look to dividends for regular income. When those years arrive, you can pull out.

As you plan your investment strategy, therefore, you might look to corporations with potential for growth plus good dividend reinvestment plans. Any dividend reinvestment plan offers the above advantages. But some offer still more:

■ With some plans you have a "cash option," the privilege of supplementing the dividend with cash and thereby purchasing additional shares at a moderate charge.

■ Some corporations not only absorb the commission costs on purchases through dividend reinvestment, but offer a discount on the purchase price of the shares. Such discounts, typically 5 percent, have been ruled taxable by the Internal Revenue Service. (The dividends themselves are taxable whether you take them in cash or reinvest them.) Note, too, that the discount may be applicable only to reinvested dividends and not to cash purchases.

Q. My 17-year-old son made a good bit of money with a lawn-care service this past summer and would like to buy some common stock. My stockbroker says he can't do so until he is legally an adult. Is this true?

A. Yes. Because a minor can't be held to a contract, stockbrokers generally won't assume the risk of selling them securities. You could make the purchase in your son's name, but he could run into problems in selling the shares. Until your son becomes a legal adult (the age depends on the state in which you live), the solution may be ownership of securities under the Uniform Gifts to Minors Act, with you or another adult as custodian. The shares would legally belong to your son, but you would have to act on his behalf in buying or selling.

Keeping Records

If you participate in a dividend reinvestment plan you will receive quarterly statements of your account: how many shares are held by you, how many shares or fractional shares have been purchased with the latest dividend, how many shares altogether the company has in your account. This information is important for tax purposes.

Your broker and the corporations in which you've invested (whether or not you elect dividend reinvestment) will send you other forms, also important for tax purposes. A confirmation of purchase and of sale will document your profit or loss for purposes of income taxes; these confirmation slips should be retained and kept on hand for at least three years after the filing of the tax return for the year in which you sell the stock. (That's how long the IRS has for a regular audit, as described in Chapter 23.) Year-end forms will document the interest you've received during the year, whether you take it in cash or reinvest it in additional shares. The interest must be reported and income tax must be paid.

It's also wise to keep your own records as the year goes by. Set up a notebook in which you record each dividend as it is received. This way you'll know if a check gets lost in the mail. Record extra dividends, stock splits, and any other relevant information in your notebook, and you'll have a running tally of your investments.

Q. After my father's death we were unable to find the certificates for some stock he owned. Can the certificates be replaced?

A. Consult your father's stockbroker to make sure that he still owned the securities at the time of his death (he might have sold them) and that he actually had possession of the certificates (sometimes a broker keeps them). If the certificates have actually been lost, the corporation must be notified. Most companies will put a "stop transfer" notice on the account for a three-month period during which the stock cannot be sold. You will have to file an affidavit of loss and buy a surety bond, for a premium of about 3 percent of the market value of the securities, which protects the company against any financial loss. After these steps are completed, new certificates will be issued.

Preferred Stock

Preferred stock, like convertible bonds (see p. 122), combines some characteristics of both stocks and bonds. It is subordinate to any debt (bonds) which a corporation has outstanding. But, as the name implies, it usually has a claim ahead of the common stock upon the payment of dividends and upon the assets of the company should the company be dissolved. Preferred stock also has these characteristics:

- The dividend is usually at a set rate, so that preferred stock, like bonds, is a fixed-income investment.

- Where bonds almost always have a final maturity date, preferreds do not. But many preferreds, like most bonds, can be called in at prices set when the security was issued.

- Some preferred stocks, like some bonds, are convertible into common stock.

- Preferred stock, in general, offers steadier income, a higher return, and a lower degree of risk than investment in common stock.

Bonds

When you buy a share of common stock, you're becoming a part owner of the corporation. When you buy a bond, on the other hand, you are becoming a creditor of the corporation (or of the governing body, since bonds are also issued by state and local governments). You are loaning money to the corporation, usually in $1,000 increments; in exchange you will receive the principal sum, at maturity date, plus interest for the use of the money.

When you buy a share of stock, as an owner, you can expect to share in the fortunes of the company. If the company does well, your dividends may increase and the shares themselves may be worth more money. When you buy a bond, you are buying a fixed-rate security. The company may prosper but your rate of return is set from the beginning.

Bonds used to be called the investment of widows and orphans; their fixed rate of return made them both safe and stable. In recent years, however, investment in bonds has not been a sure thing at all. As inflation escalated in the late 1970s, new bond issues had to have higher and higher nominal yields in order to attract investors. As yields on new issues increased, older bonds lost a great deal of their value. Investors who wanted or needed to sell their bonds before maturity often sustained significant capital loss. "Bond," in some quarters, became a nasty four-letter word. In other, less conservative, quarters, bonds became a vehicle for aggressive investment.

Bonds of one sort or another will probably still play a role in your investment strategy. How big a role depends on your investment goals, your age, and your attitude toward risk. Here are the varieties of bonds to consider:

Corporate Bonds

Corporate bonds, as indicated, represent a corporation's debt to you. That debt may be backed by collateral, as when a corporation issues mortgage bonds. Or it may be backed, in bonds called *debentures,* by a promise to pay and the full faith and credit of the issuing company. Although bondholders take precedence over stockholders when it comes to repayment out of diminished assets, it's still wise to check the financial standing of a corporation before buying its bonds.

When bonds are taking a beating from inflation, corporations increasingly try innovative methods to spur investor interest. Corporate bonds generally pay more interest than municipals, although municipal issues (see p. 123) usually have the advantage of tax exemption. Some bonds are being issued with shorter maturities, five to seven years, perhaps, instead of thirty. Some are being issued with "call protection" (see p. 126) so that high yields are guaranteed for a longer period of time. And some are being issued on a variable-rate basis.

In considering variable-rate bonds, the most important factors are the rate used to adjust the interest and the frequency of the adjustment. Look, too, for ceilings and/or floors on the variable rate. And be careful; some authorities caution that you may forgo potential capital gains (if interest rates fall and the market prices of fixed-rate bonds rise to compensate) in exchange for adjustable interest rates.

DISCOUNT BONDS

New bonds are issued at a fixed price and fixed interest rate. Discount bonds are older bonds whose prices have declined since they were issued because interest rates have risen in the interim. So-called "deep discount" bonds are those with a significant discount. Discount bonds generally offer lower current income than new issues. But when you determine the yield to maturity, adding in the capital gains that will stem from redemption at face value, the overall return looks much better.

For example: A 40-year AT&T bond, due in June 1987, was selling in mid-1982 for $665 and yielding 4 percent. But you could count on a long-term capital gain of $335, in just five years, boosting the actual yield to 12 percent.

Q. I've been saving about $500 a year toward my son's college education, with $5,000 on hand so far and eight years to go. Another $4,000, even with interest, isn't going to go very far. What kind of investment would you recommend?

A. You might use the $5,000 to buy bonds issued some time ago and now available at a discount. Such bonds often have a fairly high current yield, but they aren't attractive to people who may need to sell them before they mature. If you know, and are absolutely certain, that you won't need the money until your son starts college, you can buy discount bonds with a maturity date eight years out. You might, for instance, be able to buy eight or nine bonds, worth $8,000 or $9,000 at maturity, for your $5,000. Ask your broker for specific suggestions. Tell the broker, too, that you may want to make such a purchase again as you accumulate more funds. The interest on the bonds should, of course, be reinvested as well and added to the college fund.

Or you might buy zero-coupon bonds (see below) maturing in eight years, so that you won't have to worry about reinvesting interest. Taxes are due on the accumulating interest in zero-coupon corporate bonds, even though it isn't actually paid out, but buying tax-exempt municipal zeros will eliminate the tax liability.

ZERO-COUPON BONDS

These bonds, which sprang to popularity in 1982, pay no interest at all but promise big capital accumulation by maturity. Called by such acronyms as CATS, TIGRS, and the like, zeros are available through stockbrokers. These bonds are attractive (if interest rates don't spiral upward) because the rate is locked in. But there's a catch: Even though there's no interest actually paid, the IRS assumes "imputed interest," which is taxable each year just as if it were actually paid. Zero-coupon bonds, as a result, are most suitable for tax-deferred investments such as Individual Retirement Accounts and Keogh Plans.

Zero-coupon bonds may be purchased either individually or in specially formulated bond funds. Some have also been issued by state and local governments, which eliminates the tax problem and may make the bonds suitable for tax-sheltered investment outside your retirement plan.

CONVERTIBLES

Some bonds, combining characteristics of both bonds and common stock, are convertible to the common stock of the corporation. Convertible bonds, marked with a "cv" in newspaper bond tables, pay interest, often more than the dividends on comparable common stock but less than the interest on comparable straight (nonconvertible) bonds. Convertible bonds offer appreciation possibilities linked to the earnings and growth of the company; they tend to rise and fall in value along with the company's common stock. Yet convertible bonds have an investment value above that of common stock. Most convertible bonds are convertible into stock at a fixed rate during the entire life of the bond. Sometimes, however, the conversion privilege expires at a set date.

Why buy convertible bonds? Common stock usually offers more opportunity for appreciation. Straight bonds usually offer more income. But your investment objectives (like most people's) may be mixed. You may be willing to sacrifice some capital appreciation possibilities for the sake of income or, conversely, give up higher income possibilities for a degree of appreciation potential.

WARRANTS

Warrants, like convertible bonds, are options which entitle you to purchase the common stock of the company at specified prices with the payment of cash and surrender of the warrants. With convertible bonds you turn in the bonds in exchange for the stock; with warrants you turn in just the detachable warrant, along with your cash payment, and retain the bond itself.

Most warrants are good for only a short period of time. While they are good, you can exercise them at a profit when the common stock goes up in value. You can also usually sell warrants themselves through your broker. Once they expire, however, they are worthless.

Municipal Bonds

Municipal bonds have traditionally been exempt from federal taxes and usually from state taxes in the state in which they are issued. (Some states impose a tax on out-of-state issues. If your state does so, and if it is a high-tax state, your yield will be reduced and the bond may not be worth buying. You may want to stick to bonds issued in your own state.) Muncicipal bonds come in several varieties:

General obligation bonds are backed by the full faith, credit, and taxing power of the municipality issuing them.

Revenue bonds are issued to raise money for a specific purpose (a turnpike, a utility system, a hospital, etc.) and backed by funds raised by the particular project.

Moral obligation bonds are backed not by either taxes or projected revenues but by the issuer's moral pledge to make up any capital reserve deficiency.

General obligation bonds are the safest, followed by revenue bonds, and then by moral obligation bonds. In any case, although municipal bonds are generally considered just below U.S. government obligations (see p. 127) in terms of safety and quality (and payments on more than 98 percent of all municipals were met during the Depression of the 1930s), they are only as good as the financial soundness of the issuing state or municipality. When local governments are in financial difficulty, as does happen, be sure to investigate thoroughly before you invest. Or buy only *insured* issues (labeled accordingly)—but bear in mind that insurance guarantees principal and interest only if the bonds are held till maturity; market price is never guaranteed.

Note: Under the 1986 tax legislation, bond issues where more than 10 percent of revenue is for a so-called "private purpose" (such as housing, for example, or industrial development) will be limited in number and will be subject to the alternative personal minimum income tax (see p. 497).

SHOULD YOU BUY MUNICIPAL BONDS?

If sheltering income from taxes is of major concern in your investment strategy, then tax-free municipal bonds may be right for you. But they'll only be right if you're in a tax bracket where the tax savings make sense —and if you'll stay in such a tax bracket, as far as you can tell, for the life of the bonds. Consider state and local income taxes, too, as you make your calculations. Interest of 12 percent on a tax-free bond is the equivalent of 24 percent taxable interest if you're in the 50 percent (combined) marginal tax bracket but only the equivalent of 16 percent if you're in the 25 percent bracket. Below the 25 percent bracket, forget it; tax-free bonds don't make sense.

To find equivalent yields of taxable and tax-free investments, the investment firm of Prudential-Bache Securities suggests, divide the tax-free rate by the reciprocal of your tax bracket (the reciprocal is the number you get by subtracting your tax bracket from 100). If, for instance, a municipal is yielding 9 percent and you are in the 35 percent tax bracket, dividing 9 by 65 shows that you would have to receive 13.8 percent in a taxable issue to be competitive. You can do the same thing in reverse—multiply a taxable yield by the reciprocal of your tax bracket —to get the tax-free equivalent. You can accomplish the same thing, without the arithmetic, by asking your stockbroker for an equivalency table like the one in Table 1.

TABLE 1: Tax-free vs. taxable yields.

Tax-exempt yields	Equivalent taxable yields at tax brackets of:		
	33%	28%	15%
7%	4.69%	5.04%	5.95%
8	5.36	5.76	6.80
9	6.03	6.48	7.65
10	6.70	7.20	8.50
11	7.37	7.92	9.35

(Source: United States League of Savings Institutions)

Municipal bonds may be attractive, but don't borrow to buy them. The IRS forbids deducting interest on loans made for the purchase of tax-exempt securities. If the bonds are used as collateral for a loan, moreover, then the interest paid on the loan must be offset against the income on the bond for tax purposes. You can't exclude earned interest while deducting owed interest. And don't buy municipals for your IRA or Keogh Plan, designed to shelter retirement funds from taxes. It makes no sense to erect a tax shelter over tax-exempt securities.

Before You Buy Bonds

Here are the basic facts you should know before you invest in bonds:

BOND ISSUANCE

Bonds may now be issued only in registered form, issued in your name and with interest mailed directly to you. Bearer bonds, which were an alternate form until the 1982 Tax Act specified that all new bonds with maturities of more than one year must be registered, have coupons to be clipped on specified dates and surrendered in exchange for interest payments. Older bearer bonds are still available as resales.

RISK AND RATINGS

Some bonds are safer investments than other bonds. Those issued by the U.S. government are probably the safest investments in the world. Those issued by municipalities and corporations run the gamut from very safe to very risky. Good guides for the investor are the ratings published by Moody's and Standard & Poor's; for minimum risk stick to bonds rated A and better. Lower-rated bonds may offer higher yields but with considerably higher risk.

Note: A high rating does not guarantee a return on your investment. All it does is assure you that the issuer is, as far as is known, creditworthy with respect to the particular bond issue.

MATURITY

Bonds are issued for set periods of time. Long-term bonds may have maturity dates twenty or thirty years in the future. Intermediate-term bonds may mature in five to ten years. You are guaranteed the return of your principal if you wait until maturity to redeem the bonds; if you need the money sooner, you may lose some money. You may, looking ahead to retirement in fifteen years, buy bonds scheduled to mature in fifteen years. This is a good investment strategy, but only if you can be reasonably certain that you won't need the money in the interim. You can sell most bonds at any time, but you can never be sure of the price. If you know you'll need the money at a specific time, therefore, look for maturities on or before that date.

YIELD

Return on bonds is calculated in terms of both *current yield* and *yield to maturity*. If you buy a newly issued bond and hold it to maturity, your yield is fixed. But bonds are bought and sold, sometimes at a premium and sometimes at a discount. As the price changes, the yield changes as well. If you pay more than the face value of the bond, the excess amount is prorated annually over the life of the bond and subtracted from the yield. If you pay less than the face value, then the discount, also prorated, is added to the yield. Seventy dollars in interest on a $1,000 bond yields 7 percent, but $70 interest on the same bond, priced at $1,100, yields 6 percent. Exact yields, including the impact of compound interest, are found in the bond tables of most newspapers. Here's a sample bond quotation:

Bonds	Cur Yld	Vol	High	Low	Close	Net Chg
ATT 8¾00	10.8	210	81	80⅝	81	+¼

Bond prices are quoted as a percentage of the par or face value of the bond, represented as 100. The name of the issuing company is in the first column, followed by the original coupon or interest rate and the last two digits of the year of maturity; the above bond pays interest at the original rate of 8¾ percent and matures in the year 2000. Its current yield, because the price is below the par value of $1,000, is 10.8 percent. The High, Low, and Close (or Last, in some newspapers) columns refer to the bond's price during the day's trading; Net Change is the difference between the day's closing price and the previous day's closing price. The Volume column simply indicates that exactly 210 of these bonds were traded on the New York Stock Exchange on this particular day.

CALLABLE BONDS

Some bonds are subject to call, which means that the issuer may redeem the bond at a stated price before maturity, often after a specified number of years. Always ask whether a bond is callable and when, and in order to reduce the risk of loss, don't buy a bond at a price well above that at which the company can call the bond for redemption.

Note: If you hold registered bonds you will be notified of a call; if you hold bearer bonds, and don't read the financial press, you may not find out until you present a clipped coupon for interest. You may, as a result, lose some interest.

"AVERAGING" THE COST OF BOND PURCHASES

It's possible to adopt a technique with bond purchases similar to dollar cost averaging in stock purchases. With bonds, it entails buying a series of bonds that will reach maturity in different years. Every time a bond is redeemed the resulting cash can be reinvested to stretch the cycle still further. In addition to achieving a constant cash flow, this procedure tends to average out the effect of market price changes.

COMMISSIONS

You may find that your broker doesn't recommend bond purchases as often as stock purchases. One reason: Brokerage commissions are far smaller on bonds, and, of course, the broker is in business to make money. You can save on even this commission by buying newly issued bonds; here the broker's commission is paid by the issuer of the bond and not by the buyer.

United States Government Obligations

You can also derive income by lending money to Uncle Sam, either directly through Treasury issues or indirectly through various agency obligations. Both are fixed-income investments, with yields calculated in advance and no opportunity for growth of capital. They are ideal for people seeking both safety and guaranteed income.

Treasury Issues

The U.S. Treasury raises money through three different vehicles: bills, notes, and bonds. All are direct obligations of the U.S. government, and the safest possible investment. All are exempt from state and local income taxes, but not from federal income tax.

Treasury bonds are issued with maturity periods of ten to thirty years, with the minimum purchase price set at $1,000, and interest payable twice a year.

Treasury notes are issued with maturity periods of one to ten years. Those with maturities four years or less are usually offered in a minimum denomination of $5,000; when maturities are longer than four years, the minimum denomination is usually $1,000. Interest is payable twice a year.

Treasury bills are issued in 3-month, 6-month, and 1-year maturities, each priced at $10,000. T-bills are sold at a discount, with the interest deducted in advance from the purchase price, so that the actual yield is increased.

Q. I have $30,000 from the sale of a business and would like to invest it for a few months while I decide on a new business venture. I can put it in a time deposit or a money market deposit account at a bank, I can buy a 6-month Treasury bill, or I can put it in a money market mutual fund. Which would be best?

A. Since time deposits usually have fixed maturity dates and early withdrawal penalties, and you're not sure when you'll need the money, don't put it in a time deposit. Either a money market deposit account or a money market mutual fund would provide the liquidity you need while paying a market rate of interest. But T-bills, which can readily be sold, may be your best bet. That's because T-bills are sold at a discount which increases the effective yield. The interest, which is subject to federal but not to state or local income taxes, can also be invested during the six months to earn additional income. Check current rates before you make your decision.

HOW TO BUY TREASURY ISSUES

Treasury bills, notes, and bonds may be purchased directly from the Department of the Treasury, Bureau of the Public Debt, Washington, D.C. 20226, or from any of the twelve regional offices and their local branches of the Federal Reserve Bank (see list). There is no charge to purchase Treasury issues through the Federal Reserve Bank, and the process is reasonably simple (although the Treasury Department harbors some thoughts of cutting off direct sales). Write to the nearest Federal Reserve Bank and ask for the necessary forms; submit the forms, together with full payment, by the date given for the offering in which you are interested.

WHERE TO FIND THE FEDERAL RESERVE BANK NEAREST YOU

Federal Reserve Bank of	Address (mark envelope "Attention: Fiscal Agency Dept.")
ATLANTA	104 Marietta Street N.W., Atlanta, Georgia 30303 (404) 586-8500
BOSTON	600 Atlantic Avenue, Boston, Massachusetts 02106 (617) 973-3000
CHICAGO	230 South LaSalle Street, P.O. Box 834, Chicago, Illinois 60690 (312) 322-5322
CLEVELAND	1455 East Sixth Street, P.O. Box 6387, Cleveland, Ohio 44101 (216) 241-2800
DALLAS	400 South Akard Street, Station K, Dallas, Texas 75222 (214) 651-6111
KANSAS CITY	925 Grand Avenue, Federal Reserve Station, Kansas City, Missouri 64198 (816) 881-2000
MINNEAPOLIS	250 Marquette Avenue, Minneapolis, Minnesota 55480 (612) 340-2345
NEW YORK	33 Liberty Street, Federal Reserve P.O. Station, New York, New York 10045 (212) 791-5000
PHILADELPHIA	100 North Sixth Street, P.O. Box 66, Philadelphia, Pennsylvania 19105 (215) 574-6000
RICHMOND	701 East Byrd Street, P.O. Box 27622, Richmond, Virginia 23261 (804) 643-1250
ST. LOUIS	411 Locust Street, P.O. Box 442, St. Louis, Missouri 63166 (314) 444-8444
SAN FRANCISCO	400 Sansome Street, P.O. Box 7702, San Francisco, California 94120 (415) 544-2000
If unsure, write to:	Board of Governors of the Federal Reserve System, 20th and Constitution Avenue N.W., Washington, D.C. 20551 (202) 452-3000

You may, instead, buy Treasury issues through your stockbroker or through many commercial banks. If you buy in this convenient way, there will be a handling charge, depending on the institution, of about $50; this will reduce your yield.

You may also invest in Treasury issues by investing in a money market fund which, in turn, invests only in U.S. government securities. These funds have grown in recent years in response to investor awareness that money market funds are not insured. A fund that invests solely in government issues is as safe as the U.S. government itself.

Agency Obligations

The U.S. Treasury issues the bills, notes, and bonds described above. A wide range of other government agencies issue notes and bonds to finance their own projects. Treasury issues are backed by the full faith and credit of the U.S. government. Agency issues generally are not (although it's not very likely that the government would allow one of its agencies to default), so the yield on agency obligations is often a bit higher than that on Treasuries.

Some of the agencies raising funds via public offerings include the Farm Credit Bank, the Federal Home Loan Bank, and the Federal National Mortgage Association. These obligations cannot be purchased directly from the issuing agency; you must buy them from a commercial bank or stockbrokerage and pay a handling fee. You do not receive a certificate—computer records are kept by the issuer—but you do receive interest payments by check. The interest is subject to federal income tax. Interest on most issues, but not all, is exempt from state and local income tax. Ask your broker for details on different issues.

"GINNIE MAES"

Securities issued by the Government National Mortgage Association, familiarly called Ginnie Mae, are being bought by many small investors. A Ginnie Mae certificate represents a share in a pool of government-guaranteed mortgages and, unlike many other agency obligations, is backed by the full faith and credit of the U.S. government. The minimum size of original individual certificates is $25,000, but existing certificates may be purchased for substantially less. You may also buy shares, at $1,000 apiece, in a Ginnie Mae fund sponsored by a securities firm.

Although mortgages typically run twenty-five to thirty years, GNMA yields are projected to an average life of twelve years. Sometimes mortgages are prepaid and the life of the pool is shortened, increasing the yield to the investor. The yield, however, is not guaranteed.

Each month, as a Ginnie Mae investor, you receive both interest and a partial return of capital representing partial amortization of the principal on all the mortgages in the pool. These regular payments—although they will vary, depending on how many mortgages are paid off in a given month—make Ginnie Maes an ideal long-range investment for steady income, attractive to many retirees.

Options and Commodities

U.S. government obligations are the safest of all investments. They are also very conservative, in the sense that your money will grow through interest but not through capital appreciation. At the other end of the investment spectrum, for the investor with nerves of steel, are the risk-laden but potentially profitable areas of options and commodities.

Options

If you wanted time to make up your mind about the purchase of a piece of real estate, you might buy an option. You would pay the seller a specified amount in return for his holding the property for you at a specified price for a specified period of time. If you chose not to buy the real estate, you could simply let the option expire at the end of the time period —but the seller would keep the option fee as payment for keeping the property available to you for that length of time. If you did buy the property, the price you paid for it would be over and above the price you paid for the option.

Options on securities are a bit more complicated but work on the same principle. A price is paid, for instance, for the right to buy 100 shares of a given stock at a specified price within a specified period of time. If the right is not exercised, the option expires. The purchaser hopes, meanwhile, that the stock's price will go up (if he bought a "call," the right to buy) or down (if he bought a "put," the right to sell) by an amount large enough to pay the premium, fees, and commission on the transaction— and to provide a profit as well. If the price holds steady or moves in the unhoped-for direction, the price of the option is lost. The option itself is a contract to buy or to sell, applied to a particular security.

Buying options offers a potentially large profit from a relatively small investment (the price of the option, rather than the price of the stock), with relatively little risk (the most you can lose is the price of the option). Selling options provides a hedge against a decline in stock prices. If the price of your stock goes down, you can sell it at the price set by the option. Selling options is a conservative move, if you own the stock on which you are selling the option. If you don't, then you are playing a speculative game. With a "naked" option, one where you don't own the underlying stock, you may lose your bet and have to purchase the stock for delivery at a very high price.

Either way, you should be prepared to follow the market closely, via the closing option prices listed in the daily newspapers; options have a short life span and are much more volatile than common stock. If you want to get involved, you should also find a broker who is knowledgeable about this specialized area. And be prepared: commissions are sizable.

Note: Options on stock date only from the 1970s, but new variations, mostly tied to commodities (see below), are already in the works. For the highly sophisticated risk-seeker, options may be considered on gold and silver, coffee and sugar, Treasury bills and bonds, and so on.

Commodities

Commodities are another highly technical and speculative investment, one where a lot of money can be made or lost. An investment in commodities or commodity futures is an investment in the future price of some basic commodity: coffee or sugar or pork bellies, Treasury bonds or gold or foreign currency. If you buy commodities, you are gambling on government policies, international market developments, and the buying patterns of consumers around the world. You can put up just 10 to 15 percent at the outset, but you can lose much more, sometimes in a matter of hours; 85 to 90 percent of all the players lose money, often considerable amounts of money, in this game. This is not an investment for anyone trying to accumulate money for homebuying, college tuition, or retirement.

It is possible, however, to invest in a commodity fund, a form of limited partnership, for $5,000 to $10,000 (a lot less than it takes for individual participation in this high-stakes game). With a fund (unlike the margin trading of individual accounts), you can't lose more than your original investment. But you can, and very well may, lose that. At the same time, fees and commissions can run more than 20 percent. Even purchased via a fund, commodities are not for the faint-hearted.

FINANCIAL FUTURES

A new wrinkle in commodities trading is the futures contract without an actual underlying commodity. It is now possible to enter into futures contracts on Treasury bonds, on foreign currency, and on the action of the stock market itself, via an index of stock market prices. The Kansas City Board of Trade, for instance, has used the Value Line Index; the New York Futures Exchange uses the New York Stock Exchange Composite Index. Financial futures are a form of betting on interest rates and are not a game for amateurs. If you want to gamble, go to Las Vegas; the stakes are not as high.

A word to the wise, from the Securities and Exchange Commission, concerning any investment:

- Before buying . . . think!

- Don't deal with strange securities firms. (Consult your broker, banker or other experienced person you know and trust.)

- Beware of securities offered over the telephone by strangers.

- Don't listen to high-pressure sales talk.

- Beware of promises of spectacular profits.

- Be sure you understand the risks of loss.

- Don't buy on tips and rumors . . . get all the facts!

- Tell the salesman to put all the information and advice in writing and mail it to you. Save it!

- If you don't understand all the written information, consult a person who does.

- Give at least as much consideration to buying securities as you would to buying other valuable property.

Hard Assets: Gold, Gems, and Collectibles

When inflation rates are high and the economy looks a bit unsteady, some investors turn to tangible assets. Gold and precious gems and fine art appear immune to the ups and downs of the stock market, the uncertainties of the bond market, and the speculative vicissitudes of options and commodities. But are they, really? Let's look at these assets as investments (apart from their role in any take-to-the-hills survival strategy) and at their possible role in your investment strategy.

One important point to remember about all tangible assets: You earn no interest and no dividends while you hold them; your only opportunity for profit is when you sell—*if* prices are up and *if* you can find a buyer. At that time you'll face dealer commissions or premiums on the sale (on top of the premiums paid when you bought). Meanwhile, you'll probably have safekeeping charges in the form of vault fees—unless you keep these assets at home, which poses other risks.

Gold

Gold, the classic hedge against disaster, rose from $125 an ounce in 1975, when Americans could legally own gold for the first time since the 1930s, to $850 an ounce in January 1980. It then proceeded to move down, with periodic fluctuations, until it hovered around $335 in early 1986. If you had bought it at or near its low and sold it near the top, you could have made a great deal of money. But then, that's true of any investment, and easier to say than to do. The truth, in any case, is that many people who buy gold do so less as an investment than as a cushion against an uncertain future.

If you want to buy gold, here are the varieties to consider:

Gold coins, minted by several countries and sold at a small markup over the actual value of the gold content, are the safest and easiest way for the small investor to buy and own gold.

Bullion bars come in sizes from half-ounce wafers (that's a Troy ounce, the official measure of gold) to bars weighing hundreds of ounces. Buy from a reputable dealer, one who will give you a written promise to repurchase the bullion, to be sure that the bar is at least 99 percent pure. Gold in bars has two major disadvantages: You can't sell off part of a bar to raise needed cash; and when you want to sell the bullion, you will have to have it assayed, a procedure which will reduce any profit you might make. (However, you can avoid assaying and the accompanying charge if you leave the bars in the dealer's safekeeping instead of taking possession.)

Gold certificates are another way of buying bullion without taking physical possession. The certificate, whose value fluctuates with the underlying price of the gold, is your evidence of ownership; it is easily sold.

Gold mining stocks are a way of investing in gold and securing dividend income as well as the chance of capital appreciation. Gold stocks, however, are susceptible to government policy and political disruption, and come complete with a significant amount of risk.

Mutual funds also offer a way to specialize in gold shares, a way to diversify and to leave day-to-day management to others.

Two cautionary notes:

- Don't buy gold jewelry as an investment, not unless you like the jewelry and will enjoy wearing it. The reason: You'll be paying for the design and workmanship as well as for the gold itself.

- Don't speculate on gold; that's *really* a game for thick-skinned experts who can afford to lose. If you buy gold, buy it with money you won't need, and be prepared to hold on. Otherwise, when you need the cash, the price of gold could be at an all-time low.

Diamonds

As a tangible asset and hedge against inflation, diamonds share some of the disadvantages of gold: no interest or dividends, the cost of insuring and safekeeping, and dealer premiums on both purchase and sale. They also have another disadvantage: When you buy a diamond, you pay the retail price, since the dealer has to make his profit, but when you sell a diamond (assuming that you can find a buyer), you get the wholesale price, so that the purchaser can make a profit when he resells the stone. You can't win, unless prices rise enormously.

Investment-grade diamonds (not the same as jewelry-grade) were a popular investment in the late 1970s, when a top-quality "D-flawless" 1-carat stone rose from $6,000 to over $60,000 in three years. But look what happened in the next two years: Between 1980 and 1982, the wholesale price of that same flawless diamond fell to about $15,000. Diamonds, like gold, are a risky investment.

If you do want to put some diamonds in your investment portfolio here are some tips:

- Know the four keys to diamond value: color, clarity, carat, and cut. The best diamond has the least *color,* with ranks ranging from D (virtually colorless) down to X. Investment-grade diamonds range between D and J. Forget the term "blue-white"; it doesn't mean a thing. *Clarity* measures freedom from imperfection; "flawless" is best. *Carat* is the international standard for diamond weight, with 142 carats to an ounce. Each carat weighs two-tenths of a gram, but diamonds are so valuable that each carat is further divided into "points." A point is less than one ten-thousandth of an ounce. And *cut* is the design (round, emerald-cut, pear-shaped, etc.) and the perfection of that design. An investment stone should be round, rather than a shape that may be only temporarily fashionable.

- Know the company. Never buy from a salesman or company totally new to you. Do some investigation. Ask for trade references, bank references, supplier references.

- Be sure that any verbal claims are in writing. Does the company promise to buy back the stone? Within what time period and at what price?

- Look for certification from an independent laboratory, such as the Gemological Institute of America. This certification is not an appraisal and does not assign a value; it is an identifying report on the specific features of the stone and verifies that the diamond you buy is indeed the one you receive.

- Get an appraisal, too, from an independent source. An appraisal from the people who sell you the diamond is worthless.

Colored Gems

Diamonds may be risky, but colored gems are riskier still. There are certification standards set for diamonds. If you buy from a reputable dealer, you can be reasonably certain that an E-flawless diamond is an E-flawless diamond. But there are no objective standards for colored gems, and even reputable dealers have trouble telling some varieties apart. Leave investment in colored gems to the professionals, unless you're prepared to become a professional yourself.

Collectibles, Antiques, and Art

There are stories of vast profits in a wide range of tangible items, from mint-condition comic books to contemporary lithographs. There are also stories (the ones you don't hear at cocktail parties) about losses when the wrong collectible is purchased. Such stories have become more common. In 1980, inflation had lifted prices of all types of collectibles to record highs. By 1986, with disinflation in the economy as a whole, most collectibles had fallen on hard times. The prices of rare coins, stamps, photographs, antiques, etc. have fallen drastically.

If you are interested in collecting for profit:

- Become knowledgeable in a particular field and concentrate on that field.

- Pick a field you like, so that you'll enjoy living with your collection before you sell.

- Look for quality and rarity as keys to value. ("Instant" collectibles and "limited" editions, whether plates or medallions or prints, are widely advertised and sold; they seldom increase very much in value.)

- Be prepared to hold your collection for some years before you sell. When you do sell, expect to pay commissions ranging up to 25 percent.

- Understand the tax treatment of collectibles. Capital gains tax applies to profits from a resale, but a loss cannot be deducted unless you can prove that you intended to make a profit. Without such proof your collection will be considered, for tax purposes, as a hobby.

KEY POINTS

- Investment in mutual funds permits diversification without a major commitment of money. Your best bets are no-load funds in a "family" of funds, with free exchange-by-telephone privileges.

- Purchases of common stock make you a part owner of the corporation issuing the stock; the value of your investment will rise and fall along with the fortunes of the company.

- Purchase of bonds makes you a creditor of the issuing corporation or governing body, entitled to interest for the use of your money.

- Fixed-income Treasury issues provide safe guaranteed income but no opportunity for capital growth.

- Options and commodities are highly risky investments, suitable only for the knowledgeable investor who can afford to lose considerable sums.

- Tangible assets, such as gold and precious gems, are attractive when inflation rates are high; even then, however, they provide no income, only the chance of a profit when you sell.

Tax Shelters

In recent years, inflation drove more and more "average" Americans into tax brackets previously reserved for the well-to-do. Along with higher tax brackets, inevitably, came an interest in sheltering income from taxes. Such sheltering, however, should never be an end in itself. Instead, tax advantages should be considered as part of your overall investment strategy and lifelong financial plan.

This has always been true but is even more true today. Tax acts of 1981 and 1986 have made tax shelters as pure tax shelters considerably less attractive. First, the 1981 Act removed the distinction between earned income (formerly taxed at a maximum rate of 50 percent) and unearned income (formerly taxed at a maximum rate of 70 percent). Then the 1986 Act reduced the maximum tax to 28 percent (with a surcharge for some taxpayers bringing it to 33 percent, see p. 474). Second, the changes in both the tax rate and tax brackets mean that you could overdo your quest for shelter. If you're married and filing a joint return, you reach the 28 percent federal income tax bracket for 1986 at a combined income of $32,270; in 1988, when you'd still expect to be receiving deductions from any tax shelter you entered in 1986, you'll need a joint income of just $29,750 to hit the 28 percent bracket—an income at which it hardly pays to shelter. Third, under rules of the 1986 law, paper losses (so-called "passive income") from shelters can't be used to offset taxes due on other income. And, lastly, income tax returns with tax shelters are now being scrutinized by the Internal Revenue Service with great care. Any shelter you choose must be a legitimate investment, with a reasonable expectation of profit, and not just a shelter. If the IRS thinks otherwise, tax penalties could wipe out any benefit.

What Is a Tax Shelter?

The term "tax shelter" generally refers to an investment structured for its tax advantages; most such investments take the form of limited partnerships. But income can be removed from the tax collector's grasp in several ways. It can be removed altogether, via tax-exempt investments such as municipal bonds. It can be partially sheltered if you can arrange to have it taxed at a lower rate, as through income splitting. Or the day

TABLE 1: Marginal federal tax rates on ordinary income, 1986–88.

SINGLE FILER			JOINT FILER		
If your income is over this bracket:	You will pay a base tax of:	Plus this percent of amount over the bracket:	If your income is over this bracket:	You will pay a base tax of:	Plus this percent of amount over the bracket:
1986			**1986**		
$ 0	$ 0	0%	$ 0	$ 0	0%
2,480	0	11%	3,670	0	11%
3,670	130.90	12%	5,940	249.70	12%
4,750	260.50	14%	8,200	520.90	14%
7,010	576.90	15%	12,840	1,170.50	16%
9,170	900.90	16%	17,270	1,879.30	18%
11,650	1,297.70	18%	21,800	2,694.70	22%
13,920	1,706.30	20%	26,550	3,739.70	25%
16,190	2,160.30	23%	32,270	5,169.70	28%
19,640	2,953.80	26%	37,980	6,768.50	33%
25,360	4,441.00	30%	49,420	10,543.70	38%
31,080	6,157.00	34%	64,750	16,369.10	42%
36,800	8,101.80	38%	92,370	27,969.50	45%
44,780	11,134.20	42%	118,050	39,525.50	49%
59,670	17,388.00	48%	175,250	67,553.50	50%
88,270	31,116.00	50%			
1987			**1987**		
$ 0	$ 0	11%	$ 0	$ 0	11%
1,800	198	15%	3,000	330	15%
16,800	2,448	28%	28,000	4,080	28%
27,000	5,304	35%	45,000	8,840	35%
56,000	15,454	38.5%	90,000	24,590	38.5%
1988			**1988**		
$ 0	$ 0	15%	$ 0	$ 0	15%
17,850	2,678	28%	29,750	4,463	28%

(Source: Joint Committee on Taxation)

of reckoning can simply be postponed by deferring the payment of taxes, which you can do by rolling over the profit from the sale of a home or by investing in an annuity.

Some tax shelters are very conservative; some are extremely risky. Judith H. McQuown, in her excellent book *Tax Shelters That Work for Everyone* (McGraw-Hill, 1979), describes five different types of investor risk:

Risk as function of tax bracket. As described above, this refers to the degree of risk the government picks up as compared to your actual exposure (when the top bracket was 70 percent, the government could assume 70 percent of the risk; today your own risk is considerably increased).

Psychological risk. This means how much risk you are comfortable in assuming.

Business/investment risk. If there were no risk to the investment, Congress wouldn't have made tax shelters attractive with a tax incentive, but you should go into a shelter anticipating a reasonable profit.

Tax risk. This refers to the risk of an audit, especially if there is overly aggressive depreciation, plus the risk that changing tax laws will adversely affect your investment.

Inflation risk. Will the investment keep pace with inflation?

Shelters for Everyone

Before you consider any of the riskier tax shelters, be sure you've taken full advantage of the safe and sure shelters at your disposal; your own home, income-splitting, tax-free investments, and retirement accounts.

Your Own Home

Homeownership is still one of the biggest and best tax shelters of all, as Chapter 15 indicates. When you own your own house or condominium you may deduct both mortgage interest and property taxes from your income when calculating your federal income tax. You may defer payment of taxes when you sell the home, if you put the profits into another home. And you may exclude $125,000 of profit from taxes altogether if you are over age 55 when you sell.

Your first tax shelter, therefore, is your family shelter: the roof over your head. If you're concerned about high taxes and you don't own your own home, see what you can do to become a homeowner.

VACATION HOMES

While your primary residence offers the most tax shelter, a second home (see p. 311) has tax advantages as well, since mortgage interest and property tax payments are tax-deductible. However, taxes on profit when you sell may not be either deferred or exempt; this particular benefit applies only to your principal residence.

If you rent out your vacation home for added income, special rules apply. If you use the home most of the time yourself but rent it to others for more than two weeks a year, you may also be able to deduct other expenses, such as depreciation, maintenance, and utilities, up to the amount of the rental income. (These deductions are worth less, however, with the lower tax rates and longer depreciation schedules of the 1986 tax law.) If your personal use is less than two weeks a year, you may treat the income as a business for tax purposes. And if you rent it for only fourteen days or less each year, you don't have to report the rent as income.

Income-Splitting

Income-splitting means sharing income with a famly member in a lower tax bracket, in order to reduce income taxes due. Income can be shared with minor children over age 14, by saving money for that child's college education via a custodial account in the child's name (see p. 392). Interest is then reported in the child's name, and the taxes due are based on his or her (generally low or zero) tax bracket. The same technique can be used if you are financially responsible for a parent.

Again, tax advantages are only a part of your financial plan. You shouldn't put money into a child's name in order to save taxes if you're going to need that money yourself. You shouldn't put money into a child's name in order to save on taxes if you can do better by investing it in another way. Always calculate all the factors: the return you can get from various investments, your need for the money, your investment temperament, and your tax bracket.

Tax-Free Investments

Municipal bonds are generally not called tax shelters, but the interest income is usually tax-free. If you buy Treasury issues, the interest earned is exempt from state and local income tax.

There are special opportunities from time to time, such as the public utility dividend reinvestment program and the All-Savers Certificate, both part of the 1981 tax law. Both programs have expired, but other such opportunities will come along and a savvy taxpayer will take advantage of them where appropriate.

"Appropriate" is a key word to keep in mind as you evaluate any investment, especially any investment specifically billed as a tax shelter.

Is it right for you, in your tax bracket? Is it right for you, at your age and stage of life? Don't be misled by what things are called. The next two shelters discussed, Individual Retirement Accounts and annuities, sound as if they are meant for older people. They are not. They are, in fact, excellent tax-sheltered investments at virtually any age.

Individual Retirement Accounts and Keogh Plans

Under the 1981 tax law, every income-earning individual in this country was permitted to open an Individual Retirement Account (IRA). Under the 1986 law, this is no longer the case. You are eligible only at specified income levels, if you are covered by a pension plan (see p. 561). But if you *are* eligible and if you have income from any source, you may open an IRA, deposit up to $2,000 a year (if you've earned at least that much), take that $2,000 off the top of your income when figuring your income tax, and defer all taxes on earned interest until you withdraw the money. At that point, if all goes according to plan, you will be past retirement age and in a lower tax bracket. If you are no longer eligible under the new law, you will still be allowed to make annual contributions to an IRA; contributions will not be tax-deductible but money earned on the account will accrue tax-free until it is withdrawn

There are pitfalls as well as advantages to an IRA, and these are discussed in detail in Chapter 25, along with appropriate investment vehicles. For now, for those who are eligible, here are some essential facts:

- If you are married and your spouse does not earn any income, you may open a "spousal" IRA, with annual contributions up to $2,250 instead of $2,000.
- If you and your spouse are each earning income, you may each open an IRA and deduct $4,000 from your combined gross annual income.
- If you are divorced and not working and if your former spouse had established an IRA for you at least five years prior to the divorce (and made contributions for three of those five years), a new special rule permits you to continue deductible contributions up to a maximum of $1,125 a year.

This shelter, while a good one, is more permanent than some. If you need the money before you turn 59½, you can't get it (unless you are disabled) without incurring tax penalties. The tax penalties may not erase all the tax savings—but you should try not to put money that you know you will need into an IRA.

Keogh Plans provide similar tax benefits for the self-employed, who may contribute up to $30,000 or 20 percent of earned income, whichever is less. You'll find details on Keogh Plans in Chapter 25.

Annuities

The traditional annuity contract is the reverse of a life insurance contract: Instead of paying regular premiums toward the day when the proceeds will be paid to your survivors, you pay (in either a lump sum or periodic payments) toward the day when monthly distributions will be made to you. Those distributions usually begin in retirement and continue for a lifetime, so that the annuity has traditionally been a retirement-planning vehicle purchased by people concerned about outliving their resources. More detail about the role of annuities in retirement planning will be found in Chapter 25.

Traditional fixed-payment annuities are very much out of favor in inflationary times. But the new annuity in its modern high-yield version is an investment vehicle as well as a way of ensuring retirement income. It is an investment with several attractive features:

- Yields are competitive, pegged to current market rates. The rate of return is generally guaranteed for the first year; then it fluctuates with the return on invested funds. There is also a guaranteed minimum return.

- Although the investment is made with after-tax dollars (unlike an IRA, where your annual contribution comes off the top of your income before taxes,) income tax on the accumulated interest is deferred until payouts start. Even then, only the amount of the payout which represents interest is subject to tax. Tax deferment makes a significant difference: A single investment of $10,000 earning an assumed annual interest rate of 8 percent would, without tax deferment, grow to $33,234 after twenty-five years for an individual in the 38.5 percent tax bracket and to $40,554 for someone in the 28 percent tax bracket. The same amount in a tax-deferred annuity would become $68,485.

- You may surrender the annuity, when you're ready, and take the entire accumulation. Or you may select one of several income options:

    Life income, under which payments are made as long as you live. (If you die after one payment, that's it.)

    Life income with a guaranteed income period, most often ten years. Under this option, if you die before the minimum period ends, payments will continue to your named beneficiary for the remainder of the period.

    Refund annuity, under which payments continue to your named beneficiary until combined payments (to you and to that person) equal the premium paid.

    Joint and survivor, with payments made to you and to a joint payee you designate for as long as either of you lives.

ANNUITIES FOR THE LONG TERM

Annuities are not good short-term investments. Because you have access to your money, however, they can be a suitable investment even when you are not contemplating retirement for many years to come. Anne H., for instance, inherited $20,000 from her childless aunt and used it to purchase a single-premium deferred annuity. Left to accumulate at an assumed 8 percent interest rate, the $20,000 reached more than $63,000 by the end of fifteen years. At that point, when her son was ready for college, she wanted to use some of the money. The contract permitted withdrawals of up to 10 percent of accumulated value, without any charge or penalty, in any one year. For four years, she withdrew a little over $6,300 each year; in those same four years, the accumulated annuity funds earned interest (at the same assumed 8 percent) of over $17,000. At the end of the nineteenth year, with her son finishing college, the annuity's total value (after the four consecutive withdrawals) stood at exactly $55,438.70. Table 2 shows the annuity plan that made this possible.

TABLE 2: An example of a single-premium deferred annuity that permits partial withdrawals.

$10,000.00	Single contribution/Joint contribution	$20,000.00
$31,721.69	Value at end of 15th year assuming 8% annual compounded growth.	$63,443.38
$ 3,172.16 × 4	Four annual withdrawals years 16 thru 19 for college (each withdrawal represents 10% of the 15th-year value)	$ 6,344.33 × 4
$ 8,686.32	Interest earned during years 16 through 19 (assumes same 8%)	$17,372.64
$27,719.37	Total value at end of 19th year.	$55,438.70

Withdrawals from interest are taxable. No penalty is assessed under this contract after the tenth contract anniversary. Any annual withdrawal above 10 percent of total accumulations, under this contract, is subject to a surrender charge of not more than 7 percent of the amount above 10 percent.

(Source: Principal Mutual Life Insurance Company)

Note: Tax penalties on withdrawals can be avoided under current law (post-1987 rules are not yet clear at this writing) if a withdrawal is made at periodic intervals over at least five years. If you have money you can spare and want to help a grandchild, you can establish a deferred annuity as a custodial account in the child's name. You are allowed to give up to $10,000 a year ($20,000 if you give as a couple) without gift tax consequences, and the interest will then be taxable to the child once the child is over age 14.

You can start an annuity plan with as little as $1,500, although, of course, you'll see better results with a larger investment. You can also make installment payments rather than a single payment, but you may have to accept a slightly lower yield in return.

Before you invest: Compare fees (sales charges, redemption fees, annual administrative costs, withdrawal penalties), operating rules, minimum investment requirements, and the rules on if and when you may add new money. Also compare the yields from municipal bonds; if your income—and your taxes—will be just as high when you want your money, you might be better off with a slightly lower but fully tax-exempt yield.

Tax Shelters for Upper-Bracket Taxpayers

You may not be rich. You may not even consider yourself affluent as you buck the tide of rising prices. But you may still be tempted to think about tax shelters beyond the ones described in the preceding section. If so, think twice: The lower tax rates of the 1986 tax law, coupled with restrictions on deductions, significantly reduce the attractive features of most shelters. Under the new law you can no longer (subject to a phase-out period of five years) use paper losses of most tax shelters to offset income from other sources. More than ever before, therefore, tax-shelter investments should be evaluated as investments, not just as shelters; look carefully at the potential for income and for profit.

Then, if you decide to invest, look at shelters offered by reputable dealers. Your best bets are probably either limited partnerships or self-managed real estate investments.

Limited Partnerships

Limited partnerships have been most often (and most successfully) established to invest in real estate, oil and gas exploration, equipment leasing, or research and development. Others—in movies, cattle, coal mines, and so on—are called "exotics," and increasingly stringent Internal Revenue Service policies make them far less desirable for the average investor in search of a shelter. In fact, a shakeout is anticipated in just about all forms of tax shelters, at this writing, because of the stringent provisions in the new tax law.

In a limited partnership, whatever its investment vehicles and goals, a general partner is responsible for the business decisions; the limited partners—that's you—put up most of the money. In exchange for your investment, you used to receive the right to claim tax credits or deductions based on the partnership's business expenses, but that is generally no longer the case (see below). Today you're better off looking for income. You'll receive a share of the profits, if the enterprise has any profits. If it fails, your liability is limited (hence the term "limited" partner) to the amount of your investment.

Tax Advantages

The tax benefits stem from the partnership structure. When you own shares in a corporation, you share in the corporation's profits via the dividends you receive; you pay income tax on those dividends. You don't, however, share in any of the corporation's losses (except in the sense that the value of your shares may diminish). In a partnership, by contrast, both profits and losses are passed along to the partners. You pay income tax on your share of the partnership's taxable income; you also get the tax write-offs stemming from any losses. Those write-offs, however, can now (subject to the five-year phase-out period) be claimed only against income from similar "passive" investments. To claim tax losses against other income, you would have to actively participate in management—a provision which would rule out most limited partnerships. Note, though, that unclaimed losses don't disappear; they can be carried over and used to offset similar income in a following year, or they can be claimed when the property is sold.

Here's how your tax picture might look, taking a real estate limited partnership as a typical example:

- Mortgage interest is deductible. Since mortgage payments consist largely of interest in the early years, and since real estate purchases are highly leveraged, deductions are extensive at the beginning and much smaller later on. (In a gas and oil partnership, similarly, high drilling costs in the early years run up big losses, allocated to the limited partners in proportion to their investments.) These losses can be used to offset your taxable income from the partnership itself and from other passive investments.
  Note: Don't expect large tax losses to continue for the life of the investment. Ask to see projections several years down the line. And be prepared to owe more in taxes, later, if and when the partnership shows a profit.
- Depreciation—the recognition, in tax law, that buildings eventually wear out—is also deductible. But depreciation schedules, which were very favorable under the 1981 law, have been greatly lengthened so that expenses are spread out over a longer period of time.
- Operating expenses—taxes, upkeep, management fees, etc.—can be offset against rental income, giving you extra deductions.

   Q. My broker has recommended that I put $5,000 to $10,000 in a limited partnership investing in shopping centers. Is this a good investment?

A. It can be, but you don't say whether these are new, to-be-built shopping centers or already existing and occupied properties. Yet-to-be-developed properties are much riskier as an investment, although they offer significant potential gain. Existing properties have a track record; you can look at occupancy levels and examine operating costs over a period of time. Evaluate the partnership as carefully as you would any investment, and get advice from your own tax adviser.

IRS Requirements

The tax benefits of a limited partnership have been so extensive that abuses have existed. If you don't want to run the risk of substantial penalties (as much as 30 percent of taxes deemed due) plus interest on back taxes (changing semiannually and, in late 1986, pegged at 9 percent), be very careful. The IRS scrutinizes two elements:

- You should not claim deductions larger than the risk you assume. A tax write-off several times larger than the amount you invest is sure to draw attention and will very likely be disqualified.

- There must be economic justification to the shelter. You must expect gain from the investment as an investment, in other words, and not be going into it solely for the anticipated tax deductions.

Investment Requirements

There are two types of limited partnerships:

Public offerings are registered with the Securities and Exchange Commission and, often, in the states in which they are sold. This registration does not imply approval or endorsement, but it does mean that the partnership must meet certain standards. Public offerings, described in a prospectus, can usually be purchased in $5,000 units.

Private offerings, which are not registered or regulated, are described in an offering statement. They take fewer partners and usually require an investment of upwards of $25,000. Potential rewards may be greater; so is the risk.

Both public and private offerings often state minimum income and net-worth standards for investors. You may think you need a tax shelter, in other words, but if you have taxable income under $20,000 and net worth (without counting your house and car and furnishings) of under $75,000, you probably won't be permitted to invest. Some states, and some partnerships (especially the riskier private offerings), set tougher standards.

Should You Invest in a Tax Shelter?

Assuming that you meet the minimum income and net-worth requirements, is a limited partnership right for you? There are two factors to consider:

LIQUIDITY

Selling a tax shelter is far more difficult than buying one, for two principal reasons:

- The tax write-offs are, as noted, far greater in the early years. There's less incentive, as a result, for anyone to buy a secondhand shelter.

- Until the properties are sold and the partnership terminated, it's almost impossible to value your holdings.

Termination is usually scheduled for a fixed date, but in many cases the partnership may sell off its properties and end its existence earlier. Even so, real estate partnerships typically stay in existence for a minimum of four years, sometimes much longer. If you're going to need the money sooner, a limited partnership is not for you.

FINANCES

Tax shelters, especially under the new tax rules, don't make sense for most people. Unless you will actually do better with a limited partnership than you would in any other form of investment, there's little point in taking on the complicated bookkeeping and the potential tax audit.

In addition, both the cash flow and the yield tend to vary from year to year on most tax shelters, along with the deductible losses. You need to look at the general partner's past record of performance on similar deals. And you also need to discuss all the ramifications with a skilled tax adviser. This is not a region in which it's wise to wander without help.

Questions to Ask Before You Invest

If you do decide that you require shelter from taxes and that you can afford an illiquid investment—that is, one that you can't convert quickly to cash—there are a number of questions to ask before you invest in any particular tax shelter:

- Is it a legitimate business deal, with an expectation of profit? Do the assumptions about operating revenues and operating costs, as set forth in the prospectus or offering statement, support income and cash flow projections?

- How much of your money will actually be invested and how much will be eaten up in sales commissions, property acquisition fees, administrative charges, and the like? The expenses can be very large on a limited partnership, but a rule of thumb offered by the Research Institute of America suggests that a maximum of 25 percent should go for commissions and fees, with the rest allocated to the property itself. Better shelters put even more of the proceeds directly into the operation.

- Will you receive a minimum return before the general partner takes part of the cash flow? That's good. Will the general partner be paid substantial fees, in advance, for services to be performed? That's bad.

- Do the projected tax benefits conform to tax law? Or are you likely to have to fight for your deductions? Look for a lawyer's opinion (it should accompany the prospectus) saying that the shelter rests on solid legal ground. Be wary of one that says the IRS "is likely to take a contrary position."

- What are the income/expense projections several years down the road? Remember: In most tax shelters, taxes are deferred rather than eliminated. If you're likely to be in a still-higher tax bracket when those taxes become due, the tax shelter may not be right for you.

- What is the background of the general partners? Have they managed similar projects, and managed them well? Do the general partners have a financial stake in this project, with their own money invested? If so, they are more likely to pay close attention and to manage it well.

- What is your own personal tax situation? Can you derive enough benefit from the tax savings to make the accompanying risk worthwhile? Remember, you can derive the benefits of tax-sheltering through the relatively risk-free vehicles of municipal bonds or deferred annuities.

All tax shelters are risky. You can reduce your risk by (1) investing in a diversified partnership (one that invests in several shopping centers, for instance, rather than just one), and (2) investing consistently over a period of years.

Q. Recently, after a lot of sales pressure by telephone. I sent $8,784 to a company promising to invest it for me in oil and gas lotteries. I've filled out eight lottery forms and had all of them returned, which means they did not win the lottery. But this company (which called so many times before I sent the money and now won't even return my calls) said the loss would be tax-deductible. Is it? And was this a legitimate investment? Or have I been taken for a complete fool?

A. I'm afraid you have been taken. There is a Government Oil and Gas Lottery, run by the Bureau of Land Management of the U.S. Department of the Interior. You may participate in this six-times-a-year lottery for a small filing fee (eight lottery forms should cost no more than a few hundred dollars). None of the leases offered in the lottery are for lands known to contain oil or gas, but leases can sometimes be sold to developers. Companies selling filing services, such as the one which contacted you, can sometimes improve a leaseholder's chances of making money on a lease; they can't, according to the Better Business Bureau, improve the chances of winning the lottery in the first place. Widespread criminal activities in this field, in fact, prompted the Secretary of the Interior to suspend the lease program for several months in 1980. It was then reinstituted with new rules, but those rules haven't kept filing companies from charging excessively high fees. You might report this particular company to the Better Business Bureau, your local Consumer Affairs Office, and the Federal Trade Commission. And next time, investigate before you send money.

Tax-Shelter Traps

Legitimate tax-shelter investments contain enough risk; stay away from those that are all risk and little shelter. For example:

- Shelters urged on you by mail or by telephone. Do you really want to entrust thousands of your hard-earned dollars to someone who picked your name out of a telephone book?

- Long-distance shelters. Can you even look at the property half a continent away, much less tell if it's well managed?

- Shelters with "paper" loans that investors are not obligated to repay, set up just to increase deductions. Do you really want to run the risk of an intensive IRS audit for the sake of inflated deductions?

- Deals generated by year-end shelter panic. The shelter you're told you need in December is really the one you needed last spring. Don't you want to wait, if it's now almost year-end, and investigate before you invest?

Real Estate

If you have more money to invest, and more time to devote to your investment, you might look to the profit-making opportunities and tax-sheltering incentives of a self-managed real estate investment. There are a number of substantial benefits:

- The possibility of *appreciation*. Real property has traditionally been one of the best hedges against inflation. Even though prices have leveled off and, in some areas, actually declined, careful choice and careful management can still yield profits.

- *Leverage.* Real property, unlike some other investments, can often be purchased with as little as 10 percent of the purchase price. The smaller the down payment, the more someone else's money is working for you and the greater your potential profit.

- *Cash flow* can be consistent, although the quality of your tenants (will they stay put? pay their rent on time?) and your operating costs will determine the actual amounts.

- *Equity buildup.* As the existing mortgage balance is reduced, your equity in the property—and your potential profit—increases.

- Tax losses stemming from *depreciation* (the recognition, in tax law, that buildings eventually wear out). The Accelerated Cost Recovery System established under the 1981 tax law permitted real estate to be depreciated over a fifteen-year period; the 1986 tax law establishes a 27.5-year depreciation period for residential real property, and a 31.5-year period for nonresidential real property. These extended periods reduce the tax advantages of real estate investment.

- The possibility of *tax credits.* Tax credits are even better than tax deductions, because they directly reduce the amount of tax you owe, not just the amount of income on which you pay tax. They are available if you invest in historic property. The 1986 tax law provides a tax credit of 20 percent of the costs of restoration and rehabilitation. Don't let this tax credit blind you, however, to the true investment value of a property.

Managing Real Estate

In order to invest actively in real estate, you need cash, time, and good advice.

- While you can buy into a limited partnership for as little as $5,000, you'll need considerably more than that to do your own personal investing in real estate. You'll need enough money at the outset (money you won't need for anything else, because real estate is one of the least liquid of investments) to make a cash down payment. You may also need money for upkeep. And you may want to allocate funds to pay a professional manager, and to secure professional advice.

- You aren't likely to make money from a property that isn't closely supervised. Even if you hire an on-site manager, you'll need to keep close tabs on your investment. That means frequent visits and regular supervision.

- Good advice is essential. You'll want financial advice from your accountant and your attorney. You may want technical advice from an architect, an engineer, and/or an appraiser. And you may want to deal with a Realtor who specializes in investment property, perhaps one who is a CCIM, a Certified Commercial Investment Member of the Commercial

Investment Council of the Realtors National Marketing Institute, a division of the National Association of Realtors.

How to Invest in Real Estate

If you have the cash, the time, and the inclination, then, how do you go about investing in real estate? With the help of your real estate broker, investigate properties *in your home town*. While it's true that property is appreciating more in some areas of the country than in others, it's also true that you can't really keep tabs on an investment located in another city. You also can't really know the score. In your own home community, you know which areas are coming up and which may be sliding inexorably down. You know what's what in terms of shopping, schools, and plans for new highways. You can make a reasonably intelligent investment, based on your own knowledge, and then supervise it closely.

What type of investment? Some people have done very well with one-family houses, especially with run-down houses that can be rehabilitated and then sold at a handsome profit. Others swear by multifamily units, especially small apartment houses. And some think that profits lie in commercial buildings, in a medical office building or small shopping mall. You can do well—or badly—with any of these. Look at all the facts and figures on any particular investment possibility before you make your decision.

Note: Be careful about investing in second mortgages, especially those not sponsored by a regulated financial institution. With the stabilization (even decline) of house prices in recent years, many investors have lost their life savings.

RAW LAND

They may not be making any more of it, as the saying goes, but that does not mean that raw land is good investment. Quite the contrary, in fact, according to those in the know. Here are the problems:

- Raw land has no intrinsic value. Its worth lies in what happens to it. Will residential development move in that direction? Will the land turn out to be a prime location for a shopping center? Might a new highway be built? The answers to all of these questions—and the potential worth of the land—are tied to political decisions and demographic factors over which you have no control.

- Raw land yields no current return and, in fact, costs money to hold. You'll have taxes to pay, year after year, whether or not the land is ever developed. You'll have interest to pay, if you took a loan to buy the property, and those interest rates may be very high. You'll be taking your money out of circulation, if you buy with cash, and earning no return.

Raw land can be profitable, but you're best off considering it speculation rather than investment.

When You Sell

Your profit on investment property, with the elimination of special capital gains tax rates, will be taxed as ordinary income. But your tax liability can be reduced via one of two methods:

- Under the Installment Sales Revision Act of 1980, taxes can be paid as the money is received rather than in the year of the sale, with no limitations as to how much must be paid to the seller in any one year. You can reduce the tax bite by taking installment payments over several years, possibly raising the sale price of the property in exchange for allowing the purchaser to keep more of his money for this period of time. For more details, see IRS Publication No. 537.

- You can defer taxes by swapping your property for one of "like kind," instead of selling it. The new property doesn't have to be identical, but it should also be investment property. It's even possible for sophisticated investors, with the help of attorneys specializing in real estate tax law, to get into three-way or four-way exchanges. Some cash may actually change hands, and some taxes may be due, but the bulk of that tax can be deferred.

Real Estate Investment Trusts

Another way of investing in real estate is through a Real Estate Investment Trust (REIT). These pooled investments operate somewhat like mutual funds, but the funds are invested exclusively in real estate. REITs are traded on the stock exchanges, so there is always a market and your investment is liquid.

REITs got a bad name in the mid-1970s, when a great many went under. Those that failed were primarily mortgage-based, however, and the credit crunch did them in. Today's successful REITs are equity-based, owning and managing properties rather than buying and selling mortgages. They offer some of the advantages of real estate ownership, without some of the pitfalls. Dividends tend to be good, since REITs are required to distribute to shareholders at least 90 percent of all ordinary income generated each year. Your initial investment, moreover, may be lower in an REIT than in almost any other form of real estate investment; some shares sell for as little as $9 or $10.

KEY POINTS

- Home ownership and Individual Retirement Accounts, for those who are eligible, are appropriate tax shelters at every income level.

- Ownership of tax-free municipal bonds and income-splitting with lower-income family members may also be useful ways to shelter income from taxation.

- Upper-income taxpayers may want to consider specially structured shelters, including limited partnerships and self-managed investments.

- Both recent tax legislation and increased IRS attention to "abusive" shelters make it extremely important to investigate any shelter closely before investing. Steer clear of shelters established solely as shelters; stick to investments with a real potential for profit.

PUTTING YOUR MONEY TO WORK: CREDIT

Getting Started

Several years ago a well-known statesman arrived in Washington, direct from an overseas assignment for the U.S. government. When he arrived at the airport, he tried to rent a car for the trip home. He had a pocketful of cash and ample identification (including his diplomatic credentials), but no credit cards. The result: no car.

Credit—paying for goods and services after they've been used—is a way of life for most Americans. We use credit when we pay a dentist's bill the month after a cavity has been filled. We use credit when we finance the purchase of a car or take out a college loan. We use credit when we take a long-term mortgage to buy a house. Credit is so much a way of life that it's extremely difficult to do some things, including renting a car, without it.

For better or for worse, the American economy is built on the use of credit. Outstanding consumer debt (excluding mortgages) totaled $541.4 billion in December 1985, up almost 20 percent in a single year.

But the credit picture has changed. After a period of high interest rates in which credit was temporarily difficult to secure, creditors are once again offering unsolicited credit cards. But interest on credit, despite declining rates in general, has not come down very much. In the last few years, lenders have successfully pressured state legislatures to raise or remove state usury laws, the limits on how much you can be charged in interest; legal interest rates in many states now approach (some would say exceed) what used to be considered criminal usury levels. Indeed, at the end of 1985, when the prime rate (the basic lending rate to business) hovered between 9 and 10 percent, interest rates on bank credit cards averaged 19.4 percent.

Today, "easy credit" may be easy, but it is more expensive than ever before. So, while you'll probably still use credit, it's more important than ever to do so carefully and as part of your overall financial plan. This chapter describes the fundamentals of establishing and using credit. The next chapter describes using credit well; fitting it into your financial plan, and keeping it manageable.

You can use credit, via borrowing, when you need something and don't have the cash on hand. And you can use credit for convenience, when you do have the cash but prefer to postpone payment. But you can't use credit, in either form, unless you first establish a credit rating.

Establishing Credit

Jodi L. prides herself on always paying cash for everything, including the secondhand car she drives to her teaching job. Credit cards are a trap, she thinks, leading to impulsive buying, and she's deliberately steered clear of them. Now Jodi wants to buy a house and, with no credit history and no credit rating, is having great difficulty securing a mortgage. Jodi has learned, a little late, that it's easier to get a small first loan than a large one, easier to establish a credit rating before it's needed than at the last moment.

Getting Started

The two key factors in establishing credit are (1) your *ability to repay,* based on your income and on your other indebtedness (a large paycheck, already committed to a host of other bills, does not make you a good credit risk), and (2) your *willingness to repay,* based on your previous credit record (how often you borrow, how prompt you are at repayment). Many credit grantors also look for evidence of stability: how long you've held your current job, how long you've lived in your current home, whether you own or rent that home. Some creditors use a statistical profile in making a credit decision, others rely on their own experience. Either way, the higher your income, the longer you've been in one place, and the more you own, the easier you'll find it to secure credit—especially if your previous credit is good.

Credit grantors are not all alike, however, and it's easier to secure credit with some than with others. A good place to start, when you're seeking credit for the first time, is by maintaining checking and savings accounts without bounced checks or other evidence of irresponsibility. Then take a small loan from your bank or thrift. Repay it promptly and you will establish a credit history. Another good starting point is at a local retailer or department store. Once you have the card, use it regularly and pay the bills promptly, and you will establish a credit history. Then you can apply for a national bank card, with a reasonable chance of success.

Here are some additional tips, from New York's Citibank:

- Answer every question on a loan or credit application. An unanswered question will usually count against you more than a not-quite-acceptable answer.

- Don't assume that the lender already has the answer, even if you have previously applied to the same lender for a different loan. The information may be in the lender's computer, but a new file is usually opened for a new application.

- Offer as much information as you possibly can. If you don't have an established credit rating but you've lived in the community for a long time and have a stable employment record, be sure to point it out.

Credit Bureaus

Credit histories are maintained at credit bureaus. Contrary to what many people think, however, credit bureaus do not make decisions about granting credit. Such decisions are made only by the grantors of credit, by the stores and banks and oil companies that actually permit you to buy now and pay later. Those credit decisions, however, are often based on the material in your credit file. That file contains information about how promptly you pay your bills, about any rejection for credit, about any court judgments or bankruptcies. The file is accessible to you, under consumer protection laws. You'll find a discussion of seeing your credit file and correcting any omissions or errors on p. 162.

Although credit files contain a lot of information, they don't necessarily have everything. Oil companies, for instance, typically don't report accounts unless they are delinquent. So you could hold two or three oil company credit cards and be rejected for a bank card because you "have no credit history." If this happens, you can correct the file.

Note: Credit bureau files on consumer repayment, contrary to what some people believe, do *not* include reports of moral character. They are simply a report of credit activities. Investigative reports, which do involve interviews with acquaintances about your life-style and your character, are sometimes prepared in connection with insurance or job applications. You should be notified in writing if such a report is requested.

There are approximately 2,000 credit bureaus around the country, several large bureaus and hundreds of small local ones. To find your file, look in your local Yellow Pages under Credit Reporting Agencies or ask your bank or a department store. If you move, your credit history should follow you.

Q. My husband has a nephew with identical first, middle, and last names. In the past month, two local stores have asked my husband

NAME AND ADDRESS OF CREDIT BUREAU MAKING REPORT

☐ SINGLE REFERENCE   ☒ IN FILE REPORT   ☐ EMPLOY & TRADE REPORT   ☐ TRADE REPORT
☐ FULL REPORT   ☐ PREVIOUS RESIDENCE REPORT
☐ OTHER _____

CREDIT BUREAU OF ANYTOWN
1131 MAIN ST.
ANYTOWN, ANYSTATE 12345

crediscope® REPORT

● Member
Associated Credit Bureaus, Inc.

Date Received	4/11/86
Date Mailed	4/11/86
In File Since	APRIL 1970

Inquired As: JOINT ACCOUNT

FOR

FIRST NATIONAL BANK
ANYTOWN, ANYSTATE 12345

REPORT ON: LAST NAME	FIRST NAME	INITIAL	SOCIAL SECURITY NUMBER	SPOUSE'S NAME
CONSUMER	ROBERT	G.	123-45-6789	BETTY R.

ADDRESS:	CITY	STATE:	ZIP CODE	SINCE:	SPOUSE'S SOCIAL SECURITY NO.
1234 ANY ST.	ANYTOWN	ANYSTATE	12333	1973	987-65-4321

COMPLETE TO HERE FOR TRADE REPORT AND SKIP TO CREDIT HISTORY

PRESENT EMPLOYER:	POSITION HELD:	SINCE:	DATE EMPLOY VERIFIED	EST. MONTHLY INCOME
XYZ CORPORATION	ASST. DEPT. MGR.	10/81	12/81	$ 2500

COMPLETE TO HERE FOR EMPLOYMENT AND TRADE REPORT AND SKIP TO CREDIT HISTORY

DATE OF BIRTH	NUMBER OF DEPENDENTS INCLUDING SELF:	☒ OWNS OR BUYING HOME	☐ RENTS HOME	OTHER: (EXPLAIN) ☐
5/25/50	4			

FORMER ADDRESS:	CITY:	STATE:	FROM:	TO:
4321 FIRST AVE.	ANYTOWN	ANYSTATE	1970	1973

FORMER EMPLOYER:	POSITION HELD:	FROM:	TO:	EST. MONTHLY INCOME
ABC & ASSOCIATES	SALES PERSON	2/80	9/81	$ 1285

SPOUSE'S EMPLOYER:	POSITION HELD:	SINCE:	DATE EMPLOY VERIFIED	EST. MONTHLY INCOME
BIG CITY DEPT. STORE	CASHIER	4/81	12/81	$ 1200

160

WHOSE	KIND OF BUSINESS AND ID CODE	DATE REPORTED AND METHOD OF REPORTING	DATE OPENED	DATE OF LAST PAYMENT	HIGHEST CREDIT OR LAST CONTRACT	PRESENT STATUS			NO. MONTHS HISTORY REVIEWED	HISTORICAL STATUS TIMES PAST DUE			TYPE & TERMS (MANNER OF PAYMENT)	REMARKS
						BALANCE OWING	PAST DUE AMOUNT	NO. OF PAYMENTS		30-59 DAYS ONLY	60-89 DAYS ONLY	90 DAYS AND OVER		
2	CONSUMER'S BANK B 12-345	2/6/86 AUTOMTD. 12/85		1/86	1200	1100	-0-	-0-	2	-0-	-0-	-0-	INSTALLMENT	$100/MO.
3	BIG CITY DEPT. STORE D 54-321	2/10/86 MANUAL 4/81		1/86	300	100	-0-	-0-	12	-0-	-0-	-0-	REVOLVING	$ 25/MO.
1	SUPER CREDIT CARD N 01-234	12/12/85 AUTOMATD. 7/82		11/85	200	100	100	1	12	1	-0-	-0-	OPEN 30-DAY	

PUBLIC RECORD: SMALL CLAIMS CT. CASE #SC1001 PLAINTIFF: ANYWHERE APPLIANCES AMOUNT $225 PAID 4/4/82

ADDITIONAL INFORMATION: REF. SMALL CLAIMS CT. CASE #SC1001--5/30/82 SUBJECT SAYS CLAIM PAID UNDER PROTEST. APPLIANCE DID NOT OPERATE PROPERLY.

to take care of bad checks actually written by his nephew. Are there any precautions we can take, before this nephew does anything further, to keep our name and our credit record good?

A. You should get in touch with all your creditors, your banks, *and* the credit bureau to explain that you have no responsibility for debts incurred by this nephew. Point out any identifying features (an address or a Social Security number) which might be used to differentiate between your nephew and your husband. And ask the creditors, the banks, and the credit bureau to note your record with these distinguishing characteristics.

If You're Rejected

The creditor's written acceptance or rejection of your credit application must be given to you within thirty days of your application. If you are rejected, the creditor must tell you why. If you have been denied credit because of information furnished by a credit bureau, you have the right to find out (at no charge) what information is in your credit file. You also have the right to ask the credit agency to recheck the information. If it proves inaccurate the credit bureau must remove it from your file and, at your request, notify all creditors who received the incorrect information in the past six months that the file has been corrected. If you disagree with the credit bureau's record or if the information is accurate but incomplete—if, for instance, your late payments on one account stemmed from a dispute with a merchant over defective merchandise and payments resumed once the dispute was settled—you can write an explanation (of 100 words or less) which must be added to your credit file.

If you're turned down one place, try somewhere else. Every lending institution sets its own standards for acceptance. But don't apply for too many cards at one time. Creditors may view this as an overextension of your ability to repay.

If you do in fact have a poor credit history, you should know that it will not last forever. It does, however, last for seven years, which may seem like forever if you need credit. Try, therefore, to take on no more debt than you can responsibly handle.

Women and Credit

Q. I'm a full-time homemaker but I would like to have credit in my own name. Is there any way I can do so?

A. Credit grantors may not discriminate against women. But anyone, man or woman, must have the ability to repay in order to be creditworthy. Do you own any assets, such as stocks or bonds or an automobile, in your own name? Have you received an inheritance which you keep in a bank account in your own name? Do you work, or have you worked, part-time? Do you receive a regular monthly income from your husband? All of these factors must be considered in an application for credit. Without any of them, however, your best bet is to add your name to your husband's accounts, so that the credit history will be reported in both your names.

Under the Equal Credit Opportunity Act of 1975, you should not have any difficulty securing credit because you are a woman. The same criteria of ability to repay and willingness to repay must be applied to both women and men. Credit grantors are not allowed to ask about birth-control methods or child-care provisions, they may not consider sex or marital status in evaluating creditworthiness, and they must take all income (including alimony and child-support payments, if you choose to declare them) into account.

Although discrimination is illegal, women may still encounter problems in applying for credit. Here's what you, as a woman should know:

- Use your own name on any credit application. "Mrs. John Jones" is a social title and can apply to any wife of John Jones; Mary Jones refers to a specific person. Use your own name, and use the same name all the time. Be consistent.

- If you get married (or remarried) after establishing credit, and plan to take your new husband's surname, write to each of your creditors and tell them you want to maintain your own credit separate from your husband's.

- Have joint accounts with your husband if you like, but see that the credit history is reported in both names. This should be done automatically on new accounts. If you have accounts opened before June 1977, notify each creditor (store or bank or mortgage lender) that you want the history of the account reported to the credit bureau in each name; then check with the credit bureau, after a couple of months, to be sure that these accounts are being reported in your personal credit file. In the event that you are widowed or divorced (and 85 percent of American women are left alone, one way or the other), this credit history will be very important.

Q. I moved after my husband died, after years of paying telephone bills promptly, and when I tried to get service in my own name the telephone company wanted an advance deposit. Isn't this discrimination?

A. A utility account is a credit account (you get service now and pay for it later), and utility companies keep track of good and bad payment patterns. They may ask for a deposit if you have a bad utility credit history *or* if you're a new customer and if the company routinely requires all new customers to pay deposits. They may think you're a new customer because your name was not on your husband's account. If this is the case, tell the company that you had earlier service in your husband's name. The company must then consider his credit history as well. (It would be much easier, of course, if marital partners put both names on such accounts.)

- Creditors cannot close accounts because of a change in your marital status. They can, however, ask you to file a new application if they have reason to believe your ability to repay has changed—if, for instance, you have divorced and the original account was based on your former husband's income.

- You may have a credit card with your first name on it that is still an adjunct to your husband's account. The only way to be sure is to ask the credit bureau for your credit history. It will cost a few dollars (unless you've been turned down for credit, in which case it's free), but it's well worth the cost.

- In traditional community property states (Arizona, California, Idaho, Louisiana, Nevada, New Mexico, Texas, and Washington), and under new Wisconsin law, where husband and wife are legally responsible for each other's debts and obligations, creditors will consider the credit history of both husband and wife in an application for an account by either one if the application bases ability to pay on jointly owned property or the income of both parties. You can still apply for credit as an individual, by specifying that you wish to be judged on your own, and you should still be sure that your credit history is maintained in a separate file under your name.

In a community property state (and in any state if you choose to have a joint account with your husband) it will be counted against you if he fails to pay his bills—and, of course, vice versa. If you divorce a spouse who has demonstrated an inability to pay bills on time, don't expect to continue your own credit based on a history of this joint account.

Q. My ex-husband won't pay charge account bills that he was ordered to pay in our divorce settlement. The stores are coming after me because my name was on the accounts too. Is there anything I can do, before my credit rating is ruined?

A. The judge's order, unfortunately, is not binding on the stores. Both you and your husband continue to have contractual responsibility for jointly held accounts until they are closed, and information on the accounts will continue to be reported to credit bureaus in both names. Get in touch with your creditors and explain the situation. Ask to have your explanation attached to your credit report. If your husband can't be found and made to honor his debt you may have to pay up (you can sue him later), but the stores should be willing to make a payment schedule you can meet. Then be sure that the accounts are closed so that no further debt can be added.

Young People and Credit

While credit discrimination against women has probably received the most attention, young people (and older ones as well; see the following pages) also face particular problems with credit.

Most children are exposed to the use of credit at a very early age. They watch parents pay with plastic. Sometimes they buy cash-free schoolday lunches at a local luncheonette or pizza parlor under an agreement that a parent will pay for it later. Sometimes, too, older children borrow a parental credit card and, together with a note of authorization, use it to shop in local retail stores.

Q. My daughter charged $340 worth of clothing on my department-store account after I told her not to use the card. Do I have to pay the bill?

A. If you told the store that your daughter did not have permission and the store allowed her to use your card anyway, you do not owe anything. If you did not tell them in advance, you must pay $50 of the bill, the limit of your liability for unauthorized use even by a family member. If the youngster had been using the card on a regular basis, however, the store was justified in assuming your continued permission and may well take action to get the full payment.

Local retailers occasionally offer teenagers their own charge accounts. Limited in amount, such accounts can offer teens an introduction to credit responsibility. But the cards will extend the wrong lesson if parents pay all the bills. When a youngster uses credit, whether a personal account or a parent's account, the youngster should be responsible for paying the bills. That's the only way to learn to stay within a budget, to charge no more than can be comfortably repaid.

Once young adults are on their own—out of school and at work—establishing credit assumes the same dimensions as for any first-timer. Creditors are not allowed to judge an applicant by age, although they may ask age. But they do look at length of time on the job, length of residence, and the existence of checking and savings accounts. Because both time on the job and time in one residence may be short, young adults, even with responsible jobs, often have difficulty securing that first account. But there are some programs designed for the newly independent. American Express, for instance, says it will grant credit to graduating college seniors who have been promised a job paying at least $10,000 a year. The application must be on a special form and must be filed no more than one year after graduation.

Older People and Credit

Older men and women have complained about being denied credit just because they were over a certain age. Others have found credit suddenly cut off or sharply reduced just because they've retired from full-time jobs. But credit discrimination on the basis of age is illegal, under the Equal Credit Opportunity Act. A creditor may ask your age. But a creditor, under the law, *may not* turn you down or decrease your credit just because of your age, ignore your retirement income in considering your application, close your credit account, or require you to reapply for it just because you reach a certain age or retire.

Your age may be considered only when it is directly relevant to your ability to repay. At the age of 60, as an example, you might be denied a 30-year mortgage with a small down payment. But the denial would have to be based on the fact that your income is about to drop after retirement; it cannot be based solely on your age. If you are denied such a loan, you may still be able to secure a smaller loan with a larger down payment, especially if you have good collateral.

If a potential creditor points to reduced income as a disqualifying factor, be sure to point out any compensating factors. You might, for instance, have a long and solid credit history indicating willingness to repay. You might have assets beyond your retirement income.

Sometimes creditors insist that older borrowers take out credit insurance (see p. 183). It is, however, illegal for a creditor who requires such insurance to deny credit to you if you can't get credit insurance because of your age.

Sources of Credit

You use credit when you make a purchase of goods or services with the promise to pay at a later date. With this form of credit you often have the choice of paying in full upon receipt of the bill or spreading payment over a period of months. You also use credit when you borrow money. Here, however, you agree in advance to a fixed repayment schedule. Both types of credit are available from a variety of sources.

Retail Stores

Local stores and national chains alike issue credit cards, typically good only at their own outlets. (But the lines are blurring: The new all-purpose Sears Discover card functions like a bank card and is accepted in many places.) These cards usually do not cost anything to get or to maintain, as long as bills are paid promptly. When payment is extended, however, finance charges are levied on the unpaid balance.

Oil Companies

Oil companies, similarly, issue credit cards to their customers, cards which are good only at their own stations. (Some oil-company cards are also usable at certain hotels, but most are single-purpose cards.) Like retail charge accounts, these may be paid in full without a charge or paid over an extended period with interest.

CASH DISCOUNTS

In an effort to discourage the use of credit, because it costs them money, many oil companies are now offering discounts for cash (and at least one major company, in early 1982, stopped accepting any credit cards at all). It's a good idea, in fact, to ask any merchant whether a discount is offered for cash. Federal restrictions on cash discounts, formerly limited to 5 percent, have been lifted. Any reduction may be offered, as long as it is offered to every cash customer.

Although consumers might think merchants would happily offer discounts to dispense with both the paperwork and the delayed payment associated with credit, many merchants think credit cards justify their use by the added business they generate. As a result, they do not give discounts for cash. But it never hurts to ask.

Q. I heard about a company that will keep track of all my credit cards, and contact all the companies for me if my cards are lost or stolen. Is this service worthwhile?

A. If making a single telephone call to report loss or theft, instead of calling each of your creditors, is worth the annual fee (usually about $12), then it's worth it to you. But the most tedious chore—making a list of all your accounts—is still one you must do for yourself. You either do it to submit to the card registry, or you do it for your own records. Keep this in mind before you sign up. And remember: Federal law limits your liability on any lost or stolen card to $50, if charges are made before the card is reported missing. If you report a loss promptly—or if the creditor fails to give you a postage-paid preaddressed form to use in notification—you won't be responsible for any charges.

Bank Cards

These credit cards—Visa and MasterCard—are issued by banks and by thrifts. They are honored at a wide range of establishments, from restaurants to retail stores to travel agencies and airlines. With these cards, which used to be free but now often have annual and/or transaction fees, you have a choice of paying the full amount right away (usually, but not always, without any interest charges) or paying the bill, with interest, in installments. These cards are issued with a preset spending limit, based on your credit history. The average line of credit for most bank customers is around $1,200; whatever your initial limit, however, it is often raised and raised again as you demonstrate your ability to repay.

Bank cards may also be used to secure a cash advance, often at an interest rate lower than the interest rate on purchases. But the finance charge starts immediately on a cash advance; on purchases you often have a grace period before finance charges commence.

EXCEEDING THE SPENDING LIMIT

When you reach your spending limit you'll be denied use of the card until you've paid at least part of the outstanding bill. This can be embarrassing —especially if your card is rejected in front of a friend or a business colleague—so it's a good idea to keep track of your credit purchases and your available credit limit.

You may use more of your authorized credit line than you know you're using, however, because of a little-known practice called "credit hold." Some creditors, mostly car rental agencies and hotels, may freeze $200 or so above the billed amount as a deposit against potential damage. They should tell you they are doing so, but may neglect to do so. They should also "unfreeze" the excess amount promptly once you've returned the car or left the hotel, but may neglect to do so. (A New York State law, which other states should emulate, requires notification, customer consent, and prompt release of any amount over $25.)

"SPECIAL" BANK CARDS

A new "prestige" bank card is now available. It combines a much higher line of credit ($5,000 to $25,000) with a package of financial services: high cash advances, card registration, a monthly billing date of your choice, automatic credit life insurance on an unpaid balance up to $25,000, automatic travel insurance of $200,000 when the card is used to buy transportation, and so on. This card, accepted in the wide range of places that accept bank cards, has a bank card rate of interest on unpaid balances. It also has an annual fee on the level of a travel and entertainment card.

Travel and Entertainment Cards

These charge cards—American Express and Carte Blanche and Diner's Club—are sometimes called pay-as-you-go cards because bills must be paid, in full, when presented. They are predominantly used for travel, entertainment, and leisure, and are not accepted in as many retail stores as bank cards.

These T&E cards differ from bank cards in several ways:

- There are no preset spending limits, which makes them useful in emergencies.

- Issuers often require a fairly high income, and these cards can be somewhat more difficult to secure.

- They have annual fees but no finance or interest charges, because payment is expected immediately. When payment is not received within 30 days, a note is made. At 60 days a late charge is assessed. American Express, as an example, charges either $10 or 2.5 percent of the unpaid balance, whichever is greater. At 90 days, when a bill is still outstanding, the account is subject to cancellation. It will then be very difficult to reinstate.

"Extended payment" plans are available from the issuers of T&E cards under some circumstances, such as the purchase of airline or cruise tickets. Interest is calculated at 12 to 18 percent a year on these plans, with payment permitted over periods ranging from three months to two years. The interest is precalculated, however, so if you decide to pay early after setting up such a plan, be sure to notify the creditor so that a credit can be issued on the unearned interest.

Q. I always thought bank cards were less expensive than charge cards, but with the new annual fees some banks are charging I'm not sure. How should the two be compared?

A. Look at your own spending patterns. Do you pay your bank card bill in full immediately or accrue finance charges on an unpaid balance? And look at the practices of your bank. Does the card have an annual fee? When do finance charges start? Even if a bank card is free, you may face interest at 18 percent (or more) a year. If you accrue finance charges on many purchases, you could, as shown in Table 1, spend more on such a card than on the charge card with an annual fee of $30 to $40. (With a charge card, of course, you'll be expected to pay in full when the bill is presented. So forget the comparison if you would be unable to do so.)

How Many Cards Should You Have?

A California man applied for, and received, 1,098 credit cards. He got his name in *The Guinness Book of World Records*. He also got a major headache in terms of storing and protecting his cards.

Nobody needs over 1,000 cards. But how many do you need?

One of the major bank cards is useful, not only for making purchases but for check-cashing identification. (Try to pay for an airplane ticket by check, with no credit card for identification.) You might even want two,

TABLE 1: Bank cards or charge cards?

Average monthly balance	ANNUAL PERCENTAGE RATE				
	12%	15%	18%	22%	24%
$300	$36	$45	$54	$66	$72
$250	$30	$37.50	$45	$55	$60
$200	$24	$30	$36	$44	$48
$150	$18	$22.50	$27	$33	$36
$100	$12	$15	$18	$22	$24
$ 50	$ 6	$ 7.50	$ 9	$11	$12

In the boxed area, annual finance charges for bank cards may exceed the yearly fee for charge cards. But be sure to compare annual fees as well as the annual percentage rate.

(Source: The American Express Company)

a Visa and a MasterCard, issued by different banks. (Don't put all your credit records in one computer; banks do make mistakes.) A local department-store card, one or two oil-company cards, and, perhaps, a travel and entertainment card should round out the package. Few people need more. And most people find too many credit cards a temptation to overspend.

However many cards you have, take care to protect them. Don't leave your cards in your glove compartment or in your desk; these are the first places a thief will look. Make a complete list of all your cards and their expiration dates; a good way to do this is to simply make a photocopy of all your cards. And don't give a credit card number to anyone who solicits you by phone or calls to tell you that you've "won" a contest that you didn't know you'd entered. Even though your liability on any one card is limited to $50, your bank may refuse to issue a new card if there is reason to believe you've been careless.

Loans

When you want to borrow money outright, your credit rating also comes into play, but your sources are different.

Relatives and Friends

These personal loans are very useful, especially if you don't yet qualify for a standard loan. But it's important to treat such loans in a businesslike way. Even if no interest is being charged, sign a note indicating the terms of the loan: how much, when it is being loaned, and when it is to be repaid.

If you are making the loan, put the signed note in your safe deposit box; should you die, your family will know—and be able to prove—that money is owed. If you are making the loan, too, don't count on declaring the loss as a casualty deduction on your federal income tax should your relative fail to repay; the IRS often considers such loans as tacit gifts.

Q. Last year I lent a boyfriend $1,200 to repair his van. I trusted him and did not ask him to sign an IOU. We're not seeing each other anymore and he won't answer letters or phone calls. Is there any way I can get him to pay me back?

A. Possibly, if you take the matter to court. In most jurisdictions the amount is too large for Small Claims Court and you'll have to go to local district court. For a nominal filing fee, however, you can handle the matter yourself. You are more likely to win, however, if you have some kind of proof: a canceled check, a money order receipt, a witness who knew about the loan. It's always best, even within your own family, to have a signed document for any loan you make.

Passbook Loans

Your own savings can provide collateral for a relatively inexpensive loan, if you can afford to freeze the amount of the loan in your account for the period of the loan.

With a passbook loan, you are borrowing against the money in your savings account. The rate is generally lower than for other bank loans because the bank holds your savings as collateral. In return for the lower rate, however, you temporarily lose access to your funds. The advantage: You continue to earn interest on the savings account while it is frozen, effectively reducing the amount you pay for the loan.

Life Insurance Loans

Whole life insurance, if you have policies that have been in force for some time and have accrued cash value, can be a low-cost source of money. The interest rate on older policies ranges from 5 to 8 percent; newer policies may charge more. Life insurance loans do not have to be repaid, although any outstanding loan will diminish the amount of the death benefit. Whether or not you repay the loan balance, you should pay the interest due. See p. 420 for details.

Banks and Thrifts

Both commercial banks and thrifts are authorized to make consumer loans. So are credit unions, to their members. Such loans may be secured (by some asset, such as the automobile to be purchased with the loan) or unsecured (issued on the basis of your credit rating alone). Interest rates vary with the type, amount, and duration of the loan, as well as whether or not you provide collateral and where you take the loan.

OVERDRAFT CHECKING

Overdraft checking, sometimes called reserve checking, is a line of credit offered by banks. You must apply for overdraft checking just as you would apply for a credit card or an installment loan. It then comes into play as an automatic loan if you overdraw your checking account. The service is free, until you use it; then interest charges are applied.

With overdraft checking, you will never bounce a check. But you should be cautious:

- While a few banks will lend you the actual amount of the overdraft, most lend specified amounts, often in multiples of $100. You could wind up borrowing, and paying interest on, more than you actually need.

- Some banks will automatically repay your loan from your next deposit. But some will deduct a portion, such as 1/20th, each month so that your payments and the interest due are stretched over a much longer period of time. And some banks will not credit any portion of a deposit toward the loan unless you specifically request that they do so. Be sure you understand the terms of your overdraft checking before you use it. It may cost you less, under some circumstances, to use a credit card instead.

HOME EQUITY LOANS

Your bank or brokerage house may offer an "open credit line" with instant loans secured by the equity in your house. These loans, now that deductibility of other consumer interest has been curtailed, are expected to become increasingly popular. Be careful. A home equity loan may be cheaper than other loans, and the interest may be tax-deductible if you itemize, but it also means putting your home on the line.

Note: If you took a home equity loan before August 17, 1986, interest on the entire loan is deductible. For mortgage debt (home equity loans, second mortgages, or refinancing) assumed after that date, deductible amounts are limited to loans up to the original purchase price of the house plus any home improvements. The only exception will be mortgage debt assumed for medical or educational expense.

Stockbrokerage Firms

Personal loans are available from stockbrokers, often at a lower interest rate than may be available elsewhere, if you keep securities in a brokerage account. The catch: If the securities (your collateral) decline in value, they may have to be sold to pay off the loan.

Finance Companies

Finance companies were traditionally the source of money for the "little guy," the consumer who couldn't get a loan elsewhere. But times have changed. Where only 8 percent of borrowers from finance companies in 1979 had incomes over $24,000, 29 percent were in this category in 1983. There has also been a massive shift, according to the American Financial Services Association, toward larger loan amounts and toward secured loans, particularly second mortgages. In 1979, second mortgages accounted for 38 percent of all finance-company loans; by 1980 the figure was 52 percent. At least two major finance companies, in early 1982, stopped making loans to people who do not own their own homes.

If you do own your home, you can apply for a second mortgage from a bank or a finance company. Such loans are risky, since you may lose your home if you cannot repay the loan on schedule.

Finance-company loans have traditionally been more expensive than loans from banks and thrifts. Today, with the lifting of interest rate limits in many states, this may or may not be the case. As always, you should shop around and compare rates before you make a commitment.

Q. My 18-year-old niece has asked me to cosign a loan for her. What will I be getting into if I say yes?

A. You will be legally obligated to repay the full amount of the loan if your niece fails to do so. Don't cosign any loan unless you know the borrower well, have good reason to believe he or she will repay it, and are prepared to repay the loan yourself if necessary. If you do sign, make sure the contract is completely filled in and also that it specifies that you will be notified if any payments are missed. The contract should not pledge your house or car as security for the loan unless you expressly agree to such a provision. State laws vary and so do contracts, but a cosigner anywhere assumes a definite risk. Remember: Lenders ask for cosigners only when the principal borrower is a poor credit risk or has no credit rating at all.

Installment Loans

In addition to borrowing from a relative, a bank, or a finance company, you can arrange for a loan as you buy big-ticket items such as automobiles, appliances, and furniture.

Always compare terms carefully. Look at both the price of the item and the cost of financing the purchase. You may be able to negotiate one or the other to your advantage. Reducing the interest rate by 2 or 3 percent, for instance, may have the same net effect as cutting the price of a car by several hundred dollars. In an example by Purdue University for the Credit Union National Association, a 3 percent difference in loan rates equaled a 5 percent difference in the price of a car. A $7,097 loan at 15 percent with monthly payments of $197.50 for four years is exactly the same as a $6,724 loan at 18 percent. In this case, if you can bargain more than $373 off the price of the car, 18 percent is as good as 15 percent.

Variable-rate loans, available in some areas, often start at a lower interest rate and run for a longer term. Initial monthly payments are usually lower, but be sure to ask how often and how much interest rates can change.

Pawnshops

If you have no other source of funds, if you are in need of money for a short period of time, and if you have an asset to leave as collateral, you might look to a pawnship or loan office. One such company, in Beverly Hills, California, does business with wealthy customers in temporary need of extra funds. At a time when bank loans ran about 20 to 21 percent, it charged 26.7 percent interest on an annual basis. But pawnshops generally keep pawned items for shorter periods. Jewelry is most often pawned, with silver and furs as runners-up. The amount of the loan varies according to the resale value of the item, and loans may be renewed by paying off the accrued interest. Pawnshops are legitimate places of business, and are regulated by federal law, but they should not be your first source of funds.

The Cost of Credit

Credit costs money. It's important to shop for the best buy in credit as you would shop for the best buy in anything. Federal Truth-in-Lending laws require that creditors give you certain basic information about the finance charge and about the annual percentage rate.

The Finance Charge

This is the total dollar amount you pay to use credit. It includes interest charges and other costs such as transaction fees, service charges, and points.

These "extra" charges used to be relatively rare on open-end credit, such as bank cards and retail charge accounts. Today, especially with bank cards, extra charges are becoming more common. Most bank cards, now charge an annual fee, typically from $15 to $25. A few banks charge transaction fees instead of an annual fee. At 12¢ a transaction, an average of five transactions a month would give you a yearly charge of $7.20. For the infrequent user, therefore, transaction fees might make more sense than an annual fee.

Some states don't permit annual fees. Even in states that do, competition among banks means that you probably can, with shopping around, still find a free bank card. You may be able to secure a free card at a bank where you have an account. But be sure that there is no hidden cost—some banks freeze your account in exchange for the extension of credit. And, at some banks, finance charges begin to accrue from the date of purchase. Be sure you understand the rules when you apply for a particular card.

Note: Under 1986 tax legislation, the deductibility of finance charges is gradually reduced. In 1987, 35 percent of consumer interest is disallowed; by 1990, 90 percent will be off limits for tax-reduction purposes.

Q. I'm being billed for a suit I returned to a department store. The finance charges are adding up and I'm afraid my credit will be ruined. How can I straighten this out?

A. Don't panic. And don't pay for merchandise you did not keep. Under the Fair Credit Billing Act, you need not pay the portion of a bill with which you disagree. You must, however, pay all other parts of the bill. In filing a complaint you must write to the creditor (phone calls don't count) within 60 days, with your account number, a description of the error and why you believe it is an error, and the dollar amount in question. If you have a receipt for the returned merchandise, enclose a copy (keep the original) with your letter. The creditor must acknowledge your letter within 30 days; he must either correct the bill or explain why he believes it is correct within 90 days. If an error has been made, finance charges on the disputed amount will be dropped. In the meantime, he may not report you to a credit bureau for nonpayment, bill you for the amount, or take any action to collect.

The Annual Percentage Rate

This is the key figure in the cost of credit, the true cost on a yearly basis; it's worthwhile to look at it closely.

The annual percentage rate (APR) is not usually the same as the interest rate, although it might be under some circumstances. If, for instance, you borrow $100 from a friend at 8 percent interest and repay your friend $108 at the end of the year, you are actually paying 8 percent. But installment lending, where you repay a loan in equal monthly installments, does not work this way. If you borrow the same $100 at the same 8 percent from a commercial lender and repay it in twelve equal monthly installments of $9 each, you don't really get to use the entire $100 for the entire year. In fact, you get to use less and less of it as you make each monthly payment. Because this is so, the APR on this loan works out to 14.5 percent.

Lenders of all kinds are required to state the cost of credit in terms of both the finance charge and the APR. Both figures must be shown to you before you sign a credit contract.

While the APR is the key figure, be sure that you also compare the dollar amount you will pay for credit. That dollar amount is affected by the length of the loan as well as by the finance charge and the APR. For example: A $4,000 loan for three years at an APR of 12 percent, with monthly payments of $133, will cost you $783 in interest charges. A four-year loan at the same 12 percent, with monthly payments of $105, will cost you a total of $1,056.

Q. My banker said the APR was all I had to know in comparing the cost of a loan. Then he started talking about an "add-on" loan. What's he talking about?

A. The APR *is* the most important thing, but it will vary according to whether the loan is figured on an add-on or a discount basis.

Look at a $1,000 loan at 6 percent simple interest, with $60 as the annual interest. With an add-on loan, the bank would add the $60 to the $1,000 loan amount at the beginning. You have the use of the entire $1,000, at the outset, but must pay back a total of $1,060 in equal monthly installments of $88.30 for an APR of 10.75 percent. With a discount loan, by contrast, the $60 in interest would be deducted in advance, leaving you an actual loan of $940. You pay a little less each month—$83.40—but, because you are paying the same 6 percent interest on $1,000 while you have only $940, your actual cost or APR is 11.75 percent.

Finance charges and annual percentage rates apply to all kinds of consumer borrowing: auto loans, home mortgages, bank cards, etc. There are also specific factors to consider in open-end or revolving credit.

Open-End Credit

This is the kind of credit, typically found in bank cards and retail charge accounts, which allows you to make credit transactions again and again, usually up to a predetermined borrowing limit. You have a choice, when you receive your monthly bill. If you pay the entire amount in full, there will be no finance charge (for exceptions on bank cards, see below). If you pay the designated minimum amount and defer payment on the rest, interest is charged on the unpaid balance.

When interest is charged, there are two things to consider:

When does interest begin? Most creditors allow a 25-to-30-day period in which you may pay your balance in full without interest. With this provision you can take advantage of the delayed billing; by making a purchase right after the billing date you can have up to two months before payment is due.

But some bank cards no longer offer a free ride even to customers who always pay their bills in full. With some bank cards, purchases now accumulate interest from the date they are posted by the bank, even if there is no balance carried over from the previous month.

Note: Some banks have advertised "free" bank cards when, in fact, they impose immediate finance charges. These charges, if you use the card frequently, can add up to more than an annual fee.

TABLE 2: What it costs to finance $1,000.

(All figures are rounded to the nearest dollar.)

Annual % rate	Length of loan	Monthly payments	Total finance charge	Total cost
8%	1 year	$87	$ 44	$1,044
	2 years	45	86	1,080
	3 years	31	128	1,116
	4 years	24	172	1,152
10%	1 year	88	55	1,056
	2 years	46	108	1,104
	3 years	32	162	1,152
	4 years	25	218	1,200
12%	1 year	89	66	1,068
	2 years	47	130	1,128
	3 years	33	196	1,188
	4 years	26	264	1,248
14%	1 year	90	77	1,080
	2 years	48	152	1,152
	3 years	34	230	1,224
	4 years	27	312	1,298
16%	1 year	91	89	1,092
	2 years	49	175	1,176
	3 years	35	266	1,260
	4 years	28	361	1,344
18%	1 year	92	100	1,104
	2 years	50	198	1,200
	3 years	36	302	1,296
	4 years	29	410	1,392

(Source: Federal Trade Commission)

How is the finance charge calculated? Depending upon which of three methods is used, the same annual percentage rate can yield very different monthly interest charges. Let's say you have an account with a monthly finance charge of 1.5 percent (18 percent a year). Let's assume further that your previous balance is $400 and that you pay $300 on the account. Here's what can happen:

- On the *adjusted balance* method (the best for the consumer), the charge is based on the amount you owe after substracting your payment from your previous balance. The 1.5 percent interest on $100 yields a finance charge of $1.50 for the month.

- On the *previous balance* method (the least favorable for the consumer), you get no credit for payments made during the billing period; interest is simply calculated on your balance at the beginning of the period. Thus 1.5 percent interest on $400 yields a charge of $6.

- On the *average daily balance* method, creditors add your balances for each day in the billing period and then divide by the number of days in the billing period. Now, assuming that you made your $300 payment on the 15th day of a 30-day billing cycle, your total balances for the month are $7,500 (15 days at $400 and 15 days at $100). Divide the $7,500 by the 30 days in the billing cycle and you get $250. The average balance of $250 times 1.5 percent yields a finance charge of $3.75.

All these calculations will become infinitely more complicated if a move toward variable interest rates on credit cards takes hold. In mid-1982 a few banks began to charge interest rates indexed to U.S. Treasury bills, so that rates to holders of bank cards fluctuated along with the bank's own costs of doing business.

Q. I charged $95 on my bank card when I had my carburetor repaired. But the car is functioning as badly as it did before, and I don't think the repair was made properly. Do I have to pay the bill?

A. Until a few years ago the answer would have been yes. Once the debt was turned over to a third party, such as the bank which issued your card, you would have been responsible for paying the bill no matter how defective the product or service. Your only recourse would have been to sue the garage. No more. Under the Fair Credit Billing Act, you can refuse to pay the bill (or any remaining portion of it, if you've already paid part) if (1) the amount of the bill is more than $50, (2) the charge was made in your home state or within 100 miles of your home, (3) you tried to resolve the dispute with the merchant, and (4) you send the bank written notice that negotiations with the merchant have failed.

This law applies only to payments owed a third party, such as a bank. You'd be out of luck if you had charged the repair on a card issued directly by the garage, or if your dispute was with a department store and involved its own charge card.

Usury Laws

Federal legislation, such as Truth-in-Lending, protects consumers across the country by requiring that creditors give accurate information about interest charges. The amount that may be charged, however, is left to state legislation (although, at this writing, Congress has been asked to override all state interest-rate limits on consumer loans).

All but a dozen states currently have some limits on the amount of interest that may legally be charged (although those limits have been going up with great rapidity). The highest interest "ceiling" is 36 percent, in Indiana and Idaho. But remember, there are no ceilings at all in a dozen states. If you live in Arizona, which removed almost all limits in 1980, you might find yourself paying over 50 percent in interest under certain conditions.

State-imposed limits, in any case, have more impact on consumer loans than they do on credit in general. That's because the governing law on credit cards is the law of the state in which the card is issued rather than the state where the consumer lives. Many bank-card operations have moved to states (such as Delaware and North Dakota) where the law is favorable . . . to them. The best word for the consumer: Shop around. And hope that competition reduces the cost of credit.

Note: In a number of states there have been split interest rates with, for instance, 18 percent charged on the first $500 of your outstanding balance and 12 percent on the rest. If this is so in your state, or on your bank card, you might be better off lumping your purchases on one card rather than making a number of small purchases on two or more cards. If your credit limit permits you to do so, a larger balance on a single card results in lower interest charges.

Should You Prepay a Loan?

It doesn't make sense to many consumers, but it *can* cost money to pay off a loan early. Here's why:

Prepayment Penalties

Many loan agreements, both installment loans and mortgage loans, include a specified prepayment penalty. If you pay such a loan early you'll have to make an additional lump-sum payment. The reason: Lenders make long-range plans based in part on loans being repaid at specified intervals. If the loans are repaid early, the plans are disrupted.

Prepayment penalties are not universally applied to all kinds of loans. And they are not permitted in every state. On the disclosure statement required by Truth-in-Lending legislation, the lender must indicate whether you "may" or you "will not" have to pay a penalty (see Figure 2). If you may face a prepayment penalty, you have a choice: Shop

FIGURE 2: A sample Truth-in-Lending form.

Friendly Bank & Trust Co.
700 East Street
Little Creek, USA

Lisa Stone
22-4859-22
300 Maple Avenue
Little Creek, USA

ANNUAL PERCENTAGE RATE The cost of your credit as a yearly rate	FINANCE CHARGE The dollar amount the credit will cost you	Amount Financed The amount of credit provided to you or on your behalf	Total of Payments The amount you will have paid after you have made all payments as scheduled
12 %	$675.31	$5000 –	$5675.31

You have the right to receive at this time an itemization of the Amount Financed.
☐ I want an itemization.   ☐ I do not want an itemization.

Your payment schedule will be

Number of Payments	Amount of Payments	When Payments Are Due
1	$262.03ᵉ	6/1/86
23	$235.36	Monthly beginning 7/1/86

Late Charge: If a payment is late, you will be charged $5 or 10% of the payment, whichever is less.

Prepayment: If you pay off early, you ☒ may   ☐ will not   have to pay a penalty.

Required Deposit: The annual percentage rate does not take into account your required deposit.

See your contract documents for any additional information about nonpayment, default, any required repayment in full before the scheduled date, and prepayment refunds and penalties.

e means an estimate

This form illustrates an installment loan of $5,000, at a 12 percent simple interest rate and a term of two years. The date of the transaction is expected to be April 15, 1986, but the first payment amount is labeled as an estimate because the transaction date is uncertain. The odd days' interest ($26.67) is collected with the first payment. The remaining 23 monthly payments are equal.

(Source: Federal Trade Commission)

elsewhere for credit, or take the loan and pay it over the predesignated period.

The Rule of 78s

Although not strictly a prepayment penalty, this mathematical formula used by some creditors sometimes (especially when applied to loans longer than four or five years) has a similar effect. This formula, sometimes also called the "sum of the digits" (because the sum of the digits 1 through 12, representing a 12-month loan period, add up to 78), is applied when all of the interest on a loan is computed in advance. When you sign a loan agreement based on this advance computation, you agree to pay the principal plus interest in equal monthly installments.

When you decide to pay off such a loan early, the creditor uses the Rule of 78s to determine your "rebate"—the portion of the total interest charge you won't have to pay. This rebate, however, is seldom as much as you might think. That's because you pay more interest in the beginning of a loan, when you have the use of more of the money, and less interest in the later months.

The Rule of 78s has been called a form of prepayment penalty. With a short-term loan it really won't make much difference if you pay early. With a long-term loan, however, the picture changes dramatically. With a long-term loan the amount of interest due in the early months may actually exceed the monthly payments. The difference is added to the loan principal so that, if you pay the loan early, you may owe more than you borrowed in the first place.

For example: You take a $10,000 loan for fifteen years at an annual percentage rate of 18 percent. You make your monthly payments as scheduled for four years and then, after receiving an unexpected inheritance, decide to pay off the rest of the loan. You know that most of your early payments represented interest, but you still think you've made a dent in the principal. Not so. In this case, according to the Rule of 78s, you would have to pay $11,026 to pay off the balance of your $10,000 loan.

Federal Truth-in-Lending legislation requires additional disclosure by the lender in credit sale transactions. The lender must indicate if you "may" or "will not" be entitled to a refund of part of the finance charge if you pay early. If you will be entitled to a rebate, find out whether it is based on the Rule of 78s or on the frequently more favorable actuarial method. Read the disclosure statement, and ask any necessary questions, *before* you sign a loan agreement.

Q. I've been trying to make two payments a month on my auto loan, when I can, to pay it off faster. But friends tell me I'm losing money by doing this. Are they right?

A. Early payments don't lessen the finance charges on each payment, and by paying off the loan before it's due, you may face a prepayment penalty (specified in some loan agreements). If you can afford to pay more (not necessarily double) on a regular basis, you should consider renegotiating the loan for a shorter term, which will lessen finance costs over the life of the loan. If you can't, it would be better to put any occasional spare cash into an interest-bearing account until you have enough on hand to pay off the balance of the loan. This way, the interest you've earned will offset any prepayment penalty. Either way, talk to a loan officer and find out the best way to save on finance charges under your particular loan agreement.

In a few states, consumer loans are made on a simple-interest basis, with the interest portion of each payment calculated on the outstanding principal (the way mortgage payments are calculated). With this arrangement, there are no late charges or prepayment penalties; you simply pay interest for the precise period of time involved and the Rule of 78s does not come into play. If your payment is a couple of days late, you pay a little more interest; if you pay early, you pay less. Lenders, not surprisingly, balance their books more easily when they can collect late charges and prepayment penalties.

If you're offered a choice between two loans, one at simple interest and one with precomputed interest based on the Rule of 78s, don't make a snap decision. Compare the APR on each loan, and inquire about other prepayment penalties. If still in doubt, ask each lender how much you would owe if you paid off the loan at a specific date before its maturity.

Credit Insurance

Credit insurance, which pays off a loan in the event of your death or disability, is frequently offered as an adjunct to installment loans. Credit insurance benefits the lender. It can benefit your family as well, because loan payments will not have to be made on a reduced income.

But credit insurance has been criticized by consumer advocates. Before you buy it, here are the things you should know:

Credit insurance is usually optional. If a creditor requires that you purchase credit insurance, the cost must be included in the finance charge. Most creditors, as a result, do not require it, but borrowers may think that they do. Don't be pressured. Make an informed decision about whether or not to make this purchase.

Credit life insurance is term insurance. Credit life insurance, the most widely sold form of credit insurance, is usually a form of declining term insurance. That is, it is issued in an amount which then declines with the outstanding balance over the life of the loan. The premium stays the same, but the face amount of the policy declines along with the amount you owe. It is usually less expensive, however—unless you are ill or over age 50—to buy decreasing term insurance directly from an insurance company. The Consumer Credit Insurance Association points out, on the other hand, that it can be difficult to buy an insurance policy for $1,000 or $2,000. If you feel that you need insurance to cover a small loan, and if you don't have other insurance or other assets that will enable your family to repay the loan, then credit insurance may be your only choice.

The Cost of Credit Insurance

The price of credit life is usually expressed as cents per $100 of initial coverage over the life of the loan, with maximum premiums set by the respective states. The range is from about 40¢ per $100 to $1 per $100, with a national average of around 60¢ per $100. (At credit unions, where the cost of credit life insurance is usually built in and not paid by the borrower, costs run about 32¢ per $100.)

Whether the cost is reasonable, as the industry claims, or excessive, as consumer advocates believe, it does add to the cost of credit. Credit life insurance has been estimated to add 1 percent to the interest rate of a loan, and credit disability (or accident and health) insurance to add 2 percent. If you take both credit life and disability, according to Stephen J. Brobeck, executive director of the Consumer Federation of America, a 15 percent loan will become an 18 percent loan.

Q. I'm taking a $10,000 loan to put an addition on my house. The loan is at 18 percent, for a ten-year period. How much will credit insurance add to the cost of the loan?

A. At the average national cost of 60¢ per $100 of indebtedness, you would owe an extra $10.82 a month—or almost $1,300 over the life of the loan. Some creditors will accept payment on a monthly basis; most want the entire premium up front. The premium is added to the amount you borrow, so you're paying finance charges on the insurance as well as on the loan itself.

Credit insurance can, nonetheless, be worth buying under certain circumstances. Think about it if:

- Your family will be heavily burdened by paying off your debts.
- You don't have enough other life insurance and can't afford to buy it.
- You are ineligible for other life insurance because of ill health.
- You are at an age—generally over 50—where credit life insurance might be less expensive than other term insurance.
- You want to cover a small short-term loan, an amount so small that a commercial insurance company will not be interested.

If you do buy credit insurance, however, compare prices carefully and know what you're buying. And leave a note with your loan papers;

otherwise your family, despite the insurance, might continue paying the loan after your death.

CREDIT TIPS

- Shop around for the best terms. Remember that finance charges may differ depending on the method the creditor uses to assess them.
- Make sure you understand all the terms of your credit card or loan agreement before you sign.
- Pay bills promptly, to avoid high finance charges and to keep your good credit rating.
- Keep a list of all your credit card numbers in case of loss or theft.
- Keep accurate records of all your purchases and payments.

Staying Afloat

The use of credit has definite advantages:

- You don't have to carry large amounts of cash, or pass up a good buy because you're short of cash.
- You don't have to worry about whether a personal check will be rejected.
- You get a detailed record of all your purchases.
- You receive a single bill, for any number of small purchases, payable with a single check.
- You can pay for essential purchases, and some luxuries too, over an extended period of time.

But the use of credit has a negative side as well:

- The availability of credit may lead you to spend more than you should.
- Impulse buying may become a chronic problem.
- The spread between income and outgo may become narrower and narrower, until
- Debt becomes a way of life.

Establishing credit is one thing; using it wisely is, for many of us, something else.

Credit Trouble

People of all ages, occupations, and income brackets run into credit trouble, as is clearly shown by the records of credit counseling agencies and bankruptcy courts. More and more people in what used to be called comfortable circumstances are running into trouble as incomes are effectively reduced by increased taxes and an inflated cost of living. Trouble comes when credit is used as an extension of income, in an attempt to maintain an accustomed life-style. Unless income takes a substantial jump, the day of reckoning is bound to come. That day is sometimes hastened by one of life's misfortunes—unanticipated surgery, a job layoff —that reduces income.

Trouble often comes when a family relies on multiple incomes to keep up with inflation, and one of the jobs is lost. Ironically, many families get into trouble when a homemaker wife first goes back to outside employment. The costs of her going to work—commuting, clothes, child care, meals eaten out and convenience foods eaten in, plus an additional tax bite (see p. 475)—may be misjudged in relation to her actual take-home pay. The couple may look at the added income and, discounting the added expenses, live up to the added income by charging still more.

Trouble also comes when boom times lead people to think that times will always be good. An example: The inflation psychology of the last decade, in which homes steadily increased in value, led many people to tap that increased equity. Many of those who took second mortgages have found themselves overextended. The short-term loans are coming due and the value of the homes on which they are based has stopped rising. With new financing either unavailable or unaffordable, many owners have been forced to the wall.

And trouble comes when people simply spend without regard to income, using credit to fulfill emotional needs. Credit counseling offices are heavily booked in February and March with people who have overbought for Christmas. One such couple spent over $400 on gifts for their children, ages 6 and 2. Not much, perhaps, except that they were already committed, before Christmas, to $11,000 in prior debts on an income of $30,000 a year.

And, of course, trouble doesn't wait for Christmas. Some people spend heedlessly all year round, using money (or, in this case, plastic) to win friends, seek status, cure depression, raise self-esteem.

How can you stay out of trouble? How can you use credit within your lifelong plan for financial management?

When to Use Credit

Credit can fit into your overall financial plan if you use it to get ahead. A prime example: buying a house. Few Americans ever buy a house without the help of a mortgage loan, a use of credit which produces a significant asset with relatively little cash. A comparable use would be the financing of an education through loans; here, too, the asset outweighs the indebtedness.

Credit also makes sense in other situations: If you can earn 16 to 18 percent on your money, as you could in 1981 and 1982, it wouldn't make much sense to use that money to buy a car that you can finance at 12 to 15 percent—especially if you filed an itemized federal income tax return and could deduct the interest you pay. It's another story when you can earn 8 to 9 percent on your money and consumer credit costs 18 to 21 percent, as in early 1986, and when you can no longer deduct all of the interest, as in the case in 1987. Still, if a washing machine will eliminate endless costly and inconvenient trips to the laundromat, it makes sense to buy it on a time payment plan. It will make still more sense, of course, if you can buy the machine on sale. A saving of 20 to 25 percent justifies finance charges of 18 percent.

But credit has become a way of life. Where once the major family debt was the household mortgage, and that was to be paid off at the earliest possible opportunity, today we think it's foolish to pay off a mortgage. And we owe money, across the board, for all kinds of consumer purchases. After all, why not buy now and pay back with deflated dollars? One good reason: Because deflated dollars are still dollars—and a deflated salary may have to pay the bills.

Ask yourself: Will you still have the item in question by the time the final bill comes due? (An education yes, a vacation no.) Will you be able to pay the bills, as they come due, out of current income? (If you are counting on a bonus that is not guaranteed, think again.) Are you assuming that creditors won't grant you credit that you can't handle? (Don't. A lending institution looks at your past record of payment; only you know your future ability to repay.) Could you save enough, over a period of time, to make the purchase in cash? (If not, don't make it on credit or you may not be able to pay the bills.) Can you comfortably manage the debt you already have? (Manageable debt differs from family to family, but everyone needs a margin of safety.)

Q. We are a family of five with annual income (before taxes) of $27,000. Our debts consist of $45,000 owed on our house (worth perhaps $56,000), loans of $1,350, and a credit card balance of $1,685. We own two cars (both paid for) but have no savings. Are we in too much debt?

A. You may not be in too much debt, but you do have a serious problem. With no savings, you have no cushion for an emergency. Try to cut back on credit card use and develop a regular savings program until you build up your assets.

How Much Debt Is Too Much?

Most people can easily handle short-term debt—installment loans, retail credit, etc. (everything but a mortgage)—amounting to 10 percent of take-home pay. While still manageable, 15 percent is not quite so comfortable. And 20 percent is the danger level.

But generalizations are just that: generalizations. What is your own comfort level? How much can you manage without the stress that goes with uncertainty about paying bills? There are two ways to evaluate your situation: You can look for the warning signs that indicate you're heading for trouble, and you can calculate your own personal debt ratio.

Warning Signs

In addition to a general diffused sense of anxiety, there are specific warning signs that should tell you you're heading for trouble. Are you:

- Unable to save?
- Paying your bills a little later each month?
- Borrowing to meet current bills?
- Relying on overtime or bonuses to meet regular bills?
- Charging everyday items like groceries?
- Using savings instead of current income to pay these bills (for everyday items) when they come due?
- Using a large number of credit cards and juggling payments?
- Always paying the interest due, but never making a dent in the principal?
- "Shaving" your bills, by paying just a little less than is due?

Any or all of these symptoms means it's time to get your spending under control.

Your Debt Ratio

Here's a simple way to figure the percentage of your annual after-tax income now committed to repaying installment loans. Write down your total income for this year, after tax and other payroll deductions. Then divide your total installment payments by your take-home pay and you'll get your current actual debt ratio. Determine your manageable commitment by dividing your annual take-home pay by 10 (if you believe a 10 percent debt ratio is safest), or by 6.7 (if you believe that you can live with a 15 percent debt ratio), or by 5 (if you want to live dangerously and sustain a 20 percent debt ratio). Compare the two. How does your actual debt ratio compare with your ideal (theoretically manageable) debt ratio?

Beyond a manageable debt ratio, in percentage terms, you also need a margin of safety in dollars. Determine your current margin of safety by subtracting your current debt commitment from your theoretical manageable commitment. If your current commitment leaves only a narrow margin of safety, an almost imperceptible cushion against disaster, it's time to take stock. If it is larger than your manageable debt ratio, you're already in the danger zone.

You probably know if you're in that danger zone. The real use of these calculations is to help you determine whether or not you can safely assume additional debt. Suppose you have monthly take-home pay of $1,500 and monthly expenses, including your mortgage, of $1,200. If you have other monthly loan payments of $300, you clearly have no safety margin at all. You should not borrow again until one or more of your current loans is paid off.

Look at your current loans. The $300 in debt breaks down, let's say, into a $40 installment loan payment which will be paid off in four months, an $80 payment which will take another eleven months, and a $180 payment which runs for another year. In four months, then, you'll reduce your monthly outgo on loan repayment to $260, leaving a safety margin of $40. Should you take on another loan at this point? Maybe, but first look at two factors: your take-home pay and your cost of living. If your income has gone up (perhaps you've received a raise) you might consider a loan to buy the dishwasher you've been wanting. But you'd best recalculate your committed outgo of funds first; with the price of just about everything going up at a steady rate, you may not have the margin of safety you think you do.

WHEN YOU START TO FALL BEHIND

When the warning signals start flashing, when your personal debt ratio leaves no margin of safety, don't ignore the situation and hope it will go away. It won't, not unless you take action. There are a number of things you can do once things get out of hand, from credit counseling to debt consolidation to a declaration of bankruptcy. Before taking any of these routes, however, take a good hard look at your own situation and try to establish your own debt management program.

Debt Management

Personal debt management is a three-part plan: reducing your use of credit, identifying income and outgo, and establishing your priorities.

Reducing Your Use of Credit

The first, and absolutely essential, step in any debt management program is to stop incurring debt. Put your credit cards away (you don't have to destroy them, as long as you have some willpower) until you have reduced your current debt. You will never get your head above water if you continue to commit yourself to new debt before you make a dent in the old. So put the cards away. Use cash. You'll be surprised how it will reduce your spending.

Identifying Income and Outgo

Income-outgo calculations are an essential part of all financial planning and play a particularly important role in debt management. The very first step in gaining control of your finances, whether for simple budgeting or for getting out of debt, is finding out exactly where you stand. So, now, repeat the exercise from Chapter 2: Write down all your sources of income, and total them up (after taxes). Then write down all the ways in which you spend money, with a total in each category.

You'll probably find it easiest to determine income and outgo on a monthly basis. If you are paid weekly, you can figure monthly income as 4⅓ times your weekly rate. It would be wiser, however, to use the four-week figure in your calculations. This leaves an "extra" four weekly (or two biweekly) paychecks each year as a "bonus" that can be set aside for savings, used to meet emergencies, or put toward a vacation. (For tips on budgeting on an uncertain income, see p. 32.)

Once you identify income and outgo, analyze both. Look at income first. Can you identify any additional sources of income, funds that will help get you out of the credit trap? Do you have any U.S. Savings Bonds tucked away? How about a cash-value life insurance policy? Could you have a tag sale, and get rid of accumulated possessions while taking in some cash? Do you have time, at least temporarily, for a second job? If you do find these or other sources of funds, use them to pay off current debt. Don't take on more.

Now break down the outgo category into essential and optional. If you're over your head in debt, you'll have to cut down on those optional expenditures. But first you have to determine your own priorities.

Determining Your Priorities

One person's luxury is another person's necessity. If you're going to make a debt management plan you can live with, you have to clearly identify your own optional and essential expenditures. Be realistic. If dinner out once a week, just you and your spouse, is essential to save both your sanity and your marriage, don't treat it as a dispensable luxury. But do consider a less expensive restaurant. Or if you are so far in debt that dinner out is temporarily out of the question, schedule personal time for dessert and coffee. Meanwhile, look at other areas in which you may be able to cut back. Do you really need a new suit for business wear? Or is your current wardrobe usable for another season? Is the family's second car essential? Or is it a convenience which, with a little juggling of schedules, you could do without? Are cigarettes or soft drinks or lunches out adding unnecessarily to the outgo side of your ledger?

The *only* way to gain control of your spending is to identify your personal priorities ("personal" in this instance includes your spouse as well; if you don't agree on priorities, you have some negotiating to do). Look at your life-style. How much of the way you live, and the things you spend money on, is a result of habit? How much really matters to you?

There's another important sorting out of priorities to do, if you're already beyond your depth in debt: You must decide which creditors should be paid first when you can't manage to pay them all. Many people in this situation play by some instinctive rules—they continue to pay the mortgage and the installment loan on the car, juggle department-store bills, and put off the doctor and the dentist. Don't act by instinct. Make a plan.

DEALING WITH CREDITORS

Make a list of all your creditors, with the amount of the loan, the monthly payment, the balance due, whether or not the loan is secured by your property, and the amount of interest you're being charged. This last point is important. Some loans are at a level rate of interest. Others may have no interest at all until they are overdue, and then accrue significant amounts. Now determine how much you can manage to repay. Can you pay any of the loans in full? Or would you be better off attempting to reduce and extend payments across the board? Figure out what will work best for you.

Then discuss the situation, face to face, with each creditor. Tell your creditors the facts: that you're having difficulty (and give them the reason: that you've lost your job, are facing extensive medical bills, or are simply overextended), and that you would like to work out a repayment plan you can manage.

Most creditors will go along with a reasonable plan. They would prefer to be paid, even if slowly, rather than repossess your furniture or take you to court. And if you've been a good customer in the past, they have reason to hope that you will be so again.

You may find, however, that not every creditor will go along with your own carefully worked out plan. You may have to do some rearranging if Creditor A insists on being paid in full, while Creditor B wants a percentage of the balance due before consenting to extended payments. If you've worked out your own plan and then talked to your creditors, you should be able to rearrange things to everyone's satisfaction. Whatever you do, don't ignore bills due or notices from creditors. Doing so will only make matters worse.

Dealing with Debt Collectors

Once an overdue bill has been turned over to a debt collection agency, trouble assumes serious proportions. Now, unless you can come up with a satisfactory repayment plan, you face the possibility of legal action.

Debt collection agencies may pursue you in an effort to collect. They may write to you and they may telephone. But they are not permitted to harass you. Federal law (the Fair Debt Collection Practices Act) is very clear on this point. A debt collector may:

- Contact you in person, by mail, telephone, or telegram
- Contact other people, including your employer, in order to locate you

A debt collector may *not:*

- Call you repeatedly, or at night, or at work if you ask him not to do so
- Tell your employer or anyone else that you owe money
- Use a postcard or an envelope which would identify the writer as a debt collector
- Threaten or abuse you, use obscene language, or misrepresent who he is and what he is doing

If a debt collector violates the law, don't be intimidated. Report the illegal practices to the Federal Trade Commission, Debt Collection Practices, Washington, DC 20580.

Note: The federal Fair Debt Collection Practices Act defines a debt collector as anyone, other than the creditor or the creditor's attorney, who regularly collects debts for others. The federal law does not apply to creditors (although the laws of some states do). If a department store is after you for nonpayment of its bills, this means that its credit department may legally call you at work. If the store has turned the account over to a debt collector, however, the collector may not call you at work once you advise him that it is inconvenient for you to receive calls there.

If you fail to pay your bills, for whatever reason, and fail to work out a satisfactory repayment plan, debt collectors may take additional measures—repossession or garnishment.

Repossession

If your debt is secured by an article of property—a car, for instance, or furniture—that property may be repossessed. This may not, however, be the end of your problems. Sometimes (especially when the creditor is a little less than honest) the article is sold after repossession, at a price that will not pay off the loan. You are then without your property *and* you still owe the creditor the balance due.

If repossession appears inevitable, see if you can sell the item your-self, particularly if it's an automobile with some resale value. This way you'll be able to repay the loan with the cash from the sale and, not incidentally, you'll keep repossession off your credit history.

Garnishment

When the loan is not secured, and when the creditor sees no other means of collecting, wages may be garnisheed. Through a legal procedure, your employer must then withhold a portion of each paycheck and remit it to the creditor. Although you can't be fired for garnishment for a single debt, employers don't like the paperwork . . . and they may also lose their good opinion of employees who get in such a fix. It also does your credit record no good.

Before you get in such a fix, see what you can do about setting up a debt management program. If you can't do it alone, get outside help.

Q. About five years ago, before I knew my husband, his wages were garnisheed. Now no one will give us credit. Is there any way we can clear this from his credit record? Or, since I had good credit before I married my husband, would I be able to get credit through my name even though I'm not working now?

A. The fact that your husband's wages were garnisheed will remain on his credit record for a full seven years, although he may find a cred-itor willing to extend credit before the time is up. Another possibility: You may be able to secure credit on your own if you currently have a dependable source of income *or* if you continued your credit his-tory from before your marriage. Write to your local credit bureau, giving your maiden name, and ask for a credit report (it will probably cost a few dollars). Tell the credit bureau that you want to continue this good record under your married name. Then apply for a credit card (your best best is probably with a local department store). Make sure you apply for an individual account; if you apply for a joint account with your husband, his negative record will be counted against you. And once you get the account, be sure to pay the bills promptly.

Credit Counseling

Howard A. knew he was getting in over his head when he owed over $13,000 to eleven different creditors. Instead of looking at his finances or dealing with the debt on any kind of realistic level, he went out and got a second job. That didn't do the trick—not surprisingly, since he continued to use his credit cards—so he took a second mortgage on his house. In effect, Howard was trying to borrow his way out of debt. He finally sought help, at a consumer credit counseling agency.

Consumer credit counseling agencies exist in cities, large and small, across the country. Over 240 are part of a national network headed by the National Foundation for Consumer Credit (for the one nearest you, if you can't find a local listing, write to the National Foundation for Consumer Credit, 8701 Georgia Ave., Suite 601, Silver Spring, MD 20910). Others are affiliated with Family Service Agencies (look in your local telephone directory) and other social service agencies. Still others are profit-making ventures.

Many of the credit counseling agencies affiliated with the National Foundation for Consumer Credit have a two-part program: They will help the slightly overextended individual or family develop a workable plan for managing finances. This is often done at no cost. And they will help the seriously overextended develop a repayment plan. Under the repayment or debt liquidation plan, usually for a nominal fee (typically $10 to $12 a month), the agency may actually take monthly payments from you and channel them to your creditors. The agency may get the creditors to agree to delayed payment or to a reduced schedule of repayments. One such prorated plan is based on a "fair share" percentage of the regular payment. Suppose you have the following debts:

Creditor	Balance owed	Monthly payment
Second National Bank	$3,000	$100
Ace Finance Company	1,500	60
Dr. Welby	300	20
Fred's Collection Service	200	20
TOTAL	$5,000	$200

After subtracting necessary living expenses from income, you can only make $150 per month available for debt payments. This is 75 percent of regular payments. Therefore, each creditor is offered a prorated payment, 75 percent of the regular monthly payment:

Creditor	Regular payment	Prorated payment
Second National Bank	$100 (× .75)	$75
Ace Finance Company	60 (× .75)	45
Dr. Welby	20 (× .75)	15
Fred's Collection Service	20 (× .75)	15
		$150

Whether you go for budget counseling or for debt liquidation, the consumer credit counseling agency will do two things:

■ Request complete information about your income and about your debts. Just making this list will help you see where you are, an essential first step in making any financial plan.

■ Cut up your credit cards; the only road to fiscal solvency is a cash-only road.

The National Foundation for Consumer Credit and its affiliated agencies have received some criticism because they are funded by business. They are therefore most interested in seeing that creditors get their due and less likely, some observers feel, to suggest bankruptcy (see following pages) even when it might be the right solution. But this network of agencies has, nonetheless, rescued a great many people. Howard A. was able to get back on his feet over a three-year period. He made regular monthly payments of $370 to the agency. The agency, in turn, arranged with Howard's creditors for delayed payments and canceled penalty charges, and paid the creditors from Howard's monthly payments.

Note: Watch out for profit-making agencies and so-called "credit clinics" that charge large fees. (They are prohibited in some states but still exist in others.) They will only put you further in debt.

Debt Consolidation

When the consumer credit counseling agency took over payment of Howard's debts, as he paid the agency a monthly sum, the effect was debt consolidation. But there's another form of debt consolidation, one that may or may not work to your benefit. This is when you take a new, large loan in order to pay off all your outstanding loans.

Consolidation loans can serve a worthwhile function, but it's important for you to do the arithmetic, before you take out a new loan or refinance an old one. What will your monthly payments be? for how long? If your payments are going to go up, when you were having trouble paying the existing debt, a consolidation loan won't make sense. Don't be victimized into rolling a loan over and over, for an eternity of debt.

Bankruptcy

Can a man who owns a personal residence valued at $300,000 be bankrupt? Yes. This particular case occurred in California, in early 1982, as the result of a second mortgage which could not be refinanced when it came due. But this upright citizen is not alone. There's the $22,000-a-year printer who decided to open an ice cream shop—and failed. There's a county administrative assistant who was out of work for ten months after a knee injury. There's a policeman faced with the overwhelming cost of divorce. People of all income and educational levels have declared bankruptcy in recent years. Personal bankruptcies skyrocketed between 1978, when 179,223 Americans filed for personal bankruptcy, and 1981, when about 450,000 people filed.

There were a number of reasons for the increase: double-digit inflation, deepening recession and rising unemployment, increasing reliance on credit, an increasing acceptance of debt as a way of life . . . and, in addition, a federal law that made it a lot easier to declare bankruptcy. Now that law has been tightened, inflation has eased, and personal bankruptcies in 1985 totaled approximately 343,000.

There are two forms of bankruptcy and, while you may choose, the bankruptcy court may override your choice; it may require you to file under Chapter 13 and, at least in part, repay your debts.

CHAPTER 7 BANKRUPTCY

This is straight bankruptcy, under which your assets will be sold to repay as much of your debt as possible, with a court-appointed trustee overseeing liquidation. It's not quite as harsh as it sounds, however, because the federal bankruptcy law permits you to keep specified property, including (double each figure for a husband and wife filing jointly):

- Up to $7,500 in equity in your home (if this is not used, up to $3,750 may be applied to other property)
- $1,200 in a car
- $750 in professional implements or tools
- Household goods, clothes, appliances, and books, up to a total of $4,000
- Up to $500 worth of jewelry (but jewelry and other luxury goods bought within 40 days of your filing the petition for bankruptcy may not be eligible for this exclusion)

State law may allow different exemptions, either more or less generous. In some states you may choose between allowable federal and state exemptions; in other states you may not.

CHAPTER 13 BANKRUPTCY

Under Chapter 13 of the Bankruptcy Code, you get to keep your property. In exchange, a portion of your income will be assigned to repay your debts. You must submit a monthly budgeting plan to the court, indicating how much you can afford to pay after living expenses are met. The actual decision is made by the bankruptcy judge, after reviewing all the information about your assets, income, and obligations. Sometimes debtors repay as little as 10¢ on the dollar; sometimes they are required to pay their debts in full (in which case the only thing they have to show for the filing is additional debt, for the lawyer's fee, and a blot on their credit record). Repayment under Chapter 13 is generally for a three-year period, with occasional extension to five.

Note: If you've had friends or relatives cosign any credit application, those cosigners will be liable for your debts when you file for bankruptcy.

Under Chapter 7, your creditors can demand immediate repayment from your cosigners. Under Chapter 13, they must wait until it becomes clear that they will not be fully repaid under the court-approved plan. They may then collect the amount required to make up the full amount of the loan.

Consumer Protection

Whichever way you file, the law includes consumer safeguards:

- Creditors must leave a debtor alone. As soon as a petition for bankruptcy is filed, under either Chapter 7 or Chapter 13, creditors may no longer contact you about missed payments or other financial obligations.

- Debtors still have the option of reaffirming their debts (agreeing to pay them, despite the bankruptcy), but the affirmation must be public and the bankruptcy judge must agree that it is in your best interests. Even then you have sixty days in which to change your mind and rescind the agreement. This provision forestalls pressure to pay off old, legally discharged debts in exchange for the promise of new credit—an exchange that could put you right back in deep water.

Q. I understand that I can file for bankruptcy by myself, without a lawyer. Is there any reason why I should use a lawyer?

A. You can file by yourself, for a nominal fee. But if you have any property, a lawyer can show you how to protect it. A lawyer may also be able to tell you whether Chapter 7 or Chapter 13 would be best in your circumstances. If you do use a lawyer, be sure to select someone who:

—discusses the alternatives to bankruptcy, such as counseling,

— tells you how to retain secured property,

— advises you fully about both Chapter 7 and Chapter 13 (Chapter 7, because it's a one-step procedure, is sometimes recommended by lawyers reluctant to embark on a time-consuming Chapter 13 proceeding; your lawyer should recommend what's best for you),

— informs you about both federal and state exemptions, and

— is open about his or her fees.

If You File for Bankruptcy

Chapter 13, if you must file at all, is probably preferable to Chapter 7. It indicates to creditors a desire to pay your debts and hence may not be as severe a blot on your credit record. But bankruptcy under either Chapter

7 or Chapter 13 should be considered only as a last resort. It's never as easy as it looks. Here are some of the pitfalls:

- The slate can never be wiped completely clean. Even under Chapter 7 (Chapter 13 is more lenient), some legally enforceable debts, such as taxes, alimony, or child support, are never forgiven. Debts linked to property, such as a home or an automobile, must be paid in full or you will lose the property. If most of your debts fall into either or both of these categories, bankruptcy won't help.

- Six years must elapse before you can declare bankruptcy again. Unless you learn to keep your finances under control, bankruptcy will provide only temporary relief. (Some 20 percent of those who declare bankruptcy do so again. Some 50 percent face financial problems within two years.)

- The fact of a bankruptcy declaration remains on credit records for ten full years. During this ten-year period, you may find it very difficult to take out a loan, open a charge account, or establish credit in any form.

- You may not be ready for the psychological fallout of going bankrupt. Bankruptcy may not have the stigma it used to, but it doesn't exactly boost your self-esteem either. Nor does it do much for family relationships.

Circumstances sometimes make bankruptcy inevitable. If this happens to you, use the bankruptcy law and start again. But don't use it unless you must. Those who've been through bankruptcy tend to agree that it isn't quite as easy to live with as it is to declare.

Reestablishing Credit

Q. I *had* to declare bankruptcy several months ago, after an extended period of hospitalization left me with loads of bills and no income. It was the worst decision I ever made, but I simply had no choice. But no one cares about that. First my lawyer said I would have to wait about four years to get some credit back again. Now he says seven. What's the real number? And is something I did out of desperation, not out of a desire to get away with something, going to ruin my chances for home ownership or any credit at all forever?

A. Not forever, but probably for ten years. That's the amount of time that bankruptcy remains on credit records. (Other delinquencies—a repossession or a wage garnishment—stay on file for seven years.) But you may be able to explain your circumstances to potential creditors (they do care that your bankruptcy was the result of hospitalization rather than high living), and you may be able to reestablish your credit rating without waiting the full ten years. The best bet: Talk, face to face, with a local retailer and explain your situation.

Bankruptcy may mean a fresh start, but that start means doing without credit, at least for a while. Some debtors seem to believe that they should immediately be entitled to credit. Not so. Why should a creditor, given a demonstrable record of nonpayment of debts, want to throw money away? Why should he think he'll be repaid?

In order to reestablish credit, you have to demonstrate to creditors that you will repay your debts. There are several steps you should take:

- When you have built up your savings, take a passbook loan and pay it back promptly. The loan will be secured by your savings (your account —or at least the amount you've borrowed—will be frozen for the duration of the loan) so you should obtain it without difficulty. Prompt repayment will demonstrate your intent to handle credit responsibly.

- If you have access to a credit union, you may be able to borrow money and repay it via a payroll deduction. This, too, would demonstrate your intent to be responsible.

- When you are ready to apply for a credit card, do so with a local retailer. Save the national bank cards for later.

- You may have to be willing to make a larger down payment (on, for instance, an auto loan) or to provide a cosigner.

All of these steps, you'll notice, closely resemble the steps you take when you establish credit the first time around. That's because you're in precisely the same position, after your "fresh start," except that you're actually one step further behind. You now have a blot on your record that you must erase. But you'll be able to do so, if you're patient *and* if you're responsible. Don't bounce a check. Don't take a loan, any loan, unless you can repay it promptly.

Note: If you are in fact a responsible citizen whose bankruptcy was caused by a serious but temporary problem (such as your own illness or the need to care for aged parents), tell your creditors. They will be responsive. If you've gotten into trouble out of sheer irresponsibility, however, don't expect the welcome mat to be out the next time around. You really will have to prove yourself.

KEY POINTS

- Most Americans use credit, and it's a useful thing to have. But misuse can disrupt the best-laid financial plans, and care must be taken to manage it well.

- Use credit when it fits into your long-range financial plans. Try not to use it on impulse, or to buy things you really don't need. Try not to leave yourself without a margin of safety.

- If you do start to fall behind, try to follow a structured debt management program. If you can't do it alone, seek help from a not-for-profit consumer credit counseling agency.

- If you must deal with a debt collector, be aware of your legal rights. And if you reach the point of considering bankruptcy, be sure to consider all its implications. It won't be easy to reestablish credit.

SPENDING
YOUR MONEY:
HOUSING

Housing
Decisions

Homeownership is the American dream. The dream takes different shapes—from a white frame house with a picket fence to an urban brownstone with Victorian stained glass and a fireplace in every room to a condominium unit with a shared recreational complex—but the dream itself has held true for forty years.

Today the dream is threatened by high home prices and volatile mortgage interest rates (to be discussed, in detail, in Chapter 13). Yet it's also reinforced by the realization that today, more than ever, a house can be much more than a home. It can be a major investment, a tax shelter, and a hedge against recurring inflation. It is also, surely, the biggest purchase you will ever make.

Before you buy your first house, or your second, you owe it to yourself to evaluate your personal housing needs, determine where you want to live, and decide whether to rent or to buy. First, however, a quick look at the American housing scene today may prove helpful.

Housing in the 1980s

The 1980 census revealed a number of new housing patterns, most of them directly related to the changing social and economic patterns of American life:

- Fewer people are living in each household, down from an average of 3.11 people per household in 1970 to 2.75 in 1980.

- Smaller households lead to a need for more housing; the population rose by 11 percent from 1970 to 1980, but the number of households increased by 24 percent.

- More people lived in apartments and in mobile homes in 1980 than in 1970. Condominium purchases are way up.

All of these findings are interrelated, and all of the patterns hold true as we move toward the end of the decade. But one thing has changed. That is the seemingly ever-higher cost of housing, the spiral that became the norm in the late 1970s. Even while monthly housing costs seem to reach dizzying new heights, the purchase price of houses has in fact slowed its incessant rise. In the early 1980s house prices were up on paper but down in fact, after adjusting for inflation and for price discounts offered as incentives to move stagnant inventory. In 1986, with inflation at a low, house prices actually leveled off in many parts of the nation. That last phrase is key; there is enormous regional variation in house price appreciation.

If you are looking for a house when or where the market is depressed, you're at an advantage, because bargains may be available. If you are trying to sell a house, however, you may find that your selling price must be reduced, and that your investment has not appreciated quite as much as you had expected.

The building industry, meanwhile, is fighting for survival. In addition to reduced prices on newly built homes, there is also often attractive dealer financing (see Chapter 13). Balancing a move toward "affordable" homes—smaller houses and condominium units, smaller lots, cluster zoning, and finish-it-yourself construction—is a move toward costlier trade-up housing.

The result: If you want to buy a house, you should be able to do so.

Your Personal Housing Needs

Before you decide where you want to live or what kind of housing you want to live in, take a look at your housing needs in terms of your position in the life cycle.

Singles and Live-Togethers and the Newly Married

At this stage, you seldom need much space, probably prefer simplicity of living, and want to minimize costs. The solution, for most, is a rental apartment.

But you may want to buy a house or a condominium. Although homeownership has long been associated with meeting the needs of a growing family, both childless couples and singles of all ages are more and more often becoming homeowners. In 1970 it was relatively rare for a single individual to buy a house; in 1985, according to the United States League of Savings Institutions, over 25 percent of all homebuyers were single. And single women make up one of the fastest-growing segments of the homebuying market. Such buyers want space to entertain, are willing to "do it themselves" to keep costs down, and see a home purchase (even if they must join forces to make it possible) as the only way to fight inflation.

THE MINGLES MARKET

More and more people, both same-sex friends and opposite-sex couples, with platonic relationships and romantic ones, are teaming up to find affordable housing. Some share the rent on apartments. Some buy detached homes or condominium units. Some are moving into new "tandem" units, specially designed for unrelated owners, with two equivalent master-bedroom suites for privacy and shared living space for affordability.

State laws on such purchases vary a great deal, so it's vitally important to check the law in your state. In addition, says Kristelle L. Petersen, author of *The Single Person's Home-Buying Handbook* (Hawthorn/Dutton, 1980), sign a contract with your partner before you take title to the property. The contract should spell out:

- How the property will be owned. (In most states, the best ownership arrangement for unrelated owners is as tenants in common, without the right of survivorship.)

- Each person's contribution to the purchase price and each person's contribution to the mortgage, insurance, taxes, and maintenance.

- What happens if either partner falls behind in payments.

- Who will be allowed to live in the house (both partners' consent should be secured before either can bring in another resident).

- What happens if the house is sold: How will the property be divided? What happens if only one partner wishes to sell? The other partner should be given the first option to buy, with the method of payment designated in the contract.

- What happens to the property if one partner dies. (Be especially careful here if one of you has children and the other does not.) If title to the property is without right of survivorship, be sure that you each write a will.

- What happens in the case of the disability of one partner. (If you give each other a power of attorney with respect to the property, each will be able to make necessary decisions without the other should it become necessary.)

- What happens if you no longer wish to live together, but both wish to remain in the house. Will you flip a coin, with the winner to buy the other out?

■ Who owns property within the house, such as appliances purchased either individually or jointly.

Q. I bought a house jointly with a friend and then, almost immediately, her job required a move to another state. I can't handle the payments alone and don't know anyone who might want to share. Will I be forced to sell?

A. Not if you're fortunate enough to live in an area with a house-matching service sponsored by a community or public agency. Most of these services are designed to find housing for people who need help in finding reasonably priced housing—initially mostly older adults, now often younger ones as well—while providing a source of income for homeowners who face mounting bills. Most, as a result, match renters with owners. Through such a service, however, with its careful screening of applicants, you should be able to find a renter to share the financial burden. If you prove compatible, you might then move on to a co-ownership arrangement.

Families

Families with children begin to need more space; they also want good schools and adequate play facilities. Apartment living may seem too cramped, and apartment landlords all too often reject children, so homeownership becomes increasingly desirable. Incomes are often up at this stage (unless one income has been suspended with the arrival of children) but the demand on income is great. Among married couples buying a first house in 1985, more than two-thirds were two-income families. It usually takes two incomes today to make owning a first house possible. Then, as children grow and as income nears its peak, a larger home may become both desirable and affordable.

SINGLE-PARENT FAMILIES

Single parents are also child-oriented in their search for housing but, after the death or divorce that has created single parenthood, may find it necessary to move from a larger home to a smaller one. Profit from the sale of a first house, even if it must be divided, may make it possible to buy a second house, but the ability to make mortgage payments is often limited by the need to support a family alone.

THE EMPTY NEST

Once the children are grown, you may choose to move to more compact quarters. Move or not, money freed from child-rearing may be spent on more lavish living. "Adult" communities may be popular among those who want to shed the cares of individual homeownership; most, but not all, of these communities take the condominium form of ownership (see Chapter 17). Such communities, however, fail to interest those who prefer the stimulation of mixed-age living.

Older Adults

The elderly, alone or as a couple, generally want reduced housing costs and ease of maintenance. Some move to a moderate climate. Most, contrary to popular belief, prefer to stay exactly where roots have been put down. But maintaining the family home can be difficult, both physically and financially. Once income is fixed, housing costs consume an ever-larger proportion of that income. Even when a mortgage has long since been paid off, rising taxes and the costs of maintenance (especially when doing it yourself has become difficult) are forbidding obstacles to home ownership. (See pp. 271–72 for information on tapping the equity in a house you own.)

ACCESSORY APARTMENTS

The empty nest can provide a golden egg, as the National Council on Aging puts it, if empty space in the hard-to-manage houses of older adults is converted to rental apartments. Such "accessory" apartments are being created in suburban houses across the country, often in violation of local zoning codes, as people in need of both income and companionship put in second kitchens and rent out space.

There is a lot of opposition in some communities, as residents fear lowered property values from rental units. But the trend seems sure to grow—current estimates range from 500,000 to 3 million such apartments —and communities can control the growth with laws regulating conversion. Some such laws provide that either owner or renter must be over 62, prohibit absentee landlords, and require a renewable permit.

Conversion benefits young adults eager to find affordable suburban housing as well as older adults in need of income. The existence of rental apartments also benefits young families otherwise unable to afford the purchase of a house.

Where Do You Want to Live?

Americans are, by and large, a mobile group. We move to meet changing family needs. We move to secure new job opportunities. In 1983, 15.6 percent of the adult population changed residences. Younger adults move still more; almost 32 percent of those in the 20-to-29 age group moved during the same period. Put another way: The average length of residency per house, measured by mortgage length, is frequently reported as seven years.

So your first housing choice probably won't be your last. Nonetheless, your housing priorities deserve careful thought. Work out your personal and family needs before you look at your first house or apartment: How much space do you want? How much space do you actually need? Is more than one bathroom a must? What about storage space? Do you need a garage? Do you entertain frequently?

Some of the answers to these questions will dictate where you want to live. If you need a garage and want lots of outdoor play space for the children, a high-rise apartment or an urban brownstone may not be for you. If you like the stimulation of city life and prefer compact easy-to-care-for quarters, on the other hand, you might find an apartment, owned or rented, just fine. If your family is large, you may require the kind of living space that only an older suburban house can offer. If there are just two or three of you, however, you can probably find suitable housing just about anywhere.

In making your housing choices, look at region, at city or suburb or exurb, and then at particular communities and neighborhoods.

Choice One: Region

Unless you are locked into one area because of family or job commitments, you may want to think about a long-distance move. Maybe you'd prefer the Southwest to the winter cold of the North Central states. Maybe you could find cold weather exhilarating and would like to live in New England. Maybe, on the other hand, the Pacific Northwest has the combination of ingredients you'd like to call home. Think about your personal inclinations. Think, too, about costs.

THE COST OF HOUSING

House prices vary by region, with a 1985 high median cost of $144,100 in the area around San Francisco Bay and a low median cost of $46,300 in the Buffalo, New York, area. But median prices tell only part of the story. What if you want to compare the same house on the same-sized lot in the same sort of middle-income suburb in different parts of the United States? Where would you get the best value for your housing dollar?

In a study of 130 communities released in 1985, Coldwell Banker evaluated the cost of a three-bedroom, two-bath, 2,000-square-foot detached house with a family room, dining area, and adjacent two-car garage. The cost of this house ranged from a low of $69,000 in Fort Wayne, Indiana, to a high of $450,000 in Beverly Hills, California. Interestingly, these prices are virtually the same as those reported one year earlier; house prices are leveling off.

But prices remain high. And California, with a few local exceptions, remains the most expensive housing market in the continental United States. The same house that cost $450,000 in Beverly Hills cost $77,750 in Norfolk, $95,000 in suburban Chicago, $126,500 in Denver. Some of the lowest-cost housing areas are in the Snow Belt, but some, surprisingly, are in the South; this house cost $77,500 in Columbia, South Carolina, and $81,500 in Columbus, Georgia.

Rental prices vary by region and city as well as by type of building. The typical 850-square-foot apartment in an elevator building rented for $599 a month in Boston in 1984, according to the Institute of Real Estate Management, while a comparable apartment in Cleveland rented for $398. In general, units in elevator buildings cost more (at a national median rent of $493) than units in low-rise garden apartments (at a median of $357).

Q. I've been offered a promotion which requires a move to another state. Since I have an 8 percent mortgage on my current home, with monthly payments (without taxes) of $603, I'm wondering if I can afford to take the promotion. What kinds of things should I negotiate with my employer?

A. I assume that a hefty raise goes along with the promotion. Beyond that, if the move is to a high-cost area, these are the things to discuss: (1) A "mortgage interest differential" to pick up some of the gap, for a period of years, between your old low-rate mortgage and the more costly one you'll have to take. (2) A "settling-in" allowance, equivalent to one to three months' salary, to cover the out-of-pocket costs of moving, such as hooking up utilities and appliances; this would be in addition to moving costs themselves. (3) Duplicate costs of carrying two dwellings, if such becomes necessary, for a specified period of time. Better still, if possible, is getting your employer to sell your present home. All of these points, along with a general "cost-of-living" adjustment for new and higher living costs, should be negotiable . . . if you company wants you in that new position.

THE COST OF LIVING

Look beyond the cost of housing to the cost of maintaining your style of living in different areas. You won't have many heating bills in much of the South, for example, but your air-conditioning bills may be substantial. You may not need to own a car in New York City, if you rely on mass transit, but housing costs will be high. The Bureau of Labor Statistics indicates in its regular regional comparisons that the Northeast has the highest overall living costs, while the South has the lowest.

To live in moderate comfort, according to the Bureau of Labor Statistics, an urban American family of four—a 38-year-old husband working full time, a wife who does not work outside the home, a boy of 13, and a girl of 8—needed $25,407 in the fall of 1981 (the most recent figures available). A "lower-level" budget, more than subsistence but still bare minimum, required $15,323. And a "higher-level" budget, one providing more creature comforts, called for $38,060.

All of these figures are national averages; local figures vary considerably. Where the national "moderate" budget called for $25,047, for instance, the same family would need $29,540 in New York City and northeastern New Jersey. The differential on the higher-level budget was even greater. When the national "higher" budget called for $38,060, the same family would need $47,230, fully 24 percent more, to live as well in New York City. To live well, by comparison, in Dallas, Texas, took $33,769, 40 percent less than New York City.

Within each region, large metropolitan areas are generally more expensive than smaller ones. On its index of comparative living costs for an intermediate budget, the Bureau of Labor Statistics uses a countrywide urban average figure of 100; metropolitan areas in general rank at 102, while nonmetropolitan areas, places with population of 2,500 to 50,000, rank at 91. Cities in the Northeast range from a low of 97 (Pittsburgh) to a high of 116 (New York and northeastern New Jersey); cities in the South range from a low of 89 (Dallas) to a high of 108 (Washington, D.C.). State and local taxes are a major reason why people with comparable incomes can't afford the same life-style in different locations. Before you pick a state, if you're not already settled, look at:

Income Tax Forty-three states have a personal income tax. The exceptions (in 1985) are Alaska, Florida, Nevada, South Dakota, Texas, Washington, and Wyoming. But the taxes are very different. Some states

TABLE 1: An index of comparative living costs on an intermediate budget for a four-person family, autumn 1981.

URBAN UNITED STATES	100	SOUTH	
Metropolitan areas	102	Atlanta	92
Nonmetropolitan areas	91	Baltimore	99
		Dallas	89
NORTHEAST		Washington, D.C./Md./Va.	108
Boston	115	Nonmetropolitan areas	86
Buffalo, N.Y.	104		
New York/Northeastern N.J.	116	WEST	
Pittsburgh	97	Denver	98
Nonmetropolitan areas	102	Los Angeles/Long Beach	98
		San Francisco/Oakland	107
NORTH CENTRAL		Seattle/Everett	102
Chicago/Northwestern Ind.	100	Nonmetropolitan areas	96
Cleveland	101		
Kansas City	97		
Milwaukee	106		
Nonmetropolitan areas	91		

tax all income at a flat rate, others assess a flat percentage of the federal income tax in a piggyback tax, and some have a steeply progressive tax on graduated income. With states facing financial crises, actual tax rates are changing rapidly. But you can be sure of one thing: where there are state income taxes, your take-home pay will be noticeably lower.

Sales taxes. Levied by most but not all states, these also make a noticeable dent in your budget. Two things to look for: the *rate* of the tax and *what it covers*. Some states exempt food, clothing, and prescription drugs; others exempt one or another but not all three. Some municipalities add a local sales tax over and above the one set by the state. To compare sales tax figures, look at the IRS tables for allowable sales tax deductions on your federal income tax. These tables showed a $408 sales tax deduction for a family of four in Connecticut in 1985 and a $283 deduction for a comparable family, with the same income of $38,001 to $40,000, in North Dakota. (As of the 1987 tax year, however, sales tax is no longer deductible on federal income tax returns.)

Property taxes. These vary from place to place; so does the method of valuation. Consider tax rate, full or partial valuation, and frequency of reassessment.

Inheritance and estate taxes. These vary considerably and may be of particular interest if you are picking a retirement home.

Special taxes. Connecticut, for instance, has a capital gains and dividend tax. New Hampshire and Tennessee, in 1985, tax interest and dividends. Some localities also turn to special use taxes, such as an automobile tax, to raise funds.

The combination of state and local taxes turns out to be a major part of your tax burden. State and local general tax collections averaged $1,216 per capita in 1983, according to the Tax Foundation. Alaska collected the most in taxes from each of its residents, and Arkansas the least. Taxes are lower in the South, as a rule, but per capita income is lower too.

Choice Two: City or Suburb or Exurb

There's a trade-off in convenience. There's also a trade-off in costs. You'll get more for your housing dollar, as a rule, the farther you are from a major population center. An Associated Press survey of real estate markets in spring 1981, when the median price for a single-family home was $65,000, found that $65,000 bought a lot more house outside almost any city line than within. In Atlanta, for instance, $65,000 bought a three-bedroom split-level with no garage in a city neighborhood in the process of restoration. Twenty-five miles outside Atlanta, the same sum would buy a three-bedroom with eat-in kitchen, full dining room, fireplace, and a two-car garage, all on a half-acre wooded lot. The specific figures have changed but the disparity remains.

If you move too far, however, to a remote rural area ("exurbia"), you may find that your commuting-to-work costs increase significantly. You'll also probably find that the costs of transportation may make food and clothing and all the necessities of life very costly. In a big city, converging transportation lines and large numbers of consumers combine to make goods available at less cost.

In the suburbs, where most Americans have congregated in recent years, there are no hard-and-fast rules . . . except that it may cost a considerable amount to heat a rambling suburban home and to get from that home to your job. Other costs will depend on the size and density of your community, its closeness to distribution centers, and its economic level. High-income suburbs, not uncommonly, have stores with prices geared to those high incomes.

Choice Three: Community

What's the most important factor when you buy a home? Location, location, and location, say real estate authorities. Consider your location carefully before you move. Making a mistake can be costly.

One young couple were, wisely, more cautious than most. They had long dreamed of a certain Connecticut community as their ideal location. But they weren't quite sure enough to go out and buy, so they rented an apartment first. They learned several things: The commute was long and tiring. The neighbors were intensely dissatisfied with the schools. The parks were vandalized by bored local youngsters. And the picture-postcard rural community was simply too isolated to suit their tastes. They bought a house, when they bought, in suburban New Jersey.

Once you've narrowed your choice by region and by state, you'll have to look at particular communities. If you have no ties and are picking blind, here are some hints that may help:

- Subscribe to a local newspaper for several weeks or months before you make a final decision. A careful reading of the news and features will show you the prevailing politics of the community, the variety of religious groups on hand, the social and cultural activities which can be found. An equally careful reading of the ads will show you what merchandise is available and what prices are like.

- Talk to people in the local planning and zoning and tax offices. What's happening to the population? Is it growing, with younger families, so that educational and recreational facilities may become crowded and money will have to be raised (via taxes, of course) to build new schools and playgrounds? Is the population getting older, so that the school you are considering for your children may be closed for lack of enrollment within a short time after you move in? What's the tax base of the town? Is there industry, light or heavy? Are there shopping centers and office buildings?

Or does the entire tax burden fall on homeowners? Are sewers and side-walks in place? Or will you face this cost as well? Does the community have zoning regulations? Or could a factory be built on the nicely wooded lot directly behind your prospective home?

- What amenities and services does the community offer? Do the schools have a good reputation? Are there parks and recreational facilities? Is there a good library system? Your property taxes may be higher, depending on the tax base, to support such services but the value of your property may be higher as well. Is there an adequate police force? A paid professional fire department? A volunteer fire department (no matter how dedicated and how diligent) may cost you less in property taxes, more in fire insurance.

- How stable is the neighborhood? Look for well-maintained property. Be careful, if you plan to buy, about an area with a great many "for sale" signs sprouting on the lawns, or a lot of rental property in an area of one-family homes. Be alert to rapid turnover and/or many vacancies in an apartment building or development. All may be a sign of deterioration.

To Rent or to Buy

Until the end of World War II the majority of Americans lived in housing owned by others. Since the late 1940s, however, the scale has tipped dramatically in the other direction. Today almost 64 percent of Americans own their own homes. Some, probably a minority, own throughout their adult lives. Others, more typically, rent, then own, then, perhaps, rent again. Some choose to rent as a permanent way of life. Many factors, some financial and some not, enter into the decision. Here are some things to consider.

If You Rent

Renting may be a first step as you save money on the way to homeown-ership. Renting may also be appropriate if you are located temporarily and expect to move. Renting may be the solution for small households. And renting, for some of you, is simply a perfect way of life.

There are both positive and negative aspects to renting:

IN FAVOR OF RENTING

You'll have more control over your living expenses. And those expenses, in many parts of the country, will be lower than the expenses associated with ownership. Your rent, if you have a lease, will probably remain stable for several years. Your commitment will be limited to the term of your lease.

If you rent an apartment, moreover, you can call on someone else to shovel walks, remove trash, and fix balky plumbing. If you rent a house, you may be responsible for routine maintenance and minor repairs, but the landlord will probably assume responsibility for major items such as roof or plumbing repair; be sure to clarify responsibilities before you sign the lease. Apartment or house, you'll be unlikely to sink money into costly improvements to property that is not your own. You can invest your savings in high-return liquid assets instead of tying up your money in not-necessarily-easy-to-sell real estate.

NEGATIVE ASPECTS OF RENTING

As a renter you do without the investment value of real estate; you build no equity and you take no tax deductions. You usually can't alter the unit to suit your preferences. You may well have less space and less privacy in an apartment than in a house. You may also be subject to restrictions imposed by the owner. Rental units, moreover, are becoming increasingly scarce (and often increasingly expensive) as fewer multiple-unit buildings are built, more and more buildings convert to condominium ownership (see Chapter 17), and more and more single-person households come into being.

THE FINANCIAL COMMITMENT OF RENTING

Although your financial commitment to rental housing is usually far less than your financial commitment to a house of your own, there are pitfalls for the unwary. Be sure that you:

- Read your lease carefully. What happens if you must move before the lease expires? Are you allowed to sublet the apartment? What are your obligations with respect to maintenance? What is the landlord's obligation? Is there a clause permitting the landlord to pass along increases for fuel, utitlities, taxes, etc.?

- Consider the cost of utilities if they are not included in your monthly rent. Will your apartment be separately metered, or will an allocation of costs be made by the landlord or the utility company?

- Understand any applicable rules and regulations. Are you allowed to paint or paper the apartment? to add shelves? to put in a washing machine or a dishwasher? If you're not, and you do, what will be your financial liability?

- Know local laws with respect to health and safety in residential housing. Most cities now have housing codes which set minimum standards, and tenants in many areas are allowed to repair defects ignored by the landlord and then to deduct the cost of those repairs from the rent.

- Understand any deposits you are requested to make. A *damage deposit* must be returned when you leave unless you caused physical damage beyond normal wear and tear or, depending on the terms of your lease, unless you caused economic damage to the landlord by failing to give adequate written notice about moving. A *security deposit* is sometimes used the same way, but it can also be more complicated; it might require that you rent the unit for a specified period of time in order to receive a refund of the deposit. A *cleaning deposit* is a separate deposit, usually not refundable, used for cleaning the premises after you move out. Local laws may regulate deposits and their return; in some areas, landlords must keep deposits in interest-bearing accounts with the interest payable to the tenant.

Inspect any rental premises thoroughly before you move in, making a written record of any damages. Ask the landlord to attach a copy of this record to your lease, and keep a copy yourself. This record will document the condition of the apartment, and substantiate your claim for return of a damage or security deposit when you move out.

Q. I sublet my apartment, in accordance with the terms of my lease, when I went away for the summer. Unfortunately, my subtenant has proved to be unreliable. He neglected to pay the rent, and the landlord is dunning me. Do I have to pay?

A. If your landlord agreed to an "assignment" of your lease to your subtenant, then the subtenant is legally responsible along with you. If, however, you turned the place over as a straight sublease, you remain completely responsible.

If You Buy

Ownership also has its positive and negative aspects:

ON THE POSITIVE SIDE

With homeownership you'll find, as a rule, greater space and privacy along with the freedom (within local zoning laws and building codes) to improve and change your property. You'll also secure tax advantages and the opportunity to realize a profit when you sell. You'll have an investment that provides a hedge against inflation as long as property values continue to increase.

You won't, under current adjustable mortgage forms (see Chapter 13), have the two-part inflation hedge that combined a true increase in the value of the house with a fixed-rate loan that was paid off in ever-cheaper dollars. But you will still own a tangible asset and benefit from any appreciation in the value of that tangible asset. Note, however, that lower inflation and a slower economy have dramatically reduced house price appreciation. Annual increases in house prices averaged 9.5 percent between 1968 and 1975, rose to about 12 percent between 1976 and 1980, and hovered at just about 3 percent from 1981 to 1985. Living in a house may be nice, but at these levels it is no longer a surefire investment.

TABLE 2: The median price of houses, 1969–84.

	New homes	Existing homes		New homes	Existing homes
1969	$25,600	$21,800	1977	$48,800	$42,900
1970	23,400	23,000	1978	55,700	48,700
1971	25,200	24,800	1979	62,900	55,700
1972	27,600	26,700	1980	64,500	62,200
1973	32,500	28,900	1981	68,800	66,400
1974	35,900	32,000	1982	69,300	67,800
1975	39,300	35,300	1983	75,300	70,300
1976	44,200	38,100	1984	79,900	72,400

(Source: National Association of Home Builders)

TABLE 3: House price changes compared to inflation.

	PERCENT INCREASE	
	Consumer Price Index (all items)	Average sales price of new homes
1970	5.9%	2.8%
1971	4.3	5.4
1972	3.3	6.5
1973	6.2	8.7
1974	11.0	9.3
1975	9.1	10.7
1976	5.8	8.6
1977	6.5	12.7
1978	7.7	14.5
1979	11.3	14.2
1980	13.5	11.0
1981	10.4	8.4
1982	6.1	2.6
1983	3.2	2.5
1984	4.3	3.9
1985	3.6	2.1

(Source: Michael S. Johnson, University of New Orleans)

NEGATIVE ASPECTS OF OWNERSHIP

But homeownership also entails some disadvantages. Both the initial and the ongoing costs are high. Some, if not all, of the costs are variable, making it difficult to plan and to budget. And you should make a commitment to stay for an extended period of time—at least four years, according to some studies—if your initial costs are to be recovered and equity realized. If you must move earlier you may lose part of your investment.

THINGS TO CONSIDER BEFORE YOU BUY

When you buy, rather than rent, the financial equation becomes more complicated. After the initial purchase price and related transaction costs (to be discussed in detail in Chapter 12) you'll have to look at:

- Monthly mortgage payments
- Utilities
- Heat
- Property taxes
- Property insurance
- Services, such as trash pickup and snow removal
- Landscaping and maintenance
- Possible assessments for streets, sidewalks, and sewers
- A reserve against repairs

Some of these costs, of course, are affected by where and what you buy. Insurance, for instance, may cost more on a frame structure than on a brick one; it may also cost more in areas without a professional paid fire department. Services are provided by municipal taxes in some communities; elsewhere you'll pay separately, for instance, for private trash removal. The larger house costs more in property taxes, more to heat. The older house costs more for maintenance and repairs.

The key factor, however, may be that very few of the costs of homeownership are fixed. Monthly mortgage payments used to be a stable element in the homeowner's budget; with the new adjustable-rate mortgages, monthly mortgage payments have become unpredictable. Electricity and heating oil and the gasoline used for commuting have all risen sharply in recent years. Do the best you can to come up with an all-inclusive list of expenses before you decide to buy.

The "Real Costs" of Owning vs. Renting

You could simply compare monthly rent to monthly homeownership costs, and make your decision accordingly. But economists don't simply look at dollar outlay, or even at interest rates, in calculating real costs. These hard figures have to be modified by other factors before a valid financial comparison can be made between monthly rent and monthly homeownership costs. You should look at other factors as well:

IMPUTED RENT

"Imputed rent" is the value of your owned house as living space, the amount you might pay for it in rent if you were renting instead of buying. Because you are, in effect, paying yourself when you own, that is money gained. But there's more to the equation: If, instead of living in your own house, you rented it to someone else, you would have to pay income tax on your rental income (after deducting operating expenses). If you live in the house yourself, you don't pay this rent and you don't pay the taxes on rental income. This can be a saving of several thousand dollars a year.

OPPORTUNITY COSTS

If you decide to buy a house, however, you forgo the opportunity to invest the money you commit to the house in other ways. If you commit $10,000 to a down payment on a house, as an example, and you could have earned 10 percent a year in interest on that $10,000, that's a first-year opportunity cost of $1,000 (minus, of course, the income taxes due on that interest income). If the interest was reinvested each year, for a compounded return, your lost-opportunity costs would be significantly greater over time. Your home may, of course, appreciate in value by at least as much. But there's no guarantee that it will, and even if it does, you won't realize the gain until you sell.

Q. I'm retired, living comfortably on a total of almost $1,800 a month from Social Security, pension, and stock dividends. I also have $62,000 invested in a money market fund. I rent an apartment, for $445 a month, but am thinking of buying a $55,000 condominium to cut my income taxes. Would this be a good idea?

A. Don't look to tax savings without regard to anything else. If you buy a condominium unit, you'll be reducing your yearly income by the interest on the sum you use for the purchase. You'll also have to face costs—rising costs over the years—for taxes, assessments, and utilities. You may well be better off continuing to rent.

TAX CONSIDERATIONS

Because interest costs are deductible, costs of ownership are directly affected by your income tax bracket. (If you rent, your landlord gets the tax breaks and your get none.) The higher your income, and the higher your tax bracket, the more you will save by owning your own home. The married couple filing jointly with a taxable income of $50,000 is, according to 1986 federal tax tables, in the 38 percent bracket. If a dollar of mortgage interest payments is deducted from their taxable income, they will reduce the amount of taxes they pay by 38¢. The married couple with a taxable income of $15,000, by contrast, has a marginal tax rate of 16 percent. Reduction of their taxable income by a dollar's worth of mortgage interest, therefore, reduces their income tax bill by only 16¢. In 1987, the first couple is in a 35 percent bracket and the second in a 15 percent bracket; in 1988, the applicable tax rates on these income levels will be 28 percent and 15 percent.

Much is made of the tax advantages of homeownership. However, Michael S. Johnson, formerly of Cornell University's Department of Consumer Economics and Housing, points out that you receive the tax benefits of ownership only if you itemize deductions. More important, the full tax benefits are available only if your other itemizable deductions are at least as much as the standard deduction. The standard deduction for a married couple filing jointly in 1986 was $3,670. In 1988, it will be $5,000. Unless your non-housing-related deductions (for state and local taxes, charitable expenses, medical bills, and so on; see Chapter 23) exceed $3,670, you're not getting the full benefit of your housing-related deductions. The reason: The housing-related deductions may push you over the $3,670 mark and thus make it advantageous to itemize, but some of those deductions would be covered by the $3,670 standard deduction if you didn't itemize; only the amount of deductions *over* $3,670 can be considered an extra saving of tax dollars.

Assuming that you can and do itemize your tax deductions, however, the advantages of home ownership are substantial. During the early years of a mortgage, a much greater share of the monthly payment goes to interest than to the principal. The interest is directly deductible. A simplified comparison, taking two families of four each earning $28,000 a year, makes the point: In 1980, Family A, living in a rental apartment, paid $4,344 in federal income tax. Family B, however, bought a $70,000 house at the beginning of 1979 with a 10 percent downpayment and a 30-year-mortgage at 13 percent. Family B paid $2,737 in federal income tax in 1980. Other deductions, of course, have an impact. But it's easy to see why homeownership has been called the greatest possible tax shelter for middle-income people.

LENGTH OF OCCUPANCY

How long you expect to stay in one place is also a critical factor in your decision to rent or to buy, not only because it may not seem psychologically worthwhile to buy a house if you're planning to move again shortly but because it may not be economically sound to do so. The longer you will stay in one place, economists agree, the more cost-effective it is to own your residence.

One way of viewing the decision to buy or to rent is to ask what the rent would have to be to equal the same return on the investment you would receive from owning. What, in other words, is the break-even point in terms of your personal finances? Table 4 shows the rent you would have to pay, at various income levels and for varying lengths of occupancy, to make renting a better investment than buying.

TABLE 4: Break-even rents for $80,000 house.

Income	1 year	2 years	3 years	5 years	10 years
		EQUIVALENT RENTAL COST OF OWNING IF THE HOUSE IS SOLD AFTER THIS NUMBER OF YEARS:			
$20,000*	$1,460	$1,059	$922	$806	$704
40,000	1,362	960	823	709	611
60,000	1,283	881	744	631	536
80,000	1,236	833	697	585	491

Figures are based on a fixed-rate mortgage at 11% for 30 years, with a downpayment of 10%. Other assumptions include an inflation rate and house appreciation rate of 4%, and a pre-tax yield on alternative investments of 7%. Tax savings are based on 1985 tax rates for filing a married, joint return. Figures include maintenance, utilities, insurance, and property tax costs.

* A household with income of $20,000 could not qualify for the assumed mortgage. Figures are included for comparative purposes only.

(Source: Michael S. Johnson, Dept. of Economics and Finance, University of New Orleans)

THE IMPACT OF INFLATION

You might, although this is more difficult, also consider an inflation factor in your calculations. One of the advantages (to homeowners, but not to lenders) of the traditional fixed-rate mortgage has been in paying off a mortgage loan in cheaper and cheaper dollars. With the new and far more prevalent adjustable-rate mortgage loans, this advantage disappears.

But you can still adjust your mortgage loan, mentally, to get a "real" cost of interest in terms of inflation. For instance, if your mortgage loan is at 13 percent in a year when the Consumer Price Index is at 8 percent, then your real rate of interest is 5 percent. Figure in the tax savings and your real rate of interest is lower still. With inflation plus tax deductions, in fact, your real rate of interest may even be negative. At the same time, the value of your house will probably continue to rise. Although appreciation has slowed (4 percent annual rate in 1986, as against 8 percent in 1981, 11 percent in 1980, and 14 percent in 1979), any increase in value must be calculated. If your "real cost" is below the annual increase in value, you are making money by owning your own home.

Should You Buy a House as an Investment?

The spiraling price increases of the late 1970s made many Americans scurry to get on the homeownership carousel, or to move on to the next and larger house. No matter how insane the price of housing, it seemed, you couldn't lose. The spiral just kept moving upward as houses became more and more valuable. But the carousel has slowed. Houses in some parts of the country are worth less today, in some instances, than they were a year ago. People who bought at the height of the price spiral, and who now must sell, are forced to take a loss.

Should you, in view of these developments, continue to look on homeownership as a worthwhile investment?

Yes. Even when mortgage interest rates exceed the annual appreciation of a house, the National Association of Realtors points out, that house still has value as an investment. For example, if you are in the 18 percent marginal tax bracket at a time when appreciation in house prices is a modest 6 percent, you can realize a competitive return on your investment even with a mortgage interest rate of 10 percent on a 30-year fixed-rate mortgage. If you buy the house and live in it yourself (renting it out is another story) for ten years, your after-tax rate of return would be 13.5 percent. The rate of return includes these three elements:

- The gross rent you would have paid for the use of the house if you did not own it, based on an annual rent of 10 percent of the house's value
- The price appreciation on the house over the holding period
- The tax deduction for mortgage interest payments and property taxes

The rate of return is improved substantially by either a faster rate of appreciation or by a lower interest rate on the mortgage. When both appreciation rates and interest rates are down, as was the case in 1986, the rate of return on housing-as-investment is also down and housing should be viewed primarily as shelter. Even so, its investment potential should not be overlooked.

In looking at a house as an investment, be sure to realistically evaluate ongoing expenses for maintenance. Be sure to compare the rate of return with the rate you can secure on other investments. In summer 1986, when housing appreciation had slowed and mortgage interest rates were down, rates of return on other investments were down as well. Both long-term corporate bonds and high-quality stocks (including both dividends and appreciation) were yielding a pre-tax return of 8 to 9 percent. And be sure to consider both your current (and, insofar as possible, future) tax situation. With lower tax brackets and a larger standard deduction under 1986 tax legislation, both housing costs and the after-tax return on housing are greatly affected.

Don't speculate when you buy your home. Be aware that the rate of appreciation of house prices is likely to continue to be slower than it was, and that the adjustable mortgage forms prevalent today (see Chapter 13) mean that you don't keep as much of the appreciation in value as you might have in the past.

Look at the purchase of a house as a shelter for your family first and an investment second, and you'll be making a wise purchase.

KEY POINTS

- Don't make any housing decisions until you evaluate your personal housing needs. Your age and your stage in the life cycle are important factors in where and how you live.

- Different regions, states, and communities have different things to offer. Look at both the quality of life and the impact on your pocketbook before you decide where to make your home.

- Renting living space may be appropriate for you at one stage, ownership at another. Look at all the positive and negative aspects of each before you decide what to do at any particular time.

- Homeownership is an investment, but look at it first as an investment in a way of life rather than as an investment for capital appreciation.

12

Buying
a House

You've evaluated your personal housing needs, decided where to live, and determined to buy rather than rent. Finding an affordable mortgage may be the next thing on your mind. But there are other factors to consider before you seek a mortgage: What, besides mortgage payments, should you look at in doing your arithmetic? What kind of house do you want to buy? Should you use a real estate agent? How do you negotiate a price? What, at last, will happen at the closing on the house, when you actually take title? This chapter will focus on these matters; the next will deal with financing your purchase.

How Much Can You Spend?

You may have heard that you can afford to buy a house costing two to two and a half times your annual income. With the escalation of home prices in recent years, this long-time guideline is meaningless. What matters now, above all, is your ability to manage the monthly expense of owning a particular home.

Another time-honored rule of thumb is that monthly expenses on housing should run no more than 25 percent of your take-home pay. Forget it. In today's housing picture, 30 percent is common, 35 percent is typical and some people are spending 40 percent or more of their take-home pay on a place to live. If you bought a house some years ago you are probably spending far less of your income on housing. If you buy a house today, you must expect to spend more. Fully 34 percent of the homebuyers surveyed in 1985 by the United States League of Savings

Institutions reported spending over 25 percent of their income on housing (a sharp drop from the 45 percent of 1981).

What you must ask is this: How much can you spare each month, month after month, with some cushion for emergencies, and how much can you commit to housing? Your answer will not be the same as your neighbor's. One 28-year-old, with a wife, a child, and another child on the way, earned $39,000 a year when he set out to buy a $92,000 house. According to his bank, he should have been able to manage $970 a month on housing. He convinced the bankers, however, that he could manage over $1,500 a month on housing. It meant no movies, no meals out, no extra clothes, and a carefully drawn budget projected several years into the future. It didn't hurt that the 28-year-old was an accountant.

You must draw up your own budget, establish your own priorities. You can't stretch to the limit to buy a house if you're already deeply in debt for your Alfa Romeo and the clothes on your back. Most lenders still prefer that the portion of your income committed to housing not exceed 28 percent. Another common prescription is that your total monthly debt payments, including mortgage payments, should not exceed 36 percent of your income.

These rules, like all rules, are somewhat elastic and depend a great deal on the size of your family and on the life-style you choose. A two-person, two-income household, assuming that the two incomes are stable, can safely spend a larger proportion of income on housing than a one-income family with several mouths to feed. If you like macaroni, moreover, you can devote more of your income to housing than if you insist on roast beef. And if owning a house is more important to you than anything else, you may, like the 28-year-old above, be willing to forgo almost all luxuries for its sake.

As always, where you live makes a difference. You'll spend more on housing, as a rule, if you live in a large city and less if you live in a small town.

What you buy makes a difference as well. Condominium units generally cost less than individually owned houses. Mobile homes cost less than condos. Older houses cost less, by and large, than new ones.

The amount of money you decide you can spend will influence your decision about the type of housing you buy. Condominium ownership is very popular today, particularly among first-time buyers and among older adults with empty nests, because condominium ownership (see Chapter 17) can be both less expensive and less troublesome than conventional ownership. If you want the traditional individually owned single-family detached house, you'll have to decide, at the outset, between an old house and a new one.

In general, older houses can be purchased for lower prices than brand-new houses. The median national selling price in June 1986 was $89,600 for new houses and $82,300 for existing ones. This difference

TABLE 1: A profile of homebuyers and homebuying, 1977–85.

	1985	1981	1979	1977
CHARACTERISTICS OF BUYERS				
Median age	35.8 yrs.	34 yrs.	33 yrs.	32 yrs.
Unmarried	25.2%	29.6%	22.4%	17.0%
One- and two-person households	59.9%	57.4%	51.9%	45.8%
First-time buyers	39.1%	13.5%	17.8%	36.3%
Medium household income	$42,396	$39,196	$28,110	$22,700
Importance of second income*	56.5%	52.1%	53.9%	47.2%
Median household net worth	NA	$70,519	$52,277	$31,800
TYPES OF HOUSING				
Condominiums	13.4%	21.5%	11.0%	NA
New homes	22.1%	26.1%	30.8%	25.4%
Homes 25 or more years old	33.9%	29.5%	27.5%	23.7%
Median size of home (sq. ft.)	1,461	1,450	NA	NA
COSTS				
Median purchase price	$75,000	$72,000	$58,000	$44,000
Median down payment	$14,100	$16,100	$12,282	$ 9,000
Median total monthly housing expense	$770	$816	$550	$400
Mortgage payment	$573	$624	$401	$273
Real estate taxes	$ 75	$ 72	$ 58	$ 54
Utilities	$100	$100	$ 75	$ 60
Hazard insurance	$ 22	$ 20	$ 16	$ 13
Less than 20% down payment	55.9%	30.9%	42.9%	32.1%
Housing expense exceeding 25% of household income	33.5%	44.9%	45.7%	38.1%

* Percentage of households with two adults in which income contributed by a second earner accounted for 10% or more of total household income.
(Source: United States League of Savings Institutions)

may account for the recent surge in buyers of older homes (see Table 1). Determine your own preference, then shop your own market carefully, keeping the following information in mind.

The New House

In general, new houses may be more expensive, but a lower down payment may be possible and easier financing may be available. Builders and developers have their own steady sources of financing and can save you the time and trouble of shopping around to secure a mortgage commitment. In today's housing market, in fact, many builders are offering special financing (see Chapter 13). With the one-to-one arrangements in purchasing an older house, you're often left to do your own legwork (although here, too, today, sellers are often helping with financing).

New houses are also up-to-date. Appliances will be new, kitchens and baths will be modern, air conditioning may be built-in. New systems, however, may need a shakedown period before they function faultlessly. And, in some ways, there will be additional costs with a new house that there might not be with an older one. Builder-provided landscaping is often sketchy, and you may have to spend a good bit on your grounds. Screens and storm windows and such necessities as trash cans won't be available from a previous owner; you'll have to buy your own.

If you decide to buy a new house, there are two subspecies to consider:

THE BUILDER-BUILT HOUSE

Far and away the most common, these houses may be in a massive tract of look-alike houses or in a handful of houses tucked into an existing neighborhood. Builder-built homes have a lot to offer. Because a builder deals in quantity, he can keep prices down on everything from lumber to appliances; because a builder-built house is built on speculation (built, that is, before it has a buyer), it is designed to appeal to as many people as possible and will therefore be easier to resell. But don't fall for the model home with all its appealing extras; try to be realistic about the house you'll actually buy.

Note: The average size of builder-built houses is creeping up again, after some years of small and "affordable" new housing, but you may still be able to find a small starter home.

THE CUSTOM-DESIGNED HOUSE

This is a new house built just for you by a builder or an architect. A builder will tailor stock plans to suit your preference; his profit will be built into the cost of the house. An architect will design a house expressly for you, with a fee based on a percentage of the building cost; fees vary, but you can expect to pay about 15 percent. A skilled architect, however, can save you that much and more.

Either way, the custom-designed house is built just for you and is likely to suit you better. But it may be more difficult to resell. Your pet greenhouse or hot tub may represent a pain rather than a plus to a potential buyer.

The individually designed and built house is also likely to be more expensive. Construction materials will not be bought in quantity; they'll have to be bought as needed. As their prices rise, so will the cost of your house. Your natural inclination, too, will be to build the best, and the best, as a rule, costs more.

If you embark on either a builder-built or a custom-designed house, try to restrain the impulse to change things as you go along. It is extremely expensive to move doors or windows or closets once they are even roughly in place.

A Tale of a New House

Buying a new house, even from a reputable builder, requires vigilance. One couple, very happy with their development house on one and a half acres in rural northwestern New Jersey, tells what happened:

- Construction was slower than expected (as it often is), and closing was postponed from March 1 to July 20. Since the couple had given up their apartment on July 1, and since storing furniture was very expensive, they put their furniture in the basement of their unfinished house while they moved in with her parents. The furniture was not insured and they were lucky to have only minor water damage.

- Construction workers are human; they make mistakes. Regular visits by this couple—and early detection of mistakes—made corrections possible. "We realized one day, even though the ceiling sheet rock wasn't in place yet, that there was no cathedral ceiling in the living room. If we hadn't caught it then, the builder might not have been able to correct it." If you can't keep track during construction, or have someone do it for you, you're bound to run into trouble.

- Some things always remain to be done after moving day, and the New Jersey couple, wisely, had $1,500 of the purchase price put into an escrow fund until work was complete. Even so, it took several months before the front porch, the driveway, and promised plantings were finished. Nails will continue to pop and walls to crack for quite a while. Workmen will come back after the house has settled, in about a year, to do the necessary repairs, which will mean more plaster dust, more mess.

This couple had relatively little trouble. Post-construction defects were minor, and their builder made the necessary corrections. Not all homebuyers are so fortunate. You, as a homebuyer, should (1) seek a reputable builder (see p. 230) and (2) look for a house with a warranty.

Warranties

If you buy a can opener and it turns out to be defective, you can take it back to the store and ask for a replacement; most stores, although not obligated to replace the can opener (they could refer you to the manufacturer), will do so. But what happens if you buy a new house and it proves to be defective? Beyond the obvious impossibilities of returning a house for a replacement, what are your chances of getting the builder to set things right?

There have been many complaints about builders over the years, from the builder, who can't be bothered to come back to fix sticky windows to more serious instances of a builder's refusal to mend leaky roofs or cracked foundations. One Federal Trade Commission survey indicated that the average newly built house has defects costing nearly $1,000 to repair; 62 percent of new-house owners in this survey had at least one construction problem that the builder wouldn't resolve; and 20 percent reported a "serious disagreement" with a builder.

THE **HOW** PROGRAM

In 1974, in an effort to combat consumer dissatisfaction with builders (and to forestall government regulation of the industry), the National Association of Home Builders established the Home Owners Warranty (HOW) program. Now an independent corporation with 11,500 builder participants, HOW has provided warranties against structural defects for 1.4 million houses. The program isn't perfect; some homeowners complain bitterly that their problems remain unresolved, and some builders have dropped out in dissatisfaction or been dropped for failure to respond to the homeowners' complaints. Nonetheless, HOW does offer protection where little existed before.

For example, in a case from the HOW files, a newly built Florida house with a cathedral-ceiling-high stone fireplace began to settle. The fireplace separated as much as a full inch from the walls; the frightened homeowners were justifiably afraid that it would topple.

Because the builder refused to repair the damage, HOW insurance came into force. The insurance investigation revealed that the foundation had been laid without footings and with one of the essential supporting piers in each row omitted. The insurance carrier had the house moved from its foundation, the old foundation bulldozed out, and a new one installed. The home was then moved back and the interior damage repaired. The total cost amounted to some $36,000. The cost to the homeowner: $250.

HOW is not the only warranty program for new homes, but it is by far the biggest, available to consumers in every state but Alaska. As a combination warranty and insurance program, this is the way it works:

A warranty covers the first two years. In the first year, the builder warrants the home to be free from defects in workmanship and materials in compliance with the program's standards. This is the time, under the "free from defects" provision, for the homeowner to catch those persistent problems of sticking windows or blistering paint or incomplete landscaping. During the second year the builder continues to warrant against major structural defects and against malfunctioning of the wiring, piping, and ductwork in the electrical, plumbing, heating, and cooling systems.

In these first two years, the builder is required to come back and repair the covered defects. If, however, the builder fails to perform—if he's gone out of business or is simply uncooperative—the warranty is backed by the HOW Corporation above a $250 deductible paid by the homeowner and HOW makes the repairs.

In the third through tenth years, the home is directly insured against major structural defects with a deductible of $250. If your foundation shows signs of cracking, HOW insurance should take care of repairs.

Other things you should know:

- HOW coverage is available through builders; it is not available directly to consumers.

- The builder who enters the HOW program pays the fee for coverage. The fee may, of course, be passed on to the buyer in the price of the house.

- HOW coverage is transferable. If you buy a covered house within the warranty/insurance period, the coverage will transfer to you. If you sell, similarly, your buyer will pick up the protection.

- When a builder does not agree that any repairs are necessary, the homeowner may refer the disagreement, at no cost, to HOW's dispute settlement procedure. For more information call toll-free 1 (800) CALL HOW (in Pennsylvania, 1 (800) 222-3380), or write to HOW, 2000 L Street N.W., Washington, DC 20036.

- Builders must meet HOW standards in order to join the program. If a builder fails to perform he is expelled from the program, although he can continue in business. In New Jersey, with a tough state-mandated warranty program, builders who fail to perform may lose their registration and therefore their right to do business in the state.

- Some builders advertise their participation in HOW, but some do not; you'll have to ask. Be sure, in any case, to choose a builder very carefully, as outlined below. Building houses is an economically perilous way to make a living. Many builders, even with the best of intentions, fail to make a go of it. These are the builders who may cut corners in an effort to stay afloat. These are also the builders who may simply go under, leaving their buyers to fend for themselves.

Q. I've heard several terms applied to joint ownership of property. Can you explain the difference?

A. The biggest difference among the three forms of joint ownership is what lawyers call the "right of survivorship." When one joint owner dies, in other words, depending on the form of ownership, the other owner may or may not automatically own the property. There are three types of joint ownership:

Tenancy in common does not have the survivorship right, and is more often used by business partners than by spouses.

Joint tenancy has a right of survivorship, but either owner can sell his or her interest and force a division of the property.

Tenancy by the entirety, permitted only between spouses, has the right of survivorship and also requires joint action. Neither partner can sell his or her share, so that this form provides the most protection to both. Tenancy by the entirety, moreover, is the assumed form of ownership by husband and wife in some states, unless the ownership papers specifically spell out a different arrangement.

Picking a Builder

Choosing a builder isn't quite as important as choosing a good surgeon, says the National Association of Home Builders, but it's far too important a decision to trust to a walk through the Yellow Pages. You've heard the stories of endless construction delays, lost deposits, and badly built houses. You've seen the need for a Home Owners Warranty program. So don't trust to luck at all. Do your homework:

- Check out the builder's reputation. Talk to previous customers (ask for names of people in houses built earlier and knock on doors if the development you are considering is already partially occupied); find out what these homeowners think of the builder's skill and performance, especially post-sales performance.

- Ask the builder how he stands behind his work. If he offers a warranty, ask what it does and does not cover. Ask him what responsibility he assumes for subcontractors and others who work for him. Find out if he belongs to the Home Owners Warranty program or any other organized warranty/insurance program.

- Find out how long he has been in business and under what name. A family name is a better indication of permanence than a corporate name; be especially wary of a builder identified only through his current project . . . how will you find him once the project is completed? Find out where his main office is located, and don't do business with a builder who operates out of a truck. Ask your local Home Builders Association and/ or Better Business Bureau about his reliability and professional standing. Ask local suppliers about the builder's reputation. You might even ask your bank to run a financial check; it may cost you a few dollars but they will be dollars well spent.

Your Agreement with the Builder

Once you've satisfied yourself about the desirability of the house and the reliability of the builder and are ready to make a commitment, get everything in writing. Don't rely on spoken promises. The contract itself should spell out all the details:

- The total sales price and how it is to be paid
- The completion date for the house and the date title is to be transferred
- Any special features to be included in the house; any changes from stock plans
- Any builder-provided amenities, such as streets, sewers, or sidewalks, and when they are to be completed.

Then, when the house is finished and you're ready to move in, be sure you have the necessary documentation: a Certificate of Occupancy, warranties from all manufacturers for equipment in the house, approval of plumbing and sewer installations, and any applicable certificates of code compliance.

The Older House

Strictly speaking, an older house is any previously occupied house. A one-year-old custom-built house thus qualifies as an "old" house although it is technically more correct to call it a resale. The significant difference in buying an older home of any vintage: You buy from an individual. This means two things:

- The purchase price is negotiable. An individual seller, eager to sell and to move on, may come down several thousand dollars from the original asking price—especially if the house has been on the market for some time or if a death or a divorce has disrupted the family.
- You must secure financing on your own rather than rely on a builder package. This financing, these days, may be obtained with the help of the seller. Many of the so-called "creative financing" techniques, described in Chapter 13, are available almost entirely on resale homes.

THE ADVANTAGES OF AN OLDER HOUSE

The true older house, several years old and in an established neighborhood, has certain advantages. For one thing, the neighborhood *is* established. You're unlikely to be surprised by the need for new sewers or new schools; taxes are therefore more stable. The house itself is probably complete with lawn and trees, screens and storm windows. It may offer considerably more space for the money than a new house, and may (although not always) be better constructed. The house, if it is an older design, may also offer more interesting architecture, spacious rooms plus nooks and crannies, maybe even the charm of an old-fashioned front porch.

A *young resale* is considered by many to be a "best bet." Under five years old, these houses are contemporary and up-to-date. Yet such a house has been through its shakedown cruise and the quirks, if any, are out of its systems.

THE DISADVANTAGES OF AN OLDER HOUSE

You may find, on the other hand, that considerable work is needed to bring an old house up to your standards. The kitchen and bathrooms may be outmoded and in need of expensive modernization; they may also have been remodeled by someone without your taste. There may not be a bathroom on the main floor. Closet space may be inadequate. Basic systems, if the house is over twenty years old, may be in need of repair or renovation; even the best heating plant doesn't last forever. That interesting architecture may mask hollow walls, with no insulation to keep heating bills down.

The disadvantages of an older house will be most apparent in the *handyman's special*, the house that may strike you as having considerable charm at low cost, well worth the trouble and expense to fix it up.

Many homeowners, indeed, have reaped profits by improving run-down houses. But go into such a venture with your eyes wide open. Find out, before you buy, exactly what will need to be repaired or replaced and how soon. Hire an engineer or home inspection service to give you a written report. Then find out exactly what it will cost to make the essential changes; add that figure to the cost of the house to determine what you are actually paying for the house. And don't forget your own sweat. You may not be able to put a dollar value on it . . . or want to, when it's your dream house over which you're laboring. But stripping woodwork can lose its charm when weekend after weekend is spent doing little but stripping woodwork. At that point, you may feel driven to hire help. Will you have the funds to do so?

Appraisals and Inspections

If you're thinking of buying an older house, you may want to have it appraised, to be sure a fair price is being asked. You should have it inspected, by a qualified structural engineer or architect, to be sure there are no hidden defects. You may buy a house even if you know the electrical system has to be replaced, but you should be able to buy it at a lower price. In any case, if you're forewarned by an inspection, you won't be faced with a costly surprise later on. The inspection itself will cost approximately $150 to $300, well worth it considering the magnitude of the purchase.

Q. We're thinking of buying a charming mid-nineteenth-century house, but we're concerned about possible structural deterioration under the charm. How can we find a qualified home inspector to give us an objective report?

A. Look for an inspector who belongs to the American Society of Home Inspectors. These well-trained inspectors (they don't give appraisals, although they may provide an estimate of restoration costs) go over a house from top to bottom, evaluating heating, plumbing, and electrical systems as well as the condition of the roof, walls, ceilings, and foundation. They'll explain to you as they go along, and will give you a detailed written report. If you can't find an ASHI member near you, write to ASHI at 1629 K St., NW, Suite 520, Washington, DC 20006, and ask how to find a qualified inspector.

RESALE WARRANTIES

The HOW program, described earlier, applies only to newly built houses. There have been repeated efforts to start a similar program for resale houses, but this is a much more complicated endeavor. Two programs once sponsored by the National Association of Realtors have fallen by the wayside. Other programs, however, have been organized by real estate brokers. Most are local, but at least one, sponsored by ERA Real Estate, is offered through ERA-affiliated brokers in every state. ERA's Buyer Protection Plan provides a one-year warranty on plumbing and electrical systems, heating and cooling systems, water heaters and water softeners, and built-in appliances. The cost to the homebuyer averages around $300 and there is usually a $100 deductible.

Your best bet with a resale house, with or without a warranty, is to hire an independent inspector and have the house given a thorough inspection.

The Agreement to Buy

When you have found the house of your dreams and agreed on a purchase price, you will make a deposit and sign a purchase agreement (called by various names: a binder, bid, contract, or offer to buy). That agreement is a legally binding document that will govern your title to the house; be sure it itemizes every condition of the sale:

- The purchase price and how it is to be paid
- The date title is to be transferred, and any contingencies that may delay that transfer (you may want to be sure you have sold your current home,

the seller may want to be sure his new house is ready, but don't leave the date of transfer open-ended)

- What is to be included in the purchase price, with a specific list of fixtures and furnishings the seller has agreed to leave for the buyer as part of the sale (appliances, curtain rods, lawn furniture, and so on)

- Responsibility for fire and other possible damage until the date of the closing

- A provision that your deposit will be held in escrow until you take title to the house

- The condition that the purchase is subject to your obtaining a mortgage commitment within a specified period of time.

Q. I signed a purchase agreement to buy one house, then found another house I like better. The owner of the first house does not want to return my deposit and, in fact, is insisting that I have to go through with the purchase. Do I have to?

A. You might. Buyers and sellers alike often look at the binder or purchase agreement as simply a temporary agreement pending the formal contract of sale. But, and it's a very big but, courts in some states have held that a binder is in itself a legal contract. One buyer unwittingly agreed to an all-cash deal because only the purchase price, and no mention of financing, appeared in the binder. Another signed a binder that committed him to paying the seller's share of closing costs. And a New York seller who changed his mind about moving was forced by the courts to complete the transaction initiated by the binder, to sell the house, and to move. Talk to your lawyer about the agreement you signed; you may find a way out. And next time, make up your mind before you sign any document that can be legally enforced.

Real Estate Brokers

It is possible to buy or sell a house on your own. Most people, however, find it helpful to use a broker.

When You Are the Buyer

A broker knows the community, and the houses, in the area you prefer. He or she can give you information about taxes, schools, zoning, etc. (But confirm these facts elsewhere. Brokers have been known to refer to the "one train a day" on nearby tracks; homebuyers later learned, after they moved in, that the trains were considerably more frequent.) He or

A. No. But the commission you paid, along with money spent on permanent improvements in the house over the years you owned it, reduces your profit on the sale. Be sure to keep receipts documenting such expenditures.

If you're a seller, clearly, you'll save money by dealing with a discount broker. You may also negotiate fees with any broker; as home prices escalate, inflating commissions, sales are harder to make and brokers are more willing to be accommodating. At the same time, in a tight real estate market, brokers are working very hard to make sales, and many feel that they fully deserve the commissions they charge. But find out, before you sign any listing agreement, just what services the broker provides for the fee.

HOW TO LIST YOUR HOUSE FOR SALE

You can list your house in several ways:

- You can give the broker an *exclusive agency listing,* usually for a period of three to six months. This gives the broker considerable incentive to sell the property. Be careful, though, that you don't give an exclusive right to sell; under this arrangement, you could owe the broker a commission even if you sell the house with no assistance at all from the broker.

- With an *open listing,* the house may be listed with several brokers at one time; only the selling agent gets a commission, so that brokers tend to devote the same effort to such listings.

- *Multiple listing services,* under which brokers pool house listings, provide wide exposure to potential buyers. The commission is shared between the office obtaining the listing and the office arranging the sale. (But multiple listing services have been criticized, in a number of areas, for excluding discount brokers.)

You can also sell a house yourself. But you have to be prepared for unfamiliar and time-consuming chores. You have to be available at all times, to all comers. And you have to take the chance that the effort will cost you money rather than save you money, unless you are a good negotiator and a skillful salesperson.

When You Take Title

You've found your house, negotiated its price, obtained a mortgage (Chapter 13), and now you're ready to take title. You'd also best be ready to spend some more money.

Settlement Costs

Settlement costs, or closing costs, include all those miscellaneous items that go with taking title to property. They vary from region to region, and from lender to lender, but often include:

- A title search, to be sure the seller has the right to sell
- Title insurance, to protect the mortage lender (you may want to buy a separate policy to protect your own interests; see below for details)
- Attorney's fees (you may have to pay for the lending institution's attorneys as well as your own)
- A survey, to determine the precise location of the house and the property
- An appraisal, to satisfy the lender about the value of the property
- Preparation of documents, by the lender or by the lawyers
- Closing fees, for handling the transaction
- A credit report, on you, for the lender
- Points or an origination fee (a one-time charge, sometimes called a loan discount, to increase the mortgage yield for the lender; each point equals 1 percent of the mortgage amount)

You may also be required by the lender to have a termite inspection, to pay for recording the documents, to pay for keeping funds in escrow pending adjustment of taxes, and so on and on.

It can add up to a not-so-pretty penny, with fees totaling 1 percent to almost 7 percent of the purchase price of a house. The exact amount depends on where you live. It also depends on whether you shop around, and whether you negotiate. The seller might be willing to pay for the termite inspection, or to share the cost of transfer taxes. As an example, however, the purchaser of a $95,000 house in Illinois in 1984 paid out $4,644 in closing costs; the seller paid $1,048 over and above the real estate broker's commission.

KEEPING CLOSING COSTS DOWN

Some closing costs are required by law; some are pretty much fixed in price. But some can be greatly reduced, maybe even eliminated, by careful shopping and by thinking ahead. You may be able to skip a new survey, for instance, if you can get the seller to give you the existing survey plus an affidavit that no changes have been made to any structures that would overlap the boundaries. A title insurance company may give you a lower rate if it recently wrote a policy on the same property or if it writes your policy at the same time it writes the policy for the lending institution. Insist on choosing your own lawyer, title company, and surveyor—don't leave this choice to the broker—and discuss their fees before you make a final selection.

The lender must inform you of the anticipated closing costs, in writing, three days after receiving your mortgage application. You'll receive a final statement at the closing itself, and may review it the day before. You'll have to have the money in hand on the day of the closing. (In most parts of the country, you'll meet face to face with the seller on closing day; in some places, however, the transaction is handled by a third party called an escrow agent.)

You'll also have to adjust various costs with the seller when you take title: for the oil in the tank that he paid for and you'll use, for the taxes he's paid on the house you'll now occupy, and so on. And you'll have to pay a mortgage insurance premium, if mortgage insurance is required by the lender, and a premium for hazard or homeowners insurance as well. You may be able to include all of the payments in a single substantial check, or you may write check after check. Either way, you'll need enough money in your checking account to cover the closing costs in full.

Note: Some mortgage lenders won't give a mortgage commitment until they're assured that you can cover these closing costs.

SETTLEMENT COSTS IN TERMS OF YOUR MORTGAGE

Settlements costs, although they are paid just once, can be considered in terms of the interest rate on your mortgage loan. A rule of thumb developed by the Department of Housing and Urban Development holds that one-time settlement charges equaling 1 percent of the loan amount increase the interest charge on that loan by 0.125 percent.

For example: On a loan of $50,000, one lender (A) charges two points (at 1 percent each), a $250 application fee, and $500 for legal fees, for a total of $1,750 or 4.5 percent of the loan amount. Since each 1 percent of the loan amount in settlement charges is the equivalent of 0.125 percent in interest, the effective interest rate from Lender A is the quoted rate plus 0.56 percent (4.5 times 0.125 equals 0.5625). A quoted mortgage interest rate of 10 percent would thus become 10.56 percent. If Lender B charges three points on the same interest rate, but no application or legal fees, you would be better off taking the mortgage from Lender B.

Bear in mind, however, that these calculations assume a pay-back period of about fifteen years. If you'll live in the house just five years before you move, paying off the loan at that time, the increase in interest rate will equal 0.25 percent instead of 0.125. Try to figure out how long you'll stay in a given house before you make settlement cost and mortgage comparisons.

Note: Advertisements for new-home developments sometimes say "no closing costs, just prepaid items." This means that the developer is absorbing the costs . . . but they are probably passed on to you anyway in the cost of the property. You'll be better off, if you can afford to part with the cash, to have the builder separate these items so that you pay them when you close the sale. Otherwise you'll pay interest on these costs, as part of the loan balance, for the life of the mortgage. Developers often do, however, put together a package deal and thereby keep closing costs down.

Title Insurance

You may look at title insurance as just one of the many nuisance items for which you write a check on the day you take title to your house. But title insurance deserves a somewhat closer look, because it can, under certain circumstances, protect your investment in your property.

A title search should clear up most questions about clear title to the property, and some consumer advocates claim that a title search is all that's necessary. But there can be problems despite the most careful search: An anxious seller may conceal unpaid debts to contractors; those contractors may be able to place a lien on the property. The existence of an estranged wife may similarly be "forgotten"; under the law in some states, she would continue to have certain rights in the property. A not-quite-valid will two generations back could cast doubt on the legal transfer of title. Mistakes may simply be made. In a Long Island, New York, situation that recently came to light, a parcel of land that had actually been deeded to an heir of the seller was also mistakenly included in acreage sold to a developer. Five families who had purchased houses in the developer's subdivision were ordered by a court to return the land, including the improvements (their houses), to the rightful owner.

These things don't happen often, given the vast number of real estate transactions that take place in the country, but they do happen. That's why your mortgage lender takes a title policy (for which you pay) protecting his investment in the property. That's also why you may want to consider a title insurance policy of your own. Your lender's policy does not protect you. It doesn't even cover the full value of the property, just the amount of the mortgage loan. You should consider a policy that will protect your title—it's inexpensive, as a rule, if taken at the same time as the lender's—and you may want to consider a new form of title insurance with built-in inflation protection.

INFLATION ADJUSTMENT OF TITLE INSURANCE

The face amount of an owner's title insurance policy traditionally covers the original purchase price of the home. In recent years, however, home values have risen extremely rapidly. If a title defect is discovered just two years after purchase the owner could suffer a sizable loss.

Inflation adjustment in title policies is now available nationwide; if you're buying a house, check and be sure that it's included in your policy. If you've already been in your home for several years, however, forget it. Most claims take place within five to six years, according to the American Land Title Association, and it's very rare indeed to have a claim after ten years of occupancy. In any case, if you were to request an upgrading of the policy, you might have to pay for another title search.

The five Long Island families ordered to return their land had court costs paid by the developer's title insurance company. But that land included their homes and they still faced substantial loss. Four of the five families had their own title insurance policies, but the amounts were no longer adequate. The fifth did not have an owner's policy. In the end, after considerable anxiety, the legal owner agreed to a settlement and the settlement was paid by the title company.

Other Costs

The 28-year-old with the $92,000 house described at the beginning of this chapter faced monthly payments for mortgage and taxes of just over $1,000. His total out-of-pocket housing costs, however, month after month, come to over $1,500. He had to include—and you might too—the costs of utilities, garbage removal, homeowners insurance, and mortgage insurance. He also had monthly dues (required, not optional) for a community recreational facility.

Be sure that you include every possible expenditure as you look at housing. Use the Personal Housing Cost Worksheet (p. 242) to determine how much money you can comfortably spend. Be honest with yourself about outgo on housing, and about your own income. Do not commit uncertain income, such as overtime or bonuses.

In addition to ongoing costs, there are also up-front costs that you should be sure to consider. These include moving, decorating, and an emergency fund.

Moving Costs

Although the trucking industry has been deregulated and moving companies can now compete for business, moving may still cost more than you expect. About one in four moves, according to a 1980 report by the Interstate Commerce Commission, is underestimated by at least 10 percent of the eventual cost. Be sure that you shop around. Some movers will now offer binding estimates, some give discounts, some will guarantee pickup and delivery within a specified number of days.

PERSONAL HOUSING COST WORKSHEET

STEP 1. CALCULATE MONTHLY INCOME.

Income from employment after deductions	+ $_____
Interest and dividends	+ $_____
Other income (second job, business, etc.)	+ $_____
Total income	= $_____

STEP 2. CALCULATE MONTHLY NONHOUSING EXPENSES.

Food, beverages (home and work)	+ $_____
Entertainment and recreation	+ $_____
Clothing and grooming	+ $_____
Transportation and automobile expenses (auto loan, insurance, gas, oil, etc.)	+ $_____
Medical care	+ $_____
Child care	+ $_____
Education	+ $_____
Gifts	+ $_____
Insurance (life and health)	+ $_____
Installment loans (charge accounts, credit cards)	+ $_____
Savings	+ $_____
Other	+ $_____
Total monthly nonhousing expenses (add)	= $_____
Subtract nonhousing expenses from total of Step 1.	= $_____

STEP 3. ESTIMATE MONTHLY EXPENSES.

Proposed mortgage payment or rent	+ $_____
Allowance for property taxes	+ $_____
Allowance for utilities (heat, water, phone, electricity)	+ $_____
Allowance for maintenance and repairs (including garbage removal, gardening and lawn service, etc.)	+ $_____
Allowance for insurance	+ $_____
Other (association dues? street/sidewalk assessments?)	+ $_____
Total monthly housing expenses (add)	= $_____

STEP 4. Compare estimated monthly housing expenses (Step 3) with income available for housing (Step 2). If income available from Step 2 does not equal or exceed monthly housing expenses, then you must reevaluate your budget and resources.

WAYS TO SAVE ON A MOVE

- Do it yourself, if you have the time and the energy.
- Get at least three estimates if you decide to use a professional mover.

- Pack as much as you can yourself (although it's not a bad idea to let the movers pack fragile items and take the responsibility for them).

- Be there when the moving truck is weighed, both before and after your belongings are loaded. On the first weighing, be sure the fuel tanks are full and that heavy equipment such as dollies and chains are in place. At the second weighing, see that no husky movers jump aboard at the last moment.

- Arrange for adequate insurance. Many moving companies offer three choices: "Limited liability" insurance costs you nothing, but you will be reimbursed for damage at a flat fee per pound, regardless of value. "Added value protection," at a small premium, reimburses actual value less depreciation. A new "full value" plan, which costs varying amounts depending on the deductible you accept, pays the full cost of repair or replacement without depreciation.

- Don't sign a receipt for delivery until after you check the inventory and make sure that everything has been delivered in good condition.

Q. My washing machine hasn't worked properly since I moved, and now it's failed altogether. I'm sure it was damaged in the move, but the mover denies responsibility. Is there anything I can do to collect the cost of repairs?

A. Under a program of the American Movers Conference, the industry trade group, you and the mover can agree to submit your dispute to binding arbitration. As long as you submitted your initial claim to the mover within nine months after delivery, you can request arbitration by writing to the American Movers Conference, Dispute Settlement Program, 2200 Mill Rd., Alexandria, VA 22314. The move must have been made interstate, the mover must participate in the program, and you must write within sixty days of the company's denial of your claim. Include your name, address and phone number, the identification number of the shipment, dates and location of pickup and delivery, and any assigned claim number. You'll hear from the mover within fifteen days. Most cases are decided on the basis of written documents submitted by both parties; sometimes an oral hearing is arranged.

Decorating Costs

You'll have to make your new home livable, so, unless you already own a complete houseful of items that will fit in your new surroundings, be sure to calculate the cost of furniture, appliances, carpeting, wallpaper, etc. You may be able to postpone some purchases (many a family has lived in the family room, with an empty living room, for months or years), but you may need to make others right away. Figure out these costs as realistically as possible, before you commit your funds.

An Emergency Fund

Don't allocate every penny in advance. As you should realize by now, homeowning is an expensive proposition. An emergency fund, to pay for everything you didn't expect, should be part of your financial plan. No matter how carefully you estimate, there will be unanticipated expenditures. Be sure you have a cushion of at least several hundred dollars, more if you can manage it, to soften the impact.

KEY POINTS

- New houses, in general, cost more than resales but may be easier to finance. Older homes cost less, as a rule, but may cost more to put into livable shape.
- Your purchase contract, for new house or old, should spell out all the details; don't leave anything to unwritten agreement.
- Real estate brokers can be very helpful, but remember, if you are the buyer, that the broker (unless you use a special "buyer's broker") represents the seller.
- Evaluate how much you can spend on housing in terms of your entire budget, and remember to allow enough money for settlement costs, for moving and decorating, and for an emergency fund.

Financing
a House Today

There have been drastic changes in housing finance in the last few years, and homebuyers have ridden a roller coaster of high interest rates and high home prices. When mortgage interest rates peaked at 18 percent in 1982, fewer than 5 percent of all American households could afford to buy a median-priced house.

By spring 1986 inflation was down and interest rates had dropped significantly. As a result, for the first time in several years, a family with the median income ($27,940) could afford to buy the median-priced house ($75,500). Nonetheless, there's an apparent contradiction: At the same time that housing has become more affordable (prices in some parts of the country aren't rising at all), many first-time buyers are still either priced out of the market or relying on two incomes in order to buy a home. More than two-thirds of all first-time buyers, according to a 1985 study by the U.S. League of Savings Institutions, needed a second income to qualify for their mortgage loan.

If you're shopping for a second house (and can manage to sell the first), you are, relatively speaking, on easy street: You can put the appreciated value of your first house toward your second. Repeat buyers, as a result, can and usually do buy more expensive homes. But what if you've not yet bought your first house? Can you afford to do so? And is now the time to try?

Economists speak of affordability on a national scale. But you have to look at your own personal situation, at your income (both current and potential), and at your life-style. What do you have in current savings to apply toward a home purchase? How much of your current monthly income can you spend on housing? Is your income likely to grow? Or

FIGURE 1: The cost of the house that a $500 monthly mortgage payment will buy, assuming a down payment of 20 percent, at various rates of interest.

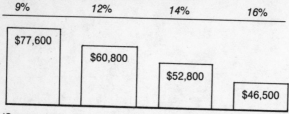

(Source: National Association of Home Builders)

have you reached a life stage where income expectations have pretty much leveled off?

As you answer these questions, also look at what homeownership can do for you. With the tax benefits that Uncle Sam provides for home-owners (see Chapter 15), you can effectively reduce your taxable income. At the same time you are building equity in a tangible asset.

But should you think about buying a house right now? Won't interest rates come down still further, making a purchase easier? Interest rates may indeed come down, although no forecaster has a clear crystal ball, but it can be argued that it won't help if you wait until they do. The reason: While you wait, house prices may very well continue to rise, requiring larger down payments, larger mortgage loans, and, even at lower interest rates, larger monthly payments.

A lot depends on your expectation of interest trends (and your willingness to gamble), but you may, if you postpone a purchase till rates fall still further, find yourself in the position of racing after a bus you've missed. When mortgage interest rates fall and more money becomes available, more people will be ready to buy; increased demand, in turn, will inflate housing prices once again.

Whether interest rates rise or fall, however, the legacy of the last few years has been a dramatic shift from fixed-rate mortgages to adjustable-rate mortgages. With these new mortgages (see later in this chapter for details), you won't gain by waiting; your mortgage will, over time, reflect whatever current interest rates exist. Unless you have to wait because you can't afford to get a toe in the door at all, think about buying now. Think about buying in terms of your two major financial commitments: the down payment and the mortgage loan.

The Down Payment

A down payment may be 20 percent or more of the purchase price. It may be 10 percent. And it may, under certain programs (such as VA and

FHA guaranteed mortgages and mortgages secured by private mortgage insurance), be 5 percent or less. Which is right for you?

Small Down Payment or Large?

The lower down payment has significant advantages. Its biggest advantage, clearly, is that it may make it possible for you to buy a house. With a 20 percent down payment on a $70,000 house, you would need $14,000 in cash right up front; with 10 percent down, you'd have to come up with just $7,000. Beyond this simple arithmetic, however, a lower down payment may make sense if you would otherwise borrow at still-higher installment loan rates to buy, as an example, new furniture for your new home. You would also come out ahead if you were able to invest the difference between a high and low down payment in a high-yielding investment.

You may also find that a lower down payment actually increases your rate of return on the house as an investment. That's because the increase in value of the house is calculated in terms of money you've actually invested in the house. This is what real estate investors call leverage: using small amounts of money to make large amounts. It works like this: If you buy a $60,000 house with a $6,000 down payment, and later sell the house for $84,000, your profit, $24,000, is four times your cash investment. If you've bought the same house with a 20 percent down payment of $12,000, your profit on the sale is only twice your actual investment. (This is a simple example. In fact, the higher monthly payments on a low-down-payment loan would reduce the profit.)

The majority of home buyers in the last few years have purchased houses with down payments of under 20 percent. If you want to do so, however, you may find it difficult. In the wake of rising numbers of mortgage defaults, as people in financial difficulty walk away from homes in which they have little invested, mortgage lenders and insurers are pulling back, tightening the rules and making fewer loans with 5 percent down payments.

A lower down payment, in any case, has disadvantages as well as advantages. Chief among them: You will pay a lot more each month to carry a larger mortgage loan; be sure you can manage these higher payments before you elect the lower down payment. Remember that the larger payments will go on month after month until the mortgage loan is paid up or until you sell the house; the difference over a period of years may be many thousands of dollars. Many mortgage lenders, moreover, charge a slightly higher interest rate for low-down-payment loans, thereby increasing your monthly costs still further.

Q. My husband and I have found a house we like for $75,000. We can manage the monthly mortgage payments, but we haven't saved enough to make the required down payment of 20 percent, or $15,000. Have you any suggestions?

A. There are three possibilities: (1) VA-backed loans, which require no down payment at all, are available for eligible veterans. (2) FHA-backed loans typically require a down payment of 5 percent. (3) Private mortgage insurance, if you can secure it through your mortgage lender, may enable you to reduce your down payment to 5 or 10 percent. Private mortgage insurance, at a fee, is available in every state; most lenders have master policies with one or more companies. If neither your lender nor your real estate agent can help you, however, write to the Mortgage Insurance Companies of America (MICA) for names of lenders in your area who offer private mortgage insurance; the address is 1725 K St., NW, Washington, DC 20006.

Note: Don't confuse private mortgage insurance with mortgage life insurance, which pays up your mortgage if you die. Private mortgage insurance protects the mortgage lender if for any reason you default on your mortgage payments.

Sources of Funds for a Down Payment

If you have enough cash on hand to choose between a low down payment and a higher one, be sure you consider all the factors (including the other costs involved in a home purchase; see Chapter 12) before you make your decision. If you have to scrape the money together for any sort of down payment, however, look at all the available sources of funds (but bear in mind that lenders are increasingly wary when borrowed money is the source of down payments):

YOUR OWN SAVINGS

Money you've saved and invested is still your primary source of funds for the purchase of a house. If you are looking forward to your first house (this is where life cycle planning proves its worth), you should be putting aside all surplus funds, in the highest-yielding investment possible, toward that down payment. Even with inflation eroding the value of savings, compound interest works: If you can save just $2,000 a year toward your house, by brown-bagging your lunch and seeing fewer movies if that's what it takes, you would have a $6,500 down payment in just three and a half years. That's if you put your money in the mattress and it earns no interest. If the money is invested at money market rates, you could have your $6,500 a lot sooner.

LIFE INSURANCE LOANS

If you've been paying premiums on a whole life insurance policy, that policy has been amassing cash value. That cash value is yours. You may borrow it, under the terms of most older contracts, at an interest rate of 5 to 8 percent; the precise rate is spelled out in your insurance contract. (The insurance industry is raising interest rates on policy loans, so new policies may no longer be an inexpensive source of money, but if you have an older policy, the rate can't be changed.) Chapter 21 has the details on life insurance and life insurance loans. All you need to know here is that (1) an older life insurance policy is an excellent source of low-cost funds, and (2) a life insurance loan does not have to be repaid.

RELATIVES

First-time buyers often find it necessary, especially in today's housing market, to turn to parents for help with a down payment. The trend has become so widespread that some economists have referred to it as the new G.I. Bill: Generous In-laws.

But generosity sometimes has strings attached. If you do need parental help:

■ Try to keep the arrangement businesslike. Borrow the money, and sign a note agreeing to the terms. Your parents may decide to forgo repayment when the time comes, but then again they may need the money and find it awkward to ask for it. This breeds resentment and ill-feelings. Put your agreement on paper.

■ Take them with you, if you can, while you look for a house. Otherwise they may be shocked and disapproving at the amount of house you are able to buy for the amount of money you are spending. They may be reading the newspapers about today's housing crunch, but it won't hit home until they compare your first house with their own. Cushion the blow by taking them along so that they see what is actually available and what it costs.

■ Think about a formal "partnership mortgage," with relatives or with outside investors, to ease the financial burden of the down payment and/or the mortgage itself; see pp.264–65.

The Mortgage Loan

There was a time, not very long ago, when an individual in search of a mortgage loan would go to a financial institution (usually a savings and loan association or mutual savings bank, traditional mortgage lenders) and secure a commitment. It was a good idea to compare interest rates and provisions at different institutions, but the basic terms didn't differ very much. Today this is no longer the case. The mortgage picture in the 1980s is so new, in fact, that it has no precedent in American homebuying history.

In the face of enormous pressure generated by the higher-than-ever interest rates being paid out to depositors, the nation's financial institutions have been forced to develop new mortgage forms to generate higher rates of return on their investments. Most of these new mortgage forms shift the risk of fluctuating interest rates to the buyer, making it all the more important to compare mortgage provisions. It's also important to investigate all the possible sources of mortgage money.

Sources of Mortgage Loans

Bear in mind, as you start your search for financing, that not every type of mortgage is available from every lender. Federally chartered institutions operate under one set of rules, state-chartered institutions under another. Then there are private mortgage lenders. Some want to make mortgage loans; others, when the cost of money is high, do not. You'll have to do considerable shopping around (1) to get a mortgage commitment at all, when high interest rates restrict the flow of funds, and (2) to get the best possible terms. Look into these sources of funds:

- Savings and loan associations, savings banks, and (in the seventeen states where they exist) mutual savings banks, traditionally the consumer's source of mortgage financing

- Credit unions, beginning to make mortgage loans in increasing numbers

- Commercial banks, moving more intensively into mortgage lending

- Mortgage bankers, often a little more expensive, but likely to have mortgage money available when others do not

- The seller of the house you want to buy (seller financing, at times when other mortgage money is unavailable or overpriced, is a popular option; see pp.267–71).

Q. I earn $23,000 a year and my husband earns $29,000. We made a bid on a $73,000 house and were turned down for a mortgage on the basis of "insufficient income." I suspect the bank just didn't want to count my income. Is there anything I can do?

A. If you are right, you may have a complaint under the Equal Credit Opportunity Act, a federal law which prohibits discrimination against an applicant for credit on the basis of sex, marital status, race, color, religion, national origin, or age. You should know that:

- You can't be refused credit just because you're a woman . . . or single, or married, separated, divorced, or widowed.

- You can't be refused credit because a creditor won't count income you receive regularly from alimony or child support.

- You can't be discouraged from applying for a mortgage loan.

- You can't be offered a loan on terms different from those offered to other people. You can't be asked for a 20 percent down payment, for instance, when others are offered mortgages with a 10 percent down payment.

- Your income, if you are a married woman, must be counted in full, even if you work part-time (but you should be prepared to show that your income is reliable). The lender, moreover, may not ask you about birth-control methods and/or childbearing plans.

ECOA requires the lender to notify you about the status of your loan within thirty days after your application is complete. It also requires you to be given a specific reason if your loan is denied. If you are not satisfied with the reason, you should have an opportunity to challenge the lender and make your case again. And, if you are convinced you are the victim of discrimination, you may file a complaint with the Federal Home Loan Bank Board (for savings and loan associations) or the Comptroller of the Currency (for national banks) or the Federal Reserve Bank in your district (for a state-chartered bank).

Mortgage Calculations

If you find mortgage payments confusing, you're not alone. But the arithmetic is simpler than it may seem. Each monthly mortgage payment consists of two parts: (1) the interest, which is what you pay the lender to borrow the money, and (2) the principal, which is the portion of the loan itself you are paying back. With your principal payment, you are increasing the portion of the house you own and decreasing the portion the lender owns. But it is the interest payment that is the key to understanding how most mortgages work.

The interest portion of your monthly payment is the monthly interest rate on your loan times the outstanding balance of the loan. The monthly interest rate is simply the annual interest rate divided by 12. If your mortgage rate is 12 percent, your monthly rate is 1 percent.

As an example, supplied by the National Association of Home Builders, suppose you have a $50,000, 30-year fixed-rate loan at 12 percent. Your monthly payment would be $514.31. This payment remains the same for 30 years, but the portions you pay toward principal and interest change each month. In the first month, you owe the lender an interest payment of 1 percent of $50,000, or $500. The remaining $14.31 goes toward reducing your loan balance, making it $49,985.69. For your second payment, you owe the lender 1 percent of $49,985.69, or $499.86. The remainder of your $514.31 fixed payment, which is $14.45, is used to reduce your loan balance to $49,971.24.

The same thing happens throughout the life of the mortgage loan

TABLE 1: Monthly principal and interest payments for a 30-year fixed-rate mortgage at different interest rates and loan amounts.

Interest rate	Loan amount					
	$50,000	$60,000	$70,000	$80,000	$90,000	$100,000
9%	$402	$483	$563	$ 644	$ 724	$ 805
10%	$439	$527	$614	$ 702	$ 790	$ 878
11%	$476	$571	$667	$ 762	$ 857	$ 952
12%	$514	$617	$720	$ 823	$ 926	$1029
13%	$553	$664	$774	$ 885	$ 996	$1106
14%	$592	$711	$829	$ 948	$1066	$1185
15%	$632	$759	$885	$1012	$1138	$1264
16%	$672	$807	$941	$1076	$1210	$1345

(Source National Association of Home Builders)

(whether you have a fixed-rate or an adjustable-rate mortgage) until the final payment, consisting almost entirely of a contribution to principal, is enough to pay off the loan. Because the initial payments go almost entirely toward interest, most of your mortgage costs at the outset are tax-deductible. Later, as the loan matures, you have less tax deduction but more equity in the house.

Fixed Rate Mortgages

Fixed-term, fixed-rate mortgages are the traditional mortgage loans, the loans that made housing available for generations of Americans and that have made housing such a rich investment. With a fixed term (often thirty years, although fifteen-year terms are increasingly popular) and a fixed interest rate (established when the contract is written, and remaining stable for the length of the mortgage), these mortgages provide budgetary stability for homeowners. They also act as a cushion against soaring inflation and soaring interest rates. When interest rates were high, this type of loan became increasingly difficult to secure, for one very simple reason: As lending institutions had to pay ever higher interest rates to entice depositors (thereby making money available for mortgages), they became ever more reluctant to commit investment dollars to investments with a rate of return locked in place for many years. (Commitments to old single-digit mortgages, in fact, were largely responsible for the plight of many savings institutions in the double-digit 1980s and, some forecasters fear, may cause similar problems if the interest rate drop of the late 1980s is temporary.)

Fixed-Rate Terms

Fixed-rate mortgages are making a comeback as interest rates stabilize (accounting for one-third of all mortgages issued in 1985), and you should know how they work as a point of comparison in your mortgage shopping.

When you take a fixed-rate mortgage you agree to pay the same amount toward the mortgage principal and interest each month; if interest rates go up after you take the mortgage, you're ahead of the game. The lender agrees that the rate of interest and hence the monthly payments will remain the same over the life of the loan; if rates subsequently fall, the lender benefits. It's a gamble. But the biggest single benefit that the fixed-rate mortgage loan offers to the homebuyer is its predictability. With this mortgage, you can budget your biggest housing expense and know exactly where you stand.

FIFTEEN-YEAR MORTGAGES

If you want to dramatically reduce the amount of interest you pay over the life of your mortgage loan, while building your equity much faster, you may want to consider one of the increasingly popular 15-year mortgages. Monthly payments are higher, but more of each payment goes toward reducing the principal. In the example we used earlier, of a $50,000 mortgage at 12 percent, the monthly payment would be $600.08 (instead of $514.31, on a 30-year loan); the initial interest payment would still be $500, but the initial payment to principal would be $100.08. As the principal is paid down, subsequent interest payments are smaller and smaller. With a mortgage rate of 12 percent, a borrower with a 15-year loan will accumulate seven times more equity in five years just by loan repayment than will a neighbor with a 30-year loan. With interest rates at 10 percent, the equity build-up is still five and a half times greater with a 15-year mortgage.

But don't leap into a 15-year mortgage. Interest savings may be advertised as being many thousands of dollars over the life of the loan. And they are. But those interest savings have to be measured against two other factors: (1) your tax bracket, because the higher your bracket the more you have to gain from making larger interest payments and the less you have to gain from reducing those payments, and (2) the amount of investment income you'll forgo by putting money into your mortgage instead of into another investment.

The 15-year mortgage may still be right for you, if (1) you can meet the higher monthly payments (for some people, this may mean buying a less expensive home), (2) you won't invest elsewhere and your mortgage is a form of forced savings, or (3) you want to pay off your mortgage before retirement or before, for example, a child starts college.

If you are intrigued by the idea of a short-term mortgage, but already have a mortgage, take heart. Unless your mortgage contract contains prepayment penalties (check with your lender to be sure), you can accomplish much the same thing by making extra payments toward principal. The advantage, in fact, is that you can put in varying amounts at varying intervals, as your pocketbook permits.

FHA AND VA MORTGAGES

Government-backed FHA and VA mortgages are fixed-rate mortgages that should also be considered when you are mortgage shopping. Both are essentially like conventional mortgages, with these exceptions:

- There is a ceiling on the amount of an FHA mortgage loan (in 1985 it was $90,000 on a one-family house), which makes these loans particularly appropriate for people buying a starter house.
- Lower down payments (in some instances, on VA mortgages, no down payment) are required.
- Interest rates are often lower than prevailing rates, but points may be added by the lender to raise the actual rate.
- There is no prepayment penalty, so if mortgage rates drop, you can refinance the mortgage at a lower rate (although you may have to pay additional closing costs if you refinance).

One drawback to FHA and VA mortgages is the extensive paperwork they require, which makes lenders reluctant to issue them, the mortgages themselves slow to obtain, and sellers often unwilling to wait.

Figure 2 shows monthly mortgage payments at various interest rates under a fixed-payment loan. When interest rates are high, as shown, you may not be able to afford much house for your money—especially since you must also manage monthly outlays for taxes, insurance, heat, utilities, and maintenance. When house prices are also high, you may be squeezed out of the market altogether . . . unless you look into one of the new mortgage forms.

Q. We were eager to buy a house, and we thought interest rates would keep going up, so we took a mortgage loan at 16 percent. Then rates fell. Are we stuck with our high-priced mortgage, or can we somehow take advantage of the new lower interest rates?

A. You can, and you probably should, refinance if the mortgage interest rate differential is at least 3 percentage points. Ask your current lender, first, if it will renegotiate your loan and, if it will, whether it will reduce or eliminate closing costs and prepayment penalties.

Do some careful arithmetic. Monthly payments on a fixed-rate

FIGURE 2: Monthly mortgage payments.

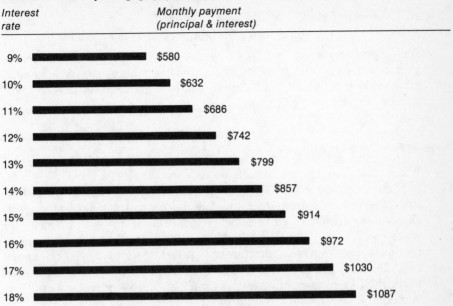

Interest rate	Monthly payment (principal & interest)
9%	$580
10%	$632
11%	$686
12%	$742
13%	$799
14%	$857
15%	$914
16%	$972
17%	$1030
18%	$1087

Monthly payments on a $72,000 30-year mortgage at 15 percent are $914, requiring an annual income of $43,226. The same mortgage at 11 percent costs $686 a month, a $228 decrease, requiring an annual income of $33,458. At 9 percent interest, monthly payments are reduced even further—to $580, more than 36 percent less than the same mortgage at 15 percent. To qualify for the loan at 9 percent, an income of $28,917 is sufficient—that's $14,309 a year less than for the same loan at 15 percent interest. (Source: NAHB Economics Division)

$72,000 mortgage are $972 at 16 percent and $686 at 11 percent. Balance the difference of $286 a month against any fees and penalties. How long will you have to stay in the house to come out ahead?

**WHEN YOU COMPARISON-SHOP FOR
A MORTGAGE LOAN, FIND OUT:**

- What additional fees or charges must you pay? These may include charges for appraisal, credit report, photographs, various statements or papers, or an origination fee or service charge.
- Are you required to carry property, life, or disability insurance? If so, must you obtain it from a particular company? You might prefer not to carry such insurance, or to obtain it elsewhere.
- Is there a late-payment charge? How late may your payment be before the charge is imposed?

- If you wish to pay off the loan early, must you pay a prepayment penalty? Does this apply when you move and sell the house?

- Will the lender allow the loan to be assumed by someone else (see pp. 267–68)? At what interest rate? Will there be an assumption fee?

- Will you be required to pay into a special escrow account from which the lender will pay your property taxes and your homeowners insurance premiums? If so, how large a deposit will be required at the closing? Will interest be paid on the account?

Adjustable-Rate Mortgages

When interest rates are as volatile as they have been in recent years, reaching unprecedented highs in the early 1980s, lending institutions suffer enormously from being locked into long-term fixed-rate mortgage loans written when rates were low. During the high-interest-rate years of the late 1970s and early 1980s, fearing still-higher rates, many mortgage lenders were understandably reluctant to issue fixed-rate mortgage loans. Their answer: adjustable-rate mortgages (ARMs) which share the risk of fluctuating interest rates between lender and borrower. Although interest rates have subsided since the heady days of 1982, and increasing numbers of fixed-rate mortgages are currently being issued, adjustable-rate mortgages still made up two-thirds of all newly issued mortgages in 1985.

Adjustable-rate mortgages are generally offered at lower initial interest rates than fixed-rate mortgages, but that rate, by definition, is not guaranteed for the life of the mortgage. It can and will change, according to the adjustment period specified in your contract, as prevailing interest rates change. When rates do change, you may see the change reflected in the payment amount, the outstanding principal, and/or the term of the loan. As you compare mortgage loans, consider the following factors:

THE INDEX

The index will be the keystone of your mortgage interest rate, and it's very important to ask which index will be used, how often it will change, how it has behaved in the past, and where it is published. Possibilities (although almost any public index of interest rates may be used) include:

- The "national average mortgage rate," which is an average of rates on loans closed during a specified period

- The Federal Home Loan Bank Board's "cost-of-funds" rate

- The 3-month or 6-month Treasury bill rate

- The yield on Treasury securities maturing in one, three, or five years

Note: Do not accept an index pegged to the individual institution's cost of borrowing or a regional cost of borrowing.

Which index you choose can make a considerable difference. The Consumer Federation of America, in a study of what would have happened under existing interest rates if an adjustable mortgage had been issued in 1976, found that payments on a $60,000 mortgage starting at an initial rate of 9 percent would have risen by 1981 by a minimum of $117 a month (when tied to the FHLBB's cost-of-funds rate) to a maximum of $389 a month (when tied to the 3-month T-bill rate).

It's not necessarily true, of course, that one index will always lead to smaller increases and another to larger ones—although you should ask the lender to show you some recent examples of how each index has moved. It depends on both the volatility of the index and the state of the economy. Some indexes reflect short-term changes in interest rates; others reflect longer-term trends. Short-term indexes usually fluctuate more sharply than longer-term indexes, so mortgage payments may change dramatically. Longer-term interest rates and indexes tend to be more gradual in their movements, but also tend to be higher than the short-term indicators. There's a trade-off between the volatility of interest and payment levels and locking in payments for a longer period at possibly higher levels. You will have to make the choice.

THE ADJUSTMENT PERIOD

The interval at which rate adjustments will be made is also significant. In theory, under the ARM, payments could change every month. In practical terms most ARMs are written with an adjustment period of one year, three years, or five years.

Think about your income potential, about the frequency with which you can reasonably expect your income to increase, before you agree to frequent unlimited changes. Remember, if the payments increase beyond your capacity to meet them, you could run the risk of default. But think, too, about the length of time you anticipate living in the house. If this is your "starter" house and you expect to move on in a few years, it might be worth securing an adjustment period long enough to lock in your payments for those few years—even if you have to pay a slightly higher rate of interest to do so. It depends, of course, on what you think interest rates will do.

THE MARGIN

The margin, which is usually fixed for the life of the loan, is added to the index rate by the lender to determine the interest rate on the loan. Different lenders use different margins, and these will determine your payments. On a $65,000 loan when the index is at 10 percent, for example, a

2 percent margin will produce an interest rate of 12 percent and a monthly payment of $668.60; a 3 percent margin will produce an interest rate of 13 percent and a monthly payment of $719.03. It's just as important to check on the margin as on the index.

CAPS

Interest-rate or payment caps, currently built into ARMs by most lenders, reduce the risk of major fluctuations in your monthly payments. An *interest-rate cap* may limit the interest-rate increase from one adjustment period to the next, it may limit the interest-rate increase over the life of the loan, or it may do both. Fairly typical caps are 2 percent per adjustment period and 5 percent over the life of the loan. *Payment caps* limit the amount of payment increase at each adjustment to a percentage of the previous payment.

Caps are an important consumer safeguard. But they do have one possible drawback in the form of negative amortization—an increase in the outstanding balance of your mortgage loan. This can happen (although it's relatively rare) when payment caps do not permit monthly payments to be large enough to pay all of the interest that is due. When this happens, the interest shortfall is added to the debt and interest may be charged on that amount, so that you may owe the lender more later in the loan term than you did at the outset.

SHOULD YOU TAKE AN ARM?

There is little doubt that the fixed-rate, fixed-payment mortgage offers stability that the ARM does not. But the ARM does have some advantages:

■ Lenders are, in many cases, offering much lower initial interest rates as an incentive to borrowers to take an adjustable mortgage. That lower rate can mean considerable savings. In an example provided by the Federal Home Loan Mortgage Corporation (see Table 2): A $55,000 30-year fixed-rate mortgage at 13.5 percent would have monthly payments of $630. An ARM for the same amount at 12.25 percent (a typical spread) would cost $576 a month. If the ARM were written with a three-year adjustment period, you would save close to $2,000 over the three-year period. That $2,000, plus interest (assuming that you were able to save it rather than spend it), could be applied to future rate increases. The initial savings, in fact, could carry you through all but a sustained period of high interest rates.

■ There are less likely to be additional points, which add to the effective interest rate, on an adjustable mortgage.

TABLE 2: Borrower's approximate monthly payments on a $55,000 mortgage.

Mortgages	Principal and interest	Assumed taxes and insurance	Total monthly payment	Savings to the borrower compared to a fixed-rate mortgage	Annual qualifying income*
Fixed-rate at 13.5%	$630	$100	$730	NA	$31,286
Five-year ARM at 12.75%	598	100	698	$32 per month; $1,920 over five years	29,914
Three-year ARM at 12.25%	576	100	676	$54 per month; $1,994 over three years	28,971
One-year ARM at 11.25%	534	100	634	$96 per month; $1,152 over one year	27,171

* Assumes monthly payment equal to 28% of gross monthly income.
(Source: Federal Home Loan Mortgage Corporation)

- Rates come down if interest rates fall (unless the loan has a built-in "floor"; be sure to ask). If you accept a fixed-rate mortgage when interest rates are high, on the other hand, you'll be locked into those rates for a long time. (You could refinance, but that in itself is expensive.)

- You may be able to negotiate individual terms, including assumability of the mortgage (so that you can guarantee a buyer a mortgage when you sell), and portability (so that you can get a new loan if you move).

In the long run, whether an adjustable mortgage loan turns out to be a good buy or a bad one depends on (1) whether interest rates are on their way up or down when you obtain your loan, and (2) what happens to interest rates over the life of your mortgage. With an adjustable mortgage loan, you have to be a bit of a gambler.

Questions to ask before you take an ARM

1. What index will be used to adjust the payments? Ask the lender for a table showing movements in that index over several years, to give you an idea of how your payments might change.

2. What is the initial mortgage rate? Does it reflect a special discount? Some initial discount rates are lower than the sum of the index and the margin, so that the rate may rise at the first adjustment period even if the index remains the same. If this is the case, you may be in for "payment shock" when your payments increase sharply. Don't take this kind of loan without thinking about your ability to make payments in the future.

3. How often will the mortgage be adjusted? The shorter the adjustment period, the more you and the lender share the risk of fluctuating rates; in return for your sharing that risk, you may have a lower interest rate on a shorter adjustment period. The longer the adjustment period, the better you will be able to plan ahead.

4. Which elements of the loan can be adjusted? The lender should give you a full explanation of how interest rates, payments, the loan balance, and the term to maturity may be adjusted and how adjusting one element may affect the others.

5. Is the loan assumable, so that you can pass it on to a qualified buyer when you are ready to sell? Is it convertible, so that you can change it to a fixed-rate loan at designated times?

6. What is the margin? Are there payment or interest-rate caps? Can negative amortization take place? Are there prepayment penalties?

Q. My adjustable-rate mortgage has just been adjusted for the first time, and I'm baffled by the new payment figure. How can I determine if the lender is correct?

A. It isn't easy, especially since regulators find that many lenders have been making mistakes with the complex calculations. First, check the published index figure and be sure the lender used the correct date. Add on the lender's margin, and be sure it's rounded in accordance with the terms of the contract; an eighth of a percentage point can make a substantial difference over 30 years. Then, and this is important, ask a senior lending officer for a full explanation.

MORTGAGE WORKSHEET

Ask your lender to help fill out this checklist.

BASIC FEATURES FOR COMPARISON	MORTGAGE AMOUNT	
	Mortgage A	*Mortgage B*
Fixed-rate annual percentage rate (The cost of your credit as a yearly rate which includes both interest and other charges)	$_____	$_____
ARM annual percentage rate	$_____	$_____
Adjustment period	$_____	$_____
Index used and current rate	$_____	$_____
Margin	$_____	$_____
Initial payment without discount	$_____	$_____
Initial payment with discount (if any)	$_____	$_____
How long will discount last?	$_____	$_____
Interest rate caps: periodic	$_____	$_____
overall	$_____	$_____
Payment caps	$_____	$_____
Negative amortization	$_____	$_____
Convertibility or prepayment privilege	$_____	$_____
Initial fees and charges	$_____	$_____

MONTHLY PAYMENT AMOUNTS

What will my monthly payment be after twelve months if the index rate—

stays the same	$_____	$_____
goes up 2%	$_____	$_____
goes down 2%	$_____	$_____

What will my monthly payments be after three years if the index rate—

stays the same	$_____	$_____
goes up 2% per year	$_____	$_____
goes down 2% per year	$_____	$_____

Take into account any caps on your mortgage and remember it may run 30 years.

(Source: Federal Reserve Board/Federal Home Loan Bank Board)

Making a Decision

As you decide which mortgage form is right for you, these are some of the factors to weigh:

- Your age and your income potential. If you are in your twenties, with relatively low current income but great expectations, an ARM with a low introductory rate might be right for you. If you're in your fifties or sixties, with fixed-income years looming ahead, you might prefer a short-term fixed-rate mortgage even if it costs a bit more.

- The number of years you will stay in the house. If you'll be there only a short time, again, it could be preferable to take an adjustable-rate mortgage, especially one with a rate fixed for three to five years. If you're planning to stay for the foreseeable future, however, and are worried about the long-range prospects for interest rates, you might try to secure a fixed-rate mortgage with its guarantee of stability.

- Your willingness to accept risk. Are you a gambler? Or does uncertainty make you nervous? If you think interest rates will come down, and are willing to gamble on that assumption, you'll take your chances with an adjustable-rate mortgage. If the inability to budget definite mortgage payments from year to year will give you sleepless nights, you might pay a bit more to get a fixed-rate mortgage.

If you take an adjustable-rate mortgage and interest rates continue to rise, housing may consume more and more of your income. If interest rates come down, however, you could be better off with an ARM than with the fixed-rate variety (especially if you got stuck with a fixed-rate loan at an interest peak). It's not an easy decision, since no authorities, least of all economists, agree on the direction interest rates will take.

Evaluate your own needs and your own temperament, then shop around in your community. Remember, as you shop, that financial institutions are governed by a variety of federal and state regulatory agencies; some permit one mortgage form, some another. Remember, too, that rates may vary widely within the same community. In today's economic climate, it's imperative to shop around.

Other Mortgage Forms

A great many other mortgage forms were introduced in the wild and woolly days of 16 to 18 percent mortgages. Most—and it's just as well—disappeared when interest rates dropped. In certain locations, some are still available. And some, of course, may well return if interest rates go up once again. Here's a brief rundown:

The Graduated Payment Mortgage (GPM)

One of the first of the alternative mortgage forms and one which is still available, the GPM is a fixed-rate mortgage (an adjustable version is also sometimes offered) designed for homebuyers who expect their incomes to rise. It has monthly mortgage payments which start low, then rise gradually over a period of five to ten years before leveling off for the rest of the mortgage period. Payments change, in other words, but you know in advance exactly when and how they are going to change.

The lower initial payments enable you to qualify for a GPM with less income than you would need for a comparable level-payment loan. Put another way, you can buy more house for your money. This is attractive to young homebuyers with low salaries and high potential.

But there are some drawbacks. Your income may not rise as expected, so that increased payments are difficult to meet. Or one of your two incomes may turn out to be less stable than expected. Even if incomes continue and increase, you'll pay out considerably more over the life of the loan (if you stay in the house that long) than you would with a traditional fixed-rate mortgage. If you sell early, on the other hand, you may not have much equity, maybe not even enough to make a down payment on another house. If you sell early enough, you may even owe the lender additional interest because of negative amortization.

The Growing Equity Mortgage (GEM)

Sometimes called the Rapid Payoff Mortgage, this is a fixed-rate, fixed-schedule mortgage with payments that change over time, but there is no uncertainty about how they will change. The major difference between the GEM and the GPM is that you start paying the same amount as you would for a level-payment fixed-rate mortgage, with increases in payments used entirely to reduce the principal. The increases in payments enable you to pay off a 30-year mortgage in fifteen to twenty years.

A variation on this theme is the *biweekly mortgage,* under which half of the monthly payment is made every two weeks, for a total of twenty-six payments a year or the equivalent of thirteen monthly payments.

Whether payments go up in amount (as in the GEM) or in frequency (as in the biweekly mortgage), the extra payments to principal greatly reduce the amount of interest you owe. Neither mortgage is widely available. But you can accomplish the same end, assuming that your mortgage does not contain prepayment penalties, by making extra payments toward principal when you have some extra cash. The advantage, in fact, is that you have the option of stopping the extra payments; just remember that even if you've made extra payments, you can never skip a regularly scheduled mortgage payment.

Partnership Mortgages

High home ownership costs (whether high in fact or high in terms of a potential purchaser's pocketbook) can be made manageable if someone else shares the burden. That someone else can be a third party, such as a lender or an outside investor. Or it might be (and more often is) a family member.

THE SHARED APPRECIATION MORTGAGE (SAM)

Shared appreciation or equity participation mortgages, like graduated payment mortgages, are designed to help first-time homebuyers get a foot in the homeownership door. With a SAM (not widely available today), the mortgage interest rate paid by the borrower is reduced in exchange for a share of the home's equity given to the lender. A one-third reduction in interest rate might be exchanged, for instance, for a one-third participation in the appreciated value of the house. The lower interest rate, because it would require a lower annual income to manage the monthly payments, would make homeownership accessible to a lot more people.

Q. We would like to help our daughter and her husband buy a house, but we can't afford to make them a gift of several thousand dollars. Is there some way we can help them out and be sure of repayment, without setting the scene for a family squabble?

A. Yes. If you use a "pledged account" you can reduce your daughter's cost of homeowning, while keeping your funds in your own name and earning a fair return on your investment. Here's how it works: You place your "contribution" in a certificate of deposit at the lending institution that grants your daughter's mortgage loan. You earn an agreed-upon rate of interest (if you take a lower rate of interest, your daughter's monthly mortgage payments will be lower) and, depending on your agreement with the lending institution, may be able to withdraw the interest on a periodic basis. At the end of the term, you can withdraw your funds from the CD, and your daughter's mortgage rate will be renegotiated. Or, if you wish to continue to help, you can roll over the CD and maintain the below-market interest rate on the mortgage. Talk to your daughter, her real estate broker, and her lender, to see if a pledged account can be arranged.

THE SHARED EQUITY MORTGAGE (SEM)

A younger and livelier brother of the shared appreciation mortgage made its appearance in the form of the shared equity mortgage. With the SEM, it's not the lender but an outside investor, often a relative, who shares in the cost of buying the house, in its potential appreciation and, meanwhile, in the tax benefits of ownership.

THE RISKS IN PARTNERSHIP MORTGAGES

This method of purchasing a house is extremely complex and should not be undertaken without sound legal advice and a carefully drawn agreement. That agreement should specify the ownership share and form of ownership ("tenants in common" is the usual approach), the terms of the rental agreement (the occupants must pay a "fair market rent" for their share of the property or the IRS may disallow tax deductions), when the arrangement will end in the form of sale or refinancing (seven years is typical, with a provision to extend the agreement by mutual consent), how profits will be split at that point, and what happens, meanwhile, if either partner defaults. All of these points apply whether the investor-owner is an outside investor or a relative. But a relative has an interest, other than financial, in the occupant-owner. An outsider does not. If you enter into a partnership mortgage with an outsider you should ask some additional questions:

- What happens if you, the homebuyer, want to make improvements in your home and the investor does not agree? Some shared mortgages give the investor veto power over home improvements, and you might wind up living with kitchen cabinets you don't like and without the patio you want.

- What happens if the house fails to appreciate in value, or to appreciate very much? Will whatever profit there is be shared equally? Or will either the house's occupant or the investor come out with a loss?

- What happens if the investor needs to sell? Can his share of the property be sold without forcing the house's occupant to sell as well?

Look at all aspects of equity sharing very carefully, and get competent advice. Either turn to an experienced real estate attorney, one who has handled this kind of arrangement before, or turn to one of the organizations (such as the Family Backed Mortgage Association in Oakland, California) that packages partnership mortgages among family members.

Mortgage Insurance

Q. We are taking on a massive mortgage commitment with our new house, and I'm concerned about what will happen to my family if anything happens to me. I was all set to take out a mortgage insurance policy when I heard that there's more than one kind. What are the differences and which is the type I should buy?

A. Mortgage insurance is essentially a type of decreasing term insurance; you pay the same amount in premiums each year but the amount of the policy decreases along with the mortgage. You can buy this kind of coverage in three ways: via a group mortgage policy issued by your lender, via an individual mortgage policy you take on your own, or via a regular decreasing term policy. The first two would be tied to the amount of your mortgage; the last could be taken out in any amount you choose.

Before you buy any policy, however, consider these facts:

- It's more important to have adequate life insurance, to cover all your family's needs, than to buy mortgage insurance alone. Even with the mortgage paid off, your survivor would still have to pay taxes, utility bills, and all the other costs of running a household.

- On a group policy issued by a lender, the lender is usually the beneficiary. Should you die, the mortgage would be paid off. But what if your survivor would prefer to continue making mortgage payments and use insurance money for other costs of living? An individual mortgage policy or regular decreasing term would permit that choice.

Buy-Downs

In order to reduce the financing costs on a new house, and thereby enlarge the pool of potential homebuyers when interest rates are high, a builder (buy-downs are primarily offered by builders but may also be arranged by the buyer) may turn over a portion of the sales price to a lending institution; the lender then uses the money to offset interest payments on the buyer's mortgage. (The mortgage itself may be either fixed-rate or adjustable.)

The lower rate, typically, applies for a limited period such as three years; it may remain level for the three years or be reduced each year. Either way, after the discount period, the homebuyer assumes the full mortgage payments. Buy-downs are particularly attractive, therefore, if you expect your income to grow (you're in a stable field with regular salary increases) or if you expect a major expenditure to end (your children will be finished with college).

Note: The buy-down may represent a discount on the price of the house, but only if the money saved on the mortgage is not added into the price somewhere else and only if the house is worth the full price in the first place.

Land Leasing

Another way of reducing housing costs involves separating the house and the land. With a land-leasing arrangement, you buy the house alone and pay annual rental on the land. This reduces your down payment by as much as 25 percent, as well as your monthly carrying costs. If a house with its land is priced at $95,000, the house alone might be priced at

$75,900. A down payment on house plus land, at 10 percent, would be $9,500, while a down payment on the house alone would be $7,590.

In addition to monthly mortgage costs on the house, however, you would have to pay monthly lease charges on the land. The total may be less than a mortgage on both house and land, but be wary: Lease charges usually start out low, so that the total monthly payments are lower, at the beginning, than they would be with a conventional mortgage, but the rental portion (often tied in with an option to buy) often has an escalation feature. If the rate is tied to inflation, you could find rapidly rising costs. Ground rents, moreover, unlike mortgage interest payments, are not tax-deductible.

Land leasing is still relatively rare in the United States. Where it is offered, it is generally by developers of new homes. Before you decide on a land lease, however, ask some hard questions: When and how often can the payments increase? at what rate? Does the contract include an option to buy the land? at what price? with what limitations? Are local mortgage lenders willing to finance a home with a land lease? And, not least, what are the resale prospects?

Q. After several months of seeking a house, we are totally bewildered by today's financing terms. If and when we actually decide on a particular house, will anyone explain all the financial details so that we can understand them?

A. Your lender, if you secure a conventional fixed-rate or adjustable-rate mortgage, should explain the details. If you use seller financing through a builder or an individual, however, you may be largely on your own. Protect yourself: Refuse to sign any contract until you fully understand the annual percentage rate (with all extra fees, such as points, factored in), the total financing charges (over the entire course of the loan, even if earlier payments are lower), and the amount of the final payment and when it is due (you don't want to be surprised by a large "balloon" payment due at the end).

Owner Financing of Resale Homes

So-called "creative financing" played a major role in home sales in the early 1980s, as owners who were desperate to sell and move on became involved in providing mortgage financing through a variety of innovative techniques. Seller involvement is far less common when interest rates are down, but you may still encounter one or more of the following:

MORTGAGE ASSUMPTIONS

When the buyer can take over an existing mortgage with a lower rate of interest, it can be very helpful to both the buyer and the seller. Mortgages used to be readily assumable. Today this is not necessarily the case, as lenders press to enforce the "due-on-sale" provisions that say a mortgage must be paid off when the property changes hands. Adjustable-rate mortgages are often assumable, but it isn't much help when the interest rate will reflect rising rates. Fixed-rate mortgages are sometimes assumable, but you'll have to check with the lender to be sure.

Even where an assumption is permitted, the old mortgage may be fairly small by the time the house is sold. The buyer must, therefore, either come up with additional cash for a substantial down payment or find additional financing, which may be secured via a second mortgage.

SECOND MORTGAGES

The purchase money mortgage or second mortgage involves the assumption of a first mortgage by the buyer and the issuance of a second mortgage (or deed of trust, as it is called in some parts of the country) by the seller to cover the difference between the first mortgage and the amount the buyer owes. The seller-issued mortgage is usually at an interest rate lower than that on a new mortgage, and is issued for a shorter term. (Second mortgages may also be obtained from lending institutions, but then the rate will usually be higher than that on a first mortgage.)

When the seller issues (takes back) the second mortgage, the buyer pays the original mortgage lender the monthly amount due on the first mortgage and pays the seller a monthly sum on the additional loan. The combined mortgage loans create a financing package that is generally (but not always) less expensive than a new mortgage would be. A second mortgage may make it possible for you to buy (or sell) your house. But be aware that:

- Payments are generally calculated on a 25-to-30-year basis but with a single large payment, a "balloon," due at the end of an agreed-upon loan period, which is usually three to five years.

- The terms of the first mortgage on the property may forbid secondary financing without the lender's consent. If you go ahead anyway, you may find yourself in default.

- The IRS requires that mortgage interest payments be reported; if you receive mortgage interest, therefore, you will have to issue a year-end statement to the borrower.

THE LEASE-PURCHASE OPTION

These "contract sales" allow a buyer to occupy a house before actually taking title. Under an option agreement, typically for twelve months, a sales contract may be executed with a closing date which coincides with the expiration of the lease. In this case the price of the house is set in advance, and the seller should try to assess realistically, as far as possible, what the house may be worth in a year's time. The buyer pays option money, which can be applied to the down payment, and can move into the house without a major expenditure. The buyer also forgoes the tax advantages of ownership during the lease period; rent is not tax-deductible (although, depending on the terms of the agreement, it may be applied in whole or in part to the purchase price of the house). The seller gets the option money as well as the lease or rental payments, and keeps the tax benefits of homeownership until the option is executed and the house is sold.

The Risks of Being Creative

Creative financing is an invention born of necessity. You won't be likely to use it when conventional financing is both affordable and available, but if it becomes necessary, you should be aware of the risks involved and do what you can to protect yourself.

TO PROTECT YOURSELF, IF YOU'RE THE BUYER

- Negotiate. Take advantage of the seller's eagerness to sell, and get the lowest price possible. See if the seller will accept a completed deal, at a lower price, rather than embark on creative financing.

- Evaluate what you can afford at each critical point: for the down payment, when a balloon payment is due, etc. Don't overestimate your ability to pay, or count on bonuses or overtime that may not happen.

- If you sign a balloon payment loan, make the period as long as you possibly can; five years is better than three, seven is better than five. (Seven is considered optimum by some analysts because it's the length of most business cycles, thereby taking in low interest rates as well as high.) Try to include a clause providing that the loan will be extended for a specified period if interest rates haven't dropped to an affordable level by the time the loan comes due.

- Ask for the right of prepayment without penalty, so that you can refinance the loan when money does become available.

- Insist, meanwhile, on notification by the primary lender if the seller fails to make any payments for which he is still responsible. If the seller moves away, skips payments, and you're not informed, you could lose your house.

IF YOU'RE THE SELLER

- Think about reducing your price instead of getting involved in creative financing, if it will mean that the buyer can get his own financing and you can invest the cash for a comparable return. If you do help the buyer:

- Insist on an adequate down payment, at least 10 percent, 20 percent if you can get it. The more stake the buyer has in the property, the more likely he is to keep up payments.

- Don't be patient with chronic late payments. Insist on prompt payment, and have your loan agreement include a provision for a penalty when payments are late.

- Find out if the buyer is creditworthy. Ask for credit references.

- Keep the term of the loan as short as possible.

- Realize that if you need the cash before the loan is due, you may have to sell the note to an investor at a substantial discount.

- Be aware that foreclosure, if you're forced to that point, is both slow and very unpleasant. If you hold a second mortgage, moreover, you're second in line after the holder of the first.

- Think about including a due-on-sale provision so that the buyer can't sell the house, and your loan along with it.

FOR BUYERS AND SELLERS

Whether you're the buyer or the seller, consult a knowledgeable real estate attorney before embarking on any creative financing arrangements. The attorney should help you:

—be sure that the particular form of financing is legal in your state,

—determine that your financing is acceptable to the primary lender, if any, under the contract terms,

—find out whether there is any conflict with state usury laws where they exist (when a private seller sets the interest rate on a mortgage loan, there is the potential for such conflict),

—assess the degree of risk and be sure that it is acceptable, and

—draw up documents to protect your interests.

With creative financing there are no standard mortgage documents. Each deal is negotiated individually. Whether you are the buyer or the seller, therefore, you'll want to protect your interests in this very complex negotiation. Don't rely on a real estate agent to protect your interests; many are simply not trained in the complex mathematical and legal ramifications of creative financing. Use a lawyer skilled in real estate transactions in your state.

Q. After living together for three years, we would like to buy a house. We talked to a real estate agent, who said we should conceal our unmarried status in applying for a mortgage. We see no reason to lie. What do you think?

A. Don't lie. Not only is the purchase of real estate by unmarried live-togethers accepted almost everywhere, you may even find it easier to secure a mortgage. Some lenders will be delighted to find buyers with two incomes and separate credit identities.

Equity Conversion

A 72-year-old widow, a retired laboratory technician, lives in a Northern California house worth $152,000. But she lives on Social Security and a small pension and can barely make ends meet. That is, she could barely make ends meet until she became one of the first recipients of a "reverse" mortgage which will pay her over $500 a month, based on the value of her home, for the next ten years.

First-time homebuyers are not the only people with problems of housing affordability. Elderly homeowners, buffeted by rising costs and fixed incomes, often have difficulty remaining in their homes. A house may be worth a great deal, but that value can't be tapped to keep the household going. A number of plans have been developed to make it possible for homeowners to tap this equity and use it for living expenses without having to sell or to move.

The Reverse Annuity Mortgage (RAM)

Under this plan, the first of the equity conversion programs to get under way, an elderly homeowner with a paid-up mortgage applies to a lending institution for a loan secured by the value of the house. The loan may be paid to the homeowner all at once, in equal monthly installments over a specified period of years (usually five to ten), or in a combination of lump sum and monthly payout. In the original version of this plan, the version which gave it its name, the loan proceeds were used to buy an annuity for the homeowner. That annuity would provide regular monthly income. In another version (sometimes called a reverse equity mortgage), the monthly payout is made by the lending institution itself.

For example: You bought a $35,000 home in 1958 and it is now, thanks to inflation, worth $80,000. Under one RAM plan you could borrow up to 80 percent of that appreciated value, or $64,000, and take out the proceeds over a period of ten years. If the interest rate on the reverse mortgage is 10.5 percent (the precise interest rate would depend on prevailing interest rates, on your age, and on the length of the loan), your monthly check from the bank would be $303.58.

The major drawback of the RAM: The loan must be repaid. The interest could be repaid monthly, even while you receive the payments, but in a period of high inflation, there would be little left to use. Or the loan could be repaid at the end of the designated loan period. Then the homeowner must either refinance the loan, for a larger amount (assuming that the home has continued to appreciate in value), or must sell the house to raise the necessary cash. RAMs, as a result, are best suited to elderly homeowners who anticipate remaining in their homes for less than ten years. Even so, there are such complicated mathematics involved in making these loans—and such sensitivity to the potential problem of evicting elderly homeowners when the loan comes due—that relatively few lenders have offered the reverse annuity mortgage.

Sale-Leaseback Plans

Under this plan, developed by a California firm, an investor or group of investors will purchase the house (at a discount from full market value) and will then enter into a leaseback arrangement with the owners, guaranteeing them occupancy and an income for life. The investor also often takes care of taxes, insurance, and repairs.

At the time of the agreement, an annuity is purchased from an insurance company. If the original homeowner outlives the amount of money raised from the sale of the house, the annuity will continue the same monthly payments. Should you, the homeowner, die before receiving the full purchase price in monthly installments, your heirs will receive the balance.

The size of the monthly checks will depend on your age and on the value of your home; the older you are (and the fewer monthly checks you expect to receive), the larger each check will be.

Note: Under the Grannie Mae program, sponsored by Family Backed Mortgage Association, the loan is strictly between relatives and the house stays in the family. Some public agencies and nonprofit community organizations are sponsoring similar programs, taking title to a house in exchange for a lifetime stipend.

Lifetime Income

A third plan, developed by a New Jersey firm, is available through banks and savings and loan associations in some states. A loan will be made, secured by a first mortgage on your home, with monthly payments guaranteed until you move, sell the property, ask that payments be stopped, or die. At that point, you (or your heirs) will owe the lender the total amount of the monthly checks, interest on those checks (at a rate lower

Table 3: A summary of mortgage varieties in the 1980s.

Type	Description	Considerations
Fixed-rate mortgage	Fixed interest rate, usually long-term; equal monthly payments of principal and interest until debt is paid in full.	Offers stability and long-term tax advantages. Interest rates may be higher than other types of financing. New fixed-rate mortgages are rarely assumable.
Adjustable-rate mortgage	Interest rate changes are based on a financial index, resulting in possible changes in monthly payments, loan term, and/or principal. Most plans have rate or payment caps.	Readily available. Starting interest rate is slightly below market, but payments can increase if index increases. Payment caps prevent wide fluctuations in payments but may cause negative amortization. Rate caps limit amount total debt can expand.
Renegotiable-rate mortgage (rollover)	Interest rate and monthly payments are constant for several years; changes are possible thereafter. Long-term mortgage.	Less frequent changes in interest rate offers some stability.
Balloon mortgage	Monthly payments based on fixed interest rate; usually short-term. Payments may cover interest only, with principal due in full at end of term.	Offers low monthly payments but possibly no equity until loan is fully paid. When due, loan must be paid off or refinanced. Refinancing poses high risk if rates climb.
Graduated payment mortgage	Lower monthly payments rise gradually (usually over 5–10 years), then level off for duration of term. With flexible interest rate, additional payment changes are possible if index changes.	Easier to qualify for. Buyer's income must keep pace with scheduled payment increases. With a flexible rate, payment increases beyond the graduated payments can result in additional negative amortization.
Shared appreciation mortgage	Below-market interest rate and lower monthly payments in exchange for a share of the profits when property is sold or on a specified date. Many variations.	If house appreciates greatly, total cost of loan jumps. If house fails to appreciate, projected increase in value may still be due, requiring refinancing at possibly higher rates.
Assumable mortgage	Buyer takes over seller's original, below-market-rate mortgage.	Lowers monthly payments. May be prohibited if due-on-sale clause is in original mortgage. Not permitted on most new fixed-rate mortgages.
Seller take-back	Seller provides all or part of financing with a first or second mortgage.	May offer a below-market interest rate; may have a balloon payment requiring full payment in a few years or refinancing at market rates, which could sharply increase debt.

TABLE 3: A summary of mortgage varieties in the 1980s. (*cont.*)

Type	Description	Considerations
Wraparound	Seller keeps original low rate mortgage. Buyer makes payments to seller, who forwards a portion to the lender holding original mortgage. Offers lower effective interest rate on total transaction.	Lender may call in old mortgage and require higher rate. If buyer defaults, seller must take legal action to collect debt.
Growing equity mortgage (rapid payoff mortgage)	Fixed interest rate but monthly payments may vary according to agreed-upon schedule or index.	Permits rapid payoff of debt because payment increases reduce principal. Buyer's income must be able to keep up with payment increases.
Land contract	Seller retains original mortgage. No transfer of title until loan is fully paid. Equal monthly payments based on below-market interest rate with unpaid principal due at loan end.	May offer no equity until loan is fully paid. Buyer has few protections if conflict arises during loan.
Buy-down	Developer (or third party) provides an interest subsidy which lowers monthly payments during first few years of the loan. Can have fixed or flexible interest rate.	Offers a break from higher payments during early years. Enables buyer with lower income to qualify. With flexible-rate mortgage, payments may jump substantially at end of subsidy. Developer may increase selling price.
Rent with option	Renter pays "option fee" for right to purchase property at specified time and agreed-upon price. Rent may or may not be applied to sales price.	Enables renter to buy time to obtain down payment and decide whether to purchase. Locks in price during inflationary times. Failure to take option means loss of option fee and rental payments.
Reverse annuity mortgage (equity conversion)	Borrower owns mortgage-free property and needs income. Lender makes monthly payments to borrower using property as collateral.	Can provide homeowners with needed cash. At end of term, borrower must have money available to avoid selling property or refinancing.
Zero-rate and low-rate mortgage	Appears to be completely or almost interest-free. Large down payment and one-time finance charge, then loan repaid in fixed monthly payments over short term.	Permits quick ownership. May not lower total cost (because of possibly increased sales price). Doesn't offer long-term tax deductions.

(Source: Federal Trade Commission)

than that prevailing in the mortgage market when the loan agreement was signed), and an agreed-upon share of the appreciated value of the house. Repayment will be made from the proceeds of the sale of the house. If the house has declined in value, the lender will take the loss.

Equity conversion in any of its forms is still a relatively new concept, but it is likely to become more widely available.

KEY POINTS

- Because mortgage loans are available from a number of different sources with varying down payment requirements, interest rates, mortgage terms, and fees, comparison shopping is vitally important.

- Fixed-rate, fixed-term mortgages offer certainty in monthly payments, but adjustable-rate mortgages, usually available at a lower initial interest rate, are a popular alternative.

- Interest or payment caps can protect you against excessive interest rate swings on an adjustable-rate mortgage, but it's also important to understand the index, the margin, and the adjustment period in order to assess your ability to make larger payments in the future.

- Creative financing, unnecessary when mortgage loans are affordable and available, may become useful once again if interest rates rise. But creative financing has pitfalls for both buyer and seller; before embarking on any form of creative financing, be sure to secure competent advice.

Insuring
Your Property

★ Your kitchen catches fire and newly installed cabinets are destroyed.

★ A neighbor's child runs across your lawn and trips over a garden hoe. A concussion leads to impaired vision, and the child's parents sue.

★ A burglar ransacks your home, vandalizing what he doesn't steal.

★ You're on vacation and your luggage is stolen.

★ While your daughter is walking the family dog, several blocks from home, the dog bites a passerby.

★ A massive tree limb cracks and falls, severely damaging your home's roof and chimney.

These events have just one thing in common: Protection against financial loss stemming from any of them is provided in a homeowners insurance policy.

Whether your kitchen catches fire or a tree limb falls on your roof, you need protection against *physical damage* via a homeowners policy. Whether your neighbor's child is injured on your property or your dog bites someone anywhere, you need protection against *liability* claims via a homeowners policy.

Homeowners Insurance Forms

If you own your own house you have a choice among several homeowners insurance packages. All include protection against liability claims, with a standard $100,000 limit which you may raise (and probably should;

see p. 288 for details). All also include protection against physical damage to your property resulting from fire, theft, windstorm or hail, explosion, riot or civil commotion, aircraft and vehicles, smoke, vandalism and malicious mischief, and the breakage of glass.

This coverage is provided in the Basic (HO-1) policy. Progressively more expensive policies cover more of what the insurance industry calls "named perils." Table 1 will help you to sort out the details of the various plans but, briefly, the Broad (HO-2) Form adds to the basic list with falling objects, weight of ice and snow and sleet, collapse of building,

TABLE 1: Perils against which properties are insured under the various homeowners policies.

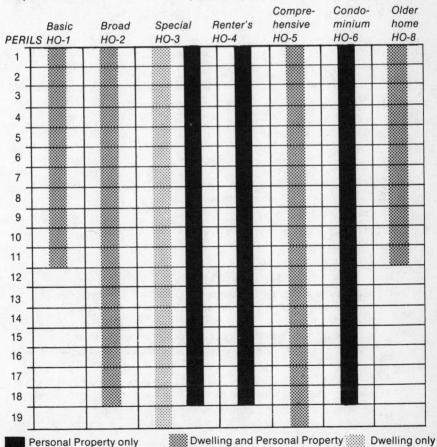

PERILS	Basic HO-1	Broad HO-2	Special HO-3	Renter's HO-4	Comprehensive HO-5	Condominium HO-6	Older home HO-8
1							
2							
3							
4							
5							
6							
7							
8							
9							
10							
11							
12							
13							
14							
15							
16							
17							
18							
19							

■ Personal Property only   ▨ Dwelling and Personal Property   ░ Dwelling only sudden breakage of a heating system or plumbing system or appliance, freezing of plumbing, heating, and air-conditioning systems, and sudden injury from electrical appliances or wiring. The Comprehensive (HO-5) Form, sometimes called "all-risk" coverage, insures you against property damage from everything except specified exclusions: flood, earthquake, war, nuclear accident, and whatever else your particular policy excludes. There is no insurance policy, whatever the title, that really covers absolutely everything.

The Comprehensive Form is probably your best bet for complete protection. If it's a bit too expensive (you'll have to make a specific price comparison based on where you live), look at the Special (HO-3) Form; it includes comprehensive or all-risk coverage on your dwelling and

PERILS

1. Fire or lightning
2. Loss of property removed from premises endangered by fire or other perils*
3. Windstorm or hail
4. Explosion
5. Riot or civil commotion
6. Aircraft
7. Vehicles
8. Smoke
9. Vandalism and malicious mischief
10. Theft
11. Breakage of glass constituting a part of the building
12. Falling objects
13. Weight of ice, snow, sleet
14. Collapse of building(s) or any part thereof
15. Sudden and accidental tearing asunder, cracking, burning, or bulging of a steam or hot water heating system or of appliances for heating water
16. Accidental discharge, leakage or overflow of water or steam from within a plumbing, heating or air-conditioning system or domestic appliance
17. Freezing of plumbing, heating and air-conditioning systems and domestic appliances
18. Sudden and accidental injury from artificially generated currents to electrical appliances, devices, fixtures and wiring (TV and radio tubes not included)
19. All perils except flood, earthquake, war, nuclear accident and others specified in your policy (check your policy for a complete listing of perils excluded)

* Included as a peril in traditional forms of the homeowners policy; as an additional coverage in the simplified (HO-76) policies.

(Source: Insurance Information Institute)

Broad Form coverage, which is not quite as complete, on your personal property (a new version is available with an all-risks contents endorsement).

If you've amassed possessions over a number of years, carefully evaluate those possessions before settling for less-than-complete coverage. One suburban house went up in flames when a spark from a gas water heater ignited a solvent being used to put down floor tile. Insurance enabled the family to rebuild the house, but the standard contents coverage (50 percent of the insurance on the house itself) was far less than adequate. See pp. 286–87 for more details on coverage of contents.

Be careful, in any case, about the "bargain" coverage of the Basic (HO-1) and Broad (HO-2) Forms, especially if you live in the northern states. Neither of these policies covers water damage to ceilings and walls caused by leakage. The HO-2 policy does cover water damage, but only if your roof actually collapses from the weight of snow and ice; most damage is caused by water seepage. If you upgrade your policy to HO-3, you'll increase your yearly premium in most states by just about 5 percent.

Q. My employer is now making homeowners insurance available on a payroll deduction plan. The price looks right, but I already carry my own insurance and wonder if I should switch. What do you advise?

A. Compare policy provisions, as well as premiums, and then find out:

- Is your employer subsidizing the premium as well as making the plan available? Most provide a small subsidy, often $3 to $8 a month.
- Will service be prompt and fair? It should be, because the insurance agent wants to retain this sizable number of customers.
- What happens if you change jobs? Usually the policy can be continued at the same price, without employer subsidy, billed to your home on a six-month basis.

The Elements of Homeowners Insurance

All homeowners forms have basic elements in common, although specific details will differ in accordance with state law and the issuing company. All include both property insurance (usually with a built-in $250 deductible; you pay the first $250 it takes to repair any damage) and personal liability coverage (with no deductible). All cover:

- The house itself, in the amount you designate (that amount should be at least 80 percent of the replacement value of the house; see p. 281).
- Other structures on the same property, such as a detached garage or a toolshed, to 10 percent of the value of the home (*Note:* If you maintain

an office or a business in a separate structure on your property, it is not covered by your homeowners insurance)

■ Personal property, the general contents of your house, usually up to half the insured value of the house (unless you arrange for more; see p. 301), but with a strict dollar limit on valuable items such as furs and jewelry

■ Additional living expenses, should you have to house your family elsewhere while repairing damages caused by an insured risk

■ Damage to trees, shrubs, and plants (but not from wind) up to 5 percent of the value of the dwelling, with a maximum of $500 per item

■ Losses of personal property away from home, usually up to 10 percent of value and limited to certain conditions

■ Personal liability, in case someone slips on your icy sidewalk or trips over a garden tool, at a minimum of $25,000 to $100,000 per occurrence

■ Medical payments to people injured on your property, without regard to fault, up to $1,000 per occurrence (this amount, too, may be increased)

■ Damage to the property of others, regardless of fault, up to $250 (useful if your child puts a softball through a neighbor's window)

Table 2 shows the type and amount of coverage for a typical dwelling under a Broad Form (HO-2) homeowners policy. Special insurance packages are designed for condominium owners (see p. 329), for mobile home owners (see p. 342), and for tenants (see p. 293).

Q. A delivery truck ran out of control down our street and across my lawn, destroying an old and beautiful oak tree that shaded our house. How can I establish the value of the tree for an insurance claim?

A. Your insurance company will probably want to send someone to look at the downed tree, so don't have it removed before you call your agent or the company. You might also want to call a local nursery or landscaper for an independent appraisal. It will help, too, if you have pictures showing the tree shading your house. The tree might be worth a great deal and, if it was very large, be impossible to replace, but an appraisal will focus on its species, size, condition, and location.

Property Damage Coverage in the Homeowners Policy

Whichever homeowners package you choose, it is absolutely vital that you buy enough insurance in the first place and that you keep your coverage up to date. "Enough" insurance means at least *80 percent* of the *replacement value* of your house. Don't settle for the amount of insurance required by your mortgage lender to cover the mortgage loan. If you

TABLE 2: Coverages under a Broad Form (HO-2) homeowners policy, assuming a house with an $80,000 replacement value.

	Insured to replacement value	Insured to 80% of replacement value
PROPERTY COVERAGES		
Dwelling	$80,000 (full value)	$64,000 (80% of full value)
Other structures on property	8,000 (10% of dwelling)	6,400 (10% of dwelling)
Unscheduled personal property	40,000 (50% of dwelling)*	32,000 (50% of dwelling)*
Additional living expenses	16,000 (20% of dwelling)	12,800 (20% of dwelling)
Trees, shrubs and plants	4,000 (5% of dwelling, subject to maximum of $500 per item)	3,200 (5% of dwelling, subject to maximum of $500 per item)
LIABILITY COVERAGES		
Personal liability	$100,000 (each occurrence)*	$100,000 (each occurrence)*
Medical payments to others (regardless of fault)	1,000 (each person)*	1,000 (each person)*
Damage to property of others (regardless of fault)	250 (each occurrence)	250 (each occurrence)

* Larger amounts are available; some policies may have lower standard amounts.

Amounts of coverages are the same under the Basic Form (HO-1), the Special Form (HO-3), and the Comprehensive Form (HO-5) except that additional living expenses under the Basic Form are covered only up to 10 percent of the amount of coverage on the dwelling.
(Source: Insurance Information Institute)

do and disaster strikes, the bank will be protected by insurance but your own investment may be unprotected. "Up to date" means regular review and increase for inflation (see below) *and* for any improvements, especially any additions you make to your house.

The amount of coverage you purchase on your dwelling becomes the base for the percentage amounts assigned to other structures on the property, to household contents, to additional living expenses, and so on. More important, *the amount of insurance on the dwelling itself determines whether you will receive full or partial reimbursement in the event of a partial loss.* With a total loss of your property, of course, you are covered up to the face amount of the policy. But most insurance claims are for partial loss: a kitchen fire, an electrical storm that topples a tree onto the roof, and so on.

THE 80 PERCENT RULE

If your house is not insured to 80 percent of its replacement value, then you will be reimbursed only for the actual cash value of depreciated property at the time of loss. With 80 percent coverage, you'll be sure of reimbursement for the full cost of repairing any damage or replacing any damaged item, without regard to depreciation, up to the full face amount of the policy.

It makes a significant difference. For example: If it would cost $80,000 to rebuild your house from the foundation up, then $64,000 of insurance would meet the 80 percent requirement. If a fire damages your kitchen, with its 8-year-old cabinets and appliances, the insurance company will pay the claim on the basis of what it costs to put the kitchen back together at today's prices. If you have less than 80 percent coverage on the house, however, payments for partial loss are reduced, with the calculations made in one of two ways. If you are carrying $40,000 in insurance, instead of the $64,000 you should have to meet the 80 percent rule, you would collect either forty sixty-fourths of the loss (on a $5,000 loss, that would be $3,125) or the actual cash value (replacement cost less depreciation), whichever is larger.

If you sustain a total loss—if, for example, your house burns to the foundation—you will be reimbursed only up to the face amount of the policy. If it will cost $80,000 to rebuild and you are insured to $64,000, you'll be out of pocket for the difference. Total disaster, fortunately, is rare, but it's devastating when it does occur. Consider full coverage.

REPLACEMENT VALUE

Don't think about the market value of your house when you think about insurance. Replacement value, or rebuilding cost, is the key. On a brand-new house, replacement value may be close to market value. In most cases, however, it's not at all comparable.

Your home may very well be underinsured because market prices have leveled off but repair costs have continued to rise. From 1975 to 1980, home purchase prices rose more than 10 percent a year; in 1981 the rise was a scant 1.2 percent. Home repair costs, however, according to a report by the Kemper Group, rose an average of 9.04 percent each year from 1975 to 1980 and continued to rise by 9.2 percent during 1981. A similar pattern has prevailed in succeeding years.

Inflation Protection

You can keep your homeowners coverage in line with current replacement costs in one of two ways:

- Review your coverage on a regular basis, upgrading it as necessary.
- Buy a policy with an "inflation-guard" provision, or add such a rider to an older policy.

It's safer by far, given human nature and our disinclination to pay attention to such things, to have the increases built into the policy. With inflation-guard protection, depending on the practices of your insurance company, your coverage will be automatically increased in one of two ways:

- By a predetermined amount, ranging from 8 to 12 percent a year
- According to an index of actual construction and labor costs

With today's volatility in construction costs, a number of insurance companies are recommending specific evaluation every three years with an index-based adjustment in the intervening years. Specific evaluation, by an insurance agent or real estate appraiser, is based on square footage, number of floors, type of construction, and additional features such as extra baths, fireplaces, and central air conditioning. Total rebuilding cost is then adjusted for locality, to reflect the tremendous differences across the country in the cost of labor and materials.

A COST ANALYSIS

Here's how a typical cost analysis might look, based on data supplied by Marshall & Swift Insurance Information Group, which prepares computerized analyses of individual home replacement value for insurance companies. This particular system is based on a square foot cost, a cost which would be different for different types of homes. In this example, the house is a two-story Colonial, frame construction, with 1,200 square feet of living space on the ground floor (not including deck or garage). The base figure in 1986 is:

1,200 square feet × 80.90 = 97,080

Additional features add to this base figure:

A half bath	$ 1,120
One-car attached garage	6,350
Brick fireplace	3,340
Deck, 100 square feet	450
Full unfinished basement	7,760
TOTAL REPLACEMENT COST	116,100

This figure, almost $1,100 more than the replacement cost for the same house in 1985, is a national average. Using the "location modifiers" supplied by Marshall & Swift, here's what the same house would cost to rebuild in three sample locations:

Shreveport, LA:	$ 94,041
Spokane, WA:	106,812
Pittsburgh, PA:	116,100

These locations are not the extremes. The lowest replacement cost, in 1986, was to be found in Valdosta, Georgia, where this same house would cost $70,821 to rebuild. The highest cost in the continental United States (Alaska and Hawaii, because so much must be imported, pose special situations) was in San Francisco, $139,320.

The Marshall & Swift service is not available to consumers; talk to your insurance agent about securing an analysis of your home. Should you want to do the arithmetic to get an idea of your home's current replacement value, however, here is a simplified formula to use; it is based on the "unit method" and does not require square foot calculations. (Remember, though, it will only approximate the actual replacement value of any individual house; the square foot method is more accurate.)

1. Determine the construction grade and quality closest to your house:

   a. Economy. Low-cost tract homes, with minimum materials and workmanship. No extras, such as dens or family rooms.

   b. Standard. The majority of homes. Standard plans, simple design, with average-grade materials and workmanship. Has extra rooms, such as dining room or den, and ornamentation.

   c. Custom. Built from special plans or modified standard plans, with good-quality materials and workmanship. Exceeds building codes.

2. Count each full room and each of the following as one unit: finished basement; full bathroom(s); brick or stone exterior; central air conditioning; aluminum siding; attached two-car garage; a full-wall fireplace; large enclosed porch; other special features. Count each of the following as a half unit: half bath (powder room or lavatory); large open porch; standard fireplace; unfinished basement; attached one-car garage; utility or laundry room; brick or stone veneer on the front only; unfinished attic with full headroom. Then adjust your count to reflect extra rooms or extra large rooms.

3. Use Table 3 for the type of construction and the number of units in your house; the figure shown will be the approximate replacement cost. However, note that this calculation provides a very rough estimate. It is not as accurate as a calculation by the square foot method, and it does not include location modifiers, so it is an average figure rather than one specific to your location. Also, this calculation won't work at all for houses over forty-five years old or worth more than $175,000, or for multifamily dwellings.

> **Q.** We bought an old Victorian house, with built-in cupboards, carved stair posts, and original gingerbread trim. The house cost us $66,000 but would probably cost three times that to restore if it were ever damaged. There's no way we can insure it to 80 percent of its replacement value. What can we do?

TABLE 3: Calculating replacement cost.

Select the amount shown opposite the number of units.

Construction units	Economy	Standard	Custom
5	41,800	52,500	64,500
5½	45,100	55,800	68,200
6	48,500	59,400	71,900
6½	51,700	62,700	75,500
7	54,900	66,100	79,300
7½	58,300	69,500	82,900
8	61,500	72,900	86,500
8½	64,800	76,300	90,200
9	68,000	79,700	93,800
9½	71,400	83,100	97,500
10	74,600	86,500	101,100
10½	77,900	90,000	104,700
11	81,100	93,200	108,400
11½	84,300	96,600	112,400
12	87,400	99,900	116,200
12½	90,600	103,300	120,100
13	93,600	106,500	124,100
13½	96,900	110,000	127,900
14	99,900	113,200	131,800
14½	103,000	116,500	135,800
15	106,100	119,800	139,700
15½	109,400	123,200	143,500
16	112,400	126,400	147,500
16½	115,600	129,800	151,300
17	118,500	133,000	155,100

For construction grades falling "in between," interpolate on a judgment basis. Costs include markups for contactor's overhead and profit, taxes, insurance, and general conditions.
(Source: The Travelers Insurance Companies)

A. Depending on where you live, you have a choice. You may be able to buy a Market Value homeowners policy (HO-8) which would provide for reconstruction with materials used today. The policy insures against all the risks covered by the Basic (HO-1) policy but with the special provision that property will be returned to usable condition rather than to its original condition. This means that you may wind up with wallboard after a fire rather than with the plaster walls of the original, but you will have a usable home and a policy with a manageable premium. Or, in most states, you can add an endorsement to a standard replacement cost homeowners policy to reduce, without penalty, the amount of insurance required. Coverage can be modified to 50, 60, or 70 percent instead of the usual 80 percent. With this endorsement, you would recover the full cost of replacement in case of partial loss or damage to the house up to the policy limit, as long as the agreed-on percentage was met. If there were a total loss, the policy would cover the cost of rebuilding using modern materials and methods. Talk to your insurance agent about what is available in your state and which approach is best for you.

When You File a Claim

If you do suffer a loss to your home or property, the New York State Insurance Department suggests that you take the following steps:

- Notify your agent or insurance company, without delay. They will arrange for an adjuster from your insurance company to look over the damage and give you an estimate on the cost of repairs or replacement. They will also help you fill out the claim forms and gather the materials you need to prove your loss.

- You should also get an estimate from your own contractor, to compare with the company's estimate. Your contractor may charge a fee for this service, but he probably will credit it to your bill if he gets the repair job.

- If there is considerable fire damage, you may want to call in a public adjuster, a licensed professional who will act as your agent in negotiating a settlement with your insurance company. The fee for this service is generally a specified percentage of your insurance settlement, based upon a retainer you agree on in advance in a signed contract. Be cautious, however, about signing up with the first public adjuster who appears on the scene after your house burns down. Gather your wits before you sign a binding agreement.

- Protect your property against further damage. If windows are broken, for instance, have them boarded up to protect against vandalism and weather damage. The cost should be covered by your homeowners policy.

- Be patient. Don't have permanent repairs made until the insurance company has inspected the property and you both agree on the cost of the repairs. The company has a legal right to inspect the property in its damaged state and can refuse to reimburse you for any damage repaired prior to its inspection.

Insurance on Household Contents

The standard coverage of household contents under every form of homeowners policy is limited to 50 percent of the amount of insurance on the house itself. You can, if you elect to do so, increase contents coverage to 70 percent. Whatever the maximum, however, these are the limits:

- Some types of personal property, such as motorbikes or golf carts, may be excluded under some policies. Other types of property, such as coin collections or silverware, may be severely limited in the dollar amount of coverage. A separate personal articles floater, described on p. 289, may be obtained for such items.

- "Mysterious disappearance" is covered under some policies, typically the more inclusive policies, and not under others. If you're not quite sure what happened to a gold chain—did you lose it because the catch broke, or did someone steal it?—you may or may not be able to collect.

- Business-related property may or may not be covered. Talk to your agent if you run a business from your home.

> **Q.** I bought a small computer which my children use for both homework and video games and I use for my part-time business of writing advertising copy for local merchants. Is the computer covered under my homeowners policy?
>
> **A.** Until recently, no. But new policies issued by many companies now cover home computers used for business, up to a total of $2,500. Some companies have higher limits. Check with your own company or agent.

- If you leave your house vacant for more than thirty consecutive days before a loss, you may not be covered. If you plan extensive travel, therefore, you might want to consider hiring a responsible house-sitter.

REPLACEMENT COST COVERAGE

Coverage of household contents is generally based on current value less depreciation, an amount which may not be nearly enough to replace cherished possessions. Today, however, more and more companies are offering replacement cost coverage. If you elect to pay the additional premium (roughly 15 percent more on a standard homeowners policy), this insurance would generally provide enough to replace the stolen or damaged item at current prices.

Under some policies, however, the insurer has the option of either paying for repairing a damaged item or reimbursing you for an amount up to four times the actual cash value of the property. With the latter provision, as an example, your living room furniture may have cost $1,800 and now be worth $350 (used furniture is worth very little). Yet it would cost at least $3,200 to replace at current prices. The insurer could, however, offer just $1,500 or four times the actual cash value. If you elect this coverage, be sure to check the terms of the policy.

Liability Coverage in the Homeowners Policy

All forms of the homeowners policy include liability coverage designed to protect you against financial loss resulting from personal liability, medical payments to others, and physical damage to the property of others.

The liability coverage in your policy will protect you against a claim for damages if you misjudge the distance in taking down a diseased tree in your backyard and the tree falls on your neighbor's house. It will protect you if someone is injured on your property and files suit. Legal defense is provided under the terms of the policy whether or not you are legally at fault. But damages are not paid unless it is determined, often in a court of law, that you are legally responsible.

The standard limit, as noted earlier, is $100,000. This may well not be enough. Damage awards in personal injury suits today are very often considerably more. If your savings might be wiped out by a personal injury lawsuit, or your future earnings threatened, it's worthwhile to consider taking out extra liability coverage. You can take extra coverage under your homeowners policy. Or, if you are a professional or a business executive with high or potentially high earnings that might be susceptible to a lawsuit, you should consider a separate umbrella liability policy.

UMBRELLA LIABILITY COVERAGE

These policies, which sell for about $100 for the first $1,000,000 in coverage and $10 for each addiitional $1,000,000, pick up where your homeowners and automobile policies stop. If your homeowners policy has the basic $100,000 in liability protection, that $100,000 will be the deductible under the umbrella policy. These policies also provide primary coverage for situations not covered by other insurance. If you're sued for libel or wrongfully evicted, for instance, an umbrella policy would provide protection above a specified deductible.

For example:

★ A school board member, along with the rest of the board, was sued by a teacher for defamation of character. The member was covered by her umbrella liability policy.

★ While driving a rental automobile in Jamaica, British West Indies, a vacationing American was involved in a fatal accident. He had limited coverage from the rental company, and his own automobile policy excluded foreign coverage. The personal liability policy provided coverage.

★ A tourist browsing in an antique shop broke a valuable Chinese vase. Her homeowner's policy would have paid just $500 toward the damage; her umbrella liability policy paid the full $11,700 cost of the vase.

Q. Because I work full-time, I hire a baby-sitter to be with my 7-year-old son after school every day. Should I be carrying any special insurance in case she's hurt in my home?

A. It's important for you to be financially protected in case anyone you hire—baby-sitter, handyman, houseworker—is injured in your home. Outside contractors should have their own insurance; check to be sure. Regular workers need to be covered by you, but the type of protection you need depends on where you live. In some states your homeowners policy will provide coverage; in others you need a separate compensation policy. Ask your insurance agent.

Additional Insurance You Might Want

The homeowners policy, even in its broadest form, has certain limits. It covers personal property only up to designated amounts. It does not cover damage from flood or earthquake at all. It may not be available in high-crime areas. Special policies fill the bill in these circumstances.

Personal Articles Coverage

The homeowners policy has a strict dollar limit on coverage of valuables. Jewelry, for instance, might be covered only up to $1,000, silver flatware to $2,500. If you own valuable items such as furs or jewelry or camera equipment, you may want a personal articles floater.

Issued either separately or as an endorsement to your homeowners policy, a floater covers listed items, to the designated amounts, wherever they are located when a loss occurs. If a diamond falls out of your engagement ring on your way to the movies, your homeowners policy will not provide reimbursement; a personal articles floater will. If a camera is destroyed by water when an overeager amateur photographer aims at the surf, your homeowners policy will not provide reimbursement; a personal articles floater will.

Most personal articles floaters contain a provision for automatic coverage of newly acquired property (within already listed categories) for thirty days. If you forget to notify your insurance agent before leaving for your vacation about a newly purchased camera, and it's lost or stolen or hit by a wave, you will be covered—*if* you notify your agent of the loss right away.

The personal articles floater also contains a "pair and set" clause, under which coverage on certain items is limited to the difference between the actual value of the intact pair or set and the actual cash value of what's left after a loss. If, for instance, you own a set of five irreplaceable commemorative medals, each of which is worth $500 but which together are worth $5,000, the loss of one would make the insurance company liable for $3,000. That's the difference between the value of the entire set ($5,000) and the value of the remaining medals ($500 × 4, or $2,000). The same principle applies to a pair of earrings; you may not be able to wear a single earring, but you haven't lost full value with the loss of just one.

THE COST OF COVERAGE

Premiums are based on value but vary according to the items listed and where you live. Insurance on silver flatware, for instance, generally costs about 20¢ per $100 of value. Jewelry coverage runs about $2 per $100 of value, in most parts of the country, but costs considerably more in high-risk urban areas. Insurance companies set their own rates, and it may pay to shop around.

Your insurance company will probably want an appraisal to back up your opinion of the value of the listed items (on newly purchased items, the bill of sale should be sufficient). And you'll probably want to update that appraisal regularly, especially with regard to jewelry, in an era when gold and silver prices fluctuate with the daily papers.

Pick your appraiser carefully (membership in the American Society of Appraisers is a good sign) and stay away from those who charge a percentage of the appraised value. Such a fee—instead of the preferable flat fee or hourly rate—is a temptation to the appraiser to inflate the value. You'll then wind up paying more than necessary, both for the appraisal itself and for your insurance.

Q. I increased the insurance on my gold jewelry when gold went to over $800 an ounce. Then the price fell and it's been up and down ever since. Should I reduce my insurance when the price goes down? If my jewelry were stolen, would I collect the amount it's insured for even if it's worth less?

A. You will never make a profit on your insurance, because you can collect only the actual value of the jewelry in case of a loss (up to the amount of the coverage). The insurance company would, if possible, replace the missing item through its own wholesale sources. If replacement weren't possible, it would pay you the market value, as long as it wasn't more (it might be less) than the face amount of the policy. Don't worry too much about the per-ounce price of gold, but do keep an up-to-date appraisal on file with your insurance agent or company.

Safe Deposit Coverage

If you keep your valuable jewelry in a safe deposit box, you probably won't need full-time insurance coverage. But if you don't insure it, what happens when you take it out to wear? Few, if any, companies still write insurance combining inexpensive long-term in-vault coverage with short-term out-of-vault coverage for occasional wear. Ask your agent about this coverage, but if you wear valuable jewelry often, you'll probably want a personal articles floater.

Although a safe deposit box is the safest place for your valuables, thefts do occasionally take place. The contents of your box are not usually insured by the bank. Your homeowners policy, as noted earlier, limits coverage of jewelry and of securities, so you may want to check into safe deposit coverage. Or leave your securities with your stock-broker and take out a personal articles floater on your jewelry.

Flood Insurance

Q. Recent hurricane warnings off the coast have made me worry about our low-lying home. If a hurricane were to come through here, would we be covered for damage under our homeowners insurance?

A. Homeowners insurance covers wind damage from a hurricane but not flood damage. The only way to secure insurance against flooding is via a special federal program, if your community qualifies. If you're eligible (you can find out by calling, toll-free, 800-638-6620), you can buy flood insurance from any insurance agent.

If hurricane-driven flood waters damage your home, and you don't have flood insurance, you may collect under your homeowners policy only if you can prove that wind damage occurred first and made it possible for the water to gain entry. If you live in an area susceptible to flooding, ask your insurance agent about the federal flood insurance program. If you build or purchase a home located in a designated flood plain, you may be required to purchase flood insurance. Otherwise, it's optional, but, very possibly, a good idea.

Coverage is provided in two phases. In the first, or emergency, phase, limited amounts of insurance are available at fixed rates. In the second, or regular, stage, which begins once a community has undertaken a comprehensive flood-management program, increased coverage is available at rates determined by amount of risk. There are deductibles on both building and contents.

New rules instituted in mid-1982 reduce the coverage on vacation homes located in flood-prone areas. If you occupy the house less than 20 percent of the year, full coverage can't be claimed. Instead, only actual cash value, which takes depreciation into account and is less than replacement cost, will be provided.

Earthquakes and Volcanic Eruptions

Earthquakes, like floods, are specifically excluded as insured risks on standard homeowners policies, even on the "all-risk" variety. But earthquake coverage may be readily obtained, wherever you live, as an endorsement to your homeowners policy. Rates will vary in accordance with state regulation and with your actual exposure to earthquakes.

Damage from volcanic eruptions has also been specifically excluded from most older homeowners policies, although some simply fail to mention the possibility. Insurers, like homeowners in the continental United States, had always thought of volcanic eruptions as rather remote . . . until Mount St. Helens caused considerable damage in the Pacific Northwest in May 1980. Much of that damage was covered under the policy wording for "explosions," but insurers are now clarifying the situation. Policies written since July 1, 1981, if they cover damage from volcanic eruptions, spell out the coverage. If your policy omits this coverage or is vaguely worded, and you live in an area where an eruption is a risk, talk to your insurance agent.

Crime Insurance

Residents of high-crime areas, such as inner cities, have often had difficulty securing theft insurance. Under the Federal Crime Insurance Program, if you have the required protective devices on your home, you may qualify for subsidized insurance against robbery or burglary. If your state is one of the twenty-six enrolled in the program (which also includes the District of Columbia, Puerto Rico, and the Virgin Islands), you may apply for coverage no matter where within the state you live. Suburban residents have taken advantage of this low-cost coverage too.

Maximum coverage is $10,000, for an annual premium (which will probably be increased) of $120. There is, presently, a deductible of $100 or 5 percent of the loss, whichever is greater. Since July, 1980, coverage of jewelry, art objects, furs, and collections is limited to a total of $500 per occurrence. That's not very much, but if you're unable to secure private insurance because you live in a high-risk area or because you've had too many claims, the federal program is a useful substitute. It may be purchased from any insurance agent or directly from Federal Crime Insurance, P.O. Box 41033, Washington, D.C. 20014

Note: The program may be reduced or phased out altogether if federal budget-cutters have their way.

FAIR Plans

If you have trouble getting property insurance at all, for any reason, ask an insurance agent or your state insurance department about a FAIR

Plan. FAIR Plans, comparable to assigned risk pools for automobile coverage, are available in twenty-six states plus the District of Columbia and Puerto Rico. They are generally limited to fire and extended coverage, although some, depending on the state, offer full homeowners insurance.

Tenants Insurance

If you rent your dwelling, you still need insurance. A lot of tenants don't seem to think so. While 93 percent of owner-occupants carry property insurance, only about 28 percent of the tenants surveyed by the Insurance Information Institute in 1984 carried fire insurance and a similar proportion insured their household contents.

Yet a landlord's policy covers only the building and any property belonging to the landlord. Your own possessions, should there be a fire (and a fire can start in someone else's apartment and spread throughout the building), will have no protection at all unless you have your own insurance. The tenant's form, HO-4, will provide reimbursement for loss of your worldly goods, from the risks itemized in HO-2. It will also provide additional living expenses should you need to seek temporary housing while your own premises are being repaired after insured damage. Costs are moderate; ask your insurance agent.

Owners of cooperative apartments may use either the renter's (HO-4) policy or the special form (HO-6) designed for owners of condominium units (see Chapter 17).

Q. I was flabbergasted at the belongings my daughter carted off to school: stereo, television, bicycle, as well as small appliances like a corn popper and hair dryer. Is all of her stuff insured under my homeowners policy?

A. Property owned by a member of your family and maintained in a temporary residence, such as a college dorm or an apartment, is generally insured up to 10 percent of the households contents coverage in your homeowners policy. Your household contents coverage is usually limited, unless you elect replacement cost coverage, to half the assigned value of your house. If you carry $60,000 in insurance on your house, with $30,000 in contents coverage, your daughter's belongings will be covered to $3,000. Check your policy, though, and watch for any exclusions; jewelry and cash are often covered to very limited amounts. And all coverage may cease if the student leaves property on campus during an extended vacation.

Cutting the Costs of Insurance

Insurance is an inexpensive way to protect an expensive investment. As overall housing costs have gone up and up, in fact, insurance costs continue to play a minor role. From 1979 to 1985, median national monthly homeowners insurance costs rose from $16 to $22; as a percentage of monthly costs, however, homeowners insurance hovers at just under 3 percent. Table 4 shows how proportionate housing costs have changed over the last few years.

TABLE 4: A breakdown of monthly housing costs.

Item	1985	1983	1981	1979
Mortgage (principal and interest)	$573	$524	$624	$401
Real estate taxes	75	65	72	58
Utilities	100	100	100	75
HO insurance	22	20	20	16
TOTAL	$770	$709	$816	$550

(Source: United States League of Savings Institutions)

Clearly it would be the ultimate foolishness to cut corners on property insurance. Without adequate insurance, you stand the chance of losing the biggest investment of a lifetime. A few dollars a month can make all the difference.

But this does not mean that you want to waste money on insurance either. There are legitimate ways to keep costs down while having proper coverage.

Premium Considerations

Homeowners insurance premiums are based on several factors:

- The rates approved in your state. There's not much you can do about this.

- The loss experience of your particular company; you can shop around for a company with lower premiums. Bear in mind, however, that you want a company that provides good service as well as a company with low premiums; ask friends for recommendations based on personal experience. But premiums for the same house in the same location have been found to vary among companies by as much as 50 to 60 percent; comparisons are certainly in order.

- The construction of your house. Brick or stone houses, because they are not as vulnerable to fire, are less expensive to insure. The addition of smoke and/or fire detectors to your home, whether the house is brick or frame, will probably earn you a discount; the discount is larger if the alarm is connected to a central station.

- The type of fire department and the nearness of a water supply. You'll generally pay less for insurance if your community has a paid professional fire department; you're also better off with a hydrant in front of your house.

- The type of policy you buy and the amount of coverage you select. Here's where you have the greatest control and can save the greatest amount of money. But don't stick to bare-bones protection without evaluating all your options. You can have more extensive coverage, and save some money, if you self-insure for a portion of the risk. Deductibles are the key.

DEDUCTIBLES

Take the largest deductible you think you can manage over and above the standard $250 deductible in most homeowners policies and put your insurance dollars to work against the catastrophic situation, the situation that could impoverish you and your family. A $500 deductible, depending on the amount of insurance on your house and which company you use, might save you from 10 to 20 percent of the annual premium.

For example: The annual premium on a $100,000 frame house in a Long Island suburb of New York City, according to the Insurance Information Institute, would be $508 with the standard $250 deductible. The cost would go up by 10 percent, to $558, with a $100 deductible. It would come down by 20 percent, to $464, with a $500 deductible, and by 25 percent, to $431, with a $1,000 deductible. The savings might be used to buy additional liability protection (remember, an umbrella liability policy costs only about $100 for $1 million of protection) or a personal articles floater.

Once You Have Insurance on Your Property

It's not enough to buy insurance and put it aside. In addition to periodic updates to compensate for rising home values, you should:

- Read your policy, and understand your coverage. It isn't always easy, even though more and more policies are now written in what the insurance industry calls "plain English." But it's worthwhile to understand your policy before you're faced with filing a claim.

- Keep your coverage up to date, notifying your company or agent of changes or improvements to your home.

- Keep track of your possessions with an ongoing inventory. Itemize what you buy, when, and for how much. Write down serial numbers of appliances, photographic equipment, etc. Keep the list, along with purchase receipts and a photographic record of valuables, in a safe place away from home. In case of theft or fire, you'll need this documentation for the insurance company. Without an up-to-date inventory, in fact, you'll find it almost impossible to reconstruct the contents of your own home. Try to picture one entire room, right now, from memory, and you'll see, upon checking, how much you've probably missed.

■ Buy whatever extra coverage you need. If your inventory shows, for instance, that you have valuables that won't be covered beyond minimal amounts on your homeowners policy, take out a personal articles floater. It doesn't cost a great deal, and it's worth it for peace of mind.

■ Keep your policy, or a copy of it, in a safe place away from home. You can get a copy from your insurance company, but if you do have a fire you'll want to be able to refer to that policy in a hurry.

■ If you do have a loss, let your insurance company know without delay. If you suspect theft, report it to your local police department; that report, whether or not the police can do anything to recover your property, will help to back up an insurance claim.

■ If you have questions about property insurance, the Insurance Information Institute has a telephone hot line; a call to 800-221-4954 will provide you with answers to most questions about household or automobile insurance. If you are dissatisfied with insurance company service after you make a claim, contact your state insurance department.

HOUSEHOLD INSURANCE AT DIFFERENT LIFE STAGES

■ Property insurance needs relate to how much property you own rather than to your stage of life, but your insurance should be reviewed and changed as necessary as you move through various life stages.

■ As a young single or just-married, your primary insurance need, if you own a car, is probably for automobile insurance. Beyond this expensive possession, however, you may have other items worth protection. A tenants policy will cover your household contents. A personal articles floater can list a camera or a coin collection or an engagement ring.

■ Live-togethers should be particularly careful about insurance as they amass possessions. Some companies will cover you both on a single tenants or homeowners policy; others won't. It can be a shock if you discover, after a theft, that your stereo wasn't insured because the tenants policy was in your partner's name.

■ When you buy your first house, you'll get your first homeowners policy, insuring your home to at least 80 percent of its replacement value. The

Broad Form (HO-2) may well be recommended, with the standard 50 percent coverage on household contents, but you might want to consider more extensive coverage with a larger deductible to reduce premium costs. You may also want a floater policy, covering individually valuable items such as jewelry or furs.

- As you move to a bigger house and more possessions, you may want a Comprehensive Homeowners Form (HO-5), or its new equivalent, the HO-3 plus an all-risk contents endorsement, with 70 percent contents coverage and a larger deductible. Replacement cost coverage on contents will be more desirable. You'll still need a floater policy and you may want safe deposit coverage as well. Umbrella liability coverage may become necessary, if you haven't purchased it earlier.

- If you sell your house when you retire and move to a condominium or to a rental apartment, you will change your property insurance to the Condominium Owners Form or to the Tenants Form. You'll also want to consider reducing insurance costs by self-insuring to a greater extent. Drop the umbrella coverage, if you're no longer vulnerable to expensive lawsuits. Reduce your personal articles coverage. That fur coat you've been insuring for fifteen years may no longer be worth very much in dollars and cents even though it would cost a good bit to replace.

Taxes and Homeownership

Owners have tax advantages over renters. Why? Not because Uncle Sam loves homeowners (although it sometimes seems that way) but because the income tax structure of the United States has long favored borrowers of money. Most people borrow money, in the form of a mortgage, to buy a house or a condominium. Mortgage payments consist partly of principal and partly of interest; the portion that is interest may be deducted from your taxable income, thereby reducing the taxes due.

The deductibility of mortgage interest is probably most important, but there are other reasons why owning a home is financially more appealing, for most people, than renting:

- Property tax payments are deductible.

- The tax due on profit from the sale of a house may be deferred.

- Sellers over age 55 may sell their homes without paying any tax on sizable sums.

All these benefits hold true despite the massive changes in the 1986 tax act. Virtually all other areas of the tax code have undergone dramatic change, but the tax advantages of homeownership, with one exception, escaped unscathed. That exception: Lower tax rates, across the board, mean that Uncle Sam pays a smaller share of your homeownership costs.

Nonetheless, there are tax advantages when you buy a house, while you own it, and when you sell. Overlook any of them, and you can be out considerable sums of money.

When You Buy a House or Condominium

Right at the outset there are two major tax benefits: the tax-deductible portions of closing costs and the potential tax deductions if you've moved for job-related reasons, both available to all buyers who itemize deductions.

Closing Costs

The costs of taking title fall into three categories. Some may be deducted from your taxable income in the year you make the purchase. Some are totally nondeductible. And some may be added to the "basis," the initial cost of your house for tax purposes; this figure becomes important when you sell the property.

DEDUCTIBLE CLOSING COSTS

The closing costs you may deduct in the year you take title include real estate taxes, interest, and points.

Real estate taxes are usually divided between buyer and seller. If you take title on September 1 and the seller paid the year's property taxes on August 15, your settlement costs would normally include a proportionate share of those taxes for the period you own the house. You may deduct that share on your federal income taxes for the year. Even if you don't reimburse the seller for that amount, you are still permitted to deduct it on your return. If you don't reimburse the seller, however, you must reduce the basis of your property by the amount the seller paid on your behalf.

Interest charges on the mortgage to the date of settlement also normally appear on the closing statement and are deductible.

Points charged by a lender are deductible if they are solely for the use of money and therefore constitute interest. If the points are compensation for specific services such as an appraisal fee or document preparation, then the payment is not interest and may not be deducted. The determination depends, to some extent, on established practices in your area. As in other complex tax areas, it is always wise to consult a knowledgeable tax adviser.

NONDEDUCTIBLE ITEMS

The settlement-day checks you write that are purely out-of-pocket expenses, with no tax benefit, include homeowners insurance premiums, mortgage insurance, charges for the use of utilities, and other fees or charges for services related to the occupancy of the house.

CLOSING COSTS THAT AFFECT YOUR TAX BASIS

Just about all other closing costs may be added to your basis, the official cost of your house for tax purposes, thereby reducing the capital gains tax due when you later sell the house at a profit (see p. 308). These items include attorney's fees, abstract fees, surveys, transfer taxes, title insurance, and anything actually owed by the seller but that you agree to pay, such as recording or mortgage fees, charges for improvements or repairs, and a commission to a real estate agent.

House-Hunting and Moving Costs

Q. I accepted a new job 600 miles away, without thinking about how expensive it would be just to find a place to live and make the move. Are any of these costs tax-deductible?

A. Yes, if your move is necessitated by a job you've already secured, you may deduct the cost of house-hunting trips, of temporary living expenses, and of the move itself, up to specified limits. You don't actually have to buy a house to make a house-hunting trip deductible, but the trip's principal purpose must be to find a place to live.

If you move because you've changed the place where you work, you may deduct certain allowable expenses, but only if you itemize the deductions on your federal income tax return. You may do so even if you are a tenant rather than a homeowner. See pp. 480–81 for details.

Note: The costs of selling and buying a house or condominium may be applied to your tax advantage in one of two ways: You may deduct them as moving expenses, or you may use these costs to reduce the gain on the sale of your old home or to increase the basis on your new home. The IRS suggests that it may be preferable to deduct them as moving expenses; if you reach the allowable ceiling on moving expenses, then turn to the second choice. But do the arithmetic and see what works best for you.

While You Own a House or Condominium

The big tax advantage of homeownership is the deductible interest you pay on your mortgage loan. Another advantage lies in the deductibility of real estate taxes from federal, state, and local income taxes. The higher your marginal tax bracket, the more you save. Other tax benefits for some homeowners include casualty loss deductions and an office at home.

Property Taxes

Local taxes on real property pay for schools, for police, for fire protection and parks, and all the expenses of running local government. Some towns keep residential property taxes down by encouraging industrial and commercial development; others keep taxes down by providing minimal services; some, no matter how hard officials try, can't keep taxes down at all. Evaluate your prospective community carefully before you decide to buy, because local real estate taxes can be a major ongoing expense of home ownership.

Q. Property taxes on our house and quarter acre come to about $2,000 a year, or $500 every three months. We've always scraped the money together when each payment is due. Now the bank that holds the mortgage on our house has offered to collect money each month, along with the mortgage payments, to hold and apply to our quarterly tax payments. Is this a good deal for us?

A. If you find it difficult to make the payment each quarter, you may find it easier to pay your taxes to the bank in monthly installments. Find out, however, whether or not your bank will pay interest on money held in the property tax escrow account. If it does not, you could be better off (if you can discipline yourselves to do so) putting the money each month into an interest-earning savings account.

Note: If your monthly payment to your mortgage lender includes an amount placed in escrow for real estate taxes, you may not simply deduct the total of these amounts as your real estate taxes for the year; you must report the amount actually assessed and actually paid. Ask your lender to supply you with this figure if you don't receive it at year-end.

After you own your home, you'll probably see your property taxes rise steadily, although, if it's any consolation, the Tax Foundation indicates that (1) the rate of increase has slowed, and (2) even higher taxes take a smaller share of your income than property taxes did just a few years ago.

You may also face some specific property tax issues:

THE EFFECT OF DECLINING PROPERTY VALUES

Local real estate taxes are based on assessments of market value. Periodic assessments (the degree of frequency depends on the local community) establish market value; the tax (at so many dollars per $100 of value) is then pegged at full market value or at a specified percentage thereof.

Either way, assessments usually lag behind volatile real estate costs. The lag helped homeowners, by keeping taxes down to earlier levels, when home values were rising rapidly. In a housing recession, however, values rise less rapidly, level off, or even fall, and today's assessments may be based on yesterday's higher market value.

You may, as a result, find your property overassessed and overtaxed.

THE IMPACT OF "CREATIVE FINANCING"

Assessments are often pegged to the going prices for houses, as recorded. But the recorded price may be considerably more than is actually paid when below-market mortgage rates are arranged through innovative financing techniques. For example: A house may be sold for $75,000, with that $75,000 the recorded price on which taxes are based. But the seller is actually holding a 25-year mortgage at 12 percent, five full points below the prevailing rate at the time of the sale. The buyer's monthly payment, as a result, is $230.76 less than it would have been at 17 percent. Over the life of the loan, the buyer saves $16,050. If that actual saving is deducted from the recorded sales price, then the actual price, and the price, according to the International Association of Assessing Officers, on which a cash-equivalency assessment could be based, is $58,950.

When houses do sell in a recessionary market, they often do so only with the benefit of seller-assisted financing. With less use of creative financing, as mortgage rates have come down, there are fewer problems with assessments based on sales price. If you have a problem, however, and feel that your assessment is higher than it should be, you can appeal.

When You Want to Appeal Your Assessment

Many towns reevaluate assessed values of houses more frequently these days, in an effort to stay abreast of changing real estate values. What can you do if, for any reason, you believe that your home has been unfairly assessed?

THE STEPS IN AN APPEAL

1. Find out if your house has been accurately evaluated. It's not uncommon for homeowners to discover, when they ask, that their house has been listed as, for example, larger than it actually is. It's not uncommon to find a half bathroom listed as a full bathroom, or a brick facade translated into an all-brick house. Some busy appraisers simply don't take all the time they should.

2. Then, if the evaluation has been accurate and you still believe that your assessment is too high, you have to provide evidence to change the assessor's mind. Talk to neighbors with similar houses and find out if

their appraisals were similar; look at property tax records in your town office to see comparable houses and their assessments; review records of recent sales in the office where deeds are recorded, again looking for comparable houses and their valuations; talk to real estate agents for an estimate of current market value.

If you believe that there are specific physical conditions which should reduce your assessment, take pictures to show the assessor. A flooded basement, cracked walls indicating settling, old plumbing fixtures . . . all may prove your contention that your assessment is too high. (Financial problems, such as unemployment or overindebtedness, are not grounds for the reduction of an assessment.)

3. Then request a meeting with the assessor. Explain your case, and show your evidence. Your appraisal may be reduced right then and there. If not, and if you are not satisfied, you can appeal upward, first (depending on the community and state in which you live) to a county board and then perhaps to the state level. Your last resort is the courts.

Be sure to follow the timetable set by your town. And don't decide, without a try, that it's not worth the effort. The appeal procedure is simple. You don't need a lawyer (unless you choose to go to court). And, it's estimated, a significant proportion of this country's homeowners are paying more property tax than they should be.

Q. My husband is only 38 but he's been disabled and unable to work for over two years. My friend said we don't have to pay property taxes because of his disability. Is she right?

A. It depends on where you live. Some communities have property tax exemptions or, usually, specified reductions for senior citizens and/ or the disabled. Look on the back of your next tax bill, or call your local tax assessor for information.

Casualty and Theft Losses

If you're unlucky enough to suffer financial loss via casualty or theft, you can, at least, claim certain tax deductions.

CASUALTY LOSS

To qualify as a casualty loss, damage, destruction, or loss of either real or personal property must result from an identifiable event that is sudden, unexpected, or unusual. Some qualifying events: earthquakes, fires, hurricanes, tornadoes, floods, storms, sonic booms, vandalism, and volcanic eruptions. Structural damage from termites is not a casualty loss because it takes place over a period of time; structural damage from a flash flood, however, generally qualifies. Smog would not, as a rule, qualify. But it may, if a sudden and severe concentration of chemical fumes in the air damages the paint on your house.

Q. I had some jewelry soaking in a cleaning solution, in a glass by the kitchen sink. When my son washed the dinner dishes, he dumped the jewelry into the sink and turned on the garbage disposal. The jewelry, which was not insured, was ruined. Can I take a casualty deduction?

A. In a similar case the IRS said no, because the person dumping the glass was negligent, but the Tax Court reversed the decision and allowed a full deduction. The IRS itself gives a similar example of a qualifying deduction. A car door is accidentally slammed on your hand, breaking the setting of your diamond engagement ring (the IRS doesn't mention what happens to your hand). The diamond falls from the ring and is never found. The loss of the diamond is a deductible casualty (with the deductible amount determined by its value in relation to your adjusted gross income).

The 1982 tax law greatly restricts allowable casualty deductions. Until the passage of this law, uninsured losses exceeding $100 could be deducted in full on your federal income tax return. Now, although the $100 base remains intact, losses are deductible only to the extent that they exceed 10 percent of your adjusted gross income. If your adjusted gross income is $30,000, your loss has to exceed $3,000 before you can claim a deduction. This means that it's now more important than ever before to carry adequate insurance.

Here are the current rules for claiming a casualty loss:

■ Reduce the loss by $100 and by any insurance compensation. If you have $400 of storm damage, and your insurance company settles your claim for $300, you are left without a casualty deduction.

■ Deduct the loss in the year the casualty occurs, unless you expect reimbursement that is later refused. In this case, you may deduct the loss when your claim is rejected.

■ Prove the loss, by collecting appropriate documentation as soon as possible after the loss occurs. Pictures of the damage, or newspaper photographs and reports, are helpful.

■ The amount you may claim is based on the decrease in fair market value of the property after the loss. Bear in mind, however, that no matter how much your property may have increased in value since its purchase, you may never claim a loss greater than the original cost. Keep purchase slips, appraisals, photographs, and any evidence which will document property value.

THEFT LOSS

To qualify as a deductible theft loss, personal property must have been unlawfully taken under the laws of your state via larceny, robbery, embezzlement, extortion, or other criminal means. Accidental loss or disappearance may sometimes qualify if it results from a sudden or unusual event or if circumstances strongly indicate that theft may have occurred.

The same rules apply for theft as for casualty losses: The loss must be reduced by $100 and any insurance reimbursement; the loss must be deducted in the year it occurs; the amount you may claim may never be more than the original cost of the property; the deductible amount of the loss must exceed 10 percent of your adjusted gross income.

Proof may be even more important where theft is concerned, since the IRS does not generally allow accidental loss to qualify. Make a report to the police if you suspect a theft, even if neither you nor they can prove a theft actually took place. The police report itself will provide documentation.

Q. I gave a builder a $5,000 deposit on a new house. The foundation was dug; then the builder went bankrupt. It doesn't look as if I'll get my money back. Can I claim a theft loss on my income tax return?

A. You can't claim a theft loss unless fraud was involved, but you can claim a nonbusiness bad debt deduction. Even though your deposit was not actually a loan to the builder, you do have a legitimate claim for repayment of your money. As tax experts at Prentice-Hall point out, that creates a debtor-creditor relationship and you can take the deduction. A nonbusiness bad debt is treated as short-term capital loss and is deductible to the extent of any capital gains you may have plus $3,000 of ordinary income. Any excess can be carried forward from year to year, reducing taxes due, until it is used up.

If You Maintain an Office at Home

If you work at home, you may qualify for a home office tax deduction. But you must, according to the IRS regulations, meet stringent requirements: The part of your home that you use for business must be used exclusively as your principal place of business or as a place of business used for meeting with patients, clients, or customers. The only business which does not have to meet the exclusive use test is use of your home as a day-care facility.

This means that if you use a den in your home to prepare legal briefs for a part-time legal practice but also occasionally use it as a guest room, you may not claim a tax deduction for its business use. If you work at another location five days a week and at home on evenings and weekends, you can't claim a deduction for work you do at home for your employer (unless work at home is required by your employer), but you can claim a deduction if your home office is your principal place of business for a sideline business.

Q. In addition to my full-time work as a nursery school teacher, I've just set up a typing service in my home. If I start keeping records now, will I be able to deduct expenses for my home office?

A. Not long ago, the answer would have been no. But recently relaxed Internal Revenue Service regulations make it possible to take home office deductions for a secondary business. You must follow the same rules as if you ran a full-time business from home: You must set aside a portion of your home to be used exclusively and on a regular basis for your typing service. And you must make some money for your efforts; deductions may not exceed your income.

If you qualify, you may deduct *direct expenditures* in full; an example would be electrical wiring installed in your office. (Some direct business expenditures, such as the purchase of equipment and supplies, are deductible as business expenses whether or not you qualify for the home office deduction.) You may deduct *indirect expenses* in an amount proportionate to the percentage of your home that is used for business. That proportion may be figured as square footage or on a per-room basis. If you use one room out of ten as an office, you may deduct one-tenth of such items as real estate taxes and mortgage interest, outside painting, fuel costs, and so on. But you must make your deductions in sequence: (1) taxes and interest, up to the extent of income; (2) operating expenses allocable to the office; (3) allocable depreciation.

For example: You set up a former breakfast room, one room out of ten in your house, as an office for your typing service. Net income from the typing service in your first year is $500. You had the following expenses:

	Total	10% for business
Taxes	$1,500	$150
Interest	2,500	250
Operating expenses of home	1,500	150
Depreciation	1,000	100

According to the IRS, you figure your deductions for business use as follows:

	1. Business net income		$500
Less:	2. Taxes	$150	
and	3. Interest	+250	400
	4. Balance		$100
Less:	5. Operating expenses of home		$150
and	6. Depreciation		100
	7. Total		$250
	8. Deduction (line 4 or 7, whichever is less):		$100

Your total home office deductions in any one year may not exceed your net income from the business.

You'll have to file a Schedule C, Profit (or Loss) from Business or Profession, along with your federal income tax return. And because this area is extremely complicated, you would do well to consult a competent tax adviser. You might also want to consult IRS Publication No. 587, Business Use of Your Home, one of a lengthy series of specialized tax advice booklets published by the IRS and revised annually.

WHEN YOU SELL YOUR HOUSE

When you sell a house on which you are taking a home office deduction, your tax situation will be complicated. You have to treat the sale as if you sold two pieces of property, one a residence and the other a business. The deferral of tax applicable to the residence portion (see p. 309) will not be applicable to the business portion; you will have to pay any tax due in the year of the sale (except that, if the home office deduction is not taken in the year of the sale, no matter how many years it's been taken before, the entire profit from the sale may be rolled over into a new residence). And, just to go a step further, if your new home will contain an office, you must treat the purchase (for tax purposes) as if you were buying two pieces of property.

When You Sell a House or Condominium

★ The Landons bought their Brooklyn brownstone in 1971, when the area was just reverting to single-family occupancy, for $26,000. They've put another $30,000 or so into the house over the years, putting in new plumbing and an entirely new kitchen, stripping and refinishing walls and floors, and so on. It was a financial struggle for a long time, with rent from a basement apartment helping to defray the costs. Now, however, the neighborhood is very desirable and the house is worth $220,000.

Here's the big tax payoff, the place where Uncle Sam really demonstrates his affection for homeowners. Under normal circumstances the sale of property on which you've made a profit leads to a substantial tax liability; profits, after all, are grist for the tax man's mill. If the Landons' $56,000 investment had been an investment in the stock market, they would owe tax on the $164,000 in profit. But when the profit is made on a house, there are a number of legitimate ways to reduce the tax, postpone the tax, or avoid it altogether. First, however, you have to understand how the profit on a house is calculated.

How to Calculate the Profit When You Sell Your House

Don't just subtract the purchase price from your sales price, or you'll pay more tax than necessary. The Landons paid $26,000 for their house and sold it for $220,000, which looks like a profit of $194,000. But they also put additional money into the house. Even if you haven't performed the extensive renovations necessary on an old brownstone, you've put money into your house too.

Here's how to perform the calculations:

1. Determine the *basis* or tax cost of the house you've sold. Take your original purchase price and add to it (a) fees paid at the closing for title insurance, legal services, etc., and (b) the cost of any capital improvements (a new deck, central air conditioning) that enhanced the value of the house. Reduce the basis by any tax credits or deductions previously claimed for residential energy credits or casualty losses.

2. Determine the *adjusted sales price* of the old house by taking the sales price and subtracting broker's commissions, legal fees, and any allowable fix-up costs (such as painting the house, within ninety days of entering into a sales contract, to make the house more salable).

3. The difference between the basis and the adjusted sales price is your taxable profit.

> **Q.** After a contractor quoted almost $1,300 to insulate our basement walls, I did the job myself for under $600 in materials. I've also done a lot of other work around the house. How do I determine what to add to the tax cost of the house?
>
> **A.** Do-it-yourselfers have to resign themselves to saving money on their original work. The IRS won't recognize the value of your own labor or the market value of the job. All you can add to the basis of the house is the actual cost of materials for improvements that enhance the value of the house.

REDUCING THE TAX ON HOUSE-SALE PROFITS

If you find yourself in the position of owing taxes on the profits in your home, the rules on installment sales may prove helpful. Under the Installment Sales Revision Act of 1980 you pay tax as the money is received, and you can spread the tax payments over two or more years. As long as you receive at least one payment after the tax year in which the sale took place, the transaction qualifies as an installment sale. The size of the down payment no longer matters, as it once did. Nor do you have to report your decision to the IRS; the installment method of reporting will be assumed unless you state otherwise.

This means that you can arrange the sale of your house to suit your tax picture. If you are under 55 and if you do not plan to buy a larger house (see below), you might arrange to spread the payments for your house over a period of time. You might even sell the house this year and choose not to receive any money at all until next year. The whole flexible arrangement (spelled out in IRS Publication No. 537) allows you to minimize the tax bite on the sale of a house.

DEFERRING THE TAX ON HOUSE-SALE PROFITS

Tax on the gain from the sale of your home is postponed if you buy another house whose price is at least as much as the adjusted sales price of your former house. Here are the rules:

- Both the old house and the new must be your principal residence. A condominium, a cooperative apartment, a mobile home, or a houseboat qualifies as well as a single-family detached house. A vacation home does not.

- You must move into the new residence within two years of the sale of the old. There are no exceptions to the time test; if the house you are building burns down just before you are ready to move in, the Internal Revenue Service will not take pity on you. (Certain adjustments are possible only if you are on active duty in the armed forces.)

- Your investment in the new house must equal or exceed the selling price of your old house, the adjusted sales price defined earlier, if you are to defer tax on the entire gain. If the cost of the new house is less, you are taxed on the difference. You may count capital improvements to your new house (such as landscaping or a new roof) as part of its costs, as long as they are paid for within the two-year period.

You may defer the payment of the tax no matter how many times you buy and sell (except that, unless a move is job-related, you are limited to one deferral in a two-year period), as long as each new house is at least as expensive as the one before. You don't have to invest the cash proceeds from the sale into the new house either. The deferral takes place even with a no-down-payment mortgage. When the time comes for a smaller and less expensive house, the tax will be due . . . unless you are then over age 55.

THE OVER-55 EXCLUSION

Eventually, for most people, the time comes when you want a smaller house instead of a bigger one. This time typically comes when the children are grown and you're looking ahead to retirement. The tax code, oddly enough, recognizes this particular human need; tax on up to $125,000 of profit is eliminated altogether if either you or your spouse is over 55 on the date of sale. (However, you may still owe state tax; consult your tax adviser.) Here are the rules for the federal exemption:

- The 55th birthday must take place before the date of sale; if your birthday is in April, don't sell your house in February.

- You must have owned and lived in the house, as your principal residence (vacation cottages and rental property don't count), for at least three years out of the five years preceding the date of sale.

- You and your spouse must agree on the exclusion, even if you file separate returns and even if only one of you owns the house.

- You must never before have taken this exemption. This is a once-in-a-lifetime deal for you and your spouse. You can't use part of the $125,000 on one house and part on another. You can't use it with one spouse and then, after widowhood (or divorce) and remarriage, use it with another. If you're over 55 and planning to marry someone who's already used the exclusion, be smart: Sell your house and take your tax exclusion before you marry. Otherwise, you'll lose it forever. (*Note:* If you take a loss when you sell your house, it is not deductible.)

Q. I inherited a house which my parents had lived in for thirty-five years. I'm planning to sell and know that it will bring many thousands of dollars more than they paid for it back in the 1940s. How do I calculate the tax?

A. Any increase in value between the date of original purchase and the date of the owner's death is forgiven for tax purposes. You must calculate your tax on the basis of the increase in value between the date of death (or six months thereafter, as determined by the estate's executor) and the date on which you sell the property.

Special Situations

There are other tax ramifications of property ownership. The biggest, perhaps, is that associated with the death of a property owner. Estate planning with respect to property ownership, including the sticky question of who should own what (it's no longer always necessarily wise to own property jointly, even if you are happily married), is discussed in detail in Chapter 24. Tax questions also arise in cases of divorce and around the ownership of vacation homes.

Divorce

Do you own your family home jointly? Are you getting a divorce? Watch out for the tax consequences.

Several different things can take place. Sometimes one spouse (perhaps the husband wants to remain in the family home while the wife takes an apartment) will buy out the other's share. This is a clear-cut purchase by one and sale by the other, and the appropriate taxes are due.

In other instances, one spouse (often the wife) will take sole title to the house as part of the divorce settlement in place of alimony or of other portions of the marital property. When this is the case, until recently, the IRS treated the transaction as a sale and a purchase; a tax based on appreciated value of the property was immediately payable—even though no cash changed hands and the "seller" might not have the means to pay. Today the rules are different. There is now no gain or loss to either party when property is transferred as part of a divorce settlement. The transfer is considered a gift. Should the recipient sell the property, however, tax will then be due.

There are also state tax ramifications, but they depend on where you live. In some situations, if you and your spouse are on relatively good terms, it may be wise to split property before you split the marriage. In others it would be a big mistake. Be sure, if you are contemplating divorce, to get good legal and financial advice. It's extremely difficult to change agreements once they are made.

Vacation Homes

A second home can provide a welcome change of scenery; it may also provide a valuable tax shelter. But the shelter has been leaking a bit since the Tax Acts of 1976 and 1986 greatly tightened the tax deductions that could be taken on second homes. Here are the rules:

PERSONAL USE

If you use your second home solely for your family's personal pleasure, you may deduct interest, taxes, and casualty losses as you do on your year-round home. Personal use should be more popular since lower tax rates and restricted tax advantages curtail investment benefits.

RENTAL PROPERTY

If you own the home primarily as a profit-making venture and don't use it yourself for more than fourteen days during the year (or 10 percent of the time the house is available for rent), then you may also, in addition to these deductions, shelter some income via deductions for depreciation and maintenance. If your expenses exceed your income for the property, in other words, the loss may be used to offset some of your other income. The 1986 law phases out this benefit over a five-year period, and will end it altogether for anyone earning over $150,000.

You are allowed to visit the property to fix it up, without counting such time as part of your "personal use" time. You're even allowed, since the IRS relented a bit, to have family and friends along while you work.

BOTH PERSONAL USE AND RENTAL PROPERTY

If you use the house for more than fourteen days yourself *and* if you rent it out for more than fifteen days during the year, then matters (and the taxes you owe) get complicated. Here's what you have to do:

1. Determine the amount of expenses attributable to rental activity. To do this, multiply the number of rental days by your total expenses and divide by the total number of days the house is in use.

2. Then figure out what proportion of these rental expenses are deductible. The amount deductible is equal to the gross income from rental minus allowable rental deductions. You can't deduct more than you earn in rent.

Be careful in your calculations. Vacation home deductions are carefully scrutinized by the Internal Revenue Service.

Q. I own a cottage which I used to use as a family weekend and summer retreat. It's winterized and perfectly suitable for year-round living. We don't use it much anymore, however, and I'm thinking of renting it out on a year-round basis and taking the tax deductions that go with rental property. At the same time, my wife's parents need a place to live. Am I allowed to rent the cottage to them and still take the deductions?

A. The IRS has had a very tough policy of disallowing deductions on rental to relatives, but that policy, after a lot of protest from taxpayers, has recently been amended. Now, as long as you charge a fair market rental (the equivalent of rents charged on similar accommodations in the local marketplace), the property should qualify for all normal deductions. Keep accurate records, however, and be able to show the IRS that no special favors changed hands.

Record-Keeping

There's so much money at stake in your home, so much potential tax liability, that record-keeping is enormously important. You may never run a business from home or sustain a casualty loss. But virtually everything you spend on your home (other than normal maintenance) will have some tax impact, either now or when you sell the house.

From the day you move in, therefore, keep a file with bills and receipts for every penny you spend on anything related to the purchase itself and to improvements to the house. Document every expenditure from closing costs to new storm windows to a deck or swimming pool. That documentation may well reduce your tax liability when you sell the house.

Under most circumstances, documents to substantiate tax claims need be kept for only three years after the date of filing. But receipts for the purchase or improvement of property on which taxes may be due when the property is sold should be kept until three years after that property is sold. With a house, where the basis of your old home is used for computing the basis of a new home, thereby postponing tax on the profit from the sale of the old home, keep the relevant records indefinitely. Those records include the purchase contract, settlement papers, and receipts and canceled checks for any improvements and additions to the property.

KEY POINTS

- The income tax structure of the United States is designed to encourage the owning of property.

- The biggest tax deductions most people have are mortgage interest and property tax payments.

- Taxes may be deferred when a primary residence is sold, as long as another residence of at least equivalent value is bought.

- People over age 55 may avoid paying tax altogether on up to $125,000 of home-sale profit.

- Adequate records are essential if you want to take full advantage of home-related tax deductions.

16

Remodeling and Renovation

The Stantons felt very fortunate when they moved from an apartment to their first house in 1976. The house wasn't perfect—it was, after all, a "starter" house, with three bedrooms and one bath—but it was just right for a young couple with one small child. Today the Stantons have three children, and a growing sense of frustration over their inability to afford a larger house. They feel lucky, by comparison with friends who failed to buy a starter house at all. But they also feel trapped in a house that is too small for a growing family.

The solution, for the Stantons as for ever-increasing numbers of other Americans: Give up thoughts of moving, at least for now, and expand the house you have.

You can protect your investment in housing by keeping your home in good repair. You can also enhance your investment, as well as your comfort, by modernizing and expanding your home. You'll have lots of company. Over $39 billion was spent in 1984 on additions and alterations to existing residential property. But which improvements are most cost-effective in terms of adding to resale value? How should you finance expansion? How can you find workmen who are both competent and honest?

Improvements to a home fall into several broad categories: You can *add space,* by building outward or upward or by converting little-used areas to functional space. You can *modernize* your home and bring living areas up to date. You can *save money* by conserving energy or adding new energy sources. And you can add a wide range of *amenities,* from a greenhouse to a sauna to a swimming pool, to make your home more livable.

Whatever you do in the way of home improvement, some general rules apply:

- Don't improve your house so much that it's far above neighboring homes in value. You shouldn't expect to sell a $115,000 house, when it comes time to move, in a neighborhood of $80,000 homes. An appraiser's rule of thumb: Don't improve a house by more than 30 percent of its current value.

- Improvements should be consistent with the character of the house and of the neighborhood. A modern addition on a Colonial-style home may never blend into its surroundings. A swimming pool, in a neighborhood that has no others, may be a drawback rather than a plus.

- Keep resale value in mind, if you expect to move in a reasonably short time; otherwise design your improvements to suit your family. If you are sprucing up your home in order to make it appeal to potential buyers, then cosmetic improvements are the most cost-effective: the quick coat of paint, higher-wattage light bulbs, a new bed of flowers. If you are remodeling in order to postpone the financial ordeal of moving, however, then added value is almost beside the point; what you want is a house to live in comfortably. Don't expect a dollar-for-dollar return on any home improvement; do expect added enjoyment in living.

- Keep accurate records of home improvements, because money spent to improve a house (as contrasted to money spent on maintenance) reduces the taxable gain when the house is sold (see Chapter 15).

Cost-Effective Improvements

Although you'll improve your house to suit your family you will also, if you plan wisely, get a portion of your expenditure back when it's time to sell. Some improvements, of course, add more to resale value than others. Those that will enhance any family's way of life, logically enough, provide the most financial payoff; most people want at least three bedrooms and are willing to pay for them. Those that fit a purely personal interest have the least; a hot tub, to many people, is a liability rather than an asset.

Additional Living Space

Added space is the biggest plus on the home improvement menu. An extra bedroom or a den may be the most cost-effective improvement you can make. In some parts of the country (regional considerations always play a major role), you may actually get full value back when you sell. If your house already has four bedrooms, however, adding another may overprice the house for a contemporary market consisting mostly of smaller families. If you do need a fifth bedroom, think about placing it so that it can function as a study or a den. You may not use it that way just now (although you might look ahead to an eventually emptying nest), but the next owners may like the idea.

Be imaginative as you consider extra space. You may not need to add a wing, and you may not spend as much money, if you can convert an unused attic or little-used garage to a bedroom or study. (Watch local ordinances, however; you may have to have a garage.) If you don't have convertible space, you may save some money by making use of existing exterior walls. If your house forms a corner, for instance, would it make sense to tuck an extra room into that corner, thereby using two existing walls? Could you, perhaps, raise the roof to secure extra living space above? Talk to an experienced home improvement contractor before you make a final decision; tips on choosing one will be found on pp. 322–24.

Modernization

Kitchen and bath modernization rank high on the home improvement list for many homeowners, but there's some division of opinion here about the return on your investment.

Adding an additional bathroom is highly cost-effective, sometimes returning more than its cost. Modernizing is something else. Home improvement contractors say that modernization is a sound investment, returning about 80 percent of the cost when it comes time to resell. Real estate appraisers, on the other hand, believe that such modernizations are seldom cost-effective, unless the original room is so antiquated as to be virtually useless. The reason: While an old-fashioned kitchen or bath is viewed as a negative by potential buyers, a modern room is simply taken for granted.

Bring your house up to date if it will make it possible for you to continue living there happily. Don't do so in the expectation of getting the costs back when you move.

Personal Choice

The least cost-effective home improvements are those that may be categorized as personal interest items. Some people like hot tubs and saunas, greenhouses and tennis courts; others find them an expensive nuisance. Your family may relish a backyard swimming pool; a potential buyer, small children in tow, may look on it as dangerous and unnecessary. So put in such amenities if you will stay in the house for a while to enjoy them, but don't expect to recoup your investment.

Energy-Saving Improvements

Energy-saving improvements are cost-effective on two counts: reducing your living costs right now and attracting potential buyers when you are ready to sell. But energy-saving improvements are far more attractive when energy costs are high. And they were far more attractive when federal income tax benefits applied. For example, adding insulation still returns from 75 to 85 percent of its cost—but this yield, according to one survey, was 17 percent lower in 1985 than in 1982.

Cost-Effective Energy-Savers

You can probably reduce your annual heating bills by significant sums if you add insulation (attic insulation is both effective and easy to install) and put in storm windows and doors. Such improvements cost some money at the outset, but pay for themselves in fuel savings in a fairly short period of time.

You can also find dramatic payoffs by making simple, inexpensive adjustments to your surroundings and in the way you live. Don't spend a lot of money on energy-saving improvements until you:

—have the burner on your furnace tuned so that it operates at top efficiency,

—install a shower flow restrictor, which will cut the cost of heating hot water,

—air-dry the dishes in your dishwasher instead of consuming the fuel to dry them by machine,

—caulk and weatherstrip leaky window frames,

—install insulation around your hot water heater, and

—use an automatic thermostat to lower the heat at night and, if you're out at work, during the day as well.

Solar Energy

Some homeowners go still further and install equipment to tap alternate sources of energy, especially solar energy. Are these improvements cost-effective? It depends on what equipment you install, where you live, and the price of electricity and home heating fuel in your area.

The energy generated by the sun may be tapped in two basic ways: via active technology and via passive applications.

ACTIVE SOLAR TECHNOLOGY

When you see solar collectors on a roof, you are looking at an active solar installation. Collectors, along with pumps, pipes, and a storage tank, harness the sun's energy and convert it to household energy. Active solar installations designed to heat water (the most practical current application in most of the United States) currently sell, installed, for an average of just over $3,000 for a four-person household.

Active solar is at its most efficient when it saves 50 percent to 70 percent of what you would otherwise spend on heating hot water for domestic use. Depending on where you live and the climate in your area, 25 percent of your annual heating bill may go for heating hot water. If you currently spend $1,200 a year on fuel oil or natural gas for heat (don't count fuel used for cooking or drying clothes), $300 (25 percent of $1,200) might go toward heating hot water. If you can save 50 percent of that, your apparent saving is $150. At $150 a year, it would take twenty years to recover an installation cost of $3,000. This is the "payback period," the period of time in which an expenditure pays for itself.

Before you install active solar technology, evaluate how much sunlight you receive; in some areas of the United States payback periods are relatively quick while in others active solar is simply not cost-effective. Look at all the factors involved: the initial direct cost, the "opportunity cost" of the money you'll spend (the loss to you of interest on that money if it were invested), and the cost of any additional insurance that may be required. Evaluate the total cost against the cost of fuel, how much energy you'll save, and your income tax bracket. In general, active solar installations are more likely to pay for themselves when the price of fuel is escalating faster than the general rate of inflation.

PASSIVE SOLAR APPLICATIONS

Passive solar involves the deliberate use of construction elements to make direct use of the sun's energy. It is most effective when built in during the original design and construction of a house. For example, a house can be placed on its site so that large window areas on the south-facing wall take advantage of the winter sun. Masonry and concrete can be used in walls and floors to act as heat storage systems.

Passive systems, because they are less expensive to install, may be more cost-effective in most parts of the country (in solar energy, even more than in other home improvements, regional considerations are important). But the same economic considerations apply to passive solar design as to active solar installations; you should look at all the factors before you decide on any home improvement. Remember, though, that the resale value of any solar-equipped house may be higher. For example: In Starkville, Mississippi, where a builder put up a group of passive solar homes, the resale price of these homes, to date, has been at least 5 percent more than the price on nearby homes of comparable size . . . solely because the sellers have utility bills to prove that it really costs less to heat and cool these homes.

SOLAR ENERGY NOTES

- Don't expect solar energy, either active or passive, to provide all your heat and hot water. No matter where you live in the United States, you will need a conventional backup system.

- Federal energy tax credits have ended, but many states offer some energy-related tax credits. Provisions vary a great deal from state to state, and you should check with your accountant or with your state's tax or energy office for details.

- Local tax assessors have traditionally increased property taxes to reflect the value of any home improvements, including fuel-conserving measures. As we become more energy-conscious, however, changes are being made and exemptions are being granted. To avoid unpleasant surprises after the fact, find out your community's policy before you begin.

- Be sure to choose a contractor experienced in this new technology, or you may make an expensive mistake.

- If you add an active solar energy system, check with your insurance agent to be sure that your homeowners insurance provides adequate coverage.

How to Finance Home Improvements

Improving your home may add to its value in the long run, but it does call for an initial outlay of funds. Credit, including installment loans, is discussed in full in Chapters 9 and 10, but specific sources of home improvement funds will be detailed here.

Before you embark on any home improvement project, find out what it will cost. Get several bids, and understand your financial commitment. Then, if you need to borrow money, you'll be able to be specific with the lending institution. You may be able to borrow as much as $8,000 to $10,000, depending on your credit rating and the policy of the lender, on an unsecured basis. A larger loan, however, may have to be secured by the equity in your home.

Variable-rate home improvement loans are also now available. If you think interest rates might come down over the life of the loan, you might want to consider a variable-rate loan. If rates go up, however, you could wind up owing more than you bargained for.

Q. Five years ago we paid off the mortgage on our small but comfortable home. Four years ago we replaced the roof, installed metal siding, painted, and put in new windows. The cost: $6,000, obtained through a bank loan. Now, looking at retirement two years ahead, we'd like to add a spacious master bedroom and bath. We think it will greatly increase the value of the house. But how should we meet the cost? Through a bank loan for the entire amount? Through borrowing against insurance policies? Or should we use cash savings in our money market fund to pay for as much as possible, then borrow for the rest?

A. Carefully evaluate the relative cost of each method of financing and then make your decision. If you take cash from your money market fund, you have to calculate the value of lost interest. If, on the other hand, you take a bank loan or a life insurance loan, you'll have to pay interest. A home equity loan, a revolving line of credit based on the accrued equity in your home, might be the best bet. You can take such a loan, establishing a line of credit up to the original purchase price of your home plus the cost of any home improvements, and the interest on the loan will be fully tax-deductible. Moreover, because it's actually a line of credit, you can draw on such a loan as needed, for home improvements or any other purpose.

Unsecured Loans

Before you use your house to raise money for home improvements (or for anything else), consider other sources of funds. Unsecured loans may be obtained from banks, thrift institutions, and credit unions (although when interest rates are high and money is tight, unsecured loans may not be easily available anywhere).

Credit unions, traditionally one of the least expensive sources of funds, are now authorized to charge up to 21 percent in interest. That's a ceiling, however, and in December 1984 the average interest rate hovered around 14.6 percent. Federal credit unions must adhere to national standards; state-chartered credit unions follow state rules. And individual credit unions set their own policies with respect to length of loan, amount of loan, and interest rate.

Banks, where the average 1983 home improvement loan was for $6,995, were by late 1985 charging about 16 percent on unsecured loans. Rates have come down since then, however, and some banks always do better for full-service customers.

FHA-insured home improvement loans, also available from banks and thrifts, are limited to $8,750 for unsecured loans and to $17,500 for loans secured by a deed of trust. FHA loans tend to be a little less expensive than conventional loans, but (as seems to be standard when government is involved) paperwork makes them somewhat slow to obtain.

Secured Loans

If you're willing to put up your house as collateral, a loan will be much easier to obtain. It may even, in view of the risk, be too easy. Even banks, traditionally conservative financial institutions, joined finance companies in the early 1980s in urging consumers to tap the equity in their homes for home improvements, college educations, vacation travel, virtually any reason at all. Think long and hard before you do. If you can't make the payments, for any reason, you stand to lose not only the amount of the loan but your entire investment in your home. If the inflationary spiral continues to level off, moreover, you may not have as much equity as you think you do.

If you do want a secured loan, here are the types to consider:

Refinancing your first mortgage, when interest rates are high, may be the most costly way to finance a home improvement. If you need $15,000, you may be borrowing $50,000 and at interest rates that may be considerably higher than your original mortgage loan. You'll be paying for many years. You'll also have closing costs to pay.

When interest rates are low, however, refinancing a first mortgage may be a smart move. In early 1986, as home mortgage interest rates dropped to their lowest point in years, homeowners flocked to lending institutions for refinancing. As a rule of thumb, an interest rate at least 2 points below your original rate makes refinancing worth considering. You can reduce your monthly costs, while raising money for home improvements. Just be sure to consider all the related costs (points, etc.) before you make your decision.

Taking a second mortgage, once frowned upon, has become increasingly popular as the rapid rise in home values has begun to represent collateral that can easily be tapped. Banks will usually lend 75 to 80 percent of the appraised value of a house minus the amount outstanding on the first mortgage, for a term of five to ten years. Interest rates are generally a point or two above the rate on first mortgages. Finance companies, with similar terms, generally charge still more. Note that several states do not permit second mortgages, or permit them only under certain stringent conditions.

An equity access loan, providing revolving credit based on the equity in your home, is another option. These loans, available from banks, thrifts, and stockbrokers in most states, resemble second mortgages in that they provide access to 70 to 80 percent of the appraised value of your house less any amount outstanding on a first mortgage. They differ from second mortgages, however, in several important ways (with variation from institution to institution): Once the line of credit is established, you often secure funds as needed by writing checks on a special account. You pay interest only on the amounts actually borrowed. You may have the option of making interest-only payments for a specified period. And, in many cases, the loan may be extended at its maturity without reapplication and without additional closing costs.

About one-third of the equity access loans being written in early 1986 were variable-rate, with interest rates adjusted monthly or quarterly. If you take a loan with a variable rate, look for some limit or cap on how much the rate may be raised.

A pilot Home Improvement Loan program by the Federal Home Loan Mortgage Corporation (Freddie Mac), while not dealing directly with consumers, is making home improvement loans more widely available. By purchasing home improvement loans from participating lenders, Freddie Mac frees additional funds for additional loans. The program has specific limits on amount and duration for condominiums and for single-family homes.

Choosing a Contractor

Whatever home improvement you contemplate, you have a basic choice: do it yourself or hire a contractor. You can save money by doing many things yourself, if you know what you're doing. For most major jobs, however, most homeowners are better off hiring professional help.

But make sure that the help you hire is both competent and honest. Only 7 percent of home improvement contractors are dishonest, says the Federal Trade Commission, but those 7 percent do a lot of harm.

Q. My brother had central air conditioning installed in his house. It never did work properly, so he told the contractor he would stop paying until repairs were made. The next thing he knew, he received a foreclosure notice on his house. He had to pay the contractor or he would have lost his house, even though the contractor never did make the repairs. How could something like this happen?

A. Your brother must have signed a contract which included a "lien-sale" provision. This clause allows a contractor to foreclose on a house if the customer fails to pay his bills. It is being used increasingly by dishonest contractors who do shoddy work. The Consumer Federation of America, in a detailed report on home improvement frauds, points to lien-sale contracts as a major problem. When they lead to foreclosure, as they can, the consumer stands to lose the entire investment in his house. Once foreclosed, the house is sold to repay the debt. In theory, at least, the homeowner should receive the difference between the debt and the selling price of the house. But some swindlers go a step further: In the "private sales" permitted by many states, the house is sold, at a very low price, to the creditor or to a friend of the creditor. The loan is paid off, the consumer gets nothing, and the swindler sells the home for a huge profit. California state law (much of this fraud has taken place in California) now protects the consumer from having a lien placed on a home by a contractor; it does not offer the same protection to loans placed with financial institutions. The result: Some contractors are now marching homeowners to financial institutions for direct loans.

Your brother had little choice once he signed this contract; he had to pay the contractor or lose his house. The best defense against this kind of practice is to be an alert consumer and not sign such contracts in the first place.

Comparison-Shop for Price

Ask several contractors to submit bids for the specific job you want done. But don't jump at the lowest bid; it may omit essential work or be based on less than the best in materials. If four contractors submit bids ranging from $8,500 to $9,500 to remodel your kitchen, and a fifth quotes $6,200, you should probably stay away from the fifth. You'll get what you pay for. Reputable bids should be reasonably close, so you may want to drop the lowest and highest you receive, if they are far apart from the others, and concentrate on selecting one from the middle range.

Buying home improvements is not like buying a car. You can't pick out the model you want with the options you want, and price it at a number of dealers. Each remodeling contractor has a different way of arriving at the price. You may have to probe to find out just how each bid has been figured. In an example supplied by Peter Johnson, former president of the National Remodelers Association, a homeowner secured three bids for insulation. One was $1,700, the second was $1,550, and the third was $1,200. He eliminated the lowest bidder, because he suspected that the bid was too low to assure good quality. Then he had to decide between the other two contractors. After further investigation, the homeowner discovered that the highest bidder had specified six inches of insulation, while the other bidder had specified four. It turned out, in this instance, that the best value was found in the highest bidder. Sometimes, however, estimates are simply miscalculated. And occasionally a good but busy contractor will deliberately overestimate a job to discourage a homeowner from adding to his workload.

Comparison-Shop for Quality

Price is far from the only factor to consider. Before you select a contractor, find out:

- Does he have an office in your community? (Stay away from itinerant workmen operating out of the glove compartment of a car; stay away from traveling salesmen offering "bargains" . . . they'll travel and you'll be left with the "bargain.")
- Will he give you the names of satisfied customers? (Talk to them and be sure he did the work both satisfactorily and on time.)
- Who are his banks and suppliers? (Talk to them, and to the Better Business Bureau as well, about the contractor's reputation.)

- Is the contractor a member of a trade association or professional group? of local civic or fraternal organizations? (You want someone who has roots in the community, and a reputation to protect.)

- Does he carry adequate insurance, both workmen's compensation and property damage/liability? (If he does not, and there is an accident, you can be financially liable.)

- Is the contract specific, spelling out the work to be done, the materials to be used (by brand name), and the date for completion? (Verbal promises are worth the paper they're written on.)

- Does he give you a precise cost for the job? And is that cost reasonable? (It should be within 10 percent of most bids submitted, and include the materials you specify.)

- Will the contractor secure all the necessary permits? (A major renovation usually requires several permits; your contractor should know what's required in your town and should do the paperwork.)

- Does he take part in a warranty or arbitration program? Many good contractors do not, but if your contractor does, you have an added assurance of quality. Home Owners Warranty has a five-year warranty-plus-insurance program for remodeling contractors; the Better Business Bureau, in conjunction with the National Association of the Remodeling Industry, has an arbitration program to resolve disputes.

Q. A contractor has bid $14,500 to add a family room and bath to our house. We think the bid is reasonable and are prepared to go ahead. But he wants half the money—$7,250—before he starts work. He says he needs it to buy materials, but we're uneasy. Should we give him the money?

A. No. If he's an established contractor, suppliers will deal with him on credit. A payment schedule should be spelled out in your contract, with payments geared to the amount of work completed. A deposit may be made in advance, but it should be no more than one-quarter to one-third of the total cost. If you pay a great deal up front, you are extending an invitation to the contractor to take the money and run. At best, he won't have any incentive to move ahead with the job with dispatch. Either stick with the contract or refuse to deal with this contractor at all.

After You Sign a Contract

Once you've picked your reputable contractor and signed a contract, there are additional things you should know:

- The contractor may offer to secure financing for you. Compare the terms of this loan with the terms of loans from other sources before you agree;

the convenience of the contractor's loan may be a trade-off for additional cost. Be sure, if you take the contractor's loan, that you receive all the written information required by law: notice of your right to rescind (see next item), and information about the terms of the transaction—the annual percentage rate, the finance charge, the amount financed, the total number of payments, and the payment schedule. Note that if the contractor arranges the loan, with your approval, the money will probably be paid directly to him. This may deprive you of the leverage you need if the job is not done as promised.

- If you do sign a contractor's contract which includes financing and uses your home as collateral for the loan, federal law gives you three business days in which to change your mind. If you decide the next morning that you didn't check the contractor's references sufficiently or you realize a day later that you can get a better interest rate elsewhere, you may cancel the contract and get your money back. During those three days the contractor should not start work or deliver any materials. A law which took effect in April 1981 makes it easier for you to give up this right of cancellation (technically known as the "right of recission"). Don't do so, unless you have a genuine emergency—such as a damaged roof which needs immediate repair—and unless you have satisfied yourself that the contractor is reputable.

- If work is to be sublet, the contractor should post a bond assuring that he will pay his subcontractors. If he does not do so, you may pay him but he may not pay his subcontractors. They could then put a lien on your home to collect.

- To protect yourself further, match your payments to the progress on the job. *Never* make a final payment or sign a certificate of completion unless and until the work is entirely completed according to the terms of the contract.

KEY POINTS

- Additional living space is the most cost-effective home improvement, returning almost dollar for dollar of your investment.
- Personal-choice additions, such as swimming pools or greenhouses, are the least cost-effective.
- Energy-saving improvements will continue to be important throughout the 1980s.
- Get bids from several reputable contractors and compare financing terms carefully before you sign any home improvement contract.

Condominiums, Cooperatives, and Mobile Homes

Housing choices go well beyond the issue of whether to rent or to buy. Once you decide to buy, you may want to consider a condominium unit, a cooperative apartment, or a form of manufactured housing. There are fundamental differences among these housing forms, both in financial and in physical terms.

The Condominium

A condominium is actually a form of ownership, not a type of housing. Condominium ownership is found in high-rise apartment buildings, in attached townhouses and garden apartments, in vacation lodges, and in all forms of housing in retirement or "adult" communities.

If you buy a condominium, you will individually own and maintain the enclosed space you occupy. You will also share ownership, along with your neighbors, of the "common elements" of the property—the exterior of the building or buildings, hallways and utilities, landscaping and recreational facilities.

In many ways, owning a condominium is like owning a conventional single-family detached house: You secure your own mortgage and pay your own taxes (taking the appropriate tax deductions), you have a deed to your property, you may remodel and decorate its interior as you please, and you may sell it when you choose to move. In another way, owning a condominium is more like renting an apartment: You'll be in close proximity to neighbors; you will have to abide by community association rules about exterior decoration, use of the grounds, and so on; you won't have to care for those grounds yourself. Shoveling snow and mowing lawns will be the responsibility of the condominium owners association. You will have to pay a monthly maintenance fee toward the upkeep of the common elements, and you may also face periodic special assessments. If the roof or furnace needs replacing, you, as one of the owners, must share in the bill. (And if your neighbors fail to pay their assessments, you may have to pay their share as well. You will not, however, be responsible for their mortgages if they default.)

The Wide Appeal of Condominiums

★ Jean holds a responsible job and works long hours. She wants to build equity instead of continuing to pay rent but does not, as a single woman with little leisure time, want to cope with home maintenance and repair. Her solution: a townhouse condominium.

★ The Stulls have had many years of home ownership, upkeep, and repair. Now, as they near retirement, they want their own space (with room for grandchildren to visit) but they also want to be free to pick up and travel without worries about leaving property untended. Their solution: a garden apartment condominium.

★ Marylou and Paul have their hearts set on a single-family detached house with a fenced play yard for the family they've just begun. But housing prices and mortgage interest rates are beyond even Paul's solid income as a corporate comptroller. Their solution, as a "starter" house: a detached condominium unit in a development.

Condominium purchases peaked in 1981, when they accounted for 21.5 percent of home purchases. After dropping to 10.9 percent of the market in 1983, they are now beginning to be a popular option once again. On the West Coast, where housing prices are highest, nearly 20 percent of all 1985 purchases were condominiums.

The typical condominium purchaser is older than buyers of other types of homes, has a higher income and greater net worth, and has a smaller household. Just about half of all the condominium purchasers in 1985 were unmarried, either singles or live-togethers. But many buyers, like the Stulls, are older adults looking for a simpler life-style. And many, more and more in fact, are young couples who would rather be buying a conventional house but can't afford to do so. (See Table 1.)

Price Factors in a Condominium Purchase

Condominiums, in general, cost less than individually owned houses. (They also, very often, contain less living space.) The 1984 median price of single-family detached homes was $72,962 (newly built houses alone had a median price of $79,900), while the median price of condominium units was $61,698. Apartment condominiums, however, are often far less

TABLE 1: A profile of buyers of condominiums, 1981 and 1983.

	1981	1983
CHARACTERISTICS OF BUYERS		
Median age	37 yrs.	42 yrs.
Unmarried	50.7%	48.7%
One- and two-person households	76.1%	71.1%
First-time buyers	16.1%	32%
Median income	$44,210	$83,848
Importance of second income*	49.4%	50.1%
TYPES OF HOUSING		
New homes	29.2%	25.5%
Homes 25 or more years old	10.9%	4.1%
Median size of home (sq. ft.)	1,071	1,154
COSTS		
Median purchase price	$66,875	$69,565
Median downpayment	$13,600	$12,000
Median total monthly housing expense	$819	$823
Mortgage payment	$616	$567
Real estate taxes	$ 68	$ 66
Utilities	$ 60	$ 95
Hazard insurance	$ 20	$ 20
Homeowners association dues	$ 55	$ 75
Housing expense exceeding 25% of household income	38.6%	43.1%

* Percentage of households with two adults in which income contributed by a second earner accounted for 10% or more of total household income.

(Source: United States League of Savings Institutions)

expensive; these units, frequently the result of apartment conversions, play an important role as starter homes.

Mortgages on condominiums are exactly like mortgages on conventional housing, and median monthly housing expense for condominium owners is almost exactly the same as for house owners. Many of the costs are lower, according to one U.S. League survey, but mandatory monthly assessments make the total just about the same: a median of $819 for the condo owner and $820 for the owner of an ordinary house. Recent increases in utility costs, maintenance and repair costs, taxes, insurance, and overall operating expenses have forced assessments up. Median monthly assessments for high-rise condominium unit owners, according to the Institute of Real Estate Management, are about $170.

THE CONDOMINIUM ASSESSMENT

As a condominium owner, you face two distinct sets of costs: assessments for upkeep, and maintenance of your own unit. As an owner, you are responsible for a proportionate share of operating and maintenance expenses on the common elements, including . . .

- Utilities
- Heating and air conditioning
- Management costs
- Garbage removal
- Janitorial service
- Grounds maintenance
- Security services
- Maintenance of recreational facilities
- Reserves for future expenses

Find out, before you buy, exactly what your assessment will cover. Is there a security patrol? Are new recreational facilities in the works?

The most important thing to know: *Your assessment must be paid.* It is not voluntary. If you don't want a swimming pool and don't use it but your monthly assessment includes swimming pool maintenance, you must pay your share.

Q. My husband has been out of work for some time, following an accident. My own salary isn't enough to pay all our bills. What will happen if I pay the mortgage but put off paying the monthly assessment on our condominium?

A. You run the risk, in many states, of losing your unit through foreclosure by the condominium association. If your assessment is what the courts would define as reasonable (your association hasn't decided to put in an Olympic-size swimming pool), you are obligated to pay or you'll put an unfair burden on the other owners who will have to pick up your share. Talk to your association's board of directors, and work out an arrangement to pay your assessment over a period of time.

In addition to the assessment, you will be responsible for the costs of maintaining your own unit. This includes your mortgage payments and real estate taxes, remodeling and decorating, interior repairs and maintenance, and homeowners insurance.

Insurance on Your Condominium

The owners association should carry insurance on the common elements, the structure itself and the areas you share with your neighbors. Be sure that your association does carry fire, theft, worker's compensation, and liability insurance. Be sure, too, that you secure your own insurance to fill in any gaps.

You'll probably want HO-6, the Condominium Owners Form of homeowners insurance, to cover your own unit, including any additions or alterations not covered by the association's policy. When you own a condominium, even one that looks like an apartment, you are not simply renting an apartment. You may own, and need to protect, depending on the bylaws of your particular condominium, all the space in your unit within the outer walls of your building. That could include interior walls and fixtures such as kitchen cabinets in addition to your household goods.

You also need adequate liability insurance, including a clause that will protect you if the association itself is sued for more insurance than it carries. If this should happen—if someone is seriously injured, for instance, in a diving accident in the community-owned pool—each unit owner could be assessed to cover the amount of damages above and beyond the association's insurance. A loss assessment provision, now a standard part of most HO-6 policies, will protect you against such potentially costly loss. It will also protect you against loss from physical damage to the common property, above and beyond the association's coverage. An example might be the bursting of a hot water heating system or extensive roof damage from ice. Ask to see the association's policy, then arrange for your own coverage to pick up where it leaves off.

Note: If this provision is not part of your policy, ask your insurance agent about adding a loss assessment endorsement.

Before You Buy

The condominium form of ownership, although it dates back to ancient Rome, is relatively new in the United States. It frequently, as a result, falls between the cracks of state statutes, leaving consumers unprotected. Quick-profit developers in some parts of the country have left some buyers with badly built and ill-managed housing. Some have simply never finished promised recreational facilities. Some ran out of money and never finished building at all. Some have raised maintenance fees sharply as soon as all the units were sold. And some have taken far too long to turn management over to unit owners.

A model state consumer protection law, the Uniform Condominium Act of 1978, has been adopted in several states and is under consideration in others. It will provide that builders must make full disclosure of projected assessments and possible future expenses, and of just what (such as pictured swimming pools or golf courses) will be completed at the builder's expense and what will not.

With or without consumer protection laws, however, it's up to you to protect yourself. Remember that a condominium purchase is a home purchase. It may be even more complex in its legal aspects than the purchase of a conventional house. Take at least the same time and care in buying a condominium unit that you would in buying any house.

READ ALL THE DOCUMENTS

Read the master deed or declaration (the "constitution" for the condominium community, requiring unanimous vote for change), the bylaws (the operating rules and regulations), and the sales contract. Together these documents will probably amount to hundreds of pages of fine print, but this fine print will, if you buy, govern the way you live. Hire a lawyer, experienced in the specialized field of condominium law, to review the documents before you sign anything.

A careful reading of these documents will provide the answers to a number of important questions. Just what, for instance, will you actually own? A balcony may be part of the individual unit or it may be a common element; if it's a common element you may not be able to fix it up as you choose. Parking spaces may be individually owned, or they may be common elements, in which any owner may park in any spot. The land and recreational facilities may be owned as a common element or leased to the owners association by the developer at a cost which may become increasingly prohibitive. Find out before you buy.

Familiarize yourself with the association bylaws. They may restrict your right to have visitors or to keep pets, to put up a fence or to paint your front door in a color of your choice. They may restrict your right to rent your unit to someone else, or they may simply require that any tenant abide by the rules and regulations. The homeowners association may amend these bylaws by majority vote, but don't count on amendment in a direction of your choice; you will have to abide by the regulations in force when you make your purchase and those enacted after your move in, by majority vote of all the owners.

SCRUTINIZE THE OPERATING BUDGET

The Warners calculated their budget to the last penny before they signed an agreement to buy their high-rise condominium unit. Within the first year, however, their careful calculations—and their budget—were obsolete. A structural engineer found that stonework on the building's facade was cracked, posing a danger to pedestrians below. Repair work was urgent, and repair bills, which had to be apportioned among the unit owners because the association lacked an adequate reserve fund, were high.

It's very important to analyze the operating budget and see if it's realistic. Look at both operating costs and reserves. Maintenance costs on a new project are sometimes "lowballed," deliberately underestimated by a developer eager to attract buyers; they may then rise sharply when the development is fully sold. Reserve funds on an existing project may also be low, in part because the association board tries to keep assessments low and in part because it simply fails to realize that every building needs repairs after a certain number of years. Either way, if the reserve fund is inadequate, special assessments will almost certainly become necessary later on.

Median annual reserves, according to the Institute of Real Estate Management, run close to 15 percent of total operating expenses. An older building should probably have a higher reserve.

You'll find it easier to analyze the operating budget if you look at a comparable document and compare assessment rates.

FIND OUT HOW THE HOMEOWNERS ASSOCIATION FUNCTIONS

What are your rights and responsibilities as a voting member of the association? A very large association may hire a full-time resident manager. Medium-sized developments may contract with an outside management firm for specific services. Small condominiums may rely to a larger extent on the volunteer labor of residents, with rotating teams of snow shovelers, sidewalk sweepers, and trash emptiers.

The kind of services you receive, and the amount of your assessment, will depend on the kind of management; the management, in turn, depends on the association. You can participate in the association in a number of ways: by voting for the board of directors and on community issues, by serving on a committee, by running for office yourself. But you should plan to participate, on some level, because the association will be your local government, maintaining and protecting the way of life you have chosen by moving into a condominium.

Q. We own a condominium unit in a development with eighty owners. Last year, after a fire destroyed the roof of our clubhouse, we were each assessed sizable sums to cover the cost of a new roof over and above the amount of insurance the association received. Shouldn't the insurance have covered the entire cost?

A. Standard policies cover only depreciated value. Suggest to your board that it purchase a replacement-cost policy, which will cover repair or replacement at current prices, and save on costs by taking a sizable deductible.

Condos: New, Old, or Conversion?

When you buy a condominium unit, you may purchase a new unit in a new development. You may purchase a resale unit. Or you may buy into a building being converted to condominium ownership. All of the above guidelines apply in each case. But there are also special conditions:

THE NEW CONDOMINIUM UNIT

Before buying a new condominium unit, try to evaluate the quality of construction. If the unit is in a multi-unit building, and the building is already occupied, talk to residents; ask, particularly, about noise transmission between units. Or visit a development built earlier by the same company and talk to residents there. Consult the local Association of Home Builders, the Better Business Bureau, and consumer protection agencies to determine if there have been complaints.

Look closely at management. Is the developer, in a new condominium, acting as manager? Has he hired a management firm? When control is transferred to the owners association, will the association be free to make its own arrangements? Or will it be locked into a "sweetheart" agreement made by the developer? When, exactly, will unit owners take control?

THE PREVIOUSLY OWNED UNIT

If you buy a condominium unit as a resale, be sure to get all the documents that the original owner received at the time of purchase; ask for them if they are not offered. Consult the association to be sure that all outstanding assessments have been paid. And find out if the previous owner has made any unapproved changes; if so, you may find yourself paying to remove the glass enclosure on the balcony or to repaint the front door. Ask hard questions about the financial condition of the association. Are there any special assessments pending? Any upcoming repairs or improvements which will add to your costs?

Find out, too, whether the owners association has the right of first refusal when you want to sell. Although this is no longer permitted under federal regulations, some condominiums, especially those built in the mid-1960s and early 1970s, restrict sales by including this right (common to cooperatives) in the bylaws; the association can then buy a vacant unit itself or refuse a potential buyer.

THE CONDO CONVERSION

If you're considering buying a unit in a building being converted from rental to condominium status, an engineer's report could be your most important document. Buildings twenty years old or older have the best potential for conversion, from the landlord's point of view, and may also provide a good buy for you, but they may also be in serious need of repair.

Hapless residents have discovered, sometimes after purchase, that heating plants or wiring need a major overhaul to extend the building's useful life. Insist on an engineering report that estimates remaining useful life and replacement cost for plumbing and electrical systems, the heating plant, and the roof over your head. Be sure, too, that there is an adequate reserve fund against repairs; this is particularly important in an older building.

Coping with Conversion

If you currently rent an apartment which is being converted to condominium ownership and you think you might like to buy your apartment, here's what to do:

- Read the offering plan very carefully; it spells out both the sponsor's offer to sell and all the legal ins and outs of the offer.
- Get together with your fellow tenants to find out as much as possible about the plan and its impact on you. Ask for a meeting with the sponsor, as a group, to get the answers to all your questions.
- Understand that the first plan is usually an offer, subject to negotiation, and be prepared to negotiate. "Insider" prices, the selling price for tenants, may be cut; reserve funds may be raised; debt burdens may be lowered . . . but you have to negotiate.
- Evaluate the economics of the deal. Look at the building as a whole: Is the estimated budget adequate? What kind of loan burden will the association face at the outset? And figure out what your own apartment's net carrying cost will be if you buy. Don't just compare the purchase price with the purchase price of other available apartments, or the monthly carrying charges with the rent you now pay. Look at your purchase price and your monthly maintenance costs and adjust them for the tax benefits you'll secure as an owner. Then compare that net cost to the costs of other housing.

IF YOU DON'T WANT TO BUY

If you currently rent an apartment which is being converted to condominium ownership and you can't afford to buy or simply don't want to buy, what (other than moving) can you do? Consider the following steps:

- Form a tenants organization. Work together to get information and to negotiate with the landlord. Hire a lawyer to represent the group. Hire an engineer to inspect the building, *before* you enter into negotiations.
- Ask your attorney, your state attorney general's office, a local consumer protection agency, or a real estate board about local law with respect to condominium conversion. Some jurisdictions require that a specified per-

centage of tenants agree to conversion; others protect the rights of tenants, or of certain groups of tenants such as the elderly, who want to stay on as renters.

You may be able to delay the conversion. Or you may be able to negotiate, as a tenants group, so that the purchase price becomes manageable. You will, in any case, gain some time in which you can make a reasonable decision about whether to buy or to move.

Time-Sharing

The Drews enjoyed their week's vacation on Florida's West coast so much that they decided to return. They also decided to buy a time share, a January week every year, in a one-bedroom condominium apartment. The purchase price was $9,000 and the annual maintenance cost was $198. The price was right but a problem arose the very first year: Dan couldn't get his usual week off in January and they were unable to use the apartment. They were also unable to rent it to anyone else.

Time-sharing is based on a simple premise: Instead of paying many thousands of dollars to own a vacation home that you may use for a couple of weeks a year, you pay a small fraction of that amount to use the property for a specified week or weeks each year for twenty or thirty years. The concept has grown in popularity, and sales have reached $1.8 billion a year.

Q. For $12,500 plus annual maintenance costs of $450 we can buy two weeks a year for twenty-five years at a vacation resort we enjoy. Would this be a good buy?

A. The only way to tell is to look at the weekly rates charged by other resorts and apartments in the vicinity. A time-share price should be about ten times the weekly rate for comparable accommodations. If it's more, you might think about simply renting instead of buying. Be aware, too, that those maintenance costs are far from fixed; as the cost of maintenance rises, which it will, so will your assessment.

WHAT TO EVALUATE BEFORE YOU BUY

- There are two kinds of time-sharing arrangements. Under one, you actually take title to the property; you get a deed and have some rights even if the developer disappears. Under the other, you buy the "right to use" the property and should be sure that you're reserving a specific unit; you should also be reasonably certain that the developer is going to remain in business.

- Outright ownership is preferable. If you can't get title, however, ask for a "nondisturbance clause" in the contract. With such a clause, you should retain the legal right to use your unit even if the developer goes under and someone else takes over management. In a Florida case, however, a federal bankruptcy judge overruled the nondisturbance clause. Time-share holders were forced to get in line with other creditors when a resort went into bankruptcy. The only protection, if this decision holds, will be the financial strength of the developer.

- The developer's reputation is more important than anything else. Talk to buyers at other resorts operated by the same developer; if there are no others, be wary. And stay clear of high-pressure sales tactics; some developers are notorious for strongarming potential buyers.

- Exchange privileges are often promised, under which you may swap your unit for someone else's somewhere else. But such exchanges are not guaranteed; they depend strictly on someone else's interest in your unit. If you want to be able to exchange, you'd best buy in a popular area at a popular season.

- If you don't plan on swapping or are unable to do so, be sure to pick an area you're going to enjoy year after year. The money you spend on your share may preclude your vacationing anywhere else for some years to come. And the nicest vacation area can begin to seem dull when wanderlust strikes.

- Buy your time share to enjoy and not as an investment. You may make a profit when you sell, but time-sharing, although it's growing fast, is too new to be sure of a resale market.

The Cooperative Apartment

When a brownstone building on Manhattan's West Side was converted to cooperative apartments a few years ago, the Smarts bought a two-bedroom duplex apartment, with the use of the rear garden, for $45,000. The building corporation, with eight apartment units, has 4,000 shares assigned by the developer. Because the Smarts occupy the largest apartment, they own the largest number of shares in the corporation, 785. Their monthly mortgage-and-maintenance assessment, therefore, is considerably more than that of their neighbors, as the necessary outlay is divided by 4,000 and then multiplied by each resident's shares. The building is small, so the residents do most of their own maintenance, keeping costs down. And Dorothy Smart, because she is a writer who works at home (and because she is a natural organizer), sets up the building schedules for trash removal, sidewalk sweeping, and snow shoveling. The co-op has increased in value. It has also turned out to be a satisfactory way of life.

Cooperatives are relatively rare, found primarily in major cities such as New York and Chicago, and mostly in older buildings. Most new construction in shared housing takes the condominium form. The two are vastly different.

When you buy a condominium unit, you buy an actual piece of property. When you buy a cooperative apartment, you buy a share in a corporation which owns the building. The share sometimes, but not always, is based upon the size of the unit you occupy. (The Smarts own 785/4,000ths of their building; they could, if ownership was per-unit, own one-eighth.) There is a single mortgage and a single tax bill for the entire building, with payments toward each divided among the residents; a proportionate share of the mortgage interest and taxes may be taken by each resident as a tax deduction.

With a co-op, unlike a condominium, you are not taking individual title to a specific piece of property. You are becoming a joint owner, with rights as a lessee. You are, in effect, your own tenant. This joint ownership, however, creates special complications:

Aspects of Cooperative Ownership

- Instead of a mortgage (because you have no individual real property to pledge as collateral), if you need financing you may have to take a personal loan. Such a loan may be (1) difficult to secure, and (2) more expensive than a mortgage (although some New York City banks, for example, do offer co-op loans similar to conventional mortgages). The interest on the loan, however, along with your proportional share of the interest on the corporation's mortgage, will be a deductible item on your federal income tax. (A cooperative corporation may conduct a stringent review of your financial situation before allowing you to purchase shares, and may require that you finance no more than 50 percent of the purchase price.)

- Monthly carrying charges, because they include the building's mortgage loan and real estate taxes, are generally higher than monthly carrying charges on a condominium unit. According to the Institute of Real Estate Management, for example, the median monthly assessment for a cooperative townhouse is $190, the median monthly assessment for a condominium townhouse is $87. If one resident defaults, moreover, the others must make up that share or the mortgage on the entire building will go into default. This is not the case with condominium ownership, where each owner has a separate mortgage.

- You may have to secure permission from your co-owners before making structural changes to your own unit.

- You may not be totally free to sell your unit when you want to move out; the corporation, in the interests of protecting a mutual investment, may want to screen potential purchasers (as you may have been screened before your purchase). Some cooperative apartments, moreover, built under specific provisions of the law, limit the amount of profit a seller can make.

- The corporation may impose a "flip tax" whenever an apartment changes hands. This fee helps to build the corporation's financial reserves.

When You Buy a Co-op

Buying a cooperative, however, is in some respects like buying a condominium unit. You will be buying into a community. Before you buy a cooperative:

- Review the operating budget and financial statements. There should be adequate reserves for repairs and replacement of building systems.

- Ask if there are any liens on the building, any litigation against the corporation, and unpaid property taxes. Any of these situations may result in extra assessments against tenant-owners.

- Find out how often the carrying charges have been increased. What are provisions for future increases?

- Read the bylaws. Can you live with the rules and regulations?

- Talk to residents and see if they are satisfied with management. How much control do residents have over management decisions, if there is an outside manager? How willingly do residents pitch in if they've agreed to do the work themselves?

- Find out if you can remodel your unit, sublease it, and freely sell it when you are ready to move on.

Q. We are all set to buy a cooperative apartment but have been told that the corporation owns only the building and not the land beneath it. Our lawyer advises us not to buy into a building on leased land. What should we do?

A. Buying a co-op on leased land can pose certain problems. The cooperative corporation itself may find it difficult to secure financing for improvements to the building. You, as a tenant-owner, will have to pay real estate taxes on both the land and the building but may be able to claim as a tax deduction only a proportionate share of the taxes on the building. Most important, even though such leases typically run for ninety-nine years, the value of your investment may be significantly diminished. At the end of the lease period all rights to the property and anything on the property (including the building itself) revert to the landowners. Unless the cooperative corporation has purchased the land in the meantime, the apartment may be worthless. If the apartment is a good buy, however, and if you don't plan to live there forever and then pass it on to your heirs, you may be justified in making the purchase. Just think it through carefully, and get good legal advice, before you do.

Co-op Conversion

Most new construction of shared housing takes the simpler condominium form. In cities where cooperatives are well established, however, older apartment buildings are often converted to cooperative ownership. Such conversions may be good for you if you are a potential buyer. But what if you are a tenant faced with a conversion? Whether or not you want to buy your present rental apartment, consider the suggestions, on pp. 334–335, for those faced with conversion to condominium ownership.

Bear in mind, too, that if you buy you will become your own landlord as well as your own tenant. The mix can take some adjustment. You may have to take care of your own plumbing repairs, and you may have to agree with assorted neighbors on the pattern of the wallpaper for the lobby. If you prefer to call the superintendent for repairs and complain about the wallpaper the landlord selects, don't buy a co-op; stick to renting an apartment instead.

Manufactured Housing and Mobile Homes

Manufactured housing is factory-built housing; it is also sometimes called prefabricated housing. This does not mean that manufactured housing is all alike or instantly identifiable; it does mean that each house is built in the factory, trucked to its site, and assembled. The house itself, once assembled, may look like a ranch house or like a two-story Colonial or, as you might expect, like a mobile home on wheels.

Manufactured housing is affordable housing because it costs less to mass-produce in a factory than to build individually on site. It costs less to buy materials in bulk and to install those materials in assembly-line fashion. As the prices of conventional houses move ever upward, factory housing is increasingly attractive. Look at the figures: The average conventional site-built house, with three bedrooms, two baths, and about 1,780 square feet of living space on a one-quarter-acre lot cost about $78,080 in 1984. The average factory-built house, with furniture and appliances in its 1,050 square feet of living space, was $21,500 in 1984. The price of the site-built house is complete with land. To get an accurate price for the manufactured house, add land and foundation, for a total price of $32,000 to $33,000. With all these extras, however, the factory-built house still costs less than half what the site-built house does.

Manufactured housing, especially mobile homes, has traditionally been associated with the young and with the old. Forty-five percent of all sales are made to people in their twenties and thirties, a third to those over age 60. But manufactured housing is, because of its sheer affordability, appealing to more and more people. One simple statistic tells the tale: More than 82 percent of all the new houses sold in the United States in 1980 for under $40,000 were factory-built homes.

There are two broad categories of manufactured housing: modular and mobile. Both are made in the factory and transported, virtually complete, to the site where they will be installed. Both come in units 12 to 14 feet wide and 36 to 70 feet long; both can be doubled or tripled in width and in living space by placing units side by side. Both have just about everything in place before leaving the factory, from the heating system and plumbing to the carpeting on the floor.

But there are major differences as well.

Modular Houses

Modular houses are usually purchased and financed, like conventional site-built housing, along with land. They are treated in all respects, in fact, as conventional housing: They must be placed on a permanent foundation, they must conform to local construction codes, they are taxed as real property. Modular houses, like other houses, generally appreciate in value. Their assembly-line construction, at the same time, results in costs considerably less than conventional site-built housing: $20 per square foot (plus about $3 a square foot for foundation and setup) instead of $40 to $45.

Transportation costs sometimes eliminate the price advantage. With high interest rates, however, builders are interested in speed; the faster a home can be occupied, the lower the carrying costs and the higher the profit margin. More and more builders, therefore, are teaming up with manufacturers to offer modular housing.

A factory-built modular house may appeal to you if you're looking for less expensive housing. It may also appeal to you, if you want a new house, on the basis of speed. From foundation to completion, a site-built house can take six to nine months; a factory-built house, by contrast, can be in place within a few weeks.

Because modular housing is exactly like conventional housing, with the exception of construction techniques, financing and insurance considerations are exactly the same. The information in Chapters 13 and 14 applies to factory-built homes as it does to site-built homes.

Mobile Homes

The mobile home variety of manufactured housing is another story. These homes, although they are seldom mobile at all, are built with a chassis and wheels, axles and brakes. Mobile homes have traditionally been regarded as motor vehicles; they've been placed on rented lots, financed with short-term high-interest installment loans, and taxed as personal property, depreciating in value. All of this is beginning to change.

■ Mobile homes are now being built in a variety of styles, including luxury models with cathedral ceilings, sunken bathtubs, and fireplaces. Some cost $50,000 and more. Some, with pitched roofs and shingle siding, look very much like conventional houses.

■ Some states are beginning to tax mobile homes as real estate, especially when they are placed on individually owned land. In mobile home parks, on rental lots, homes are still more often taxed as personal property. Either way, mobile homes are now more likely to appreciate in value (although still not as much as conventional houses). So you won't necessarily lose money when you sell.

■ Some states, too, have ruled that exclusionary zoning is illegal. In these states a community cannot exclude a mobile home or restrict its location just because it is a mobile home. Local jurisdictions may, however, require that all the houses in a given area (including mobile homes) conform to compatible standards.

■ New mobile home developments are more and more often planned to look like suburban housing developments, with sidewalks, underground utilities, and recreational areas. Increasingly, too, residents own their land as well as their homes. More than half of all mobile homes are placed on individual lots, usually in rural areas. Mobile home subdivisions involve the sale of land with homes, and mobile home condominiums, like other condominiums, involve individual ownership of home-plus-lot and joint ownership of common elements.

All of these changes in mobile homes have led to changes in the financial picture as well.

FINANCING A MOBILE HOME PURCHASE

Mobile homes, like automobiles, have generally been financed with relatively short-term installment loans. Down payments are usually 10 to 20 percent, sometimes as much as 25 percent. Most maturities run ten to fifteen years. Interest rates are often 2 or 3 percentage points above those for conventional home mortgages. Loans are available from mobile home dealers or from lending institutions; many purchasers take the easy route and finance through the dealer, although it's always best to compare terms and interest rates.

As mobile homes become more and more like site-built houses in their size and the amenities they offer, there is a national trend toward financing them like site-built houses. This is particularly true when the mobile home will go on land you own, and where it is a larger multi-section home. There is a trend toward simple interest (rather than the add-on interest of installment loans) and toward longer maturities. There is also, according to the Manufactured Housing Institute, a steady increase by savings and loan associations into the business of financing mobile homes. Although savings and loans are allowed to make 30-year loans on mobile homes, however, few are doing so.

If you are financing a mobile home purchase, shop around:

■ Go to savings and loan associations, banks, and credit unions as well as to the mobile home dealer.

■ Find out how your state taxes mobile homes. In the states where they are taxed as real estate rather than as personal property, it is more likely that you will be able to finance your purchase through a loan resembling a conventional mortgage. The loan may still have a maturity of twenty years rather than thirty but it will be a significant improvement over the installment loan arrangement.

■ Be aware that you will probably owe a sales tax on the purchase of a new mobile home. If you buy a used mobile home directly from an owner, you may or may not, depending on the state, owe a sales tax. If your home must be moved to its site, however, new or used, you will have to pay a motor vehicle registry fee.

■ Do not sign any financing agreement unless the terms are carefully spelled out. The lender must tell you the annual percentage rate you are being charged, in simple interest terms.

■ Look into FHA- and VA-backed financing. Both guarantee loans on mobile homes; both steadily liberalize their criteria. The FHA, as of mid-1985, will insure up to $40,500 for twenty years on a single-wide or multisection unit; it will insure up to $54,000 for twenty years on a single unit plus land and the same amount for twenty-five years on a multisection unit plus land. For eligible veterans, the VA will guarantee up to 50 percent of a loan to a maximum of $20,000; maturities are twenty years on a single-wide unit, twenty-three years on a multisection. The FHA requires a small down payment, the VA none at all.

■ There are generally no closing costs or attorney's fees to pay in financing and insuring a mobile home. A title search is not required either, unless you are buying land as well as the home itself.

Q. We've bought a new double-wide mobile home which will be placed on a lovely grassy site in a well-run park. What kind of insurance do we need?

A. You want protection against damage to your personal property, the contents of your home, as well as against damage to the home itself. If your home is at least 10 by 40 square feet, you can get a package policy similar in its coverage to HO-2, the Broad Form Homeowners. Differences in construction, especially susceptibility to wind damage, make mobile home policies more expensive than comparable policies on conventional houses. Having a properly installed tiedown may reduce your premium. Older mobile homes, bought used, are even more difficult and more expensive to insure.

ONGOING COSTS

If you decide to buy a mobile home, you will be responsible for:

- Monthly payments of the principal and interest on either an installment loan or a mortgage
- Monthly rent, if your home is in a park or development (and this rent can go up very steeply)
- Property taxes, if you own your own lot
- Property and liability insurance
- Utilities
- Maintenance and repairs

The Ealings—he is a $17,000-a-year computer repairman, she is a housewife and mother of two—live in a 24-by-60-foot mobile home in a mobile home park in Virginia. With a 15-year FHA mortgage on their $15,000 secondhand unit, they pay $164 a month toward the mortgage, $129 a month in rent for the lot, $27 for homeowners insurance, and about $88 for utilities. Although they look at mobile home ownership as the only kind of homeownership they can afford, they feel they've made a wise investment. Paying rent, for them, was throwing money away.

Before You Buy a Mobile Home

Mobile homes, despite vast improvements, are still not the precise equivalent of conventionally built homes. Despite advances in construction, for example, the average life of a mobile home has been estimated to be fifteen years. So you may not pass a mobile home on to your children and your grandchildren. But it may provide reasonably comfortable and affordable housing right now. Before you buy:

- Be sure you have a place to put your home. Local mobile home parks may be full, or may require that a home be purchased through the park. Zoning regulations may not permit placement on private property.
- Understand the rental fee if you will rent a lot. Rentals vary from $50 to $300 and more a month, with most communities ranging from $80 to $150 a month. Get a lease if you can, and find out how often the lot rental has been raised and can be raised. (One of the persistent complaints about

mobile home living has been the arbitrary authority of mobile home park operators. In most cases, residents have little say about regulations and little redress if rents are raised.)

- Understand the rules and regulations of any mobile home community you are considering. Will you be permitted to have children? (The Ealings' park permits up to three, with rent increases for each birth; some parks permit none.) Will you be able to have a pet? (The Ealings are allowed one small pet, up to 10 inches high at the hips and 26 pounds, at an extra $5 in lot rental per month.) Will you be required to buy all equipment from the park operator? Can you be evicted at the owner's pleasure?

- Find out what the base price includes, which appliances and what furnishings. If you don't want to buy the furniture, you may get a discount, but it won't be equivalent to the retail value of the furnishings.

- Find out what extras you will have to cover. Many mobile home communities require steps with handrails, skirting to conceal the wheels, foundation supports, anchoring to the ground. These costs, typically, add about 15 percent to the purchase price of the home.

- Decide what other options you might like. Air conditioning and a patio are pleasant additions, but be sure to calculate their cost before you commit yourself to a purchase.

- Be sure that your home conforms to the 1976 standards enacted by the Department of Housing and Urban Development, providing for fire safety and wind resistance. A newly built home will meet the standards; an older home bought as a resale may not. Multi-sections, in general, are sturdier than single-wides. Also note that formaldehyde, widely used in manufactured housing construction, is now suspected of cancer-causing emissions. Watch for either federal rulings or industry action to safeguard consumers.

- Find out what warranty you have on the house itself and on any appliances and equipment. Find out who will honor the warranty if any work is required. And be aware that a used mobile home may have no warranties at all, on either the home itself or its contents.

- Inspect any mobile home carefully before you buy. Most mobile homes, according to the Federal Trade Commission, contain defects. And most warranties exclude transportation and setup from warranty. If your home is damaged while in transit or while it is being installed on your site, you may wind up with leaking ceilings, buckled walls, inoperative doors or windows . . . and no satisfaction from either the manufacturer or the dealer.

When You Want to Sell

When you're ready to sell your mobile home and move on, you'll probably have little difficulty if you own the land on which it stands. If you are renting in a mobile home park, however, you may have to obey the regulations of the park. Find out what those regulations are (recognizing that they are subject to change) before you move in.

As mobile homes are becoming more and more the nation's affordable housing, eager buyers are likely to be found. The problem in selling, if there is one, will stem from the home's location.

KEY POINTS

- A condominium may look like an apartment or like a house. It is a form of ownership which combines the ease of apartment living with the advantages of homeownership. When you buy a condominium unit, you buy an actual piece of property.
- Cooperative owners do not own individual units. When you buy a co-op, you buy a share in the corporation that owns the building.
- Factory-built housing includes modular or prefabricated houses built in a factory but assembled on an individual lot and sold, financed, and taxed as individual homes.
- Factory-built housing also includes mobile homes, factory-built and factory-assembled, and placed on an individually owned lot or on a rental lot in a mobile home community. Mobile homes, although more and more resembling conventional houses, are still often financed with short-term installment loans and taxed as either vehicles or personal property.

SPENDING YOUR MONEY: AN AUTOMOBILE

Owning, Renting, or Leasing an Automobile

If home ownership is the number-one American dream, automobile ownership must rank a close second. In fact, 85 percent of households in the United States have at least one car; 37 percent have two or more cars.

Yet owning and operating a car is taking more and more of the family budget. As the cost of owning and operating a new car rises even faster than the overall rate of inflation, more and more people are refraining from buying new cars, holding on to their old cars, and driving less.

What about you? Are you in the market for a new car? a used car? Should you have a car at all? This chapter will focus on the costs of car ownership, on alternatives to ownership in the form of renting and leasing, and on how to buy and pay for a car if you decide to do so. The next chapter will describe the ins and outs of automobile insurance.

What It Costs to Own a Car

In 1950, according to the Hertz Corporation, motorists spent an average of 8¢ a mile and drove an average of 9,032 miles, for an annual cost of $724.

In 1972, the last full year before the Arab oil embargo, driving cost 12.1¢ a mile and cars were driven an average of 10,362 miles a year. Total cost: $1,256 for the year.

By 1985, when per-mile costs were up to 47.6¢, the average motorist had reduced miles per year to 8,586. Total costs, nonetheless, were more than $4,000.

These figures, of course, are averages. New cars cost still more to operate. A 1985 compact sedan kept just one year will cost its owner an estimated $5,469 or about 66¢ a mile. The same typical car, driven the same 8,586 miles a year but kept for ten years, will cost just $3,476 (in constant dollars) in its tenth year or less than 41¢ a mile. There are some lessons in these figures:

■ It will cost you less to run an old car than a new one. Most Americans have learned this lesson well. The average age of cars currently on the road is 7.6 years, the highest average since the Korean War years of the early 1950s.

■ As more and more people keep their cars longer before trading them in for newer models, it's becoming increasingly difficult to buy a good used car.

The costs of automobile ownership come in two parts: purchase price and operating costs.

Initial Purchase Price

The average 1985 *new car,* with the most popular options (power steering, power brakes, automatic transmission, and air conditioning), sold for $9,834; in 1979 the average car sold for $5,079. In buying a new car, depending on what you need and what you want, you can still spend under $8,000—but you'll get a subcompact with few extras. You can also spend over $30,000 for a fully loaded luxury-size car. Prices don't go up, these days, in a simple progression from small car to large. The kicker in today's marketplace is that smaller cars with better gas mileage ratings may cost as much as larger, more comfortable models. Dealers won't negotiate very much on small easy-to-sell cars. You may find a lot more price flexibility on cars sitting on the lot and eating up overhead.

Purchase prices on *secondhand* cars are considerably less. A pick-of-the-crop year-old car with relatively little mileage on it may sell for 20 to 25 percent less than the same car brand-new, while a seven-year-old model may run a full 90 percent less. Specific prices, of course, depend on the age and condition of the car, but the average price of a secondhand car in 1984 was $5,406. This typical car was 4.5 years old and had been driven 45,434 miles.

Operating Costs

The costs of maintaining your car, once you own it, can also be viewed in two parts: fixed and variable.

FIXED COSTS

These "standing" costs are those that remain essentially the same whether your car is driven 15,000 miles a year or left sitting in your driveway. They include licensing, taxes, insurance, interest, and depreciation (the difference between the resale value and the initial purchase price). They may also include such ongoing expenses as monthly garage rent or inspection fees. These figures are fixed, once established, but they are affected initially by the kind of car you buy (taxes, licensing, insurance, and depreciation) and by the way you buy it (interest costs). Fixed costs usually amount to two-thirds to three-fourths of your total annual outlay; the more you drive, however, the lower fixed costs become on a per-mile basis.

VARIABLE COSTS

These "running" costs are those directly related to how much or how little you drive: gasoline and oil, service and repairs, tires, batteries, sparkplugs, as well as bridge and tunnel tolls, sporadic parking charges, and traffic tickets. Some of these costs, of course, are also tied to the kind of car you buy. Fuel efficiency, in particular, can have a significant impact on the amount you spend on gasoline in the course of a year. But fuel efficiency, despite the considerable attention it's received in recent years, is but one of several factors and should be weighed accordingly. If you get hung up on fuel efficiency, you may wind up spending more overall on automobile operating costs.

For example: Suppose you are trying to decide between a new $10,000 car that is supposed to average 26 miles per gallon and a used $5,000 car that may average 13 miles per gallon. Suppose, also, that gasoline costs $1.00 a gallon. If you drive 10,000 miles a year, you would spend about $384 on gasoline per year for the $10,000 car and $764 per year for the $5,000 car. Clearly, your gasoline expenditures will be cut by about half if you buy the more fuel-efficient vehicle. But what about the initial purchase price of the car? the additional interest charges on a bigger loan? the higher insurance premiums on a new and expensive car? You will have to drive the fuel-efficient car for seven years before you recover the additional cost in savings on gasoline alone. And if you drive fewer miles, fixed costs will be proportionately more important than variable costs such as gasoline; the operating cost differential between large and small cars becomes, as a result, less significant.

Q. We don't use our family car for business. Is there any way that any of the owning and operating costs might be tax-deductible?

A. Yes. If you use your car for *medical* (trips to the doctor) or *charitable* (including volunteer activity on behalf of a charity) purposes, you may deduct either the actual costs of operating the car (gasoline, oil, and maintenance) *or* the standard per-mile rate permitted by the IRS. (In 1986, the rate was 9¢ a mile for medical care and 12¢ per mile for charity.) You may also claim tolls and parking fees. Accurate records are essential.

If you decide to buy a car, after calculating how much it will cost (use the worksheet to do your calculations), several elements will enter into your calculations: how much you can afford, what size car you need, how to get the most car for the best price (old car or new), and how to pay for your purchase.

WORKSHEET TO CALCULATE CAR OWNERSHIP COSTS

COSTS IN YOUR LOCALITY

1. Amount paid for your car — $_____
2. Cost of accessory items — $_____
3. Cost of a tire to fit your car — $_____
4. Price of gasoline per gallon (including tax) — $_____
5. Price of oil per quart (including tax) — $_____
6. Annual cost of your insurance — $_____
7. Estimated cost of your daily parking — $_____
8. State registration fee for your car — $_____
9. Sales/titling, and/or personal property tax — $_____
10. Mechanic's labor charge per hour — $_____
11. Monthly interest cost (monthly payment × number of months for loan less amount of loan / number of months for loan) — $_____
12. Term of your auto loan — _____
13. Your mileage for the year — _____

ESTIMATED FIRST-YEAR COST

Ownership costs (first year)	Total	Cost per mile (total column ÷ line 13)
14. Depreciation (25% of line 1)	$_____	_____
15. Accessories (line 2 ÷ 12)	$_____	_____
16. Insurance (line 6)	$_____	_____
17. Registration fee (line 8)	$_____	_____
18. Financing (12 × monthly interest cost)	$_____	_____
19. Sales/titling, and/or property tax (line 9)	$_____	_____

Operating costs (first year)		
20. Gasoline (annual gallons used × line 4)	$_____	_____
21. Oil (line 13 ÷ owners manual change requirements × line 5)	$_____	_____
22. Snow tires (2 × line 3 × .25)	$_____	_____
23. Maintenance and repair (based on line 10)	$_____	_____
24. Parking (250 × line 7) or actual days parked × daily cost	$_____	_____
25. Tolls	$_____	_____
26. Total cost (add lines 14–25)	$_____	_____

(Source: Federal Highway Administration)

How Much Can You Afford?

The answer to this crucial question depends on your budget (see Chapter 2), which, in turn, depends at least in part on your stage of life.

Average driving costs per year are close to $4,600, over and above the initial purchase price of the car. Where does this figure fit in your income-outgo picture? And, beyond the dollars-and-cents answer to that question, beyond your practical need for transportation, how important is it to you to own a car? What are your other goals? If you're single, with few responsibilities, you may be willing and able to put more money into an automobile than cold hard figures would otherwise indicate. If you've just started a family, a car may be essential but strictly on a no-frills basis. And if you've retired on a limited and fixed income, transportation may play a definitely secondary role.

How Much Car Do You Need?

Will you be using the car for daily stop-and-go commuting? Or solely to transport camping gear on an occasional weekend jaunt? Do you stick to superhighways? Or travel a rutted country road to a retreat in the hills? Must you accommodate only yourself? Or must you also comfortably seat a spouse, a car pool crowd, a couple of small (or large) children? Smaller cars are generally less expensive to operate (see Table 1), but the answers to all these questions should dictate the size and type of the car you buy.

TABLE 1: The costs of car ownership for different sizes of new cars.

Car type	Gasoline, oil, etc.	Mainte-nance	Depreciation, interest	Insurance, license, tax	Total
Subcompact 4-cylinder	$ 718	$430	$1,886	$1,058	$4,092
Compact 6-cylinder	728	430	2,413	1,193	4,764
Intermediate 6-cylinder	878	538	2,358	1,252	5,026
Full-size 8-cylinder	1,045	538	3,194	1,321	6,098

Estimates are based on 10,000 miles per year, for a car in good trade-in condition in five years with 50,000 miles. Financing is at 33 percent down and a 5-year loan at 13.32 percent interest. Insurance is $500 deductible and $100/300 thousand injury and $50,000 property damage insurance.
(Source: The Hertz Corporation)

Look at all your needs, at how often you do what. Don't buy a wagon or a van to hold your camping gear if you go camping once a year; a roof rack may do just as well. Don't buy a small car with a small engine, in the interests of fuel efficiency, and then find that the steep road to your favorite vacation hideaway is an almost insurmountable obstacle. Don't buy a sporty two-door model when you know that you'll be taking three or four passengers back and forth to work each day; the trip will become distinctly uncomfortable.

Q. My husband has always put the family car in his name alone. Is there any reason why our car shouldn't be registered in both our names?

A. It's generally not a good idea to own an automobile jointly. The reason: If either of you is involved in an accident and the car is jointly owned, you could both be sued. Assets belonging to each of you individually could then be subject to any court judgment. It's best to have the family car registered in one name, either name.

PSYCHOLOGICAL NEEDS

A two-door car may be uncomfortable for your car pool, but if it's the only model that suits your racing-car self-image, you may buy it anyway. Emotional needs often play a major role in automobile selection.

A "psychographic" marketing study by the Opinion Survey Center of Toledo, Ohio, measured the elements that go into the decision to buy a particular car. Just about half the car-buying population, the survey found, is practical, making logical step-by-step pocketbook-in-mind decisions. The other half, which tends to be younger but includes people of all ages, is more emotional, swayed by newness, snob appeal, or image.

Are you practical? Do you focus on price and value, reliability and durability, over and above the image a car conveys? Do you look at a car as first and foremost a means of transportation? Then you may be happy (and your budget will certainly be better balanced) with a modest sedan, new or secondhand.

Or are you more emotional, seeing your car as a personal statement, a reflection of your self? Are sexy looks more important than practicality? the newest model better than the tried-and-true? Then you're likely to want the sporty two-door model, regardless of your passengers' comfort.

It's possible, of course, to buy the same car for different reasons. A sports car may be racy to one driver, a well-engineered automobile to another. But if you understand your own motives when it comes to buying a car, you'll do your pocketbook as well as your ego a favor.

Old Car or New?

Fixed and variable costs for brand-new cars, taken together, range upward from 40.9¢ a mile for subcompacts to 62.9¢ a mile for full-sized cars. That's an average, based on 10,000 miles a year for five years (even though people have cut back on their driving, it's still easier to do the calculations based on 10,000 miles a year). If you drive more over the same five years, the per-mile figure drops while the dollar outlay rises. If you keep your car longer, your overall costs go down.

Used cars are about 45 percent less costly to buy and run than comparable new models. Ownership and operating expenses for second-hand cars, again depending on how long you keep the car and how far you drive, range from 12 to 50 percent below charges for new cars in similar driving. In an example provided by the Hertz Corporation: A 1984 compact costs an estimated 47.1¢ a mile to run 10,000 miles a year for four years. The same car bought used as a four-year-old vehicle and driven 10,000 miles a year for another four years would cost just 26.8¢ a mile, for a saving of 43 percent.

An American car, well maintained, should provide 100,000 miles of driving. Forty to 45 percent of all cars are still on the road after ten years of operation, with a sharp drop-off between the tenth and the fifteenth year. With regular maintenance and good driving, and the luck to stay clear of accidents, you should be able to expect ten years and 100,000 miles from almost any car.

Whatever type of car you drive, regional considerations will affect your operating costs. Urban areas are generally more expensive places to keep automobiles, but urban areas are not all alike. Variables include the factory-to-destination price of the automobile, the risk of accident and hence the cost of insurance, repair and maintenance costs, parking costs, and tolls. In 1985 it cost 47.6¢ per mile to operate a domestic compact, as a national average. In Los Angeles, the most expensive city for car ownership, it cost 62.7¢ a mile, while in Detroit, according to a study of twenty large cities, it cost 46.2¢.

Buying a New Car

If you've decided to buy a new car you'll have, in addition to a choice of models, a choice of options. Here, too, you'll be best off thinking it through before you set foot in a showroom. Is air conditioning a must? What about power steering? A basic no-frills car costs considerably less, a couple of thousand dollars less, than the same car "loaded."

Your initial choice of automobile, moreover, will affect the options you need. Expensive extras on some cars are basic included-in-the-sticker-price elements on others. A careful reading of the annual automobile issue of *Consumer Reports,* published each spring, will spell out the details and help you decide what's worthwhile. The dealer may offer you a "package" of options at a bargain price. The price may indeed be lower than all the options purchased separately, but it won't be a bargain unless you need and want all the individual items.

Once you know what you want in a new car, be prepared to negotiate. Most car prices are negotiable, although some are more negotiable than others. If it's the end of a month . . . if a model is moving slowly

. . . if the dealer has a lot of cars on hand . . . you're more likely to find a better price. Comparison-shop among different dealers, and don't be pressured into buying before you're ready.

Remember:

- Finance costs, if you're borrowing money from any source, must be figured in the total cost.

- Dealer preparation charges, taxes, licensing fees, and destination charges, which can add up to hundreds of dollars, must also be added in.

- A trade-in of your old car, if any, should be negotiated separately. Find out what the bottom-line price is on the new car you want; then talk trade-in value (and sell privately if you want top dollar and don't mind the hassle).

- You're going to want service from the dealer as well as delivery; keep this in mind if you find the best price at a dealer 30 miles away or through a discount buying service.

TACTICS TO AVOID

In your price-shopping, be wary of the high-pressure sales tactics engaged in by some dealers:

- In *lowballing* the dealer meets your price, then suddenly "remembers" some extra charges he failed to include. Don't agree to a price that goes up after a deal is made.

- In *highballing,* by contrast, the salesperson offers you a terrific trade-in price on your old car, then turns around and increases the price on the new car to make up the difference.

- *Turnover* tricks involve wearing you down with sales pitches from one salesperson after another.

- You're *locked in* when you turn over a temporary "deposit" or the keys to your old car; then, when you decide you've had enough, you may not be able to retrieve your property to leave. Don't sign anything or turn over keys (you can go along on a test drive) until you're sure the deal is the one you want.

Q. My new car has been at the dealer for repairs more often than it's been in my driveway ready for use. They can't seem to make it work properly, and I know I've got a lemon on my hands. Is there anything I can do?

A. The manufacturer's warranty should provide repairs of defects, but it does not oblige the manufacturer to replace the car or offer a refund if the defect can't be fixed. You do have the right, under federal law (the Magnuson-Moss Warranty Act of 1975), to sue for a replacement or a refund, plus attorney's fees, if the car remains defective after a number of attempts at repair. You may do better, however, if you live in one of the states that have begun to provide consumer protection for new-car purchasers. Under a Connecticut law, for example, failure to repair substantial defects in four attempts means that the manufacturer will be required to either refund the purchase price or replace the vehicle. If he fails to do so, the buyer can sue for refund or replacement after first submitting to arbitration.

Buying a Used Car

Used cars, as noted, cost considerably less than new cars, both in initial purchase price and in operating costs. The average 1985 car, bought new, sold for about $9,115. The average used car bought in 1984, when it was four and a half years old, cost just about $5,400. No wonder most people, especially most younger people, buy and drive secondhand cars.

But there are other factors to keep in mind:

- A new car can be ordered with the options you want; a used car will be an as-is proposition.

- As people keep cars longer, to avoid the costs of trading up, good used cars are both harder to find and more expensive.

- Repair costs increase along with the age of the car, although the slowed rate of depreciation, in many people's opinion, does a lot to compensate. (If you keep the car past the first set of repairs, moreover—past the three-year mark—you probably won't face major repairs again for another three or four years.)

- Warranties, where available at all (it depends a great deal on where you buy the car; see below), may provide minimal coverage.

- Financing may cost more on a used car (although overall costs will be lower) because some lending institutions charge higher rates and offer shorter loans on older cars.

WHERE TO BUY A USED CAR

All things being equal, however, you will save money by buying a secondhand car. If you decide to do so, comparison-shop among new-car dealers, used-car dealers, rental or leasing agencies, and private individuals. Keep the following distinctions in mind:

- A new-car dealer resells the best of the used cars he takes in trade-in. His prices are often higher than those of other used-car sources, but he has service facilities and may offer a written warranty.

- Used-car dealers often have a wider variety of cars on hand, from the best to the worst. They often do not have service facilities and are less likely to offer a warranty.

- The big rental agencies (Hertz, Avis, and National) sell their used cars directly to the consumer after about a year of use. Rental cars tend to run up 18,000 to 22,000 miles in a year, but they are also well maintained and come with warranties. Prices are generally lower than dealer prices, but they are also generally nonnegotiable.

- If you buy from an individual car owner you may strike a better deal, but you're also completely on your own—no service, no warranty, no recourse if things go wrong. Your best bet if you buy privately: Buy from someone you know, someone who has probably kept the car in good repair.

Q. I bought a used car and the brakes failed almost as soon as I left the lot. The salesman says I bought the car "as is," but isn't the dealer responsible for repairs when something happens so soon?

A. That depends on the terms of your sales contract and on the state in which you live. If the contract says that the dealer "disclaims all warranties" or that you bought the car "as is," then the dealer is not responsible. The only exception: Some states require dealers to make cars fit to pass inspection. If you live in one of these states, the dealer will have to repair the brakes; otherwise you must foot the bill yourself.

Paying for Your Car

Sixty percent of all cars, new and used, are financed at the time of purchase. If you're planning to take a loan to pay for your car, you should know that:

- Automobile loans, like other loans (see Chapter 9 for a full discussion of credit), are available from a number of sources. If you take the financing agreement offered by the auto dealer without first comparing costs at a variety of lending institutions (banks, savings and loans, credit unions), you may spend more than necessary . . . except, of course, if the manufacturer or dealer is offering a temporary bargain rate as an incentive to sales.

- Interest rates vary from lender to lender. The figure to get, and to compare, is the annual percentage rate or APR. Federal law requires lenders to give you this figure.

- Look at the total interest cost over the life of the loan; don't be misled by monthly figures, which will vary with the length of the loan and with the APR. For example, if you finance $9,600 at 11 percent for three years (which used to be the standard length of an auto loan), you will pay $314.29 a month or $1,714.50 in total interest over the life of the loan. If you finance the same amount at the same rate for five years (rapidly becoming the industry standard), you will pay $208.73 a month and a total of $2,923.64 in interest over the life of the loan. That's $1,209.14 extra for the privilege of spreading payments over the additional years. At higher interest rates (and a five-year loan often costs 0.5 percent more), the differential is greater still.

- Think carefully before taking a loan of more than three years. Recognize that, with depreciation, you may face a period of well over a year when the actual value of the car is less than the amount outstanding on your loan. If you trade the car during this period, you probably won't get enough to pay off the loan. If the car is wrecked or stolen during this period, your insurance (see Chapter 19) will probably cover only the depreciated ("book") value of the car (less any deductible); if the book value is less than you owe, you will be liable for the difference.

- You do not, as a rule, have to accept or pay for credit insurance as part of your loan. If a lender tells you that it is required, check with your state insurance department or consumer affairs department. In most cases, for most people, credit insurance is overpriced and unnecessary.

Paying Cash

Skipping a loan and paying cash for your car, if you have it to pay, may or may not save you money. Look at:

- The interest you will lose on the money you withdraw from investments to pay for the car

- The rate of inflation, and your own opinion about paying back a loan in what may be less valuable dollars

Whether you pay cash or take a loan, you can reduce your dollar outlay for a car by paying as little as possible for the car in the first place. Some places to shop: consumer buying services such as CarPuter which offer automobiles at cost-plus-a-specified-amount; travel and automobile clubs, which often offer special dealer arrangements to members.

Q. A local automobile dealer is offering a 5 percent rebate on the price of new cars. Another is offering a special financing program at 12.8 percent. Which arrangement is the better deal?

A. You have to compare the dollars-and-cents (and warranty provisions) of each offer, but, in general, you may be better off with lower financing terms. As an example, a $10,000 car financed for four years at 16.5 percent would have monthly payments of $228.73 with a 20 percent down payment. The monthly payments would stay the same with a rebate, unless you used the rebate to increase the down payment. The same car, if you can finance it at 12.8 percent, would have monthly payments of $213.83 for a saving of almost $700 over the life of the loan.

Do You Need a Car?

If you live in a community with good, safe, dependable mass transit, you may very well be able to do without a car. If you live in a built-up urban area, moreover (the kind of area most likely to have good mass transit), you will probably find the costs of car ownership prohibitive. Parking garages alone, in New York City, can cost more than many people are accustomed to paying for housing. If you can walk to the supermarket, bank, and library, and use a bus or subway or bicycle to commute to work, you probably don't need a car. Your occasional need for a car, largely on weekends and for vacations, can probably be met, less expensively, by renting (see below).

If you find yourself behind the wheel virtually every day, however, chances are that you do need a car . . . unless a lot of the driving is more from habit than from necessity. This may be particularly true if you're driving the household's second car. Would it be worth it to you to consolidate errands, share a ride to work, and generally do without the convenience of car ownership in order to save some money?

Should You Rent?

The car that you own costs you money twenty-four hours a day, 365 days a year, whether you are using it or not. You continue to pay for insurance, interest, and the intangible but very real depreciation even while the car sits idle in your driveway or at the curb. The only car that costs you money only while it's actually being used is a rental car.

Most people think about renting for personal use only while on vacation. But if you live in a city where garaging is expensive, you may save money by renting even if you use a car every single weekend plus two weeks a year. However, it's impossible to look at owning vs. renting in financial terms alone. There's a psychological element as well. The cost of renting for the year may be favorable, but you are likely to look at the cost per weekend and decide that your planned activities are not worthwhile. If you are going to spend $30 or more to rent a car for a day, a picnic in the country may begin to look like expensive fresh air.

If you do decide to rent, whether for vacation or for year-round use, be very careful to compare costs carefully. The biggest companies, with the most convenient locations, are sometimes the most expensive. The smallest companies, tucked away in a single location in a single city, may be the least expensive. But if you'll be renting in one city and leaving the car in another, you'll probably find that you're better off with the larger companies. A small company may well charge an extra fee for drop-off elsewhere, resulting in a higher overall charge. A small company may also be unable to provide quick on-the-road service if the car breaks down.

Rental Costs

There are three kinds of rates to compare before you rent a car:

- Time plus mileage, in which you pay so much per day plus so many cents per mile.

- Unlimited mileage plans, now much more common, under which you'll pay more per day or per week, but that's it. With no extra mileage charges, these plans are often (depending on how far you'll drive) more economical than time plus mileage. There are also some combination plans available, under which a specified number of miles is included with extra charges for extra miles driven.

- Special rates. Every car rental company has a confusing variety of special plans. Rent a car in Florida during vacation season and you'll probably find a special rate. Rent a car on your way to a city where the rental company needs the car and you may get a special rate. Watch the ads, and ask the rental companies, to see what's available when you plan to rent a car.

COST-CUTTING ON RENTALS

You'll save money if you compare rates carefully, in terms of your own particular needs. You'll also save some money if you:

- Take advantage of discounts. Almost every corporation, association, and fraternal group seems to offer a car rental discount to its members. But don't take a discount without making some comparisons: The largest car rental companies, with the highest base rates, offer the largest discounts; you may under some circumstances be better off with a different company and no "discount." You also can't take both a special rate and a discount; in some cases you'll save more money with a special rate.

- Rent the smallest car you can comfortably use. Rates at all companies go up with the size of the car. (If you've reserved a specific size car ahead of time, you get the rate for that car, even if the company gives you a larger car.)

- Understand all the terms of the agreement. If you're an hour late in returning the car, will you be charged for an extra day? How much insurance is included (see below)?

- Rent an older car, if you don't care too much about looks. In many cities mechanically sound older cars are available at much lower cost from rental agencies going by such names as "Rent-a-Wreck" or "Lease-a-Lemon."

Insurance on Rental Cars

The major car rental agencies carry personal injury liability insurance, which protects you, up to specified limits, in case of an accident. (Some smaller agencies force you to rely on your own insurance, which may or may not be adequate to cover a rental car.) But these large agencies will also ask you to waive collision coverage or to pay an extra $7 to $9 a day for this coverage. Before you decide, find out whether your own auto insurance covers you. Also ask about the extent of your potential liability if you sign the waiver; in some cities it can be $1,000 or more. If you're going to be driving an unfamiliar car in unfamiliar territory, in an urban area with heavy traffic, the extra insurance might not be a bad idea.

Whether or not you take the collision coverage, keep the basic liability coverage in force by:

- Having everyone in your group who might drive the car sign the rental agreement. Others, especially family members, are sometimes allowed to drive without advance signature. But drivers under 21 or, sometimes, under 25 may not be allowed to drive your rental car at all. Be sure you read the contract carefully before you turn the wheel over to your child.

- Understanding and abiding by the basic provisions of your rental agreement. It may, for instance, forbid towing. It may not allow driving in another state. Read the small print in your rental agreement, even if you're in a hurry.

Should You Lease?

Renting makes sense when you need a car once in a while. It isn't practical for an extended period of time. Leasing a car may make sense if you need a car but don't want the headaches of ownership. At one time, leasing was pretty much restricted to corporate fleets and to individuals such as salespeople who were on the road much of the year and who could deduct a leased vehicle as a business expense. Today, with rising new-car prices and interest rates more and more individuals are leasing cars for personal use.

THE ADVANTAGES OF LEASING

- Leases are written on the basis of assumed mileage. If you drive less than 10,000 miles a year, leasing probably does not pay. If you lease a car and drive more than the agreed-upon amount, you will pay a surcharge.

- If your driving is business-related, leasing provides documentation for income tax purposes and may be slightly more convenient than owning your own car. On the other hand, if you buy a car for business use, you can take advantage of depreciation deductions.

- Do you need or want a bigger, more expensive, or newer car than you can otherwise afford? By eliminating the down payment (although you may have to pay up to two months' leasing fee as security), leasing makes it possible to buy more car for the same monthly payment.

- If you don't want to worry about eventually selling the car, then you might want to think about leasing.

- Can you earn a substantial return on money otherwise committed to a down payment on a car? If so, leasing may make financial sense for you.

THE DISADVANTAGES OF LEASING

Leasing may appear more attractive now that sales tax and interest charges on an automobile loan are no longer deductible on federal income tax returns. But leasing has drawbacks as well. Unless you drive a lot, leasing may work out to be more expensive than owning. And, of course, when you've finished with the lease, all you own is a piece of paper. When you finish paying off an auto loan, you own a physical asset that can be sold.

Leasing Contracts

If you think you might want to lease an automobile, these are the types of arrangements to consider:

An open-end lease is the least expensive on a month-to-month basis, although it may cost you slightly more at the end of the leasing period. In effect, you're making a bet with the leasing company: If the resale value of the car is higher than the company expects it to be at the end of the lease, you come out ahead; if the car is worth less, you'll owe some additional money (but usually no more, according to federal law, than three times the monthly lease payment). If you're going to consider an open-end lease, do so only with a car known to hold its resale value. And consider a lease with an option to buy. If you like the car, at the end of the lease period, you'll be able to acquire a good (because you've taken care of it) used car.

Q. I've been happy with the car I've leased for three years. But how do I decide if it makes good financial sense to buy it when the lease period ends? Might I be better off leasing another new car instead?

A. Good financial sense in buying a leased car depends on whether the residual value of the car (the amount you agreed upon at the outset) is approximately the same as the current market value. If you're going to owe another $400 or so anyway, do you want to pay the money and then not have the car? Start checking newspaper classified ads a month or two before your lease ends to see the retail value of the car you have; then compare that figure to the figure on the lease. But remember: If you're happy with the car, if it's running well and serving your needs, that may be the most important factor.

A closed-end lease will cost you somewhat more, perhaps an additional $15 to $20, each month. When it's over, however, you can hand in the keys (assuming that the car is undamaged) and walk away. You won't have to be concerned with its current market value.

With any lease you will assume at least some of the variable expenses of car ownership: gasoline, oil, and so on. You will pay sales tax on the lease payments, and you may have to pay state registration fees as well. You also, under some if not all leases, buy your own insurance.

Where the leasing company provides the insurance, be sure that it covers everyone who may drive the car. Sometimes drivers under 25 are excluded; such a clause can be a real nuisance if you need your 24-year-old to drive you to the airport.

Leases also vary with respect to *maintenance:*

- A full-maintenance lease has the leasing company providing complete service, from batteries to tires.
- A nonmaintenance lease leaves you in charge.
- There are also some partial maintenance plans.

The more maintenance you have the leasing company assume, the more you will pay. A general rule of thumb is that maintenance packages don't become cost-effective unless you will put more than 20,000 miles a year on a car.

Cost Comparisons

It's very difficult to make dollar-for-dollar comparisons between owning and leasing. Too much depends on whether or not you finance a purchase, and at what interest rate; too much depends on the number of miles you drive and the kind of insurance you buy. But the Hertz Corporation, which is in the business of leasing cars, provides this example:

For a $6,500 domestic subcompact, a three-year full-maintenance lease would cost about $3,400 annually, including licensing and insurance. This is equivalent to 22.65¢ per mile for 15,000 miles a year. And it is about $95 more a year than the $3,306 you would pay as the owner of this car for fixed costs and maintenance. (Variables of gas and oil remain the same whether you own or lease.) That $95 could easily be wiped out for an owner by an extra 1 percent in interest charges, by a big repair bill, or by a lower trade-in allowance than expected. At the same time, it's important to remember that at the end of the leasing period the driver owns nothing; at the end of the loan period the same driver does own a car.

If you decide to lease, after weighing all the variables that apply to your situation, you have several choices of leasing agent, among them banks, rental companies, leasing companies, and automobile dealers. Some offer only one type of lease; others offer you some choice.

Consumer Protection in Auto Leasing

Federal law, in the form of the Consumer Leasing Act, protects you when you lease personal property such as automobiles, furniture, or appliances for more than four months. The law has the following provisions:

- You must be given, before you agree to any lease, a written statement of its *costs*, including (1) the amount of any advance payment, such as a security deposit; (2) the number of payments, the amount of each one, and the dates they are due, as well as the total amount of those payments; and (3) the amount you must pay for license, registration, and taxes, as well as for any other fees such as maintenance.

- You must be told the *terms* of the lease, including (1) what kind of insurance you need; (2) who is responsible for maintenance and service; (3) any penalty for default or late payment; (4) how you or the leasing company may cancel the lease, and the charge for doing so; and (5) whether you can buy the property and, if you can, when and at what price.

- You must be helped to *compare* the cost of buying on credit with the cost of leasing, by being told the total amount you are responsible for under the lease, the value of the property at the beginning of the lease, and the difference between the two. For example, a three-year open-end car lease might show:

36 monthly payments of $125	$4,500.
+ Estimated value of car at end of lease	2,000.
Amount you are responsible for under the lease	6,500.
− Value of car at beginning of lease	5,800.
DIFFERENCE:	$ 700.

You could compare this "difference" of $700 with the finance charge if you bought the car on credit.

In addition, if the lease is open-end:

- The leasing company must tell you that you may face extra charges (a "balloon payment") at the end of the lease, and how that payment will be calculated.

- The balloon payment, unless otherwise agreed upon, may equal no more than three times the average monthly payment.

- At the end of the lease you have the right to obtain an estimate of the property's value from an independent appraiser; both you and the leasing company must abide by the estimate.

Note: If you are leasing a car exclusively for personal use, don't agree with a salesperson's suggestion that you may also occasionally use it for business. Business use, such as calling on clients, excludes you from the protection of the Consumer Leasing Act.

KEY POINTS

- It costs less to buy and to run an old car than a new one.
- Compare financing costs carefully before you buy, especially when rebates and special deals are offered.
- Think about whether you need a car at all. It may be cost-effective to rent a car on an as-needed basis instead of owning one all year round.
- Leasing a car is another option, and may be worthwhile if you drive more than 10,000 to 12,000 miles a year. Compare costs carefully, however, before you decide to lease.

Automobile Insurance

Insurance, according to some estimates, is the second most expensive item in car ownership (depreciation, unless you buy an older car, is the first). If you keep your car for four years, use it to commute, and have a youthful male driver in your household, you might pay about $850 a year for auto insurance. Specific rates vary widely, according to where you live and other factors (see pp. 372–74), but this figure breaks down to 8.5¢ a mile for 10,000 miles of driving.

Automobile insurance *is* expensive. But don't try to do without it. Automobile coverage protects you against potentially tremendous financial loss stemming from accidental injury to other people or to property. Most states require motorists to carry some automobile insurance; others have "financial responsibility" laws instead. Whatever the law in your state, you should carry automobile insurance, and you should carry more than the mandated minimum.

Basic Auto Insurance Provisions

Automobile insurance comes in six basic parts, some of which are essential and some of which are optional.

Bodily Injury Liability

Bodily injury liability coverage is absolutely essential (and required in most states). It provides financial protection against legal liability (up to the limits of your policy) for injury or death resulting from an accident involving your automobile. It applies whether the injured person is in your car, in someone else's car, or a pedestrian. It applies to injury caused by your car, no matter who is driving, as long as the person driving your car has your permission to do so. And it applies when you or members of your family are driving someone else's car, as long as the driver has the owner's permission.

Bodily injury liability is often written in two parts, as 15/30, 50/100, 100/300. In each case the first figure is the maximum amount, in thousands of dollars, that the insurance company will pay for the injuries of any one person in any one accident. The second figure is the maximum amount, in thousands of dollars, it will pay for all of the injuries resulting from any one accident. Some policies are written with a "single limit," under which the maximum amount that will be paid for all losses in any one accident is stated as a single figure.

Suggestion: Buy as much bodily injury liability protection as you can afford. Jury awards in accident cases can be very high, and without enough insurance you can be wiped out.

Q. May I use my car in a car pool, without changing my automobile insurance policy?

A. Yes. As long as the car pool is not a business conducted for profit (it's okay to collect expenses from your passengers), your insurance will apply. If you are regularly carrying several passengers, however, it might be a good idea to consider increasing the limits on your bodily injury liability coverage.

Property Damage Liability

John intended to back out of his driveway, but put his car in drive by mistake. As he shot forward, he demolished his neighbor's fence. The fence was rebuilt with money received from John's automobile insurance company.

Property damage liability applies, up to the stated limits in your policy, when your car damages the property of others. Damaged property is most often a car (John could have sideswiped his neighbor's car), but the coverage applies to any property (except your own): fences, lampposts, buildings, etc. Protection is in force no matter who is driving your car (with your permission) and while you or members of your family are driving someone else's car (with the owner's permission).

Property damage coverage is often expressed as the third part of the liability formula: 10/20/5; 50/100/10. Again, your state may have minimum requirements, but you may want to consider additional coverage.

NO-FAULT INSURANCE

Your automobile insurance policy will pay personal injury and property damage liability claims when you are at fault. In many accidents fault is not easy to ascertain (three cars pile up in an intersection and you're caught in the middle; whose fault was it?), leading to extensive and expensive lawsuits. Many states, as a consequence, have adopted "no-fault" auto insurance.

Under no-fault laws, your insurance company will pay for bodily injury losses resulting from an accident, including medical and hospital expenses and lost income, no matter who is at fault. Details of coverage vary from state to state, especially with regard to the amounts to be paid and conditions governing the right to sue.

Medical Payments

This coverage in the basic automobile policy covers medical, dental, and surgical bills resulting from injury sustained in an auto accident; it's generally available in amounts ranging from $500 to $10,000 per person per accident. It covers you and all members of your family (who live with you . . . not an adult son or daughter resident elsewhere) while riding in your car or someone else's car, or when struck by a car while walking. It also applies to guests in your car.

Medical payments are made without regard to fault, and the coverage is not available in some states where no-fault insurance is the norm.

Protection Against Uninsured Motorists

This coverage applies mainly to bodily injuries for which an uninsured motorist or a hit-and-run driver is legally liable. It also applies, in most states, to injuries caused by an insured motorist whose insurance company becomes insolvent.

Despite state financial responsibility laws and mandated liability coverage, some estimates indicate that at least one of every eight motor vehicles on the road today is not insured. Unless your state has no-fault insurance, in which case you will be compensated by your own insurance company, becoming the victim of an uninsured motorist can leave you financially destitute as well as physically injured. Uninsured motorists protection is optional (as is *under*insured motorists coverage in some places). Unless you live in a no-fault state or are adequately covered under other forms of insurance for any potential financial liability, give serious thought to including it in your basic automobile policy.

There is no excuse for being an uninsured motorist. Every driver can get insurance. If insurance is not available on an individual basis because of a poor driving record, lack of experience, or the situation in your state (many companies refused to write any auto insurance in New Jersey, for instance, when the state refused to allow rate increases), it is available through an "assigned risk" plan. Shop around first and then, if necessary, ask an insurance agent about assigned risk. Rates may be higher, depending on the state and on your own record, but you will have insurance. And you may be able to move to regular coverage after an accident-free interval.

Q. My 22-year-old son, who is on his own and working and living in another city, does not have his own car and drives ours when he comes to visit. Should we still carry him on our auto insurance?

A. As long as he is no longer a student and is living away from home, you probably don't have to keep him on your policy; he should still be covered if anything happens while he is driving your car. But check with your own agent or company representative to make sure.

Collision Insurance

Steve was slowing for a red light when the driver in front jammed on his brakes. With quick reflexes, Steve was able to stop, without hitting the car in front. But the driver in back was not so lucky, or so skillful. His left front fender tangled with the right rear fender of Steve's car. The repairs to Steve's 1980 Chevrolet cost $1,380. Steve filed a claim with his own insurance company and collected $1,180 (the cost of repairs less a $200 deductible) under his collision insurance. He'll collect the rest, later, when the other company settles.

Collision coverage pays for damage to your car regardless of responsibility, whether you run into a tree or another driver runs into you. If you are involved in an accident in which the other driver is legally at fault, the collision insurance you carry on your own car will enable you to collect from your own insurance company and have your car fixed without delay. Without collision coverage you have to wait for payment until the other driver's insurance company agrees to a settlement.

If you do collect under your own collision coverage when another driver is at fault, your own company will then "subrogate" your claim— that is, submit it to the other company for payment. When it is paid, you will receive your deductible.

Collision coverage, which is optional, is written on a deductible basis, with premiums based on the year, make, and model of your car. It is generally worth carrying when your car is new and not worth carrying on a car that is several years old and greatly diminished in value.

Comprehensive Physical Damage

Mary's windshield was cracked by a flying stone. . . . Andrew's car was stolen from a busy suburban shopping mall. Both were covered under the physical damage portion of their auto insurance policies.

Comprehensive, as it's usually called, protects you against financial loss stemming from a wide array of perils: fire, theft, glass breakage, flood, falling objects, missiles, explosion, earthquake, windstorm, hail, water, vandalism or malicious mischief, riot or civil commotion, or collision with a bird or animal. It does *not* apply to damage incurred in a collision with another car or object and it does not include wear and tear, engine failure, or mechanical difficulties.

The coverage is written with a deductible, most commonly $50, and with premiums based in part on location. There are more car thefts in some areas than in others. Wind and hail storms, similarly, are more frequent in some areas than in others.

Replacement Cost Insurance

When Marilyn took a skid on an icy Nebraska road, her yearly budget hit the skids too. She learned it would cost her more to repair her 1982 auto than it was currently worth. Her insurance company totaled the vehicle and gave her a claim settlement of $5,500, its current value, but less than she still owed on the loan she had taken to buy the car. Marilyn had to dip deeply into an already none-too-healthy savings account to purchase the 1986 model of the same car for $11,374.

A car is deemed a total loss by an insurance company not only when it is impossible to repair but also, as Marilyn found out, when it would cost more to repair than the car is currently worth. With escalating repair costs, this situation is confronting more and more drivers. In 1971 only 3.5 percent of all damaged autos insured by one major carrier were totaled; by 1984 the figure was 9.9 percent. According to the Alliance of American Insurers, a 1985 two-door sport coupe that cost $10,682 new would cost $37,014 for parts and paint alone, without labor, if it had to be rebuilt.

The answer: replacement insurance, similar to the replacement insurance on household contents described in Chapter 14. Under a Kemper plan, for example, the insurer will pay to repair the car even if repair costs exceed its current market value, up to the cost of a comparable new car. If the car cannot be repaired for less than the price of a comparable new car, the company will pay the cost to replace the damaged auto with a new car of the same make with the same equipment.

How would this coverage work for Marilyn? Because a replacement car of the same type cost $11,374, the insurer would have paid up to $11,374 for repairs to her car even though the car was "worth" only $5,500. If repair was not possible, the insurer would have provided up to $11,374 for the purchase of a replacement vehicle.

Replacement insurance must usually be elected within 30–90 days of your purchase of a new car. It does not apply to damage caused by fire, theft or larceny. Replacement coverage is not available in every state. Where it is available it is offered, at this writing, by only a few insurers. It may, however, be worth investigating. At a modest additional cost— Kemper's policy is priced at an extra 10 percent of the combined comprehensive and collision premium, or an average of $15 per six-month policy period for the average mid-size car—you could be protected against the significant financial loss you could face if your car was severely damaged. That loss could entail both the inflated price of a new car, while your old car was still providing good transportation, and the continuing cost of paying off an auto loan on a car you no longer have.

Q. I may drive to Mexico for vacation and I was told that I need special automobile insurance. Doesn't my regular insurance apply?

A. No. Mexico has special rules, requiring that nonresident drivers purchase auto liability insurance from a Mexican insurance company. The rules are very stringent (a Mexican endorsement attached to a U.S. policy is not sufficient), and failure to comply could leave you in serious trouble. Your car could be impounded, your driver's license could be revoked, you could even be imprisoned. You can buy a short-term "Special Automobile Policy for Tourists" from a Mexican insurance company in most American border cities. Don't leave home without it.

If you're crossing the border in the other direction, however, and traveling to Canada, you'll find life a bit easier. Your American insurance policy does apply, although you'll need a "Non-resident Inter-province Motor Vehicle Liability Insurance Card." This card, which proves that you do have auto insurance, may be easily obtained from your own insurance company or from a provincial or territorial government office of Canada.

Auto Insurance Rates

Insurance may be a sizable chunk of the costs of owning a car. But insurance can also be considered a bargain. In the decade of the 1970s, when the overall cost of living rose by 106 percent and the cost of automobile repair and maintenance rose by 119 percent, the cost of auto insurance rose by a relatively modest 96 percent. In addition, of course, the cost of insurance is a bargain compared to the cost of settling most claims.

Many motorists, nonetheless, are feeling the pinch of rising premiums. It's possible to keep your own automobile insurance premiums down. It helps, to start with, if you understand how rates are established.

How Auto Insurance Rates Are Set

The overall cost of insurance is determined by the experience of insurance companies: the number of claims they receive and the cost of resolving those claims. Because this claims experience varies from place to place, automobile insurance rates have traditionally been based in large part on where you live. Another important factor is driver classification.

WHERE YOU LIVE

A rating territory may be an entire city, or a part of a large city, a suburb, or a rural district. Rates are based on the claims involving cars kept in the particular territory, regardless of where an accident actually takes place. A Tennessee driver responsible for an accident in California affects Tennessee rates, not those levied in California.

In general, for obvious reasons, it costs more to insure a car in Los Angeles, California (or any large city), than in Clinton, Iowa (or any small town or rural district). There have been arguments, however, that the whole territorial classification system is unfair. Why should a middle-aged driver in Newark, New Jersey, with a spotless driving record, have to pay more for auto insurance than a younger (and more careless) driver in a Princeton suburb?

DRIVER CLASSIFICATION

Claims experience also varies in accordance with categories of drivers: driving record, age, sex, and marital status. In general, the younger the driver, the higher the rates, with still-higher rates for single males and the highest of all (based on nationwide accident experience) for young single males who own and operate their own cars.

The classifications can get complicated. One company, for instance, lists its rates as follows:

"Base" rates apply to:

— married men age 25 or over,

— married women of any age,

— single men over age 30 who are owners or principal drivers,

— single women age 25 to 30.

Higher rates apply to:

— married men under 25.

— single women under 25,

— single men under 25 who are not owners or principal drivers,

— single men under 30 who are owners or principal drivers.

Lower rates apply, for this company, to:

— drivers over 65 (unless there are youthful drivers in the household),

— women ages 30 to 64 who are the only drivers in their household.

There's been a lot of discussion about whether this age, sex, and marital status categorization is fair; at least one state legislature has outlawed this method of computing rates, and at this writing Congress is considering action which would eliminate sex as a factor in all insurance rates. But insurance companies point out in their own defense that it's been well documented that unmarried males under the age of 25 are responsible for proportionately more accidents than young women or older adults of either gender. True, but, again, the careful teenager is penalized just by virtue of being a teenager.

Until this controversy is resolved (if ever), bear in mind that insurance companies set their own rates. If you shop around, you may find very different premiums charged for a person who fits your description.

OTHER FACTORS

Where you live and what you're like are not the only factors that enter into the setting of rates. Other factors include:

■ Whether the vehicle is driven for business (and exposed to more traffic and more potential accidents) or solely for pleasure

■ The number of miles driven each year (less is better)

■ Whether or not the car is kept in a garage (and thereby protected from the elements and, somewhat, from theft)

■ Your occupation (considered as a rating factor by some companies, in some states)

■ The specific loss experience of the type of car you buy (now a basis for rates in more and more companies). Some companies offer a discount or impose a surcharge on collision premiums only; others apply discounts and surcharges, often ranging from 10 to 30 percent, on both collision and comprehensive.

Typical rates are shown in Table 1.

TABLE 1: Sample automobile insurance rates.

	Average student living at home	Good student living at home	Average student away at school	Good student away at school
50/100/25 0 ded/comp $100 ded/coll	$342	$289	$289	$237
50/100/25 $100 ded/comp $200 ded/coll	313	265	265	217
100/300/50 0 ded/comp $100 ded/coll	364	307	307	256
100/300/50 $100 ded/comp $200 ded/coll	335	283	283	232

Comparative rates on automobile insurance for a Columbus, Ohio, family of three—a 42-year-old husband, a 40-year-old wife, and their 19-year-old son. The father, who is the principal driver, commutes 12 miles to work in the family's 1984 Ford Escort. The son has taken a behind-the-wheel driver education course. Each of the three drivers has a good driving record. Rates are for six months, effective 2/86. (Ohio has a 10 percent account credit for insureds who have auto and homeowners coverage with the same company.)

(Source: Aetna Casualty & Surety Co.)

Keeping Costs Down

You can keep your automobile insurance costs down by driving less, by garaging your car, and by buying a well-rated model. Talk to an insurance agent while you're car-shopping, and find out what it will cost to insure the model you're considering. Ask if you might get a discount or, conversely, whether a surcharge might be imposed. Be aware, too, that some cars, notably high-performance and sports cars, may cost you more in insurance; the assumption is that you won't buy all that power unless you mean to use it. Luxury cars, too, attractive to thieves and expensive to repair, may also cost more to insure.

You can also keep your auto insurance costs down in a number of other specific ways:

DISCOUNT PLANS

Take advantage of any and all discounts for which you may be eligible, and ask your company (it may not volunteer the information) which discounts it offers. These might include:

- Safe driver plans, for drivers with good records
- Specific model discounts, if you drive a car with good crash-resistance
- Farm discounts, for cars or trucks owned by a farmer or rancher
- Anti-theft devices, and airbag or automatic belting systems
- Driver education discounts, for high school and college students who maintain good grades
- Away-from-home discounts for students living at school over 100 miles away (this discount does not apply to students who own their own cars and carry their own insurance; it's always less expensive to register your child's car in your name and to include the child on your insurance policy)
- Good student discounts, for high school and college students who maintain good grades
- Multiple-car discounts, for households owning two or more passenger cars and insuring them with the same company
- Nonsmoker and nondrinker discounts, offered by some companies
- Senior citizen discounts, offered by some companies
- Car pool discounts, for those who share the driving to work

CAR POOLING

Car pooling saves money, in several ways:

- On auto insurance. Premiums may drop from 10 to 25 percent if you share the driving with others. Even with companies which do not offer specific car pooling discounts, lowering driving mileage may place you in a lower premium classification.
- On dollar outlay. If you drive a one-way distance of 10 miles, in a standard-size sedan, you save at least $500 a year by sharing the driving with just one other person. Rotating drivers among a larger group would save proportionately more.
- On time. Many cities have car-pool lanes on highways and toll bridges, speeding commuting time to work. Many employers, too, now offer preferential parking to car poolers.
- On car upkeep and maintenance. Driving your car less means less wear and tear.

SELF-INSURING

Think about how much you can afford to self-insure and buy insurance with the appropriate deductibles. Collision insurance, for example, is usually written with deductibles ranging from $100 to $500. A deductible of $200 instead of $100 could mean a savings of 10 percent on your collision insurance; a $500 deductible could mean a savings of 25 percent. Comprehensive insurance may be written with deductibles from $50 to $250; choosing the $50 deductible instead of full coverage could save you 8 to 12 percent.

DROPPING UNNECESSARY COVERAGE

Drop collision insurance altogether when your car is four or five years old. Chances are that its book value at this point is far less than you would collect should the car be damaged. The car may provide adequate transportation for your family, and therefore cost a good bit to replace, but its book value is what counts. No company will pay more in repairs than the car was worth before the accident, minus any salvage value (unless you have replacement insurance; see p. 371).

Don't duplicate coverage. If you carry umbrella liability insurance (described in Chapter 14), you may not need as much personal injury liability coverage. If you have adequate health and accident insurance, you may not need medical payments coverage. If you belong to an auto or travel club, you may not need towing insurance (or, if you have towing insurance, you may not need to belong to an auto or travel club). Review all your policies carefully to narrow any gaps while reducing overlapping coverage.

SHOPPING AROUND

Rates vary widely; it pays to comparison-shop (but look at a company's claims record as well as its rates). It may also pay to give one company both your auto and your homeowners insurance business. As a bigger customer, you may get better service. And you will avoid the gray areas that can occur between coverages . . . the kind of situation, for instance, that might develop if a passenger trips while getting out of your car and injures himself in your driveway, and two insurers fight over who will pay.

But don't be penny-conscious to the extent that you leave yourself vulnerable. Keep your coverage in step with inflation, particularly in the areas of property damage liability, medical payments, and uninsured motorists coverage.

KEEPING YOUR INSURER UP-TO-DATE

Keep your insurance agent or company informed of changes in your life that may change your insurance premiums. Tell the company if you move, stop driving to work, join a car pool, reach the age of 25, get married, or have a child go away to college. All of these things make a difference.

KEY POINTS

- Automobile insurance is absolutely essential, whether or not it is required by your state.
- Buy as much bodily injury liability protection as you can afford, against the risk of injuring anyone with your car.
- Save money on auto insurance by taking sizable deductibles on collision and comprehensive protection, and dropping these coverages altogether as your car ages.

SPENDING
YOUR MONEY:
HIGHER EDUCATION

Financing
an Education

Bill Taylor is the father of three children, ages 10 through 14. He's aware that college costs a lot of money, but never sat down to actually calculate what college will cost. Now he's learned, to his horror, that four years at the average state university currently cost about $26,000 while four years at the average private university are in the neighborhood of $50,000. If all three children attend a state university, the total cost, at today's fees and without regard to inevitable yearly increases, would be $78,000. But today's costs, as Bill well knows, won't be tomorrow's costs. What's more, with three children in a span of four years, the Taylor family will face overlapping expenses. With Bill's current income of $34,200, the next ten years look bleak indeed.

Education beyond high school is an expensive proposition. But it is also an investment in the future. Whether you are a parent planning for the higher education of your children or an adult planning your own advanced education, you'll want to think through the best ways to finance that education and to make the most of the opportunities open to you. This chapter will focus on college costs and on ways to meet those costs. The first section of the chapter deals with funding your children's educational expenses; the second focuses on economical ways to educate yourself.

What Does College Cost?

College comes in many shapes and sizes, from the highly selective and high-priced institutions of the Ivy League to local low-cost community colleges where students live at home. In between are universities and colleges in a wide range of sizes, of quality, and of cost. Whatever school you look at, however, whatever kind of school it is and wherever it is located, there's no doubt about one thing: College costs are *up*.

For a number of years, despite surging inflation, college costs rose at a rate well below the rate of the Consumer Price Index. In the decade starting with the 1972–73 academic year, total expenses at four-year colleges rose by 95 percent at public colleges and 100 percent at private colleges; in the same decade the Consumer Price Index rose by 123 percent. For hard-pressed parents, of course, the difference may be slight. In any case, financial pressures have caught up with colleges and in 1982–83, when inflation had slowed to about 6 percent, the overall cost of college increased by an average of 11 percent. In 1985–86 costs increased by about 7 percent.

Nonetheless, many experts insist, income has risen more than college costs. According to the College Board, a family with an income of $20,000 in 1971–72 was expected to contribute $3,900 to a child's costs. A decade later the same family, earning $46,000, was only expected to pay $6,400 toward college. Put another way, today's parents are paying for a smaller proportion of total college costs.

Why, then, does it hurt so much? Because while we're earning more we're also spending a lot more on taxes, on housing, on energy costs . . . on living. And because college costs, despite what the experts say, are high. On a nationwide basis, for the 1985–86 school year, according to the annual survey taken by the College Board, resident students at public four-year colleges paid an average of $5,314 a year for tuition and fees, books and supplies, room and board, personal expenses, and transportation. At private four-year colleges, the average total reached $9,659 a year. Two-year colleges are less expensive, with commuting students at public institutions spending about $3,627 a year and those at private colleges about $6,470. Commuting students spend less, as a rule, at any school . . . between $800 and $1,000 less than their on-campus classmates.

There are regional variations as well; colleges in New England, by and large, are more expensive, and those diagonally across the nation, in the Southwest, are less expensive. In 1985–86, an average four-year private college in New England (not Harvard; it cost over $15,000) cost $11,903 while a comparable college in the Southwest cost $7,784. (See Table 1.)

MISCELLANEOUS EXPENSES

Many parents, understandably, focus on paying for the major elements of a college education: tuition, room, and board. But there's a lot more at stake when young people are sent off to live on their own. Figure on $1,500–$2,000 for transportation, books, and supplies, and personal

TABLE 1: Expenses, by region, for resident students, 1985–86.

	Public 2-year	Private 2-year	Public 4-year	Private 4-year
NATIONAL				
Tuition and fees	$ 659	$3,719	$1,242	$ 5,418
Books and supplies	355	367	373	384
Room and board	*	2,591	2,473	2,781
Personal expenses	*	667	836	694
Transportation	*	351	390	382
TOTAL	$ *	$7,695	$5,314	$ 9,659
NEW ENGLAND				
Tuition and fees	$ 897	$5,033	$1,496	$ 7,153
Books and supplies	410	364	399	370
Room and board	*	3,553	2,608	3,419
Personal expenses	*	570	780	625
Transportation	*	243	220	336
TOTAL	$ *	$9,763	$5,503	$11,903
MIDDLE STATES				
Tuition and fees	$1,127	$3,770	$1,583	$ 6,115
Books and supplies	362	355	375	404
Room and board	*	2,604	2,977	3,102
Personal expenses	*	779	681	662
Transportation	*	*	308	309
TOTAL	$ *	$ *	$5,924	$10,592
SOUTH				
Tuition and fees	$ 498	$3,281	$1,323	$ 4,366
Books and supplies	318	352	379	386
Room and board	*	2,316	2,173	2,487
Personal expenses	*	680	736	669
Transportation	*	375	349	461
TOTAL	$ *	$7,004	$4,960	$8,369
MIDWEST				
Tuition and fees	$ 907	$3,414	$1,375	$ 5,194
Books and supplies	348	391	354	368
Room and board	*	2,329	2,236	2,514
Personal expenses	*	625	861	678
Transportation	*	389	341	358
TOTAL	$ *	$7,148	$5,167	$ 9,112
SOUTHWEST				
Tuition and fees	$ 461	$2,550	$ 773	$ 3,644
Books and supplies	368	425	380	359
Room and board	*	2,170	2,342	2,411
Personal expenses	*	875	925	841
Transportation	*	425	659	529
TOTAL	$ *	$6,445	$5,079	$ 7,784

TABLE 1: Expenses, by region, for resident students, 1985–86. *(cont.)*

	Public 2-year	Private 2-year	Public 4-year	Private 4-year
WEST				
Tuition and fees	$ 342	$3,350	$1,021	$ 5,582
Books and supplies	375	333	375	406
Room and board	*	*	2,813	2,950
Personal expenses	*	542	932	847
Transportation	*	458	427	439
TOTAL	$ *	$ *	$5,568	$10,224

* Sample too small to provide meaningful averages.
(Source: *The College Cost Book*, the College Board)

items. Some students, of course, spend considerably more. Some of the big dollar items: food (those late-night pizzas and their accompaniments can add up to several hundred dollars a year) and telephone calls (today's students call their far-flung friends, sometimes to the tune of $50 a month; they don't seem to write). Owning and maintaining a car on campus, for those who do, is another major expense.

What's the best way for parents to handle this outgo? Encourage your child to plan spending over a semester. If you're supplying spending money, do so on a semester basis and don't plug the gaps that may occur. If the youngster is depending on his or her own earnings (summertime or year-round part-time) it will be even easier; you can just bow out of the personal-spending question and let the student manage. It won't necessarily be good management—middle-class college students are notoriously irresponsible about spending money, especially while they're busy adjusting to college life—but it's the only way they'll learn. If you supply money on an as-needed or as-requested basis, life in the real world after graduation will be a tremendous shock.

Q. My daughter will need a checking account for the first time when she goes off to college. What's the best way to set it up? Should we have a joint account, at a bank near home, so I can make deposits for her when necessary? Or would it be better if she opens an account at school?

A. Long-distance management is difficult. If her account is near her school, where she'll be living most of the year, she'll easily be able to verify her balance and handle any problems that arise. She'll also find it easier to cash checks from the same community; out-of-state check-cashing can be very difficult. Wherever the account is opened, however, tell your daughter how important it is to keep accurate records and to balance her checkbook. Tell her, too, that it's better to keep her money in an interest-earning NOW account, to make the most of what she has. But she should compare minimum balances and service charges before picking a bank or savings and loan.

More and more college students use credit cards, often a second card on a parent's account. On many campuses, too, bookstore purchases (which typically include far more than books) may be billed directly to parents. This may enable parents to keep costs down—or it may encourage the student to spend. Better, I think, to have students pay their own bills and learn to be financially responsible.

How Will You Meet These Costs?

If your income is low and your children are bright, you probably won't have a problem; financial assistance should be available. If you're well-to-do, you'll probably be able to pay the bills as they come due. If you're a member of the vast middle class, however, even if you're at the high-income end of the middle class, you're likely to find college costs a burden.

Before you decide how to shoulder that burden in the least painful way, decide how you feel about paying for college.

Some parents want to provide everything, including a college education, to get their children off to a good start in life. Others believe that some things, including college, mean more to the child who contributes to the cost. Most college financial aid offices today require contributions from both parent and child. Decide on your own position.

As your child earns money during the high school years, for instance, will the child be able to spend that money? Or will you insist that some portion of the child's earnings be set aside for college? (If you do, be sure that college is the child's goal as well as your own.) Once your youngster is in college, will you continue to provide a regular allowance? Or will the student be expected to contribute to his or her social life, if not to tuition itself?

Some parents have always scrimped and saved to put money aside toward college education for their children. Others, out of choice or necessity, have spent money on current need while assuming that college costs would somehow be met. Under many college aid formulas, as we'll see a bit later in this chapter, the parent who has saved and accumulated assets may be penalized. Even without penalties, however, the combined influence of higher college costs and widely available financial aid has created a fundamental shift: Parents who used to believe in the virtue of savings, in paying for college out of past income, are now increasingly turning to borrowing, to paying for college out of future income. Where do you stand? And will the recent cuts in federal funding force you to change your mind?

Where you stand may depend, to some extent, on the ages of your children. If you have pre-schoolers and are told that the current cost of college, at a state-supported public institution, may run to a minimum of $20,000 for each child for four years, you may just throw up your hands and assume that you can't possibly save enough to meet the dollar figure that those costs will reach in fifteen years. If you have teenagers, on the other hand, you may already have had lengthy discussions about meeting college costs in the almost-here-and-now, and you may have decided that you've missed the boat, that it's too late to start saving in any meaningful way.

But whatever the ages of your children, now is the time to start planning ahead. If you have pre-schoolers, it's not too soon. If you have teenagers, it's not too late. Start now.

TABLE 2: Projected college costs, 1986–90.

Type of institution	1986/87		1987/88	
	Resident	Commuter	Resident	Commuter
4-Year Private	$11,224	$9,633	$12,346	$10,596
2-Year Private	8,794	7,804	9,673	8,584
4-Year Public	6,283	5,058	6,911	5,563
2-Year Public	5,146	4,582	5,660	5,040

Type of institution	1988/89		1989/90	
	Resident	Commuter	Resident	Commuter
4-Year Private	$13,580	$11,655	$14,938	$12,820
2-Year Private	10,640	9,442	11,704	10,386
4-Year Public	7,602	6,129	8,362	6,742
2-Year Public	6,226	5,544	6,848	6,098

(Source: *Don't Miss Out,* Octameron)

ESTIMATE COLLEGE COSTS

The place to start is with an estimate of what costs will actually be for your children when they are ready for college. Table 2 shows estimated costs beginning in 1986. If you have several years before your children start college, your estimate may be more of a guesstimate, but it's still worth doing, to give yourself a savings goal. Determine your personal estimate of future costs, therefore, based on:

■ Where your children will get the best education to meet their particular needs. If you have a budding physicist, one type of school may be indicated; for the average nondirected teenager, the choices may be more extensive.

■ Current college costs at the type of school each child will need. Add an inflation factor of 5 to 6 percent (inflation may subside, but it's unlikely to be totally eliminated).

■ How many children you will have in school, for how many years. Overlapping years need extra weight in your calculations.

Here's the way college costs shape up for the Taylor children. Based on a steady inflation rate of 6 percent, four years at a public college for the three children will require a total outlay of $99,376. That's if the Taylor family pays each bill as it comes due, without advance planning. Table 3 shows how the figures look, based on an analysis prepared by Ziedins & Company, financial consultants in Denver, Colorado.

TABLE 3: Projected college expenses for the three-child family discussed in the text.

Child's name: Present age: Year	Chris, 14	Nikki, 12	Barry, 10	Total annual outlay
1987	0	0	0	0
1988	0	0	0	0
1989	0	0	0	0
1990	$ 6,709	0	0	$ 6,709
1991	7,111	0	0	7,111
1992	7,538	$ 7,538	0	15,076
1993	7,990	7,990	0	15,980
1994	0	8,470	$ 8,470	16,940
1995	0	8,978	8,978	17,956
1996	0	0	9,517	9,517
1997	0	0	10,088	10,088
TOTAL	$29,348	$32,976	$37,052	$99,376

A range of $6,709 to $17,956 per year will be required between 1990 and 1997 if costs are paid as they become due.
(Source: Aivars Ziedins, President, Ziedins & Company, Ltd.)

With three children two years apart (bad planning to begin with, if the Taylors had looked ahead to college) and consequent overlapping costs, twelve years of college will have to be paid within a span of eight years.

Even with Wendy Taylor's returning to paid employment, and a consequent boost in the family income from $34,200 to $48,000 before taxes (a figure which should rise along with inflation), the outlay of $17,956 in 1995 will be hard to meet. What steps can the Taylors (and you) take now to meet future college costs? What can you do to keep those costs down?

Keeping Costs Down

An essential part of meeting college costs is keeping those costs as manageable as possible. In recent years parents and students have been told to pick the best school for the student, regardless of cost, and then figure out how to pay for it. The rationale for this approach is that schools will create financial aid packages for students they want, in a "need-blind" approach to admissions. This has been true and is still so at many schools, although to a lesser extent. But because (1) not every student has a single "best" school (most don't) and because (2) federal aid to education is being drastically curtailed, it's not a bad idea to look at ways to keep those costs down. Here are some tips.

ACCELERATED PROGRAMS

Bright students, in particular, may get as much as a full year's college credit on the basis of Advanced Placement courses and examinations completed in high school. Diligent students may do four years of college in three, or make up a semester by attending a lower-cost summer school.

COOPERATIVE EDUCATION

The federal government has cooperative education opportunities (also being curtailed in the budget-conscious '80s); so do some private institutions. With some variation among individual programs, a student may alternate semesters of work and study, work part-time during the school year, or, in rare instances, even work solely during summer vacations. Under most of these programs, the course of study takes a bit longer but savings are considerable.

ATTENDING A SCHOOL IN YOUR HOME STATE

This can be a double money-saver: First, if you go to college within your home state, especially a public institution, you'll probably find tuition and fees lower for state residents. And, second, within your home state you may be eligible for grants, scholarships, or loans offered only to residents.

COMMUNITY COLLEGES

These two-year institutions are generally the least expensive educational option of all. Many students live at home and hold down a part-time job while attending a community college. Then, armed with an associate degree after two years of study, the able student can transfer to a four-year institution to complete work toward a bachelor's degree.

Note: While tuition and fees are generally much less at a community college, it is not necessarily true that living at home with parents costs less than living in a dormitory or apartment on a college campus. Food costs may actually be higher: The student will consume his or her usual quantities at the family table and will also need on-campus meals (when there's no time to get home between classes or between class and an evening activity) and snacks (for social time). Transportation, to and from campus on a regular basis, may cost another $200 to $300. Do your arithmetic carefully before assuming that commuting to college is cost-effective.

EMPLOYER-PAID PLANS

If you work for a company with generous tuition benefits, you can attend school at your employer's expense. Some such programs reimburse job-related study; others recognize that all learning is valuable. The ambitious high school graduate can seek a job with educational benefits, and save almost the entire burden of college costs.

Note: Some tuition assistance may be taxable as income.

THE MILITARY

The highly competitive service academies (West Point, Annapolis, and the Air Force Academy) are free but open to very few. But there are other ways to use military assistance for education. There are ROTC scholarships, educational benefits for joining the Reserves or the National Guard, and educational programs for enlisted men and women.

CORRESPONDENCE COURSES

Expensive on-campus time can be shortened if a student moves ahead via home study. Be sure, however, that the correspondence school is accredited and that its credits will be accepted for transfer at the college you plan to attend.

SPECIAL PROGRAMS

Some colleges reduce tuition costs for siblings (and some allow parents of students to attend school free). Some, eager to attract able students, reduce tuition for good grades. Some even guarantee the four-year cost of education, if the entire bill is paid in advance. In asking questions of colleges, ask about such special programs as well.

Paying for College

Once you have an idea of what higher education will cost, and of ways to cut these costs, then you have to decide how you'll come up with the necessary funds. There are several methods, from systematic savings through loans and grants. Perhaps the most important point to bear in mind, however, is that the methods are not mutually exclusive. You should draw on a variety of methods and sources. The College Funds Worksheet lists a wide range of possible college funds. Which are applicable to you?

COLLEGE FUNDS WORKSHEET

Fund source	Amount you can expect per year
SAVINGS	
Parents	$_____
Student	$_____
INCOME	
Parent	$_____
Student, summer	$_____
Student, school year	$_____
SCHOLARSHIPS/GRANTS	
Need-based	$_____
Academic merit	$_____
Special interest/talent	$_____
Athletic	$_____
Community	$_____
LOANS	
Government-backed	$_____
College	$_____
Private	$_____
OTHER	
GI Bill	$_____
Military (ROTC, etc.)	$_____
Borrowing against life insurance	$_____
Refinancing a home	$_____
Home equity loan	$_____

Savings Plans

Systematic savings can work for you, no matter when you begin, although the earlier you start the easier you will find the task. If you start to save just $40 a month at just 5.25 percent when your child is 8 years old, you'll have $8,000 saved in ten years. If you wait until the child is

13, you'll have to save $145 a month to reach the same goal. A mere $8,000, of course, won't go very far. But if you already have it on hand when your child starts college, you won't have to take it out of current income that year.

TABLE 4: A possible solution for the three-child family described in the text, based on an annual contribution to an investment fund earning 9 percent.

Year	Opening balance	Annual deposit	Annual withdrawal	Annual earnings	Closing balance
1986	$ 0	$8,219	$ 0	$ 533	$ 8,752
1987	8,752	8,219	0	1,100	18,070
1988	18,070	8,219	0	1,704	27,993
1989	27,993	8,219	0	2,347	38,558
1990	38,558	8,219	6,709	2,596	42,665
1991	42,665	8,219	7,111	2,836	46,609
1992	46,609	8,219	15,076	2,576	42,328
1993	42,328	8,219	15,981	2,240	36,806
1994	36,806	5,023	16,939	1,613	26,503
1995	26,503	5,023	17,956	879	14,450
1996	14,450	2,341	9,517	471	7,746
1997	7,746	2,341	10,088	0	0

(Source: Aivars Ziedins, President, Ziedins & Company, Ltd.)

Look at it another way: The $99,376 that the Taylor family will need to pay college bills as they come due becomes $80,480 if annual deposits, as shown in Table 4, are made from 1986 through 1997. The assumed rate of return, before taxes, is 9 percent. Had they started when 14-year-old Chris was 8, even if the rate of return was considerably less, they would have had to save much less to reach the same goal.

Start as early as you can to save as much as you can. Be methodical. Get in the habit of regular deposits. Choose a bank or thrift with a special college savings plan and you may earn higher interest. Or put small sums into a regular passbook savings account until you have large enough sums to place in higher-yielding investments. Or, perhaps better yet, purchase U.S. government Series, EE bonds in your child's name; they pay a variable rate of interest and the tax due on the interest can be eliminated or deferred (see p. 71 for details). Virtually any of the investments discussed in Chapters 6 through 8, depending on the amount of risk you want to assume, might be appropriate for an educational fund.

Setting Up a "Tax Scholarship"

Systematic savings in your name will grow, but they will just as systematically be reduced by the income tax due on interest earnings. Until recently, you could amass considerably greater income, on the same initial investment, by putting savings in your child's name. With a so-called "tax scholarship," via a custodial account or a trust, income would be taxed at the child's tax rate. Since small children generally have little other income, taxes were minimal.

The 1986 tax law has changed the picture. You can still put savings in your child's name, but until that child reaches the age of 14, any earnings over $1,000 a year will be taxed at the parent's rate. The only way to set up a tax scholarship, therefore, is to do so for your children over the age of 14; investment earnings will then be taxed at the child's rate.

If this makes sense in your particular situation, these are the alternatives:

OUTRIGHT GIFTS

You could make an outright gift to your child or grandchild, subject only to the gift tax restriction of $10,000 per person per year. (You can give more, of course, if you pay the necessary gift tax.) You and your spouse can jointly give $20,000 tax-free to each child each year, if you have the money and if you want to relinquish control of the money to your child. You can give securities that have appreciated in value, let the child sell the asset, and reduce the tax due on the profit. But gifts are irrevocable. Most parents do not want to make outright gifts to their children.

Q. I would like to use some securities I've accumulated over the years to pay my grandson's way through college. I don't want to give him the money. I also don't want to sell the stock and pay the tax. Can you suggest an approach that will help my grandson, while minimizing taxes due?

A. Donate the stock itself to the college, with the provision that the earned income be used to fund your grandson's tuition and that income earned after his graduation be used to establish a scholarship fund. You'll get several tax breaks. The gift itself is a charitable contribution. The income will be taxed at your grandson's marginal tax rate, not your own. You're removing the asset from your taxable estate. And, if the university sells the stock rather than your selling it, you won't have tax to pay on the appreciated value. Any college or university will be happy to help you make the necessary arrangements, but be sure to get good legal advice as well, since such arrangements are subject to challenge by the IRS.

CUSTODIAL ACCOUNTS

When an Ohio couple inherited $25,000 in 1976, they thought ahead to the college education of their two children, then ages 16 and 13. They established four custodial accounts for each of the children. Each account contained $3,000 and took the form of a bank certificate of deposit; each CD was timed to mature in each of the four years of college for each child. Interest rates were much lower in 1976 than in the early 1980s, especially on short-term time deposits. Not one of these accounts paid over 8 percent. Nonetheless, when the first $3,000 account matured after a year and a half in August 1977, in time for their son's first year at college, it returned $3,393. The fifth certificate, redeemed in August 1981, in time for their daughter's first year of college, returned $4,278. Since the son's first year cost about $7,000 and the daughter's almost $9,000, each maturing CD paid just under one semester's bills. The interest earned, meanwhile, was taxable to the children.

You can establish custodial accounts under the Uniform Gifts to Minors Act (UGMA), in your state; the account is in the child's name with a designated adult as custodian. The interest is taxable to the child if that child is over age 14. Younger children may earn up to $1,000 a year in investment income and have it taxed at their own rate; on higher amounts the parents' tax rate applies. The parent retains control of the funds until the child reaches legal age (unlike an outright gift, where control is immediately transferred to the child). At that time, no matter how you may feel about it, the money belongs to the child. Money and securities are most often given under a custodial arrangement; some states also permit gifts of insurance policies or real estate.

It's easy to open a custodial account (maybe too easy; don't do it without thinking it through). All you have to do is secure a Social Security number for your child and fill out the forms available at any bank or stockbrokerage. If the original custodial account is in the form of securities, you'll also need a custodial account in which to deposit dividends (unless, of course, you arrange to have any dividends reinvested). You'll also have to be sure that a tax return is filed for the child.

Before establishing a custodial account, find out what UGMA regulations apply in your state. In most cases, the custodian may retain control of the funds until the child turns 21 (even if the legal age of majority in the state is 18), but some states require that control be relinquished at the child's 18th birthday. Do you want your youngster to control the money then?

If you use the money set aside in a custodial account, meanwhile, to pay for food, clothing, or shelter, you'll lose the tax advantage; such expenditures are considered your obligation as a parent and the money may then be taxed to you. College expenses, although a gray area in the eyes of the IRS, have generally been considered acceptable (although state law varies . . . be sure to check).

TRUSTS

Both Clifford trusts and spousal remainder trusts, which offered ways to have income taxed at a child's rate while principal eventually reverted to the donor, have been wiped out by the 1986 tax law. Such trusts are now taxed to the grantor, so that parents or grandparents or whoever establishes the trust would have to pay the tax.

If you already have such a trust in effect, consult your tax adviser.

IF YOU TAX-SHELTER

If tax-sheltering education dollars sounds good to you, get competent legal and accounting advice. And remember:

- Money, once given, stays given. You can't put money into a child's name and then take it back again. Don't give money you can't afford to give.

- Even if you retain control over the funds during your youngster's childhood, under most tax shelter arrangements the child will take control upon becoming a legal adult. If you suspect that your youngster may want to run off to Europe to take up motorcycle racing instead of completing an education, and if you would disapprove of the use of these funds for this purpose, don't put the money in the child's name.

- If you name yourself as custodian for your child, and die while the custodial account is in effect, the money becomes part of your taxable estate. If your taxable estate will be $600,000 or more in value, large enough to be subject to federal estate taxes, think about naming someone else as custodian: a relative (required in some states) or a trusted friend.

- If assets in a student's name earn enough income (once the child reaches age 19, and with or without his or her own earnings) to provide more than half of the student's support for the year, you lose the student as a dependent on your federal income tax return.

- If you do use the tax shelter of income-splitting to fund education, then you'll want to put your money in investments yielding the highest possible return. Forget about tax-exempt investments for this particular purpose; they make no sense.

Apply for Financial Aid

The moment of truth will dawn during your youngster's senior year of high school. If savings (both taxable and tax-sheltered) don't add up to enough, you'll have to turn to other sources. One such source might be a second mortgage on your house or an equity access loan, used directly for college tuition (mortgage deductions are permitted, even beyond the cost of the house, for educational expenses). Another might involve borrowing against life insurance, although interest on such loans is no longer tax-deductible. But the first step, for many people, will be an application for financial aid.

Q. My parents are divorced and each says the other should fill out the financial aid application for my colleges. What do I do now?

A. Tell the parent with whom you lived for the greatest part of last year that it's his or her job to fill out the form. If you lived on your own, or shared your time equally between your parents, then the job falls to the one who provided the bulk of your basic support (housing, food, clothes, medical care, etc.). An individual college may also require a financial form from the other parent, and may consider that parent's current marital status and other obligations.

Most schools today have financial aid offices. Most will help you to meet what's called "demonstrated need," the difference between total college expenses and the amount your family is able to contribute. Note that demonstrated need is not a fixed amount; since the sum the family can contribute remains essentially the same, a student will usually receive more in aid from a more expensive school.

Whatever the amount, financial aid generally comes in three forms: jobs, grants, and loans. The proportion of each in the total package depends on the amount of demonstrated need. It also depends on the philosophy of the particular college. Some, believing in student self-help, give jobs and loans first; others start out with grants.

THE NEED ANALYSIS

All financial aid is based on a need analysis, a detailed (very detailed) look at your family's financial profile. The need analysis, based on your honest answers to a long list of questions (backed up, in case you're tempted to fudge, by your tax returns), provides the answers to the fundamental questions: How much can you, as parents, contribute to your child's yearly educational costs? How much can the child contribute? And how much remains to be made up from outside sources?

The forms are complex and are based on tax data, but don't put off submitting them until tax-filing time in April. Check each school's filing dates and follow instructions.

How much you can contribute is not a question answered simply by a look at your annual income. Other factors include the number of children in your family, and how many of them will be in college at the same time; your age, and how close you are to the fixed-income years of retirement;

special expenses you may have, such as medical bills for an aged or chronically ill member of the family.

How much you can contribute is also linked to your assets, and here is a point of some controversy. Should the parents who have saved toward college costs, perhaps depriving themselves along the way, be expected to fork over much more than the parents, with an identical income, who have lived life to the hilt, spending every penny? (If you've saved toward college, on the other hand, why not expect to spend for college?) Should home equity be counted as an asset, so that parents who are house-poor may be relied on for a far larger contribution than those with more limited but more liquid funds? (If you own a home, on the other hand, you may not have liquid cash, but you do have more financial flexibility.)

Note: Colleges have two choices when it comes to determining your contribution: They may use the need analysis approach or, if you are applying for a Guaranteed Student Loan and nothing else, and if your income is between $30,000 and $75,000, they may use a simple "look-up" table (see Table 5) supplied by the Department of Education. That table is based on income alone; it ignores your assets. If you are asset-rich (perhaps because you live in an area with inflated real estate values), then financial aid authority Robert Leider has a suggestion: Ask the financial aid office to determine your contribution both ways, and to use the way most favorable to you. (It's advantageous to the college too, because your college loan will come from outside sources.) You'll forfeit your right to other aid, but you may very well come out ahead.

TABLE 5: What parents are expected to contribute annually to college costs.

Family size	ADJUSTED GROSS FAMILY INCOME						
	$35,000	$40,000	$45,000	$50,000	$55,000	$65,000	$75,000
Family Contribution for a Dependent Student from a Two-Parent Family							
3	$4,060	$5,430	$6,820	$8,180	$9,450	$11,950	$14,300
4	3,220	4,510	5,890	7,270	8,540	11,060	13,410
5	2,560	3,660	5,020	6,410	7,700	10,240	12,590
6	1,930	2,850	4,040	5,420	6,730	9,270	11,640
Family Contribution for a Dependent Student from a One-Parent Family							
2	$3,500	$4,710	$6,050	$7,280	$8,450	$10,770	$12,980
3	2,890	3,960	5,300	6,560	7,740	10,070	12,280
4	2,260	3,160	4,380	5,680	6,850	9,200	11,410
5	1,760	2,530	3,570	4,850	6,030	8,380	10,590
6	1,270	1,940	2,800	3,880	5,080	7,430	9,660

(Source: *College Loans from Uncle Sam,* Octameron)

How much your children are expected to contribute hinges on both earning power and assets. Most students are expected to be able to save $700 to $900 toward college costs from summer earnings just before the freshman year and at least $1,000 in each succeeding summer. If there is need for financial aid, moreover, the student may be expected to work part-time during the school year as well (and a job may be provided by the college).

Assets are another matter. Students are expected to contribute a sizable portion of their accumulated assets to the cost of education. The assumption is that students, unlike parents, have few other demands on assets combined with greater long-term replacement potential. The result may be, however, that assets placed in your child's name to save tax dollars may later reduce the amount of outside financial aid available.

Your remaining need, the difference between college costs and the amount that you and your child can jointly contribute to the costs (not what you think you can contribute, but what the colleges think you can contribute), is the amount that needs to be made up in a financial aid package. That package, as noted, consists of jobs, loans, and grants. Jobs may come from the financial aid office or, for the motivated, from an independent job search. Grants and loans are more complex.

Q. My son has been offered financial aid from two schools. Either school would suit him fine. But the aid packages are so different that it's like comparing apples and oranges. What should we focus on in making a decision?

A. Assuming that your need is fully met by each college and that your estimates of reasonable family contributions agree with the figures used by each college, then look at the proportion of each package made up of gifts (scholarships and grants which do not require repayment) and of self-help (loans, which must be repaid, and work opportunities). And remember two things: (1) Your first choice should be the college which best meets educational needs. (2) A financial aid package can be appealed. If the package at the first-choice school has more self-help and less outright help, for instance, talk to the financial aid office and see if the package can be changed. If not, or if your son would really be equally happy (and equally well educated) at either school, go with the school offering the best overall aid package.

STUDENT GRANTS

Scholarship grants are available from a number of sources. Some are based purely on merit, but most are based on need, with specific income limitations that vary from time to time.

- Uncle Sam's Pell Grants (formerly called the Basic Education Opportunity Grants, or BEOG), the foundation of student aid, are restricted to applicants from families below a specified income level ($28,000 in 1985, with sharp cuts forecast) and are limited in amount (the maximum award in 1985–86 is $2,100). It's important to apply for a Pell Grant, even if you think you're not eligible, because the application itself may make you eligible for other grants and loans. Apply early (a good word of advice for all grants and for loans as well); available funds can run dry.

- Supplemental Educational Opportunity Grants (SEOG) provide additional funds (amounts range from $200 to $2,000) to needy students. Funds are provided by the federal government but distributed by the colleges.

- State governments also offer need-based grants, many restricted to in-state study; contact your own state office of higher education for details.

- Colleges offer individual grants as well. Most, again, are based on need, but some, particularly at middle-level colleges eager to attract top-of-the-line students in a buyer's market, are based strictly on merit.

- National Merit Scholarships, which have both college sponsors and corporate sponsors, are awarded on the basis of scores in the Preliminary Scholastic Aptitude Test given each fall to high school juniors.

- Employers, civic and fraternal organizations, professional and trade associations, unions and alumni organizations . . . all may also be potential sources of grants. Many are open only to those involved in some way with the sponsor: the sons and daughters of employees, of union members, etc. Others are open to anyone, based on need or on the writing of an essay, on citizenship, or on athletic ability.

Grants, unlike loans, do not have to be repaid (although a portion may be taxable); clearly you are ahead of the game if grants make up a larger portion of your financial aid package. Some advisers suggest that once you're accepted at the college of your choice, the proportion of grants to loans can be negotiated with the financial aid office.

Note: Don't think the game is finished once the freshman year is under way. More aid becomes available to students once they have demonstrated ability on the college level. Keep grades up, and apply again.

STUDENT LOANS

College loans are available from a variety of sources, including some colleges; some schools, in fact, are developing innovative programs to fill any gap left by reduced federal spending. But the biggest programs by far are two federally subsidized loan programs: National Direct Student Loans and Guaranteed Student Loans.

National Direct Student Loans are need-based loans subsidized by the federal government but distributed directly by the colleges. They carry the lowest rate of any loan program, currently 5 percent, and repayment need not start for six months after the student leaves school. Federal funding for NDSLs has been sharply curtailed, with appropriations of new funds reduced from $286 million to $200 million. But these loans are made from a revolving fund; as students repay their loans, directly to their colleges, more money is available for loans. There is some $1 billion in the existing fund as this is written; that money, plus the new appropriations, is available for new loans as long as existing loans are repaid. *Moral:* Don't default on a student loan. It isn't legal, it isn't moral, and it isn't fair to other students.

Guaranteed Student Loans are the biggest student loan program of all. Although the rules for GSLs keep changing, the outline is the same: The loan is provided to the student (not to parents) by a local bank or thrift institution, guaranteed by a state agency, and insured by the federal government, with an interest rate generally below market rates (the government makes up the difference to the lending institution). Repayment, as with the NDSL, does not begin until six months after the student leaves school.

From 1965, when the GSL program began, until 1978, GSLs were available only to students below a specified income ceiling. Then all ceilings were removed and GSLs became available to all students. The rationale was good: Only a small percentage of students had been excluded under the needs test and the necessary paperwork made banks and thrifts reluctant to become involved in the program at all. But the result, in an era of rising interest rates, was that many families realized that they could borrow at GSL's 7 percent interest rate and put the money into a money market fund earning 17 percent. The outlay of federal funds grew enormously and, in 1981, income ceilings were reimposed. At the same time, interest rates were raised to 9 percent and origination fees of 5 percent (which effectively reduce the loan amount) were imposed.

Note: Interest rates on GSLs do vary—the rate fell to 8 percent in fall 1983—but whatever rate is in effect when you take your first loan is the rate that remains in effect for all subsequent loans under the program.

If your family is below the income ceiling, however (or if you are a graduate student or an independent undergraduate), a Guaranteed Student Loan is still a very good thing to have. And if you are above the income cutoff but need the loan (because you have more than one child in college at a time, because you are supporting aged parents, because you have very high medical bills . . .) your child may be able to obtain a loan anyway. Don't refrain from applying just because you think you're not eligible.

For example, in 1985 (the rules may have been tightened still further by now), a two-parent family of four with an adjusted gross income of $75,000 and only one child in college would be expected to pay $13,410 toward that child's college costs. Even at the most expensive Ivy League universities, that student would be ineligible for a Guranteed Student Loan. But if the same family had two children in college at a cost of $12,000 each, the expected family contribution for each child would be half of $13,410 or $6,705 and each student would be eligible for a GSL.

Q. Banks seem to write college loans only for their depositors. But my bank doesn't write them at all, and the bank where my son has an account will make loans only to college juniors. We must have help or he won't be able to start school. Is there anything we can do?

A. Contact your state's Department of Higher Education, probably in the state capital, for the name of the agency supervising government-guaranteed student loans in your state. (A complete list of guaranteeing agencies may be found in *College Loans from Uncle Sam,* available for $2.25 postpaid from Octameron Associates, P.O. Box 3437, Alexandria, VA 22303.) That agency should be able to tell you which institutions in your area are making loans. In some states, the agency will actually match student and lender. Lending institutions, while they must meet federal standards, can decide whether or not to participate and set their own rules about eligibility. Don't wait until the last moment. Shop around before you need a loan, and if you'll have to open an account, do so as early as possible.

REPAYMENT OF STUDENT LOANS

One of the reasons that loan programs are being restricted is that too many people have walked away from this obligation; too many have looked at the loans as a free gift from Uncle Sam. Student loans must be repaid, and the government is taking legal action against defaulters. The minimum annual payment on a Guaranteed Student Loan is $600, and repayment may be made over five to ten years (see Table 6).

Repayment on federally subsidized student loans may be deferred under certain conditions, such as service in the armed forces or the Peace

TABLE 6: Monthly repayments under a Guaranteed Student Loan of various sizes at 8 percent.

Loan amount	Monthly payment	Number of months	Total interest	Total payment
$ 2,500	$ 50.69	60	$ 541.40	$ 3,041.40
5,000	60.66	120	2,279.20	7,279.20
7,500	90.99	120	3,418.80	10,918.80
10,000	121.33	120	4,559.60	14,559.60
12,500	151.66	120	5,699.20	18,199.20

(Source: Octameron Associates)

Corps. Cancellation is another story. Under most circumstances, only death or permanent total disability eliminates the responsibility to repay the loan; bankruptcy does not. Student loans, in other words, must be taken seriously as a debt obligation.

Loans, especially low-interest loans, are an appealing way to finance college. But interest on college loans is no longer tax-deductible. And a great many young adults, especially those with post-college graduate or professional education, are starting their working lives with an extremely heavy debt load. "Manageable" debt for someone with a bachelor's degree in business might total $7,000, according to the Educational Testing Service, while a graduate with a degree in computer science might be able to manage $10,000. While loans may be the only way you can attend school, be sure you understand what you're taking on. You don't want to be paying for your own college education up until the time your own children apply for college loans.

PARENT LOANS

These "auxiliary" loans are meant to provide additional funds for educational expenses. Known as PLUS loans (also occasionally called by their former title, Auxiliary Loans to Assist Students or ALAS loans), they are open at this writing (further tightening is planned) to parents, graduate students, and independent undergraduates. The interest rate is closer to market rate, hinged to the rate on 90-day Treasury bills; it was 14 percent until November 1, 1982, then fell to 12 percent. Repayment must begin within sixty days.

Parent borrowers must start to repay the entire loan, both principal and interest, within sixty days, so this type of loan program is primarily a way of easing the cash flow problems generated by twice-a-year college bills. Full-time students may defer the payment of principal until they leave school but must make monthly payments of interest. Even so, PLUS loans are considerably more expensive than GSLs of the same size, the result of a "double whammy" of higher interest rates and no in-school interest subsidy. A graduate student, with several years' worth of loans, could face monthly interest payments of $400 to $500 while still attending school, a sum that would be virtually impossible to pay on most graduate student budgets.

PLUS loans may be more help to parents than to students themselves. They should, nonetheless, be on your list of avenues to investigate. If local banks cannot provide information, consult your college financial aid office or your state office of higher education.

Q. If I declare myself financially independent of my parents, can I secure more financial aid for college?

A. Independent undergraduates may be eligible for more aid, because their resources are generally limited, than students who receive help from their parents. If you want to be considered independent for federal financial aid (colleges may set their own rules), you must meet certain strict criteria: You must not be listed by parents as a federal income tax exemption (and should not have been listed last year), and, if you are under age 24, you must have earned at least $4,000 in each of the past two years. If you are at least 24, married, or a veteran, under new regulations you are automatically considered independent. Financial aid administrators may exercise their own judgment in unusual circumstances.

Tuition Payment Plans

While not strictly financial aid, any plan that allows parents to spread out the burden of college costs is a big help. Remember, college bills are usually due twice a year, once for each semester. With costs of $7,000 or more, much more, per year, you face a hefty out-of-pocket cost every few months (usually in August and then again in December). Tuition payment plans can help.

There are a number of prepayment and installment plans available, through colleges themselves or through private agencies. For example:

- Some colleges offer parents the opportunity to pay the year's costs in eight or ten monthly installments. There may be no interest at all, just a nominal administrative fee. (The college starts getting its money two to four months earlier than it otherwise would, so it comes out ahead.) If spreading payments over a longer period of time will be important, look for a college which offers this option.

- Some commercial programs do charge interest, but may allow you to spread payments over additional years. Some of these programs are limited to students at particular colleges (you'll get a mailing on these once your child has enrolled); others are open to everyone. One of the best-known nationally available plans, administered by the Knight Agency of Boston, offers two programs. In one, a prepayment plan, you make monthly payments and the plan in turn pays the college. In the other, a loan program, you have ten years to repay the costs of four years. Another program, called Collegaire, is run by Students' Financial Services in Atlanta. This plan, a savings account plus credit line, reduces effective interest costs by offsetting finance charges on the credit line with interest earned on your savings. (Remember, though, that interest charges are no longer tax-deductible.)

- Some commercial banks offer tuition payment plans via a line of credit and extended repayment. Interest on these loans—and they are loans—is charged when checks are written against the line of credit. The interest, however, may be at the rate of interest being charged on other consumer loans; in 1985, one such program charged 18 percent.

Note: Most installment plans offer an insurance feature, either built-in or as an optional extra. If the parent who signs the loan dies or becomes disabled, the remainder of the bills may be forgiven. This insurance feature means that it's a good idea to have just one parent, preferably the parent with the larger income, sign the installment agreement.

When You Are the Student

One-third of all the college students in the United States are over the age of 25. Whether you are attending college for the first time, seeking a second degree in a different field, or going back to school to resume an interrupted education, you are part of a growing movement.

Forget age, however, and there's not much difference between older students and students of "traditional" college age. Most of the financial advice extended earlier in this chapter applies equally to the adult student. Federal grants and loans, as one instance, have no age limitations. But there are some special things to say as well:

- The student with dependents, at any age, has special needs and must make those needs known to the college financial aid office. Extra money can sometimes be made available for expenditures such as child care which may make it possible for an adult to attend school, but the school must first know that the need exists.

- You do have to attend school at least half-time in order to qualify for most financial aid programs. A course at a time won't count, although some programs require as few as six credits a semester to qualify. Under many programs, where aid is available to the part-timer, it may be available for a longer period of time. Find out if the institution or program to which you are applying will extend aid eligibility beyond the usual four years.

- Each school has its own policy when it comes to awarding aid to part-time students. Many restrict scholarships and grants to full-timers, leaving only loans to help the part-timer. Others simply allocate about 10 percent of available funds for part-time applicants. Be sure to apply to a number of schools that meet your educational needs, recognizing that you may receive financial aid from one and not from another.

- Some financial aid programs are expressly designed for adults returning to school. You owe it to yourself to find out about such programs and apply for the ones that are appropriate. You'll find a sampling below.

High School

If you had to leave school before completing 12th grade, you can earn a high school equivalency certificate through the General Educational Development (GED) program, administered through local school systems. GED exams, which measure the ability to think clearly rather than knowledge of specific facts, are given in English, social studies, mathematics, literature, and natural science. They may be taken in English, Spanish, or French. For information about the exams themselves and about preparatory courses, contact your local superintendent of schools.

College

There is an almost bewildering array of options open to the adult student seeking a college education. Some are accepted by one school and not by another. Narrow your choice of schools in terms of the education you want to receive. Then see which of the schools you would like to attend accept which of the following:

- The College Level Examination Program (CLEP), like the GED, tests knowledge acquired outside of the formal classroom and gives college credit for that knowledge. The tests, given at regular intervals at testing locations around the country, include two types of examination: General Examinations in five broad areas (English composition, humanities, social science/history, mathematics, and natural science) and Subject Examinations in a wide array of specialized subjects from accounting to Western civilization.

- External degrees are granted by programs in several states; you may enroll in these programs no matter where you live. In New York the Regents External Degree program and in New Jersey Thomas A. Edison College, as examples, offer degrees for all kinds of documented learning: courses taken at other colleges, noncollegiate courses evaluated and found comparable to college courses, military education programs, correspondence courses, proficiency examinations, and individual assessments of knowledge and skills. CLEP exams usually result in a year or two of credit, so that a student can enter an on-campus program at an advanced level; external degree programs make it possible to earn a college degree without ever attending college in person.

- "Life experience" is given credit at a number of colleges. Students, under the guidance of academic counselors, usually prepare a presentation documenting what they have learned through work or volunteer experience. A longtime bookkeeper might get credit for a course in accounting, while a nursing home volunteer might amass credits in gerontology and in administration. Each school decides how much educational credit is given for life experience.

■ Weekend programs have been designed by some colleges specifically to aid the person who is attending school while holding down a full-time job. Such programs typically entail intensive on-campus work one weekend a month, with extensive home study assignments in between. Such programs are available for specialized graduate work as well as for undergraduate studies.

If you take advantage of one or more of these programs, you can save a lot of money. A 54-year-old Connecticut man, for example, had dropped out of high school to enlist in World War II. Thirty-five years later he took, and passed, a high school equivalency examination and signed up to "take a few courses" at a local community college. There he heard about CLEP and about the external degree program. Within eighteen months, via a combination of night courses and examinations based on life experience, he earned a Bachelor of Arts degree. Total cost: $598.

In addition, consider the following:

■ There are special grant programs designed for women (particularly women in midlife returning to school) and for members of minority groups. Consult your college financial aid office and community organizations for the names of specific programs.

■ If you are a veteran, or the dependent of a deceased or disabled veteran, you may be eligible for some educational benefits under the G.I. Bill.

■ If you want to take a couple of courses rather than enroll as much as half-time, and if you are over the magic age called "senior" (which may be as low as 60 in some areas), you may be eligible for free courses or reduced tuition. Ask at the college you want to attend. (And don't forget courses given by local libraries, community centers, Ys, museums, recreation departments, evening high schools . . .)

■ Employer-paid tuition benefits are particularly appropriate for the older student. Ask your personnel benefits office about your employer's policy.

As an employed adult, you may also enjoy tax breaks by furthering your education. If the courses you take are required by your employer or by law, or if the course maintains or improves skills needed on your present job, you may deduct the costs of tuition, fees, books, and necessary travel on your federal income tax return (you must file an itemized return). You may not deduct educational costs if you are unemployed or if the courses will equip you for a new and different job.

If you are a full-time student, with a working spouse and children under age 15, you may claim a tax credit for a portion of child care expenses. Tax credit may also be claimed for out-of-home but noninstitutional care of an aged or disabled dependent; a day care program for an elderly parent would count. You do not have to itemize deductions to claim this credit.

KEY POINTS

- College costs can be cut in a variety of ways: accelerated high school programs, attendance at local community colleges, correspondence courses, etc.

- College costs can be met, via a systematic savings program started well in advance. Savings can be compounded, once children are 14 or over, if you know you won't need the money and if you trust your children's judgment, by putting the money in your children's name, to be taxed at their lower bracket rate.

- Financial aid, although reduced, is still available via grants, loans, and jobs. Be sure to file an application, and file it early, even if you're not sure you qualify.

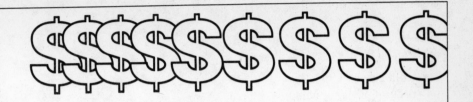

PROTECTING YOURSELF: INSURANCE

Life
Insurance

★ Jonathan T., new Bachelor of Science degree in hand, is solicited by a life insurance salesman. The message: Buy protection cheap, while you're young and insurable.

★ Anne and Will K. are both 28 years old, both climbing the executive ladder. An insurance salesman Will meets at the gym tells him that each should carry life insurance to protect the other.

★ Eric P., 32 years old and a first-time father, receives several telephone calls from eager salesmen while his wife and newborn son are still in the hospital. The message: You have responsibilities now, responsibilities you can carry out through life insurance.

★ The Taylors, in the midst of calculating college costs for three teenage children, are told that life insurance can build an education fund.

★ The Elmers, now that the nest is almost empty, are thinking about a divorce. In addition to the already-in-force life insurance that Mrs. Elmer will take over as part of the property settlement, an insurance agent suggests that she buy additional insurance on her husband's life. Then, if anything happens to him, her income will continue.

★ Tom A., twelve years from retirement, hears that life insurance can provide retirement income.

★ Peter M., the owner of a small business, is 67 and has been urged to carry life insurance to pay estate taxes, thereby protecting the business for his heirs.

Does life insurance actually fulfill all of these functions? Do all of these people need life insurance?

Life insurance may be used to meet a variety of financial planning goals. New types of life insurance, in fact, are being promoted as investment vehicles. But life insurance is fundamentally one thing and one thing only: *income protection.* If and when you buy life insurance, buy it to protect the people who are dependent on you from financial loss resulting from your death. Other purposes are strictly secondary.

When you buy insurance—of any kind—you are entering a pool with other people. All of the people in the pool pay a specified sum (based, in the case of life insurance, primarily on expectations of mortality), and the insurance company pays out, from the combined premiums of all the policyholders, the benefits due to those who die while they are insured.

The same principle applies to all insurance. In automobile insurance, an insured individual can repair a damaged car with insurance proceeds; the proceeds come from the reserves built up by the insurance company from premiums paid by all policyholders. In the case of life insurance, of course, the insured is no longer present to collect. Policy proceeds are paid to the person or persons the insured has named as beneficiary. Life insurance can't keep you alive; it can ease the damage done to your survivors' lives by your death. Life insurance, to repeat, is income protection.

The purchase of life insurance, almost more than any other part of your personal financial plan, is tied to your life stage. Your age and, even more important, the number of your dependents affects not only how much life insurance you need but whether you need it at all.

How Much Life Insurance Do You Need?

You have dependents you'd like to protect. You've decided that you do need life insurance. Now you'd like someone to tell you how much you need and what kind to buy. There are no pat answers to either question. How much life insurance you need depends on your personal situation: what you want life insurance to do and what other assets you have. What kind to buy is a related but separate question, to be considered a bit later. The first decision you should make is the basic decision: how much.

INCOME REPLACEMENT

There was a time when a flat income multiple, such as five times annual income, was offered as the all-purpose solution. But to look solely at income is to ignore the fact that one $30,000-a-year woman is supporting two children and an aged mother while another, at the same income level, is supporting only herself. Their insurance needs are clearly different, and an all-purpose answer does not work.

Another form of income multiplier has been developed, however. It ties the multiplier to both age and income, with built-in assumptions about family size as well. This "income replacement" approach has as its objective the replacement of 75 percent of after-tax earnings from date of death to date of retirement. The assumptions are that 75 percent of a wage-earner's after-tax income is sufficient for the family, once work-related and personal expenditures are gone, and that earned income would be reduced at retirement age.

Table 1 represents the amount of life insurance needed when the worker is not covered by Social Security and/or has no children eligible for Social Security survivor benefits. This makes a considerable difference in the amount needed. A 30-year-old worker earning $15,000 needs 13.5 × $15,000 or $202,500 of life insurance to replace 75 percent of after-tax earnings for thirty-five years.

TABLE 1: Multiple of annual pay to determine amount of insurance that will replace 75 percent of take-home pay, with no Social Security benefits.

Gross annual pay	\multicolumn{7}{c}{Age of insured}
	25	30	35	40	45	50	55
$9,000 ×	15.4	14.3	13.1	11.6	9.9	8.0	5.7
15,000 ×	14.5	13.5	12.3	10.9	9.3	7.5	5.4
18,000 ×	14.2	13.2	12.1	10.7	9.1	7.3	5.2
20,000 ×	14.0	13.0	11.9	10.6	9.0	7.2	5.2
25,000 ×	13.7	12.7	11.6	10.3	8.8	7.1	5.1
30,000 ×	13.4	12.5	11.4	10.1	8.6	6.9	5.0
40,000 ×	13.1	12.2	11.1	9.9	8.4	6.8	4.8
50,000 ×	12.8	11.9	10.8	9.6	8.2	6.6	4.7
60,000 ×	12.4	11.5	10.5	9.3	8.0	6.4	4.6

(Source: Principal Financial Group)

Table 2 illustrates what happens when the worker is covered by Social Security survivor benefits. It assumes two children, born when the insured is 26 and 29 (Social Security benefits are payable until a dependent child reaches 16). At ages 25, 50, and 55, this table is exactly the same as Table 1, because at these ages this family does not include an eligible child. But a 30-year-old worker earning $15,000 now needs only 5.4 × $15,000 or $81,000 of life insurance.

Note: On both tables, the multiples decrease with added income, because higher rates at greater income levels mean that after-tax income is a smaller percentage of the gross.

TABLE 2: The effect of Social Security survivor benefits, assuming a child born when the worker is 26 and another born when he is 29, on the multiple of annual pay in Table 1.

Gross annual pay	Age of insured						
	25	30	35	40	45	50	55
$9,000 ×	15.4	5.8	6.7	7.7	8.8	8.0	5.7
15,000 ×	14.5	5.4	6.3	7.3	8.3	7.5	5.4
18,000 ×	14.2	5.3	6.2	7.2	8.2	7.3	5.2
20,000 ×	14.0	5.3	6.1	7.1	8.1	7.2	5.2
25,000 ×	13.7	5.6	6.5	7.4	8.1	7.1	5.1
30,000 ×	13.4	6.3	7.1	7.7	8.0	6.9	5.0
40,000 ×	13.1	7.6	7.9	8.1	8.0	6.8	4.8
50,000 ×	12.8	8.2	8.3	8.2	7.9	6.6	4.7
60,000 ×	12.4	8.5	8.4	8.2	7.7	6.4	4.6

(Source: Principal Financial Group)

"PERSONALIZED" NEED

While it's possible to decide how much life insurance to buy on the basis of this income replacement formula, there are a couple of things missing in this approach. First, it does not consider the actual income needs of your family at specific times and for specific purposes. Second, it does not enter your other assets into the calculation. A "personalized needs" approach does both. The personalized approach looks beyond income replacement to specific needs. Here are some of the things life insurance can do:

■ Provide ready cash for final expenses. These could include funeral costs, any uninsured medical expenses, probate fees, and estate taxes.

■ Pay off any debts left after your death. In addition to uninsured medical and hospital bills, this might include a mortgage on your home (if continuing to pay the mortgage would be a burden for your survivor and if the family wanted to continue living in the home), an automobile loan, or any other consumer debt.

■ Provide money to cover housekeeping expenses. If you are the homemaker, it will cost your surviving spouse considerable sums to provide day care for children, cleaning and laundry services, and so on. If you are a wage-earner with a stay-at-home spouse, your survivor will incur these costs upon return to the labor market. If both of you are currently working, the costs of these services may already be built into your budget. But will they be manageable on a single income?

■ Provide replacement income for your family, in different amounts at different intervals:

1. A readjustment period of two or three years after your death, during which the family reshapes its financial affairs and during which your spouse might secure additional training to reenter the job market or might move from part-time to full-time employment. (Even if your spouse is already working full-time at a substantial income, there will be a period of readjustment while the family adjusts to one paycheck instead of two—and to the added expenses that might result from your absence. If, for instance, you were handy around the house, an electrician or a carpenter might now have to be hired for occasional tasks.)

2. The period while children are still at home and dependent, and Social Security survivor benefits may supply part of the family's income needs.

3. The college years, when Social Security comes to an end just as expenses become heavier.

4. The years between the time the youngest child becomes independent and the surviving spouse reaches retirement age. For most people, there are no Social Security benefits during this period and, as a result, there is additional need for life insurance to fill the gap.

5. After the survivor reaches retirement age and starts to receive Social Security retirement benefits and/or regular pension checks.

You'll find a worksheet on which to make your own personal calculations on pp. 414–15. Before filling it in, however, evaluate all your sources of income.

OTHER SOURCES OF INCOME

Life insurance is not the only source of support for your family. You'll need just enough life insurance to plug any gap between existing assets and your family's needs. (As assets grow, in fact, the need for life insurance diminishes.) So, at this point, you must evaluate those existing assets. Consider:

- Cash on hand, in bank accounts and money market funds, which could be used to pay final expenses
- Securities, such as stocks and bonds, which your family might sell or might retain to add to regular income
- Existing life insurance, including any on-the-job group life insurance provided by your employer, group insurance purchased through a fraternal group or trade association, and any already-purchased individual policies
- The value of your home, if it would be sold, and of other potentially salable assets such as jewelry or coin collections
- Lump-sum pension benefits, such as the balance in an Individual Retirement Account, payable to your survivor

- Social Security benefits for a surviving spouse and dependent children. These benefits can be substantial, adding up to more than $1,000 a month for a family in which the wage-earner has always earned the maximum amount subject to Social Security tax.

Q. Do you recommend buying a life insurance policy on an infant?

A. Some people believe that buying life insurance for a baby gives him or her a start in life—by building cash values, ensuring insurability, and providing low insurance rates. Or parents may want to have money for final expenses if the baby should die. But, really, your first responsibility to the baby is to provide for the future if anything should happen to you or your spouse. Before you spend money on insuring the baby, be sure that you both have adequate life insurance so that the baby would be cared for into adulthood.

Your Life Insurance Needs

Needs change, and this exercise can't be performed just once and then forgotten. But the only way to determine how much life insurance your family will need is to make calculations based on the assumption that you will die tomorrow. If you did, how much money would your family need to carry on? Make your best estimates as you fill in the following worksheet.

INSURANCE NEEDS WORKSHEET

FINAL EXPENSES (lump sum)
Funeral costs $_____
Uninsured medical expenses $_____
Probate fees $_____
Estate taxes $_____

DEBT REPAYMENT (lump sum)
Mortgage $_____
Auto loan $_____
Other $_____

HOUSEKEEPING EXPENSES (monthly amount × number of months)
Child care $_____
Other $_____

REPLACEMENT INCOME (monthly amount × number of months)
For a readjustment period $_____
For dependent children $_____
For the college years $_____
For a surviving spouse,
   pre-retirement $_____
For a surviving spouse,
   post-retirement $_____
                    TOTAL $_____

This total represents your best guess as to the amount of money your family will need. The largest sums will be for ongoing expenses of housekeeping and replacement income. But, as mentioned earlier, you already have assets on hand to meet some of these needs. Add up these assets:

```
ASSETS ON HAND
Cash on hand                      $_____
Securities                        $_____
Existing life insurance           $_____
Lump-sum pension benefits         $_____
The market value of your house
  and other possessions           $_____
Social Security survivor benefits
  (monthly amount × number of
  months)                         $_____
                        TOTAL  $_____
```

Now subtract your total assets from the total needs you calculated above. The result is the amount of life insurance your family needs . . . if your spouse is not employed. If there is another income in the family, calculate that income for the number of years the children will be dependent.

```
Income needs:                     $_____
 −Assets on hand:                 $_____
 −Spouse's income
   (yearly income × number of
   years of children's depen-
   dency)                         $_____
 =ADDITIONAL INSURANCE NEEDED:  $_____
```

AN EXAMPLE OF ONE FAMILY'S INSURANCE NEEDS

★ Jim, now age 30, earns $25,000 in a middle-management corporate job. His wife Mary, age 27, is a teacher but is currently at home with two children, ages 4 and 1. Jim has $20,000 of on-the-job group life insurance and an individual policy in the amount of $20,000, purchased five years ago. How much additional life insurance should Jim carry?

Based on the *income replacement* approach (Table 2, p. 436), Jim needs life insurance, after allowing for Social Security benefits, of 5.6 times gross earnings, or about $140,000. Of this amount, $20,000 is already in force through Jim's group life insurance and $20,000 through his individual policy. If the family wants the 75 percent of earnings on which Table 2 is based, then an additional $100,000 in life insurance should be purchased.

The *personalized needs* approach is a bit more complicated, but this is the way Jim and Mary do the calculations:

- Lump-sum needs, for funeral expenses and an emergency fund, are estimated at $7,500. (This includes probate fees, based on an estimated 4 percent of the estate. There won't be enough of an estate to make federal estate taxes a factor in their calculations. And, with Jim's excellent group health benefits, there should be minimal uninsured medical expenses.)
- Income replacement needs are estimated as follows:

1. For a two-year readjustment period: $1,750 per month is needed.
2. After readjustment, but while children are still dependent: $1,375 per month is needed.
3. While the children are in college, additional need is estimated at $600 per month per child.
4. After the children are grown and until Mary is 65, it is assumed that she will return to work. Her supplemental income needs are estimated at $450 per month.
5. During Mary's post-retirement years, in addition to her own pension and Social Security, it is estimated that she will need $800 per month.

Social Security survivor benefits will help to meet these income replacement needs, with $1,198 per month while the two children are dependent, $1,026 per month while one child is dependent, and $684 per month after Mary turns 65. Nevertheless, Jim needs an additional $100,500 of life insurance, less his other accumulated assets. This figure is remarkably close to the figure achieved through the income replacement formula, so close that it looks unnecessarily tedious to go through all these calculations. But there are times when the answers won't be quite so similar. Let's look at the same family in five years. They're all five years older. Jim is now earning $30,000 per year, and has $25,000 of group life insurance. Mary has returned to teaching, earning $15,000 a year, and has $10,000 of group life insurance. Jim has his original $20,000 of individual life insurance plus a $100,000 policy bought five years ago, at the time of the family's first evaluation.

The problem with using the income replacement method now is that the tables do not recognize that the surviving spouse is employed. Since Social Security benefits are lower when a surviving spouse works, the insurance amounts determined from Table 2 will be somewhat low. Let's see how it works out: Using Table 2, with Jim at his current age, 35, the appropriate multiple is 7.1. $30,000 of gross annual income times 7.1 yields a total insurance need of $213,000. Since Jim currently carries $145,000 of insurance, he needs an additional $68,000.

But what happens under the personalized needs approach? Lump-sum needs are estimated at $9,000. Replacement income is estimated to be $1,200 per month for a one-year readjustment period, $950 per month after readjustment but while the children are still dependent, $400 additional per month per child during the college years, a supplemental income for Mary of $300 per month after the children are grown and before she retires, and nothing during her post-retirement period since it is now assumed that she will have sufficient income from her pension plan and Social Security. It will take $145,000 to meet these needs (in addition to Social Security benefits). Since Jim already owns $145,000 of life insurance, no additional purchase is indicated.

WHEN A WIFE IS A WAGE-EARNER

Now that Mary is working outside the home, she has insurance needs as well. Let's compare her needs, using both approaches:

Using income replacement and, again, Table 2, the appropriate multiple at her age, 32, is about 5.8. Multiplying this by her gross annual income of $15,000 indicates a total insurance need of $87,000. Deducting the $10,000 of group life insurance that Mary currently owns leaves an unmet insurance need of $77,000.

Using the personalized needs approach, however, the answer is different. If Mary dies, Jim will need $600 per month for a one-year readjustment period, $500 per month after readjustment but while the children are dependent, $200 per month per child while the children are in college, plus an immediate lump sum of $4,500 for the funeral and related costs. Total insurance needs: $30,000. Since Mary already has $10,000 of insurance, she needs an additional $20,000. Again, existing assets should be subtracted from this total.

In performing these calculations for your own family, you may find it helpful to enlist the help of a professional insurance agent (see p. 434). Whether you use an agent or not, however, it's very important to decide how much life insurance you need before you think about what kind to buy.

Q. I let my life insurance lapse when I lost my job, but now I have another job and want coverage again. Can I get the old policy back?

A. You can usually reinstate a lapsed policy within five years by paying the back premiums plus interest and passing a physical exam. It's worth doing if you initially took out the policy some years back, because yearly premiums will be much less. A $50,000 whole-life policy for which you paid $672 a year starting at age 25 could cost you $1,290 yearly if you take it out at age 47. If you decide to reinstate a lapsed whole-life policy, you can still turn it in for the remaining cash value or convert it to a paid-up policy in a reduced amount. Whatever you do, don't ignore that policy; it probably still contains some valuable benefits.

What Kind of Life Insurance Should You Buy?

Life insurance goes by a lot of names but comes in two basic varieties: permanent and term. It's important to understand the difference.

Permanent Insurance

Lifelong, level-cost protection is provided by permanent insurance, also called whole life or straight life. Both the face amount of the policy (the death benefit) and the premium (the amount that you pay) are fixed at the time you buy. Neither will change, despite the fact that the chance of death increases with age. Insurance companies compensate for this increasing risk of death by charging more than necessary in the early policy years, less than necessary in the later years. Thus the premium remains level.

CASH VALUE

The "extra" premiums that you pay in the early years contribute to the reserves that the insurance company is building up against the increasing likelihood of paying out a death benefit. They also, in part, form your cash value in the policy, an amount that accumulates with interest and that is always available to you either as cash surrender value should you cancel the policy or as a policy loan while the insurance remains in effect.

Life insurance agents often like to call this cash value element of permanent insurance a "savings" feature. The cash value earns interest. That interest is tax-free while the policy remains in force, when you cash the policy in (except to the extent, if any, that the cash value exceeds the premiums you've paid over the years), and when your beneficiary receives it as income.

VARIATIONS ON PERMANENT LIFE INSURANCE

Limited payment plans still provide lifelong protection, but the premium period is shorter. Under 20-payment life, for instance, the policy would be fully paid-up after twenty years. You'd pay more in premiums in each of the twenty years, however, because there are fewer payments overall. Another example is paid-up-at-65, under which you pay premiums each year until you reach age 65, then have paid-up insurance in force; again the premiums are higher. With the higher premiums under limited payment plans, there are also higher cash values.

Endowment policies guarantee that a specific sum of money is available on a specific date. If you know, in other words, that you will want $50,000 to pay for college expenses when your 8-year-old daughter reaches 18, you could buy an endowment policy that would mature in ten years. You would pay higher premiums than you would under a comparable limited payment plan (and considerably more than under straight permanent life); you would also have higher cash values. Your family would receive the $50,000 face amount if you died before the ten-year endowment period was up; you would receive it at the end of the ten years if you were still alive. Either way, your daughter would be able to attend college.

Neither limited payment plans nor endowment policies are particularly good buys in inflationary times. If you want a savings plan, you can find a more effective way of saving. If you want life insurance with cash value, you might just as well spread the payments over as long a period as possible and pay your premiums with deflated dollars.

Variable life (not the same as variable premium insurance; see p. 437) offers the opportunity for a policy to grow in value. With premium dollars (the fixed regular premium of whole life) invested by the insurance company in equities (such as common stock) or in a money market fund instead of in such fixed-rate instruments as long-term mortgages, both death benefits (the face value) and cash values can grow. They can also decrease, but the death benefit won't fall below a floor fixed in the policy; the investment risk is concentrated in the cash value. There is, as a result, no guaranteed cash value.

Variable life, like any investment based on the performance of the stock market, is a gamble. Before you decide to take that gamble, ask yourself these questions: Do you expect the stock market to go up or down? (Variable life may be a good buy in inflationary times, a poor risk in a recession.) Do you want an insurance company to manage your investments for you? And are you willing to pay the charges (administrative expenses, brokerage fees, ongoing annual sales charges . . . all in addition to a first-year sales commission of as much as 50% of the premium) associated with that management?

While variable life policies permit you to borrow against the cash value, such a loan may permanently reduce the possibility that the death benefit will grow.

If you are interested in a variable life policy, look for an exchange provision under which you may exchange the policy, usually within a specified period of time, for a traditional whole life policy. And if you don't exchange the policy, keep tabs on performance; you may want to switch, if you have a choice, to a different fund within the insurance company's portfolio.

Characteristics of Permanent Insurance

Permanent insurance, in any of its forms, has several advantages:

POLICY LOANS

You may borrow against the accrued cash value, at relatively low interest rates. Policy loans on older policies are available at interest rates ranging from 5 to 8 percent; newer policies may have higher rates. Some of the newest policies may have variable interest rates, tied to current market rates and fluctuating periodically during the life of the loan.

Policy loans do not have to be repaid, although any outstanding loan will be deducted from the death benefit. Because a permanent life policy is a ready source of cash, many policyholders have taken advantage of these low-interest loans, especially when interest rates are much higher elsewhere and loan proceeds can be reinvested at those higher rates. (But critics point out that the cash value is your own money. If it represents "savings," they say, why need you pay interest at all?)

Q. I'm thinking of borrowing against my life insurance and investing the money to earn more. Before I do, are there any hidden charges on such a loan?

A. There are no hidden charges; the interest rate quoted in your policy is a simple interest rate. But there are a couple of things you should know: The interest on the loan is no longer tax-deductible. But it's important to pay the interest each year, if at all possible. If you don't pay the interest on the loan as it comes due, the company will deduct the interest from the policy's remaining cash value, adding it to the principal of the loan, so that you'll end up paying interest on the interest and, possibly, losing any advantage you may have gained.

AUTOMATIC PAYMENT

Automatic premium provisions in most policies permit you to fall behind on premium payments and have an automatic loan drawn against accrued cash value to keep the policy in force. Such provisions take effect only if there is sufficient cash value built up in the policy. They can be useful if, for instance, you fall ill and forget to make a scheduled payment. (You also have a "grace period" of thirty-one days, after each premium due date, in which to make the payment without penalty.)

LONG-TERM RIGHTS

Nonforfeiture provisions reinforce your rights to the cash value in the policy. If you drop a permanent life insurance policy, in other words, it doesn't just lapse. You retain rights to the accumulated cash value, and may tap those rights in one of several ways:

- By taking the accumulated cash value in a lump sum payment
- By using the cash value for as long as it lasts to pay premiums and keep the full amount of the insurance in force
- By using the cash value to fully pay a policy with a smaller face value

These rights may be exercised at any time (although they won't make much sense early in the policy, before much cash value has built up). They may be particularly useful at retirement, when you no longer wish to pay premiums.

Note: If you let the policy lapse without choosing one of these options, the company will automatically use the cash value, as long as it lasts, to pay premiums and keep your coverage in force.

DISADVANTAGES OF PERMANENT INSURANCE

Permanent life insurance, once the mainstay of the entire industry, has claimed a decreasing share of the market in the last couple of years. One company halted its sales of permanent insurance entirely in 1982, asserting that permanent life is obsolete, that it no longer meets consumers' needs.

While few companies would take this step, consumer advocates continue to criticize the "savings" aspect of whole life insurance. While the tax-free nature of the interest helps the cash value in any comparison with savings accounts (where interest is taxable), the rate of return is still appallingly low, often below 3 or 4 percent. The Federal Trade Commission has pointed out that because the cash value builds very slowly (administrative costs and sales commissions bite very deeply at the beginning), the average annual return is actually negative until the policy is at least ten years old. Since almost half of all purchasers let their policies lapse within the first ten years (they didn't really need all that insurance, they can't afford the premiums, they gave in to the urgings of a salesman . . .), the only winners are the insurance companies.

The insurance industry, of course, disagrees. So do some impartial observers, pointing out that cash value should not be considered savings but should be regarded as similar to equity in a house, building slowly and available to you when you need it. But there's another parallel: The longer you live in a house the more of your own money (as contrasted to the mortgage lender's) is invested in the house and the smaller the return you receive when you sell. The longer you live, similarly, the more of your own money will be returned to your survivors in the life insurance death benefit. The cash value, even if you never touch it, is not added to the policy proceeds paid to your beneficiary; it is used by the insurance company, along with other reserves if necessary, to pay those proceeds. The insurance company, in other words, assumes more risk earlier in the policy, less later on. Put another way, you're buying more protection at the beginning, less and less with the passing years.

Suggestion: Do your savings elsewhere. Use your life insurance to protect your family.

Term Insurance

Pure protection, without any cash value, is provided via term insurance, an increasingly popular choice among savvy consumers. As its name implies, term insurance is written for a specific term; the term may be one year or five years or more. The death benefit is payable if you die during the term period. If you don't, that's it. There is no cash value, no "savings" feature, no built-in loan arrangement. Term insurance, as a result, is less expensive than permanent insurance. That is, it's far less expensive when you are young. Premiums are based on age and rise at each renewal interval, rising sharply later in life.

Term insurance may be:

—renewable, without regard to your health, up to a maximum age of 65 or 70, and

—convertible, without a medical exam, to permanent insurance; this option must usually be exercised at a specified interval before the term period ends.

Both features, although they may increase the premium by a small amount, are worthwhile.

Q. I'm raising three sons alone and am worried about what will happen to them if anything happens to me. I have some group life insurance through my job but probably should have some individual insurance as well. I can't afford very much. What would be the best kind to buy?

A. You'll get the most protection for the least amount of money—which is what you need while your sons are dependent—from term insurance. Buy guaranteed renewable term, so you'll be able to renew it when the term expires. Buy term with a conversion privilege and you'll be able to convert it to a whole life policy without a medical examination should you decide to do so when your children are grown and your life insurance needs change.

VARIATIONS ON TERM INSURANCE

Declining balance term insurance, also called decreasing term, keeps the premium the same each year for the specified period while the face amount of the policy declines. This kind of policy is often used as mortgage insurance, to cover the decreasing balance of the mortgage on your home. It may be used for other purposes as well, such as insuring a homemaker's life during the diminishing period when children are dependent.

Ideally, the money needed by your family to pay off the mortgage should be included in your total insurance needs, rather than covered separately. If you plan carefully, and buy one large policy instead of several small ones for different purposes, you may save some money.

If you do buy decreasing term insurance to cover a mortgage, perhaps because you already have an insurance program by the time you buy a house, be sure that the beneficiary is your family and not the bank that holds the mortgage. If the bank gets the proceeds it will pay off the mortgage. But perhaps your family would prefer to keep the mortgage in force, live in the house, and invest the money elsewhere for a better return. You should give your family the option of making the choice.

If you buy decreasing term insurance, be sure to find out when and under what circumstances you may convert the policy to whole life or renewable term.

Credit life insurance, often sold (with or without your full awareness) as part of a consumer loan, provides insurance for the loan balance. The idea is to pay off the loan if you die, sparing your survivors the burden of debt (and sparing the lender the burden of collecting). Credit life insurance tends to be expensive and most people can accomplish the same purpose at less cost via regular term insurance.

Combination Policies

Permanent life insurance serves certain purposes. Term insurance serves other purposes. Which should you buy? Just to muddy the waters (and your decision), there are also combination policies to be found:

Whole life insurance may be bought with a term insurance rider, thus offering both permanent protection and cash values along with a larger death benefit at a lower total premium. The term rider can be level term to boost your total protection package. Or it can be decreasing term, to cover, for instance, the declining risk of dying before your children are grown.

Family income policies use a combination of permanent life insurance, to provide a death benefit, and declining balance term insurance, to provide monthly income during the years when children are small. The declining balance in this instance is pegged not to the amount of a mortgage, but to the declining years of dependency. As, each year, the number of years of dependency diminish, so the need for insurance diminishes. The monthly benefit remains the same, depending on what you purchase, but the number of years over which it will be paid diminishes with the life of the policy.

Note: Don't confuse the family income policy with so-called family plans. The latter provide insurance in varying amounts on each member of the family; you want to concentrate your insurance on the breadwinner(s).

Changing Policies to Meet Changing Needs

The hottest new items on the insurance shelf are flexible policies which allow you to adapt your life insurance to your changing needs.

ADJUSTABLE LIFE

Adjustable life is a policy designed for change. With a one-policy combination of permanent and term insurance, the holder of an adjustable life policy can raise or lower premium payments, increase (subject to certain limitations) or decrease the amount of coverage, lengthen or shorten both the protection and premium payment periods. This flexibility is attained by varying the period of the term component. The decision is based on what you can afford. Two 25-year-olds might each have $25,000 worth of coverage. One, spending $1,000 in premium dollars per year, would have that coverage to age 68. The other, able to afford $300 a year in premiums, would be covered to age 38—although annual policy dividends could be used to extend the period of coverage. As the second insured becomes able to afford more insurance, moreover, premiums can be increased and coverage extended.

The idea is that a single policy can provide the coverage you need when you need it: as a young married, a parent of young children, a middle-aged parent of college-bound youngsters, and an older person looking forward to retirement. Adjustable life, not surprisingly, started out under the name "life cycle insurance."

UNIVERSAL LIFE

Universal life combines insurance with a high rate of return on earnings. The vehicle: a combination of term insurance and a cash value account that resembles a money market fund. The insurance company guarantees a minimum return on the cash value portion, usually not less than 4 percent, with actual rates depending on investment performance (in 1985, rates were running about 10 percent). The policy offers a number of advantages in addition to its potentially high yield:

- It is extremely flexible; it's possible, for instance, to skip premiums without causing the policy to lapse. And it's possible to change the face amount of the policy, to raise and lower premiums, and to withdraw part of the cash value without interest charges.

- Disclosure is far beyond typical life insurance practices, with universal life issuers sending policyholders an annual statement spelling out the amount of protection you have, the fees, and the interest rate.

    Universal life clearly has advantages; it made up 38 percent of individual life insurance sales in 1985, up from just 2 percent in 1981. It also has some disadvantages, less likely to be noted in promotional material:

- There is often a first-year charge of several hundred dollars plus annual administrative fees of 5 to 7 percent of your premium. These charges, like those on a load mutual fund, reduce your effective yield.

- It's difficult to compare policies, and make the best buy, because both rates of return and administrative charges vary over time.

- The term insurance portion may cost more than separate term insurance would cost. The yield on the investment fund may counterbalance this, when interest rates are high. When interest rates fall, as they were doing through 1985, universal life loses its competitive edge. Perhaps, as the National Insurance Consumer Organization suggests, it's best to buy term insurance to meet your life insurance needs and do your investing separately.

Q. When I took out a life insurance policy recently, I was 34 years old. Why did my policy list my age as 35?

A. For insurance purposes age is often calculated on the nearest birthday, which may not be the last one. If your next birthday was less than six months away when you took out the policy, your age was correctly listed as 35.

SINGLE PREMIUM LIFE

A combination tax shelter and life insurance policy, single premium life allows depositors to buy life insurance with a single sizable deposit (usually a minimum of $5,000) and then accrue tax-deferred interest at a rapid rate. Most policies offer a fixed return for an initial period (in early 1986, returns ranged from 8 to 10 percent), after which returns are adjusted in accordance with a market index. An advantage of these policies is that you can borrow against the accumulated earnings at a net cost of zero. A disadvantage is that terminating the policy means that income taxes are due on the accumulated earnings, and cashing in the policy within the first few years may mean an early-surrender charge to the insurance company.

Policies vary from company to company so be sure to compare initial and adjusted interest rates and how they are set, along with loan features and surrender charges.

Which Is the Right Insurance for You?

Permanent life insurance has some advantages, outlined earlier; you'll pay for those advantages—for the cash value, the loan provisions, and all the rest—with higher premiums.

Term insurance is far less expensive and provides only one thing: the guarantee that your death during the term period will provide your family with the insurance proceeds.

And then there are the combination policies. Which should you buy? Before you make any decision:

ANALYZE YOUR INSURANCE NEEDS

As a general rule, the younger family needs the most insurance. At younger ages, term insurance costs far less than permanent. Term insurance costs a great deal, far more than permanent insurance, as you near retirement age. But you probably won't need life insurance when you are no longer relying on current income as a source of funds. Remember: Life insurance is designed as income replacement. Also remember: Despite the argument by many life insurance agents that permanent insurance is lifelong insurance, most holders of permanent policies let them lapse before age 65.

ANALYZE YOUR BUDGET

What can you afford? If you have $200 to spend on life insurance and you are a 35-year-old male, you could buy about $15,000 worth of whole life insurance. With the same $200 you could buy almost $80,000 of five-year term insurance, convertible, without a medical examination, to permanent insurance. Clearly, if $200 is all you can afford, you'll buy more protection for your family with term insurance.

ANALYZE YOUR ABILITY TO SAVE

Permanent insurance provides forced savings through the buildup of cash value. But the rate of return on these savings is low. If you have the self-discipline to buy low-cost term insurance instead of high-cost permanent insurance, and invest the difference (instead of spending it) in high-yielding investments, you'll come out way ahead. If you can't trust yourself to invest the difference, however, permanent insurance may provide you and your family with some savings.

ANALYZE YOUR TAX SITUATION

The cash value in permanent insurance is sheltered from taxes while it is building, making permanent insurance a reasonable purchase for some people in high tax brackets. Investment yields on self-managed investments, if you pursue the course of buy-term-and-invest-the-difference, will have to be adjusted for taxes. You could, of course, invest in tax-exempt securities. But your tax-sheltered buildup in a life insurance policy will be immediately available at time of death; tax-exempt securities (or any securities) can be sold but the time might not be right for a profit.

ANALYZE YOUR BASIC OPTIMISM/PESSIMISM QUOTIENT

If you think that double-digit interest rates may reappear, then you may well want one of the new variable or universal policies with their high rate of return pegged to current market rates. If you think the nation's economy may take a downward turn, you may want to stick with traditional forms of insurance, either with the pure protection of term insurance or with permanent insurance with its cash value and built-in guarantees. Permanent insurance had a good track record during the Depression of the 1930s; companies stayed in business and benefits were paid. The new policy varieties have no track record at all.

Life Stage Planning

Now let's look more closely at the cast of characters introduced at the beginning of this chapter and see where life insurance fits into their lives.

The College Graduate

Jonathan T. is 22 years old, fresh out of college, and on his way to a management trainee job he's lined up halfway across the country. His parents, who have put him through school, are in comfortable circumstances. Nonetheless, college was expensive and they're now looking forward to having money available for travel.

Does Jonathan need life insurance? No. He might, if his parents were dependent on him and his death would deprive them of needed income. Or he might want some coverage if he had few assets and his death would burden his family with debts and last expenses. But Jonathan's parents are not dependent on him and he will probably have enough group life insurance built into his new job to cover a funeral and any final expenses.

What about the argument of cost and insurability? The sales agent has told Jonathan that he should buy life insurance while he's young and healthy because (1) it will be cheaper if bought when he's younger, and (2) he knows that he's insurable; if he's later stricken with a serious and lingering illness, he might find it difficult to purchase life insurance. Both statements are true, as far as they go. Life insurance is cheaper per dollar of coverage when bought at a younger age. But it won't be cheaper over a lifetime of premium payments. And why buy a product, any product, that you don't need? Most 22-year-olds are insurable by any health definition, but so are most 32-year-olds. In the unlikely event that Jonathan's health deteriorates in the next decade to the point where no individual life insurance is available to him, he should still be able to convert his on-the-job group life insurance to an individual policy. Such conversion, although expensive, can be made without regard to the policyholder's health.

Two Incomes, No Children

Ann and Will K. have no dependents other than each other. Yet each is earning a young professional's salary and could clearly continue to do so if left alone. Do they need life insurance? Probably not. But they might want to buy some life insurance if the death of one would leave the other with a major financial burden.

For example, suppose Ann and Will recently bought a condominium in ski country. They hope to rent it out part of the year and make back some of their expenses. Meanwhile, rented out or not, there are hefty mortgage payments to be made each month. Those mortgage payments would be too much for either partner to carry alone. The condominium could, of course, be sold. But if the survivor would like to keep it, life insurance may make it possible to do so.

They have several choices: They could each buy a fixed-sum policy, either permanent or term, on the other's life or on their own. They could each buy a decreasing balance term insurance policy, to cover the remaining amount on the condominium mortgage. If Ann earns $33,000 a year to Will's $25,000, and if Ann kicks in proportionately more toward the mortgage payments, then a larger policy might be taken on Ann's life.

If their incomes are roughly equal, on the other hand, they might take insurance policies in the same amounts. Or, in still another option, they might consider joint life insurance. Available in permanent or term varieties, joint life is a single policy on two people which pays the face value only on the first to die. Since Ann and Will's purpose in purchasing life insurance is to protect their mutual investment in the condominium, joint life would serve the purpose. Joint life, although it pays proceeds on only one of the two insureds, costs more than a single policy. But it costs less than two equivalent individual policies.

New Parents

Our first-time father is another situation entirely. Eric has earned a good salary. But so has Nancy, his wife. Nancy is planning to stay out of the work force for several years now, until both children (they plan to have two) enter school. What happens if Eric should die while the children are pre-schoolers? When Nancy does reenter the labor force she will have lost ground and her salary will probably be lower than it might have been; it will almost certainly be lower than Eric's. She will also face child care costs. And what happens to the family if Nancy should die, either before or after she returns to work?

This family needs life insurance, probably a good deal more life insurance than they realize. Eric needs enough insurance on his life to provide an income for Nancy and the child(ren). Nancy should have enough insurance on her life, right now, to replace her child care and household management function in the home. When she returns to work she will want enough insurance to cover both lost income and child care.

Eric and Nancy do not, however, want life insurance on the newborn child. Despite the urgings of the life insurance agent, that child is best protected by spending available life insurance dollars on protecting the parents who will raise the child to secure adulthood.

Money for College

The Taylors, with three teenage children, have been urged to use life insurance, specifically an endowment policy, to fund the children's college education. A good idea? Sometimes, perhaps, but not in a time of double-digit inflation or volatile swings in interest rates. Life insurance, with its conservative investment portfolios, cannot match other investments at such times. But life insurance, in any economic climate, admirably serves its primary purpose of income protection. That should be the Taylors' first goal.

The Taylors need life insurance for the same reason Eric and Nancy do: to provide replacement income to support the family until the children are grown. Part of that support includes funding a college education. If both Taylors live and can continue their savings plan, the children will be able to attend college. But what if a wage-earning parent dies? Life insurance on that parent's life could then make it possible for the children to continue their education. Ten years of low-cost term insurance will see the three teenagers through school.

On the Edge of Divorce

Bob Elmer has a total of $95,000 on his own life: two individual policies of $40,000 and $30,000, and a group policy of $25,000. Dorothy expects to assume ownership of the $40,000 policy as part of the property settlement. Her insurance agent has suggested that she also buy a new $25,000 policy on Bob's life, to ensure some income if he dies and maintenance payments cease. (Dorothy is working, but she just returned to work after the children entered high school; she needs some alimony to make ends meet. She also wants to be sure that their youngest child, 19 years old, will be able to finish college.)

Let's look first at the transfer of ownership in the $40,000 policy. The transfer of that policy as part of the property settlement may subject Dorothy to unnecessary and possibly sizable taxes. It may be possible to avoid that tax by transferring the policy to Dorothy *before* the divorce. But the only sure way around taxes in the transfer of ownership is via a policy with no cash value. Either Bob transfers an existing term insurance policy to Dorothy, or he takes out a brand-new policy with Dorothy as the owner. There's also another solution: Bob doesn't transfer a policy at all, but sets up an arrangement whereby his estate must use the insurance proceeds to continue alimony payments after his death.

Dorothy can also buy a policy on Bob's life, either before or after the divorce. (Even afterward she has what is legally called an "insurable interest" in Bob's life; she will suffer financially from his death.) She can buy a policy and pay the premiums. Or she can make the purchase and have Bob, under the divorce agreement, responsible for making the premium payments. Whichever course they choose, life insurance can ensure that their youngster can finish college and that Dorothy will have an adequate income.

Pre-retirement

Tom A. is 53 years old and plans to retire in twelve years. His wife, Jeannette, is 47; after staying at home while the children were young she returned to school for a master's degree in social work. Today she works three days a week on the child guidance team in a nearby school district and sees private patients at home on the other days. Tom has been carrying $100,000 of individual life insurance on his own life (in addition to the $50,000 of group life provided by his employer), faithfully paying the premiums as they come due, for twenty-eight years. Jeanette has $20,000 of group life insurance through the school where she works.

Tom has been told that life insurance can be designed to provide retirement income. It can, but just as the Taylors found in examining their need for college funds, Tom and Jeanette find that a short-term life insurance policy is not necessarily the best approach to retirement income. In fact, with no dependents and with adequate income-producing assets, Tom and Jeanette should reconsider their need for life insurance. Why should Tom continue to pay premiums for $100,000 of individual coverage? He'll have his group coverage while he works and, since his employer is progressive when it comes to employee benefits, will continue half of his group coverage, or $25,000, when he retires. Why spend other dollars on life insurance at this stage of life, dollars that could profitably be invested elsewhere?

Young families with dependent children need life insurance. Older people often do not. Yet just as many people buy life insurance and let it lapse when they shouldn't, other people buy life insurance to meet specific needs and then proceed to pay premiums forever, without a second thought, when the need no longer exists. There are other options:

- Tom might cancel his policy, take the cash value, and invest it in the money market. Or he might use the cash value to purchase an annuity, from the same or a different company, to provide monthly income during the retirement years. Such a purchase may or may not be wise, depending on the state of the economy. (More information on annuities will be found in Chapter 25.)

- Tom might keep the policy in force but convert it to a paid-up policy, reducing the amount of insurance in force but also eliminating the need for further premium payments. With this choice the built-up cash value remains intact and Tom retains the option of borrowing against it, still keeping the policy in force, or, at a later date, surrendering the policy.

The Business Owner

Peter M., widowed some years ago, owns and runs a small carpet-cleaning business. His children are grown and self-supporting. He continues to carry life insurance, primarily to pay estate taxes due when he dies. Does he need this life insurance? Not anymore. The Economic Recovery Tax Act of 1981, now that it is fully phased in, removes some 96 or 97 percent of all estates from the federal tax man's grasp. (See Chapter 24 for a full discussion of estate taxes.) His children won't have to sell the business to pay the taxes due; they may sell it, if they choose to do so, or they may carry on. Estate taxes will probably not be a factor in their decision.

But there is another factor in Peter's insurance calculation. His mother is 87 and widowed. She's managing now with the money her husband left and occasional help from her children. But what if she outlives Peter? What if she outlives her inheritance *and* Peter? He may want to continue some life insurance coverage in order to protect her. Since term insurance is prohibitively expensive for a man in his sixties, if it can be obtained at all, Peter's best bet is to continue paying premiums on one of the whole life policies he originally bought with estate taxes in mind.

Q. My husband purchased a $5,000 insurance policy in 1956 and has been paying the premiums for thirty years. Dividends are applied to purchase additional paid-up life insurance. He's 59 now and we would like to know: Should we continue to pay on this policy? If so, for how long?

A. The only reason to continue paying is if you want to keep the policy in force to provide the $5,000 to your husband's beneficiary. Otherwise (especially since most of that $5,000 is now made up of your own accumulated cash value), I would suggest that the policy be either cashed in or converted to a paid-up policy with no further premiums due. Ask your agent or the company for the necessary forms.

You and Your Life Insurance

As you calculate your life insurance needs, keep three things in mind:

- If inflation resumes at the high levels of recent years, your calculations may be quickly out of date. The amount you may now determine as adequate to provide college for your children may well not be adequate five or ten years from now. The same holds true as you project needed retirement income for your spouse. Try to include an inflation factor in your calculations, based on the number of years ahead and on whether you think the cost of living will outstrip investment income.

- Your life insurance needs will change as your family grows and their needs change. You'll probably need considerably less life insurance, as an example, once your children are finished with school and are on their own.

- Your life insurance needs also change as your assets change. Life insurance provides an "instant estate." That estate, the amount of money you'll leave to your family, should gradually be supplanted by an estate built up through growing net worth. Life insurance, in other words, should be part of your total financial plan. Your goal should be to build your income-producing assets to the point where you no longer need life insurance.

Policy Riders

A number of additional provisions may be built into insurance coverage, many at nominal cost. Some are worthwhile; some are less so.

WAIVER OF PREMIUM

These provisions are built into some policies, are available as separate riders on others. With some variation (all insurance provisions vary from company to company and from policy to policy), the waiver of premium provides that your policy will be kept in force by the company, with no further premiums necessary, if you become totally disabled before a specified age. In general this provision is worth having. But, before you buy, find out:

- What is the age cutoff?
- How long is the waiting period before the rider takes effect?

- How does the company define total disability?
- Does the waiver then continue for life? until recovery? for a specified number of years?
- How much does the rider add to the cost of the policy?

DISABILITY INCOME

This can be purchased as a rider on your life insurance policy. It provides payment of a monthly income (often stated as a percentage of the face amount of the policy) while you are totally disabled, after an initial waiting period. Before you buy this rider, ask the same questions you would ask about the waiver of premium provision: How does the company define total disability? How long is the waiting period? How long does the income continue? And compare costs. You probably will want some disability income protection. But are you better off with it as a rider on your life insurance? Or should you take a separate income replacement policy? (See pp. 451–55 for a full discussion of disability coverage.)

ACCIDENTAL DEATH BENEFITS

So-called "double indemnity" provides double or even triple benefits if you die by accident rather than by illness. Some specify multiple benefits only for death in an airplane, train, or bus.

Should you look for double indemnity? No. Such riders make very little sense, unless you have some reason to think that your family will need far more money to live on after you die in an accident than after you die in bed. Spend your insurance dollars on increasing your total coverage. The $50 that a 30-year-old woman would pay for double indemnity on a one-year $50,000 renewable term policy would buy her another $22,000 of one-year renewable term—payable no matter how she dies. (But if you already have this coverage, be sure your family knows about it. And don't bother buying special trip insurance when you travel.)

Note: If you pay for tickets via a charge or credit card, you may also have automatic trip insurance; be sure your family knows about this too.

GUARANTEED INSURABILITY

As its name implies, this provision guarantees the right to buy additional insurance, without regard to the state of your health, up to a specified age. Such riders are most often available on whole life policies, and provide for the purchase of more whole life insurance. They seldom, if ever, apply on term insurance.

Questions to ask:

- Up to what age may you buy additional insurance?
- At what intervals may the purchases be made?
- What are the minimum and maximum amounts you may purchase?
- What is the cost of coverage?

How to Buy Insurance

While your first order of business should be to determine how much life insurance you need and the form that insurance should take, you'll also have to decide how to buy it.

Choosing a Company

Many people buy life insurance from whichever company a friendly or persistent agent happens to represent. But there are great differences among insurance companies, and you'll be a wise consumer if you select your company rather than let it select you.

You'll want to consider:

- The rating given the company by Best's Insurance Report. This authoritative guide can be found in most well-stocked public libraries.
- Whether or not the company is licensed to do business in your state. You might also consider, no matter where you live, companies licensed by New York State. New York's high regulatory standards are a definite plus for any company which meets them.
- The reputation of the company for service. Ask around among friends, and check with your state insurance department. Are claims settled promptly? Are employees courteous and responsive? Can you get through to the company when necessary?

If you buy your insurance through a life insurance agent, you may have less direct contact with the company. But payments, and decisions about payments, come from the company. Pick a company that will, as far as you can tell, remain solvent. Pick one licensed in your state so that a complaint, if one is necessary, can be filed with your state insurance department. Pick a company with a reputation for good service.

Using an Agent

Most life insurance policies are bought from insurance agents . . . largely, as the industry puts it, because life insurance is sold rather than bought. While most of us recognize the value of life insurance, in other words, very few of us go out to buy it; we wait until a life insurance agent persuades us to buy. We also wait for the agent to tell us how much insurance we need and what kind of policy it should be.

Agents, good agents, serve a purpose. They can be enormously useful in helping you to analyze your life insurance needs. But you should realize that the income of a life insurance agent is based on commissions. Some types of policies, notably the permanent variety, pay substantially higher commissions than other types. Take the advice you get, therefore, but weigh it against your own best interests as you understand them. Before you consult an agent, think through the kind of protection your family needs and think through the dollars that you can afford to spend on this protection. Then, if you like, consult an agent to help you work out the best program within your own individually selected guidelines.

HOW TO SELECT AN AGENT

What should you look for in an agent? What should you expect the agent to do for you?

- Pick an agent as you would pick your attorney or your accountant: through recommendations from trusted friends, business associates, and other professional advisers, and through an examination of his or her credentials. What kind of training has the agent had? How much experience? Does the agent look at insurance as part of your total financial plan? Is he or she willing to meet with your attorney or tax adviser? Does the agent keep up, through ongoing training, with developments in insurance and in related areas such as tax legislation? Has he or she met the stringent requirements to become a Chartered Life Underwriter (CLU)? Many competent agents are not CLUs (and not every CLU would be the best agent for you), but the designation is a useful one.

- Pick an agent whose personal style you like and trust. Pick one who will spend time with you analyzing your insurance needs and objectively suggesting varying approaches to meet those needs, one who will be clear about both cost and coverage. There is no one answer, no one single ideal policy; be wary of an agent who suggests that there is.

- Pick an agent who will provide the ongoing service you need, not one who will sell you a policy and disappear. The agent should keep you informed of new developments and should keep informed of your situation; he or she should review your life insurance needs every few years in terms of your changing family or finances.

Buying Direct

Life insurance need not be bought through an agent. It can be bought directly, either through the mail or, in a handful of states, over the counter in savings banks. Both mail-order companies and savings banks claim that because they have no agent force to support through sales commissions, their policies are less expensive. In many cases this is so, but comparable policies and costs should always be compared before a purchase is made.

Over-the-counter insurance is individual insurance and may be either permanent or term. Mail-order insurance, while it's almost always term insurance, comes in two forms: group and individual. Group insurance by mail, offered to you because you belong to an association or carry a certain credit card, has two drawbacks: You lose the insurance if you leave the group, and premium rates are not guaranteed. It also has an advantage if you're in poor health: You can't be turned down. Individual policy rates are usually guaranteed and the policy itself is usually automatically renewable. Use group insurance, therefore, as a supplement to your life insurance program but not as your total program. And compare costs carefully before you decide to buy direct.

Q. A life insurance offer that came in the mail promises that I can't be turned down for insurance, regardless of my health, as long as I return the application by the specified date. Is this really so?

A. Yes, you can hold the company to its promise. Group life insurance policies, the kind offered by mail, do not usually require proof of insurability. Both state insurance commissions and the Direct Marketing Insurance Council, moreover, say that promises made in writing in any insurance advertisement or mail offering are legally binding and must be honored. Should a promise not be kept, notify your state insurance commission.

Cost Considerations

Perhaps the biggest cost differential in life insurance is the difference between permanent insurance and term insurance. You will have to decide, at the outset, which type of policy or combination of policies best suits your needs. But there are other cost considerations as well:

Participating and Nonparticipating Policies

Some policies pay dividends; they are called "participating" policies. Others do not; they are called "nonparticipating." Here are the differences:

PARTICIPATING

The participating (or "par") policy generally has a higher premium; if the investment experience of the insurance company is good (as it often is during periods of high interest yields), portions of the premium are returned to policyholders in the form of dividends. Because those dividends are a return of excess premium, they are not treated as taxable income by the Internal Revenue Service. But *interest* on dividends, if you leave the dividends with the company to accumulate, is something else; it must be reported on your federal income tax form.

The holders of participating policies have some options as to what to do with declared dividends: They may take them in cash, use them to reduce premium payments, or leave them with the insurance company to accumulate interest (that interest, as noted, is taxable). All of these options apply to dividends on both permanent and term insurance. Holders of permanent insurance have additional choices: They may use the dividends to buy additional paid-up insurance or, with some companies, may use the dividends to purchase one-year renewable term insurance. The last choice, in the opinion of many insurance authorities, is a good way to combat inflation by building up the value of your policy. Whichever option you choose, you may change your mind at a later date (although if you choose to buy additional insurance you may then find yourself having to pass an insurability test).

Note: Dividends on participating policies, because they depend on investment performance, are never guaranteed. The insurance company will show you a projection of dividends. But, if the economy stagnates or enters a prolonged recession, or if the company's investment managers lose their touch, your dividends may not be forthcoming.

NONPARTICIPATING

"Nonpar" policies do not return a dividend to policyholders. Where the holder of a par policy does not know in advance what insurance costs will actually be, because the price on these policies is the premium less any dividend, the holder of a nonpar policy has traditionally had the advantage of guaranteed costs. In recent years, when investment returns have been very favorable, nonpar policies with their fixed premiums have been a poor choice.

In a variation of the nonpar policy, designed to give issuing companies a competitive edge (after companies were criticized for failing to pass on higher earnings and reduced mortality experience to their customers), some policies are now written with a *variable premium* (not to be confused with variable life, where the premium is fixed but the investment return may vary; see p. 419). In most such policies, the initial premium is lower than it might otherwise be; this low initial premium may be guaranteed for a base period, such as two years. If the investment outlook then changes, the premium may then be raised or lowered. Limits on such policies (how often the premium may be changed, and to what extent) vary from company to company.

Group Insurance

Most of this discussion has centered on the life insurance you buy as an individual. Life insurance may also be purchased via a group. In general, although not always, group insurance is less expensive. (*Caution:* Some organizations raise money by selling insurance to their members. Instead of passing along the savings, the organization keeps the money. Buying such insurance is okay if you understand this; it's not so okay if you think you're getting a bargain.) In general, too, group insurance is limited in type (it's usually available only as term insurance) and in amount. But you may also be able to purchase insurance, as a member of a group, that you would otherwise find it difficult or impossible to buy.

You may already have some group life insurance through your employer. You may also be able to purchase additional group life insurance through professional or trade associations, fraternal organizations, labor unions, even credit card issuers.

Group insurance has these disadvantages:

■ The amount may be limited, and may not be as much as you may need.

■ As term insurance, there are no cash value buildups or loan provisions.

■ It ends when you leave the group. However, a new "perk" offered by some employers continues group life insurance after retirement, usually in an amount equal to one-quarter or one-half of the pre-retirement amount.

Group insurance has these advantages:

■ You can secure insurance simply by being a member of the group; there are usually no questions asked and no medical examinations.

■ Your cost is low because the coverage is generally term insurance and because there are savings in the administration of a group plan.

■ If the group insurance is terminated or if you leave the group, you usually have the right (for a specified period of time) to convert the policy to individual coverage. This coverage will, as a rule, be far more expensive. But it will be life insurance coverage, and if you are in poor health and unable to secure insurance elsewhere, it may be worthwhile.

Insurability

Because the cost of life insurance is based in part on mortality, insurance companies need to know the state of your health before they issue a policy. You will be asked to fill out an application, including basic information about the state of your health. It is in your interest to answer those questions accurately; misinformation, if it comes to light, could invalidate your coverage.

In many instances—with group life insurance and with relatively small individual life insurance policies—this application form may be all that's necessary. If the application form triggers some concern at the company or if you are applying for a large amount of coverage, however, you may have to have a medical examination.

If you are found to be a higher-than-average risk, you can probably still buy life insurance, but it may cost you more. Since different companies have different underwriting standards, it is entirely possible that one company would charge you a standard rate even while another charges you more. This is another good reason for using an agent. An extra premium, in any case, does not have to last forever. If your health improves, or if you have been without evidence of disease for a period of time, talk to the company; it's entirely possible that the "rating" would be eliminated or reduced (it can't be raised, so you needn't fear additional cost). If, on the other hand, you take good care of yourself, you may be entitled to lower-than-usual rates. Many companies, for instance, write special low-premium policies for nonsmokers.

Extra premiums are sometimes charged for certain occupations deemed to be risky: acrobats and astronauts, lion tamers and sand hogs, mountain-climbing guides and miners, all may be asked to pay additional premiums for life insurance coverage. But the days are past when certain occupations would exclude you from life insurance; today virtually everyone in any line of work—even astronauts—can find a company willing to write insurance.

Q. My husband was planning to take out additional life insurance just before he was advised that he needed a heart bypass operation. No insurance company will sell him regular life insurance right now, but is there any way for him to get more coverage?

A. Ask your insurance broker about short-term surgical survival insurance. Although this insurance is generally more expensive than regular coverage, it's designed for just this kind of situation. The face amount of this special policy, up to a maximum of $500,000, is paid to the beneficiary if the insured dies within thirty days as a result of the operation. The one-time premium ranges from 1 to 5 percent of the policy's face value. As soon as your husband recovers, have him carry through his resolve to buy additional life insurance.

Comparing Costs via the Interest-Adjusted Method

Perhaps the most complicated question facing any potential purchaser of life insurance is the question of price comparison. Given the differences among insurance companies and among insurance policies, how can a rational comparison be made? You can't simply look at the premium you're asked to pay. You have to be sure, first of all, that all policy provisions are the same. For example, is waiver of premium in the event of disability built in to each policy you're considering? Or will you pay for it separately?

Assuming that two policies are identical in their provisions, you can compare their costs over a period of years by looking at:

- The sum of the premiums you'll pay over the years (a figure affected by how long you live and by how long you keep the policy in force)
- Any dividends you may receive (a figure which will vary with the company's investment experience)
- What cash value is available (a sum affected by the varying rates at which cash values build up in different policies)

Then, in order to make a valid comparison, you would also have to consider an interest factor based on the "time value" of money—the interest you could earn on your money if you did not use it for this particular purchase.

All of these factors are analyzed for you, and distilled to an index number, in the interest-adjusted costs now routinely prepared by life insurance companies. Ask your company or agent to show you the "20-year interest-adjusted surrender-cost index" for the particular policy you are thinking of buying. Although the index is based on some complicated mathematics, you won't need any mathematical skill to interpret it. Just remember: The lower the index number, the lower the overall cost.

Should You Swap an Old Policy for a New?

As interest rates rose through the late 1970s, insurance companies earned more on their investments. The result: lower premiums on new policies. The holders of older policies, unless those policies were the participating variety that returned excess premiums in dividends, were often left holding an excessively expensive policy.

This development has caused consumer advocates to rethink the formerly firm advice never to switch one insurance policy for another. Today, under some circumstances, you might be wise to cancel an old policy (especially an old nonparticipating permanent life policy with a poor rate of return) and buy a new one. Such a move might save you considerable sums.

Before you say yes to the next life insurance agent urging such a swap, however, do a very careful comparison of both policy features and interest-adjusted costs. Get out your old policy and read it over, then write to the company for a detailed cost breakout: premiums, cash surrender value, death benefits, plus the index figure for this policy. Get the same information on the new policy you are thinking about buying. Then ask the agent who sold you the old policy to tell you why you should keep it in force. Weigh the arguments on both sides carefully, bearing in mind:

■ The biggest commission and administrative costs come out of your premium in the first year. This means two things: The agent may want to sell you a new policy because he gets a nice big commission, and your cash values build up very slowly at first, much faster later on. If you cancel a permanent contract before it is ten years old, you may be forfeiting much of its potential cash value.

■ Every life insurance policy has a two-year "incontestability" clause; during these first two years the insurer may cancel the contract if it turns out that you made any untrue statements on your application. During these same two years, as a rule, no benefits will be paid in case of suicide. If you take out a new policy, you'll face a new two-year period of possible challenge.

If you decide to swap policies after weighing all the arguments pro and con, be sure you've passed the medical exam and that your new policy is firmly in force before you cancel your old one. You could otherwise find yourself sadly uninsured.

Or, instead of swapping, think about (1) keeping the old policy in force and buying additional coverage at new lower rates, or (2) borrowing against the cash value of the old policy and using the proceeds to buy term insurance at favorable rates. If you're underinsured, as a great many people are, either approach might be better than an outright swap.

Keeping Premiums Down

The most obvious way to keep premiums down is to shop around among insurance companies before you buy. This is also the most significant, since some policies will cost twice as much as others (or thousands and thousands of dollars over a lifetime of coverage) for essentially the same coverage. You can also save some money, although not as much, by:

■ Paying premiums annually if at all possible. More frequent payments add up to higher premiums. (One study indicated actual interest rates on monthly premiums ranging from 4.9 percent to 29.3 percent.)

■ Buying as much as possible at one time—within, of course, the boundaries of your budget and your insurance needs. Larger policies often sell for less-per-thousand than smaller ones.

Your Beneficiary

> **Q.** I'm making a college loan to my nephew for the spring semester, and while I expect him to pay it back, I would like payment guaranteed if anything happens to him. What would you think about his taking out a life insurance policy and naming me as beneficiary?
>
> **A.** It's a good idea. Better yet, so that he can't change the beneficiary without your consent, have him designate you as the beneficiary irrevocably. You may also want to make arrangements so that you'll be notified by the insurance company if the premiums aren't paid.

You will be asked to name a beneficiary for your life insurance, the person or persons you wish to receive the policy proceeds when they become payable. It's also wise to name a contingent beneficiary, in case you outlive the first beneficiary. Make a specific election here, rather than simply having the proceeds payable to your estate; if you do the latter, the insurance money will have to go through the probate process along with the rest of your estate, delaying its receipt by your family.

Keep your beneficiary informed about the kind of insurance policy you have (a great many beneficiaries never collect because they simply never knew the policy existed) and where you keep the policy (preferably not in a safe deposit box, which in many states will be temporarily sealed at your death). Be sure your beneficiary knows the name of your insurance company and agent. Keep the company informed as to the whereabouts of your beneficiary.

You have the right to change your beneficiary (via a form obtainable from the insurance company) and should remember to do so if your circumstances change. You may, for example, name a child as a contingent beneficiary (after your spouse), and forget to add her later-born brother. But if you've looked ahead to the eventuality of having more children, you could have named "children of the insured, John Smith." If you've done this, no further change will be necessary. But be careful: "Children of the insured, John Smith" might mean that your wife's daughter by a previous marriage, whom you meant to include, is in fact excluded. If you make it "children born of the marriage of John and Ann Smith" you may be excluding adopted children. Think it through carefully.

And think through the unlikely possibility that one or more of your children may predecease you. You can anticipate this possibility by phrasing the beneficiary provision so that any children of such a child (your grandchildren) will share in the proceeds with your other children. This can be done either *per capita*, by equal shares, or *per stirpes*, along family lines. If you have two children and one of them predeceases you, leaving two children, a per capita distribution of your insurance would give one-third each to your surviving child and the two children of your other child; a per stirpes distribution would give one half to your child (the same half he or she would have received had your other child survived) and divide the other half (their parent's share) between the two grandchildren.

It's very important to anticipate as many situations as possible *and* to review your beneficiary provisions regularly. You probably won't want proceeds to go to an ex-spouse (unless, of course, such a distribution is part of the divorce agreement), but it can happen. It can happen if you (1) have your beneficiary designation simply read "wife/husband of the insured" without a specific name, or if (2) you forget to make a beneficiary change when it's appropriate to do so.

Q. I just found out that the beneficiary listed on my husband's life insurance policy is his mother. My husband says he did this in case we should both die in an accident and that his mother knows the money is mine. I say it leaves me with nothing. Shouldn't my name be on the policy?

A. If your husband wants you to receive the money, then your name should be on the policy as the beneficiary. If he is worried about what might happen if you were to die in a common accident, he can name his mother as contingent or secondary beneficiary.

Who Should Own Your Policy?

Life insurance proceeds are not subject to income tax. But they are included in your total estate for the purposes of establishing the amount of estate tax which may be due. They can be excluded from your list of owned assets if you do not in fact own the policies. For many years, therefore, financial advisers have been suggesting that people with sizeable estates have their life insurance owned by a spouse (or, in some situations, by a trust set up for the purpose).

Transfer of ownership to a spouse was worth considering, provided that the marriage was expected to last. A transfer is irrevocable. An owner has full rights to the policy: to borrow against the cash value, name the beneficiary, elect settlement options, even cancel the policy altogether. (If you transfer ownership but retain any of these rights, the IRS will conclude that the transfer is simply a tax dodge.) Transfer of an existing policy, moreover, may have tax consequences of its own; gift taxes (equivalent in amount to estate taxes) may be due on the value of the policy at the time the policy is transferred. A brand-new whole life policy, or a term policy of any age, has no cash value and hence no tax consequences. But giving up such a policy still means giving up control of an asset; this is not a step to be taken lightly.

Transferring ownership, in any case, may no longer be necessary. The Economic Recovery Tax Act of 1981 created an unlimited marital exemption, so that any amount may pass to a surviving spouse tax-free. It also increased the size of estates subject to estate tax, so that as of 1987 only estates over $600,000 (left to anyone but a spouse) are subject to federal tax. (States have their own inheritance taxes. Many exempt all or part of life insurance proceeds.) Review your own total estate carefully (see Chapter 24, on estate planning), and get expert advice to minimize any tax consequences, before you decide that someone else should own your life insurance.

Settlement Options

Your beneficiary doesn't have to take the proceeds of your policy as a lump sum. There are other choices, to be elected either by you or by your beneficiary when the time comes.

Interest income options allow the company to hold the proceeds and pay out interest on the proceeds, either for a specified period or for the beneficiary's lifetime. The interest paid will be based on a rate stated in the policy. Under some policies, portions of the principal may be withdrawn along with the interest.

Income for specified period or **income of specified amounts** may be elected to provide payouts of both principal and interest on a predetermined schedule and at a predetermined rate.

Life income provisions guarantee income for the life of the beneficiary, with the amounts based on the age and sex of the beneficiary at the time of the policyholder's death. If the beneficiary lives longer than mortality tables would indicate, the principal plus interest will be collected. If the beneficiary dies early, however, a substantial portion of the principal may be forfeited, unless the election has included a guarantee of a specified number of payments.

You may be urged to select one of these options, on the grounds that you can best determine the eventual use of your insurance proceeds. Before you do, however, bear in mind:

- Your election of a settlement option constitutes a binding contract between you and the insurance company. Your beneficiary will not be able to change your election, no matter what may happen in the future.

- Your beneficiary may do much better financially if he or she can take the lump-sum proceeds, use what is necessary for immediate need, and invest the rest for maximum return. Some insurance company interest rates are notoriously low.

- Your beneficiary will almost certainly do better psychologically by having control of that money. Either leave the decision to be made by your beneficiary, therefore, to suit his or her needs at the time, or elect a lump-sum payment, which will accomplish the same purpose.

Q. Among my father's papers after his death we found a note with the number of a life insurance policy. We never found the policy and don't know the name of the company. Is there any way to find out who wrote this policy?

A. A first step would be to look through your father's canceled checks and receipts; you may find a record of payment to the insurance company. You might also check with the personnel department of the company where your father last worked, in case it was a group policy. And, if these steps are unproductive, you might try the life bureau of the department of insurance in each of the states where your father lived.

KEY POINTS

- Life insurance serves different purposes at different times. But its most important function is to protect those who depend on you from financial hardship resulting from your death. Take care of income replacement as you plan your insurance program, before you do anything else.

- Determine how much you need and how much you can spend before you think about what kind of life insurance to buy. Compare costs and policy provisions before you make a decision, and buy as much protection for your family as you can afford.

- Review your coverage regularly, at least every five years and more often if there is a change in either your family constellation or your financial circumstances. You may find that you need a different amount or type of life insurance to reflect a new marriage, additional children, changes in income, a move to a new house, or a different job. You may need more insurance at some periods, less at others. Your life isn't static. Your life insurance program should not be static either.

22

Health
Insurance

The average family of four spent $3,708 for health care in 1980 . . . and will spend $11,900 in 1990. Younger people generally spend less; older people, especially those over 65, often spend considerably more. You have different health concerns, and different expectations of health care's place in your budget, at different life stages. But wherever you are in the life cycle, however much or little you may earn, whatever the number of your dependents, health insurance deserves a prominent place in your financial planning.

What are your current concerns?

- As a young single, leaving your parents' nest, you need first-time coverage of your own. Will you have it through your employer? If you do, will it be enough?

- As a two-income couple, your primary concern may be supplementing rather than duplicating each other's on-the-job group coverage. Do you have a choice about which fringe benefits to accept?

- A family has wide-ranging concerns, from paying the initial costs of childbearing to replacing a disabled breadwinner's earnings. Can you find adequate protection in one package? Or do you need several different policies?

- Divorced and widowed women, suddenly on their own after years of coverage under a husband's group health insurance, have special needs. Should health insurance be part of a divorce agreement? Where can you find individual health insurance at a price you can afford?

- Retirees need to supplement Medicare. And early retirees face the difficult task of filling the gap between employee benefits and the Medicare starting date. If you've thought of retiring early, have you also thought about the difficulties of finding health insurance at age 62?

Health insurance, of course, can't guarantee good health any more than life insurance can ensure that you will keep on living. Both protect you and your family against financial loss. That loss, in the health insurance arena, comes in two parts: the out-of-pocket costs of health care, which (especially for hospitalization) are outdistancing inflation; and the costs of income lost when you are ill.

What kind of health insurance do you need?

Types of Health Insurance

Health insurance, unlike automobile or homeowners insurance, comes in a bewildering variety of shapes and sizes, with no standardized forms to ease the confusion. But there are several specific types:

- Basic protection includes hospitalization, surgical, and medical benefits.

- Major medical insurance provides coverage against the financial costs of long-term illness. It is often designed to take up where basic protection stops, and may also be purchased alone.

- Hospital indemnity policies, often sold by mail, provide direct cash benefits when you are hospitalized.

- Disability income policies provide you with a percentage of your earnings if you are disabled through illness or injury and unable to work.

- "Dread disease" policies pay benefits only for a specific, named condition.

- "Medi-gap" insurance, as its name implies, provides older people with the coverage that Medicare lacks.

- Health maintenance organizations, while not strictly insurance, provide economical prepaid preventive and treatment services in one central location.

Here's what you should know about each:

Basic Coverage

Your basic health insurance package pays all or part of the medical and hospital bills associated with short-term illness or injury. It covers hospitalization, surgical procedures, and doctor visits.

Hospitalization portion includes payment toward room and board and regular nursing care while in the hospital, plus certain hospital services and supplies such as X-rays, laboratory tests, and medication.

Note: Your policy should include payment of hospital room and board charges at the full daily rate (semiprivate) for 60 to 120 days. See Table 1 for what these charges are apt to be. It's best to have a policy based on service (that is, current charges for a semiprivate room, whatever those charges are), since benefits will then rise along with hospitalization costs. When a policy has fixed "inside limits" restricting the dollar amount of reimbursement, the benefit schedule may be out of date before the ink on your signature is dry.

TABLE 1: Semiprivate room charges, 1985.

State	Room charge	State	Room charge
Alabama	$162.22	Montana	$203.02
Alaska	273.98	Nebraska	154.62
Arizona	192.59	Nevada	241.32
Arkansas	141.16	New Hampshire	199.27
California	281.20	New Jersey	182.61
Colorado	212.38	New Mexico	191.78
Connecticut	205.98	New York	223.63
Delaware	214.16	North Carolina	139.24
District of Columbia	273.71	North Dakota	175.63
Florida	181.78	Ohio	228.94
Georgia	150.72	Oklahoma	165.10
Hawaii	230.82	Oregon	230.02
Idaho	199.10	Pennsylvania	255.65
Illinois	246.60	Rhode Island	205.10
Indiana	184.23	South Carolina	140.04
Iowa	179.47	South Dakota	161.85
Kansas	184.11	Tennessee	142.26
Kentucky	175.74	Texas	158.57
Louisiana	156.31	Utah	169.09
Maine	209.04	Vermont	211.27
Maryland	187.33	Virginia	164.12
Massachusetts	228.92	Washington	228.96
Michigan	269.86	West Virginia	163.81
Minnesota	188.21	Wisconsin	166.80
Mississippi	113.56	Wyoming	166.00
Missouri	185.43	U.S. AVERAGE	212.77

(Source: Health Insurance Association of America)

Surgical procedures, both in and out of the hospital, should also be covered in this basic protection package. Some policies include a schedule of fees which will be paid for various surgical procedures. This schedule should be updated at relatively frequent intervals or it, too, may rapidly become outdated. More and more policies, instead, provide reimbursement of a surgeon's fee up to the "customary and reasonable" charge for the particular procedure. Customary charges vary by region and also by doctor. Check with the local medical society to find out what "customary and reasonable charges" are in your area and you won't be faced with an unpleasant surprise after surgery. (Many complaints stem from inadequate reimbursement . . . and at least part of what patients consider "inadequate" reimbursement comes from using a surgeon more expensive than most in the area.)

Doctor visits are the third portion of the basic health insurance policy. Reimbursement for diagnostic procedures and laboratory tests may also be covered, but preventive care, including checkups, often is not. Be sure you know just what is covered.

At one time a basic health insurance package might have been all you needed. Today, with escalating health care costs (especially hospital room and board costs), this is no longer so. In fact, it's probably more important for most people to have coverage against long-term illness. You can budget for Band-Aids, or for the costs associated with a respiratory illness. You can't really budget for open-heart surgery or the long-term expenses associated with cancer.

Major Medical

Major medical is the all-important protection that picks up where basic protection stops. It covers you against the steep and ongoing costs of a major illness or accident. It's the insurance that protects you against financial devastation. If you can afford only one type of health insurance, major medical should be the one.

DEDUCTIBLES

Major medical comes with a deductible, a fixed amount that you must pay before your benefits begin. If you carry basic health insurance, the deductible can be linked to those basic benefits so that you have no exposure at all. If you don't carry basic coverage, or if you prefer to save some premium money by having a "corridor" between your basic and your major medical coverage and self-insuring these costs, you can select a larger deductible. Deductibles on major medical policies can run from $100 to $2,000, sometimes even more; the larger the deductible, the lower the cost of your insurance. Look at the deductible amount as the amount you are willing to self-insure, the amount you can manage to pay without bankrupting your family.

The deductible should, ideally, apply to the entire year rather than to each illness. But watch out for high deductibles on each family member starting in January of each year, even if the illness began the month before. Good policies have a carry-over provision. Good policies also often apply the deductible to a family rather than to an individual. If a family of four carries a policy with a $100 deductible, for example, the insurer might pick up expenses for all family members after $200 in deductible expenditures.

CO-INSURANCE

Major medical also comes with a co-insurance feature, under which you pay a percentage (often 20 percent) of costs and the insurance company pays the remainder. With a 20 percent co-insurance provision, a medical bill of $10,000 in eligible expenses would leave you paying $2,000 (plus the deductible) out of your own pocket.

Good policies also contain a "stop-loss" provision, under which you have to pay only up to a predetermined amount and no more. If you have a stop-loss clause specifying $1,500 out-of-pocket costs, then the insurer will pay 100 percent of all remaining expenses after that level.

Major medical policies also specify a maximum amount payable, preferably in lifetime terms. Such a maximum should be at least $100,000, preferably $250,000. The costs of a catastrophic illness can be catastrophic; in the most expensive case recorded to date, twenty-six days of hospital care for a young woman with a very rare blood disease came to $358,942.88. Even the best health insurance leaves the patient responsible for a percentage of the costs; the percentage, in such a case, unless your policy contains a stop-loss clause, can be devastating.

Q. My son will graduate from college in June. Can he still be covered under my health insurance policy?

A. Maybe, if he is going on for further schooling and remaining financially dependent on you. If not, his coverage under the family policy may end when he graduates and/or reaches his 19th or 21st birthday. Your policy may have a conversion privilege, however, under which he may obtain individual coverage without a medical exam, if he does so within a specified time.

Hospital Indemnity Policies

Benefits under these policies, designed to reimburse you for out-of-pocket health care costs, are paid to you directly, in cash, on a per-day basis. You've seen the ads, in newspapers and in magazines and in your mailbox: $20 a day, $30 a day, $50 a day . . . for each day of hospitalization after the first three, or five, or eight . . .

There are a couple of things to keep in mind about these policies:

■ They are not designed to provide primary health insurance coverage. Any per-day cost, spelled out in dollars, is inadequate in an era of $300 a day and more for hospital room and board. These policies can, however, provide supplementary coverage, extra dollars that you can use as you see fit, whether for extras in the hospital or to help out at home. They can also be very useful if you are otherwise uninsurable.

■ These policies pay benefits *only* while you are in the hospital and only, as a rule, after a specified number of days in the hospital. Since the average hospital stay is just eight days (twelve days for older people), such policies prove useless to the vast majority of people who buy them. If, of course, you are in the hospital for a extended period of time, an indemnity policy could prove helpful. If you decide you want an indemnity policy with immediate or almost immediate payments, you can probably find one. But the premium cost will be higher.

Take care of your primary health insurance needs before you consider buying a hospital indemnity policy.

Disability Income

This form of insurance, important but often overlooked, provides you with an income should you become sick or injured and unable to work. It protects your family from the financial deprivation that could result if a breadwinner is out of work for any substantial period of time. Disability income protection is an essential form of health insurance. Before you rush out to buy it, however, look at other forms of disability income you already have:

ON THE JOB

Many employers provide some form of disability income. It may be a limited number of sick days with pay. Or it may be a full-scale disability income policy on a group basis. You're in good shape if your employer provides a full-scale group policy. But you should find out exactly what benefits are provided, how soon they would begin after you became disabled, and how long they would last.

Some companies do not provide disability income coverage as such, but do have group health insurance policies for their employees under which a disability income rider can be added by the individual for a modest premium. If you have this option, you should consider taking it. Disability income protection is important insurance to have, and this is an inexpensive way to make the purchase.

SOCIAL SECURITY

If you are covered under Social Security for retirement benefits, you are also covered for disability benefits. Those benefits are substantial and may be the most important part of Social Security for younger workers.

Under this program, you can count on a monthly benefit if you are disabled for an extended period. Those benefits, moreover, are calculated as if you had retired at age 65 in the year the disability began. At this writing, family benefits can run to $1,400 a month.

These are the things you should know:

- Benefits for permanent or indefinite disabilities begin with the sixth month; they continue for life, as long as you remain disabled.

- After twenty-four months of benefits you qualify for Medicare, which helps pay your medical bills.

- You must file a claim, and that claim must be approved before you can receive any benefits. It's important to file a claim as soon as you think you might be eligible, as soon as you've been told that you can no longer engage in "substantial, gainful activity." If you forget to file, you can claim retroactive benefits for up to twelve months, but you and your family may lose some benefits.

- If you have a spouse and dependent children your disability benefits are increased. In one example provided by the Research Institute of America, a 35-year-old father of two children, disabled in 1981 and remaining disabled, could find his family entitled to fully $289,000 under Social Security disability benefits.

Because of the funding problems presently facing the Social Security Administration, more stringent regulations are being applied across the board. More basic claims are being disallowed. Those who care for the children of a disabled worker no longer are entitled to benefits after the children reach the age of 16. There may well be additional changes. But even with limitations, the Social Security disability program will play an important role in your planning; don't overlook the benefits it offers.

OTHER BENEFITS

Depending on where you live, your occupation, and your background, other disability benefits may be available to you:

- Worker's compensation, for a job-related disability
- Veterans Administration pension disability benefits
- Civil Service disability benefits
- Black lung benefits
- State welfare benefits and Aid to Families with Dependent Children
- Group union disability benefits
- Automobile insurance which includes benefits for disability resulting from an automobile accident

- Credit insurance which includes the paying off of an installment loan if you become disabled

- Waiver of premium provisions under life insurance, under which you will owe no further premiums should you become disabled

Add all these benefits together. If they come to approximately 70 percent of your after-tax income, you may not need any private disability income insurance. If they fall far short, you should definitely consider the purchase of an individual policy. The risk of a disabling accident between the ages of 35 and 65 is a lot greater than the chances of dying. The risk of a *permanently* disabling accident is slim. But the risk of an accident or illness that may put you out of commission for at least ninety days is not slim at all.

WHEN YOU'RE UNDERINSURED

Carl and Ann N., in their twenties, are parents of a 2-year-old girl. Carl, a computer salesman, earns $18,000 a year and brings home $1,180 each month. Ann gave up her secretarial job to care for their daughter. All is going well . . . until Carl develops a degenerative muscle disease and is unable to work. His physician certifies that he is totally disabled. Carl has no prior military or civil service that might qualify him for government disability programs. He hasn't worked long enough to be covered by Social Security disability benefits. And the illness is not job-related, so there will be no worker's compensation.

This couple think they are covered and will be able to manage; Carl's employer, after all, provides a long-term disability benefit of 50 percent of average earnings in the past three years. But Carl has not worked long enough to qualify for full coverage, and his benefit is based on an assumed average annual salary of only $10,000. This brings in $417 a month. But Carl and Ann now have to pay $100 a month to continue their group life and medical insurance, benefits which were paid by the employer while Carl was working. This brings replacement income to $317, or 27 percent of their pre-disability income. An individual disability income policy would have gone a long way toward assuring this family an adequate standard of living.

Individual Disability Policies

There is great variation among individual disability policies offered by various companies. Here are the things you should know:

- Most individual policies require that you be totally disabled before benefits begin. Benefits for partial disability are sometimes provided, but usually only if the partial disability follows a period of total disability for the same cause.

■ The definition of disability within the policy is crucial. Be sure you find out exactly how it is defined or you may be in for an unpleasant surprise when you file a claim. There are two things to watch for. First, disability can be defined as being unable to perform your customary occupation (e.g., as a practicing dentist), any related occupation (e.g., teaching dentistry), or any occupation at all (e.g., stuffing envelopes at home). You're better off with a policy providing benefits when you can't work at an occupation you're trained for. Second, disability can also be interpreted as requiring total in-hospital or in-house confinement. Even ill people can get out for some fresh air, however, and you don't want a policy so narrowly restricted.

Q. My husband has been ill and is receiving disability payments under his company's insurance plan. I thought disability insurance benefits were not taxable, but now I'm told they are. Which is right?

A. The IRS makes a distinction between disability insurance purchased by an individual and that purchased by an employer. If your husband had bought his own insurance and paid his own premiums, the benefits would not be taxable. As it is, since his premiums were paid by his employer, the benefits are taxed as income.

■ You may select the amount of your benefit, up to a point. Most insurers will limit benefits from all sources to no more than 60 to 70 percent of your gross salary. The companies don't want to pay more because they don't want to encourage malingerers. But you won't need your full gross salary, in any case, because you won't be paying taxes or the costs of going to work.

■ You can choose a policy in which benefits start from the first day of disability or one where the benefits start six months later. (Some policies have different waiting periods for accident and for illness.) The longer you choose to wait, the lower your premium. Again, self-insurance for relatively small amounts pays off. (If you established the financial plan detailed in Chapter 2, you should have three to six months' income in liquid savings, ready to be tapped in just such an emergency. So you shouldn't need immediate-pay disability benefits.)

■ You can choose a policy in which the benefits will be paid for as little as one year or as long as to age 65 (or even longer, if you're still working full-time). Again, logically enough, the shorter the benefit period the lower the premium. While saving money is important, however, so is having adequate coverage. A longer term of benefits may be worth buying.

- Your policy should cover both accident and illness. Some policies pay only for accidents.

- Different policies are renewable under different conditions. The most desirable (although the most expensive and the hardest to find) is noncancelable, a policy that is guaranteed renewable at a fixed premium rate until a specified age such as 65. Guaranteed renewable policies cannot be canceled, but the company can raise the premium rates for an entire class of policy-holders. Optionally renewable insurance (the option is the insurance company's, not yours) is least desirable; the company can't arbitrarily cancel your policy alone, but it can, under this provision, cancel or refuse to renew an entire group of contracts.

- The kind of work you do affects both your coverage and your premium. If you change jobs, be sure to notify your insurance carrier right away.

Dread Disease Policies

Health insurance policies are sold, often by mail, for a number of specific ailments. Most prevalent, however, is cancer insurance. For a relatively small sum, these policies promise to pay the costs associated with hospitalization for cancer. Are they a good buy? Most insurance experts think not. Here's why:

- The premium may be low, but 60 percent of it, on the average, is retained by the company in salesmen's commissions, administrative expenses, and profit. Less than 40 percent, according to a study by the House Committee on Aging, is paid out in benefits. This contrasts with an average 80 percent payout on standard health insurance policies.

- Some of the sales pitches for these policies are downright deceptive. They may claim that the policies pay "extended benefits" for hospital confinements over ninety days . . . but don't say that the average stay for cancer patients is fourteen days. They may say that they pay for "definitive cancer treatment" . . . without noting that this means nothing is paid for much of the cost associated with cancer treatment: pathology reports, rehabilitation, etc.

Even where benefit payouts are good, and sales pitches are forthright and honest, most objective observers believe that any money you would spend on insurance against a single dread disease would be better spent in improving your overall health insurance. Cancer does strike a lot of people. But so does heart disease. Why insure against only one disease?

Medi-gap or Wraparound Policies

This insurance is specifically designed to meet the needs of retired men and women, for whom Medicare is not enough. Before you decide whether or not you need such supplementary coverage, however, you have to understand what Medicare does and does not do.

MEDICARE

Major changes may be in the works, as the Medicare system faces funding problems. For now, Medicare comes in two parts: Part A, hospital insurance; and Part B, medical insurance. Both have deductible and co-insurance provisions. Both become available when you reach 65 if you are retired; if you keep working between 65 and 70, your employer's group plan provides primary coverage.

Q. My elderly mother is worried about the possibility of needing long-term nursing home care in the future. Won't Medicare cover the costs?

A. No. Medicare and most private supplemental policies cover only short-term nursing home care directly following hospitalization. But special policies for long-term care are being developed and are already available in some states. Most pay $30 to $60 a day for up to four years for a monthly premium of $20 to $80, depending on the person's age when the policy is taken. Waiting periods vary from zero to 100 days. Ask your insurance agent for information.

■ You are entitled to *Medicare Part A* if you have worked long enough under either the Social Security or Railroad Retirement programs. If you retire at 65 or over, and are not eligible under one of these plans, you may buy this hospitalization protection (but only if you also buy Medicare Part B). It pays for a specified number of days of full hospital care for each illness after an initial deductible, and everything over a specified amount per day for a succeeding period. It also has lifetime "reserve" days, which you can draw on when other benefits are used up.

■ You may buy *Medicare Part B* at age 65 for a monthly premium. After you have reached the deductible amount, Medicare will pay 80 percent of doctor bills incurred in connection with illness or injury; routine check-ups are not covered. The 20 percent that you must pay, moreover, is based on what Medicare designates as "reasonable fees." You may wind up paying considerably more than just 20 percent, either because the doctors in your region charge more or simply because Medicare bases its fees on the preceding year and doctors' fees seldom remain stable from year to year.

Medicare currently covers only 35 to 45 percent of your health care costs. Some expensive items are excluded: private duty nursing, custodial nursing home care costs, out-of-hospital drugs, dental care, routine immunizations, foot care, eye examinations and eyeglasses, hearing aids, etc. That's why many older people feel the need for additional supplementary health insurance.

SUPPLEMENTAL INSURANCE

There are two types of supplemental insurance available to you after retirement:

The hospital indemnity policy, described on pp. 450–51, pays daily cash benefits when you are hospitalized. Because Medicare covers most of the early costs of hospitalization, some people set aside the early benefits of these policies against later costs.

If you are interested in this type of policy as a Medicare supplement, be careful about:

■ Limitations on pre-existing conditions. It's very difficult to reach age 65 without some pre-existing health condition; you don't want a health insurance policy that excludes all benefits for such conditions. Limitations range from two years to as little as six months. What's worse, some companies refuse all claims during the limitation period for illnesses which can be shown to have originated before the policy was purchased —whether or not you knew you had the condition at the time of purchase. At best, a pre-existing condition clause can be tricky; the longer the period, the less the policy costs, but the longer you are vulnerable to significant out-of-pocket costs.

■ The elimination period, or the amount of time you must wait before benefits begin. You will pay more for first-day coverage, and you may not need it while Medicare is paying most of your bills (unless you want to build up a reserve against later illness).

■ Duration of benefits. Most of these policies pay their cash benefits from one to two years, as long as you remain hospitalized; others will extend benefits (usually at a lower rate) to skilled nursing home care following hospitalization.

Many older people, fearful of being wiped out by illness, overinsure. Some respond to a half a dozen or more mail-order solicitations for hospital indemnity insurance. Knowledgeable sources in the industry say that if you are spending more than about $1,000 a year in health insurance premiums at an age when you are eligible for Medicare, you are probably overinsured. Take a good look at the policies you have and decide if you really need and want all that coverage. (If it makes you feel more secure to carry extra insurance, that's okay, but it's important to understand what you're doing.)

The wraparound policy is specifically designed to fill the gaps left by Medicare. Available through private insurance companies, the Blue

Cross–Blue Shield plans, and some retirement associations, these policies typically pay the Medicare deductible and co-insurance amounts. They also cover all or part of health services not covered by Medicare, such as out-of-hospital prescription drugs, medical appliances, and equipment.

Note: Most insurance policies designed to supplement Medicare tie their payments to the "reasonable" charges specified by Medicare. Unless you can get your doctor to accept "assignment" and accept the amount set by Medicare, you may find yourself paying part of your doctor bills even if you buy supplemental insurance.

Your post-retirement health insurance needs may also be met by membership in a health maintenance organization (see pp. 459–61).

WHAT TO DO BEFORE YOU RETIRE

The best time to think about the health coverage you will need after 65 is long before you reach 65, while you may still be covered by on-the-job group insurance and while you have more options. Here's what to do:

- Ask your employer whether your group insurance benefits can continue beyond retirement. Some employers will continue to pay all or part of the cost of continued coverage. Others won't, but will let you sign up yourself. It's a good idea to continue group coverage, even if you have to pay the premiums, because such coverage is cheaper than other health insurance. (You'll probably find the premiums less expensive than you expect, because Medicare will pick up much of your basic health coverage.) It may even work out to your benefit to continue a less-than-perfect group plan and take supplemental insurance to fill in any remaining gaps.

- If you cannot continue in the group health insurance plan, find out if you can convert it to an individual plan. The premiums will be higher, but the advantage is that there won't be any waiting for pre-existing conditions to meet a qualifying test of time. You also will be sure not to have any time lapse in coverage.

- Whether you continue in the group plan or convert the group plan to an individual policy, find out whether you can get additional benefits under the company policy; some have riders, for example, permitting you to buy additional days of hospital coverage. Also find out whether your spouse will continue to be covered after you die. If not, it's very important for your spouse to look into individual coverage before reaching age 65.

- Several months before you reach 65, make sure that your Social Security records are in order and that you apply for Medicare. Benefits are not automatic. You must apply, and you are well advised to do so early. If you do not sign up for Medicare Part B when you first become eligible, you may do so only during the first three months of each succeeding year. You'll also pay more with each succeeding year.

■ Think about your post-retirement plans. Medicare's coverage is limited to the United States, including Puerto Rico, the Virgin Islands, Guam, and American Samoa. If you plan to do much traveling after retirement, be sure that you have private insurance which will pick up any burdensome health care costs.

■ If you are planning to purchase a supplemental policy, do so early. Most wraparound policies do not have long waiting periods for pre-existing conditions, and some don't have any, but it may be important to you to have no lapse in coverage at all.

Q. I retired recently at age 62 and then discovered that health insurance is almost impossible to buy at this age. Supplemental policies are available, once you reach 65, to tie in with Medicare, but what about those of us between 62 and 65? I'm working fifteen hours a week (and can't work more without losing my Social Security retirement benefits) but these few hours leave me ineligible for group health insurance. What can I do?

A. You are not alone. Individual policies *are* hard to find in your age bracket. But you do have some options. Some companies do accept applicants in their sixties, usually for a major medical policy that converts at age 65 to a Medicare wraparound. You can keep your premium within reason by self-insuring with a sizable deductible, thereby putting limited dollars to work as protection against catastrophic illness. Most Blue Cross–Blue Shield plans are also required by law to offer an annual open enrollment period, when anyone may secure individual coverage regardless of age or state of health; you might look into this possibility. Health maintenance organizations also have open enrollment periods for those under 65; once you turn 65, Medicare would be accepted and the HMO would serve as a supplement. You might consider a hospital indemnity policy, which pays daily cash benefits in case of hospitalization; it won't be adequate, but it will be something. And you might look into membership in an organization, such as the American Association of Retired Persons (open, at a nominal fee, to those over 55), which makes you eligible for insurance to bridge the gap.

Whatever you do, look into post-65 health insurance before you turn 65, and secure full coverage as soon as you can.

Health Maintenance Organizations

These prepaid health service plans are not strictly insurance, but they serve much the same purpose. They also do much more. They provide comprehensive health care, both preventive care and treatment, in exchange for a fixed monthly fee. That fee tends to be less (10 to 40 percent less, according to one study) than the usual combination of insurance plus out-of-pocket medical expenses; the average family premium in 1985 was $200.61 per month. It also may be paid by your employer, since prepaid group plans or HMOs are an alternative to group insurance (an alternative that must be offered by your employer if your company has twenty-five or more employees, if any health insurance is offered as a benefit, and if there is an HMO in your area). Any extra expenses, if you belong to an HMO, tend to be small. Some HMOs, for instance, charge members a dollar or two for each doctor visit and/or a dollar or two for each prescription.

By mid-1985 there were 393 HMOs in the United States, up from 33 in 1971. Almost 20 million members of these plans receive comprehensive health services, with no worries about unexpected medical bills. In federally qualified plans these services must include:

- Physician services (including consultant and referral services)
- Inpatient and outpatient services
- Medically necessary emergency health services (if you must go to another facility in an emergency)
- Short-term (not to exceed twenty visits) outpatient mental health services for evaluation and crisis intervention
- Medical treatment and referral services for addiction to or abuse of drugs or alcohol
- Diagnostic laboratory and therapeutic X-ray services
- Home health services
- Preventive health services including immunizations, well-child care from birth, periodic adult health evaluations, family planning, and children's eye and ear examinations

Other services may also be offered (and frequently are, especially in employer-sponsored group plans):

- Prescription drugs
- Adult eye examinations
- Dental care
- Extended mental health care
- Rehabilitative services including physical and occupational therapy

The primary advantages of an HMO are low cost and comprehensive service. The elimination of the paperwork associated with insurance and Medicare claims is also a plus. The major disadvantage is the frequently impersonal nature of the service; you often have no choice when it comes to the doctor who treats you. Some health maintenance organizations provide more services than others; look into this carefully before you join. Some are strong and stable organizations, while others have folded after a promising start. Find out as much as you can before you sign up. Ask these questions:

- Are doctors board-certified? Are they well established in the community?
- Which hospital does the HMO use? Is it a teaching hospital? Is it conveniently near you?
- How are complaints handled?
- Who else uses this HMO? Are they satisfied? (Ask them yourself.)

Be aware, too, that many HMOs will not enroll people over 65, although they will continue service to those previously enrolled. Again, the time to arrange for post-65 medical coverage is before you turn 65.

Group Insurance

The most extensive and least expensive health insurance is the health insurance you buy through a group, especially the group formed by your fellow workers. (Even if you have to pay all or part of the premiums, on-the-job group insurance will generally cost you less than anything you can buy on your own.) It may be very important when you're comparing job offers, therefore, to take a close look at the fringe benefits being offered. A good health insurance package can be worth several hundred to a couple of thousand dollars in salary; an inadequate package may need to be supplemented. *Note:* Reagan Administration proposals to tax a portion of employer-paid health insurance premiums as income have, at least temporarily, been dropped.

Q. I discovered that I was pregnant just a month after my employer changed group insurance companies. Now neither company will pay my bills. The first says it is no longer responsible. The second says it is not responsible either, because the pregnancy began before the policy did. Is there anything I can do?

A. Talk to your employer's benefits department; most companies do make some provision for continuing coverage in this type of situation. Next, if your employer has not made such provision, get in touch with your state insurance department (probably in the state capital) and find out if your state is one of those that requires that a successor group-insurance plan, if it replaces an existing plan within sixty days, provide continuous coverage.

A good group policy will include the basic and major medical provisions outlined earlier. It may also contain extras (unlikely to appear in individual policies at any price) such as group dental insurance. It will be relatively inexpensive because the employer or administrator remits all the premiums to the insurance company and administrative costs are thereby reduced. The advantage to you, in addition to lower costs, is insurability. In a true group plan you won't be excluded because of problems with your health.

But the insurance provided on the job may not be adequate to protect you and your family. If, for instance, you have only basic protection in your group policy, talk to your employer about providing major medical coverage or buy it for yourself. If you do have major medical but with inadequate benefits, you should buy additional coverage. A personal major medical policy with a deductible of $30,000 (if that is the limit of your group insurance) and a maximum lifetime benefit of $250,000 should be relatively inexpensive.

COORDINATION OF BENEFITS

When 18-year-old Jack fractured his ankle playing football, it didn't cost his parents a cent, even though each of their on-the-job health insurance policies contained standard deductible and co-insurance provisions. The reason: Under a "coordination of benefits" provision, Jack's father's insurance company paid his medical bills as if it were the only coverage. Then his mother's insurance company paid the remaining charges.

Group insurance plans usually contain a coordination of benefits feature. That means that you cannot collect twice for the same ailment under different policies. You can usually collect the deductible and co-insurance amounts from one policy under the other, though some employers, trying to cut costs, are restricting this benefit. You and your spouse, if you are both employed, should watch out for overlapping and duplicative coverage but try to have one policy extend the other, if at all possible.

WHEN YOU LEAVE YOUR JOB

Don't let your group insurance lapse if you lose your job; that's just when you are most vulnerable to the costs of illness. Most policies contain a conversion provision, which allows you to convert the policy to an individual basis. The cost will be much greater and the benefits far less extensive, but if you have any pre-existing medical condition you'll find conversion very worthwhile.

Another possibility: interim insurance. You can buy short-term coverage (up to six months and, from some companies, renewable for an additional six months) to cover you for any medical claims starting during the contract period.

Q. My daughter, who will graduate from college this year, plans to travel for the summer, then start full-time employment in the fall. Her coverage under our family health insurance ends with her graduation, and she won't have any group insurance of her own until she starts work. Is there any insurance she can get for the time between?

A. Yes. Short-term policies to cover just this kind of situation (and the situation where a person is between jobs) are available in every state. With some variation, the coverage often runs for 60 to 180 days, with a deductible of $50 to $200. Premiums vary by age and by where you live, but 90-day coverage for your daughter at age 21, as an example, would cost about $150 for a policy with a $100 deductible; the company pays 80 percent of costs on the next $1,000 and pays all medical bills beyond that point. Coverage even continues beyond the policy period, up to a lifetime, for any condition contracted during the policy period.

Association Group

If you can't get a job with health insurance benefits, or can't convert your group policy when you leave such a job, you may still be able to purchase insurance through a group. If you are a member of a trade or professional association, fraternal or business group, labor union or civic organization, you may be eligible for health insurance through that group. Such health insurance will usually, but not always, be less expensive than insurance you buy on your own.

Group insurance (other than on the job) is not always true group insurance. Where an organization cannot collect and remit premiums, its members may nonetheless be seen as a natural market for solicitation. When the group agrees that its mailing list may be used, it may do one of two things: pass the premium savings on to members or use them as a money-making method for the group's treasury. There's nothing wrong with a group making insurance available to its members and at the same time enriching the group as a whole, but you should understand that mail-order insurance offered to you because you are a member of such-and-such a group may not necessarily be the best buy when it comes to insurance. You'll have to compare prices carefully to be sure.

Individual Insurance

There are a number of circumstances in which you may find yourself without group insurance. You may be between jobs, or working for an employer with no insurance plan. You may have outgrown coverage under your parents' insurance. You may have retired. Or you may have been recently widowed or divorced. Whatever the circumstances, you should be sure to provide yourself with individual coverage, preferably in advance so that there will be no lapse in protection. Just one illness or accident, when you are financially vulnerable, could wipe you out.

Individually purchased health insurance can provide essentially the same type of basic and major medical protection as group insurance, although at substantially greater cost. Individual insurance is available from local Blue Cross–Blue Shield organizations and from commercial life and health insurance companies.

Blue Cross–Blue Shield

Blue Cross covers hospital bills and Blue Shield covers the costs of medical/surgical care.

Although Blue Cross–Blue Shield exists throughout the United States, local Blue Cross–Blue Shield plans are autonomous and offer different plans in different areas. In general, "the Blues" have premiums tied to where you live and the number of people covered rather than to age, to sex, or to state of health. There is a single-person rate, a two-person rate, and a family rate. The family rate covers a family regardless of size—a pricing policy which makes the Blues a good buy for a large family.

The Blues have other advantages:

- Blue Cross plans are based on services; whatever the bill is, it will be paid directly to the hospital. With commercial insurers you may have to pay the bill and then wait for reimbursement. That reimbursement, depending on your policy, may or may not cover the entire bill.

- Policies issued by the Blues are guaranteed renewable, which is not always true of commercial insurance.

- Virtually every plan has an open enrollment period during which anyone may enroll, regardless of health. Although a pre-existing condition may be excluded from coverage for a specified period, you can never be totally excluded from a Blue Cross–Blue Shield plan.

Commercial Insurers

A number of commercial insurers write health insurance, primarily major medical, on an individual (nongroup) basis. These policies have premiums based on age, sex, and where you live as well as the deductibles and benefits you select. They are also, by and large, selective, excluding those people who may make major claims (the very people who often need health insurance most). Such policies, for these reasons, may be a better buy than the Blues for a young and healthy single person.

Most commercial insurers, moreover, because of rapidly rising costs, have pulled out of the basic protection area. If you want basic hospital/medical insurance you may have to buy it from Blue Cross (or from a health maintenance organization). But the commercial insurers do have one advantage: If you want a major medical policy (the kind of protection that's most important), you'll probably have to buy it from a commercial insurer; the Blues, with a few exceptions, offer major medical only to groups. If you want both basic hospital/medical protection and major medical insurance your best bet may be a combination of a basic Blue Cross policy and major medical coverage from a commercial insurer.

Q. My doctor charged $800 to remove my gall bladder and I got back just $425 from my health insurance policy. Am I stuck with the difference, or is there something I can do to collect the actual fee?

A. You can appeal the insurance company's decision. Under the law in most states, the company must give you a written reason when a claim is denied in part or in full. If you don't understand the reason, or aren't satisfied, call the company's customer service department for a full explanation. If you're still not satisfied, file a written appeal; include any additional information you or your doctor can supply about why the particular procedure was necessary or why the fee was this much. (If your surgeon repaired an ulcer while removing your gall bladder, through the same incision, reimbursement could be substantially more.) The company owes you a written decision within 60 to 120 days. Then you can still go a step further: If it's a Blue Cross–Blue Shield plan, write to the Consumer Affairs Division, Blue Cross/Blue Shield Associations, 1700 Pennsylvania Ave., NW, Washington, DC 20006. If it's a commercial insurance company plan, contact your state insurance department (usually in the state capital).

What to Look for

Whether you purchase health insurance through a group or on your own, through a Blue Cross–Blue Shield plan or from a commercial insurer, there are certain things you should look for. Find out:

WHAT IS COVERED?

You'll know whether the policy covers doctors bills. But you may not know, unless you ask, whether payment is limited to specific kinds of doctors. Some policies, for instance, exclude chiropractors. Other possible exclusions to find out about, in advance: Is coverage limited to certain hospitals? Are preventive or diagnostic measures covered? What about out-of-hospital treatment? Nursing home care? Are psychiatric benefits provided? Are newborn infants covered from the day of birth? At what age will children be excluded from a family policy? What about maternity costs and, more important, any complications of pregnancy? Federal law requires employers to provide employees with pregnancy benefits comparable to benefits for other medical conditions. *Wives* of employees, however, may not be covered to the same extent—although a Supreme Court ruling in June 1983 did hold that company health insurance must cover the pregnancies of employees' wives to the same extent that it covers all other dependents' medical care.

HOW ARE PRE-EXISTING CONDITIONS DEFINED?

Be sure your policy refers to conditions that you know about; otherwise, you could be refused claims for conditions that took a long time to develop but were undiagnosed when you purchased the policy.

If you're thinking of switching to a lower-cost policy, remember that you may have to start all over again to satisfy a pre-existing condition clause. Your existing policy may now cover everything, without regard to pre-existing conditions, and may be worth keeping even if it costs a bit more.

WHAT IS THE COMPANY'S LOSS RATIO?

The loss ratio is the percentage of premiums returned to policyholders in benefits. Although the figure is not definitive (a company with a favorable loss ratio may still go out of business and leave you stranded), you'll usually get a better deal where there is a higher loss ratio. The Blues, as nonprofit organizations, generally have a loss ratio of over 90 percent. Group plans written by commercial insurers should be able to show loss ratios in the 80 to 90 percent range. On individual coverage (where administrative costs are necessarily higher), look for a company with a loss ratio of 60 percent or more.

IS THE POLICY GUARANTEED RENEWABLE?

Such a policy cannot be canceled under any circumstances. Rates may be raised, but only if they are raised for an entire class of policyholders. Without a guaranteed renewable policy, you may be left at any time without health insurance protection.

Women and Health Insurance

The general principles of health insurance apply to everyone, male or female. But women do face particular problems.

INCOME PROTECTION

Are you a housewife? Have you thought it would be a good idea to carry disability income insurance, in case you are disabled and help must be hired to care for small children? Have you ever tried to buy such insurance? Have you found an insurance company that would sell it to you?

Or are you, perhaps, a freelance, running a business out of your home? Have you, as a self-employed businesswoman, tried to secure disability income protection? While self-employed men can secure disability income protection without too much difficulty, self-employed women often find it extremely difficult to do so. When disability insurance is available, premiums are often much higher for women. A typical company doing business in Pennsylvania, for example, charged $216.60 a year for disability insurance for a 35-year-old man and $328.85, or 51 percent more, for a 35-year-old woman doing the same job. A Pennsylvania woman has sued the company, and it is, at this writing, no longer doing business in Pennsylvania.

The problem is what insurers call a "track record." They don't want to insure you against loss of earnings unless those earnings (and their loss, if you are ill and unable to work) can be independently documented. They don't charge the same rate, although this is being challenged in the courts, in Congress, and in state legislatures, because experience shows that women file more claims.

The housewife, with no income to verify, has the most difficulty securing coverage, although the situation is beginning to improve. The self-employed woman may have an income but she has no employer to confirm that she is indeed on sick leave and unable to work. If you are in this position, and unable to find a company to write individual insurance, try to find and join a professional association in your field which sponsors such insurance for its members. Such association insurance, if it meets your needs, may cost less than individual insurance.

MEDICAL COVERAGE

For widows and divorcées, losing a husband often meant losing health insurance as well. A great many women have health insurance protection through their husbands' on-the-job coverage. When the marriage ends, whether through death or divorce, the health insurance has ended as well. In some instances, women with serious illnesses have been left unprotected. One such woman, whose $100,000-a-year bills for cancer treatment had been paid under her husband's policy, could not find a company willing to write a policy covering the treatment. New laws now protect both workers and their dependents.

If you are married and dependent on your husband's group health insurance, here's what you should do:

- Find out what major medical coverage you now have. If at all possible, secure your own coverage through your job or through an organization.

- If you are covered through your husband's insurance, find out what happens under the terms of the policy in case of death or divorce. New federal rules require companies to continue offering group health insurance coverage for up to eighteen months to terminated employees and their dependents, and to offer coverage for up to thirty-six months to divorced or separated spouses and the dependents of active workers, as well as to widowed spouses and dependents of covered workers. These rules should be a big help, but be aware that available coverage is not necessarily free or low-cost coverage. The law permits companies to charge a monthly premium of up to 102 percent of the cost of providing similar coverage to other employees and their dependents. Even if you've paid a portion of employer group health insurance before, a large portion was probably subsidized; now the burden of payment is on you. If that burden is too great, you may want to consider a "conversion" policy that permits you to convert the group policy to an individual one. Its cost is typically more reasonable, but its benefits are also usually far more limited.

- Consider the cost of health insurance in preparing a budget for life on your own, and be aware that individual coverage will cost you more than group coverage.

Keeping Costs Down

Good health insurance is expensive, and this is one area in which it doesn't pay to cut corners. But you can save some money if you:

- Self-insure as much as you can afford, by taking a policy with a sizable deductible. If you have no group insurance, you're probably best off self-insuring basic costs and buying as much major medical coverage as you can afford. Remember, it's the costs of catastrophic illness than can wipe you out.

- Don't overinsure. The Federal Trade Commission has estimated that over three million Americans have purchased extra health insurance coverage that they can't use and don't need. The only beneficiary of overinsurance is the insurance company that pockets the premiums. With group insurance, as a general rule, you can't collect twice for the same illness even if you have two policies; with individual insurance you may be able to collect, but what's the point? If you make an actual profit on an illness, in fact, that profit is taxable.

■ Take the appropriate tax deductions. Premiums you pay for medical-care policies (but not for hospital indemnity or disability income policies) are tax-deductible if, along with all your other deductible medical expenses (see Chapter 23), they exceed 7.5 percent of your adjusted gross income.

DOS AND DON'TS OF HEALTH INSURANCE

■ Compare policies carefully before you buy. Ask three or four companies to suggest a policy best suited for your age, income, and family situation. Then compare both benefits and costs. Remember: There are no standard forms, and health insurance policies differ greatly. Know what your policy does cover, whether you have group or individual insurance, and be sure to file claims promptly when appropriate.

■ Be sure, before you buy, that your policy cannot be canceled or the premiums raised unless the action applies to all policyholders in your class or in your state. Otherwise, you may find yourself out in the cold after an expensive illness.

■ Think about buying your life and health insurance from the same salesperson, if you have an agent in whom you have confidence. With more at stake, the agent is likely to be a strong advocate in your behalf.

■ Tell the whole truth on any application for insurance. Pre-existing conditions will usually be covered after a waiting period. If a condition is very serious, you may have to accept a policy with no coverage for that particular ailment (although you should shop around). If you lie about a pre-existing condition, however, the company may refuse a claim or even cancel your coverage.

■ Buy from a company licensed to do business in your state. Then disputes, if any, may be referred to your state insurance department.

■ Don't replace a policy simply because it appears to be out-of-date. Instead, ask your company to upgrade the policy or buy supplementary coverage. If you do buy a new policy, keep your old one in effect at least until all waiting periods (for coverage of pre-existing conditions) are exhausted.

■ Don't forget other coverage you may have. Automobile insurance policies frequently include medical benefits. Life insurance policies may include disability income riders or double indemnity provisions.

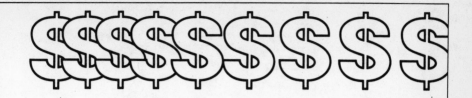

LOOKING AHEAD

Tax Planning

Taxes play a major part in financial planning. They will continue to do so despite the enactment of the 1986 tax law, an act that has been acclaimed as major reform of a complicated and cumbersome tax system. The law does reduce tax rates, and as long as rates stay down (doubtful perhaps, with the current deficit), taxes will not influence investment decisions to the same extent as in recent years. Nonetheless, although many lower-income Americans are removed from the tax rolls by this measure, one look at the tax law and at the tax forms that must now be filled out will convince most taxpayers that change is not necessarily simplification and that lower tax rates do not necessarily result in lower tax bills. Before we go further, however, a look at the new law is definitely in order.

The 1986 Tax Law

The 1986 tax law, in a nutshell, establishes just two tax brackets: 15 percent for single filers earning up to $17,850 and for joint filers earning up to $29,750, and 28 percent for taxpayers earning over these income levels. But, of course, it isn't that simple. For one thing, there are surcharges applying to some taxpayers that will bring effective rates up to 33 percent. For another, these rates don't take effect until 1988, although elimination of many deductions is effective with the 1987 tax year. For 1987, meanwhile, five "transitional" tax brackets (see Table 1 in Chapter 8) will mean higher taxes for many people.

The rules remain the same for the 1986 tax year as they were for 1985. No surprises here. But when you file your tax return for 1987 and thereafter, major changes are in store. Although all details of the new tax

FIGURE 1: Personal income tax: first and top marginal bracket rates, 1913–83.

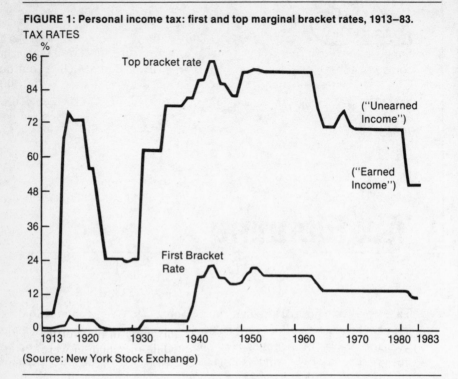

TAX RATES

(Source: New York Stock Exchange)

law are not available at this writing—be sure to consult your tax adviser for up-to-date information—here, in broad outline, is what you'll need to know.

Your Tax Bracket

Income tax rates have gone up and down since the federal income tax began in 1913, as Figure 1 demonstrates. With the 1981 Tax Act, still in effect through the 1986 tax year, federal income tax rates started at 11 percent and rose, in stages, to 50 percent. In 1987, tax rates start at 11 percent and rise to 38.5 percent. In 1988, as noted, there will be just two rates: 15 percent and 28 percent, with a 5 percent surcharge on the amount by which a single person's income exceeds $43,150 and a married couple's income exceeds $71,900. The surcharge creates an effective marginal tax rate of 33 percent. In a further complication, for couples earning more than $149,250, instead of the surcharge, a flat 28 percent rate will be charged against all taxable income. A toughened alternative minimum tax, moreover, will make it harder to escape the tax net. These income levels are for 1988 and will be adjusted thereafter with inflation.

Marginal Tax Rates

The marginal rate is the rate of taxation on the top dollar you earn. Suppose you and your spouse, filing a joint return, declare taxable income of $46,000 for 1987 on an earned gross income of $54,000. Your tax is $8,840 plus 35 percent of the amount over $45,000, for a total of $9,190. You can have a joint taxable income of up to $90,000 before that percentage goes to 38.5 percent. So all the dollars that you earn between $45,000 and $90,000 will be taxed at the marginal rate of 35 percent. This is what you mean when you say that you're in a 35 percent tax bracket.

If you live where you face a state income tax and possibly a local income tax as well, you should calculate your overall tax bracket. For example, suppose your federal tax bracket is 35 percent. You have a state income tax of 15 percent. Your combined tax rate is 50 percent, reduced by the federal tax benefit you receive from the deduction of the state taxes on your federal return. This reduction in your tax rate (35 percent of 15 percent, or 5.25 percent) gives you an actual combined tax bracket of 44.75 percent.

AN ADDED INCOME

John Black is an English professor at a university in the Northeast, and was the sole wage-earner for the family while the children were young. In 1981 his income was $30,000. Then, in 1982, his wife Nancy obtained a part-time job earning $8,000. John, meanwhile, received a $2,000 raise. The Blacks had an additional $10,000 in income . . . and wound up the year having to borrow $2,000 to pay income tax. What happened?

John's withholding assumed a maximum tax rate of 32 percent, while Nancy's withholding was based on a maximum of 16 percent. When they filed a joint tax return, however, Nancy's income added to John's was taxed at the 32 percent marginal rate from the first dollar and went up from there.

Nancy's income and John's raise actually brought their combined income into the 43 percent marginal tax bracket. If they had adjusted the amount of tax withheld from their paychecks to reflect the change in bracket, they would have been okay. Or they could have saved the money during the year to meet the tax bill. Instead they wound up in debt. Although this is less likely to happen when the new tax law is fully phased in, it can still happen in 1987. Don't let it happen to you. If your income jumps, for any reason, think of taxes before you spend.

Effective Tax Rates

You don't, fortunately, pay your marginal rate on everything you earn. It's easy, and heartening, to figure out your effective tax rate. Simply take the actual income taxes you pay, in dollars, and divide the figure by the total of your gross income for the year. Using the same example used to illustrate marginal tax rates above, taxes of $9,190 on a gross income of $54,000 equal an effective tax rate of just over 17 percent.

There are, of course, a lot of variables in this equation. The actual number of exemptions and deductions and credits you can claim, and whether or not you itemize deductions at all, will affect your taxable income and hence your tax. Where you live also makes a significant difference. Federal taxes may be the same, and may account for the bulk of your tax outlay, but local taxes, which vary enormously, also make a difference. Residents of New York City, with one of the heaviest tax burdens in the nation, pay both state and city income taxes as well as federal. Residents of Florida, at the other extreme, pay no local income tax at all.

Don't forget to consider the impact of taxes other than income taxes: sales taxes, excise taxes, property taxes, and so on. From gasoline to telephone service, a great many products and services, important in our daily lives, carry higher price tags because of hidden taxes.

Bracket Creep

Before the 1986 tax law simplified the bracket structure, even when tax rates were cut and tax brackets reduced, as happened under the Reagan economic program, taxes could take an increasingly sizable proportion of your gross income. The reason: bracket creep, an adequately eerie description of the phenomenon that occurs when inflation-generated pay increases, which don't increase your spending power because prices have also risen, push you into ever-higher tax brackets. For example, the Conference Board, a business research group, points out that in 1970 the family with a $25,000 income—a very high level in the 1970 income structure—paid $4,361 in federal income and Social Security taxes. In 1985, they needed $65,327 before taxes to maintain the same standard of living, and paid $14,473 in taxes. (See Table 1.) Although bracket creep is now less likely under the federal tax structure, state and local taxes, when added to federal taxes, can have a similar effect.

For you, personally, taxes (including state and local income taxes, sales taxes, and property taxes as well as federal income and Social Security taxes) may well be the single largest item in your budget. Take the time to figure out both your marginal tax rate and your effective tax rate. The first will help you decide how best to put your dollars to work (a high marginal rate makes tax-sheltering worthwhile). The second will tell you how much of your own income you actually have to work with after paying taxes.

TABLE 1: Pretax income needed to match the spending power of pretax income in 1970.

	$5,000	$10,000	$15,000	$25,000	$50,000
1970 PRETAX INCOME					
Less: Federal income tax	238	986	1,854	3,987	11,982
Less: Social security tax	240	374	374	374	374
Equals: Income after federal taxes	4,522	8,640	12,772	20,639	37,644
1975 NECESSARY PRETAX INCOME	6,447	13,767	20,635	34,536	70,392
Less: Federal income tax	−53	1,263	2,517	5,766	18,597
Less: Social security tax	377	805	825	825	825
Less: Amount to cover inflation since 1970	1,601	3,059	4,521	7,306	13,326
Equals: Income after federal taxes, in 1970 dollars	4,522	8,640	12,772	20,639	37,644
1984 NECESSARY PRETAX INCOME	12,132	24,482	37,602	62,922	123,838
Less: Federal income tax	557	2,278	4,685	11,268	31,712
Less: Social security tax	813	1,640	2,519	2,533	2,533
Less: Amount to cover inflation since 1970	6,240	11,924	17,626	28,482	51,949
Equals: Income after federal taxes, in 1970 dollars	4,522	8,640	12,772	20,639	37,644
1985 NECESSARY PRETAX INCOME	12,609	25,450	38,960	65,327	128,367
Less: Federal income tax	581	2,367	4,743	11,681	32,820
Less: Social security tax	889	1,794	2,747	2,792	2,792
Less: Amount to cover inflation since 1970	6,617	12,649	18,698	30,215	55,111
Equals: Income after federal taxes, in 1970 dollars	4,522	8,640	12,772	20,639	37,644

Federal income and social security taxes are computed for a married couple, only one of whom works, with two children. No allowance is made for any other taxes. Calculations use the tax laws in effect each year. Deductible items are assumed to equal 17 percent of pretax income in 1970, 20 percent in other years. For calculating maximum tax and earned income credit, all income is assumed to be earned, personal service income. Inflation is calculated from the deflator for personal consumption spending, with a 3.5 percent rise assumed from 1984 to 1985.
(Source: The Conference Board)

Taxable Income

The key to your tax bracket is your net or taxable income. Reducing the net is the way to reduce both your bracket and the amount of tax you pay. The IRS makes a clear distinction between taxable and nontaxable income, and in at least some instances you can control the category into which your income falls.

Note: Tax law is extremely complex. It also changes regularly. This chapter highlights some of the information, accurate as of this writing, that you can use in your overall financial planning. For specific advice, consult a competent tax adviser.

Q. My husband and I are in the midst of divorce proceedings. Rather than pay separate alimony and child support, he wants to make a single monthly payment for both. He claims it will be simpler. Should I accept this?

A. No. Alimony is subject to income tax, but child support isn't. If they are lumped together, you will have to pay tax on the whole amount. (Your husband, conversely, may claim alimony, but not child support, as a deduction on his tax return—a reason he may want to pay the full sum in alimony alone.)

Gross Income

Your gross income consists of every item of income, from any source, unless it's specifically excluded in the tax law. Gross income includes wages, salary, tips, business receipts, interest and dividends, rents, royalties, annuities, pensions, etc. The IRS is quite literal in its definition of source: If you make $200 (after related expenses) at a garage sale, you are supposed to report it as taxable income. If you belong to a barter club and swap your skill at upholstering for someone else's skill at dentistry (or for "credits" which you can exchange for goods or services at a later date), you are supposed to report the fair market value as part of your gross income.

To compute taxable income, gross income is reduced by exclusions and by deductions, and the resulting tax liability is reduced by credits. *Exclusions* are items not subject to tax; many need not even be listed on your tax return. *Deductions* reduce the amount of taxable income; the actual saving from a deduction depends on your tax bracket. *Credits* are a direct reduction of the tax owed; a dollar credit is a dollar saved.

EXCLUSIONS

Some "income" is excluded from gross income right from the start, although some customary exclusions have now been dropped from the list. Under the 1986 tax act, for example, all unemployment compensation is taxable as income. So are all dividends, and most awards and prizes. Still, you do not have to count:

- Accident and health insurance reimbursement. But there are always exceptions. If you deducted medical expenses in one tax year and received reimbursement from an insurance company in the next tax year, the reimbursement is includable in gross income in the tax year received, up to the amount of the deduction previously taken. Disability insurance (income replacement) payments are not taxable if you have paid the premiums; they are taxable if your employer has paid the premiums on your behalf.

- Employer-paid accident and health insurance premiums, and premiums for up to $50,000 of group term life insurance.

- Workmen's compensation and similar benefits

- Child-support payments you receive from an ex-spouse

- The gain on the sale of your home, if you reinvest the proceeds in another home within two years, or the gain (up to $125,000) if you are at least 55 years old and have used the home as your principal residence for at least three of the previous five years. See Chapter 15 for details.

- Cash rebates on the purchase of a new car or other item (the rebate simply reduces the price you pay; it is not income)

- Proceeds of damage awards, if you win a lawsuit for slander, libel, or personal injury. But interest earned on the money from the time of the award until you actually receive it is taxable, and damages for lost wages or lost profits are entirely taxable.

- Life insurance proceeds paid to you as a beneficiary. But if they are received in installments, with interest added, you may owe some tax on the amount by which the proceeds are greater than they would have been at the insured's date of death.

- Gifts and inheritances. But they may, as described in Chapter 24, be subject to gift or inheritance tax; and if property you receive through gift or inheritance later earns interest, that interest is taxable income.

- Most Social Security and Railroad Retirement Act retirement benefits

- Interest on most tax-exempt bonds issued by state and local agencies. (Interest on U.S. Treasury issues is not taxable on state income tax returns.)

Q. I won $25,000 in a sweepstakes and got a check for the full amount. What do I do about taxes?

A. Sweepstake and lottery winnings are taxable and you must delcare your winnings as ordinary income when you file your federal income tax return. Should you be lucky enough to win again in the future, you can reduce the taxes due by (1) keeping receipts for all lottery tickets you buy in the course of a year, if you buy them regularly, and deducting the cost of losing tickets, and (2) buying tickets jointly, so that income and taxes are split among several people. Meanwhile, if the winnings will increase the tax you owe this year by a substantial sum, you may have to file a declaration of estimated tax and make quarterly payments. Consult a tax adviser.

- Scholarships and grants, if you are a degree candidate and the payment is made for your education and training. If you must work as a teaching or research assistant in exchange for your grant, the amount is still not taxable as long as the money goes toward tuition and as long as all degree candidates are required to perform similar services. (If you are not a degree candidate, certain limitations apply.)

ADJUSTED GROSS INCOME

This is a phrase that crops up regularly in tax jargon. It refers to your entire ("gross") income minus specific adjustments. Examples: contributions to IRAs or Keogh Plans for those who are eligible, interest lost on time deposits because of early withdrawal, alimony payments, and some disability income payments. (Job-related moving expenses and unreimbursed business expenses, formerly adjustments to gross income, become itemized deductions under the new tax law.) The term is a technical one. You'll arrive at it, without necessarily understanding just why certain deductions crop up here and others at a later point in the tax form, simply by following the step-by-step instructions on the form itself.

Other deductions are subtracted from adjusted gross income to arrive at taxable income. Be sure to claim all allowable deductions and you'll shelter some of your income from taxes.

Deductions

Here are details on some specific deductions:

INDIVIDUAL RETIREMENT ACCOUNTS

The $2,000 a year that you are allowed, if eligible (see p. 561), to contribute to an Individual Retirement Account ($4,000 if you and your spouse both hold paying jobs, $2,250 if only one of you works outside the home) comes right off the top of your gross income. It therefore lowers your taxes. If, for instance, you are in a 28 percent tax bracket, putting $2,000 into an IRA saves you $560 in taxes. If you don't invest in your own retirement, you won't have the whole $2,000 to invest in something else; you'll only have $1,440. The same deductibility holds for Keogh Plans, which are for the self-employed. (*Note:* Depending on your income, you may be entitled to a partial deduction for your IRA contribution.)

Tax on the interest earned by your IRA funds is deferred until you withdraw the money, when, presumably, you will be retired and in a lower tax bracket. IRAs and Keogh Plans are, therefore, a superlative tax shelter for middle-income Americans who qualify. (For more on both IRAs and Keogh Plans, see Chapter 25).

MOVING EXPENSES

If you moved because you changed jobs, and the new place of work is at least 35 miles farther from your old home than your previous job location, you may deduct some related expenses: house-hunting trips, travel to your new home, temporary living expenses at the new location, moving household goods, and so on, subject to certain limitations.

Here are the requirements:

- You must be employed full-time for at least thirty-nine weeks during the year immediately following the move; if you're self-employed, you must work full-time for at least seventy-eight weeks of the two years following the move.
- The moving expenses must generally be incurred within a year after you begin your new job.
- Expenses must be reasonable.

Reasonable deductible expenses include:

- The costs of moving your household goods and personal effects, including the costs of moving those items from a place other than your old residence if it's no more than the cost of a move from your former home (this might be a good time to clear those wedding presents out of your mother's basement)
- Travel expenses, including meals and lodging, for yourself and your family (even if you don't travel together), while enroute from your old residence to your new one
- The costs of pre-move house-hunting trips, after obtaining work in the new location, for you or a member of your family
- The costs of occupying temporary quarters (meals and lodging alone) at the new location for a period of up to thirty consecutive days
- The costs of selling or acquiring a home. Such fees as real estate commissions (when you sell), escrow fees, attorney's fees, title costs, and the like may instead be used to either reduce the gain from selling your old home or to add to the basis of your new home. It may be preferable to deduct them as moving expenses, but you'll have to make a decision. You can't do both.

Both travel expenses and moving expenses are fully deductible. But the deduction for house-hunting trips, temporary lodging, and selling and buying a residence is limited to $3,000 overall, of which no more than $1,500 may be for house-hunting trips and temporary quarters.

CHARITABLE CONTRIBUTIONS

The 1981 tax law, for the first time, permitted some deduction of charitable contributions by people who did not file itemized returns. The 1986 tax bill rescinded this provision. Only taxpayers who itemize deductions may now deduct charitable contributions.

Keep track of your deductions through the year. And if you do volunteer work for a charitable organization, without pay, you may deduct as charitable contributions (if you itemize) the direct cost of doing the work: telephone calls, postage, uniforms, and travel at either 12¢ a mile or the actual costs of gas, tolls, and parking fees.

You can also benefit by donating appreciated property. Instead of donating $1,000 in cash, for instance, you might donate securities worth $1,000. You may claim a deduction for the current fair market value of $1,000, and you avoid the tax you would pay on the appreciated value of the stock if you sold it. Note, however, that donations of appreciated property under the 1986 tax law will have to be used in computing the alternative minimum tax.

MEDICAL EXPENSES

The costs of medical and dental treatment, including a wide range of services, are deductible if you file an itemized return, if they are not reimbursed by insurance, and if they exceed 7.5 percent of adjusted gross income. Drugs are no longer categorized separately; instead, prescription drugs and insulin may be lumped with other medical expenses in seeking the 7.5 percent threshold while over-the-counter medication other than insulin isn't counted at all. Travel expenses for medical care are still deductible, either at 12¢ a mile or actual out-of-pocket cost. Health insurance premiums are no longer deductible unless, together with other medical expenditures, they bring you over the 7.5 percent limit. Premiums for life insurance policies, disability income policies, and hospital indemnity (cash payment) policies are not deductible at all.

There are frequently differences of opinion between the IRS and individual taxpayers with respect to claims for medical deductions. Sometimes the IRS wins; sometimes, believe it or not, the taxpayer wins. One woman's doctor prescribed a special high-protein diet to alleviate symptoms of hypoglycemia. She claimed a tax deduction for the extra costs of the special diet. The IRS disallowed the deduction, on the basis that the food was simply a substitute for food she would otherwise consume. The Tax Court, however, disagreed. She was allowed to take the deduction.

Suggestion: Always take a deduction you believe to be legitimate, but be prepared to argue your case.

Q. My daughter is gradually going blind from an incurable illness. I know that her medical costs are tax-deductible. But what about all the special equipment she needs?

A. You may take a deduction for the cost of equipment related to her condition: special lenses, a special typewriter, a tape recorder, and so on. For specific information, consult IRS Publication No. 907.

INTEREST

Amounts paid for the use of borrowed money used to be fully deductible if you itemized your return. Millions of Americans deduct the interest payable on home mortgage loans (another superlative tax shelter), but other forms of interest have been deductible as well: interest on personal or business loans, interest on installment loans and bank credit card purchases, prepayment penalties and finance charges, and interest paid on federal income tax balances due. No more. Mortgage interest on first and second homes is still fully deductible, up to the original purchase price of the house, the cost of improvements, and amounts borrowed against the house for medical and educational expenses, as long as the total amount borrowed does not exceed the fair market value of the house. The deduction for interest on loans used to finance investments is generally limited to the amount of investment income. (But don't borrow money for a tax-exempt investment, expecting to deduct the interest on the loan while sheltering the interest you receive. You can't have it both ways.)

Interest on consumer loans is now deductible according to a gradually reducing schedule, from 65 percent in 1987 to 10 percent in 1990 and none thereafter.

Q. My bank loaned me $3,000 toward the purchase of a $10,000 certificate of deposit. The interest on the CD, of course, is taxable. But how do I handle the interest I pay on the loan? Do I just report the difference between the two as income?

A. No. You may have made a package deal with the bank, but the components are separate transactions as far as the IRS is concerned. You must report the total interest you receive on the $10,000 CD. You may also deduct some of the interest you pay on the $3,000 loan, until this deduction is fully phased out in 1991, but only if you file an itemized return.

TAXES

If you itemize your federal income tax return, you may deduct other taxes that you pay during the year: state and local income taxes, real property taxes, and personal property taxes. (Sales taxes, under the 1986 act, are no longer deductible.) You may not deduct Social Security or Railroad Retirement taxes withheld from your pay, federal gift and estate taxes, or state inheritance or gift taxes.

Note: In states that peg their income taxes to the federal tax structure, allowing the same deductions, state and local taxes may rise—

unless these states follow the federal lead in reducing tax rates. In states where the tax is a fixed percentage of the federal rate, taxpayers will find state taxes sharply dropping. Taxpayers in states with no or low income taxes and no or low sales taxes will also benefit. But the disparity may not last long, as state legislatures take action.

CASUALTY AND THEFT LOSSES

Casualty losses, as described in Chapter 14, stem from damage to property from sudden and unexpected events. Theft losses arise from the unlawful taking of property by any means. In both cases, the 1982 Tax Act made a drastic change: Formerly, uninsured losses exceeding $100 could be deducted on your federal income tax return. If a storm did $500 worth of damage to uninsured property, or if an uninsured ring worth $500 was stolen, you could have deducted $400 on your federal return. Or if the same property was insured for $200, you would have had a $200 deduction. No more. The $100 that is not deductible remains intact. But what *is* deductible is now limited to losses that exceed 10 percent of your adjusted gross income. If your adjusted gross income is $30,000, your loss would have to exceed $3,000 before you can claim a deduction. It now becomes more important than ever before to carry adequate insurance on your home, your automobile, and your valuable personal property.

The IRS has claimed that amounts that *could* be reimbursed by insurance are not deductible, even if you don't collect. The Tax Court has ruled, however, that a taxpayer can choose not to file a claim with the insurance company—you might not think it's worth higher rates or the possibility of cancellation—and still deduct the loss on an itemized return. (But the case was not decided unanimously, and there may be further challenges.)

If you do qualify for a theft deduction—a burglar made off with all your jewelry—you can't claim more than you paid for the item, no matter what its current value. (If you insure some items, such as gold jewelry, up to appreciated values, you may wind up with a taxable gain from the insurance reimbursement. But you can skip all or part of the taxes on the gain by using the insurance proceeds to replace the stolen item within two years.)

You must document your loss, with purchase receipts, appraisals, photos, and/or police reports. Since casualty and theft losses are carefully scrutinized by the IRS, it's a good idea to attach documentation directly to your tax return. Don't wait to be challenged. And be sure to keep copies of all documents submitted with your tax return.

EDUCATIONAL EXPENSES

You may deduct the costs of going to school, both tuition and transportation costs, if (1) the education is required by your employer or by the law in order to keep your job, or (2) the education maintains or improves skills used in your present work. You may *not* deduct expenses for education that is required of you in order to meet the minimum requirements of your present job, or for education that qualifies you for a new occupation.

MISCELLANEOUS DEDUCTIONS

There are other deductions available to taxpayers who itemize, from adoption expenses to union dues to fees for tax preparation and advice. Under the new law, however, expenses in this category will be deductible only to the extent that they, as a group, exceed 2 percent of adjusted gross income. Consult IRS Publication No. 17, "Your Federal Income Tax," for a complete list.

Q. What are the rules on allowable deductions at different income levels? Are there specific amounts I'm allowed to claim?

A. You may claim only what you actually spend. But you may find some guidelines in the statistical averages in Table 2, compiled by Prentice-Hall from IRS figures. If your claims are higher, you increase your chances of an audit, so be sure that you have adequate documentation. If your deductions are much smaller, you may have overlooked some things you should claim. Remember, these are just averages and you are entitled to all the legitimate deductions that you can document—no more and no less. Remember, too, that these are averages under the pre-1986 tax law.

TABLE 2: Average itemized deductions in 1984, based on federal tax returns filed in 1985.

Adjusted gross income	Medical	Taxes	Gifts	Interest
$20–25,000	$1,468	$ 1,820	$ 767	$ 3,076
25–30,000	1,339	2,184	803	3,477
30–40,000	1,749	2,698	1,156	4,023
40–50,000	1,876	3,488	1,105	4,796
50–75,000	3,127	4,768	1,546	6,492
75–100,000	6,316	7,002	2,412	9,598
100–200,000	9,494	10,641	4,234	13,704

Tax Credits

A credit is a dollar-for-dollar write-off against taxes due and is therefore more valuable than a deduction. Certain tax credits can be claimed whether or not you file the long form.

CHILD CARE

With the 1981 tax law, the credit working parents can take for child care was increased and placed on a sliding scale, ranging from $720 for one child at an adjusted gross income of $10,000 to $480 at an income of $30,000 or more. The amount is doubled for two or more children.

The law also broadened the definition of expenses to which the credit applies. Before, expenses incurred for services outside the home could be counted only for a dependent child who was under the age of 15. Now, you may also claim this credit if you incur the expenses for a disabled dependent (including your spouse or an aged parent) who spends at least eight hours of every twenty-four in your household.

Note: Under the 1981 law, too, child care can become a nontaxable fringe benefit, if your employer chooses to participate. And that's child care anyplace—at home, in a day care center or nursery school of your choice, or in an on-the-job child care center.

Q. My job keeps me away from home from eight to six. The public school my 7-year-old would normally attend has classes only from nine to three. A good private school nearby has before-school and after-school programs specifically for the children of working mothers. If I send him there, can I take a tax credit for the tuition?

A. You can't claim a credit for the tuition, but if the school will itemize its bills, you can claim a credit for the special programs before and after regular school hours.

EXCESS SOCIAL SECURITY

If you held two jobs during the year, either both at once or consecutively, you might have had too much withheld in Social Security taxes. If you did, you may claim the excess as a credit on your tax return. But if you worked for just one employer, and too much Social Security tax was withheld, you may not claim a tax credit. Your employer will have to make the adjustment.

Exemptions

The number of exemptions you claim affects the amount of tax you pay. This is a major area of change in the 1986 tax law, one that greatly reduces the taxes paid by large families. Under this law the personal exemption, which was $1,080 in 1986, rises to $2,000 by 1989. The rise is in stages—$1,900 in 1987 and $1,950 in 1988—and, after 1989, the amount will be adjusted each year for inflation.

The new law eliminates the personal exemption for high-income taxpayers, phasing it out gradually for joint filers with taxable incomes over $149,250. Like the 5 percent surtax (see p. 474), this phase-out results in a marginal tax rate of 33 percent.

There are other changes. The blind and the elderly, formerly entitled to a double exemption, are now limited to one (although this is partially offset by an increase in the standard deduction; see p. 494). And children who can be claimed as dependents on their parents' tax returns will no longer be allowed to claim a personal exemption on their own returns as well.

Note: Children over the age of five, claimed as dependents, must now have their own taxpaper identification or Social Security numbers.

You may claim exemptions for dependents who meet all five of the following tests:

- You must provide more than half of the dependent's total support during the calendar year.

- You may not take an exemption for a dependent if the person has gross income of more than a specified amount for the year, unless the dependent is your child and is either under 19 at the end of the year or a full-time student for at least five (not necessarily consecutive) months of the year.

- Unrelated people may be dependents if they are members of your household for the entire taxable year; certain relatives may be dependents no matter where they live, if they meet the other tests.

- Your dependents must generally be citizens or residents of the United States.

- You may not claim as a dependent anyone who files a joint return with someone else, unless the only reason for filing a return is to claim a refund of tax withheld. For example: You support your daughter and her husband while they attend school. They owe no taxes but file a return to receive a refund of taxes withheld on her summer job. You may claim them both as dependents, as long as the other tests are met.

    Q. We provided room, board, and spending money for a Swedish high school student from January through mid-June while she attended our local high school. May we claim her as a dependent on our income tax?

A. You can't claim her as a dependent, but you may deduct up to $50 of your costs per month as a charitable contribution. IRS rules state that the student, foreign or American, must be both a member of your household (but not a relative or dependent) and a full-time student in the 12th or lower grade (college exchange students don't qualify). You must have a written agreement with the sponsoring organization, and the purpose of the visit must be to provide educational opportunities for the student. Then itemize your deduction with the description "foreign exchange student living in my home (dates) under an agreement with (organization)." Don't attach the agreement to your tax form, but do keep it with your tax records.

Who Is a Dependent?

It's easy to list the rules, but it's not always quite as easy to interpret them. Here are some special situations in which the above rules apply:

CHILDREN

- A baby born on December 31 counts as an exemption for the entire year, as does a child adopted at any time during the year. A foster child may be claimed if he or she lived in your household for the entire year.

- College students, on the road between dependence and independence, sometimes create special problems. While age does not count, as long as the child is a full-time student, the other tests still apply. The trickiest of these, for many parents, is the issue of providing at least half of the student's support. Here are two things you should know: Scholarships do not count in calculating support; and the value of lodging you supply your child when he or she is home on vacation does count toward support. If your child has independent income which would edge just over the half-support boundary, have him or her bank the excess. As long as the money is not actually spent on the student's support, it won't count against your claiming him or her as a dependent. Be sure to calculate your youngster's earnings *and* the income from any assets you've put in his or her name to reduce taxes. If a child earns enough to go over the halfway mark, have him or her save some or you'll lose the exemption.

Q. My daughter is staunchly independent and wants to pay for as much of her own college expenses as she can. This year she's put up $4,300, from summer and year-round part-time jobs. We've contributed $3,500 to her college costs. Is there any way we can still claim the exemption?

A. Yes. If you figure in the "fair rental value" of her room and board while she is at home, you'll probably find that you still provide more than half her support. You may also figure in any major purchase, such as a car, which you make for her.

DIVORCE AND CHILD CUSTODY

There are special rules to determine which divorced parent gets to claim the exemption for a dependent child. Both *custody* and *support* come into play.

The parent who has custody usually gets to claim the exemption, whether or not that parent actually provides more than half the child's support. But there is an exception: If your divorce decree or other written agreement allows your ex-partner to claim the exemption, and if that parent actually contributes $600 a year to each child's support, then your former spouse may claim the exemption.

Suggestion: Think about tax exemptions, as well as about actual levels of support, when you draw up a divorce agreement.

PARENTS

If you get together with others to support a dependent (for example, if you and your sisters pitch in to support your father), one of you may claim him as a dependent as long as the others sign an agreement specifying that they will not do so for that tax year. You may take turns in subsequent years, if you choose to do so, as long as anyone making the claim contributes at least 10 percent of the support.

Medicare payments no longer count as support. You may claim an elderly parent as a dependent even if Medicare payments add up to much more than half the support for the year.

Income that is excludable from the dependent's gross income, such as Social Security benefits, is not counted toward the $1,000 gross income permitted. If that income is actually used for support of the dependent, however, it counts in determining whether you have furnished over one-half of the dependent's support. If your parent has over $1,000 of gross income, and therefore cannot be claimed as a dependent, you may still be able to deduct his or her medical expenses, as long as you contribute more than half the support for the year.

Q. My parents maintain their own household, with help from me. They manage on $9,000 a year, of which I contribute $3,000. Is there some way I can claim the exemption?

A. The IRS will assume that your $3,000 in annual support is divided between your parents and that you are therefore not entitled to a dependency exemption, unless you specify, in writing, that your financial contribution goes to just one parent. Since they live on $4,500 apiece, your $3,000 is clearly more than half the annual support for one parent, and you should be able to claim the exemption. It will help, however, if you can make direct payments for support items such as clothing and medical bills; ask your parent to have the bills sent directly to you, then pay by check and keep both bills and checks as documentation.

Remember, however, that you cannot generally claim a dependency exemption for anyone who files a joint return with someone else. By filing separately, your parents may end up with a greater additional tax liability than your savings from claiming a single extra exemption.

LIVE-TOGETHERS

Internal Revenue Service rulings don't pay any attention to whether a relationship is legal. But state laws do. If you live together, without benefit of matrimony, in a state that frowns upon such behavior, you can expect to have an exemption you claim for your partner disallowed.

Rules of the Tax Game

As in any game, skilled players come out ahead. You can become skilled by learning the rules.

Who Must File

You are required to file a federal income tax return by April 15 of each year, even if you owe no tax, if you meet IRS specifications. The rules apply whether you are a citizen (living in the United States or abroad) or a noncitizen with resident status.

WAGE-EARNERS

Filing requirements under the 1986 tax law have been raised. These are the new limits, for the 1987 and 1988 tax years:

If you are single you must file a return if you earn $4,470 or more for 1987 and $4,950 or more for 1988. If you are single and over 65 the income requirement changes to $5,650 and $5,700.

If you are married and file jointly, you must file a return if your combined gross income is $7,600 or more for 1987 and $8,900 for 1988. The requirement is $9,400 and $9,500 respectively if one spouse is 65 or older, and $10,000 and $10,100 if both of you are 65 or more.

If you are a "surviving spouse" you must file a return if you had gross income of $5,700 in 1987 and $6,950 in 1988; for those over 65, the threshold is $7,500.

For unmarried heads of household, the under-65 threshold is $4,470 in 1987 and $6,350 in 1988; for the over-65, it is $7,050 and $7,100.

Even without taxable income, earned or unearned, you should file a return if you are entitled to a tax refund.

THE SELF-EMPLOYED

If you are self-employed, no matter what your age or marital status, you must file a return if you had net earnings from your trade or profession of $500 or more for the year. This rule applies even if your self-employment is part-time and/or temporary.

If you are self-employed, you must also pay the self-employment equivalent of the Social Security tax withheld from an employee's wages. In 1986 the self-employment tax was 12.3 percent on the first $42,000 of earnings from self-employment. Under the 1983 changes in Social Security, the tax is the sum of employee and employer Social Security taxes, reduced, initially, by a tax credit. If you also held a paid job, the amount subject to self-employment tax is reduced by any salary on which your employer was liable for Social Security taxes.

If income taxes are not withheld from your income you must file estimated tax returns and pay your taxes quarterly. See p. 498.

Note: If you work for yourself, don't forget possible tax deductions: for an office at home, for inventory storage space, depreciation of equipment, and so on (see pp. 305–307).

Q. I don't want to work full-time while our children are small, but I am teaching piano at home and earning $88 a week. I am keeping accurate records to report at tax time but should I be setting aside some of this money each week toward taxes?

A. If you'll earn more than $500 a year in income not subject to withholding, call your local IRS office and ask for Form 1040-ES. Fill out the accompanying worksheet, and see how much you owe. If you owe more than a designated amount each year (in 1986, it is $500), you must make estimated tax payments on the 15th of April, June, September, and January. You may start at any time during the year, if you see that payments will be due, and you may change your payments if your income changes. The IRS won't remind you when payment is due, so mark your calendar. For more information, ask the local IRS office for Publication No. 505, "Tax Withholding and Estimated Tax."

SURVIVORS

If you are a surviving spouse, executor, administrator, or legal representative of someone who died during the last tax year, and if that someone had any taxable income, then you must file a federal tax return on that person's behalf. Any taxes due will be paid out of the estate.

Filing Status

Are you married? single? separated? divorced? widowed? Your social status (as legally defined by the state in which you live) determines your filing status with the Internal Revenue Service. Within the broad categories, however, you have some choice and some decisions to make. Here are the categories:

MARRIED TAXPAYERS

You are considered married for tax purposes if you are married and living together as husband and wife, if you are living together in a common law marriage recognized by your state, married and living apart but not legally separated or divorced, or separated under an interlocutory (not yet final) divorce decree. If you are married and living with your spouse, you may file a joint return or you may file separate returns. The joint return is usually preferable, because the tax rate is lower, but you might figure your tax both ways to see which is better for you.

Q. I got married on December 27. Do I still need to file jointly for federal income tax, or can we file separately? What are the rules affecting marriage so close to the new year?

A. Your filing status for tax purposes is your status on the last day of the tax year. If you are married and living together as husband and wife on December 31, then you are considered married for the entire year. But this does not mean that you must file a joint return. A husband and wife may also file separate returns. If you both had income, you should figure your tax both ways to see which way gives you the lower tax.

You may also file a joint return if your spouse died during the tax year. You may continue this preferential status for two more years if you have at least one dependent child and if you do not remarry. If you remarry during the tax year in which your spouse dies, and file a joint return with your new spouse, then you must file a return for your deceased spouse as "married, filing separately."

HEAD OF HOUSEHOLD

This is the appropriate status for most single parents, peopie who are unmarried but maintain a home for dependent children or other relatives. The tax rates for heads of households are lower than the rates for single taxpayers or for married people filing separate returns; they are higher than the rates for married people filing jointly.

You can claim head-of-household status if you have paid more than half the cost of maintaining a home for the entire year for any of the following:

- Your unmarried child (including adopted, foster, or stepchildren) or grandchild. This child must have lived with you for the entire year but does not need to be your dependent. For example: You maintain a home for yourself and your unmarried son, age 26; he is not your dependent but you do qualify for head-of-household status.

- Your married child or grandchild who has lived with you and who does qualify as your dependent

- Your mother or father, who does qualify as your dependent, whether or not the parent has lived with you

- Any other relative who does qualify as a dependent, if that person has lived with you

SINGLE TAXPAYERS

You file as a single taxpayer if on the last day of the tax year (the calendar year, for most taxpayers) you are unmarried or legally divorced or separated in accordance with the laws of your state.

What Form to Use

To itemize or not to itemize, that is the question. There are now three possible tax forms, with other variations under development, but you can itemize deductions only on the long form, 1040. Many taxpayers, put off by the complexity of the long form, file a short form instead. Even though they may be legally allowed to do so, they may be shortchanging themselves in the process. Many deductions and credits are available to you only if you file the long form. Don't just take the form the IRS sends you in the mail, therefore; it will send you the short form if that's what you filed last year. Instead, analyze your situation each year and decide which method of filing will do you the most good.

You are allowed to use the short form, 1040A, if all of your income is from wages, salaries, tips, interest, dividends, and/or unemployment compensation, and your taxable income is under a specified amount (in 1986, $50,000).

You may not use the short form if any of the following apply:

- You received income from sources other than those listed above, including annuities, alimony, self-employment income, or gain from the sale of a home.

- You can be claimed as a dependent on your parents' return and you had interest, dividends, or other unearned income of $1,000 or more.

- You want to apply any part of a tax refund to next year's tax.

- Your financial circumstances are at all complex; see IRS Publication No. 17.

You may use the new form, 1040EZ, which is even simpler than the 1040A, if you meet all of the following requirements:

- You are single.

- Your taxable income is under $50,000.

- You have no dividend income.

- Your interest income is $400 or less.

- You claim no deductions, and no exemptions for being over age 65 or blind.

You should use the long form if either of the following apply:

- You can save money by itemizing deductions. Look closely at uninsured medical expenses, interest and taxes on your home, charitable contributions, and uninsured casualty losses.

- You are entitled to adjustments or credits that would reduce your tax, including a disability pension, moving expenses, alimony, the residential energy credit, child care credit, and so on.

THE STANDARD DEDUCTION

Called the "zero bracket amount" until recently, the standard deduction is the part of your income that is not subject to tax. The 1986 tax law significantly raises the standard deduction, but the specific amount still depends on your filing status:

- If you are married, filing jointly, or a qualifying widow or widower, your standard deduction, $3,670 for 1986, will be $5,000 for 1988.

- If you are married, filing separately, your standard deduction, $1,835 in 1986, will be $2,500 by 1988.

- If you are single, or a head of houshold, your standard deduction for 1986 is $2,480; by 1988 singles will have a standard deduction of $3,000 and heads of household $4,400.

There are several things to remember about the new standard deductions:

1. All standard deductions remain the same for 1987 as for 1986, with an inflation adjustment.

2. The previous "zero bracket amount" was built into the rate tables; itemized deductions had to be reduced by the amount for your filing category. Under the new law, the standard deduction is subtracted from income before calculating taxes and before itemized deductions, if appropriate, are claimed. Many taxpayers, however, may now find that they are better off not itemizing.

3. There is a $750 increase in the standard deduction for people age 65 and over. This increase offsets the loss of the double personal exemption for the elderly, but does no good for taxpayers who itemize deductions rather than take the standard amount.

Q. We have always dreamed of retiring overseas, in some warm climate. What are the tax ramifications if we actually do so?

A. It depends on just where you retire. If you choose a "treaty" country, one with which the United States has a tax treaty (Italy, Greece, and Great Britain fall into this category), you can probably avoid dual taxation. In a nontreaty country, however (a category which includes Mexico and Spain), you may be in deep tax trouble. The United States taxes the income of its citizens, without regard to where that income is earned or where the citizens live. If you retire to a treaty country, you'll pay the higher of the taxes levied by the two countries. In a nontreaty country, you could wind up paying both. You could also wind up paying taxes on your Social Security benefits, which are at least partially nontaxable here. Giving up your citizenship, by the way, won't help. Be sure to consult a competent tax adviser, one familiar with overseas taxation, before you pull up stakes.

Withholding

Some taxpayers deliberately overpay taxes throughout the year in order to claim a refund at tax time. They do so as a form of forced savings. In fact, since Uncle Sam pays no interest on taxes withheld from your pay, this is a very poor way to save, unless you are absolutely incapable of saving any other way.

Other taxpayers deliberately underpay taxes so that they can use their money before the IRS stakes its claim. This is okay, *if* you'll actually have the money on hand when taxes are due *and* if you don't underpay by very much. If you miscalculate, interest and penalties may eat up any investment profit you might otherwise have.

The amount that is withheld from your pay each payday is determined by the W-4 form you file with your employer. This form lists the number of "allowances" you claim. The more you claim, the greater your take-home pay. Your allowances include your dependents. But don't stop there. The IRS also permits extra withholding allowances to reflect anticipated deductions and credits. You may claim an allowance for, among other things, retirement savings via an IRA and for some job-related moving expenses. Both income averaging and the two-earner deduction, which in the past could be used to reduce withholding, have now been eliminated.

Note: If your actual tax liability is greater—because, for example, you have income from interest and dividends—you may not wish to claim the full number of withholding allowances to which you are entitled.

It's up to you, within certain limits, to determine how many withholding allowances you claim. If you want to increase withholding because, for instance, you expect sizable investment income, you may do so. To have the maximum amount withheld, enter 0 for the total number of allowances you claim. And if you are married, check the box that says "Married, but withhold at higher Single rates." If you want to reduce withholding so that your taxes will come out even, you may claim as many as fourteen allowances without challenge by the IRS. You may claim more, but be sure you're entitled to them.

If you won't earn enough this year to owe any federal income tax (and you didn't pay tax last year either) you may escape withholding for income taxes (but not for Social Security) by filling in "Exempt" on the W-4 form. Then you won't have to wait for a tax refund to get your money.

Tax is also due on some pensions, on annuities, and on some forms of sick pay. If you don't have tax withheld, you will have to make quarterly payments of estimated tax.

IF YOU UNDER-WITHHOLD

Think twice before you "borrow" money from Uncle Sam by under-withholding. If you don't end the year having paid in within 10 percent of the tax you'll actually owe (except under special circumstances), you may owe penalties as well as interest. But the interest alone should give you pause: Pegged at 12 percent until February 1, 1982 (a level which made some taxpayers willing to invest the money during the year at then-prevailing double digit rates of return, and then pay the interest), it now moves twice a year with the prime rate. In 1982 the IRS interest rate was 20 percent; in late 1986, when investment returns hovered around 7 to 8 percent, it was 9 percent. At any level, moreover, interest due the IRS is now compounded daily.

Minimum tax

You can use tax breaks to reduce your tax liability, but only up to a certain point, because of what's called an alternative minimum tax. This tax, which has been toughened under the 1986 law, means that taxpayers using so-called tax preferences (such as paper losses from limited partnerships) must calculate their tax liability under both regular tax rules and under the alternative minimum tax (which adds in otherwise exempt amounts of income). The higher of the two amounts must then be paid.

Extensions

If you can't get your federal income tax return in on time, you may secure an automatic four-month extension by filing Form 4868. But the extension of filing time beyond April 15 is not permission to postpone paying taxes. Along with Form 4868 you have to send a check for the tax you think you will owe when you complete your return. When the final figures are in, you'll owe interest on any unpaid amount from April 15 until the date you file. If your estimate is low by more than 10 percent, you'll face penalties as well. Extensions beyond August 15 may be secured by filing Form 2688, along with a detailed explanation of the circumstances forcing the delay.

If your state has an income tax, find out the rules for extensions. Some states extend the due date for the state return along with a federal extension; others require a separate application.

Amendments

If you file the short form and later realize that itemizing would have cost you less, or if you file the long form but overlook a deduction, you may file an amended return on Form 1040X. Do so within three years of the time the original return was filed, submit a separate form for each year for which you claim a refund, and be sure to spell out your reasons and attach adequate documentation for your claim.

If you file an amended return, it does not necessarily mean that an audit of your original return is more likely. If any of your deductions are questionable, however, you might think twice about filing an amended return.

Estimated Taxes

If you do not pay your federal income taxes through withholding or do not have enough withheld, you may have to pay an estimated tax on a quarterly basis. Such a tax might be based on income from pensions (if tax is not withheld), alimony, self-employment, annuities, interest, dividends, rent, capital gains, and so on.

You must pay estimated tax if you will owe at least $500 in tax on income not subject to withholding. There are also certain income limitations, outlined in IRS Publication No. 505. You may pay the entire estimated tax for the year at once, or you may pay in quarterly installments. Payment dates are the 15th (or following Monday if the 15th falls on a weekend) of April, June, September, and January.

However you make the payments, your total for the year must, under the new law, equal at least 90 percent of the tax you owe, or you will be subject to a penalty. You can avoid the penalty if you pay at least as much tax as you paid the previous year, but it's a good idea to figure your estimated tax as closely as possible. You can amend your estimate, as necessary, during the year.

Self-employed people usually realize that estimated tax is due. Retirees may not. But the same rules apply to taxable income from any source, whatever your age or occupation. Failure to file can result in penalties as well as interest.

Audits and Appeals

Q. The IRS claims I made a mathematical error on my return and keeps on billing me for additional taxes. I say my return was correct, but my protests have no effect—the bills keep coming. What can I do?

A. Call the "taxpayer service information" number (it's usually toll-free) listed in your local telephone directory under U.S. Government, Internal Revenue Service. Ask for the problem resolution officer; there's one in each IRS district office. These officers won't handle tax questions or problems, but they will hack through red tape and solve administrative or procedural problems such as yours. And they try to respond within five working days.

There is a word calculated to strike terror in a taxpayer's heart: audit. An understanding of the process, however, may help you to cope.

WHOSE RETURN IS CHECKED?

The process begins with the selection of returns for audit. Here are some of the items that might flag your return for attention :

■ Arithmetic errors. Every return is screened for accuracy. If an error is found, you'll receive either a refund or a bill for additional taxes due. But you'll also bring your return to IRS attention. Check and double-check your arithmetic before you mail your return.

■ Omissions. Put down an incomplete Social Security number, don't attach all your W-2 forms, forget to sign your return . . . and you'll invite scrutiny of the entire tax return.

■ High income. While the odds against audit are very high for all taxpayers, you are definitely more likely to be audited if your adjusted gross income is over $50,000. Only about 1.5 percent of all returns are audited, but the figure is over 8 percent for those in the $50,000-plus category. (You might also secure unwelcome attention, on the other hand, by filing an itemized return, complete with wide-ranging deductions and credits, and an adjusted gross income of $10,000 or less.)

■ Excessive deductions. If you claim deductions above and beyond the average of your income bracket (see Table 2 on p. 485), your return may draw attention. Moral: claim all the deductions to which you are entitled, but have adequate documentation, and attach documentation to your return. Two areas in which to be particularly careful: casualty losses and unreimbursed business expenses for travel and entertainment.

TYPES OF AUDITS

An IRS audit may be simple or detailed. It may take place through the mail, on the government's home ground, or on yours.

A **correspondence audit** may be used when one or two relatively simple items are questioned and the necessary backup evidence may be submitted by mail. When you send such evidence, however, send copies; don't ever send the originals.

Audits in an IRS office are more usual. Here you will be asked to bring records relating to particular questions. Bring those records, but don't bring anything else. You don't want the audit to go any further afield or to open up new areas for questioning. You may ask that the meeting be rescheduled if the original date is not convenient. You may bring your accountant or attorney along, if you like, or send him or her in your place, and it may be a good idea to do so if this professional prepared your return.

A **field audit** is conducted at your home or place of business. It may also be conducted at your accountant's office. Either way, this audit is likely to delve into more details of your financial affairs.

AUDIT ADVICE

- Don't relax just because you received a refund. Your return may still be audited.

- The IRS is not responsible for advice it gives. You may fill out your return following information received directly from an IRS employee, and you may still be challenged. In the last resort only the tax law applies.

- Court rulings may not even be applicable. IRS Publication No. 556, "Examination of Returns, Appeal Rights, and Claims for Refund," contains this illuminating language: "In some instances, the official position taken by the Internal Revenue Service may differ from certain court decisions. Although the Service will follow Supreme Court decisions, it is not required to follow decisions of any lower court for cases other than those involving the particular taxpayer and issue involved in that lower court. The Service can lose an issue in a lower court and still continue to apply its interpretation of the law to other cases involving similar issues."

- The outcome of an IRS audit may affect your state income tax liability, and vice versa. If an audit results in changes in tax liability, on any level, you may want to file an amended return. The IRS exchanges information with state tax agencies.

- Don't panic. Unless you're guilty of fraud (as in any deliberate underreporting of income) the worst outcome of an audit is additional tax due, with interest and, possibly, financial penalties. But you aren't likely to go to jail.

- If you are called for an audit, be sure that you are thoroughly prepared. Have all the necessary records with you. And see if you can find any additional deductions that you failed to claim but might be entitled to. Example: You forgot, when you filled out your income tax return one year, about a ten-speed bicycle which had been stolen from your garage. So you never claimed a casualty loss. If your return for that year is audited, you can bring up the stolen bicycle.

THE TAXPAYER COMPLIANCE MEASUREMENT PROGRAM

Some tax returns are selected for audit because the IRS is tracking particular problems, such as tax shelters. (There's a difference between a tax shelter and a tax dodge. See Chapter 8.) Others are selected simply at random, under the Taxpayer Compliance Measurement Program. TCMP, as it is called, is a statistical measuring instrument for the IRS. It helps to establish taxpayer profiles, and is undoubtedly a very useful tool for the IRS. What it is for the taxpayer, however, is something else. That's because, in the process of establishing this statistical profile, the IRS challenges an entire tax return. That means that the taxpayer must provide documentation for *everything*. Are you married? Where's your marriage certificate? Do you have children? Where are their birth certificates? And so on, and on.

Some taxpayers have challenged the necessity to participate in TCMP. They've all lost.

HOW TO APPEAL

An audit does not always result in additional tax liability. You may even emerge with a refund due. But what if the IRS auditor does disallow some deductions? What if he or she asserts that you do owe more money? And what if you disagree?

Figure 2 details the IRS appeals process. Simply put, these are your options:

- The first step, if the audit takes place in an IRS office, is an immediate meeting with a supervisor. You may be able to resolve your difference of opinion right then and there.

- You can also ask for an appeals conference, which will be scheduled at a convenient time and place. Most differences, says the IRS, are resolved at this level.

- The next step is going to court. If your case is small, too small to hire an attorney but big enough to fight, you can go to the United States Tax Court's Small Tax Case Division. It has a $5,000 limit on disputes it will hear. It also offers the taxpayer two advantages: Disputes are settled with a minimum of formality and expense, and you do not have to pay the taxes at issue until the court has ruled. The regular Tax Court hears cases without regard to a financial ceiling.

- You may, alternatively, appeal your case to either the United States Court of Claims or a United States District Court. Here the rules are slightly different: You must first pay the taxes, then file a claim for a refund, and then, either after the refund is rejected or you have waited at least six months and your claim has not been acted upon, file your suit. If you lose, you may appeal to the next-highest court. You may also, at any stage of the appeals process, reach a settlement with the IRS.

Under the 1982 Tax Act, interest due the IRS (or due from the IRS) will be compounded daily. (The only exception: The penalty due for underpayment of estimated tax will not be compounded.) If the rate (which will change twice a year, in accordance with the six-month average of the prime rate) is 15 percent, tax and interest due will double in about four and a half years. It can take this long for an issue to wend its way through tax court, and so if you lose you'll owe twice as much.

FIGURE 2: Income tax appeal procedure.

At any stage of procedure: You can agree and arrange to pay.
You can ask the Service to issue you a notice of deficiency so you can file a petition with the Tax Court.
You can pay the tax and file a claim for a refund.

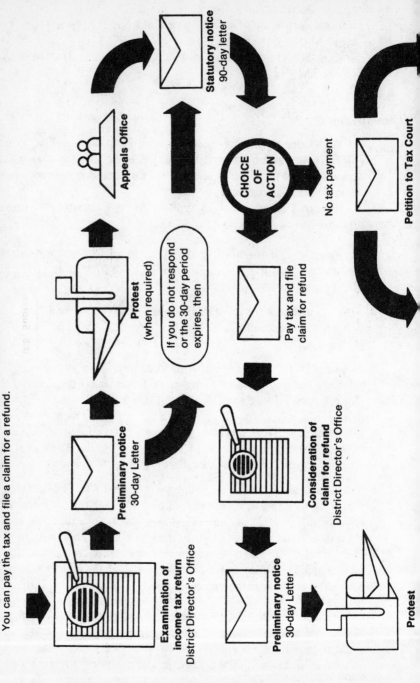

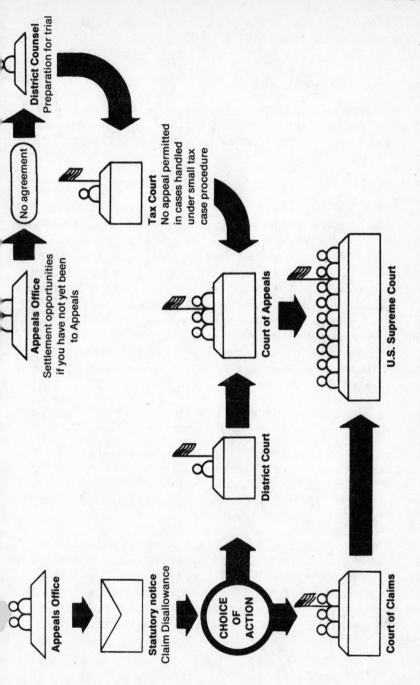

Appeals Office

Statutory notice
Claim Disallowance

CHOICE OF ACTION

Court of Claims

District Court

Court of Appeals

U.S. Supreme Court

Appeals Office
Settlement opportunities
if you have not yet been
to Appeals

(No agreement)

District Counsel
Preparation for trial

Tax Court
No appeal permitted
in cases handled
under small tax
case procedure

(Source: Internal Revenue Service)

You'll probably, therefore, think twice before fighting the IRS through the courts . . . which is exactly what the IRS wants.

Prevention Starts with Record-Keeping

The best defense, the saying goes, is an offense. And the best defense for you, as a taxpayer, is scrupulous record-keeping. Adequate records will help you when you file your returns and, if necessary, when you face an audit.

WHAT RECORDS SHOULD BE KEPT?

Every piece of paper relating to a taxable or tax-deductible item should be kept for the period of time during which that tax return may be scrutinized. State laws vary, but the IRS has three years from the filing deadline in which to audit your federal return. A return for 1987, with a filing deadline of April 15, 1988, may be the target of an audit until April 1991. If you fail to report 25 percent of your income, however, the IRS has six years in which to mount a challenge. And if you fail to file at all or file a fraudulent return, there is no time limit.

Once three years are past, assuming you've been honest, you can get rid of most of those scraps of paper cluttering your closets. But don't discard them all. Be sure to keep:

- Copies of your back tax returns. You may decide to file an amended return. And they're a useful source of reference in any case.

- Any records relating to items taxable over a long period of time. You should keep records of stock transactions, from the time a stock is purchased until three years after it is sold. And you should keep records of improvements made to your home, which will reduce the amount subject to capital gains tax when the home is sold.

Suggestion: Instead of simply filing all your canceled checks by month and year, as most of us do, why not try this trick used by financial pros: Separate your returned checks, after you balance your statement, according to purpose. File all the home improvement checks in one file, the medical expense checks in another. Then, at the end of three years, you can toss the irrelevant items and keep your tax-related items all together.

Professional Help

Have you thrown up your hands at the complexity of the tax forms? Have you decided that you need help? If so, you're not alone. Almost 40 percent of all taxpayers hire someone to prepare their tax returns for them.

If you plan to use the short form, and to forgo itemizing, chances are that you can do it yourself. But if you plan to use the long form, and if you have large deductions, you may want help.

Sources of Help

Some help is free:

■ For all taxpayers: The IRS offers a variety of free publications. Publication No. 17, "Your Federal Income Tax," is a basic guide issued each year; it is supplemented by a large number of detailed guides, some of which are listed below, that apply to specific questions. The IRS also offers in-person group counseling on how to complete tax forms. Its one-on-one tax assistance, both by telephone and face-to-face, has been drastically curtailed with federal budget cutbacks.

SOME USEFUL IRS PUBLICATIONS

463: Entertainment, Travel and Gift Expenses
502: Dental and Medical Expenses
503: Child and Disabled Dependent Care
504: Tax Information for Divorced or Separated Individuals
505: Tax Withholding and Estimated Tax
506: Income Averaging
508: Educational Expenses
521: Moving Expenses
523: Tax Information on Selling Your Home
525: Taxable and Nontaxable Income
529: Miscellaneous Deductions
547: Tax Information on Casualties, Disasters and Thefts
550: Investment Income and Expenses
554: Tax Benefits for Older Americans
559: Tax Information for Survivors, Executors and Administrators
560: Tax Information on Self-Employed Retirement Plans
587: Business Use of Your Home
588: Condominiums, Cooperative Apartments and Homeowner Associations
590: Tax Information on Individual Retirement Arrangements

- For taxpayers over age 60: Free tax help is available via volunteer programs, including those run by the American Association of Retired Persons. For information, write to Tax-Aide, AARP, 1909 K Street, NW, Washington, DC 20049.

If your return is complicated, however—if you've invested in a tax shelter or had business income or taken an aged parent as a dependent— you'll probably want the help of a paid preparer. That help comes in a variety of skill levels and a variety of costs:

- Commercial preparers range from the storefront tax offices that spring up like dandelions each spring (and close long before the dandelions in your lawn have died) to professional services that are likely to be there when you need them (should your return, for instance, be audited). At all of these agencies, however, the heaviest burden of work comes in the couple of short months before the Ides of April. That means that extra help is put on, help that may or may not be well trained.

- Enrolled agents are certified by the IRS after having worked at least five years as an IRS auditor or after passing a government exam. Enrolled agents are authorized to represent you before the IRS; if you are audited, in other words, you can have an enrolled agent who has prepared your return either accompany you or speak for you.

- Public accountants have been trained in accounting, but cannot represent you before the IRS.

- Certified public accountants (CPAs) have passed a professional qualifying exam, and are authorized to represent you. CPAs, moreover, are qualified to provide year-round tax counsel. CPAs will also cost more than the other tax preparers, but if your financial affairs are at all complex, you'll probably find the cost worthwhile. (And remember: The cost of tax advice is tax-deductible if, with other miscellaneous deductions, it exceeds 2 percent of adjusted gross income. Just be sure to keep your receipts.)

- Attorneys have passed a bar exam but may or may not have special tax training. Like CPAs, attorneys are authorized to represent you before the IRS.

WHAT TO ASK

Before you settle on any individual tax adviser, however, there are a number of questions you should ask:

- What is the adviser's training or experience in preparing tax returns? in offering tax advice?

- Does the adviser take responsibility for accuracy? Does he or she have someone else double-check returns? If so, are they reviewed for arithmetic errors only or for possible errors in interpretation of the tax law?

- Approximately how much will preparing your taxes cost? How is that fee determined?

- Where can the adviser be found later in the year?

- Can the adviser represent you if the IRS audits your return? At what charge?

WHAT TO AVOID

Stay away from a tax preparer who:

- Advertises misleadingly low rates. The preparer will either stick to the short form—a form you can prepare for yourself—or will charge you for "extras" that should have been included.

- Claims, proudly, that no client is ever audited. Many areas of the tax code are subject to interpretation; a good tax adviser will know when to claim deductions that might be challenged—and how to fight a challenge.

- Guarantees a refund, before completing your return.

- Suggests that a refund check be mailed to the preparer rather than to you.

- Suggests that you under-report income, claim nonexistent deductions, or do anything else that hints of fraud.

- Asks you to sign a blank return or one made out in pencil.

- Refuses to sign his own name to your tax form. Paid preparers are required by law to sign your return, include address and identifying number, and provide you with copies.

It's Still Up to You

Even if you hire someone to prepare your tax returns, you still have work to do. You have to gather all your tax records, and put them in order for your tax preparer. Failure to do so will cost more time during your tax session . . . and time is money. See your tax adviser early; don't wait till April (or even March), when the tax forms are piling up. If you pay a CPA for tax counsel, be sure to have a session before the end of the year, to discuss sheltering income and timing deductions and otherwise minimizing taxes that will be due. If you wait till after January 1 to think about taxes, it's too late to do anything constructive for the prior year.

And remember, even if you hire someone to prepare your tax returns, you're not off the IRS hook. You are still personally liable for any additional tax, interest, or penalty. Make sure you know what's going on your tax return, and review the return before you sign it.

KEY POINTS

- Determine your tax bracket and effective tax rate.
- Take full advantage of all exclusions, exemptions, deductions, and credits to which you are entitled.
- Maintain adequate documentation.
- Try to do a five-year projection so that you'll anticipate your income and your income tax, and be able to allocate funds for investment.
- Review your projections regularly and adjust them as necessary.
- Make tax planning part of your year-round and lifetime financial planning.

Estate Planning

★ When Ted Watson died, he left property worth $150,000 but no will. So the state, by law, stepped in and dictated the distribution of the $150,000. His wife received $50,000, his married son in medical school got $50,000, and his 14-year-old daughter got the remaining $50,000, to be administered for her by a court-appointed guardian. In some states the proportional shares would have been different. But in no state would the distribution have been just as Ted would have wanted. The only way to be sure of that was to write a will.

★ Sharon Curtis, at 27, has given no thought to wills or estates. If she did think about it, she would assume that the man she lives with would keep the property jointly purchased, the stereo and so on, while she might want her younger sister to have her jewelry. If Sharon is hit by a car, however, this is not what would happen. Her live-in lover would receive nothing . . . unless her family felt inclined to be generous. Her sister couldn't count on anything either. Just as in any case where someone dies without a will, the state would step in and dictate distribution, usually to the closest blood relatives. In Sharon's case this would be her parents. (Where there are no relatives—a live-in partner does not count—all her belongings would become the property of the state.)

What about you? How much property do you have? (Review your net worth calculations in Chapter 2.) What will happen to that property after you're gone, those assets you've worked so hard to acquire?

Estate planning is not a task reserved for either the elderly or the affluent. Anyone, at any age, who has property to leave has the right to decide how to leave it. Anyone with property, at any age, also has the right to try to minimize taxes on that property. These are the two functions of estate planning.

Leaving Your Property

Your estate consists of everything you own at the time of your death: house, savings accounts, insurance policies, stocks and bonds, pension and profit-sharing benefits, assets of all kinds. Some of this property, such as insurance and pension proceeds, will pass directly to a named beneficiary. Some of it, such as your home or bank accounts, may belong to a person named as joint owner. There is only one way to be sure that the rest is distributed in accordance with your wishes: Write a will. Whether you are single or married, male or female, age 25 or age 65, if you have any property at all you should have a will.

Why Write a Will?

Without a will, distribution of your property will be determined by state law. Your parents may get assets your spouse could use. Your minor children, more to the point, may receive funds that their surviving parent needs to raise them. Those funds will be placed under control of the law, if you leave no will, with a court-appointed guardian to watch over them; your estate will pay the guardian's fees. The children will receive the funds when they reach legal age; you might prefer them to be older and more mature.

Only with a will can you distribute hard-earned assets as you think best. Only with a will can you leave everything to your spouse, knowing that he or she will care for your children. Only with a will can you spread the distribution of those assets over a period of years, should you choose to do so. Only with a will can you leave property to a favorite charity or a favorite friend; only with a will can you disinherit a close but disliked relative. Only with a will can you leave more money to a child who needs special help and less money to another. Only with a will can you make provisions to aid an aged parent, or arrange to let a beloved aunt live rent-free in your house until her death, or skip a generation to help your grandchildren.

Only with a will can you:

—distribute your property exactly as you wish it to be distributed,

—select the person who will follow your instructions in making the distribution,

—eliminate the necessity of a court-appointed—and expensive— administrator,

—be sure that your heirs will receive the property without unnecessary delay, and

—minimize taxes and other expenses in the settlement of your estate.

Writing a Will

A will may be simple or it may be complex, but it must follow legal forms. In fact, although you are not necessarily required by law in every state to use a lawyer to draft your will, you may cause your heirs unnecessary grief and cost them more money if you try to bypass the cost of a lawyer and then leave an improperly drawn will. If you want to prepare your own will, be sure that you understand your state's requirements and follow them to the letter. A good overall guide will be found in *How to Be Your Own Lawyer, Sometimes* by Walter L. Kantrowitz and Howard Eisenberg (Putnam, 1979).

THINGS YOU SHOULD KNOW

- Anyone over legal age may write a will.

- Once written, a will must be signed in the presence of witnesses. Most states require two witnesses; some require three. Keep track of the witnesses, if you can, as they may be called to verify your will after your death.

    Q. I've written out exactly what I want done with my property after my death, because I don't see why I should have to bother with a lawyer. Now someone tells me this kind of will isn't legal. Is that true?

    A. It depends on where you live. Some states do recognize handwritten (technically called holographic) wills. Even if yours does, you have to be careful to follow its rules. Find out what those rules are. They may specify that the will be literally handwritten (no typing) or that there be no witnesses (which would put the will in another category). If you break the rules, whatever they are, the will may be invalid. Be very specific, too. Example: Don't leave "the contents of my house" to a favorite nephew and then leave a valuable coin collection in the house . . . not unless you want the nephew to have the collection too. All in all, it's advisable to consult a lawyer. A simple will is not expensive, and you will be sure that your wishes will be followed.

- A beneficiary under the will should not be a witness, or the legacy may be declared invalid.

- Think carefully before you distribute your assets. A bequest of $10,000 to a favorite relative or cause may be 10 percent of your estate at the time you write the will. What happens if your estate becomes much larger before you die? What happens if it becomes much smaller? It may be better to phrase such bequests in terms of percentages instead of dollar amounts. Think through exactly how much you want to leave, and discuss with a competent attorney the best way to phrase the will.

- Although you may leave as little or as much as you wish to people of your choice, you are restricted in one way: The law does not generally permit you to totally disinherit a spouse. If you are married at the time of your death, in fact, the law in your state may require that you leave a designated minimum to your spouse; that minimum may be what he or she would be entitled to receive if you died without a will. (But a spouse left out of a will does not receive this statutory share automatically; a suit may have to be filed.)

- If you secure a divorce, you may want to change your will immediately, to remove your ex-partner from any share of your assets. But you can't do so until the divorce is final and you are no longer legally married in the eyes of the law. What you can do, in the meantime, if you've earlier willed substantial assets to your spouse and are now in the midst of divorce, is reduce his or her bequest to the minimum amount required by state law. Then, when the decree is final, redo the will.

- If you are remarrying, you may want to sign an antenuptial agreement with your prospective spouse, to protect any children you each may have. With such an agreement, if it's signed before the wedding, you can legally agree that neither of you will make any claim on the other's estate. You can also revoke the agreement later, as long as you both agree to do so . . . if, for instance, the marriage works out well and lasts for a long time.

- If you want to disinherit blood relatives, don't just leave them out of your will or they may mount a successful challenge. Explain in the will that your omission is deliberate. But do so nicely; nastiness may lead to a lawsuit. It is not necessary, as you may have heard, to leave them a token, such as one dollar; if you do, in fact, it might be taken as an insult and lead to trouble.

- A husband and wife should each have a will. A wife who does not work outside the home and who is totally dependent on her husband may think a will is unnecessary. She would be wrong. If her husband dies and leaves everything to her, what happens when she dies? What happens if she dies almost immediately, before she has an opportunity to write her own will? The state will step in and make the distribution, regardless of either partner's wishes.

- Your will should specify what happens if an heir dies before you do, or simultaneously, and should name secondary beneficiaries. Otherwise, this might happen (and has): A childless husband and wife are killed in the same accident but she outlives him by an hour. All of his property, inherited by her during that hour, is then distributed in accordance with state law to her relatives. His get nothing.

- The wills of a husband and wife should be separate wills. A joint will, unless it is very carefully drafted, may be treated as a legally binding contract which will lock the surviving partner into a distribution of assets that may no longer be desirable as circumstances change.

- Write your will so that it will reflect your wishes if you die today. When your wishes change, redo your will (and be sure to destroy the old one). But don't, ever, amend an existing will by writing on it; the addition won't hold up in court.

- Review your will regularly, especially if you become a parent, retire, move to another state, divorce, remarry, or do anything that could affect the distribution of your estate and the validity of your existing will. Review your will when any important economic or personal event occurs.

  Q. I put all my affairs in order, including updating my will, before I retired. Now I'm thinking about getting away from cold weather and moving to the Southwest. Will I have to redo my will? Or will it remain valid?

  A. Different states have different requirements with respect to wills, and so, in general, it's a good idea to review your will when you move. Although a will made in another state may be valid, it may be costly to probate and may subject an estate to taxes from both states. Be very careful about moving your legal residence, especially if you retain any property in another state, or both your old state and your new one may attempt to collect inheritance taxes when you die.

- Involve your spouse in the planning of your will. Don't present him or her with a *fait accompli*. Estate planning is part of your overall financial planning and is a process that should be a family affair.

- Sign only the original of your will and keep that original in a safe place, where it can be easily located by your survivors. You might leave it in your lawyer's files, with an unsigned copy at home for reference. Or, in some states, you may leave it (for a small fee) with the local probate or surrogate's court. Just be sure to retrieve it if you decide to make any changes or to write a new will. And be sure to tell someone where it is.

- A safe deposit box is generally not a good place to keep a will because most states require the sealing of a box upon the death of its owner, until the tax authorities can inspect the contents. Even if the box can be opened under court order to search for a will, the process is time-consuming and unnecessarily troublesome for the survivors. One solution: his and hers safe deposit boxes, each containing individually owned assets and the other's will.

- You can put funeral directions and requests for organ donations in your will but they may not be read in time. A better way to leave such instructions is in a letter of intent left with your will (reinforced, perhaps, by your spoken instructions ahead of time and an organ donation form). This letter can also contain specific bequests—the antique chest to son Mark, the pearl necklace to daughter Anne—which might clutter up your will. It can be combined with your personal record, described on pp. 516–19.

PICKING AN EXECUTOR

When you write your will you must name an executor to see that its provisions are carried out. The executor may be anyone you choose (except that a few states require that an executor be a resident of the state), so you may name a relative, a friend, or a bank. Before you decide, look at what your executor must do:

- Prepare a complete inventory of all your assets—real estate, securities, cash, bank accounts, and so on
- Collect any money owed you in the form of salary, pension, profit-sharing, veterans benefits, Social Security, outstanding loans, etc.
- Pay off any valid debts you owe to others and challenge questionable claims
- See that life insurance companies are notified of your death
- Arrange for your family's immediate living expenses
- Liquidate assets as necessary and invest others wisely to provide income during the time that the estate is being administered
- Prepare and file, as they become due, all income tax, estate tax, and inheritance tax returns
- Distribute your estate to the people named in your will
- Make an accounting of all receipts and payments to the probate court and to the beneficiaries

The naming of an executor is clearly not a casual task. It's important to choose someone who has both the competence and the time to do the job well. Just inventorying assets and filing the necessary legal documents requires dedication. But the executor must do more. He or she (a female is called an executrix) must exercise considerable judgment if your estate is to reach your heirs in anything approaching its proper size. Just when assets are sold can make a considerable difference in their value; just when taxes are paid can affect how much is paid. An executor can, of course, secure professional assistance in making these decisions, but professional assistance costs money, and the money comes out of the estate. The executor should, therefore, be someone with financial know-how as well as someone you can trust to carry out your wishes. A spouse may be your first choice, but that spouse may do better with professional backup; if your estate is at all sizable or complicated (if, for instance, you own a family business), you might name a professional co-executor such as an attorney or a bank.

In naming an executor, remember:

- Executors are paid from the estate, with fees in many states set by law. In New York State, as an example, an executor's commission is 5 percent on the first $100,000 of gross value in the estate, with a sliding scale down to 2 percent on anything over $5,000,000. A single executor on a $300,000 estate would thus receive $13,000. This fee is the same whether a bank or an individual acts as executor, except that (1) a commercial bank may set its own minimum fee, such as (in one major New York City bank) the full commission payable on assets of $300,000, even if your estate is considerably smaller, and (2) a spouse, relative, or friend may waive the fee.

- Never name someone who has not expressed willingness to serve. If your named executor declines the post, the court may have to appoint someone.

- You might name an alternate executor, in case the first is either unwilling or unavailable when the time comes.

- Review your choice periodically—especially if you've chosen someone older than yourself.

- Many banks have trust departments that specialize in the administration of estates. But they may be structured to serve large estates best. Before you name a bank as executor of your will, have a talk with a trust officer and make sure that the bank is willing to handle your estate. (But don't underestimate the size of your estate either; inflation has probably made you worth more than you think.)

- Under the best of circumstances an estate takes some time to settle. Taxes must be paid, and federal estate taxes are not due until nine months after death; the IRS may not finish processing the return for another nine months or more. Creditors must be allowed an opportunity to come forward and file any claims. Assets may need to be sold to pay necessary taxes. All of this takes time. A simple estate may take a year to settle. If your affairs are at all complicated, a delay of two to three years is not at all unusual. However, the delay does not mean that your heirs will be temporarily destitute. Periodic distributions may be made from the estate during settlement.

- If you name a bank as co-executor but want the family to retain personal control, you can have a provision in your will that gives your spouse or adult child (or whoever is named as your personal executor) final say in any dispute.

Q. When I wrote my will, several years ago, I named my son as the executor. He has since moved out of state and tells me he can't be my executor. Is he right?

A. Your state may permit out-of-state executors (most do, some do not, some do if the executor is a close relative), but even if it's legal you could be putting a real burden on your son. An executor has major responsibilities, many of which must be performed where you last lived. Your son may or may not be able to take the time from his family and business to travel to your state to attend to these matters. Even if he is willing, the costs of his travel will be charged against your estate. Instead of naming your son alone, why not name co-executors; your son plus a local attorney or bank?

Personal Affairs Record

You can make life easier for your executor, whether relative or impersonal outsider, by leaving a complete record of your personal affairs. (You'll also make it easier on yourself, while you're living, if your affairs are organized. And you'll save money when you visit a lawyer to have your will drafted if you present a tidy package of information.)

Take some time, now, to create this personal record. (It will take some time; it's a big job—but an important one.) Then update it on a regular basis. And tell someone—your spouse, a grown child, your executor—where the record is. Preparing the record *with* your spouse, or reviewing it with him or her, is an ideal way to be sure that you are both fully informed about your financial affairs.

The personal record (use the following worksheet as a guide) should include both the facts about your finances and information about the location of all your important papers. Keep a copy in your desk drawer and another copy clipped to the copy of your will.

PERSONAL INVENTORY WORKSHEET

1. SOCIAL SECURITY NUMBER: _____
   Location of card: _____

2. LIFE INSURANCE (if more than one policy, list information for each)
Policy number	Company	Face value	Beneficiary

   Name, address, and telephone number of agent: _____
   _____
   _____

3. SAVINGS ACCOUNTS (if more than one, list for each)
   Name and address of financial institution: _____
   _____

   Account number: _____
   If joint account, name of other person: _____
   Location of passbook or statement: _____

4. CHECKING ACCOUNTS (if more than one, list for each)
   Name and address of financial institution: _____
   _____

   Account number: _____
   If joint account, name of other person: _____
   Location of canceled checks: _____

5. TIME DEPOSITS AND CERTIFICATES OF DEPOSIT
   Name of institution where purchased: _____
   Number(s) and maturity date(s): _____
   Location of documents: _____

6. U.S. GOVERNMENT BONDS
   List of serial numbers and denominations: _____
   Location of bonds: _____
   Names of any co-owners: _____

7. SECURITIES
   Name, address and telephone number of broker: _____
   _____
   _____

   Location of securities: _____

   List of stocks and/or bonds

Company	No. of shares	Certificate no.	Maturity (bonds)

   List of mutual funds

Company	No. of shares	Account no.

8. SAFE DEPOSIT BOX
   In whose name? _____
   Location: _____
   Location of key: _____
   List of contents: _____
   _____
   _____
   _____
   _____

PERSONAL INVENTORY WORKSHEET (*cont.*)

9. PENSION OR PROFIT-SHARING PLAN
    Company and account number: _____
    Name and address of employer: _____
    _____
    _____
    _____

10. KEOGH PLAN AND/OR INDIVIDUAL RETIREMENT ACCOUNT
    Where? (bank? mutual fund?): _____
    Account number: _____

11. AUTOMOBILE (if more than one, list for each)
    Make, type, and year: _____
    License number: _____
    Location of ownership papers: _____
    Insurance company: _____
    Policy number: _____

12. REAL ESTATE (if more than one property, list for each)
    Location of property: _____
    Title owned by: _____
    Location of deed: _____
    Mortgage held by: _____
    Amount of mortgage: _____
    Location of mortgage document: _____
    Location of tax receipts: _____
    Insurance company: _____
    Number of policy and its location: _____

13. PERSONAL PROPERTY (jewelry, furs, collections)
    Description: _____
    Location: _____

14. HEALTH INSURANCE (include major medical and disability)

Company	Type of policy	Policy no.	Location of policy

15. TAX RECORDS
    Name, address, and telephone number of accountant: _____
    _____
    _____

    Location of tax records: _____

16. CREDIT CARDS (list for each)

Company	Account no.	Name on card	Location of card

17. MAJOR CREDITORS (list for each)
    Name, address, and telephone number: _____
    _____
    _____

    Location of notes, contracts, or receipts: _____

18. WILL
    Location of original: _____
    Location of copy: _____
    Name, address, and telephone number of attorney: _____
    _____
    _____
    _____

This form is a rough guide to your own personal record; you may have more, or less, information to note. Either way, be sure to add a page indicating the location of other valuable documents (if they are not already listed in your safe-deposit box inventory): marriage and birth certificates, school transcripts, military records, citizenship papers, adoption papers, divorce decrees and alimony agreements, important warranties and receipts, and so on. Be specific: Are the papers in a box in the attic? In the upper-left-hand drawer of your desk? Include proof of membership in any fraternal, professional, or union organization that entitles the estate to any benefits—and leave instructions to your survivors to claim those benefits. Include information about a cemetery plot you own, if any, and funeral preferences. Be sure, too, to include a list of any outstanding debts—money you owe and money owed to you—to forestall any false claims against your estate. And attach a list of people who should be notified of your death.

Naming a Guardian

Q. My brother and I are in high school now. What happens to us if our parents die without a will? What happens to our house and our car, our parents' savings, and our education? There's nothing wrong with our parents, but we got to talking with them and they said they don't have a will. If anything should happen to them, what happens to us?

A. The only way for your parents (and you, by talking it over with them) to have a say in what happens to you and to their property is by writing a will. If they die without a will, the state will distribute the property according to its laws. Most of it would probably go to you and your brother, but because you are not yet of legal age, a guardian would have to be appointed to care for you and handle the money. The court would decide who that guardian is, and it might or might not be someone you or your parents would choose. Urge your parents to write a will, without delay.

An essential part of a will, if you have minor children, is a guardian to care for them if you and your spouse both die. That guardian should be chosen with care. A close relative may be your first thought, but similarity of child-raising beliefs may be more important than family ties. Grandparents, who may otherwise be ideal, may not have the energy to cope with youngsters. So, before you decide:

- Think about what's most important to you in raising your children. Try to select guardians who would raise your children the way you would, in terms of ethical values, religious beliefs, proper behavior, and so on.

- If your children are old enough (past the earliest school years), discuss the matter with them. It won't alarm them to have a matter-of-fact discussion about people they'd like to live with. And listen to what they have to say: There may be factors important to your children that won't occur to you. It may be particularly important, for instance, especially for a teenager, to stay in the same school and community.

- Before you make a definite decision, talk to the people you'd like to name. How do they feel about it? Are they willing to accept the responsibility?

- If you've found warm, loving people to serve as guardians for your children, but have some qualms about their financial savvy, you don't have to give them the entire burden. You can name a separate trustee to manage the money and property left to the children. That trustee could be instructed to confer with the guardian about the distribution of funds on the children's behalf.

- If you don't write a will, or don't name a guardian, a court will decide who will care for your children. The judge may ask the children their preference, but isn't obliged to do so. The court will also appoint a caretaker of the children's inheritance, whether or not you would have thought the guardian capable of handling the funds. There will be fees to be paid to the court-appointed guardian and caretaker, fees which will come out of your estate.

Probate

Q. My husband and I have worked very hard to acquire all that we have, a house, two cars, and personal belongings. We are still young: I am 27 and my husband is 34. We have a 2-year-old daughter. We are concerned about what would happen if one of us died. Is there any way to avoid inheritance tax, lawyer's fees, or probate court fees if one of us should die? Why is it important to have a will if everything ends up in probate court anyway?

A. Taking your questions one at a time: Inheritance and estate taxes are based on the amount of property you leave, and have absolutely nothing to do with whether or not that property goes through probate. Legal fees may be higher if you do not leave a will, because the court will appoint an administrator to distribute assets. Estates go through probate court whether or not there is a will, but if you have a will you can distribute your property the way you prefer and can name the executor. More important, only by writing a will can you name a guardian for your 2-year-old daughter. Write a will, just as soon as you can, and don't worry about probate.

Probate is the legal process of "proving" the will is valid. If you leave a will, your designated executor takes care of the legal formalities, often with the help of an attorney. If you do not leave a will, the probate court (sometimes called surrogate's court) will appoint an administrator to do the job; the administrator, too, will probably appoint an attorney to help.

Probate has become a swearword in some quarters, largely because of administrative delays and because of the sometimes substantial fees paid (out of the estate) to attorneys, appraisers, and others. Probate procedures differ from state to state, but probate itself is not the problem; abuse of the system is more often a problem. One way in which you can reduce abuse, and reduce excessive fees, is by picking the right attorney and the right executor and making clear to them how you want your affairs handled.

A Uniform Probate Code, which has been adopted in some states, simplifies the probate process. Under UPC an estate can be distributed without court supervision unless someone actually asks a court to protect his interests. A new model law will, if adopted, go a step further: Under the Succession Without Administration Act, heirs could file a simple affidavit and receive the assets of an estate by assuming its debts. This approach, which could be used whether or not there was a will, would eliminate many fees and commissions.

SHOULD YOU AVOID PROBATE?

Avoiding probate, meanwhile, or attempting to avoid it, may leave your heirs in worse shape. This is because the only real way to avoid probate, at present, in virtually every state, is to eliminate any need for a will. The way to avoid the need for a will, if you have any assets at all, is to pass those assets on through means other than a will. A description of some of these means—lifetime gifts, joint ownership, and trusts—is given later in this chapter.

The point to remember, however, is that every action has a consequence. If you distribute all your assets directly, your estate may not have enough cash on hand to pay final expenses. If you don't write a will, you forgo the opportunity to choose your own guardian for minor children. If you avoid probate, and the costs of probate, you may subject your estate to unnecessary taxes, you may complicate its legal distribution, and you may lose control of your assets during your lifetime. Weigh all these consequences before you decide to take elaborate measures to avoid probate.

Some property does pass directly to your heirs without going through probate. Jointly owned property is one example. U.S. Savings Bonds, when there is a co-owner or surviving beneficiary, is another. Life insurance, under some circumstances, is a third. Insurance proceeds, if there is a designated individual named as beneficiary, pass directly to that beneficiary without having to go through probate. If your beneficiary is your estate, however, the proceeds are included in your estate for probate purposes and distribution may be delayed. Either way, all of your property—including jointly owned property, U.S. Savings Bonds, and insurance—is included in your gross estate for the purpose of calculating estate taxes that may be due (see below). *Avoiding probate does not mean avoiding estate or inheritance taxes.*

The only way to keep property out of your taxable estate is not to own it. In the case of insurance on your own life the policy has to be owned outright by another person, with the premiums paid by that person. If you retain any control (such as the right to borrow against the policy or to change the beneficiary), the proceeds remain in your taxable estate.

Estate Taxes

The right to transfer property from one person to another has been taxed for many years. Before 1977 there were two different federal tax structures: one for property transferred by gift during life and the other (at a higher rate) for property transferred at death. The Tax Reform Act of 1976 created a unified gift and estate tax, with property transferred at death considered your final gift.

The Economic Recovery Tax Act of 1981 made major changes in the federal estate tax laws, changes that have now eliminated federal estate taxes from 95 percent of all estates (unless inflation continues to raise the value of estates, pushing them once again into taxable categories). Most people no longer have to worry about reducing federal estate taxes. But you should nonetheless be familiar with the new law. (And you should review a will you wrote before the new law, to make sure it still fulfills your wishes.)

Here are the highlights of the 1981 law:

TAXABLE ESTATES AND TAX RATES

- No federal estate tax return need be filed for estates under $600,000. This figure refers to your gross estate. Your taxable estate is less; it is arrived at after subtracting funeral expenses, outstanding debts (including income taxes), executor's and attorney's fees, and other allowable deductions. An estate could, therefore, total far more than $600,000 and still be exempt from tax. These amounts are also "unified." That means that they incorporate both your estate and gifts made during your lifetime after 1976. If you give $50,000 to your mother now, that gift will be added to your gross estate when you die to determine whether estate taxes are due. (For more on gift taxes, see below.)

- The maximum tax rate on estates and gifts is 55 percent, scheduled to come down to 50 percent in 1988.

Q. Since my husband's retirement, we have spent six months of each year in Vermont and six months on the Costa del Sol in Spain. We drew up our will while we were still living year-round in the States. Do we need to change it now?

A. You might. For one thing, people you've named as executors or trustees in this country might not be allowed to serve abroad. For another, the age of legal majority might be different and there might be some difficulty with bequests to children or grandchildren. And, not least, your estate may wind up paying double estate taxes, especially if you own real property in both countries. One possible solution: separate wills for the assets in each country. Before you do anything, however, show the will prepared in the United States to an attorney familiar with the law in Spain.

LEAVING ASSETS TO YOUR SPOUSE

- Any amount of money may now be given or left to your spouse, without gift or estate tax liability. This unlimited marital deduction means that you can simply leave everything to your spouse, if you wish to do so, without complicated and extensive legal maneuvers to minimize taxes. If this is your intent, your will could use the phrase "maximum marital deduction." If you wrote a will including this phrase before September 11, 1981, however, it will be assumed to refer to the old law under which the maximum marital deduction was no more than the larger of half the estate or $250,000. To obtain the new larger deduction, rewrite your will.

- Estate tax may be due later when the *surviving* spouse dies, if your estate and your spouse's total more than the exempt amount. You may want to minimize those taxes through trusts and other techniques described later in this chapter. But taxes are not the only consideration. You could, for instance, inherit from a spouse and then pass along the estate tax-free by remarrying and leaving the entire estate to your second spouse. You'd be doing Uncle Sam out of taxes this way, but you might also be doing your children out of their rightful inheritance. If your estate is more than the exempt amount of $600,000), consult a knowledgeable attorney for advice. Whatever the size of your estate, however, think about what you want your family to have. Don't get caught up in the arithmetic of tax saving to the exclusion of family considerations.

■ An estate may now be left, tax-free, for a surviving spouse without giving that spouse control over what happens to the assets when he or she dies. In the past, control had to be transferred along with assets. Now a husband might set up a trust to leave his wife income for life, while passing on the principal of the trust, on her death, to his children from a first marriage. This change in the law may be attractive to someone who has remarried after death or divorce. It also deprives the survivor (usually, by the laws of mortality, the wife) of control over the estate she inherits.

■ Where property is jointly owned by husband and wife it will now be assumed, for estate tax purposes, that each owns half the property. This is a major change from previous law, which assumed that the entire value of the property belonged to the first to die and was taxable in his or her estate. (For more on joint ownership, see pp. 526–28.)

THE GIFT TAX

■ Just as an estate tax is paid by the estate, a gift tax is paid, when due, by the giver.

■ Gift tax rules have been changed so that you may now make unlimited annual gifts of up to $10,000 each without incurring any gift tax. A married couple may, if they wish, pool their tax-free opportunities and give up to $20,000 per gift each year tax-free, even if the funds come from only one of the partners. Such gifts are a way of reducing your taxable estate. But, again, there are other considerations: Don't give assets away during your lifetime if you may need those assets.

■ It may do the recipient more good, in terms of his or her income tax, to receive the assets via your estate. That's because the cost basis for measuring capital gains of inherited assets is fixed at the time of death, while the cost basis of assets you give is fixed at your present cost basis, which is usually their purchase price. For example: You leave your daughter securities that you bought at $35 a share and that are valued at your death at $50 a share. Your daughter sells the securities for $60 a share. Because they were inherited she pays tax only on the difference between $50 (the "stepped-up basis" at the time of death) and $60. If you had made her a gift of the securities during your lifetime, the tax would be based on the difference between your purchase price of $35 and the selling price of $60.

- Unlimited gifts may be made for medical purposes or to pay school tuition, without gift tax, if such payments are made directly to a medical or educational institution for education, training, or care of a specified individual. A grandparent might be able to help a grandchild through medical school, without gift tax liability. Or a niece might be able to pay for long-term care for an elderly aunt. (But don't confuse gift and income taxes. You can pay tuition for a grandchild or a nephew free of gift taxes, but you may not take an income tax deduction for doing so.)

- Gifts made within three years of death were assumed, under pre-1981 law, to be made in contemplation of death; they were, therefore, included in the estate for estate tax purposes. No more. With certain exceptions (such as life insurance policies), most gifts, no matter when they are made, will no longer be included in the taxable estate.

State Taxes

The above information applies to federal estate and gift taxes. Most states also levy their own taxes. They don't necessarily conform. Some states don't tax gifts. Some states continue to limit the annual gift tax exclusion to $3,000 after the federal limit was raised to $10,000. And some states, similarly, do not have a full marital deduction.

An estate tax is a tax on the right to dispose of property; it is assessed against the entire estate and paid out of the assets of the estate before distribution. The federal estate tax is uniform throughout the country. State estate taxes differ, but a credit is allowed against the federal estate tax for state estate taxes actually paid. Some states, however, have tax rates that exceed that credit.

An inheritance tax is a tax on the right to receive property and is paid by the recipient after distribution of the estate. Some states have inheritance taxes that are applied differently to different beneficiaries. The closer the relationship, the greater the amount of inheritance exempt from tax and the smaller the tax assessed. A surviving spouse, as a rule, has the greatest exemption and the lowest tax. *Suggestion:* If you are planning to move after retirement, you might take a look at state inheritance taxes before you make a decision. They vary considerably.

Q. We made our wills about ten years ago. Since then our lawyer has died. Do we have to write new wills?

A. Your original will is still valid—*if* you have or can obtain the signed original. If the lawyer had kept the signed original, and if you cannot retrieve it from his office, you will need to draw up new wills. But a will should always be reviewed every few years, in any case. And the significant tax-law revisions of the last few years would make it wise for you to review your will now even if it is still valid.

Reducing Your Taxable Estate

There are several popular ways to reduce a taxable estate. They are worth a look, even though the new tax laws remove most estates from tax considerations.

Lifetime Gifts

If you give assets away during your lifetime, up to the annual exclusion of $10,000 per gift per person, they will not be included in your estate when you die. Assets that may be given include cash, securities, real estate, life insurance . . . virtually anything at all.

You might give your adult children an outright gift of cash and remove that cash from your estate. You might give a life insurance policy, on your own life, to your beneficiary and remove the face value of the policy from your estate. If the policy is term insurance or a whole life policy that has been fully borrowed against, it may have little current value and no gift tax will be due. You can then give your beneficiary an annual gift of cash with which to pay the premiums on the policy, and as long as the gift is less than $10,000, no gift tax will be due. You can give assets that may increase in value (such as securities or real estate) and eliminate further appreciation of the asset from your taxable estate.

But I can't emphasize one point strongly enough: Don't look at taxes to the exclusion of everything else. Don't give away property you may need or wish to control. Plan your finances over your anticipated lifetime and let your heirs, unless you have money to spare, worry about taxes that may become due after you are gone.

Joint Ownership

If you are married, you and your spouse may own everything jointly and assume that you don't need a will. If you are single, you may have put your assets in joint ownership with a sibling or a nephew or niece and assume that you don't need a will. Joint ownership has been called "the poor man's will" because assets that are jointly held do pass directly to the joint owner without passing through probate. But unless your estate is modest indeed, joint ownership may be a very poor substitute for a will. Here's why:

- If you own property jointly, with right of survivorship, you have nothing further to say about its future ownership. You may not leave the property (or your share of it) to anyone else in your will. (Joint ownership as tenants in common does allow you to dispose of your share, but this is a form of ownership more often used by business partners than by marriage partners.)

■ Neither owner has exclusive control of jointly owned property. If one owner is away on business or incapacitated by a stroke or simply stubborn, the other owner may be unable to dispose of securities or real estate that is jointly owned. If you and your spouse should divorce, your jointly owned property will be frozen until negotiations are complete—unless you both, as joint owners, agree to the sale.

■ Jointly held bank accounts, however, may be different, depending on state law. In some states each owner has full rights to the account. This can be convenient. It also means that one may clean out the account without warning to the other. In other states the one who cleaned out the account would owe half to the other.

■ Joint accounts pass directly to the surviving owner, but directly does not mean immediately. Joint bank accounts may be temporarily blocked (and outstanding checks stopped) until state tax authorities have reviewed the situation.

■ When you place assets in joint ownership with someone other than your spouse, you may incur a gift tax liability. If you place your son's name on your 100 shares of AT&T stock, you may be doing so simply to ensure his ownership of the stock when you die. As far as the Internal Revenue Service is concerned, however, if the gift is over $10,000, you've made a taxable gift in your lifetime. (And the gift tax is paid by the person who makes the gift.)

■ Jointly held property may be seized for the debts of either owner. Witness the elderly widow who puts all her savings accounts in joint ownership with her daughter, so that the daughter can pay her mother's bills and will not have to worry about estate taxes after the mother dies. But the daughter becomes overextended, and declares bankruptcy. Before the mother realizes what is happening, the joint bank account (never mind that it's the mother's money) has been seized to pay the daughter's debts. If you're worried about paying your bills, whether because you are elderly or simply traveling a great deal, give a power of attorney instead of joint ownership. A power of attorney may be as limited (to write checks) or as broad (to handle all your affairs) as you like, and you may revoke it at any time. Or establish a living trust, as described on pp. 530–31.

JOINT OWNERSHIP AND THE 1981 TAX LAW

The biggest problem with joint ownership in the past—the presumption that everything in a joint account was put there by the first to die (unless the survivor could prove otherwise) and was therefore includable in his or her gross estate—has been superseded by the 1981 tax law when joint ownership is between spouses. Husband and wife can now own assets jointly, even if one spouse earns no income, and each will be assumed to own half. There is no gift or estate tax problem. This modernization of the law does not, however, remove all complications.

For example: You and your spouse jointly own a house (your primary residence) for which you paid $36,000 some years ago. The house is now worth $150,000. One of you dies, and the other wants to sell the house. If the house were wholly owned by the first partner to die, it would pass free of estate taxes to the surviving partner as part of the unlimited marital deduction. In addition, the "basis" in the house for tax purposes would be the full value of the house at the time of the first partner's death, or $150,000. (This is what lawyers called "stepped up" basis—the initial cost of the property, stepped up to its value at the time of death—a provision in tax law that reduces capital gains tax due when inherited property is sold.) If the house is jointly owned, however, only half of the value is included in the estate. The remaining half of the current value ($75,000), plus half the original cost ($18,000), would be the maximum "basis" for the surviving spouse. If he or she then sells the house for $150,000, $57,000 would be taxable gain (unless the survivor is over age 55 or defers the tax by buying another house to use as a principal residence). If he or she keeps the house, instead, the value of the entire house would be taxable in his or her estate, raising the cost basis for the children who then inherit it to the value in that estate.

Some attorneys suggest, in view of the 1981 tax law, that it's a good idea to have appreciating assets, such as a house, in the name of the spouse most likely to die first. This advice assumes that you can figure out which one that is.

Whatever you do about your primary residence, however, any out-of-state property might better be jointly owned to reduce final expenses. If you live in New York and own a vacation cottage in Massachusetts, both states will insist on probating your will (since real estate is the key to probate). If you own the property jointly, it will pass to your joint owner outside probate.

Note: The change in the tax law with respect to joint ownership applies *only* to spouses. If you own property jointly with anyone else, relative or friend or investment partner, the entire value of the property will be assumed to belong to the first to die and will be included in his or her gross estate. It will be so assumed for the second to die as well and, if there is a third owner, for the third. Unless it can be proved to the satisfaction of the Internal Revenue Service that the money to buy the property came from separate funds (no easy task), the property may be subject to estate tax two, three, or more times, as many times as there are partners.

Trusts in Estate Planning

A trust, despite its forbidding sound, is simply a three-party agreement in which the owner of property (the grantor) transfers legal title to that property to someone else (the trustee) for the benefit of a third party (the beneficiary).

In a *testamentary* trust, which takes effect at the death of the grantor, the beneficiaries are the heirs to the estate. In an *inter vivos* (living) trust, which takes effect as soon as it is established, and may or may not continue after death, the beneficiaries may be anyone you designate—including yourself, the grantor of the trust. Living trusts, furthermore, may be *revocable,* subject to change at any time during your lifetime, or *irrevocable,* not subject to change.

When you make a revocable trust, you retain control; because you retain control the assets in the trust are included in your estate and are subject to estate tax if tax is due. The assets held in a revocable living trust will go directly to your beneficiaries when you die, however, without probate and its delays. With an irrevocable trust, if you part with all right to receive benefits from the assets, you gain the tax advantage of removing the assets from your estate but you lose control of your assets. Don't make an irrevocable trust unless you are wealthy enough so that (1) estate taxes will be an issue, and (2) you'll have enough other property in your control to ensure continuation of your life-style.

The Uses of Trusts

Trusts are not just for the wealthy. You might want to set up a trust for any one of a number of reasons:

- To manage your own assets, either because you are too busy during your working life to pay proper attention, you face a serious illness, or you have retired and don't want to worry about financial matters. Via a living trust, revocable when you wish, you can name a trustee to handle investments and manage your funds. You can direct the trustee to consult with you on major decisions, or you can give the trustee full power to act. This trust will not save any income or estate taxes, but that is not your goal.

- To manage assets left in your will to minor children, until the age at which you would like the children to receive the property. (If you die without a will and without making such provisions, a guardian will be named by the courts and the children will receive the funds as soon as they reach legal age, which in many states is 18.)

- To provide income to your surviving spouse (or children), and then pass your estate on to your children (or grandchildren).

■ To bypass probate, by disposing of assets outside your will.

Q. We have two children, ages 12 and 15, and are writing simple wills in which we leave everything to each other and then, when the survivor dies, to the children. But we don't want to just give each child half of whatever we leave (it won't be that much) because we can't tell at this point how much money each child will need to finish an education. We can't tell if one will have special medical needs. Is there some way we can leave our assets intact, for the benefit of both children, with a manager able to make decisions in the best interests of the children?

A. Yes. You can leave all or part of your estate in what is called a "sprinkling" trust, with a named trustee empowered to distribute the assets between the children as they are needed. That trustee may be the guardian named to actually care personally for the children. Or it may be a separate individual or institution, in which case you might require consultation with the guardian. You can also determine the ages at which you want the children to receive any money left in the trust. If remaining amounts will be sizable, you might want to stagger the distribution: so much at age 25, so much at age 30, and so on. That decision will depend on the maturity of your children and the amount of money you expect to leave.

Advantages of a Living Trust

Testamentary trusts permit you to determine what happens to your property after your death. Living trusts have additional advantages:

AVOIDANCE OF PROBATE

Living trusts permit your estate to skip probate proceedings with respect to the assets in the trust, thereby saving both time and fees.

Some advisers recommend that an entire estate be kept out of probate via the mechanism of living trusts. But this represents an unreasoning fear of probate, and can complicate affairs for your survivors. What if, for instance, you come into money upon your death that you have not foreseen? It could happen if, as one example, your death is caused by an automobile accident and a settlement is made to your estate. Create living trusts, if you like, but also leave a will for the remainder of your property.

Note: Removing property from probate does *not* mean removing it from your taxable estate. The only way to do that is to divest yourself permanently of control and enjoyment of your assets during your lifetime, via an irrevocable trust. Few people want to do this.

PROFESSIONAL MANAGEMENT

A living trust can provide professional management of your assets. If you should become ill or incapacitated—a special consideration for the elderly—your trustee can continue to take care of all your financial affairs.

You can establish a living trust for this purpose while you are hale and hearty, and do away with concerns about the financial results of disability. A living trust, controlled by you while you are willing and able to do so, works far better than a power of attorney (which, in some states, automatically ends with incapacity) or guardianship (which can go beyond financial management to remove all independence from an elderly person's life).

COORDINATION OF ASSETS

A trust can be designed to coordinate all your assets, so that securities, life insurance, pension and profit-sharing benefits, real estate, etc. can be transferred to your trust when you die and administered in one central place for the benefit of your heirs.

PRIVACY

A trust agreement, unlike a will, is a private matter. A will becomes public when it is admitted to probate. If you have a trust in effect when you die, no one needs to know what you've left or to whom.

Marital Trusts

Trusts can be tailored to meet almost any need. But that need should be evaluated as a family affair, or lingering resentment can be the result. A marital trust, for example, can be set up to administer an estate and distribute income to a surviving spouse. The purpose might be reduction of estate taxes. It might be protection of the survivor's interests. And it might be the distribution of assets in what lawyers call a "multiple marriage" situation.

Before the enactment of the 1981 tax law, a trust was often created to hold part of the husband's assets after estate tax had been paid. The trust shielded the assets from a second tax at the later death of the surviving spouse. Today, as a result of the 1981 law, total assets are passable to a spouse without estate tax. For most people, therefore, concern about successive taxes is no longer a reason to establish a trust for the surviving spouse.

But the full amount inherited tax-free by the surviving spouse will be subject to estate tax when the second spouse dies. And that spouse (unless he or she remarries and becomes entitled to another full marital exemption) will be entitled (in 1987) to a maximum exemption of $600,000. If you own sufficient property (a net worth of over $600,000) so that estate taxes will be a consideration for your surviving spouse, the use of trusts to hold what is exempt from estate tax at your death (up to a maximum of $600,000) might be appropriate to avoid tax at the second death. You should talk to an attorney who specializes in estate planning.

Note: Don't get the impression that a trust is all or nothing. You may put any proportion of your assets into one or more trusts, and do as you like with the remainder.

The marital trust has been used to care for a spouse unable to care for herself (I use the feminine pronoun advisedly, as it was most often men who felt their wives were inadequate on the financial front), a provision which deprived widows of any control over their financial futures and of any flexibility in managing assets to meet changing needs. If you feel strongly that your spouse will need help in managing finances, give her that help right now.

The marital trust can also now be used, where there has been a remarriage, to care for two families. Until the end of 1981, the marital deduction could not be used for a trust which paid income to a spouse but then passed on the assets, on that spouse's death, to someone else; until 1981 the spouse had to have the right to dispose of a marital trust at death. Now such a "terminable interest" (an interest in the assets that terminates on the second spouse's death) does qualify for the marital deduction. This means that a partner in a happy second marriage, wanting to provide for the second spouse but still leave the bulk of assets at her later death to children of a first marriage, may do so via a trust and still claim the marital deduction.

When both partners come to a late-life remarriage with sizable assets, each might execute a trust with income to the surviving spouse and the principal to the trustmaker's children. (Provision may be made for the principal to be invaded for the surviving spouse in case of need.) Both sets of children will be protected. And the trust of the first to die will qualify for the marital deduction.

Q. When my wife and I divorced, I agreed to name her and our son as irrevocable beneficiaries of my life insurance. I also want to leave my son the rest of my property. But I've been a major source of support for my mother, now almost 70, and I want to be sure that she's taken care of if I die first. What's the best way to handle this?

A. You might leave your property in a trust, with the income paid to your mother during her lifetime and the principal then going to your son at her death. You can word it so that your son must be at least a certain age before coming into the money. Then if your mother dies before he is old enough (in your estimation) to handle the funds, the trust would continue to be administered on his behalf. You can also include wording so that your son becomes the trust's sole beneficiary if your mother dies before you do. Clarify your own goals, then talk to a competent attorney.

Naming a Trustee

A trustee, like an executor, may be an individual or an institution. However, an executor has an essentially limited responsibility, ending when the estate has been distributed to the beneficiaries, but a trustee has an ongoing responsibility. The trustee must administer the assets in the trust for the duration of the trust, making wise investment decisions. Trust fees are generally regulated by state law, and are generally the same for an individual and for an institution, stated as a percentage of the trust.

SHOULD YOU USE A BANK AS TRUSTEE?

Banks frequently advertise their trust services, and those services are extensive (although they may be most effective with, and actually limited to, larger estates). A bank can offer:

- Stability. The institution will endure, where an individual might not.

- Professional administration. With computerized systems, banks can offer documentation and follow-up on an impressive scale.

- Interdepartmental efforts on your behalf. A trust officer may make investment decisions, while a custodial department handles day-to-day management of your account.

A bank, on the other hand, is not personalized. The trust officer you talk to now may not be the one who later administers your estate. The trust officer, known to you or not, may simply not appreciate the lifestyle your family enjoys and may not give them all the money you would want them to have.

More important, many institutions have had notoriously poor investment results on behalf of trust funds, especially in the recent turbulent economy. Many trust funds have lost a great deal of ground in inflationary times.

Institution or individual, a trustee should invest in a balanced portfolio, for income and for growth; and review the portfolio on a regular basis, making transactions as appropriate. Too few transactions indicate neglect.

Suggestion: If you name a trusted individual as trustee, that individual can hire a bank to provide service to the trust. Then, if the institution's performance is not satisfactory, the named trustee has the power to fire it and hire another.

Life Insurance in Estate Planning

Life insurance agents used to urge the purchase of life insurance (among other reasons) to provide cash on hand to pay final expenses, including estate taxes. Today, with most estates free of estate taxes (including the small family businesses that formerly carried large life insurance policies to ensure the continuation of the business), taxes are no longer the motivating force in the purchase of life insurance.

But there are other reasons to buy life insurance (for more on life insurance, see Chapter 21):

■ If you have not yet built assets to the level where your family will be supported in your absence, life insurance provides an "instant estate."

■ If you have assets, but not liquid assets, and you know that there may be substantial final expenses in the form of uninsured medical and hospital bills, funeral costs, income taxes, and the like, life insurance can take care of these bills, so that your survivors need not cash in other assets on a "forced sale" basis.

■ A surviving spouse with a sizable estate and no marital deduction to reduce tax liability may need life insurance to take care of estate taxes.

Note: Before 1982 it was sometimes a good idea for husbands and wives to own the life insurance policies on each other's lives. Such ownership removed the proceeds from the taxable estate. With the extended marital deduction and exemptions now provided, however, most people need not worry about estate taxes—or about ownership of life insurance. You can retain ownership—and control—of your own policy.

How Much Cash Will Be Available for Final Expenses?

Whatever your net worth, your survivors will need cash on hand to wrap things up. Give them a hand, now, by using the following worksheet to estimate what will be needed and what will be available:

ESTATE PLANNING WORKSHEET

ESTATE SETTLEMENT COSTS		CASH ON HAND	
Medical/hospital bills	————	Checking account	————
Funeral costs	————	Savings account	————
Federal estate tax	————	Money market fund	————
State inheritance taxes	————	Insurance proceeds	————
Administration costs	————	Pension or profit-sharing	
Other outstanding liabilities	————	proceeds	————
TOTAL	————	Money owed you	————
		Other assets quickly	
		convertible to cash	————
		TOTAL	————

Will there be enough?

Estate Planning Is a Family Affair

Don't think about the future by yourself; estate planning is not a do-it-alone proposition.

IF YOU ARE MARRIED

If you are married, estate planning is both a joint and an individual endeavor. You *each* need a will. You each need a net worth statement. You each need to be able to put your hands, quickly, on liquid assets. You each need to understand your financial affairs. Don't assume, whatever your age, that either one of you will necessarily die first. You simply can't tell. Make your calculations, and your preparations, to cover any eventuality.

The widow who knows absolutely nothing about financial affairs (and it's most often, but not always, a widow) may be a figure of fun in comic strips, but the joke turns bitter all too soon in real life. There is enough to cope with at the time of death, without starting from the beginning in financial management.

Couples always divide family responsibilities. Someone balances the checkbook just as someone (not necessarily the same someone) handles the investments. Someone makes the trip to the safe deposit box and keeps track of valuable papers, while someone fills out the tax forms. Someone, for that matter, knows whom to call to repair the furnace and someone knows how the household appliances work. Share this information. Don't wait until one of you must face the unfamiliar alone.

Then, after you've told each other all you know about your financial affairs, swap jobs for practice. Each of you take on the other's financial responsibilities for a couple of months: balance the checkbook, pay the mortgage, enter a running tally of dividends received, and so on. You may find it takes longer to get the job done—but it's better to have the learning period now, by choice, than later, by necessity.

Discuss, together, what you will do about:

- Writing a will. Decide how you want to distribute your property and make wills, one for each of you, saying so. Do it without delay.

- Choosing an executor. It should be someone in whom you both have confidence.

- Naming a guardian. It's even more important that you agree on this person, and that you consult your minor children before naming anyone.

- Establishing testamentary or living trusts, and naming a trustee.

IF YOU ARE A SINGLE OLDER ADULT

You may also want to share your plans with someone close, a relative or friend. If you are a widow or widower with grown children, you should tell them (roughly, not necessarily in detail) about your affairs. Don't let them put you off by telling you that you will live forever. You won't. Tell them:

- Where your will is located and why you've made any specific provisions therein.

- Where your personal affairs record is located

- Whom to contact: your lawyer and accountant and stockbroker, as well as far-flung relatives and friends

Do your estate planning as part of your lifetime financial plan—the plan that includes maximizing your assets while you're alive and distributing them when you're gone. Make your arrangements now, whatever your age, as if you might die tomorrow. Then review your plans, and change them as necessary, as you move along through life.

KEY POINTS

- Write a will. This is the only way to be sure that your assets will be distributed as you would like them to be.

- A personal affairs record and a letter of instructions, supplementing your will, will make your executor's task much easier.

- Probate is the legal process of validating a will. You can bypass probate by distributing your assets outside of a will: through joint ownership, a trust, or an outright gift while you are alive. Doing so with all your assets, however, may leave you without adequate funds while you are alive; it may also deprive your estate of the funds needed to pay final bills. By-passing probate, in any case, does not reduce or eliminate estate taxes.

- Federal estate tax returns must be filed when estates exceed designated amounts. You may, however, leave any amount to your spouse (or inherit any amount from a spouse) without federal estate taxes being due. Taxes will then be due, if the estate is large enough, on the estate of the surviving spouse.

- If your affairs are at all complicated, or your assets at all extensive, don't be a do-it-yourself estate planner. Get the professional help of a competent attorney.

Retirement Planning

★ John is 36, preoccupied with his career. On the personal front, his biggest financial goal is buying a house. The last thing on his mind is retirement.

★ Jean is 49. Finished paying college tuition for one child, she has two more children to go. With six more years of college bills, she can't think about saving toward retirement. Yet she's always wanted to retire early and travel—and she'll be 55 when the last child graduates.

★ At 62, Howard plans to keep working into his seventies. That gives him a good ten years to set the stage for retirement . . . if he stays healthy, and is able to work as long as he plans.

For most of us, it never seems to be the "right time" to think about retirement. We're too busy living in the present, making ends meet and saving for short-term goals. Sometimes, too, we're fearful of retirement, thinking of it as a time when life begins to go downhill. Yet planning for retirement is essential if retirement is to be a positive experience, the experience it ought to be. Planning for retirement is just the culmination of lifelong financial planning, the time when it all comes together.

This chapter will dispel some of the myths surrounding retirement, help you to assess how much money you'll need in retirement, and show you how to reach that goal.

The Later Years Are Good Years

Here are some facts about the retirement years:

■ A man of 65 can expect to live over fourteen more years, a woman over eighteen (see Table 1). These are averages, of course, and some people will live considerably longer. Plan your retirement with as much thought as you've given to planning your career. It may last almost as long.

TABLE 1: Expectation of life at various ages in the United States, as of 1982.

Age	WHITE			ALL OTHER			TOTAL		
	Male	Female	Total	Male	Female	Total	Male	Female	Total
0	71.4	78.7	75.1	66.5	75.2	70.9	70.8	78.2	74.5
1	71.3	78.4	74.8	66.7	75.3	71.0	70.7	78.0	74.3
5	67.4	74.5	71.0	62.9	71.5	67.2	66.8	74.1	70.5
10	62.5	69.6	66.1	58.1	66.6	62.4	61.9	69.2	65.6
15	57.6	64.7	61.2	53.2	61.7	57.5	57.1	64.3	60.7
20	53.0	59.8	56.4	48.5	56.8	52.7	52.4	59.4	56.0
25	48.4	55.0	51.7	44.1	52.0	48.1	47.9	54.6	51.3
30	43.7	50.1	47.0	39.7	47.3	43.6	43.2	49.7	46.6
35	39.1	45.3	42.2	35.4	42.6	39.1	38.6	44.9	41.9
40	34.4	40.5	37.5	31.1	38.0	34.6	34.0	40.2	37.2
45	29.9	35.8	32.9	27.0	33.6	30.4	29.6	35.5	32.6
50	25.6	31.3	28.5	23.2	29.3	26.3	25.3	31.0	28.3
55	21.6	26.9	24.4	19.8	25.4	22.7	21.4	26.7	24.2
60	17.8	22.8	20.4	16.6	21.7	19.2	17.7	22.6	20.3
65	14.5	18.8	16.8	13.8	18.2	16.2	14.4	18.8	16.8
70	11.6	15.2	13.6	11.4	15.0	13.3	11.6	15.2	13.6
75	9.0	11.9	10.7	9.2	12.2	10.9	9.1	11.9	10.7
80	6.9	9.0	8.2	7.2	9.6	8.6	7.0	9.0	8.2
85+	5.2	6.6	6.1	5.3	7.5	6.6	5.2	6.7	6.2

(Source: National Center for Health Statistics, U.S. Department of Health and Human Services)

- "Senior citizens," men and women over 65, are not all alike. Far from it. With the elderly spanning thirty years or more, the diversity is substantial. The "young old," those from 65 to 75, are often energetic, healthy, and thoroughly involved in life. The "old old," those over 75, are more likely to be slowing down, although not all do. There's no reason to anticipate illness and disability just because you reach a particular birthday. At least 70 percent of the elderly, according to one study, rate their health as good or excellent. No more than 5 percent of the elderly are in hospitals or nursing homes at any time. Most live in the community, most are independent.

- Women live longer than men. For every 100 women age 65 and over, there are only 68 men. For every 100 women age 75 and over, there are only 56 men. Most elderly men, not surprisingly, are married; many elderly women are not. But women are better survivors, adjusting to widowhood. Men, if they don't remarry after a wife dies, frequently succumb themselves within a few short years.

- With longer life expectancy (see Table 2), three- and even four-generation families are increasingly common. The result: You may be helping to support elderly parents while meeting your own retirement needs. Planning ahead is more important than ever.

TABLE 2: Expectation of life at birth in the United States, 1900–82.

Year	WHITE Male	Female	Total	ALL OTHER Male	Female	Total	TOTAL Male	Female	Total
1900	46.6	48.7	47.6	32.5	33.5	33.0	46.3	48.3	47.3
1910	48.6	52.0	50.3	33.8	37.5	35.6	48.4	51.8	50.0
1920	54.4	55.6	54.9	45.5	45.2	45.3	53.6	54.6	54.1
1930	59.7	63.5	61.4	47.3	49.2	48.1	58.1	61.6	59.7
1940	62.1	66.6	64.2	51.5	54.9	53.1	60.8	65.2	62.9
1950	66.5	72.2	69.1	59.1	62.9	60.8	65.6	71.1	68.2
1960	67.4	74.1	70.6	61.1	66.3	63.6	66.6	73.1	69.7
1965	67.6	74.7	71.0	61.1	67.4	64.1	66.8	73.7	70.2
1970	68.0	75.6	71.7	61.3	69.4	65.3	67.1	74.8	70.9
1971	68.3	75.8	72.0	61.6	69.8	65.6	67.4	75.0	71.1
1972	68.3	75.9	72.0	61.5	70.1	65.7	67.4	75.1	71.2
1973	68.5	76.1	72.2	62.0	70.3	66.1	67.6	75.3	71.4
1974	69.0	76.7	72.8	62.9	71.3	67.1	68.2	75.9	72.0
1975	69.5	77.3	73.4	63.7	72.4	68.0	68.8	76.6	72.6
1976	69.9	77.5	73.6	64.2	72.7	68.4	69.1	76.8	72.9
1977	70.2	77.9	74.0	64.7	73.2	68.9	69.5	77.2	73.3
1978	70.4	78.0	74.1	65.0	73.5	69.3	69.6	77.3	73.5
1979	70.8	78.4	74.6	65.4	74.1	69.8	70.0	77.8	73.9
1980	70.7	78.3	74.5	65.3	74.0	69.6	70.0	77.7	73.8
1981	71.1	78.5	74.8	66.1	74.5	70.3	70.4	77.9	74.2
1982*	71.4	78.7	75.1	66.5	75.2	70.9	70.8	78.2	74.5

* Provisional data.

(Source: National Center for Health Statistics, U.S. Department of Health and Human Services)

- The well-being of the retired depends in large part on the source of retirement income. Social Security benefits and some pensions are indexed to the cost of living, so that income increases over time. Investments may also yield proportionately more when interest rates are high. Fixed benefits, of course, lose much of their purchasing power with the passing years.

- Personal income is usually cut by a third to a half after retirement. Some work-related expenditures are eliminated, but more is spent on health care. Yet one of the most significant trends among the older population over the last two decades, according to the American Council of Life Insurance, has been the improvement in financial standing. Between 1959 and 1980 the median incomes of older men and women grew at a faster pace than the median incomes of men and women in the general population.

■ Retirement income, according to a study by the Employee Benefit Research Institute, comes from five major sources: (1) Social Security provides 92 percent of elderly families with retirement benefits, with an average of $4,300 in cash income in 1979. (2) Employer pensions provide an average of $4,100 per family to 34 percent of elderly families. (3) Earnings from part-time or full-time employment provide an average of $9,500 per family to 31 percent of elderly families. (4) Financial assets provide an income of $3,000 per family to 71 percent of elderly families. (5) Public assistance (including Medicare, which is not related to need, and Supplemental Social Security Income, which is) to provide an average of $2,200 to 95 percent of elderly families.

■ Older people are going to get more and more attention as the years go by, simply because they are going to make up a larger and larger share of the population. In 1940, one in fifteen Americans was over age 65. By 1980, one in nine (or 11 percent of the population) was over 65. And by 2020, when the baby-boom generation of the 1950s reaches retirement age, one in five (fully 20 percent of all Americans) is expected to be over 65.

Your Retirement Budget

Whether you are 40 or 50 or 60, you owe it to yourself to fit retirement planning in among your other financial goals. As you make investments, buy insurance, and manage your cash, look ahead to the days when the fruits of your efforts will be a comfortable retirement. The keystones of that comfortable retirement are Social Security, an employer pension, an Individual Retirement Account or Keogh Plan (if you are eligible), and your own investments.

Before evaluating any of these sources of income, however, it's important to figure out just how much you'll need. This is easier to do if you're closer to retirement, but it's important, even if you're twenty years away, to rough out a retirement budget. Then you can evaluate your sources of income and see what you need to do to fill any gaps.

How Much Money Will You Need?

The Bureau of Labor Statistics, in its analysis of budget data, looks closely at the needs of retired Americans. In its budgets for autumn 1981 (the last of the series, because funding cuts have reduced BLS programs), the average annual cost of a "lower-level" budget, excluding personal income taxes, was $7,226 for an urban retired couple. An intermediate-level budget cost $10,226 and a higher-level budget was $15,078. (See Table 3.)

TABLE 3: Annual budgets, at three levels of living, for a retired couple, autumn 1981.

Component	Lower budget	Intermediate budget	Higher budget
TOTAL BUDGET	$7,226	$10,226	$15,078
Total family consumption	6,914	9,611	13,960
Food	2,183	2,898	3,642
Housing	2,377	3,393	5,307
Transportation	553	1,073	1,960
Clothing	244	409	629
Personal care	198	290	424
Medical care	1,085	1,091	1,098
Other family consumption	275	457	901
Other items	311	615	1,118

Note: Income taxes are not included in the total budgets.
(Source: Bureau of Labor Statistics)

The three budgets are based on hypothetical lists of goods and services, specified in the mid-1960s to portray three relative levels of living. The three budgets are also national averages; there is considerable regional variation, as shown in Table 4. Direct pricing of these goods and services last took place in 1969, with annual updates through 1981 in accordance with the Consumer Price Index. Tables 3 and 4 are, therefore, not totally reflective of current costs. But they can be used to give you an idea of the proportion of your retirement income that will be spent for different budget items.

For most people, a livable post-retirement income amounts to at least two-thirds of pre-retirement income; three-quarters provides a more comfortable margin, especially in the face of rising prices. How much you'll actually need depends on how much you're used to having and on your post-retirement life-style.

Ezra P. earned a gross income of $20,000 before he retired. As a married taxpayer, filing jointly, his total tax bite (federal and state income taxes, and Social Security) came to $4,488. Work-related expenses totaled $931 and savings and investments, calculated by the President's Committee on Pension Policy at 9 percent of after-tax income, came to $1,396, leaving a net pre-retirement income of $13,185. With no taxes due on Social Security retirement benefits at this level, Ezra needs exactly that $13,185 —or 66 percent of his pre-retirement income—to create an equivalent income in retirement. The key is disposable income. The more you earn, therefore, the smaller the equivalent percentage. Don R., in contrast to

TABLE 4: Annual costs on an intermediate budget for a retired couple, autumn 1981.

Urban United States	$10,226	SOUTH	
Metropolitan areas	10,568	Atlanta	9,516
Nonmetropolitan areas	9,203	Baltimore	10,051
		Dallas	9,768
NORTHEAST		Washington, D.C./Md./Va.	11,000
Boston	11,925	Nonmetropolitan areas	8,801
Buffalo, N.Y.	10,744		
New York/Northeastern N.J.	11,623	WEST	
Pittsburgh	10,503	Denver	10,028
Nonmetropolitan areas	10,318	Los Angeles/Long Beach	10,238
		San Francisco/Oakland	10,921
NORTH CENTRAL		Seattle/Everett	11,343
Chicago/Northwestern Ind.	10,070	Nonmetropolitan areas	9,529
Cleveland	10,500		
Kansas City	9,978		
Milwaukee	10,673		
Nonmetropolitan areas	9,298		

(Source: Bureau of Labor Statistics)

Ezra P., earning $50,000, paid $17,824 in taxes, $1,931 in work-related expenses, and $4,826 in savings and investments, for a net pre-retirement income of $25,419. With post-retirement taxes figured at $1,965, Don's equivalent retirement income is $27,386 or 55 percent of his post-retirement income.

Preparing a Budget

Your own retirement budget starts with your current budget. Look at the budget worksheets in Chapter 2, and write down your current expenditures in every category. Then, and this is the hard part, project those expenditures to post-retirement. There are two considerations:

Actual dollars and cents. You'll spend less after retirement on work-related expenses: clothing, lunches out, transportation. You'll spend less on taxes, too, since some of your income (including at least half of your Social Security) will be tax-free and the rest will probably be taxed at a lower rate. Property taxes may come down, if your community has an exemption or discount for older residents. Health care (unless you can manage to continue good health insurance into retirement) may cost more. Your life-style, more or less costly, will be at least partly up to you.

Inflation. Although the rate of inflation has slowed, the decreasing value of the dollar must be a consideration to anyone planning to live on a fixed income. You can work inflation into your retirement calculations by using the worksheet and table in Figure 1. A 7 percent inflation rate is high at this writing, yet looks modest when we remember recent double-

FIGURE 1: A worksheet for adjusting retirement calculations for inflation.

	Step 1: Current expenses	Step 2: Estimated Annual retirement expenses
Food		
Housing		
Transportation		
Clothing		
Medical		
Savings and investments		
Life insurance		
Other		
TOTAL		

Step 3: Projection for inflation

Multiply the total from Step 2 by the appropriate inflation factor from the Inflation Factor Table below. For example, if you are five years from retirement, and assume an inflation factor of 7 percent, you'll use Inflation Factor 1.4 to learn how much you'll actually need that first retirement year. After that, project for five years into retirement and make any other projections you think are necessary.

Your first
retirement year: _____

Five years
after retirement: _____

Further
projections:_____

INFLATION FACTOR TABLE

Years to retirement	PERCENTAGE RATE OF INFLATION							
	5%	6%	7%	8%	9%	10%	11%	12%
5	1.3	1.3	1.4	1.5	1.5	1.6	1.7	1.8
8	1.5	1.6	1.7	1.8	2.0	2.1	2.3	2.5
10	1.6	1.8	2.0	2.2	2.4	2.6	2.8	3.1
12	1.8	2.0	2.3	2.5	2.8	3.1	3.5	3.9
15	2.1	2.4	2.8	3.2	3.6	4.2	4.8	5.5
18	2.4	2.8	3.4	4.0	4.7	5.6	6.5	7.7
20	2.6	3.2	3.9	4.7	5.6	6.7	8.1	9.6
25	3.4	4.3	5.4	6.8	8.6	10.8	13.6	17.0

(Source: U.S. Department of Agriculture)

digit inflation. Modest or not, though, an inflation rate of 7 percent would reduce your purchasing power nearly in half in a period of ten years.

You can meet your retirement needs, and resist the impact of inflation, by planning ahead, now, while you are at the height of your earning power. Your plans should include preparing a retirement budget and revising it periodically as you move closer to retirement, understanding Social Security and any pension benefits to which you may be entitled, opening and maintaining a high-yielding Individual Retirement Account, making and modifying investments to make the most of your assets, and managing cash and credit well.

Social Security

Since 1935 the Social Security system has been the foundation on which retirement plans can be made. It was never intended to ensure a financially secure retirement by itself. Nor was it ever an actual insurance program, with your contributions set aside for your future use. But despite some shakiness in recent years, the system still does exactly what it was intended to do: It provides a foundation on which you can build additional retirement security. And it does so as originally planned, via transfer taxes on the current working population to fund the benefits of current retirees.

Social Security Benefits

The Social Security tax that you pay during your working years is matched by an equal amount paid by your employer (unless you're self-employed, in which case you have paid more than an employee but less than the employee-employer total and you will, if you continue working, pay the combined amount). These taxes provide four distinct benefits:

Retirement benefits, which you can elect to receive at any time after age 62, are based on the number of years (actually calendar quarters) that you've worked and the amount that you've earned. Your spouse and, in some cases, your children may also be eligible for benefits based on your earnings record.

Survivors' benefits are a form of life insurance, providing payments to your spouse and dependent children (up to a specified age) after your death.

Disability insurance, described in Chapter 22, ensures you of a monthly income if you are unable to work because of an illness or other disability. Disability benefits are important to every worker long before retirement age.

Medicare, also described in Chapter 22, provides both hospital insurance and voluntary medical insurance for men and women over age 65.

Q. I'm working two jobs to make ends meet, and both employers withhold Social Security tax from my paycheck. Are they supposed to?

A. Yes. You owe Social Security taxes on the full "wage base" earned (the actual amount changes each year), from one or more jobs. Each employer is required to withhold the tax up to the mandated limit, without regard to whether you are working at another job as well. If too much is withheld for the year, you can apply the excess against your federal income tax. If some is still left over, you can request a refund.

How to Estimate Your Retirement Benefit

Within this system based on length of working life and the amount you've earned over the years, benefits vary enormously. A 65-year-old man retiring in 1985 could receive a maxium monthly benefit of $717. But the average retired worker, in 1985, actually received $548 a month. There are additional variations, depending on whether a worker retires later, has a spouse receiving benefits, and so on.

How much you'll get from Social Security depends, in large part, on how much you earn. Lower-paid workers have a higher "replacement ratio" than higher-paid. If you earn the maximum currently subject to Social Security tax, you can expect to receive about 27 percent of your pre-retirement income from Social Security retirement benefits. If you earn an "average" income, your ratio will be 41 percent. And if you're at the bottom of the wage ladder, you'll get about 54 percent of what you earn. These ratios, which have changed regularly, are now expected to remain constant for some time. Social Security, remember, was never designed to allow you to live in the style to which you are currently accustomed—not without help from other resources. Social Security benefits are not taxable, however (unless your total income is above a specified amount, as described on p. 553), which increases their actual value to you.

It's a complicated system, and it's very difficult to determine how much you will actually receive in monthly retirement benefits if you are still some distance from retirement—especially since the adoption of an indexing system designed to help benefits keep pace with the cost of living. But there are three things you should do:

- Every few years during your working life, ask your local Social Security office for form SSA 7004, Request for Statement of Earnings. Mail the completed form to P.O. Box 57, Baltimore, MD 21203. You'll get a statement showing past reported earnings, in total, plus annual earnings (on which Social Security tax has been credited) for each of the last three years. Compare these year-by-year totals with your year-end W-2 forms and report any discrepancy to the Social Security Administration. It's wise to do this at least every three years, because it becomes much harder to correct any errors after three years have gone by.

- When you are within a few years of retirement, ask your local Social Security office for a copy of the free leaflet "Estimating Your Social Security Retirement Check." It contains a step-by-step procedure for determining the monthly benefit you will receive when you retire.

- Apply for retirement benefits a few months before you want them to start. This will allow time for all the necessary paperwork. You'll need your Social Security number, proof of age, and evidence of recent earnings (W-2 forms from the last two years or, if you're self-employed, copies of your last two tax returns).

Important: Social Security benefits are not automatic. You must apply for them. And you must apply for Medicare before you retire (see p. 458).

Q. I want to retire at 63 but know that I will have to take a reduced Social Security benefit. Would I be better off waiting until 65?

A. Not necessarily. People who retire at 62 (the earliest permissible retirement age under the Social Security system) must accept a benefit that is 80 percent of the amount they would have received at age 65 (based, of course, on the earnings record to that date; working longer could raise the basic benefit). At 63, your benefit is 86.6 percent of your full age-65 benefit. If you wait to 64, you'll get 93.3 percent. What few people realize, according to tax publishers Prentice-Hall, is that these are generous levels. Most people who begin to collect at 62 will collect so much before age 65 that it would take twelve years of the higher "full-65" benefits to make up for what they were paid in the three years from 62 to 65. So make your retirement decision not just on the amount of Social Security you'll receive, but on the overall basis of what's best for you.

When to Retire

Although federal law for the last few years has prohibited mandatory retirement (in most fields) before age 70 (and this upper cap has recently been phased out as well), Social Security retirement benefits are still based on a "normal" retirement age of 65. You will have to decide, based on a number of factors—personal as well as financial—just when you want to retire.

You have three options under Social Security:

- Retire between 62 and 65 on a reduced benefit
- Retire at 65 on a full benefit
- Continue working and get a bonus for each year of work past your 65th birthday up to age 70

IF YOU RETIRE EARLY

If you retire at age 62 your basic Social Security benefit will be reduced by 20 percent; the reduction is smaller for each year closer to age 65. The reduction is permanent. You will never receive as much as you would have if you had retired later. But your monthly check may change, in one of three ways:

- You'll receive your share of general increases, such as cost-of-living increases, in Social Security benefits.

- If you become eligible for disability benefits after you retire but before age 65, you will probably receive a larger check. So be sure to notify your local Social Security office if you become disabled after taking early retirement but before reaching age 65.

- You can increase your monthly check by returning to work either before you turn 65 (your benefits will go up because you've received fewer early benefits) or after 65 (if your income raises the lifetime earnings average on which your Social Security payments are based). Example: Betsy retired at age 62, receiving $280 a month or 80 percent of her basic benefit of $350. She returned to work for one full year, at age 65, and when she retired again, her monthly benefit was $309.

IF YOU RETIRE AT 65

You'll receive more in your monthly retirement checks if you retire at 65 (or at whatever "normal" retirement age is the rule) than if you retire early. Not only will your benefit be the full benefit, rather than a reduced proportion thereof, but you may increase your benefit by earning more in your last years at work and dropping from the calculations earlier less-well-paid years.

IF YOU CONTINUE WORKING PAST "NORMAL" RETIREMENT

If you continue working past 65, you will receive a larger basic Social Security benefit. You'll also receive a "delayed retirement credit" which increases your benefits by 3 percent for each year between ages 65 and 70 in which you receive no benefits because you are at work.

There are "earnings limitations," changing each year, which limit the amount you may earn while still receiving Social Security benefits. Those limitations end at age 70 and you may then earn as much as you can without forgoing any benefits.

Family Benefits

Q. I was married for sixteen years and then divorced. I have not remarried but my ex-husband has. Will his new wife get all his Social Security? Or am I still entitled to any benefits?

A. Since January 1979, divorced wives are eligible for Social Security on their former husbands' earnings records as long as they were married for at least ten years and have not remarried. You will therefore receive exactly what you would if you were still married: the spouse's benefit of 50 percent of your ex-husband's retirement benefit. His new wife will be entitled to the same amount. Neither of you affects the benefit received by the other. (And either or both of you may choose to receive benefits based on your own individual earnings record if it will provide a higher benefit.)

You are not the only one to receive monthly Social Security checks based on your income over the years. Some of your dependents are also eligible for benefits.

If you are receiving retirement or disability benefits, monthly payments may also be made to your:

- Unmarried children under 18 (or under 19 if full-time high school students)
- Unmarried children over 18 who become severely disabled before age 22 and who continue to be disabled
- Wife or husband 62 or over
- Wife or husband under 62 if she or he is caring for a child under 16 or a disabled child who is getting a benefit based on your earnings

After your death, monthly payments may be made to:

- Unmarried children under 18 (or under 19 if full-time high school students)
- Unmarried children over 18 but who become severely disabled before age 22
- Widow or widower 60 or older
- Widow, widower, or surviving former spouse who is caring for your under-16 or disabled child if the child is receiving a benefit based on your earnings
- Widow or widower 50 or older who becomes disabled within seven years after your death or within seven years after the end of benefits paid as a child's caretaker
- Dependent parents age 62 or older

Checks can also go to a former spouse, married to the worker for ten or more years, at 62 for a divorced spouse, at 60 for a surviving divorced spouse, and at 50 for a disabled surviving divorced spouse. Under certain conditions children may be eligible for Social Security benefits based on a grandparent's earnings.

Note: If you have been denied benefits based on a former spouse's earnings record, because that former spouse is not making support payments and is not under a court order to do so, *reapply for benefits now.* The support requirement has been eliminated.

Q. My 14-year-old son lives with me and my second husband. His own father, my former husband, has retired and is receiving monthly Social Security payments. Is my son eligible for benefits as well?

A. Yes. In a situation like yours, where a minor child lives with mother and stepfather, the child may be entitled to Social Security benefits (for retirement or disability) from three insured adults: mother, stepfather, and natural father. Get in touch with your local Social Security office and arrange for benefits for your son. However, your son is entitled to only one benefit. He won't be allowed to collect on his father's record, on yours, and on his stepfather's all at once.

Women and Social Security

When Jerry retired at age 65 in 1984, after earning $18,000 in his last year of work, he received $669 in monthly retirement benefits. His wife, who had been a homemaker for most of their marriage, received the spouse's 50 percent, adding $334 to the couple's monthly income for a combined family total of $1,003. Jerry's neighbors retired at the same time. But Ed and Betty each earned $9,000 for a total of $18,000. Each received a monthly Social Security check of $440, for a total of $880. The same yearly family income, the same monthly contributions over the years, and $123 less every month from Social Security.

As the Social Security Administration points out, of course, Betty had some benefits that Jerry's wife never had. Because she was covered by Social Security in her own right:

- She was covered by disability insurance while working
- Her children would have received survivor's benefits if she had died while they were young
- She has a choice about when to retire. While the homemaker cannot collect Social Security benefits until her husband retires, the working wife can elect to retire at age 62 and collect a reduced benefit on her own earnings record.

But the Social Security system was designed in the 1930s, and it still, to a surprising extent, reflects the social patterns of the 1930s: lifelong marriages in which women were homemakers, dependent on the economic support of men. It may have made sense, in 1935, for retirement benefits to be based on one earner's income, with dependent spouses entitled to a proportionate share of those benefits. It doesn't seem to make as much sense today, with the majority of women working outside the home, increasing numbers of self-supporting women, and a changing view of marriage as an economic partnership.

There have been some changes. Gender distinctions within Social Security law have been eliminated. Benefits are now applicable without regard to sex. The "widow's" benefit is now a "survivor's" benefit. But inequities remain:

- A married woman worker is entitled to a retirement benefit based on her own earnings or to a benefit of 50 percent of her husband's benefit, whichever is greater. She cannot receive both. This means that the protection she earns as a worker may duplicate, rather than add to, the protection she already has as a spouse. All the Social Security contributions she makes over the years may yield no return, since she can receive just as much protection in many cases without making contributions at all.

- Some two-income couples, like Betty and Ed, receive less in benefits than a one-income couple with a comparable income. The system is still geared to man-as-breadwinner, woman-as-homemaker.

- Widowed homemakers under age 60 cannot receive benefits unless they are either at least age 50 and disabled or are caring for children. Many widows have no Social Security protection during just the period when they may face difficulty entering or reentering the labor force.

- Married women workers, in general, get substantially lower benefits than men both because women frequently spend time out of the paid labor force while they care for children and because women, on the average, earn less than men.

- Homemakers may be without disability protection just when they need it most because benefits are not provided for disabled homemakers or their children if the woman has not worked in recent years.

WHAT YOU SHOULD DO

A major overhaul of the system has been proposed to amend these inequities. Until such an overhaul takes place—and it's likely to be sidetracked by the entire system's pressing need for financial support (see below)—you have to do what you can to protect yourself. Here are a few things you should do:

- Be sure to keep Social Security records up-to-date when you change your name. Whether you are currently in the paid labor force or not, it's important to have the correct name on Social Security records. Otherwise, earnings may not be properly credited and you may have difficulty when you apply for benefits.

■ If you've earned your own Social Security credits you'll have to decide whether you'll receive a larger benefit based on your own record or on your husband's. But you'll also have other options. Suppose your husband continues to work past age 65, and earns too much to collect retirement benefits. Or suppose he's younger than you. You can go ahead and retire on your own record. Then, when he does retire, you can elect to receive the spousal benefits if they would be higher. Or, regardless of your husband's age, you can take reduced benefits on your own wage record before age 65. If you do, however, your payment will always be reduced—even if you take reduced benefits on your own record and then take wife's benefits when your husband retires.

■ Try to retain eligibility for Social Security survivors' and disability benefits, even while you're a young mother at home with children. You may be able to keep previous work credits up to date, the Research Institute of America suggests, with relatively little effort. In 1986 only $440 in earnings for the entire year entitled a worker to a quarter of work credit; $400 of net income from self-employment did the same. So if you're tied down at home, any kind of part-time work that produces this much income can help to retain your eligibility for survivors' and disability benefits, as long as you maintain careful records and file the necessary tax returns.

Problems and Solutions

Recently, the Social Security system has been in difficulty as a result of both demographic and economic factors.

On the demographic side, increasing numbers of retirees must have their benefits funded by a decreasing pool of workers. When Social Security began, in 1935, 15 workers paid retirement benefits for each retiree. In the 1980s the ratio reached 3.3 to one. By 2020 or so, when the "baby boom" generation of the 1950s will be ready for retirement, the ratio may be as low as 1.5 to one. If this happens, and if no other changes are made, the level of taxes will be intolerable.

On the economic side, the system's outgo has outdistanced income. With benefits indexed to prices while taxes are indexed to wages, and with prices rising faster than wages, benefits are outpacing the ability of taxation to keep up. By the mid-1980s, without Congressional action, prompt payment of benefits would have become impossible. That's the short-term crunch. The long-term crisis shows up around the year 2012, when the first of the baby-boomers starts to retire. In between, for a period of some fifteen years between 1996 and 2010, the funds should be solvent.

But Congress has taken action, and may yet take further steps. Among the measures which will affect your retirement planning:

- "Normal" retirement age will be raised to age 67. The change will take place gradually and only workers under age 45 in 1983, when the bill was passed, will be affected. The "delayed retirement credits" discussed earlier, currently at 3 percent, will gradually be raised to 8 percent by the year 2008 in order to encourage retirement at a later age. With longer life spans and increased good health in the later years this change, although controversial, makes a good deal of sense.

- Cost-of-living adjustments, which wreaked havoc with the system during the double-digit inflation of the late 1970s, were postponed for six months and then scheduled to take place each January starting in 1984. The delay will keep funds in government coffers and save the system an estimated $39.4 billion by 1989.

- Steeper payroll taxes on working folk will increase revenues. By 1990, if you're still working, you'll be paying 7.65 percent of wages up to an estimated $57,000 (the actual figure will depend on the inflation rate between now and then). The self-employed will be paying the combined employee-employer rate, for a total of 15.3 percent by 1990. Tax credits will soften the blow on the self-employed for the first couple of years, but then full taxation will take effect.

- Taxation of retirement benefits, above a specified minimum level, has been introduced for the first time. Beginning in 1984 up to half of Social Security retirement benefits are subject to tax if your adjusted gross income, including nontaxable income such as interest on municipal bonds, exceeds $25,000 for an individual and $32,000 for a married couple filing jointly. At the outset only a small proportion of Social Security recipients are subject to tax under this provision; by 1990, the American Association of Retired Persons estimates, fully 25 percent of recipients could be paying taxes on part of their Social Security retirement benefits. The problem is that these threshold figures are fixed, not indexed to inflation; normal growth in income over the years will push more retirees over the limit.

These measures, all incorporated in the far-reaching Social Security legislation of 1983, should keep the system solvent. There may (and probably will) be more change in later years, but you should continue to be able to count on Social Security retirement benefits to provide part of your retirement income.

Pension Plans

In 1930 only 15 percent of Americans working in private industry were covered by pension plans. By 1984, according to the American Council of Life Insurance, half of all private employees and three-quarters of government civilian employees had pension coverage other than Social

Security. Pensions are now a fact of American life, part of the fringe benefit package many employees have come to expect.

But all is not rosy on the pension scene. There are frequent tales of woe:

★ Al has followed an ever-upward career track, one that has required a considerable amount of job mobility—out of school and into a two-year management training program, then eight years at another company, followed by two more moves. Now, at 43, he's suddenly realized that he has no pension; he's moved, from a retirement planning standpoint, too much.

★ Margaret returned to the work force at age 34, after her children were all in school, and held a clerical job for the next twenty-eight years. When she was ready to retire—more than ready, in fact—she discovered that her company's plan, together with Social Security, was designed to replace a specific percentage of pre-retirement earnings. Since lower-paid workers receive a higher proportion of income from Social Security, Margaret's pension became proportionately smaller. After all those years of service, her pension totaled $29.12 a month.

★ Harold had every reason to expect a comfortable pension, after working for the same company for thirty-three years. But the company was absorbed by another company and the old pension plan eliminated. Harold was told he would have to work for another ten years to qualify for a pension, and a smaller pension at that.

★ Veronica's husband had long assured her that she would be protected by his pension plan if he died first. Joe did die, just thirteen days before his 55th birthday . . . and that's when Veronica found that the option to elect widow's benefits was presented to employees only when they had reached age 55. Despite Joe's thirty years of employment with the same company, Veronica received nothing.

If you're covered by a pension or profit-sharing plan, it's vitally important to understand its provisions long before you're actually ready to retire. You have to figure out, today, what you can expect to get tomorrow in order to plan your financial future.

Understanding Your Pension Plan

There are a number of important things to find out about your pension coverage:

WHAT TYPE OF PLAN IS IT?

There are two basic types of pension plan:

A **defined benefit** plan, under which most people are covered, either spells out what your pension will be in dollars and cents or specifies the formula which will be used to determine benefits. The company must then make whatever contributions are necessary to fund the designated benefits.

A **defined contribution** plan works the other way around, with either the contributions or the formula for determining them fixed and your future benefits based on the investment return received on the contributions. A profit-sharing plan is a defined contribution plan.

Q. I stopped working in 1971, after twelve years with one company, to become a full-time homemaker. I've heard that there's a law that says I'm entitled to some retirement benefits. Is that true?

A. I'm afraid not. If you had still been working for your company on January 1, 1976, when the Employee Retirement Income Security Act of 1974 took effect, and if your employer had a pension plan, your earlier years of service would have counted toward a pension. As it is, you've almost certainly lost pension credit for the years you worked. Even if you were to go back to that company now, such a lengthy break in service would almost certainly force you to start over again (in terms of pension credits) as a new employee.

WHAT ARE THE ELIGIBILITY REQUIREMENTS?

How old do you have to be, or how long do you have to work for your present employer, in order to qualify for pension benefits? Don't assume that you are covered just because you work for a company with a pension plan. There may be specific requirements for coverage.

If your company has a pension plan, according to the Retirement Equity Act of 1984, employees must be enrolled after attaining age 21 or one year's employment, whichever is later—except that plans with immediate vesting (see below) may require three years of employment. Part-time employees, those working fewer than 1,000 hours a year, may be excluded from coverage.

WHEN DO YOUR PENSION BENEFITS BECOME VESTED?

At what point do you retain the right to some or all of your pension benefits whether or not you keep working for the same employer, are laid off, or are fired?

Before 1974 workers had no protection against the wholesale termination of a plan or against the loss of individual benefits during, for example, an extended layoff. Today, if a company has a pension plan (no legislation requires that your employer offer a pension plan in the first place), it must meet one of three minimum vesting standards:

- 100 percent vesting after ten years on the job.
- 25 percent vesting after five years of service, plus 5 percent for each additional year up to ten years and an additional 10 percent for each year thereafter, with benefits 100 percent vested after fifteen years of service.
- 50 percent vesting when age and length of service totals forty-five years, with a minimum of five years employment, and full vesting five years later. This is also called "rule-of-45" vesting.

Effective January 1, 1985, service after age 18 (instead of age 22) must be counted. In addition, breaks in service of up to five years will not interfere with vesting.

Effective with plan years beginning after December 31, 1988, under provisions of the 1986 tax law, the minimum period for immediate vesting will be five years; an alternative method would establish 20 percent vesting after two years on the job, with another 20 percent in each subsequent year and full vesting after seven years. These provisions will ensure pension coverage to people who change jobs frequently; if you're such an employee, however, bear in mind that the pension you receive will probably be smaller than if you had stayed on at one company.

HOW IS THE AMOUNT OF PENSION CALCULATED?

Is it based on your salary? your years of employment? a combination? How old must you be to collect? What if you want to retire early?

The pension formula may reflect wages in every year of employment, or only those in the last few years before retirement. You'll probably come out ahead with the last-few-years formula, simply because you're likely to be earning more in those later years. The benefit may provide a fixed amount, or it may contain cost-of-living escalators; the latter, of course, is preferable from your point of view. Benefits may start at a fixed retirement age or at one of several optional retirement dates; benefits will vary with the option selected.

Ask about the provisions of your company's plan. How is the benefit calculated? How much can you actually expect to receive? Will it rise with the cost of living? Will it be offset by your Social Security benefits?

Some pension plans are designed to be "integrated" with Social Security, with benefit formulas designed—together with Social Security—to replace a specified percentage of pre-retirement income. When Social Security benefits go up, pension benefits under such plans often go down.

Q. I decided to keep working after 65 and then was stunned to realize that company contributions to my pension stopped at age 65 anyway. Isn't there a law against this?

A. No. In fact, when mandatory retirement at 65 was outlawed in 1978, pension laws were purposely left unchanged. The reason: Congress thought that companies might be encouraged to retain older workers if pension costs would not increase. As a result, however, only about half of the major corporations in one recent survey take into account any years worked or income earned beyond age 65. There's nothing you can do about it, unless your company changes its policy or Congress changes the law.

ARE YOUR PENSION BENEFITS PORTABLE?

Social Security is completely portable; it stays with you wherever you work. By and large, with the exception of some employees covered by union-sponsored pension plans, most private pensions are not portable. If you change jobs, you can and usually do lose the right to accumulated pension benefits.

But you do, under federal legislation, retain a vested right to certain pension benefits after specified periods. Those benefits aren't strictly portable; they don't go with you to your next job and create a cumulative pension. But they are yours, and tax law provides some relief on vested benefits. If you change jobs and if you would otherwise have to pay income tax on a lump-sum payment of the vested pension benefits, you may defer those taxes by immediately investing the lump sum in an Individual Retirement Account or by depositing money in the pension plan at your new company.

WHAT ARE THE PAYMENT OPTIONS?

Does your pension plan protect your dependents? or you alone? Will you automatically receive monthly payments? Or may you elect a single lump-sum payout if you decide to do so?

Protection for Dependents

A pension may be paid in the form of a *life annuity,* with monthly payments made for the lifetime of the retired worker. A pension may also be paid as a *joint and survivor annuity,* with monthly payments made for life to the worker and, at the worker's death, continuing (usually in a reduced amount) for the life of the designated survivor. The worker's benefit may be reduced in order to provide the continuing benefit to the survivor. Where a man might receive $100 a month under a life annuity option, as an example (specific figures will vary), he might receive $91 a month under the joint and survivor form, with the guarantee that his wife (if she survives him) will continue to receive $45.50 a month for the rest of her life.

Under the 1984 legislation, a pension plan offering annuity payments must offer a joint and survivor option, under which a continuing pension benefit of at least 50 percent of the worker's benefit is paid to the survivor when the retired worker dies; this option, furthermore, goes into effect automatically for married employees unless the employee and the spouse both reject it in writing prior to retirement.

Under the 1984 legislation, too, pension administrators must abide by divorce decrees which treat an employee's pension as divisible marital property. A divorced spouse may also begin to receive pension benefits before the employee actually retires.

If a plan offers early-retirement pension benefits, it must also under the Employment Retirement Income Security Act of 1974 (ERISA) offer a *pre-retirement survivor annuity* under which benefits are paid to a surviving spouse even if an employee dies before normal retirement age. These pre-retirement benefits, under the 1984 legislation, are payable to all vested employees. Under this option, the monthly benefits to be received at normal retirement age may be reduced.

Q. I want my son to be my beneficiary under my company pension plan. But I've been told that my husband (we're separated, but not divorced) will get my benefits after my death unless he agrees, in writing, to let them go. What can I do?

A. One of the unfortunate by-products of the Retirement Equity Act of 1984, intended to benefit dependent spouses (usually women), is that both men and women lose some control over their own pensions. If you don't know where your husband is, and can convince your pension plan administrator that you've tried unsuccessfully to find him, you may be allowed to name your son instead. If you can find him, try to get his consent to a waiver; otherwise, he will retain his interest in your pension and will receive the survivor's benefit after your death.

Lump-Sum vs. Monthly Payments

★ When Dora K. retired last year, at age 65, she was earning just over $20,000 a year. She now receives about $6,000 a year in Social Security retirement benefits and another $6,000 a year in monthly checks from her company's pension plan.

★ Anita M. also retired last year. With the same years on the job and about the same pre-retirement income, her Social Security benefits are about the same. So is her pension—or it would be, if she took it in monthly installments. But Anita's employer offered her a choice. Instead of $500 a month in pension, or $6,000 a year, she elected to take $50,000 in a lump-sum distribution.

You may be offered a lump-sum payment at the time of retirement instead of monthly payments for life. Which should you take?

There are advantages and disadvantages to each approach (although the lump sum may make more sense for the highly paid employee). Here's what you should consider:

- What rate of return would you have to earn on your lump sum to give you the monthly payments you would otherwise receive from the pension? Do you have confidence that your investment skills would provide this rate of return, even if interest rates decline?

- A lump-sum distribution is equivalent to your expected lifetime pension, reduced by the amount of interest the company could otherwise expect to earn on the money. What is your company's "discount rate"? You are more likely to come out ahead if the rate is less than current investment yields.

- How long do you expect to live? And will you need your pension to live on? With monthly payments, your income is guaranteed for life no matter how long you live. With a lump-sum payout, you run the risk of losing it all on a bad investment or simply outliving your income. Unless you have other sources of retirement income, therefore, you might be better off with regular monthly payments.

- Does your company make cost-of-living adjustments to pensions? If it does, bear in mind that a lump-sum payment, once taken, is finished; there will be no adjustments. Monthly payments, on the other hand, may be increased to help you cope with rising prices.

- Think about your family. If you take a lump-sum distribution, your survivors will have the money if you die shortly after retirement. If you take a regular pension, you have to elect a joint and survivor option (with its, usually, lower benefits) to insure income for your survivor.

Taxation of Pension Benefits

Monthly pension payments, with the exception of the amounts you contributed, are taxable as received, at ordinary rates of taxation. Taxes are automatically withheld from pension checks (if your pension totals at least $5,400 a year) unless you file a form requesting exemption.

You do not retire from paying income taxes just because you retire from work. If you do not have taxes withheld from pension payments and if you will owe income taxes at the end of the year, then you must make quarterly payments of the tax that will be due. For more information, see IRS Publication No. 575, "Tax Information on Pension and Annuity Income."

Lump-sum distributions are eligible for one-time-only special tax treatment, so that the money you receive in one year can be taxed as if it were averaged over a five-year period. Or all taxes may be deferred until you reach age 70½ if you put the lump-sum payment, within sixty days, into an Individual Retirement Account.

Pension Rights

That all-important ERISA legislation also provides some basic pension rights:

THE RIGHT TO INFORMATION

You are supposed to receive annual statements indicating whether or not you are entitled to a pension and how much that pension would be, at retirement age, if you stopped working now. In addition, as retirement nears, you should receive a detailed statement setting forth the exact dollar amount of:

- A full lifetime pension
- Your pension reduced to provide a survivor's benefit
- The amount of any survivor's benefit

THE RIGHT TO PROTECTION

Although you can lose out if your company goes out of business or discontinues its plan, you'll have some protection if you were covered under the typical defined benefit plan. The Pension Benefit Guaranty Corporation, a federal agency, provides insurance. Some plans, such as those run by church programs or local governments, may be exempt. And amounts are limited; in 1982 the maximum guaranty was $1,381 a month to a beneficiary of a terminated plan, regardless of how much more you would have been entitled to receive under the plan itself.

Q. My husband never wanted me to take a job outside the home. He always said I'd be protected under his pension plan. Now, after twenty-eight years of marriage, we're being divorced. Do I have any of that protection?

A. You very well might. While the 1974 ERISA legislation prohibited assignment of pension benefits by plan administrators, the 1984 Retirement Equity Act specifically recognizes that a pension may be considered marital property. Tell your lawyer to include your husband's pension in negotiations and, depending on the property settlement you reach, you may claim part of the pension or its equivalent value in other property.

Other Retirement Income

In addition to Social Security and on-the-job pension benefits, which together should provide 60 to 65 percent of your pre-retirement income, you can fund some of your own retirement income through an Individual Retirement Account (plus a Keogh Plan if you're self-employed) and an annuity. IRA and Keogh Plans are "qualified" retirement plans, as defined by the Internal Revenue Service, with superior tax benefits. But the amounts that may be contributed to them are limited by law. Annuities, which also provide some tax advantages, may offer you a way to save additional money toward retirement.

Individual Retirement Accounts (IRAs)

Individual Retirement Accounts were authorized by Congress in 1974, to encourage employees who were not covered by any pension plan to save toward their own retirement. Covered employees could not participate. From 1981 through 1986, any wage-earner, regardless of other pension coverage, could open an IRA.

Now the rules have changed again. Only workers without other pension coverage or with incomes below $25,000 as an individual or $40,000 as a married couple may take the full IRA deduction of $2,000 a year. A partial deduction is allowed for single individuals earning between $25,000 and $30,000 a year and for married couples earning between $40,000 and $50,000 a year. People who no longer qualify for full IRA deductions, however, are still permitted to make annual contributions to an IRA; the contribution will not be deductible but interest earned on the IRA will accumulate on a tax-deferred basis until it is withdrawn. Earned income for IRA purposes includes salaries and wages, professional fees, commissions, tips, bonuses, alimony, self-employment income, even income to a retired partner from work-in-process or accounts receivable as of retirement date. Earned income does not include rents, interest, or dividends, or income earned from sources outside the United States.

Two-income couples may set aside $4,000 each year in two separate accounts, as long as each has at least $2,000 in earned income. (If you work part-time, and earn $2,000, you may contribute your entire income to an IRA.) One-income couples may establish a "spousal" IRA, with an annual maximum contribution of $2,250; this account may be divided as you wish, as long as no more than $2,000 is allocated to either spouse.

Q. I'm a homemaker, with no outside income. My husband has established a spousal IRA, with contributions in my name, but now we're divorcing. What happens to my retirement benefits from that IRA?

A. Your retirement benefits are still your retirement benefits. In addition, your husband's IRA (like a pension) is marital property subject to distribution in divorce. If it is transferred to you, it won't be taxable even if you're under 59½. Once it is transferred, however, all IRA rules apply.

Contributions made to an IRA, if you meet the requirements, are tax-deductible. If you put $2,000 into an IRA and are in the 28 percent bracket, you save $560 in taxes; thus the net cost of the IRA is actually $1,440. The earnings also grow on a tax-deferred basis. If you put $2,000 a year into an IRA yielding a consistent 9 percent, compounded annually, after thirty years you would have $297,150. If you invested the after-tax remainder of the same $2,000 in a taxable investment with the same yield over the same period, and you were in a 25 percent tax bracket, you would wind up with $144,620. Table 6 illustrates what happens at different tax brackets.

TABLE 6: Taxable accumulations, at various tax brackets, compared with tax-free accumulations under an IRA.

	25% Tax bracket	40% Tax bracket	50% Tax bracket	IRA
Amount available to invest	$2,000	$2,000	$2,000	$2,000
Tax	500	800	1,000	-0-
Amount available after taxes	1,500	1,200	1,000	2,000
Earnings rate after tax	6.75%	5.4%	4.5%	9%
Amount at the end of 30 years	$144,620	$90,039	$63,752	$297,150

(Source: E. F. Hutton)

There are some disadvantages: If you dip into your IRA account before you reach age 59½ (unless you're totally disabled), you will lose the tax deferment on the amount withdrawn, which will then be taxed as ordinary income, and you will pay a penalty tax of 10 percent. You also must start withdrawing your money by the time you are 70½, whether or not you are still working.

Should you open an IRA? Yes. Even with these restrictions, an IRA is one of the best tax-sheltered investments that a middle-income person can have. It should, without question, be included in your plans for retirement.

Should you open an IRA if you can't afford $2,000 a year? Yes. You'll have more money for retirement if you can save more money now, while you're working. And you'll have more if you can put the maximum allowed by law into the tax-deferred vehicle of an IRA. But you'll still come out ahead with smaller contributions.

Should you open an IRA if you're still in your twenties? Yes. You may think retirement is too far away. You may think you'll need the money and be unable to get it. But you'll have a lot more money when you do retire if you start it compounding early. And if you leave the money on deposit even a few years before you have to touch it (assuming that you may need to do so), you'll still come out ahead.

Should you open an IRA if you're now close to retirement age? Yes. While you will end up with a lot more money if you start earlier, it still makes sense to start an IRA at 50 or 55 or even 65. If you are now age 55 and you put away $2,000 a year until you are 70 years old, your total investment will amount to $30,000. At 9 percent interest, however, you'll have $64,007 waiting for you at the end of the fifteen years. At age 60 your ten years of investing will add up to $20,000, and you'll have $33,120 at age 70. And if you start at age 65, with just five years to go, the $10,000 you invest will grow to $13,047. Remember, too, that when you begin to make your withdrawals, at age 60 or at age 70, the remainder of your account continues to earn interest and to grow.

Q. Together, my spouse and I earn $55,000. Only one of us is covered by a pension plan at work. Can the other open an IRA?

A. Sorry, no. The way the 1986 tax act is drafted, it appears that Congress intended that joint filers, whether they have one or two pension plans between them, are forbidden from opening an IRA for the noncovered spouse and making deductible contributions.

WHERE TO INVEST YOUR IRA FUNDS

There are a bewildering array of choices available for IRA investment. Before you decide on any specific investment, look at several factors:

■ How much risk can you afford to take? If you have other retirement income, from a company pension and/or other investments, you may choose to put your IRA funds into a risky but potentially profitable investment. If not, it's best to be conservative.

■ How much risk can you tolerate? Whether or not you can afford risk doesn't have anything to do with whether you can sleep comfortably at night. Make your IRA investment, as you make all investments, in accordance with both your pocketbook and your temperament.

■ How old are you? If you have many years before retirement, you can look to capital appreciation. If you're very close to retirement age, however, capital preservation may be more important.

■ Do you want to manage your investments yourself? And are you willing to pay fees and commissions for the privilege?

With all this in mind, and remembering that you can divide your IRA contributions among more than one account, look at these possibilities:

Financial institutions (banks, savings and loans, and credit unions) offer time deposits of varying lengths, with either fixed or variable interest rates. When interest rates are high (and if you think they're unlikely to go higher) you might consider locking in your return by using one of the longer-term accounts. But shop around. Rates and compounding intervals vary. To compare actual yields: Narrow your choices, then ask each institution to tell you how much you will earn in one year on $1,000.

The advantages of using a financial institution are convenience (there's a bank or thrift on almost every corner; your credit union, if you have one, is probably at your place of work), low cost (there are few, if any, fees), and security (accounts of up to $100,000 are insured by an agency of the federal government).

Note: If you maintain it in the same institution to compound for thirty or more years, your IRA could grow to considerably more than $100,000. If insurance is important to you, think about opening later accounts in different institutions.

There are disadvantages as well. Rates may not be as high as interest rates elsewhere. And if you need your money or want to switch it to another account after putting it into a time deposit, you'll face loss of interest and other penalties. Be very careful, in fact, before signing any time deposit form. With some institutions, you may not be allowed to withdraw your funds early even if you're willing to pay the penalty.

Mutual funds are the choice of increasing numbers of investors. With a mutual fund, opened through a brokerage firm or by mail, you can invest your IRA dollars in just about anything: stocks, bonds, Treasury issues, even (via a money market mutual fund) money itself. With a "family" of funds, in fact (see p. 109), you can switch your IRA funds, without penalty and often without cost, to meet your own changing needs and the changing investment climate. When interest rates are high, you can keep your funds in a money market mutual fund. When rates start to drop, you can look at an income fund. If capital growth becomes your primary aim, look at stock funds.

Advantages: If you choose a "no-load" fund, one without an upfront commission to an independent salesman, all of your contribution will go directly to building your own retirement income. Maintenance fees are low, typically $5 to $10 a year. Disadvantages: You can't lock in a high yield with a mutual fund as you can with a financial institution. And mutual funds are generally not insured, although you can, if you're worried, select a fund that invests solely in U.S. government obligations.

Insurance companies are attracting a share of the IRA market with new annuity products, with rates of return pegged to current interest rates. Advantages are relatively low fees, safety, and relatively high rates of return. Disadvantages are that the high rate of return is not guaranteed (rates may fall as low as 3 or 4 percent), and surrender charges are usually imposed if you terminate your account before a specified time. Moreover, the earnings in an annuity are already tax-deferred. Why put them into a tax shelter such as an IRA? If you want an annuity to augment your retirement income (see pp. 570–72), buy one separately.

Self-directed accounts allow you to manage your own investments. You can buy and sell stocks or bonds; you can invest in real estate or in oil wells or in equipment leasing. But you will pay both a start-up fee and an annual maintenance fee for a self-directed account at a brokerage house, plus brokerage commissions every time you buy or sell.

Advantage: potentially significant gains from capital appreciation. Disadvantages: potential loss, no guarantees and no insurance, relatively high fees.

Q. My employer is offering a "salary reduction" plan as a way of saving for retirement. Should I participate?

A. A salary reduction plan can be a very good thing, if you can afford to defer receipt of some of your salary. It works like this:

A percentage of your salary is set aside as an investment in your future; your employer may match all or part of your contribution. The amount you contribute is not included in your gross income, so you do not pay any income tax on it. You also don't pay Social Security tax on this amount. In addition, investment earnings accumulate without being taxed. Then, if you take the money in a lump sum at retirement, it qualifies for special income averaging over a five-year-period; money withdrawn form an IRA at retirement, by contrast, is taxed as regular income.

IRA STRATEGIES

Whether you choose professional management or your own self-directed account, there are ways to make the most of an IRA investment. Here are some hints:

- You may open as many IRAs as you like, as long as your total contribution for any calendar year does not exceed the maximum then set by law. This means that you may open different types of accounts to achieve different investment objectives. You might put part of your annual contribution into an insured deposit in a financial institution, for instance, and part into a growth-oriented mutual fund.

- You may borrow to invest in an Individual Retirement Account, and it may be worthwhile to do so and reap the tax advantages. Just be sure to do some careful arithmetic first, comparing borrowing costs and your tax-sheltered return.

- Don't forget that administrative fees connected with opening an IRA are tax-deductible if you itemize your deductions on your federal return.

- IRA contributions are, as noted, tax-deductible. You can adjust your taxes when you file your return—or you can reduce your taxes at the beginning of the year by filing an amended W-4 form with your employer. Two extra exemptions should reduce your withholding to approximately the right level.

- Stay out of tax-free investments. While you are permitted to put your IRA contributions into municipal bonds or other tax-exempts, it does not make sense to do so. As the Internal Revenue Service has noted, income from an IRA is taxable upon withdrawal and you would actually be turning a tax-free investment into a taxable one.

- Look at specialized investments. Zero-coupon bonds, for example (described on p. 121), are particularly suitable for retirement plans and not for ordinary investing. Why? Because you receive no interest but are taxed, outside an IRA, as if you do.

- You may switch your money from one IRA to another as many times as you like, as long as you don't actually take possession of the funds. This provision makes it possible to modify your investments in tune with a changing investment climate. You may also, thanks to the 1982 tax law, roll over part of the account and pay tax and penalties solely on the part you keep.

- You may also actually get your hands on your money, and use it for any purpose you like, as long as you do so no more than once a year and as long as you keep the money in your possession no more than sixty days. This makes it possible to use your IRA funds, without penalty, on a short-term basis.

- If you're locked into an old low-yielding certificate of deposit, and don't want to take the penalty for withdrawal, you have another option: Withdraw the accumulated interest—there's no penalty as long as you don't invade the principal—and use it to open a higher-yielding account for your IRA. Once you do so, you can also instruct the bank to deposit future interest on your old certificate to the new account.

- If you're in your late fifties when you open your IRA, compare institutional regulations carefully. There are no federal tax penalties for withdrawing your IRA money after age 59½, but some financial institutions have their own penalties for withdrawing funds before a stated maturity date. Banks are permitted to waive penalties if you're over 59½, but they are not required to do so. Find out your bank's policy before you commit your funds.

- If your employer offers an IRA through payroll deduction, consider the pros and cons before you enroll. On the plus side is sheer convenience. There is also an element of forced saving, which you may appreciate if you would otherwise find it difficult to put money aside for retirement.

On the other hand, you'll save far more if you can manage to put $2,000 into your IRA at the beginning of each year. While it's better to contribute monthly to an IRA than not at all, it's better still to get your money working early.

■ Upon your death, the money in your Individual Retirement Account goes to your named beneficiary. The money may be taken in a lump sum, or withdrawn over a period of no more than sixty months, unless you've already started to receive periodic distributions, which your beneficiary may then continue. The money is included in your estate for estate tax purposes, and the beneficiary will have to pay ordinary income tax on the money as received. Or, if the beneficiary is your spouse, he or she can roll over the IRA into his or her own IRA, prolonging the tax-free compounding. The annual ceiling on contributions does not apply in this instance. It also does not apply if you transfer your own accumulated pension benefits into an IRA.

Q. I opened an Individual Retirement Account early this year with $2,000 and now I need the money. I know I can't take it out yet, but can I borrow on it?

A. No, not without penalties. Any portion of your IRA used as security for a loan will be treated—and taxed—as current income. In addition, if you are under 59½ and not disabled, you'll have to pay a 10 percent penalty just as you would for early withdrawal. The penalties are not too bad when compared with the tax-deferred interest earned in an IRA over a period of several years. In your case, since your IRA is so new, you will lose out. See if you can find a less costly source of funds before you borrow against your IRA. Or use the IRA, without penalty, by returning the money within sixty days.

WHEN YOU RETIRE

You may start withdrawing money from your IRA, without penalty, at any time after age 59½. Or you may leave it untouched until age 70½, when you must start to withdraw. This is when you must make a choice: Take the money in a lump sum? Or withdraw it in installments, over a period of years?

Deductible IRA withdrawals, remember, are taxed as ordinary income when they are received. (Nondeductible contributions will be merged and a proportionate share will be taxable.) Don't take a lump sum, therefore, unless you really need the cash.

If you elect to receive the money in installments, you will have to comply with IRS tables on life expectancy; otherwise you'll face a significant penalty. The institution where you have your funds can provide you with the tables you'll need. You can base your IRA withdrawals on your own life expectancy or on joint life expectancy for you and your beneficiary. And you may recalculate your withdrawals each year, so that you won't outlive your IRA.

Remember: Your IRA account can continue to grow even while you make withdrawals. If you start your account at age 40, depositing $2,000 a year for twenty-five years, you'll have put in $50,000 of your own money. At age 65, after compounding at 9 percent, the account is worth $184,648 . . . an amount which gives an annual retirement income for fifteen years of $21,016. This is much more than $184,648 divided by 15, which would be $12,310. The reason: continued compounding of the balance left in the account. Table 7 indicates how much you can withdraw each year, starting at age 65, from IRA accounts of different sizes.

TABLE 7: Annual retirement income from an IRA.

Age IRA was started	Your total deposit	At age 65 grows to	Gives annual retirement income over 15 years of
25	$80,000	$736,584	$83,835
35	60,000	297,150	33,820
40	50,000	184,648	21,016
55	20,000	33,121	3,770

If you start an IRA at the age shown, contribute $2,000 at the beginning of each year, and the account earns 9 percent compound interest, you will accumulate the amounts shown and be able to withdraw the amounts shown.
(Source: American Council of Life Insurance)

Keogh Plans

Keogh Plans have major advantages for the self-employed. Contributions, up to $30,000 a year are deductible. Earnings, like those in an Individual Retirement Account, grow on a tax-deferred basis; accumulations are not subject to income tax until they are withdrawn. Again, as in an IRA, there are withdrawal penalties before age 59½ (unless you die or become disabled), and money must start to be withdrawn by age 70½.

THINGS YOU SHOULD KNOW

- Contributions to a Keogh must be made from earned income; "unearned" income, such as stock dividends, may not be the basis of a contribution.

- If you have any employees, you must include in your Keogh Plan those who work for you full-time, are at least age 21, and have been with the company for at least one year.

- Most Keogh Plans are "defined contribution" plans, under which contributions are based on a percentage of net income; you can decrease or skip your contribution when business isn't good. Another type of Keogh is the "defined benefit" plan under which you establish a benefit goal for yourself and make contributions accordingly; you may be able to contribute a larger percentage of income to a defined benefit plan, but you may also have to make contributions each and every year.

- Defined contribution plans are either "money-purchase" or "profit-sharing" plans. You may contribute up to 25 percent of your net income to a money-purchase plan or up to 15 percent to a profit-sharing plan. Or you may have a combined plan. Whatever your choice, under new rules net earnings must be reduced by your contribution before the contribution is made, effectively reducing the amount to 20 or 13.4 percent.

- You are allowed to contribute to a Keogh as long as you have income from self-employment, even after age 70½. You'll have to withdraw some money at that point, but you can make contributions as well. (An IRA, on the other hand, forbids contributions after age 70½.)

  Q. I'm in business as a writer, preparing advertising brochures and company reports as well as an occasional magazine article. I never know just how much my income will be. How can I make a contribution to my Keogh Plan before the year is over?

  A. You don't have to. As long as your plan is opened before the end of the year, you can make your contribution up to the time you file your income tax return for that year—April 15 or, if you get an automatic extension, August 15. You'll earn more interest, however, if you start your money compounding earlier in the year. Why don't you do this: Make a basic contribution early in the year, figured on the minimum you expect to earn; then add to it as you get a clear picture of your income toward the end of the year, with a final contribution once the year is done. Just be careful not to contribute too much, or you'll face penalties.

- If you take a salaried job after setting up a Keogh on the basis of being self-employed, you can no longer make contributions (unless, of course, you continue to have some self-employment income). But you can leave your plan in place, accumulating earned interest, until you are ready for retirement. You should leave it at least until age 59½ or you will have to pay the penalties.

- You may open a Keogh Plan in any of the vehicles described in the section on Individual Retirement Accounts. You may also switch your plan from one vehicle to another, as long as the institutions transfer the money directly and it does not pass through your hands.

■ When you reach age 70½, you must decide whether to take the money in a lump sum or in installments. If the lump-sum option is selected, five-year income averaging may be used as long as you've had your plan in effect for five years; if you take the money in installments, regular tax rates apply. This may make it worthwhile to take a lump-sum distribution from your Keogh Plan earlier, at age 59½, because then you can continue making contributions and building your retirement fund while you continue to be self-employed.

Annuities

Simply put, an annuity provides a guaranteed lifetime income. You can outlive the proceeds of your investments. You can't outlive an annuity.

You can buy an annuity to provide extra retirement income over and above your Individual Retirement Account. You can also buy an annuity with the proceeds of an IRA or of a company pension plan. You can buy an annuity with as little as $1,000, but annuities make more sense as supplemental retirement income for people who can invest considerably more. If you come into a sizable amount of money, through an inheritance or selling a business or some other windfall, you might consider purchasing an annuity.

HOW ANNUITIES WORK

■ An annuity may be *immediate,* in which case it starts as soon as you pay the premium, or *deferred,* starting at a designated later date.

■ The premium may be a single lump-sum payment, either cash out of your pocket or a rollover from an IRA or pension plan, or it may be made in periodic installments. Installment annuities are always deferred annuities, but it is single-premium deferred annuities that have received the most attention in recent years.

■ Earned interest accumulates tax-free throughout the deferral period. Payments are taxed, as you receive them, to the extent that they exceed your contribution.

■ The annuity itself may be *fixed,* providing a fixed income for life, or *variable,* with payouts above a guaranteed minimum level depending on investment return. The variable annuity may offer you a choice of investment vehicles.

■ Payout may be in one of several forms. *Straight life* provides payments to you for your lifetime. A *refund* annuity pays somewhat less than straight life because it provides for payment of at least the amount paid in premiums, regardless of when the annuitant dies; any refund will be made to the beneficiary in a lump sum or in installments. A *joint and survivor* annuity provides payments for as long as either you or your designated survivor lives. And a *certain period* annuity makes payments for life, with a guaranteed minimum number of years. For example: Larry, age 50, buys a single-premium deferred annuity with a maturity date timed for retirement at 65. Assuming that the $10,000 accumulates at 10 percent for the next fifteen years, Larry could choose:

—a lump-sum distribution of $41,772,

—a life annuity of $520 a month for life,

—a ten-year certain annuity of $490 a month,

—a refund annuity of $502 a month,

—a joint and survivor annuity, with the full amount continuing to his named beneficiary, of $390 a month, or

—a joint and survivor annuity, with 50 percent of his benefit going to his beneficiary, of $441 a month.

(These figures, provided by the American Council of Life Insurance, are based on Larry and his wife reaching age 65 together and the assumption that she, in accordance with average mortality tables, will live longer. Precise benefits from any annuity are always based on the specific age of the annuitant.)

SHOULD YOU BUY AN ANNUITY?

Annuities have long been conservative investments, with high up-front costs and low rate of return. If this were still true, annuities would not, under any circumstances, be a good investment in an inflationary period. But annuities have changed.

The rate of return on annuities is now often pegged to market rates. Formerly formidable front-end fees have been reduced or eliminated by many companies—although there may be penalties, instead, for withdrawal before a specified time.

An annuity can be viewed as an investment. But it is designed as a guaranteed income during retirement. The 1982 tax law reinforced this long-term view of annuities by providing that early withdrawals are both fully taxable and subject to tax penalty.

Think about buying an annuity, therefore, if:

■ You have a few thousand dollars to put aside as supplementary retirement income, and you'll leave the money in place until you do retire.

- You are in a tax bracket where you will benefit from the tax-free accumulation of funds.

- You want to be sure that you can't outlive your income.

COMPARE ANNUITIES BEFORE YOU BUY

Annuities are sold with many different features. Here's what to find out before you buy:

- What is the current interest rate, how often does it change, and by what index does it change? Will a currently high interest rate be in effect for five years? or just for the next few months?

- What is the minimum interest rate guaranteed in the contract? This rate may be as low as 3.5 or 4 percent.

- Is there a "bailout option" that permits you to cash in the annuity, without withdrawal penalties (there may be tax penalties), if the interest rate drops below a specified figure? That figure is usually below the current market rate but well above the guaranteed contract minimum.

- What penalties are there for early liquidation? Regardless of bailout privileges, there may be graduated penalties over a period of years. You might, for example, be penalized by 7 percent of the principal withdrawn during the first year, 6 percent in the second year, and so on, until the penalty disappears. You might, with other companies, face a constant never-ending penalty of 6 to 7 percent.

- Are there front-end load charges? And, if so, how much will they reduce the amount of money that is going to work for you? Many companies have dropped front-end charges, but some still have them. Be sure to ask.

- Are there annual administrative fees, either at a flat rate or at a percentage of the principal amount? Find out before you buy.

- How much of the cash value can you take as a loan? How long must the annuity have been in force before any loan can be made? And what is the rate of interest you will be charged? (Remember: New IRS rules will treat a loan against an annuity as a withdrawal; you may be subject to both tax and penalty.)

- What will you get for your money? The rates of payout vary considerably from company to company. Ask what rate is current . . . and what rate is guaranteed.

Adding to Retirement Income

Will your Social Security, your pension, an Individual Retirement Account, and, perhaps, an annuity be enough when combined with your savings and investments to ensure a comfortable retirement? If not, or if you'd like to do still better, now is the time to take the necessary steps. Whether you are 40 and still paying for college tuition or 60 and thinking seriously about retirement, right now is the time to get started.

You can increase your post-retirement income by reducing spending, investing the resulting surplus, taking a second job, and making productive use of property you already own. Here's how:

REDUCE SPENDING

This suggestion may appear all too obvious. But cutting back on spending well before you retire does two things: It permits you to adjust, both financially and psychologically, to a reduced budget, and it frees money, while you're still working, for investments that will augment your retirement income.

Your pre-retirement budget estimates are designed to pave the way for an easy retirement. But estimates may well have to be changed in the clear daylight of actual retirement. One way to come as close as possible in your preliminary estimates is to practice. That's right: Practice being retired. Use weekends and vacation time to rehearse your retirement living style. Here's what the Hendersons did on one two-week vacation: Instead of taking the opportunity to stay at a resort hotel, they rented a cottage. There, they lived within their planned retirement budget. They ate out, but occasionally instead of every day, and at lunch, when menu prices are often lower, rather than at dinner. They went to the movies, but they also sought free and low-priced entertainment: a musical production at the local high school, a flea market, beachcombing and long strolls along the water. They found, in fact, that they restricted themselves too much; the budget allowed room for some extras.

When you're within a few years of your planned retirement, start phasing down all your living expenses to fit within your projected retirement income. Keep track, if you haven't done so earlier, of all your "optional" spending, the money you may spend on impulse or not-really-necessary purchases of everything from candy bars to garden equipment and personal clothing. Once you keep track of such expenditures, you can begin to see what really gives you pleasure and what does not. Would you rather, if you must make a choice, buy workshop equipment or build a vacation fund?

As you reduce your spending, do so slowly, until you reach a level that you think will be comfortable after retirement. If you can't pinpoint your post-retirement income, then work toward a level of two-thirds to three-quarters of pre-retirement spending. But do so slowly. The whole point of this exercise is that a gradual cutback won't hurt; a drastic post-retirement change in life-style can hurt a great deal.

INVEST FOR EXTRA INCOME

While you are busy reducing outgo, in this retirement rehearsal, you're also still working and still earning money. Invest the surplus you'll gain by cutting back, and you'll have more income-producing capital when you actually retire. If you set a specific goal, of whatever amount you need to supplement your other retirement income, you can work toward it in the years before retirement. For example: Mike is ten years from retirement and wants to accumulate an additional $50,000. He assumes a yield of 8 percent on his savings. He will reach his goal by saving $273 a month for ten years. Table 8 shows how much you would have to save each month, at 8 percent, to achieve various nest-egg goals.

TABLE 8: Monthly deposit required to produce a given balance in a given number of years in an account yielding 8 percent.

Number of years	AMOUNT TO BE SAVED			
	$25,000	$50,000	$75,000	$100,000
10	$137	$273	$410	$547
15	72	144	217	289
20	42	85	127	170
25	26	53	79	105

(Source: United States League of Savings Institutions)

Note: There's no reason not to dip into capital after retirement—as long as you do your calculations carefully. Look at your life expectancy, double it to be on the safe side, and consult Table 9 to get an idea how much money you can withdraw for how long on a regular basis to supple-

---

TABLE 9: Monthly withdrawals possible for a given number of years from an account of given size yielding 10 percent.

Number of years	BEGINNING BALANCE			
	$25,000	$50,000	$75,000	$100,000
10	$330	$661	$991	$1,322
15	269	537	806	1,075
20	241	483	724	965
25	227	454	682	909
Unlimited (interest only each month)	208	417	625	833

(Source: United States League of Savings Institutions)

ment your other income from other sources. If Mike's $50,000 nest egg is accumulating at 10 percent, and he wants it to last for twenty years, he could withdraw $483 a month. If he wants to keep the principal intact and withdraw only the interest, he would have to limit withdrawals to $417 a month.

TAKE A SECOND JOB

Another job can bring in additional income. Just be sure, if you take a second job before retirement, that it's not costing you more in travel costs and extra income taxes than it is producing. Many people find it preferable to move into a second job after retirement, when taxable income is down. Don't sell yourself short. You can look in your own field for a post-retirement job. You can also look beyond it, to something you've enjoyed as an avocation throughout your working life. An avid gardener, for instance, might find employment in a nursery, with a landscape gardener, or as a teacher of hobbyists.

Note: You can earn several thousand dollars a year ($7,800, in 1986, for people 65 to 69, and rising each year) without affecting your Social Security payments.

LOOK TO INCOME-PRODUCING PROPERTY YOU MAY OWN

If you have a country cottage, for example, and use it just part of a year, think about renting it out in other months. Your summer hideaway may make good September-to-June rental housing for nearby college students. Or if you're not using your trailer or recreational vehicle on a regular basis, think about renting it out to add to your spending money.

Be resourceful as you plan your retirement and you'll develop other income-producing ideas of your own.

Pulling It All Together

You've spent a lifetime earning, spending, and investing your money. Once you retire you may or may not continue to earn. But you will continue to spend, and you should, if at all possible, continue to invest. Here are some of the areas you should consider:

Investments

As a young adult, with few responsibilities, you could take investment risks as you looked to capital growth. With family responsibilities building up in the middle years, there were probably fewer dollars to invest; those there were had to be conservatively invested. With the diminishing responsibilities and increased income of the years after children left the nest, it was time for solid capital appreciation. Now, with the retirement years, secure income may be the most important goal.

If you invested independently, you've adjusted your portfolio to meet these shifting needs. You probably moved from speculative securities to investing in the stock of solid established companies to a quest for tax-free income. Now, as income becomes more important, bonds may look more attractive. If you invest via mutual funds, you can make the same sort of transition, moving from a basic money market mutual fund (a good place to accumulate your investment nest egg) to a combination of money market fund plus common stock fund. You can add a tax-free fund as sheltering income from taxes becomes important. And you can shift to a bond fund when retirement income is the top priority.

The important thing, always, is to pay attention. Don't make an investment, even in a bank account, and then forget it. Review your investments, at regular intervals, and change them as appropriate to meet your changing life-style as well as a changing economic scene.

Insurance

You've probably carried life insurance over the years to protect your family. Once your children are grown and your other assets are sizable, you may not feel life insurance is necessary. Remember, though, that your pension will either come to an end at your death or, if you've elected the joint and survivor option, be sharply reduced. Your own Social Security will also stop and your surviving dependents will receive a curtailed benefit. You may, therefore, want to keep enough life insurance in force to provide a cushion for your spouse. But don't keep excess amounts. And review the possibility of reducing coverage or converting to paid-up protection; you may save substantial amounts in premiums.

If you keep any life insurance in force, be sure that the application of dividends, the beneficiary designation, and the settlement options are in line with your current wishes.

Credit

If you've somehow reached retirement age without establishing a credit rating, do so at once, before you retire. It may be very handy to have, and it may be very difficult to establish once you no longer have a regular income.

If you're a woman who has had credit only in tandem with her husband, take steps, right now, to establish your own credit identity. All you have to do is write to credit issuers and request that the record of payment on the cards you hold jointly be reported in both your names.

The Equal Credit Opportunity Act then ensures that you will have a credit identity, but it won't happen unless you first make the request.

Remember: Credit discrimination because of age is illegal, but some of the conditions that go along with age, such as reduced income, may make it difficult to secure credit for the first time.

Housing

★ Elinor and Hal sold their upstate New York home when Hal retired, and moved to an adult community on Florida's gulf coast. The climate was warm, the people friendly, the community pleasant. But the pull of family and of old friends was too strong. Within a year they made the expensive move back to New York.

★ The Martins looked forward to retirement and the opportunity to move to the community where their only daughter lived. They did move, and within six months, their daughter's husband changed jobs and moved his family to another state. The Martins could not afford to move again. They had to stay where they were and, somehow, make new friends and put down new roots.

★ Mary and George, unlike the others, have no wanderlust. They'd like nothing better than to stay right where they are . . . except that the house is too large and hard to maintain. They may, after a while, have to think about moving.

There are a lot of reasons for pulling up stakes in retirement, and a lot of reasons for staying put. If you're thinking about moving, be sure to consider every side of the question:

■ Your old house may be big and expensive to heat. But will you save any money, in an era of high home prices, by moving to a smaller house? by taking on a mortgage?

■ Remember that moving itself costs money. The movers themselves are only the initial cost. You must also consider closing costs and landscaping if you buy, appliances and furniture and window hangings even if you don't. Some of your furniture may fit; a lot of it simply won't.

■ Consider *all* the alternatives, as outlined in Chapters 11 to 17: a private house, a rental apartment, a cooperative apartment, a condominium, a mobile home. All have their good points, and their not-so-good. You have to decide what's best for you.

■ Retirement or "adult" communities deserve a word to themselves. You may be attracted to a peaceful enclave, where maintenance is provided, where a pool of potential friends of your generation awaits. Just be sure, before you make such a move, that you (1) appreciate age stratification,

(2) like the planned social activities that often go along with community living (and that you pick a community with the level of activity you prefer), and (3) that the finances will work out as planned (review the developer's credentials, and talk to residents before you make a decision).

■ Most retirees remain independent, but moving in with children may be an option that presents itself in later years. Again, think carefully before you do. Sort out the emotional implications: Will you be able to refrain from interfering in their lives? and they in yours? Will you each have privacy? And be sure to spell out the financial considerations: Will you contribute to the running of the household? Will you, in fact, help your children to buy their home? If you do, for example, provide the down payment while they take care of monthly payments, what will happen if they run into financial difficulty? Will you have to bail them out? What happens if a job change necessitates a move? Try to anticipate every eventuality, and set the ground rules, before you move in. And try, as hard as it may be, to be objective about money with your children; it's the only way house-sharing can work.

■ If you do want to remain in your own home, but finances are a problem, consider the possibilities outlined earlier in this book: You may be able to tap the equity in your house via a mortgage loan; you may want to find someone to share the house, and its costs, with you; you may find a reverse annuity mortgage or equity sharing with an outside investor your best solution. Talk to your lawyer, your banker, a real estate broker, and local community agencies before you decide you can no longer afford to remain in the home you love.

■ If you decide to move, look at all the variables: the cost of living, the presence or absence of state and local income taxes, the level of property taxes, and the range of state estate and inheritance taxes. Find out about any tax breaks to which you may be entitled, and include them in the equation as well.

■ If you decide to move, after considering all the facts, try to keep your options open. Retain ownership and rent out your current home, if you can, while you move to the new community. Then, if the move doesn't work out for any reason at all, you'll have an open door to return. Don't be in a hurry to buy in your new community, for the same reason; flexibility is important, until you're sure the move is right for you.

Suggestion: Before you do anything, try swapping homes with someone in the community you're considering. A stay of a few months, even a few weeks, will tell you a lot more about a community than a brief stay in a hotel, and it won't be nearly as expensive. You can arrange a swap through several agencies devoted to that purpose; one well-known agency is the Vacation Exchange Club, 12006 111 Avenue, Suite 12, Youngtown, Arizona 85363.

LOOK AHEAD TO RETIREMENT

- Project your retirement budget by first figuring out how much money you will need and then figuring out how much you will have. Don't forget to include an inflation factor in your estimates, and to redo your estimates at regular intervals as you get closer to retirement.

- File Form SSA 7004 with the Social Security Administration every three to four years to be sure that your Social Security contributions are accurately recorded. When you are within a few years of retirement, ask Social Security for an estimate of the benefits you will receive. Make an actual application for benefits several months before you plan to retire.

- Ask your company personnel office for details of your company pension plan. Be sure you understand when you will be vested and entitled to benefits under the plan. Find out what the payment options are and select the one most appropriate for you; discuss your decision with your spouse.

- Open an Individual Retirement Account, if you're eligible, and set aside tax-sheltered money for your own retirement. If you're self-employed, use a Keogh Plan instead.

- Think about purchasing an annuity if you believe that it fits into your retirement income objectives. Compare provisions carefully, however, before you buy.

- Augment your retirement income by reducing spending and investing the surplus, by considering a second job, and by making the most of all the assets you have.

- Review your investments, insurance, credit rating, and housing situation. Now is the time to pull all the strands of your lifetime financial plan together. Now is the time to make the most of all that you have.

26

Inflation, Recession, and You

Our spending habits are shaped by our financial know-how, by individual temperament, and by our stage of life; they are also shaped by the economic climate in which we live.

You don't have to be an economist to recognize the economic turbulence of recent years. After the post–World War II decades of economic well-being, inflation began to soar. By the end of the 1970s, Americans had almost become accustomed to double-digit inflation. Savings began to drop as prices rose, which led to some forecasts of doom (because savings provide investment money for a society's capital growth), but as long as individual incomes rose more or less in tandem with inflation, ordinary people did not seem too upset.

In fact, however, real family income did not continue to rise. The 1980 Census revealed that while real family income, excluding the effects of inflation, rose rapidly from 1960 to 1970, it was virtually unchanged from 1970 to 1980. The median family income (half of all families have income above the median and half below), adjusted for inflation, was $15,637 in 1960, $20,939 in 1970, and $21,023 in 1980. Progress, for most people, came to a halt. At the same time, with more two-income families, more families are in higher income brackets than ever before.

In 1981, at last, the inflation rate fell sharply. The Consumer Price Index (described in Appendix A), which had registered double-digit price increases for a couple of years, dipped to 8.9 percent for 1981 and 3.9 percent in 1982. That's not *deflation*, which economists describe as a dropping of prices. Instead it's *disinflation*, defined as a period in which prices rise but not nearly as quickly as they were rising. In fact, prices went up less in 1981 than in any year since 1977. Some prices, notably in the food department (sugar, coffee, chicken . . .), actually went down.

The Economy and You

What does it all mean? What does it matter, to you, personally, if we are having an inflation, a deflation, a disinflation, a recession, or, heaven forbid, a depression? (A recession has been defined, flippantly, as when your neighbor is out of work; a depression as when you yourself are out of work. A depression involves more of the population for a longer period of time than a recession. Unemployment figures are higher, people are hungrier. . . .) The meaning comes through in both psychological and practical terms.

THE PSYCHOLOGY OF INFLATION

We've grown so accustomed to rapid inflation in the last few years that we expect it to continue. Inflation, in short, has become a fact of life. When the *New York Times* conducted a survey in June 1982, it found most Americans rejecting the fact that the rate of inflation had slowed. Although *statistics* indicated a sharp decline in rising prices, *people* believed that prices were rising just as rapidly as ever.

We also tend to act on our beliefs. If we think that prices are still rising rapidly while the dollar is losing its value, then we'll think in terms of going into debt to pay off the debt with cheaper dollars. If we're convinced that homeownership is the best buffer against inflation, then we'll do almost anything to buy a house. Such actions may be dangerous, if we look more closely at what is actually happening.

THE PRACTICAL EFFECT OF DISINFLATION

Inflation has been "Public Enemy Number One" for so long that it's hard to realize that we've actually grown accustomed to living with it. But we have. In the last decade we've changed our patterns of both saving and spending to suit inflationary times. When times change, we have to adjust, or we have a problem.

Here's what can happen:

- You took on a big mortgage in the perfectly reasonable expectation, after years of merit plus cost-of-living raises, that your income would continue to grow. Now your income is not growing as fast as you expected (it may not be growing at all even if you're still doing well at the same job you've held for years, because hard-hit companies are reducing raises, freezing salaries, sometimes cutting wages as well), but those mortgage payments won't go away.

■ You've felt rich in the last few years, secure in the knowledge that the home you bought for $23,000 in 1951 could be sold for $175,000. That was a bundle of money that could be tapped by taking a second mortgage on the property, while continuing to live there. It could also be tapped by selling the house and moving up to something bigger and better. Now this is not necessarily so. The value of real estate has fallen faster than just about anything else. You can probably still get a second mortgage, but it might be very foolish to do so when repayment in more expensive dollars could be a problem. Should you want (or need) to sell, you might not easily find a buyer even if you are ready to sell at a lower price. A great many "house-rich" Americans are no longer so rich as they thought they were.

■ You invested in real estate, in fine art, in gold, in rare coins, in the type of hard-asset collectible that is very attractive when inflation rates are high. When inflation starts to slow, the value of these investments levels off or even declines. If you joined the bandwagon late, when prices were near their peak, you may have lost sizable sums.

■ You sold a home and took back a mortgage, expecting to get all your cash via a balloon payment in three years. Now the buyer can't refinance and you have to either extend the loan or foreclose on the house. Neither option will do wonders for your pocketbook.

■ You closed your savings account, after several years of hearing the "experts" tell you that money market mutual funds would pay far more interest on your savings, and joined a money market mutual fund. Now you let your money sit there, just as it did in the savings account. Don't. Your interest rate in the savings account, while low, was fixed. Your interest rate on the money market fund fluctuates daily. If rates really start to come down, you might be better off taking your money out of the money market and going right back where you started. Even if rates stay stable, you should be alert to the options offered by new savings and investment vehicles, such as the insured money market accounts now offered by banks and savings associations. You've got to pay attention.

■ You're on Social Security and you've gotten used to double-digit cost-of-living increases in your monthly check. Not anymore, not with disinflation. The 1985 increase, taking effect in January 1986, was just 3.1 percent.

None of this is meant to indicate that inflation is good and disinflation is bad. Inflation has caused a great deal of grief to the nation's economy as well as to individuals. But it does give the advantage to borrowers rather than to lenders. Anyone with large debts—the young, growing, and overextended family is a good example—can benefit from inflation because those debts are lightened by inflation. Anyone holding fixed assets—such as senior citizens living on accumulated capital—suffers when inflation makes those assets worth less and less.

Those who benefit from inflation often suffer from disinflation, as borrowers are now at a disadvantage. Lenders, however, are not necessarily better off. The homeowner who can't manage to pay his high mortgage payments is no help to the bank that is relying on his payments to keep itself solvent. It's possible that with disinflation everyone loses.

What we need is a relatively stable (not stagnant) economy. What we also need, as individuals, is the ability to adjust to a changing economy in terms of our personal money management. We have to pay attention to the world around us, even as we are preoccupied with earning a living and doing the most with our money. As I said at the outset, money management is not a one-time affair. The time to buy a house, the kind of investments we make, the amount of credit we use, the places we keep our money . . . all are affected, or should be, by our own stage of life and by the contemporary economic climate. Keep your eyes open, adjust your patterns of spending and saving and investing as necessary, and you'll come out ahead.

APPENDICES

Appendix A:
The Cost
of Living

We talk a lot about interest rates, at a time when small investors have earned the kind of interest only millionaires and corporations used to know. We start to take for granted the kind of income levels that sounded like real wealth a generation ago, even while knowing that we're not wealthy at all. But the real measure of the economic climate, as it affects our thoughts and our pocketbooks, is the cost of living.

How do we judge the cost of living, beyond the repeated onslaught of the supermarket? The most commonly accepted—as well as frequently criticized—measure is the Consumer Price Index (CPI). The CPI does more than measure change; it creates change as well.

The Consumer Price Index

The CPI, as defined by the U.S. Department of Labor Bureau of Labor Statistics, is "a statistical measure of change, over time, in the prices of goods and services in major expenditure groups—such as food, housing, apparel, transportation, and health and recreation—typically purchased by urban consumers. Essentially it measures the purchasing power of consumers' dollars by comparing what a sample 'market basket' of goods and services costs today with what the same sample market basket cost at an earlier date." The base period, the time to which current prices are compared, is 1967. An index number of 100 is given to 1967 on the assumption that a specific market basket of goods and services then cost $100. In May 1986 the CPI for urban consumers throughout the United States was 326.3, meaning that the same combination of goods and services then cost $326.30. The CPI thus is an index of changes in prices and a measure of inflation. It is *not,* as the Bureau of Labor Statistics points out, an index of the cost of living.

The CPI is not a valid measure of the cost of living, even though it's often taken to be, because:

- It looks only at the retail prices of specific goods and services; it does not look at taxes, which take more and more of everyone's income and account for an increasing share of the actual cost of living.

- It does not attempt to report changes in the style of living, or shifting consumer spending patterns. If you start to eat more chicken when beef becomes expensive, the CPI continues to report changes in the price of beef. If you eat out more often at fast-food restaurants, or buy more convenience foods to eat at home, the CPI may take several years to reflect this fact.

- It does not reflect noncash consumption, such as on-the-job fringe benefits or government services which can add to your standard of living.

In addition, the CPI includes weights for each category of expenditure, establishing their relative importance. But energy use, for instance, dropped sharply with moves toward conservation, and some analysts believe that energy should be given a lower weight. Housing, with the highest weight in the index, is a major bone of contention and will be discussed below.

Nonetheless, by charting the course of prices over a period of time, the CPI does provide a useful measure of inflation. It also has other uses, attached to it over the years.

THE USES OF THE CPI

The primary use of the CPI is, as noted, as an index of changing prices. It is also used:

- As an economic indicator. Thus it measures the success or failure of government policies.

- To escalate income payments. More than 8.5 million workers are now covered by collective bargaining contracts providing increases in wage rates based on increases in the CPI. These rising wages, some economists feel, are a cause as well as an effect of inflation.

- To determine the income of more than 50 million people receiving funds from the federal government: Social Security recipients, retired military and federal Civil Service employees and their survivors, and food stamp recipients. All of these rising payments may also fuel inflation.

- To establish the official estimate of the poverty threshold. This estimate is the basis of eligibility for many health and welfare programs.

■ To guide many private-sector agreements. Rental, royalty, and child support agreements now often include escalator clauses based on the Consumer Price Index.

So many people are affected by the CPI—approximately half of the population, by some estimates, including dependents—that every percentage point increase in the index in a single year leads to a rise in federal outlays of from $2 billion to $3 billion. Since 1981 the CPI has also been used for the indexing of income tax brackets and the setting of personal exemption amounts, with a staggering effect on government revenues.

CRITICISMS OF THE CPI

The CPI is not perfect; no statistical measure is. But because it has such a profound effect on the way we live, a lot of attention is paid to making it as accurate as possible. One of the biggest changes, made in the interest of accuracy, has been measuring the cost of housing. The cost of homeownership rose more drastically than almost anything else in the last decade. That rise was, until recently, directly reflected in the Consumer Price Index. But since relatively few people buy a house in a given year and the costs of maintaining a house bought at an earlier date are considerably lower, inclusion of current costs in the CPI skews the index and makes it unreliable.

There were several specific problems:

■ Mortgage forms have changed so drastically that the CPI, which has used the long-term fixed-rate mortgage as standard, became increasingly unrepresentative of the mortgage market. Variable rates and principal amounts simply cannot be used in a measure of comparison.

■ More and more sellers of homes have been providing some financing (the "creative" arrangements described in Chapter 13), and such financing arrangements are not reflected in the CPI.

■ Buying a house, moreover, is not like buying a hamburger; a house represents a long-term investment, a durable asset as well as consumable shelter. Even Janet L. Norwood, commissioner of the Bureau of Labor Statistics, has said that the Consumer Price Index should reflect the changing cost of "consuming shelter" rather than the rise or fall in house prices and mortgage interest rates that make a house-as-investment more or less valuable.

The housing component of the CPI has, therefore, been revised. Today housing is measured in terms of "rental equivalence" and reflects property taxes, repairs, insurance, general maintenance, and, only secondarily, housing prices and interest rates. The revision reduces the reported rate of inflation and, as a result, also reduces wage and pension increases pegged to the CPI. In the short run some people may lose out by the revision, but in the long run a more accurate measure should be very helpful.

Your Personal Inflation Index

★ A $12,000-a-year secretary, age 25, lives alone in a Manhattan apartment, has no car, keeps a tight budget, and finds that food and rent account for about two-thirds of her total expenditures.

★ A two-income family, in their early thirties, with one child in public school, live in a recently purchased home in a New York suburb. He's a manager. She's a reporter. Each needs a car. Combined income: $44,000.

Which life-style suffered more from inflation?

If you guessed Manhattan, says New York's Citibank, you're wrong.

The secretary's cost of living rose by 8.1 percent from April 1979 to April 1980, while the suburban couple's rise was 16.4 percent. The big difference: the cost of owning a home and the expense involved in running two cars.

By 1981–82, when the volatility of price movements had subsided somewhat, the figures were closer together. From May 1981 to May 1982, when the average CPI for all families increased by 6.7 percent, the secretary (now earning $14,000) saw a personal CPI of 6.3 percent and the suburban couple (now earning a total of $50,000) experienced a CPI of 7.2 percent. If we again see big price swings in fuel prices or food prices or rent or whatever, then there will be a major impact on people who have a larger portion of their budgets devoted to that item.

The Consumer Price Index may indicate an annual average rate of inflation for the nation as a whole. As these examples demonstrate, however, the national average may not apply to you. Your own personal cost of living may be higher, or lower, than the national average. It depends on where you live and on what you buy.

WHERE YOU LIVE

The national CPI is an average of twenty-eight cities, but the CPI actually rises faster in some than in others. In April 1980, for instance, high-cost New York had a CPI of 11.9 percent while the Dallas–Fort Worth area registered 19.1 percent. That's because the CPI registers upward movement in costs rather than costs themselves. With home building slower in the New York area than in the Sunbelt, as just one example, fewer people in New York paid the higher costs associated with new homes and new mortgages. Those costs, therefore, were not reflected in the regional CPI.

WHAT YOU BUY

If you spend a larger share of your money than most people do on items whose prices remain relatively constant, says the Bureau of Labor Statistics, your own rate of inflation will probably be lower than the average. Or if you spend more than most people on items whose prices are rising rapidly, you will probably experience more inflation than the national average indicates.

A second car, with the gasoline to run it, will increase your personal CPI. So will buying a first home, or heating an old home with oil, or having a substantial proportion of your income devoted to expenditures vulnerable to inflation. But you can keep your personal CPI below the national average if you walk to work, buy a used car instead of a new one, live in a moderate climate, and have a larger proportion of your overall expenses devoted to fixed expenses and/or to categories relatively untouched by inflation. Your cost of living is, to a large extent, up to you.

Appendix B: Between-Jobs Survival Skills

The money management skills outlined throughout this book will help you to survive a period of unemployment. But some are more important than others. If you're out of work, for any reason, here are the things you should do:

MARSHAL YOUR RESOURCES

Look to all possible sources of funds to get through the between-jobs period:

- Savings. Try to establish, *before* you're unemployed, a readily accessible savings "cushion" equivalent to at least six months' earnings.

- Investment income and, if necessary, sale of income-producing assets; this is the rainy day you've been saving for.

- Unemployment compensation. How much you'll get, and specific eligibility requirements, are determined by the state in which you live. But do apply; don't assume that you're not eligible because, for instance, you received some severance pay. (*Note:* Unemployment insurance, under the 1986 tax law, is fully taxable.)

- Life insurance. A loan against the cash value in an older whole life insurance policy may be available for as little as 5 to 8 percent. Life insurance loans do not have to be repaid (although the face amount of the policy will be reduced by the amount of any outstanding loan).

- Earnings of other family members. Now, if ever, is the time for you all to pull together.

■ Your own earnings from temporary or part-time or free-lance work. Can you tutor students? take in typing? do research? set up as a consultant in any field? Assess your skills carefully, and see what you can do to bridge the employment gap.

CUT BACK ON SPENDING

Don't wait until unemployment is a fact; cut back on spending just as soon as you see unemployment as a possiblity. Reduce day-to-day outlay: Brown-bag your lunch, set up a car pool, stop smoking. Defer major purchases: Put off buying a new car, or a new coat, until your income is stable. Swap services with friends: Trade upholstery for automobile repairs, baby-sitting for a haircut. Pool resources: Buy food cooperatively, set up a home repair tool center.

And take a good hard look at housing, probably your single largest budget item. Think about renting out a spare room in your house, or taking in a roommate in an apartment. Give up your own housing, as a last resort, and move in with relatives. Sublet your apartment, if your lease permits, or rent out your house, but try not to dispose of either permanently. You want to reduce expenses temporarily, not cut yourself adrift.

Note: Talk to your mortgage lender, without delay, if you'll have difficulty meeting monthly payments. Try to work out a repayment plan, acceptable to both you and the lender, under which your regular mortgage payments may be temporarily reduced or suspended, even if the payments must be extended over a longer period of time. Ask the lender, too, whether you are eligible for any government mortgage protection plan.

SET UP A SURVIVAL BUDGET

Match your reduced income against your reduced expenditures and do a six-month cash flow projection. If you can't last six months (you'll probably need more time than you think you will), go back and cut outgo some more. Most budgets contain some fat; now is the time to pare that fat, and you'll have a healthier diet when you're back to work.

Remember: You don't have to match your usual gross pay. Federal income and Social Security taxes, the devilish duo that take the biggest chunk of your gross income, will be all but eliminated when you're between jobs. So all you have to come up with is your net income minus the discretionary spending you can eliminate.

SPEND MONEY WISELY

As you do your survival budget, be sure to allocate enough money for your job search. You'll probably need at least $100 a month to get your résumé typed and printed, get to interviews, take people to lunch. You'll need more if you travel to another city in search of a job.

Some job-related expenses—including travel, placing classified ads, and the typing of résumés—are tax-deductible if you are seeking a new job in the same line of work. But you do have to spend the money first. And you do have to keep receipts.

This may also be a good time to invest money in retraining and self-improvement, to learn new skills and beef up old ones. But investigate services and prices first; a low-priced adult education course may provide the same training as a high-priced seminar.

KEEP IMPORTANT INSURANCE IN FORCE

Personal property insurance is important—now is not the time to replace your car or repair your home out of your own pocket—so keep up the premiums if you possibly can.

Health insurance, however, is even more important. With a semiprivate hospital room (*just* the room) costing an average of $226 a day in 1986, you can't afford to be unprotected. Here's what you can do:

- Find out, before you leave your job, if you can convert your group health insurance to individual coverage. The premium will go up, and some benefits may be reduced, but there will be no lapse in coverage.

- Ask an insurance agent about interim health insurance, a full-coverage short-term policy usually written for a maximum of six months.

- Check into group insurance plans offered by professional and social organizations. Most are hospital indemnity plans, paying specified amounts per day if you are hospitalized, rather than broad health insurance. They are better as supplementary coverage than as primary coverage, but they are clearly preferable to no coverage at all.

USE CREDIT WITH CARE

A line of credit may extend your financial resources, but using credit without a paycheck to pay the bills can be very dangerous. Don't use a credit card to take up the slack in your budget. You'll wind up with bills you can't pay at an interest rate you can't afford.

If you're having trouble meeting existing bills, talk to your creditors and work out a repayment plan. Don't ignore the bills, hoping they'll go away; you may do lasting damage to your credit rating. If you really don't see a way to pay your bills, get help. You can get the address of the consumer credit counseling agency nearest you by writing to the National Foundation for Consumer Credit, 8701 Georgia Ave., Suite 601, Silver Spring, MD 20910.

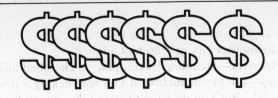

Index